**National University
of Singapore**

*Singapore's
Global University
Your Key to Asia*

Join a global university,
rooted in Asia,
focused on the future.

Plug in to a network of the
world's top centres of education,
research and enterprise.

Be part of a vibrant community
of 28,000 students from
80 countries, engaged in
a comprehensive range of
disciplines from humanities
to the sciences.

ABOUT THE AUTHORS

The Guide to the World's Top Universities is co-authored by
John O'Leary, Nunzio Quacquarelli and Martin Ince

John O'Leary is Editor of *The Times Higher Education Supplement*
and Editor of *The Times Good University Guide UK.*
Previously John was Education Editor at *The Times.*
John has a degree from Sheffield University.

Nunzio Quacquarelli is Managing Director of QS.
Nunzio is the Research Director of the THES - QS World University Rankings, assisted by Ben Sowter.
Nunzio is Editor-in-Chief of TopMBA.com, TopGraduate.com and TopUniversities.com and writes
regularly on education and careers topics for *The Times* of London, *The Times of India,*
Die Zeit, South China Morning Post amongst other newspapers around the world.
Nunzio has an MA from Cambridge University and
an MBA from The Wharton School, University of Pennsylvania.

Martin Ince is a Contributing Editor to *The Times Higher Education Supplement* and
Coordinator of the THES-QS World University Rankings.

ACKNOWLEDGEMENTS

This edition has been produced in association with Blackwell Publishing,
which will ensure distribution and availability in bookstores
and libraries around the world. We would also like to thank our official educational partners: ETS
- Toefl and IELTS.

The authors wish to give special thanks to the many individuals
who helped compile this edition of *Guide to the World's Top Universities.*
In particular we would like to thank Ben Sowter who has compiled and processed the data which
makes up the THES - QS World University Rankings. We would like to thank numerous colleagues at
THES and QS who have contributed in various ways to the book, including David Nelkin, Marie Field,
Jason Newman and Mandy Mok.

The authors would also like to thank the dozens of government and research agencies, as well as all
the universities which have provided data towards
the rankings and feedback, especially Juliette Linares of EduFrance.
Many of the official government websites are listed in the chapter on
'How to choose a university and course'.

In addition we would like to thank Evidence Limited for supplying five-year citation data. All data,
whether sourced direct from universities or from government and research agencies, has been
checked by the authors.
Whilst all efforts have been made to feature accurate information, with such huge volume of data
involved in this exercise, originating in so many different countries and languages, the authors
cannot guarantee complete accuracy. Any errors brought to our attention will be corrected in the
next edition of the guide.

What the press say

"The 2006 THES - QS World University Rankings reveal that Oxford and Cambridge are now Harvard's closest competitors after the US institution's lead slipped from 13% last year to just 3% this year... The Ranking is based on a survey of more than 3,000 academics and 736 graduate employers, and takes into account a university's student-staff ratio, its ability to attract foreign students and internationally renowned academics."
Alexandra Smith, The Guardian

"The World University Rankings... confirm Britain's position as a centre of global educational importance."
Alexandra Frean, Education Editor, The Times

"It is good for the UK to be benchmarked against the best universities in the world... It is also in the public interest to see that our higher education system remains world-class."
Richard Lambert, Director General, Confederation of British Industry

"Asian varsities rank high in world top 200 universities."
Khaleej Times

"Seoul National University has recently received outstanding international recognition. It came 63rd in this year's THES-QS World University Rankings, a surge from 93rd in 2005. Its engineering college was listed among the world's top 20 colleges by globally renowned academics."
Chosun Ilbo, Korea

"The latest THES-QS World University Rankings underline the fierce competition between leading universities across the world. The Indian Institute of Technology has made it to the league of best universities in the world, ranked 57th."
The Times of India

"A dozen Australian universities have made a table of the top 200 institutions in the world."
The Australian

"The University of Edinburgh is hoping to raise £350m from supporters and benefactors by 2011. Almost £150m has already been secured for the appeal. It is currently ranked in the top 35 of the 2006 THES-QS World University Rankings."
BBC News

What top universities say

"We're pleased to have our excellence recognized."
Marilyn McGrath Lewis, Director of Admissions, Harvard University

"The THES-QS represents perhaps the 'gold standard' of university rankings, so this kind of recognition is particularly valuable. Vanderbilt, ranked 53rd, clearly stands side-by-side with the very best universities in the world"
Gordon Gee, Chancellor, Vanderbilt University

"It is very reassuring that the collegiate systems of Cambridge and Oxford continue to be valued and respected by peers, and that the excellence of teaching and of research at both institutions is reflected in the World University Ranking."
Ian Leslie, Pro-Vice Chancellor for Research, Cambridge University

"We take pride in the special international reputation and position of McGill as an entirely fitting tribute to our remarkable faculty, staff and students. McGill University was the only Canadian university to crack the top 25 in this global guide to universities."
Heather Munroe-Blum, Vice-Chancellor McGill University

"It's pleasing that ANU's performance continues to be recognised as being up there with the best in the world."
Ian Chubb, Vice-Chancellor, Australian National University

GUIDE TO THE
WORLD'S TOP
UNIVERSITIES

THE TIMES **HIGHER** EDUCATION SUPPLEMENT · QS · Exclusively Featuring the Official **World University Rankings**

In association with

(ETS) **TOEFL.**   **IELTS**

Published by Quacquarelli Symonds Limited in association with Blackwell Publishing

Blackwell
Publishing

Published 2006 by QS Quacquarelli Symonds Limited
in association with Blackwell Publishing

QS Quacquarelli Symonds Ltd
1 Tranley Mews
Fleet Road
London NW3 2DG
United Kingdom

ISBN: 1 4051 6312 7
(978 1 4051 6312 5)

Project manager: Linda Martin
Design: Sarah Hudson, Johanna Glassborow, Ed Winder
Cover design: Anna Martin

Distributed by Blackwell Publishing
Printed and bound by Emirates Printing Press, Dubai

Discover more at
www.topuniversities.com

NOTE: The nature of our research methodology demands that we begin with an initial shortlist of
the world's leading universities. This began with a list of the world's leading universities by research
impact in 2004 and evolves each year on a case by case basis. Missing universities can be added to
our shortlist if they can supply us with justification for their inclusion relative to institutions already
included. To enquire about inclusion in our list please supply supporting evidence to research@
qsnetwork.com. Royal Holloway (University of London), the University of Essex and the University of
East Anglia have already been added to our list for 2007 on this basis.

Contents

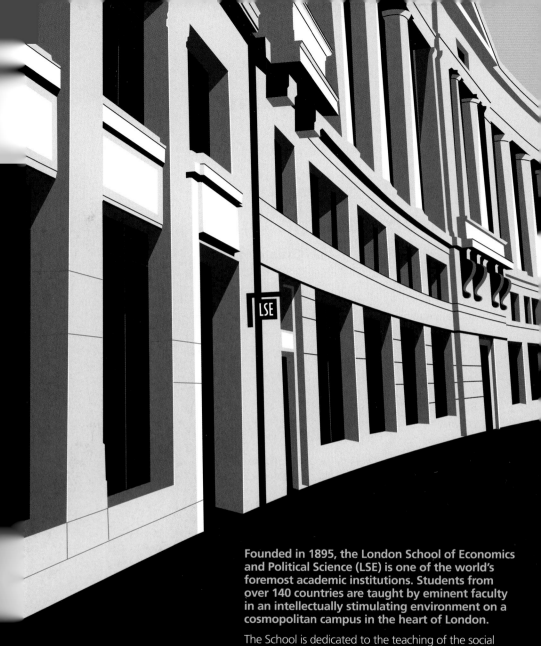

Founded in 1895, the London School of Economics and Political Science (LSE) is one of the world's foremost academic institutions. Students from over 140 countries are taught by eminent faculty in an intellectually stimulating environment on a cosmopolitan campus in the heart of London.

The School is dedicated to the teaching of the social sciences and pioneered the study of a number of subjects, including anthropology, international relations and social policy. Today 35 undergraduate and over 130 graduate degrees are available, in fields ranging from actuarial science to sociology, biomedicine to urbanisation.

LSE has produced 29 world leaders and heads of state, 13 Nobel Prize winners, and a host of alumni who are both nationally and internationally recognised. For more information on what LSE could offer you please contact us by telephoning **+44 (0)20 7955 6613**, emailing **stu.rec@lse.ac.uk** or visiting our website at **www.lse.ac.uk**

LSE
THE LONDON SCHOOL
OF ECONOMICS AND
POLITICAL SCIENCE

Welcome to the world's first top university guide

Around the world, governments are ending the free provision of local university education and, instead, are encouraging students to seek out the best university education, at home or abroad. Many governments are providing grants for international student mobility. In the US, recent Abraham Lincoln Study Abroad legislation aims to encourage a million students to study overseas, annually by 2016. The European Commission's Bologna Accord will make room for over 500,000 first degree graduates to study in other EU nations for a Masters degree, by 2010. Over three million Asians are expected to study outside their home country by 2020. The majority of these students will look to study at one of the 500 top universities featured in this guide.

The universities featured in this guide offer over 10 million undergraduate places and over 3.5 million postgraduate places. Over a million of their students come from overseas.

Graduates of these universities are consistently among the most highly paid young professionals in every country in the world. Government and industry leaders in every country covered in the guide come overwhelmingly from these same universities. The UN reports that 80 per cent of the world's 18–24 year olds are unemployed, while only 10 per cent of the world's graduates are unemployed. But for many high-flyers it is no longer enough to have a first degree from a local university. From knowledge-based industries like consulting and banking, to global concerns like the automotive and technology industries, as well as governments seeking to establish a globally minded cadre of young administrators, QS research finds that employers are increasingly focused on the best universities to recruit graduates.

In addition to being fascinating reading, we hope this guide will change the lives of tens of thousands of people for the better, by directing you to the top performing universities in the world, helping you find funding and guiding you into career paths which will allow you to achieve your full potential.

Who should use this guide?

Are you bright, well educated and looking to have a successful international career after high school?

Are you a parent looking to give your son or daughter an edge?

Are you a graduate looking for a prestigious Masters or PhD?

Are you taking your first degree and considering your 'exchange' study options?

Are you an employer/researcher refining your choice of universities to target for recruitment/partnership?

Are you an academic looking to change institution?

There is something in this book for you!

What does the guide tell you?

Based on The Times Higher Education Supplement - QS World University Rankings, this is the definitive guide to the universities around the world which truly excel.

The reason for the rankings, their methodology and how to interpret them are explained in detail. The guide discusses the results of the 200 most highly ranked universities in 2006. In addition the 100 top universities in key departments are featured: natural sciences, life sciences and biomedicine, engineering and IT, social sciences and arts and humanities.

In the guide you will also receive advice on how to choose a top university, application tips, sources of scholarships and funding, comparisons of costs and an overview of employment opportunities.

Reviews of the ten most popular country study destinations will help you narrow down feasible study options, with a detailed look at government grants and subsidies for overseas students.

Finally we provide profiles of the 100 most highly ranked universities and a directory of over 500 highly ranked universities around the world.

How to use this guide?

The guide should be your start point for choosing a top university at home or abroad.

Review the rankings but do not rely on them to answer all your questions. A university should not be selected purely based on its ranking, when relatively small variations in data can account for large positional movements.

Identify universities in the countries which match up to your study and career goals and provide a feasible study option in terms of cost and financial aid.

Cross reference the overall ranking position of each university, with its strength in the departmental ranking relevant to your study interests.

Once you have drawn up a long-list of top universities that meet your basic criteria, you can further investigate entry requirements, culture and specific subjects on offer, by reading the profiles in this guide (if they figure in the top 100) or by visiting the school website or **www.topuniversities.com**. Additional information is also available at **www.thes.co.uk**.

Once you have made your final short-list of universities, the guide will provide you with tips on how to apply and how to fund your studies, which will hopefully make the difference and enable you to gain acceptance at the university of your choice.

Good luck!

TOEFL®
Scores Open
More Doors.

The TOEFL® test is the key
to your recruitment success. *Why?*

- **It opens your doors to more international students.** Over 20 million students around the globe have taken the TOEFL test since its inception in 1964 — and those numbers continue to grow steadily.

- **It gives your institution greater visibility and reach.** Join an international education network of more than 6,000 institutions in 110 countries that includes most of the top institutions in the *Top Universities Guide*.

- **It helps you select students who are more likely to succeed academically.**

- **It is the world's best academic English test.** The TOEFL test replicates **real situations** from university classrooms and life, provides **unbiased, objective scoring** and is **accessible** in 180 countries.

Find out more

To learn more, call +1-609-683-2432, e-mail us at internationaldevelopment@ets.org or visit www.ets.org/toefl/recpacket11.html.

Listening. Learning. Leading.

Ranking the world's universities

The world's leading universities are no longer content to be recognised as pre-eminent in their own country. Higher education has become such a global enterprise that the best institutions tend to be more interested in comparing themselves with rivals thousands of miles away. The University of Manchester, for example, has set itself the target of breaking into the top 25 in the world, Bristol wants to be in the top 50.

It is easy to see why. Companies and governments mount global searches before placing valuable research contracts, top academics frequently move continents to further their careers and students, too, are increasingly mobile, particularly at postgraduate level. For some students, a move abroad may be the only way to find top quality tuition and a high standard of academic facilities in their particular subject; for others, to experience a different culture and a new way of thinking is valuable in itself and a big attraction for future employers.

Whatever the nature of their search, students and research managers want to be sure that their chosen university is truly world class. And those institutions with international ambitions need to be able to demonstrate their quality in the round. Until recently, however, there has been no way to compare universities internationally. Domestic league tables have become commonplace in virtually every substantial higher education system, but they have been constrained by national boundaries.

Huge interest in rankings

The World University Rankings, produced by The Times Higher Education Supplement and QS, represent an attempt to fill this gap. Published this year for the third time (and for the first time in book form), they have aroused huge interest and no little controversy. More than a million people viewed the rankings online when they appeared in 2005, and there have been debates on every continent since then. A UNESCO experts' group has spent more than a year poring over the methodology and, over one weekend in May, the findings were being discussed in Berlin, Seoul and Tartu, in Estonia.

As might be expected, given the nature of the project, there has been no immediate consensus. Some still insist that it cannot be done — Philip Altbach, Director of the Center for International Higher Education, at Boston College, for one. "Everyone wants a world-class university. No country feels it can do without one," he wrote when the 2005 rankings were published. "The problem is that no one knows what a world-class university is, and no one has figured out how to get one."

In all probability, there never will be agreement on a single method of comparing universities worldwide. But there has been widespread support for the objectives set in compiling our rankings: to produce an up-to-date view of the strengths of the leading institutions as they impact on research and teaching, giving credit for an international outlook. They reflect the qualities seen in practically all of the universities recognised informally as international powerhouses, institutions rooted in research but also justly proud of their teaching prowess.

David Levin, the President of Yale University, writing in Newsweek, listed the same priorities in his account of what makes a global university. "In response to the same forces that have propelled the world economy, universities have become more self-consciously global: seeking students from around the world who represent the entire spectrum of cultures and values, sending their own students abroad to prepare them for global careers, offering courses of study that address the challenges of an interconnected world and collaborative research programs to advance science for the benefit of all humanity. Of the forces shaping higher education none is more sweeping than the movement across borders," he wrote.

Different types of university

There are many other types of university, equally valuable and fit for purpose, that do not aspire to international status. They may serve their local communities, usually with an emphasis on teaching rather than research, or they may be determinedly national institutions with an eye to knowledge transfer. However, the universities in our ranking (and others like them) tend to judge themselves internationally on the power of their research, often as members of the growing number of global higher education networks, as well as recruiting both students and staff from many parts of the world.

The real difficulty facing those who seek to rank such universities is not how to define them, but where to find the data that will make for reliable comparisons. Different national systems — naturally enough — collect the data that matter to them and in the form that suits their purpose. The limited number of measures in the World Rankings reflects just how few there are that transfer across borders — and even they can present problems.

Take citations, the most common source of international academic comparisons and the least controversial of our six indicators in the various discussions of methodology. The measurement of citations in leading academic journals confers a clear advantage on English-speaking universities and on American universities in particular. English may have become the international language of higher education, as of business, but that is little consolation to institutions that work in other languages and whose academics stand correspondingly less chance of building up a competitive body of citations.

It is also clear from the figures produced by Evidence Ltd from the Thomson Scientific database that the research culture in the United States differs from other parts of the world. American research leads the world, but the sheer volume of citations registered by US universities suggests that their academics also cite each others' work more regularly than is the case in most of Europe or Asia. There is no suggestion of corruption; merely a difference in normal academic practice.

At least citations are generally accepted as a measure of research reputation in the sciences. (There is no easy equivalent in the humanities and less application to the social sciences.) But there is no international measurement of teaching quality — and almost certainly never will be. Most countries do not even attempt national comparisons. The nearest proxy, however imperfect, is the staff/student ratio. Despite the onward march of technology, with increasing use of the internet and MP3 players for teaching purposes, there is no substitute in conventional universities for face-to-face contact. Students value small teaching groups and the opportunity to consult tutors.

International activity

Nor is it easy to measure international activity. Some universities have whole campuses overseas, others have numerous partnership programmes and exchange schemes. But it is possible to be globally active and internationally minded without such formal initiatives. The proportions of international students and staff have been selected as the most universally applicable indicators, although both have been accorded a low weighting in the ranking so as not to overplay their importance.

Other possible indicators have been considered and either discarded as impractical or shelved until enough data can be collected to make them reliable sources of comparison. This was the case initially with the employers' survey, which was omitted from the first edition of the rankings, in 2004, because the sample was considered too small. Now that the pool of international employers is larger and more diverse, it is considered a valuable addition and one which will continue to grow in the years to come.

Academic opinion was already considered a vital element if the rankings were to paint the most current picture of international higher education, rather than reflecting past glories. Even citations inevitably credit universities for work which may have been carried out several years previously; Nobel prizes, which form a substantial part of the rankings published by Shanghai Jiao Tong University, often relate to research done far in the past. The thousands of academics who take

15

part in the peer review exercise conducted by QS are judging universities in their own discipline as they are today. By aggregating the views of subject experts, we avoid impressionistic judgements of overall quality and provide material for the separate faculty-level rankings.

Peer review

Peer review is the method used to assess academic quality in universities all over the world and it has formed a part of US university league tables for many years. In the absence of more precise statistical data on activities such as teaching and more up-to-date comparisons of research, it has become the central element of the World University Rankings. It is, after all, a matter of opinion which are the best universities in the world. Who better to ask than the people who work in them?

Among the other indicators considered for inclusion in the rankings have been various spending measures. Many domestic tables measure the amount spent on libraries, for example, but it was decided that — even if genuinely comparable data could be collected — too great an advantage would be conferred upon wealthy nations for the results to be meaningful. Similar objections have been raised to the use of graduate employment rates: there is a danger of comparing economies more than universities.

Entry standards provide another obvious area of comparison — and one much used in national league tables. But while business schools have an international entry standard, most areas of university life do not. Much work has been done on the equivalence of different qualifications, but it is not yet clear how this can be incorporated into a system of rankings such as these. No doubt other measures will be developed – the proportion of staff with PhDs is one area of enquiry, as is the number of PhDs awarded by each university – but, despite frequent appeals for workable additions, no glaring omission has yet emerged.

What has become clear is that the need for international comparisons is growing all the time. The travelling scholar dates back to the Middle Ages, but never have such numbers been crossing national boundaries. There were great leaps forward in student mobility in the late 1970s, when numbers rose by 30 per cent, and at the beginning of the 1990s, when the increase was even larger. But they were as nothing compared with the near- 50 per cent growth that has taken place since the millennium. UNESCO now estimates total student numbers to be beyond 132 million, almost 3 million of whom are studying abroad.

More than half of this travelling band go to four countries: France, Germany, the UK and the US (which takes by far the largest share, despite fluctuations in recent years). Australia, Canada and Japan are the other three big student destinations, although countries such as China have set their sights on joining this group. The World University Rankings illustrate vividly why this is the case

16

since these are the countries (with some honourable additions) that dominate the leading positions. In all three years of the rankings, US universities have occupied more than a third of the top 100 places, but even this is less than many critics predicted. Famous American names — led in all three years by Harvard University — take a majority of places in the top 20, but their grip is soon loosened. European universities outnumber the US contingent in the top 100, led by UK institutions, and Australasia is not far behind.

Widespread excellence

In fact, the rankings have shown that excellence in higher education is distributed more widely than many in the West have presumed. The high standing of Australian universities in Asia, for example, has helped propel seven of them into the top 100, while no fewer than 21 different countries are represented in those leading positions. Several nations have only one such institution, but it has become a matter of economic and cultural importance, as well as national pride, to compete at this level. In Germany, for instance, which has 11 universities in the top 200 but only one in the top 50, the government has set about identifying a group of elite research institutions which will benefit from considerable extra investment.

The 2006 edition of the Organisation for Economic Cooperation and Development's annual Education at a Glance report focuses particularly on international student mobility as one of the defining characteristics of 21st century activity. Over the past 12 months alone, it records an 8 per cent increase in traffic and expresses concern that some countries might be both overexposed to the international market and nearing their effective capacity in some academic areas. More than a third of postgraduates at UK universities were from overseas, for example, while foreign students accounted for 39 per cent of Masters places in Australia and 41 per cent of PhDs in Switzerland.

Such figures illustrate not only the scale of international demand for higher education, but also the need for prospective applicants to do their homework on likely destinations. Large concentrations of foreign students – especially representing a single nationality – can dilute the experience of working and living in another country. The OECD's statistics underline the dominance of English language tuition and the ability of universities in developed countries to both attract and cater for more foreign students than their counterparts elsewhere. There is no sign yet of any slowing of the trend to internationalisation, but it is easy to imagine students' choices narrowing for reasons of cost or the availability of places. Rankings should never be the sole source of information behind the choice of university, but they can be an invaluable starting point.

How to choose a university and course

Choosing a university, whether it be for an undergraduate, Masters or exchange programme, is one of the biggest decisions you will make in your life. It will determine many of the friends you will have in later life, the cultures you understand, the type of work you will do and, increasingly, people choose a university to influence the country in which they seek to live and work.

In modern complex societies, education is the most reliable route to a well-paid and interesting career, in almost any field. Yet the vast majority of people around the world still settle for a university based on the convenience of being 'close to home'. As we have seen, UN figures show that 80 per cent of the world's 18–24 year olds are unemployed, while only 10 per cent of the world's graduates in this age range are unemployed — but this 10 per cent tends to be concentrated in local universities which lack the prestige to attract top employers, or the quality of courses to provide a route to a Masters or PhD.

When choosing a university, always aim for the best institution which will accept you. Invariably, if you have the academic ability to gain a place, the funding can become available either through scholarships, student loans, part-time jobs or your parents.

There are many factors to consider when choosing a university. The decision should be complex and will take time and effort to research. But we believe this book can save you a great deal of time and open your eyes to many new opportunities, both at home and abroad.

It is not just the millions of internationally mobile students who will use this book. In addition, we know that academic staff are one of the world's most mobile workforces and seek to benchmark their current institution with others. Employers, seeking to recruit top graduates, or fund research, are also scouring universities on an increasingly international basis. Governments, anxious to place their research funding at the best performing institutions, also look to benchmark their universities with those overseas. All these groups will use this book, but it is the internationally mobile students for whom this chapter is intended.

Start with The THES — QS World University Rankings

The tables within this book are a guide to the world's top 500 universities. This should be the starting point for anyone serious about their university education. The prestige of these institutions is unmatched and passed on to their alumni, who will benefit throughout their professional careers.

We have a high level of confidence in the data contained in our tables and the methods we have used to analyse it — which has been subject to a great deal of expert scrutiny. But the information we have gathered needs to be used with thought. We encourage you to read our chapter on rankings and to dig deeper into the data to make sure a university is right for you. Not everyone should study at Harvard, or Cambridge, or Tokyo or Peking University. Every university has different department strengths, subject strengths, cultures and networks. All these have to be considered.

Our tables use evidence of excellence in teaching and research, as well as the opinions of academics and employers, to construct a ranking. In addition, they contain measures of the international commitment of universities in the shape of their percentage of overseas nationals as staff and students.

The main tables are supplemented in this book by two new forms of information. One of these is a series of profiles of the world's top 100 universities. These are intended to give the flavour of each of the world's best universities. What is its culture and history? Has it produced famous alumni? What are its main strengths? Factors such as these are important for the overall ethos of the institution and for the experience you will have as a student. The profiles also contain a wealth of more tangible information. Much of it relates to the subject specialisations of specific universities. The world's top 100 institutions tend to be good at a broad range of subjects, and excellent in many. But if your first love is philosophy, you might not be happy on a campus dominated by engineers or medics.

We have also sought out quotes from students at the top universities which capture the essence of their experience at the institution of their choice.

The second new resource we provide here is outline information on the world's top 500 universities. Space considerations dictate that we cannot provide complete profiles for all of these institutions. But we do provide web addresses for each of them which will allow you to find out more. Additional information on all 500 institutions can also be found at **www.topuniversities.com**.

Using the rankings tables

All the universities in this book are top institutions. They educate the leaders in every activity from medicine to politics, and produce new knowledge at an increasing pace in all fields.

The biggest component of their position in our tables is an academic peer review — the regard in which universities are held by other top academics around the world. This accounts for 40 per cent of an institution's possible score. Because we aggregate scores in this heading from all over the world and from all fields of academic life, an institution is likely to do well here by being good in most or all subject areas. The exceptions are a small number of highly prestigious specialist institutions such as the London School of Economics, or science and technology universities in California, London, Tokyo and elsewhere. This measure is a broad indicator of the university's standing amongst its peers, and has been gathered from a statistically robust sample of respondents.

The next column is an employer peer review, based on a sample of over 700 international graduate employers. It captures universities' attractiveness to top recruiters. This is a factor of acute interest to many students. However, all 500 of the universities we analyse here produce graduates who are in high demand. This measure is mainly designed to assess universities' attractiveness to employers operating in the globalised world. If you already know the kind of employer, career and location you intend to seek out locally, this measure might not be valuable to you. Its main use is for students wanting a higher education that will make them visible to these worldwide enterprises.

Our columns on universities' international attractiveness to staff and students represent their own commitment to globalisation. It shows that this is one area in which the United States does not have a world lead. Europe and Asia have the world's most international universities. It has been argued that the very size of the US makes it tricky for universities there to be highly international. In the Netherlands or Switzerland, whose universities have large percentages of foreign staff and students, there are half a dozen other countries within a day's drive. In the US Midwest, there are none. But we think that this is a valuable measure of the seriousness with which universities take their international role. Australia, after all, is an island continent but still brings in overseas students and academics in impressive numbers. By contrast, universities in some other Asian countries such as Korea and Japan show badly in a reckoning of their international orientation. Many now regard it as a priority to change, for example by teaching more in English. They may move radically in this part of the table in future years. Overall, we think that this factor is an important one in assessing the likely experience of overseas students. As a rule of thumb, a university with a low percentage of international students and faculty is likely to offer fewer facilities and provide less of a social network for overseas students.

Citations per faculty, our measure of the publishing performance of universities, is intended to capture their research capacity as a function of university size. We use the number of citations per staff member partly to prevent very large universities dominating the table and partly to allow us to measure the density of top research intellect in institutions. This measure is a good one for would-be research students. It might also be of value for internationally mobile lecturers and organisations thinking of homes for their research budgets. However, it has a number of biases. One is caused by the fierce publishing ethos of the biomedical sciences. A big medical school is a massive plus in terms of generating both papers and citations. There are also well-known biases in this data in favour of English-language publication and against the arts and humanities. Anyone with an interest in these subjects might pay less attention to this criterion.

Our measure of the staff to student ratio of universities is a direct look at the adequacy of their commitment to teaching. It might matter less for potential researchers than to would-be undergraduates. It is also prone to subtle influences. Oxford and Cambridge universities in the UK both teach for several weeks a year less than other nearby institutions. Some universities make extensive use of postgraduate students to teach undergraduates (which we exclude from our faculty numbers) while others frown on the practice. In some top institutions, students may never see the renowned scholars whose pictures adorn the prospectus, while in others these individuals are expected to give their fair share of nine o'clock lectures. So again, it is worth looking beyond these figures, for example at our institution profiles, to get a fuller picture.

Search for the best department and course

Within the guide we provide a detailed ranking of the 100 best institutions for five major department categories: arts and humanities, engineering and IT, life sciences and biomedicine, natural sciences and social sciences. These findings will further help you identify if a university measures up in the field which interests you. In addition, the institution profiles will tell you the top subjects at the 100 leading institutions.

These rankings contain little subject-specific information. The sheer volume of this detailed data makes it impossible to publish in the guide. This means that anyone using this book to find a place to study should regard it as only one source of the information they need. Every university featured in this guide has a searchable course listing available on **www.topuniversities.com**. You may also want to add to this information with facts from subject associations, professional societies, university websites and other sources.

Consider the location

The guide also provides detailed country reviews for the ten most popular overseas study destinations in the world: Australia, Canada, France, Germany, Japan, Netherlands, the Nordic Countries, Singapore, United Kingdom, United States. In each of these reviews you will find tips to help you identify which country will best suit your study needs in terms of quality, culture, cost and financial aid.

Sometimes there are major structural considerations which affect the country you choose. For example, most large US medical schools teach the subject to postgraduates. They may well have studied the life sciences as undergraduates, but many have not, and there are doctors in the US with first degrees in maths and English. It works well, but if you want to start studying medicine at age 18, this system may not be for you.

Look at student exchanges

If you are already a student, one way of expanding your experience and getting a flavour of overseas study is through your own university's exchange programme. Typically this might involve spending anything from a few weeks in summer to a complete year in a foreign country.

It can be useful to look at the exchange schemes offered by a university to which you are thinking of applying. Are they in countries that interest you? Do they major on the US and Europe, or has the university recognised the growing importance of Asia? And how well ranked are the names on the list? If your interest is in engineering, you might look for an exchange with MIT rather than a less prestigious university. Further information on student exchanges is also available on **www.topuniversities.com**.

Check facilities

The facilities offered by universities can vary enormously. This can have a big impact on your enjoyment of your university experience. All the universities featured in this guide offer an excellent academic experience, but you also want to check out the availability of accommodation, computer centres, sports facilities, career service and even social clubs. We aim to add this information in future editions of the guide, but in the mean time we direct you to the university websites which provide varying levels of information on these topics. Our profiles of the top 100 universities also provide some insights.

Identify the cost and funding options

Within the guide we provide a detailed review of average university course fees, for local and international students. These vary from completely free at universities in the Nordic countries, to over $50,000 at some private US universities – even before living costs. Fees act as a constraint on many people studying at a top university, especially the expensive private universities. However, graduates of the world's top universities tend to earn enough to pay back their student debts within a few short years. If you can gain entry to one of these top institutions, you will benefit from higher earnings for the rest of your life.

Will you be accepted?

There is no accepted comparison of university entry standards across borders. We have chosen not to publish this data this year to conduct further research. Each university website will provide a guide to entry requirements, usually explained based on the local education system. Comparisons within countries are also available within the government statistical sources listed at the end of this chapter.

Make a visit to the school or an education fair

If a university is nearby, there is absolutely no substitute for visiting it and, if at all possible, meeting the people who will be teaching you, as well as some students. This might happen when you visit for an interview, on a specified open day, or at your request.

Education fairs can be an extremely time efficient way to meet admissions officers from your target universities, gather brochures and obtain answers to your personal questions. There is no substitute for face-to-face contact. There are many undergraduate education fairs taking place around the world, which can easily be found by conducting a Google search. QS, the publisher of this book, organises the QS World Grad School Tour in 25 countries around the world, enabling you to meet with up to 160 universities offering postgraduate Masters and PhD programmes — more information is available at **www.topgraduate.com**. QS also runs the QS World MBA Tour, in which you can meet business schools from around the world — more information is available at **www.topmba.com**.

Talk to staff and alumni

If you cannot manage a visit, perhaps because of distance, remember that telecommunications is cheap. What happens when you ring up a university that looks good on paper, or send them an email? You will need the right answers to questions on topics such as finance, accommodation and employment prospects. But in addition, you will be able to form an impression of how important you are to them. Given the amount of time and money you are about to commit to the next stage of your studies, this is a substantial consideration.

Most universities with a significant international student body have an alumni association with branches around the world. Contacting them will put you in touch with recent (and not so recent) graduates whose experiences you might want to hear about. But their testimony should be treated with some caution. Activists in such groups are self-selected and probably had a better than average time at the university in question.

Sources for further information

AUSTRALIA	IDP Education Australia **www.idp.com**
AUSTRIA	Austrian Exchange Service **www.oead.ac.at**
CANADA	Canadian Education Centre Network **www.studycanada.ca**
DENMARK	CIRIUS Study in Denmark **www.studyindenmark.dk**
FINLAND	Centre for International Mobility (CIMO) **http://finland.cimo.fi/studying.html**
FRANCE	Agence EduFrance **www.edufrance.fr**
GERMANY	DAAD – German Academic Exchange Service **www.daad.de**
INDIA	University Grants Commission **www.ugc.ac.in/studyindia/index.html**
IRELAND	Education Ireland **www.educationireland.ie**
ITALY	MIUR – Ministry of Education, University and Research **www.study-in-italy.it**
JAPAN	JASSO – Japan Student Services Organization **www.jasso.go.jp**
MALAYSIA	Study Malaysia **www.studymalaysia.com**
NEW ZEALAND	Education New Zealand **www.newzealandeducated.com**
NORWAY	The Norwegian Centre for International Cooperation in Higher Education (SIU) **www.studyinnorway.no**

Sources for further information (continued)

SINGAPORE	Singapore Education **www.singaporeedu.gov.sg**
SOUTH KOREA	National Institute for International Education Development **www.studyinkorea.go.kr**
SPAIN	Eduespana **www.eduespa.org**
SWEDEN	The Swedish Institute **www.studyinsweden.se**
TAIWAN	Ministry of Education **www.studyintaiwan.org**
TURKEY	Study Turkey **www.studyturkey.metu.edu.tr**
THE NETHERLANDS	NUFFIC **www.studyin.nl**
UK	The British Council **www.educationuk.org**
USA	Education USA **http://educationusa.state.gov**

nurturing futures.

ai Knowled Village is the fast-growing education hub of the middle East. Its world-class structure offers educational institutions the perfect environment to create and disseminate vledge, and form a connected community of knowledge-based entities. Home to over 15 national universities and more than 300 training, HR and education service providers, Dubai vledge Village offers a vibrant learning environment for students interested in advanced national degree programmes in fields such as Engineering, computing, Technology, Business agement, Biotechnology, Life Sciences, Fashion, Media and more. If you'de like to be a part of a ng Knowledge-based community, contact us on Tel +971 4 390 1111, Fax +9714 390 1110 or www.kv.ae today.

DUBAI
KNOWLEDGE
VILLAGE

A member of
TECOM INVESTMENTS

WORLD MBA TOUR™
topmba.com

The WORLD MBA TOUR and www.topmba.com

Helping to transform business education

We recognise the contribution made by every individual and institution to the world's leading network for education and careers.

- 375,000 web visitors and TopMBA Scorecard users
- The 60,000 talented young professionals attending the Tour
- Over 370 international business schools
- Our 165 committed Media Partners
- The local partners and educational organisations across 38 host countries
- For **1** future at a time

supporting   providing

US$2.7 Million exclusive scholarships

offering   innovating

The QS team look forward to sharing more innovative solutions and un-missable events - both with you and your colleagues and friends.

2006/07 Venues

North America	Western Europe	Central Europe	Asia	India & Middle East
Miami	Paris	Moscow	Tokyo	New Delhi
Atlanta	Milan	Kiev	Seoul	Hyderabad
New York	Zurich	Budapest	Beijing	Bangalore
Boston	Frankfurt	Athens	Shanghai	Chennai
Washington DC	Munich	Istanbul	Taipei	Mumbai
Toronto	Madrid		Hong Kong	Dubai
Chicago	London	**Spring 07**	Ho Chi Minh City	Cairo
Los Angeles		Sofia	Bangkok	
San Francisco	**Spring 07**		Kuala Lumpur	
Houston	Rome		Singapore	
	Barcelona			
	Lisbon			
	Brussels			

The benefits of studying abroad

An international experience forming part of an undergraduate degree has become commonplace in recent years. For many this means a semester or term on an organised exchange programme, with a partner university in another country like the UK or the USA. However, for more than 2.5 million students in 2005 this actually means an entire programme of study being followed away from home, sometimes in a neighbouring country but very often on the other side of the world.

Though 69 per cent of all travelling tertiary-level students are currently enrolled in programmes in either North America or Europe, more and more students are seeking different destinations as the location for their international period of study. In addition to choosing a country destination, such diverse factors as location of institution, subject choice, mode of delivery, length of study, cost of programme and teaching style are all areas of concern for students thinking of pursuing a postgraduate degree abroad. With the global labour market placing more importance on postgraduate experience, getting the decision right on where and what to study is increasingly complex. A recent report by the Finnish Government indicates that employers assess studying and training abroad in three different ways. Firstly, from the perspective of occupational skills — whether the international experience increases students' skills in their field of studies. Secondly, how does the experience affect students' personal growth; and thirdly, what kind of skills and abilities do students develop abroad that can help them perform in an international setting in the future? Though the report indicates that the first category of experience is questionable, the last two provide very strong arguments for study abroad, particularly with regard to the development of superior language skills and the ability to deal with people from other countries.

More choice

So what are the benefits of studying abroad and why might you consider a period away from home as part of your degree? Listening to students who already have experienced the benefits of study abroad is one of the best ways of finding out about the tangible effects of seeking educational opportunities in another country. Many choose to study abroad because the academic programme they wish to pursue is not available at home, the emphasis or teaching method is different or simply because of the reputation of a particular international institution. Remember, not all education systems are set up the same way and many adopt a very traditional way of teaching and assessment that might not fulfil your ambitions or strengths. Jackie Wong, the Senior Education Advisor at the Australian Education Consultancy and graduate of the University of Melbourne, in Australia, chose to study abroad firstly "because of the flexibility of choice in the subjects I wanted to study. In Hong Kong I would have had to study a large number of options with very little opportunity to choose" and secondly "as there were only 20 or so students in each class the professors actually remembered my name!". Such reasons for studying abroad are common and underline the importance many attach to the learning experience and structure and approach to teaching that you may not necessarily find at home.

Quality of degrees

One of the most compelling reasons for studying abroad, however, involves the perceived quality of the degree. This is a very complex area that such tools as the QS/Times Higher Education Supplement's rankings seek to help unravel. In many societies, anything that is regarded as international is synonymous with quality and prestige. Education is no different, yet the sheer number of universities in the world today means that the notion that all are of the same quality is nonsense. Many universities in many different countries benefit from excellent government support, good infrastructure and a policy of strict quality control, ensuring that the degree programmes offered by their institutions are of an agreed and reputable standard that have international reference points. However, there is an equal number that do not have such good policies and simply offer a degree that meets a local need and has no value in the international context. True benefit for an international student is derived from studying at an institution that fulfils certain universal standards and is, at a very minimum, quality assured by a national agency and, at best, recognised by an international body such as a professional association.

Albert Luk, an Assistant Technical Analyst at OOCL, an international logistics company in Hong Kong, chose the University of York in the UK for his degree in Software Engineering for two key reasons, "firstly because UK higher education has an excellent reputation over most other countries in the world and secondly because the recognition of the degree in Hong Kong is very high." The recognition of your degree is one of the foremost reasons why you might seek a period of international study and is certainly one of the major benefits from the experience. With so many people already travelling overseas for their education, it indicates that the current labour market is far more mobile than ever before. The more recognised your degree is, the farther you will be able to travel with it. Recognition, however, is not always focused on an individual name such as Harvard or Cambridge, but can simply indicate a more general reputation of a country's system of higher education or vocational training.

Independence and new cultures

In many ways, Sameera Suri is typical of many students who have studied internationally. An Indian national, Sameera now resides in Geneva, an employee of the international agency, the World Health Organisation. In her role as a communications officer for the Diabetes Unit she utilises both the skills she gained in her degree from the London School of Economics and her experiences of being an international student in London. "There were so many advantages related to my period of study abroad. I certainly learnt to become self-sufficient and much more independent than I was in India. But much more importantly, I started to understand how many common elements there are in the world, irrespective of where you come from and where you live."

Similarly, Anuradha Bajaj, also from India, studied in the UK for reasons that are as important as any related to quality or reputation. "I wanted to get a blend of different academic approaches with the opportunities of living and working in another country. The chance to manage my life away from home – open a bank account, speak another language, cook different food and see an entirely different history were things I thought were important to help me develop." Such reasons compel many to look overseas for their university education and Anuradha's experiences represent many international students who rank experiences outside of the classroom as important as those in the process of gaining an international qualification. The ability to adapt to an alien culture, manage one's everyday life – often in a foreign language – and gain an insight into a completely new way of life are as valid reasons as any purely academic ones for a period of international study and in some ways benefit the individual much more directly. Employers, too, recognise these more esoteric reasons for studying abroad and consistently employ those graduates who have the ability to understand cultures different from theirs so that they can bring these skills to their business. In a world that has undoubtedly become smaller, the need to be more international in outlook and understanding is something that all employers wish to maintain and so the need for graduates of this kind is likely to become even greater in the years to come.

Career benefits and language skills

Others look to more tangible reasons for pursuing a degree overseas. "I participated in a degree overseas primarily to enhance my career future opportunities," says Tommy So, a personal portfolio consultant in the Credit Suisse Group. His experience of working in another language, he believes, has certainly enabled him to progress in his chosen career path. "For me, the benefits of studying abroad are not only about the gaining of an international exchange experience but the improvement of my spoken and written English. Because of this I think studying abroad helped me to get opportunities at some large international companies." Kenneth Lai, assistant to the general manager for a Japanese joint venture manufacturing firm invested in China, completed a degree in the UK in

1994. He concurs with this view: "Studying in English was important — in fact, grasping English in the UK was even more important in helping me develop an international career."

Tommy and Kenneth's experiences touch on a centrally important reason for the enormous interest in study abroad. The growth in qualifications taught exclusively in the English language, at all levels, reflects the continuing importance of the language in every contemporary international sphere. Those universities that wish to become active in the lucrative international student recruitment market increasingly have to adapt their existing academic offerings into a completely new medium — a task not to be taken lightly. Developments in such diverse countries as Finland, the Netherlands and South Korea, where degrees of all kinds are now being taught in English, underline the importance of language to international study. That said, where students have particular and non-English language ambitions, the international choice is still extremely diverse and as relevant to specific careers in certain country situations.

Life experience

There are many reasons for seeking an international education, all of which ultimately revolve around personal ambition and circumstances. The benefits derived from such an experience are similarly individual but can be summed up in a number of areas — personal development and growth, general experience, cultural experience and future employment opportunities. You may find yourself in the position where you know precisely what your ambitions are and what you need to do to achieve them and so pursue your period of international study in a more single-minded fashion. Many others, however, understand the more general benefits of the process of studying abroad and embark on the period as more of an adventure. Either way, you will discover many things when you study abroad — about yourself, about the country in which you are living and about the world — and remember and use the experiences for the rest of your life. Ross McCalden's experience of researching, applying and enjoying a degree overseas is typical of the 2.5 million students studying abroad this year. "I was drawn to the College of Europe because of the prestige of the institution, the quality of the degree and the fact that being abroad gave me a perspective with people from different cultures." Ross may well never have studied abroad if it wasn't for a personal contact and now he sees only advantages to his experience: "I think you definitely get to know yourself better and being away from familiar concepts really opens your mind to new ideas of thinking and ways of doing things. I think it is also good for character building and of course language skills. It made me a more rounded person."

Whatever your reasons for studying abroad you can be certain that the experience will be one that you never regret for the rest of your life.

What career?
Benefits of a top degree

Studying abroad is an enticing prospect — from the attraction of learning new languages and adopting and embracing different cultures, to the more functional benefits of developing occupational and personal skills, and seeking prospective employment abroad.

This chapter delves into the trends of student mobility and employment. We look at the topic from the point of view of employers and what they are looking for as part of their graduate recruitment. We then look from the point of view of international applicants to discover their aspirations and expectations, and, finally, students and alumni to see whether they met their ambitions and what benefits their mobility has brought them.

The UNESCO Institute of Statistics reported that between 1999 and 2004, the number of mobile students worldwide surged by 41 per cent from 1.75 to 2.5 million. This not only reflects the rapid expansion of higher education overall, but also the sustained growth in demand for top-quality graduates, amongst employers around the world.

What benefits can students with international experience offer and what benefits can they expect? Views will naturally vary from country to country, employer to employer, and person to person, but the overriding view is that these students develop an international outlook and maturity, often lacking in domestically educated graduates.

The employer view

As part of The THES – QS World University Rankings, QS has conducted a survey of almost 400 international employers of graduates and postgraduates around the world, as well as over 450 employers of MBAs. The employer views in this chapter draw from this annual research programme, as well as other sources.

More and more companies are global in their operations without ties to any one region.

Many of these companies have human relations managers with global or regional responsibility for hiring graduates, postgraduates and MBAs from the best universities and business schools in the world. In addition, many recruiters headquartered in one location will have responsibility for a region elsewhere. Many graduates and postgraduates in Asia, Latin America and Eastern Europe are hired through head offices in North America or Western Europe.

Although 38 per cent of responding recruiters are based in North America, 40 per cent have some responsibility for recruiting globally or in Europe, Asia or Latin America. Similarly, European recruiters make up 28 per cent of our sample, but 36 per cent also have some responsibility for recruiting globally or in North America, Asia or Latin America. This should be good news for mobile graduates, whatever your country of origin or study and your preference for international mobility.

The salary benefits of a top degree

Though salary may not be the overriding factor in choice of university or first degree course, it nevertheless helps in determining the feasibility of study abroad.

The Association of Graduate Recruiters in the UK publishes a report on graduate salaries as compared to those of non-graduates, which reveals that UK graduates, on average, achieve a 50 per cent premium over non-graduates' earnings. QS research results suggest that the premium for graduate education spans all professional sectors and continues to increase as each further degree is added. The tables below provide average reported salaries across the EU and North America, at four stages of higher education; first degree, Masters, PhD and MBA.

First degree salaries vary significantly by industry sector. Consulting, financial services and banking pay the highest starting salaries – all three sectors exceed $50,000 average starting salaries. Manufacturing and retail report the lowest average graduate starting salaries in the range of $30-40,000 per annum.

Average reported salaries in EU and North America, at different levels of higher education

	First degree	Masters	PhD	MBA
Auto	$45,787	$59,167	$72,500	$92,575
Banking	$52,200	$60,559	$74,119	$91,235
Consulting	$56,700	$65,410	$80,743	$94,664
Financial Services	$54,130	$61,750	$76,670	$93,874
Government	$35,780	$43,100	$47,500	$82,500
Healthcare	$39,945	$43,706	$45,125	$91,332
Manufacturing	$33,730	$43,558	$51,967	$85,021
Retail	$37,873	$45,225	$46,450	$87,355
Technology	$46,330	$49,318	$54,380	$92,658

Copyright: QS Quacquarelli Symonds 2006

% Variation in EU and North American average salaries compared to first degree

	First degree	Masters	PhD	MBA
Auto	100%	129%	158%	202%
Banking	100%	116%	142%	175%
Consulting	100%	115%	142%	167%
Financial Services	100%	114%	142%	173%
Government	100%	120%	133%	231%
Healthcare	100%	109%	113%	229%
Manufacturing	100%	129%	154%	252%
Retail	100%	119%	123%	231%
Technology	100%	106%	117%	200%

Copyright: QS Quacquarelli Symonds 2006

What is revealing about this QS study is the premium employers place on further higher education: Masters, PhDs and MBAs. Masters degrees can achieve anything between a 6 per cent and 29 per cent premium on a first degree, with some of the lower paid sectors at first degree level — government and manufacturing — putting a premium on Masters degrees.

PhDs are no longer just a route to a professorship. Many employers actively seek to recruit PhDs and offer salary premiums. This QS research is one of the first studies to quantify this premium, which varies between 113 per cent and 158 per cent. The automotive industry offers the largest premium for PhDs, followed by manufacturing, banking and consulting.

A discussion of higher education salaries would not be complete without referring to the world's most popular postgraduate course, the MBA. Employers continue to place the greatest salary premium on the MBA qualification, with salaries of between 157 per cent and 252 per cent of equivalent first degree salaries. The sector with the highest average reported MBA salary is consulting, at over $94,000.

International career opportunities are booming

International graduates are seen as huge assets by international employers in many sectors — from knowledge-based industries like consulting and banking, to global industries like healthcare, consumer products and automotive, as well as governments seeking to establish a globally minded cadre of young administrators.

Many international employers now focus on building relationships with universities and business schools to target the crème de la crème of international graduates.

The most straightforward source of entry for international students into companies is through internship programmes. This allows employees to become familiar with the company and its cultures, and employers the opportunity to view the candidate at close hand, without having to complete all the formal visa requirements for full-time hiring.

Procter & Gamble (P&G) hires international graduates in most countries in which it operates. P&G has an extensive internship programme which often leads on to full-time hiring. P&G's diverse workforce demonstrates the multicultural nature of business in today's society and the opportunities for international graduates. "P&G, in 2005, had an amazingly diverse year in terms of international graduates" says Alexa Barker, their Director of Diversity. The UK and Ireland head office alone has staff from 73 different nationalities. P&G's holistic approach to operations - one reflected by many blue-chip companies - opens up a wealth of opportunity for international graduates. As an example of the success of this international policy, Ms Barker cites one team of 13 people — made up of 13 different nationalities — which was the company's most successful division last year.

Other companies will hire international graduates directly. Take, for example, DMS, who, in their own words, are "embracing the international market of young academics." This multinational manufacturing company based in the Netherlands, has, until recently, focused on recruiting Dutch-based nationals. However, this focus has now shifted towards the attraction of international graduates to help diversify their management population. DMS hire directly into their structured programmes, where employees have the opportunity to work in an international environment. "We are broadening our international talent population more than ever before. We want our graduate employees to grow to become tomorrow's executives," says Jackie Cuthbert, Vice President of Executive Resourcing.

For employers around the world in any industry, success ultimately lies in the skills of their workforces. In a world which is nowadays international by nature, occupational and life skills can be accrued through international student mobility. The importance of this mobility as perceived by governments is also evident, with schemes such as the Abraham Lincoln Study Abroad Act of 2006 implemented by the US Senate which calls for a national programme to study abroad. The programme will create fellowships and scholarships for individual students and establish partnerships with colleges and universities. The goal of the programme is to create and sustain annual growth rates to achieve one million students studying abroad annually by 2016-17.

Skills from international mobility

CIMO — the government education agency of Finland — carried out extensive research into employer attitudes towards international student mobility. In her report "Study on the relevance of international student mobility to work and employment", Irma Garam of CIMO summarises three benefits that international graduates can offer: occupational skills, personal growth and internationalisation. It is the combination of these three skill sets which is the attraction for employers.

Occupational skills relate to increased skills in the students' field of study, personal growth to such factors as cross-cultural communication skills, an understanding of local customers and cultures and the ability to deal well with new circumstances, while internationalisation represents the attributes that will allow them to operate in an international environment.

International graduates are expected to bring new energy, new ideas and concepts and tend to have a good all round business acumen. Irma Garam believes that "international experience gives students the self-confidence, the ability to survive, and other general skills highly valued in the labour market".

Ms Garam adds that "there is a strong belief amongst employers that studying abroad teaches students to handle different situations, gives them a broader perspective and a greater sense of proportion".

Proctor & Gamble agrees with the view that personal growth from international mobility is a valuable asset. "International candidates bring a good dimension to our workforce, which helps with our holistic approach. We do not expect and do not disadvantage those who do not have particular language experience in a particular country — we can offer them that with the job — and working with such global products, understanding of different cultures on the job will enable employees to pick up skills which will enable them to be transferred to our offices throughout the world", says Alexa Barker.

DSM focus on a European and Asia-Pacific drive where they forecast the most substantial business growth. Jackie Cuthbert at DSM says that the attractiveness of international graduates lies in their ability to translate local values on a global scale: "Employees who have studied or worked abroad bring with them an international mindset. Different geographies have different ways of doing business, and, as with all firms, we must ensure that our corporate values remain. Our graduate employees are able to work in a global marketplace, but with a cultural sensitivity that ensures our values stay true. They are much more business savvy than yesteryear."

The applicant view

QS also conducts surveys of international applicants for postgraduate study to identify their motivations and career aspirations. In 2006, over 7,400 postgraduate applicants responded to the survey. The applicant view in this section draws from this research.

What applicants expect from international mobility

Applicants have a variety of motivations for deciding to study abroad: learning and developing language skills, quality of institutions not available at home, courses not available at home, or simply the curiosity to have an overseas experience.

The QS Postgraduate Applicants Survey 2006 is the largest poll of international postgraduate candidates. What becomes abundantly clear is that most applicants seeking an international education at the Masters, PhD or MBA level are also seeking to gain work experience abroad, at least for a period of time.

Study abroad can certainly improve your employment prospects. It is ensuring that you apply yourself and your skills in the most effective way, and that you know where and how to find the opportunities that are paramount. It is also worth looking at what you expect in return, and how you feel that international mobility will aid your career development. Also important is how to convey your international experience as a valuable marketing tool for yourself. If an employer was torn between two like-for-like candidates, this could ultimately prove a deciding factor.

On job applications and in interviews, it is important to make the distinction that your choice to study abroad was a beneficial career decision and will add to your personal and occupational attributes. How did you decide upon your location? What skills have you learned that will help in your role? How have you grown on a personal level? And how did the placement tie in with your degree? In layman's terms, you need to prove that it has given you added value and was not just fulfilling your backpacking dream. It is a common desire for young people to want to travel, so it is important to stand out from the crowd and show what you have adopted and embraced from your time abroad.

Employer selection criteria

Within the QS Postgraduate Applicants Survey, "International opportunities" stands alongside "career progression", "job satisfaction" and "training and development" as the most important employer selection criteria for postgraduate applicants. The table below shows the percentage of respondents which rated each criteria as very important.

Criteria for selecting a postgraduate employer

Criteria	Rank	% Very important
Job Satisfaction	1	68
Training & Development	2	64
Career Progression	3	62
International Opportunities	4	61
Salary & Benefits	5	48
Job Type/Function	6	46
Corporate Ethics	7	36
Corporate Culture	8	32
Industry Sector	9	26

Copyright: QS Quacquarelli Symonds 2006

Industry preferences

The QS Postgraduate Applicants Survey also looks at the sectors which postgraduate applicants see as very attractive employment destinations, as shown in the table below. Consulting is consistently the most attractive sector with applicants around the world, followed by financial services. IT and telecommunications is the third most attractive sector.

Per cent of respondents seeking to work in specific sectors

Industry sector	Rank	% Very attractive
Consulting	1	49
Financial Services, Banking & Accounting	2	39
IT & Telecommunications	3	34
Industry & Engineering	4	31
Retail, Consumer Products & Media	5	26
Non-Profit & Public Sector	6	23
Other	7	22
Pharmaceuticals & Healthcare	8	13

Copyright: QS Quacquarelli Symonds 2006

There are variations in these results in different countries around the world. In North America, consulting was even more popular, appealing to 74 per cent of respondents. Financial services followed close behind in popularity. Respondents from Latin America also favoured consulting, but industry and engineering was second choice. In Western Europe financial services and accounting was the most popular career path, followed by consulting, then industry and engineering and then IT. By contrast, in Asia-Pacific, applicants favour a career in IT and telecommunications ahead of all other sectors.

The student/alumni view

Below are some real life examples of students and alumni who have benefited from study abroad and reflections on how it has helped in their personal and professional development.

A view from...

- An MSc from Macedonia, having studied in Kuwait and now at LSE
(BSc International Relations and History and MSc History of International Relations)

What are the benefits of studying overseas?
Learning from another culture/society is the greatest benefit, as many international students who return to their country with a positive impression may assume positions of responsibility in their government or society.

Why did you choose the UK to study?
I went to an international school in Kuwait which followed the British education system (GCSEs and A-levels), so it seemed natural to choose the UK. It was also significantly cheaper and quicker than studying in the US. Unfortunately with the current status of the situation in, and international opinion of my country, a degree from the UK (or US) seems to be valued and 'worth' more at home and internationally.

What skills have you brought away from your time abroad?
Meeting people from all over the world is a bonus to education and adds a whole new dimension to your thinking. You really begin to appreciate comparing different mentalities, traditions, politics, and the best method of crossing boundaries, as well as fostering international dialogue and consensus.

- A BA from Hong Kong, having studied at the University of Melbourne

(Now senior education consultant at the Australian Education Consultancy - University of New South Wales' Hong Kong office)

Since graduating, I have worked in different fields including banking and finance, and am now with the Australian Education Agency. The network I have built from my time abroad has really helped in my career. I have also learnt to become independent, multitasking and I am able to work in an English speaking environment.

- A graduate from Hong Kong, having studied Law at LSE

(Now a solicitor for an English law firm)

Why did you choose to study abroad?

My situation was unusual in the sense that I did not have a particular country where I was familiar with the education system, which I could call home. I spent 14 years in Seoul at an international school, then another year in Jakarta, again, at an international school. Home to me was either Seoul or Hong Kong. Due to my inexperience with the education system in Hong Kong (the only formal education I had ever received in Hong Kong was pre-school) my parents and I just assumed that I would continue abroad. Whilst the financial cost of studying abroad is obviously greater, my lack of experience combined with the general reputation of certain schools in the US and the UK helped me narrow my choices.

There is also the unquantifiable element of exposure which studying abroad is able to provide. (This I will not elaborate on as the benefits of free museums, cheap student theatre tickets and classmates from all over the world, are obvious).

Has your time abroad helped with your career?

Yes, the firm I work for is an English law firm which predominantly hires from Oxbridge, LSE, Kings and UCL. Whilst it is not impossible to obtain a job here, if I had graduated from Hong Kong University, it would have certainly been more difficult. That is the case with most of the English law firms in Hong Kong.

- A graduate from Argentina, having studied at Tufts in the USA and the University of Plymouth in the UK

(BA from Tufts, MSc in International Shipping from Plymouth, now President of an Argentine shipping company)

What are the benefits of studying overseas?
Without a doubt, the education system in the United Sates and the UK far excel any other in the world. In my line of work, the ability to communicate fluently in English is fundamental.

Has your time abroad helped with your career?
Studying abroad has helped me greatly in shipping. Being international in nature, the experience of studying and working with people from different parts of the world has been most beneficial.

Career benefits in a nutshell

Demand for international graduates is set to rise, with a particular emphasis on postgraduate degrees. Candidates graduating will generally be well remunerated, so this should not be an area of concern if you possess the sought after skills and attend a top university.

Having said this, do not expect to simply walk in to a great job just because you have qualified with a first degree, Masters or a PhD. Valid experience and other personal attributes must still fit in with the role.

Today's graduates live in a world of opportunity, but will face competition from other top graduates from around the world. So it is how you convey your skills and demonstrate your ability to apply them to the job at hand that will see you succeed.

The overriding view from employers is that if you have an excellent academic track record, your nationality is no barrier to your future employment. In fact, if you can demonstrate a real passion to work in an international environment, and bring with you the mindset and outlook that can help drive a business forward, you may be more attractive than locally educated graduates.

Tips for applying to university

Applying to your local university or an international institution is not something that should be taken lightly. The competitive world in which we live makes the process of application extremely significant for those who wish to enter the best and most suitable university for their own abilities. Whether you choose to apply to one of the world's top universities in the USA or a smaller college in Denmark, the time and effort you will need to invest into the application procedure is great. However, advice is available from various sources to make the process more manageable. Look to teachers, lecturers, careers counsellors, parents and current students who are all able to provide you with tips ahead of you submitting your application material. Any of them may be able to improve your chances of admission to your chosen university.

That said, with increasing competition, the need to make the best of your application becomes ever greater. The application form and related materials consist of a number of common elements, irrespective of the university you are applying to. Each of these elements plays a role in your admissions decision and as such should be considered individually to ensure that you submit a complete, well-rounded and thorough application. The following advice is intended to give you more of a background on what admissions staff would like and expect to see in a potential student's application material.

Application materials

Many systems of application require you to submit an application form and additional material alongside. This material can take many different forms, but generally includes attested or original copies of your academic results and qualifications; the results of any standardised tests that you might have to take such as IELTS **(www.ielts.org)** or TOEFL **(www.ets.org/toefl)**; an application fee; and one or more letter of recommendation. There are exceptions to this and the UK's UCAS service is the major one, with the emphasis on a single completed form and officially no opportunity to send additional material through the administrative process. Application material varies from system to system, but is universally important to provide admissions staff with as much information as possible to enable them to make an informed decision on the quality of your application. If you are unsure of exactly what material is required, contact the institution you are interested in to get the correct information.

The content of application forms tends to be consistent across all countries: details of your name, age, address, schooling, academic achievements − including those that have yet to provide results − and the programme of study that you are interested in. These sections require precision and honesty and are regarded by admissions staff as the most basic information that qualifies your application for further consideration. Many institutions today actually ask you to submit online application forms, so the need to remember to write legibly is no longer relevant, though the care you must take in completing this information is as important no matter how your application is submitted.

References

Depending on the system of education you are applying to and the individual university, "reference letters" or "letters of support" are expected to reinforce your academic record, what you have written about yourself and to help make a judgement on your potential to benefit from the programme of study that you have applied for. UK undergraduate programmes require one reference, whereas most US degrees require two and some Australian universities do not require any at all.

Two main issues arise concerning references: firstly, and in many ways most importantly, who actually writes your reference; and secondly, what the references should say about you as a student and as a person. Choosing someone to be a referee is an extremely important task and one that may have a significant impact on the success or failure of your application. Referees have to possess a good knowledge of you as a person and as a student, and as such be able to write in support of your application in a very honest, open and direct manner. Most universities expect to receive references from teachers, tutors or counsellors, though in some situations it will be relevant to ask your employer or someone that you have had contact with in another context, such as an extracurricular activity. Most members of admissions staff will not examine who the person actually is, though they will note the relationship between you and the referee. Rather they will focus on the content of the supporting comments and so there are no particular advantages in asking well-known people to be your referees. Above all else, those who write your references should know you well and be able to describe you in a way that reflects the best of your abilities and the qualities that make you unique. Comments on your academic and intellectual strengths are particularly important in the more competitive universities. At smaller institutions, your description of the way in which you work or interact with others may be particularly important.

The style in which a reference is written is very much dependent on the individual university. Many US institutions will provide a pro-forma reference sheet that allows referees to indicate your academic abilities in relation to those in your graduating class, for example. Others will allow a more free flowing approach, encouraging referees to express exactly what they feel about you as an applicant and a potential member of the university in question. In either case, guidelines are issued along with other application materials so that the people you choose to be your referees are fully aware of exactly what is to be expected from the admissions staff at the institution you are interested in.

Your references are important because they help give a flavour of you as an individual and separate you from other students with very similar entry qualifications. References that are written positively and informed with examples of your work, your activities or your characteristics are more likely to help your application be successful than those that are routine and simply list your attributes.

Statement of purpose and the application essays

All students intending to study at university will have heard countless stories about the importance of the statement of purpose or the application essay or essays. As one of the most talked about aspects of an application it is commonly and consistently the most misunderstood part of the application process and as such causes the greatest amount of concern.

One common concern is the simple identification of the purpose of such a piece of writing as an integral element of a university application. Irrespective of the country or university you wish to apply to, the opportunity to write about something at relative length is often the only chance you have to deviate from what is essentially a rather mundane and list-like process. In the USA, Canada and throughout Asia, this piece of writing is called the application essay and serves two purposes: firstly, to demonstrate your command of the written word in English and secondly to give an insight into you as a person. It is common for universities to pose you questions in their application essays such as "Describe the defining moment of your childhood", or less prosaically "Describe how a failure in your life made you a better person", so that admissions staff can learn about your personal qualities and the way in which you think and behave. More often than not, international students interested in applying to universities that operate this kind of "scenario-type" essay will not be asked for an interview and therefore this can serve the purpose of an "interview on paper". Many universities that favour this kind of approach will ask you to write a number of essays of this kind, thus making the effort needed to apply much greater than you might anticipate.

In other parts of the world, the approach is different. The UK, Australia, the Netherlands and other countries in Europe operate a more limited essay-type format for their applicants. In the UK, for example, this is known as a Personal Statement on the Universities and Colleges Admissions Service (UCAS) application form and allows a strict one page of A4 paper for the purpose. Because space is limited, the intention is to test the applicant to see whether they are able to express themselves in a succinct fashion, capturing the important aspects of their personality and interest in an individual academic subject area. Again, because few of these universities will be in a position to interview you, admissions staff will want to see a blend of what makes you unique and what kind of contribution you will give to your chosen programme of study or university. What to include in this kind of essay is very difficult indeed and requires a lengthy period of preparation before you submit the finished piece of writing. Some universities will expect you to demonstrate knowledge of their programmes or reputation, while others will want you to exhibit strong extracurricular interests to complement your academic record. The only way of knowing what the right approach is for your application is by contacting the admissions staff of the university you are interested in and asking what they expect.

As a national or international student, the importance of the application essay cannot be underestimated. Different universities view the importance, however, in quite unique ways. Some, for example the most competitive universities in Australia, the UK and the USA, use this extended piece of writing as the defining element that separates applications from one another and ensures that some are accepted while others are rejected. This is certainly the case where many applications are received from students with very similar academic records and there is no alternative but to use other measures to select. Other universities, for example those smaller institutions in Europe and the USA with limited student numbers and applications, focus a great deal of their recruitment and admissions effort on the assessment of applications through the extended piece of writing. Why does this happen? With smaller institutions, the emphasis is often on building a particular community or atmosphere on campus and so how different individuals might be able to contribute is extremely important.

Your approach to writing one of these extended elements of an application, irrespective of the institution you are applying to, is important. It goes without saying that honesty in all that you commit to paper is essential. It is not uncommon for students to inflate their achievements or interests, only to have them questioned by a member of admissions staff via email or telephone contact, bringing their entire application into doubt. Many of the more complex "scenario-type" essays require a great deal of preparation and thought and should not be undertaken lightly. Your school or college counsellor may well be an excellent resource for you to use in order for you to develop a coherent argument in one of these essays, allowing you to draft a number of versions so that the final result reflects not only your character but also your best effort. The shorter kind of essays or personal statements will expect you to balance concrete examples of your interest in the academic subject area you are applying for as well as demonstrating that you have qualities outside of the classroom that the institution would benefit from. As a general rule, irrespective of the kind of essays expected, you should be confident that once written your friends reading your statement would be able to both recognise you and be interested in learning a little more!

Interviews

Twenty years ago it was very common for many of the world's top universities to insist on interviewing all likely candidates by asking then to attend a face-to-face session at the actual place of study. With more students choosing to leave their home country and study abroad, however, the area of interviews as part of the application process has become more complicated. Many universities recognise that it is often unreasonable to expect candidates to fly overseas for an interview in addition to the potentially high tuition fees they will have to pay when accepted, and have now abandoned the practice.

Some institutions, however, continue to interview applicants because they believe it is the fairest way of selecting the most appropriate students for their programmes. Occasionally this will require you to fly to the university, at your own expense, to undergo one or more interviews as part of your application. In many other cases, the institution is willing to travel to you for the purpose of interview, conducted either by admissions or international staff, or often by local alumni who have already graduated from the institution in question.

Depending on the institution, the purpose of the interview is to make a final selection based on the material you have already submitted as part of your application. Interviews can focus on a number of areas, including the subject that you have applied for, your extracurricular interests or the reasons behind wanting to come and study at that particular university. In an interview, an institution tends to be looking for a number of qualities in your answers that indicate that you would be an asset to them. A passion for and knowledge of your academic subject is a crucial first area that they will be looking for. Secondly, they will want to see that you have the ability to think independently and critically, and grasp complex or new issues should they be raised in the discussion. Thirdly, they will want to assess whether you are a good fit for their environment and, finally, they will want to assess your confidence and your all round abilities.

Preparing for an interview is not always easy and you will be guided by staff at the institution as to what they will expect from you. Where you are given the opportunity to meet admissions or other staff, make sure that you are sure of the reasons for your application, your own unique qualities and what you might be able to bring to the university.

Deadlines

Irrespective of what and where you wish to study it is essential that you are fully aware of all deadlines that are relevant to your application process. In almost all country's systems of education, whether the application process is managed by a central administrative service (as is the case in the UK) or direct with a university, deadlines exist for all or certain categories of students. All institutions publish these deadlines at least one year in advance and make the consequences of missing any of these dates very clear to all applicants. Deadlines really are what they indicate — the very last line passed which you cannot move. Many institutions around the world will simply not review your application if it is received after the published date — a terrible situation if all of the other elements of your application are very strong and would normally qualify you for a place.

The timing of your application can have a significant impact on whether you are successful or not. In many of the very popular programmes, such as economics, law and management, the earlier you submit a completed application the better your chances are if you have met the minimum entry requirements. Similarly, in the most popular universities programmes fill up quickly and so applications received early can increase their chances of a positive decision. This situation obviously varies from country to country, but underlines the position that submitting application material early is beneficial to you.

Applying to university can take more than a year in some cases and the preparation of all of your material can take some time. Within the application process there is never one single area that is more important than any other. Applications to all universities tend to be regarded in a very holistic sense and, as such, your preparation must be thorough and consistent to ensure that all of the elements are your best efforts and reflect your highest standards.

Opening doors, creating opportunities

Your life, your skills, your future

IELTS is the International English Language Testing System.
If you want to study or work in a country where English is the language of communication, IELTS is vital in preparing you for your future. It's designed so you can prove your English language skills, helping you open doors to international opportunities.

- IELTS is the original four-skills English language test. You can be sure that an IELTS score tests and demonstrates your true ability to communicate in English across all four language skills – Listening, Reading, Writing and Speaking.

- IELTS is truly an international English language test which reflects and respects international diversity.

- IELTS scores are trusted and recognised by over 4000 educational institutions, government agencies, employers and professional organisations worldwide as proof of candidates' English language proficiency.

- IELTS is the preferred English language test for many educational institutions worldwide. The prestigious Duke University Graduate School in the U.S. mentions on their website that IELTS is their preferred English proficiency test.

- IELTS is easily accessible for candidates worldwide. It is available up to 4 times a month in over 300 locations across the world.

- IELTS results are available 13 days after taking the test. Institutions can also access test results instantly though our online E Downloads service.

- Visit us at **www.ielts.org** to find your nearest test centre and use our Global Recognition System to search for institutions worldwide recognising IELTS.

www.ielts.org

What parents need to know — a guide to study costs and more

Introduction

With over 4,000 universities in the world and 17 million students, it is no surprise that the availability and take up of higher education differs greatly in countries around the world, as do the relative costs of study and living. Smart students and parents today can shop around to look for the best value education, which fits within a career strategy.

The importance of degree education for future employment prospects can be seen in unemployment figures. According to Dr. Ramu Damodaran of the United Nations Department for Public Information, 80 per cent of the world's 18–24 year olds are unemployed. Yet for those with a university degree, the figure is less than 10 per cent.

For any prospective students and their parents, it is important to know and understand the costs, as well as the quality, of educational institutions so that you can budget and make the best choice. You will generally face both tuition and living costs that can vary quite dramatically throughout the world.

Where will my money go?

One of the first questions on the lips of anyone who is planning to study abroad in the 21st century — students and parents alike — is "how much will it cost?". Investing in higher education is probably the most important personal investment of any individual's life. Having to study hard for several years and accumulate significant debt may seem a bad bargain, but when you review the career options for today's graduates, within this book, it becomes apparent that a good degree is almost priceless.

The world of higher education is changing. Ron Perkinson of the International Finance Corporation (World Bank) describes the "perfect storm of forces changing the shape of international education — increased importance of knowledge and credentials in the employment market, demographic increases in numbers of young people aged 18—24 around the world, reduced government funding and globalisation."

These forces are creating many changes, but the overwhelming change is that university education is no longer going to be free for many people in their home markets. Free university education is a thing of the past. As a consequence, many young people are shopping overseas for the best deals — not necessarily the lowest cost, but the best price for a given quality. These will vary according to the type of programme that is chosen, the country of choice, the length of stay, as well as other factors that can be seen in the World University Rankings, which provide a guide to institutional quality — although there are many other indicators that should also be taken into account.

Comparison of international study costs

Most institutions today are either charging, or about to introduce charges, for tuition. Private universities have charged tuition fees for many years, but in most countries public universities have recently or will soon be introducing tuition fees.

The table opposite shows average international tuition costs amongst all 500 plus universities featured in this guide, organised on a country basis. It provides a quick basis for comparison for prospective students and parents considering study abroad.

Comparison of international study costs

	Average undergraduate fees (US $)	Average postgraduate fees (US $)
Argentina	$2,250	$2,294
Australia	$11,362	$11,333
Austria	$472	$472
Belgium	$3,290	$3,993
Canada	$4,873	$3,736
Chile	$3,336	$2,725
China	$535	$343
Denmark	$10,671	$7,402
Finland	$0	$0
France	$1,038	$2,690
Hong Kong	$6,756	$7,652
Indonesia	$1,288	$1,125
Ireland	$16,870	$8,918
Israel	$1,675	$1,900
Italy	$798	$762
Japan	$2,192	$1,707
Malaysia	$994	$1,155
Mexico	$3,483	$3,390
Netherlands	$4,702	$6,648
New Zealand	$9,339	$7,289
Norway	$0	$0
Portugal	$502	$940
Russia	$1,600	$8,861
Singapore	$4,220	$5,300
South Africa	$2,775	$2,550
South Korea	$1,631	$545
Spain	$1,006	$1,126
Sweden	$0	$0
Switzerland	$769	$1,111
Thailand	$2,091	$736
United Kingdom	$13,761	$13,749
United States	$19,656	$19,525

The US has the highest average tuition fees for undergraduates and postgraduates. Public universities have average tuition fees of $13,500 per annum (in-state tuition fees are lower), but private universities are more expensive producing an average of $19,600 across all universities.

In Singapore, average tuition is $13,500. However, if a student is accepted they will be eligible for a Ministry of Education grant worth $9,000 if they sign a deed of covenant agreeing to work in Singapore for three years after graduation, reducing the net cost to approximately $4,500.

Public universities in Western Europe have fees of approximately 600 per year, which are available to domestic and international students in some countries. Several Nordic countries – Finland, Norway, Sweden - do not charge tuition fees for domestic or international students, though this policy is under review and fees are expected to be introduced in 2008.

The UK is more expensive than its European counterparts. University tuition costs an average $5,600 per year for domestic students and an average $13,700 for international students. In the UK, tuition fees are dependent upon your personal circumstances including family income. According to AimHigher, the government backed website for higher education, 30,000 international students begin under-graduate courses each year in the UK, the vast majority of who are full fee paying students.

The popularity of the UK as an international study destination is demonstrated by a recent report from the Norwegian Embassy. Norway and Iceland top the list of countries providing the most students abroad relative to the population. In 2005 there were 21,484 Norwegian students at foreign universities, with the UK as the top choice with 2,905 studying full-time in the UK in 2005 and an additional 530 students returning to the UK to complete parts of their studies, i.e. via exchange programmes.

Comparison of course fees at the top 200 universities

In each country there are private universities which typically charge higher fees than public universities. Our top 200 universities consist of both private and public institutions, explaining the wide variation in fees even within countries.

Not surprisingly, many of the most expensive universities in the world are the US private institutions which appear at the top of our rankings.

The fees below have been provided in telephone interviews with administrators at each opposite and corroborated through published information on websites. Fees can vary for different programme types. For example, many professional postgraduate degrees are more expensive than the averages quoted and, likewise, other courses are less expensive.

Tuition fees for international students

2006 rank	University	Country	Average undergraduate fees (US $)	Average postgraduate fees (US $)
1	Harvard University	United States	$27,448	$27,488
2	University of Cambridge	United Kingdom	$18,559	$18,559
3	University of Oxford	United Kingdom	$28,840	$23,707
4=	Massachusetts Institute of Technology	United States	$30,600	$30,600
4=	Yale University	United States	$29,820	$26,800
6	Stanford University	United States	$29,847	$29,847
7	California Institute of Technology	United States	$25,355	$25,355
8	University of California, Berkeley	United States	$16,476	$14,694
9	Imperial College London	United Kingdom	$25,570	$25,760
10	Princeton University	United States	$29,910	$29,910
11	University of Chicago	United States	$30,123	$31,680
12	Columbia University	United States	$30,260	$30,532
13	Duke University	United States	$29,770	$29,350
14	Peking University	China	$641	–
15	Cornell University	United States	$30,000	$30,000
16	Australian National University	Australia	$14,000	$16,000
17	London School of Economics and Political Science	United Kingdom	$20,874	$29,326
18	Ecole Normale Supérieure	France	–	–
19=	National University of Singapore	Singapore	$4,240	$3,575
19=	University of Tokyo	Japan	–	–
21	McGill University	Canada	$11,900	$8,500

2006 rank	University	Country	Average undergraduate fees (US $)	Average postgraduate fees (US $)
22	University of Melbourne	Australia	$8,900	$13,200
23	Johns Hopkins University	United States	$30,140	$30,140
24	ETH Zurich	Switzerland	$961	$961
25	University College London	United Kingdom	$23,051	$25,190
26	University of Pennsylvania	United States	$27,544	$29,386
27	University of Toronto	Canada	$2,840	$10,700
28	Tsing Hua University	China	$641	$2,051
29=	Kyoto University	Japan	$4,600	$4,600
29=	University of Michigan	United States	$25,840	$27,124
31	University of California, Los Angeles	United States	$16,476	$14,694
32	University of Texas at Austin	United States	$12,960	$11,952
33=	University of Edinburgh	United Kingdom	$19,819	$19,819
33=	University of Hong Kong	Hong Kong	$9,000	$16,300
35=	Carnegie Mellon University	United States	$30,650	$28,200
35=	University of Sydney	Australia	$21,000	$18,000
37	École Polytechnique	France	$8,973	$12,818
38	Monash University	Australia	$15,900	$15,600
39	University of Geneva	Switzerland	$820	$820
40	University of Manchester	United Kingdom	$19,011	$19,011
41	University of New South Wales	Australia	$14,920	$15,330
42	Northwestern University	United States	$29,940	$29,940
43	New York University	United States	$28,328	$23,304

Rank	University	Country		
44	University of California, San Diego	United States	$16,476	$14,694
45	University of Queensland	Australia	-	-
46=	University of Auckland	New Zealand	$12,380	$13,830
46=	King's College London	United Kingdom	$21,859	$20,129
48=	University of Rochester	United States	$28,250	$28,250
48=	Washington University in St. Louis	United States	$29,700	$29,700
50=	University of British Colombia	Canada	-	-
50=	Chinese University of Hong Kong	Hong Kong	$10,300	$5,420
52	Sciences Po Paris	France	$1,170	$641
53	Vanderbilt University	United States	$29,240	$29,240
54=	Brown University	United States	$30,672	$30,672
54=	University of Copenhagen	Denmark	$13,972	$13,972
56	Emory University	United States	$28,940	$27,770
57	Indian Institute of Technology	India	-	$4,157
58=	Ruprecht-Karls-Universität Heidelberg	Germany	$0	-
58=	Hong Kong University of Science & Technology	Hong Kong	-	-
60	Case Western Reserve University	United States	$26,500	$25,400
61=	Dartmouth College	United States	$30,279	$30,279
61=	Nanyang Technological University	Singapore	$4,200	$9,700
63	Seoul National University	South Korea	$2,734	$3,269
64=	University of Bristol	United Kingdom	$28,517	$24,904
64=	Ecole Polytechnique Fédérale de Lausanne	Switzerland	$1,038	$20,073
66	Boston University	United States	$29,988	$29,988
67	Eindhoven University of Technology	Netherlands	$1,918	$10,254

2006 rank	University	Country	Average undergraduate fees (US $)	Average postgraduate fees (US $)
68	Indian Institute of Management	India	–	–
69	University of Amsterdam	Netherlands	–	–
70=	School of Oriental and African Studies	United Kingdom	$19,011	$19,011
70=	Osaka University	Japan	$4,670	$4,670
72	Ecole Normale Supérieure Lyon	France	$200	$320
73	University of Warwick	United Kingdom	$19,011	$19,011
74	Universidad Nacional Autónoma de México	Mexico	$450	$1,000
75	University of Basel	Switzerland	–	–
76	Catholic University of Louvain	Belgium	$6,665	$6,665
77	University of Illinois	United States	$16,108	$15,362
78	University of Dublin, Trinity College	Ireland	$19,515	$14,472
79=	University of Otago	New Zealand	$9,740	$10,400
79=	University of Wisconsin	United States	$19,254	$22,978
81	University of Glasgow	United Kingdom	$17,870	$19,296
82=	Macquarie University	Australia	$13,500	$18,100
82=	Technische Universität München	Germany	–	–
84	University of Washington	United States	$17,400	$17,300
85	University of Nottingham	United Kingdom	$19,334	$19,334
86	Delft University of Technology	Netherlands	$2,201	$7,632
87	University of Vienna	Austria	–	–
88	University of Pittsburgh	United States	$19,500	$24,824
89	University of Lausanne	Switzerland	$955	$11,107

90=	University of Birmingham	United Kingdom	$18,060	$18,060
90=	Leiden University	Netherlands	$1,923	$14,100
92	Erasmus University Rotterdam	Netherlands	$13,138	$13,138
93=	Lomonosov Moscow State University	Russia	–	–
93=	Université Pierre-et-Marie-Curie	France	$208	$320
95	Utrecht University	Netherlands	$9,614	$9,614
96	Catholic University of Leuven	Belgium	$6,409	$6,409
97	Wageningen University	Netherlands	$5,512	–
98	Ludwig-Maximilians-Universität München	Germany	$1,521	$1,025
99=	Queen Mary, University of London	United Kingdom	$18,232	$18,232
99=	Pennsylvania State University	United States	$29,910	$16,654
101	University of Southern California	United States	$29,988	$24,240
102=	Georgetown University	United States	$29,808	$27,528
102=	Rice University	United States	$18,863	$25,600
102=	University of Sheffield	United Kingdom	$17,965	$15,399
105=	University of Adelaide	Australia	$13,700	$13,500
105=	Humboldt-Universität zu Berlin	Germany	$0	$0
105=	University of Sussex	United Kingdom	$15,855	$18,218
108	National Taiwan University	Taiwan	$915	$1,046
109=	University of St Andrews	United Kingdom	$20,057	$20,152
109=	University of Zurich	Switzerland	$1,298	$475
111=	University of Maryland	United States	$17,500	$12,618
111=	Uppsala University	Sweden	$0	–
111=	Wake Forest University	United States	$28,210	$24,475

2006 rank	University	Country	Average undergraduate fees (US $)	Average postgraduate fees (US $)
111=	University of Western Australia	Australia	$15,700	$13,800
115	University of Twente	Netherlands	$5,640	$9,357
116=	Fudan University	China	$641	$1,282
116=	University of Helsinki	Finland	$0	$0
118	Tokyo Institute of Technology	Japan	$4,670	$4,670
119	Hebrew University of Jerusalem	Israel	$2,275	$2,275
120	Keio University	Japan	$9,000	$6,700
121	University of Leeds	United Kingdom	$25,475	$25,475
122	Lund University	Sweden	$0	$0
123	University of North Carolina	United States	$16,303	$16,661
124=	University of Massachusetts, Amherst	United States	$9,937	$9,937
124=	University of York	United Kingdom	$18,593	$18,593
126	University of Aarhus	Denmark	$15,638	$15,638
127	Purdue University	United States	$16,867	$18,980
128=	Kyushu University	Japan	–	–
128=	Nagoya University	Japan	$4,600	$4,600
130=	Tufts University	United States	$30,377	$30,982
130=	University of Virginia	United States	$21,172	$18,672
132	University of Durham	United Kingdom	$18,735	$18,735
133=	University of Alberta	Canada	$13,800	$5,900
133=	Vrije University Brussels	Belgium	$647	$1,288
133=	Hokkaido University	Japan	–	–

Rank	University	Country		
133=	University of Newcastle upon Tyne	United Kingdom	$18,726	$17,167
137	Radboud Universiteit Nijmegen	Netherlands	$3,365	$8,716
138	Vienna University of Technology	Austria	$1,461	$1,461
139	University of Liverpool	United Kingdom	$16,825	$18,060
140	Cranfield University	United Kingdom	–	–
141=	University of California, Santa Barbara	United States	$16,476	$14,694
141=	Cardiff University	United Kingdom	$17,937	$17,937
141=	University of Ghent	Belgium	$647	$647
141=	University of Southampton	United Kingdom	$18,156	$18,156
145	Georgia Institute of Technology	United States	$20,272	$20,244
146	RMIT University	Australia	$12,800	$13,700
147=	Chalmers University of Technology	Sweden	$0	$0
147=	Tel Aviv University	Israel	$1,880	$2,550
149	Freie Universität Berlin	Germany	$0	$0
150=	Korea University	South Korea	$7,178	$8,698
150=	Texas A&M University	United States	$11,415	$10,284
152	University of Notre Dame	United States	$29,070	$28,970
153	University of Bath	United Kingdom	$19,011	$19,011
154	City University of Hong Kong	Hong Kong	$7,725	$10,815
155	McMaster University	Canada	$9,600	$10,600
156=	Curtin University of Technology	Australia	–	–
156=	Georg-August-Universität Tübingen	Germany	$1,730	$1,730
158=	Technion – Israel Institute of Technology	Israel	$2,363	$3,070
158=	Universität Ulm	Germany	–	–

2006 rank	University	Country	Average undergraduate fees (US $)	Average postgraduate fees (US $)
158=	Waseda University	Japan	$8,800	$7,900
161=	Chulalongkorn University	Thailand	$8,145	$9,402
161=	Université Louis Pasteur – Strasbourg I	France	-	-
163	Michigan State University	United States	$17,336	$15,168
164	Saint-Petersburg State University	Russia	-	-
165=	Université Libre de Bruxelles	Belgium	$8,011	$8,011
165=	University of Science and Technology of China	China	$2,500	$3,800
165=	State University of New York at Stony Brook	United States	$10,610	$10,920
168=	George Washington University	United States	$34,000	$15,768
168=	Tohoku University	Japan	-	-
170=	University of California, Davis	United States	$16,476	$14,694
170=	Eberhard Karls Universität Tübingen	Germany	$1,282	$1,282
172=	Rheinisch-Westfälische Technische Hochschule Aachen	Germany	$1,282	$1,282
172=	University of Maastricht	Netherlands	$7,691	$10,254
172=	Royal Institute of Technology	Sweden	$0	$0
172=	Yeshiva University	United States	$22,200	$22,178
176	Queen's University	Canada	$13,775	$10,185
177	University of Oslo	Norway	$0	$0
178	University of Bern	Switzerland	$1,077	$327
179	Shanghai Jiao Tong University	China	$641	$1,400
180	Nanjing University	China	$590	$897
181=	Kobe University	Japan	-	-

Rank	University	Country		
181=	University of Montreal	Canada	-	-
183=	Jawaharlal Nehru University	India	-	-
183=	Free University of Amsterdam	Netherlands	$2,350	$10,575
185	Universiti Kebangsaan Malaysia	Malaysia	-	-
186	University of Innsbruck	Austria	$897	$897
187=	Brandeis University	United States	$30,160	$30,160
187=	Johann Wolfgang Goethe Universität Frankfurt	Germany	-	-
187=	University of Minnesota	United States	$12,320	$15,272
190=	University of Barcelona	Spain	$913	$2,692
190=	University of Reading	United Kingdom	$18,441	$21,863
192=	University of Malaya	Malaysia	$874	$2,488
192=	Queensland University of Technology	Australia	$12,400	$13,200
194	Technical University of Denmark	Denmark	$0	$0
195	University of Aberdeen	United Kingdom	$18,330	$18,330
196	University of Wollongong	Australia	$13,000	$16,700
197	Università degli Studi di Roma - La Sapienza	Italy	$974	$923
198=	University of California, Irvine	United States	$16,476	$14,694
198=	Korea Advanced Institute of Science & Technology	South Korea	$5,600	$7,200
200	Université Paris-Sorbonne (Paris IV)	France	-	-

Study costs do vary considerably throughout the world, which could play a part in your choice of university. Looking at the World University Rankings will help put these costs in perspective relative to the course and institution.

Comparison of living costs

In addition to tuition fees, you will need to take into consideration a variety of costs when budgeting and deciding on where to study. The living costs of moving abroad, or even moving out of the family home to study at a domestic university, will form a large part of your expenditure. You will often find, especially with US institutions, that they collate these variables into a single figure — so as a student, or as a parent, it is vital to research what costs are included in quoted figures and what additional costs will be incurred. These costs include essentials such as accommodation, food, travel and study books. It is also important to remember that exchange rates will fluctuate, affecting your budget.

So how can you find out about these costs of living? Where is the most expensive place to study? And where can you afford?

There are numerous public sources and publications providing you with tables of the costs of living throughout the world. These tend to have slightly varied results, as differing criteria is used for each, but they generally give an equal overall "big picture", so browsing any of the widely published ones will give you a good idea of the expenses you may face.

World's ten most expensive cities

2006	2005	Country	2006	2005	Country
1	(3)	Oslo	6	(5)	Copenhagen
2	(1)	Tokyo	7	(7)	London
3	(8)	Reykjavik	8	(6)	Zurich
4	(2)	Osaka Kobe	9	(8)	Geneva
5	(4)	Paris	10	(10)	Helsinki

Source: February 2006 Economist Intelligence Unit

According to the Economist Intelligence Unit, Oslo this year took over as the world's most expensive city, replacing Tokyo's 14 year stint at the top. This follows the trend of eight of the priciest locations being in Europe, while the US has dropped significantly — their highest city being New York in 27th place.

Although these listings can act as a guide to the cost of study abroad, they are merely that, and actual costs will also be dependent upon your lifestyle and ability to budget. Salaries are likely to be commensurate to the costs, so a part-time job could be a solution, and one that is becoming a trend. A recent Royal Bank of Scotland survey published by the BBC shows that students in the UK work an average of 16 hours a week (with 20 per cent doing more than 20 hours), and almost half of the UK's students take on part-time work in term time, in a £2.3bn a year industry.

You are, however, not just comparing like for like goods, as different cultures will encourage you to spend in different ways, and student environments usually have lower cost accommodation, restaurants, sports facilities and entertainment, than the city as a whole. In many cities, students are also eligible for large concessions on transport and other items. Reading online blogs and real-life accounts can give a more real picture of the costs you may face.

Another good way to compare living costs is the Big Mac index – which measures the purchasing power parity (PPP) between two currencies and provides a basis for showing how market exchange rates affect a similar basket of goods (e.g. a Big Mac hamburger) in different countries.

Country	Big Mac price local currency	Big Mac price US dollars	Over(+)/under(–) valuation % against the dollar
Argentina	Peso 7.00	2.25	-27.23
Australia	A$3.25	2.45	-20.87
Brazil	Real6.40	2.96	-4.69
Britain	Sterling1.94	3.65	+17.59
Canada	C$3.52	3.15	+1.94
China	Yuan10.50	1.32	-57.39
Euro area	Euro2.94	3.74	+21.00
Hong Kong	HK$12.00	1.54	-50.27
Hungary	Forint 560	2.60	-15.95
Indonesia	Rupiah14,600	1.60	-48.52
Japan	¥250	2.13	-31.44
Malaysia	M$5.50	1.49	-52.05
Mexico	Peso29.0	2.64	-14.96
New Zealand	NZ$4.45	2.92	-5.35
Poland	Zloty6.50	2.08	-32.70
Russia	Rouble48.00	1.79	-42.13
Singapore	s$3.60	2.28	-26.48
South Africa	Rand13.95	1.89	-38.92
South Korea	Won2,500	2.58	-16.85
Sweden	Skr33.0	4.54	+45.80
Switzerland	SFr6.30	5.04	+62.44
Taiwan	NT$75.00	2.28	-26.47
Thailand	Baht60.0	1.61	-48.09
United States	$3.10	3.10	–

Source: The Economist – 25th March 2006 Big Mac Prices

As a general rule, the cost of living is higher where the US dollar is weak relative to the local currency and vice versa. In most of Asia living costs are low in dollar terms, with currencies being undervalued against the dollar from -16.9 per cent in South Korea to -57.4 per cent in China. Central Europe also has low living costs in dollar terms, with Poland undervalued at –30.7 per cent and Russia at –42.1 per cent. Latin America shows quite a substantial variation in its rating of countries compared to other regions, with Brazil only slightly undervalued by –4.7 per cent, whilst Argentina is undervalued by -27.2 per cent.

At the other end of the spectrum, Britain has a high cost of living in dollar terms being overvalued by 17.5 per cent, and the Euro area is even more expensive, being overvalued by 21.0 per cent. Heading the list, the Nordic countries are the most costly region in which to live, with Sweden overvalued by 45.8 per cent.

So what does all of this mean?

Broadly speaking, study in developed countries will be more costly than in developing countries. However, the reputation of universities, as exemplified by the World University Rankings, tends to far outweigh study and living costs, when people make their study choices.

Few students choose to move from developed countries to study in developing countries. By contrast, huge numbers of students from developing countries choose to study abroad, due to the comparative increased quality of education away from their homeland. Indeed, the UNESCO Institute of Statistics' (UIS) Global Education Digest 2006 reports that tertiary students from sub-Saharan Africa are the most mobile in the world, with 5.6 per cent studying abroad, while at the other end of the scale, only one out of every 250 North American students (0.4 per cent) studies overseas, making this group the least mobile.

Costs will vary according to your destination country, the type and length of your programme, and what is included in the programme cost, as well as further costs which may include your passport, visa, airfare, medical costs, transportation, meals, books, insurance and accommodation, to name but a few.

However, do not let these facts scare you off. They are mostly costs you would encounter at home, and the extra ones involved will generally be worth it, especially with the financial aid available and the fact that you will more than likely be remunerated upon employment (see What Career? Benefits of a top degree). The true cost of your study will be dependent upon a multitude of factors as discussed, and this value is part of the overall acclimatisation of studying abroad.

Financing and scholarships for overseas study

How do people pay for their studies?

For 18 year olds about to embark on their first degree, the answer is often that parents pick up the bill. QS recently surveyed 4000 applicants to university graduate schools around the world and for those with no work experience, parents and scholarships were the most usual sources of funding.

However a rapidly growing proportion of graduate students around the world return to university after a period of work experience. These students are willing to use their personal savings and loans from global financial institutions to fund their study abroad. In fact, worldwide 70 per cent of respondents in the QS applicant survey reported that they would use personal savings or loans to fund their studies.

Below we look at scholarships and funding available on a country by country basis. But there are several international bodies which provide scholarships around the world.

The Rotary Foundation is one of the largest scholarship providers. Since 1947 nearly 37,000 men and women from 100 nations have studied abroad under the Ambassadorial Scholarships programme. Today it is the world's largest privately funded international scholarships programme. Nearly 800 scholarships were awarded for study in 2005-06, totalling approximately US$500 million, for undergraduate and graduate students as well as for qualified professionals pursuing vocational studies. While abroad, scholars serve as ambassadors of goodwill to the people of the host country and give presentations about their homelands to Rotary clubs and other groups. Upon returning home, scholars share with Rotarians and others the experiences that led to greater understanding of their host countries. (www.rotary.org/foundation/educational/amb_scho/)

The Ford Foundation provides an International Fellowship Programme for PhDs and other potential leaders, targeting individuals in countries without systematic access to higher education. (www.iie.org)

The Bill and Melinda Gates Foundation, although primarily concerned with disease control, also funds some educational scholarships through partnerships with specific universities. The foundation awards "Millennium Scholarships" to promising students who don't have the financial means to attend college.

Do top universities provide scholarships to overseas students?

Almost all universities featured in this guide offer scholarships for international students.

Are loans available for overseas study?

Banks are geared towards providing student loans for domestic study in most countries of the world, but they can be more wary about funding overseas study. There is a risk that candidates will not return home and it will prove difficult to collect the loan outstanding. In order for a bank to provide such a loan, they may well ask for some form of parental guarantee — which at least avoids the need for parents to have the cash ready and available from day one.

In the US, FedMoney.org is the most comprehensive FREE full-text online resource on all US government grants and student financial aid programmes. There are Federal Direct Student loans and federal Family Student Loans for people seeking to study within the US. Sallie Mae offers loan facilities for people to study abroad and at home, for undergraduate and graduate studies. (www.salliemae.com)

In addition there are private loan providers who will underwrite high potential candidates who meet selection criteria (usually based on acceptance to a top tier institution).

In Europe most of the major banks provide student loans, but will require some form of guarantees for study abroad. The UK is probably the most mature market in this respect. By contrast, in Germany banks are still getting used to the idea of student loans and are only just beginning to offer these types of products.

Are scholarships available for study in the US and Canada?

An attraction for international students is the large number of scholarships and financial aid packages available at the many well-endowed universities in the US. Despite this large availability of scholarships, competition is fierce. The World Bank estimates that 70 per cent of foreign students in the US pay full fees.

The US also offers the most sophisticated financial support, being able to offer discounted rates for delayed payment and other solutions to meet needs of people with lesser means. Many US universities' financial aid departments ask for a statement of your family's financial situation. If they decide that your family can only contribute $1,000 per year that is all you will have to pay — if they want you. Alternatively they may have international student loan schemes.

There are, however, many charitable bodies which can provide partial scholarships. The most prominent provider of scholarships is the Fulbright Commission. The Fulbright Program supports educational exchanges at the graduate level that strengthen understanding and communication between the United States and over 140 countries. The work of the programme is developed and facilitated by the US Department of State and binational Fulbright Commissions and US embassies overseas. Selection is carried out in the student's home country with applications via the local Fulbright office. **(www.fulbright.org)**

There are also a large number of corporate sponsored scholarship schemes for study in the US. For example, the Adobe Multi-National Scholarship Program, funded by Adobe Systems, provides scholarship awards to meritorious secondary school students attending a post-secondary degree programme in business, design studies, education, engineering, graphic art, graphic design, maths or sciences and who need financial assistance to achieve their educational goals. **(www.iie.org/wcoast/adobe.html)** USAID provides scholarships for women in technology, sponsored by CISCO. **(details available at www.iie.org/wcoast/wit.html)**

Are scholarships available for study in the UK?
The British Council provides a comprehensive website of scholarships available on a university by university basis in the UK. **(www.educationuk.com)** Oxford University offers Rhodes Scholarships, while the Bill and Melinda Gates Foundation has funded numerous scholarships at Cambridge.

In addition there are the Chevening Scholarships which are available for outstanding applicants to British institutions. These scholarships, funded by the Foreign and Commonwealth Office, enable overseas students to study in the United Kingdom.

Scholarships are offered in over 150 countries and enable talented graduates and young professionals to become familiar with the UK and gain skills which will benefit their countries. The Chevening programme currently provides around 2,300 new scholarships each year for postgraduate studies or research at UK Institutions of Higher Education. **(www.chevening.com)**

Marshall Scholarships finance young Americans of high ability to study for a degree in the United Kingdom. At least 40 scholars are selected each year to study either at graduate or occasionally undergraduate level at an UK institution in any field of study. Each scholarship is held for two years.

The Association of Commonwealth universities **(www.acu.ac.uk)** provides the Commonwealth Scholarship and Fellowship Plan. The plan was designed as a system of awards to men and women from all Commonwealth countries chosen for their high intellectual promise and their capacity to return to make a significant contribution to life in their own countries.

Are scholarships available for study in the European Union?

There are three main sources of scholarship funding within the EU; national associations geared towards encouraging study in their home country, the individual universities and the EU itself.

The largest university scholarship scheme identified by the authors is that offered by Politecnico di Milano, worth over 2 million for candidates entering their postgraduate programmes in design, architecture and management.

National bodies like DAAD in Germany, Edu France, Nuffic in Netherlands and the many others around Europe all offer some scholarship funding. DAAD concerns itself primarily with funding living costs for overseas students.

The French Government makes approximately 22,000 grant awards each year to foreign students. There are scholarships offered under bilateral assistance programmes between French and overseas governments, accounting for about 80 per cent of the 22,000 grants. Information can be obtained from French embassies in each country **(www.diplomateie.gouv.fr)**. The French Ministry of Foreign Affairs also provides grants for specific programmes, run from its head office in Paris.

The European Union is also a major provider of scholarships for study within EU member nations (including the UK). The European Union Programme Alban aims at the reinforcement of the European Union – Latin America co-operation in the area of higher education and covers studies for postgraduates (in the context of Master and Doctorate degrees) as well as higher training for Latin American professionals/future decision-makers, in institutions or centres in the European Union. Participant countries are the member states of the European Union and the following 18 countries of Latin America: Argentina, Bolivia, Brazil, Chile, Colombia, Costa Rica, Cuba, Ecuador, El Salvador, Guatemala, Honduras, Mexico, Nicaragua, Panama, Paraguay, Peru, Uruguay and Venezuela. **(http://ec.europa. eu/comm/europeaid/projects/alban/index_en.htm)**

The European Union also offers EuropeAid. This programme offers a wide range of funding for educational institutions and also includes individual scholarships. The website is not particularly user friendly and in the best EU tradition, changes frequently, so it is best to visit the home page and search for up-to-date information. **(http://ec.europa.eu/comm/europeaid/index_en.htm).**

Are scholarships available for study in Australia?

According to IDP, the official universities body representing study in Australia, most international students in Australia are full-fee paying students who are not covered by a scholarship. The number of scholarships available for international students is limited and the competition is intense. IDP manages a range of scholarships for the Australian Government, foreign governments and private organisations.

The Commonwealth Learning Scholarships Programme was introduced in 2004 to assist students from poor backgrounds, particularly those from regional and remote areas and indigenous students, who are Australian citizens or holders of permanent humanitarian visas. Both are awarded on a competitive basis, are non-repayable and target students from low socio-economic status backgrounds. Over the five-year period, 2005-9, the AUD $406 million that the government will provide will help about 43,000 students meet the costs associated with participating in higher education. **(www.dest.gov.au)**

There are also AusAID scholarships for students from partner countries, deemed to require financial support. These countries include, but are not limited to, Pacific-Rim nations.

Are scholarships available for study in Asia?

The Ministry of Education in Singapore has one of the most extensive scholarship programmes in the Asia region. The Asian Scholarships aim to provide the young people of Asia with opportunities to develop their potential and train them in the skills that will enable them to step confidently into the new millennium. **(www. moe.gov.sg/aseanscholarships/)**

Malaysia also offers a wide range of education scholarships for postgraduate and undergraduate study. A detailed listing of these scholarships can be found at **www.malaysia-scholarship.com**.

Korea is making a concerted effort to attract more foreign students. In part, this is through co-operative arrangements with overseas universities. Scholarships and grants are available through KOICA **(Korea International Cooperation Agency – www.koica.go.kr)**. Additional information can also be found from KAFSA .**(Korean Association of Foreign Student Administrators – www.kafsa.or.kr)**

Japan has one of the largest communities of foreign students. Some 62,000 students from approximately 160 countries and regions around the world have studied in Japan under the Japanese Government (Monbukagakusho) Scholarship programme established in 1954. In 2004, there were 9804 foreign students studying in Japan as Japanese government scholarship students. **(www.japan. org.au/Monbukagakusho.htm)**

Other Asian countries are following suit. China and Thailand are embarking on major expansion plans to attract overseas students and will be making funds available for scholarships.

The world's top 200 universities

Understanding the World University Rankings

The publication of The Times Higher Education Supplement (THES) — QS World University Rankings has generated vast interest around the world, becoming generally accepted as the standard for benchmarking university quality across borders. The Top Universities Guide uses these rankings as the basis for comparing these leading institutions around the world and it is important that readers understand the methodology adopted in order to interpret the rankings correctly.

The following tables rank the world's top 200 universities. They are the third edition of The THES — QS World University Rankings (published in The THES on October 6, 2006. The two previous versions, published in The THES on November 5, 2004 and October 28, 2005, can be seen at **www.thes.co.uk**).

In addition, this book contains details on a further 300 plus universities which feature prominently in the research of the World University Rankings, but missed out on a place in the top 200 — these institutions appear in the directory, alongside further information on the top 200.

Basis for comparison

Because universities are a magnet for the most talented people in any country, any attempt at ranking them is bound to be subject to intense scrutiny by highly intelligent analysts. The growing internationalisation of higher education means that these tables are of great interest and importance to academics, employers, parents and prospective graduates around the world.

All rankings are subjective and are very sensitive to the factors and weights applied. Every prospective student needs to dig beneath the ranking and study the underlying data and read profiles in this book and online, to see if a particular university really represents the best choice.

The data used to compile these tables has been drawn from a wide range of sources. But it has a single intention, to provide a measure of the world's top universities on as even a basis as possible.

Within a single national system, it is often possible to collect a vast amount of highly comparable data on universities and colleges. In the UK, The Times Good University Guide ranks universities on nine criteria. The US News and World Report ranking of universities in the US uses 18 columns of data to produce its main analysis and also publishes a host of subsidiary data on colleges of different types.

By contrast, the World University Rankings use a smaller number of highly robust criteria which, we hope, mean something similar whether the question is asked in Norway or Brazil.

A peer review by academics, as well as a recruiter peer review, account for 50 per centage points of the World University Rankings. These measures are designed to provide up-to-date insight into which are the top universities, as judged by the people who really know — the academics reviewing the current research output and the employers seeking to hire the best graduates. Like the other measures we show here, they are presented with the top-scoring institution normalised to 100, and to three significant figures.

The remaining 50 per centage points of the ranking are allotted on the basis of quantitative criteria designed to reflect universities' excellence in teaching and research, and their international focus.

Academic peer review

Of the six columns we show, the most significant is peer review. We believe that active academics are the best judges of university quality, and their opinion accounts for 40 per cent of the final score in this ranking. QS obtained their opinion by building up lists of active academics in approximately equal numbers in North America, Asia, Europe and the rest of the world, and with approximately equal numbers in each of the five major areas of scholarly life — arts and humanities, engineering and IT, life sciences and biomedicine, natural sciences, and social sciences. These academics were asked to name up to 30 top universities in the fields they know about. We are confident that this approach allows us to pinpoint the world's most intellectually lively universities.

In three years we have obtained data from 3703 individual academics and these have been aggregated for this presentation, with duplicates removed so that only the most recent response from any individual is used. But in future years, older data will drop off and we shall not use any responses older than three years. This data is weighted so that the various subject groups and the various regions of the world — the Americas, Europe, the Middle East, Africa and Asia, including Australia and New Zealand — are of equal importance in the final result.

Recruiter peer review

The next 10 per centage points of our score were obtained by a similar peer review of the other group with substantial inside knowledge of the world's universities, the employers. The employers we sought out are ones who recruit internationally from top universities. They are spread across every field from consultancy and banking to transport and manufacturing. This measure was introduced in 2005 and includes responses from 736 employers. Much as QS asked the academics which they regard as the top universities for research and scholarship, so it asked employers where they look for the top graduate employees.

Faculty/student ratio

We measure teaching excellence by the simple and widely-accepted criterion of staff/student ratio. This is a robust measure and is based on data gathered by QS from universities or from national bodies such as the UK's Higher Education Statistics Agency, on a prescribed definition of staff and students. We believe that this measure is an important one for anybody considering the likely student experience at a university they are considering attending, and allot 20 per cent of the total score to it.

Citations per faculty

We assign a further 20 per cent of the total to another measure designed to tease out the density of academic brain-power in widely differing institutions. This is the number of citations in academic journals per staff member which the institution has obtained in the previous five years. While published papers in journals are vital to academic careers, the number of other papers that cite them is the generally accepted measure of a paper's importance and originality.

The staff numbers used to produce this indicator are the same as those used for the staff/student ratio. (This has the advantage of discouraging cheating. An institution which minimised its declared staff numbers would do well on this measure but worse on the staff/student ratio, while one which exaggerated staff numbers would achieve the opposite effect.)

The other half of this equation, the number of citations received, is more controversial. The figures are generated for us by Evidence Ltd, a UK-based firm which carries out analyses of this type for clients across Europe. It is produced from information gathered by Thomson Scientific in the United States, the world's leading supplier of citations data. Evidence analysed five years of data contained in Thomson's Essential Science Indicators database to produce the number of papers and citations for every university in the world generating significant quantities of research.

The Essential Science Indicators database has the advantage that it points to institutions generating the most highly cited papers, and therefore to the leading research groups. However, we recognise that it has some drawbacks. It discriminates against non-English publication, although this problem is easing as researchers in Asia and elsewhere publish increasingly in English, and as Thomson broadens the range of journals it samples. It also disadvantages some subject areas such as the arts and humanities, where publication in refereed journals is less significant than in fields such as life sciences and biomedicine. In the UK and elsewhere, efforts are under way to measure the impact of research in these areas. It may be possible to make use of this work in our future rankings.

International student ratio and international faculty ratio

The final 10 per cent of the ranking scores uses measures designed to capture the international commitment of universities around the world. We believe that this is important partly as a direct measure of the appeal of an institution, and partly for what it reveals about different universities' attitude to globalisation.

We assign five per cent to the ratio of overseas staff in each university, and another five per cent to the ratio of international students. It has been argued that it would be possible to staff a university with ill-paid and underqualified staff and do well on the first of these criteria. Perhaps so, but a university that acted in this way would be unlikely to figure in these pages. It would do too badly on our other measures to appear.

We believe that these measures are simple and understandable, and that the exercise is one in which it is difficult for universities to cheat.

Measures and institutions not included

The World University Rankings are just that — a ranking of universities. Because our interest is in universities that teach a broad variety of subjects to a full range of students, we do not list institutions that do not teach undergraduates. This means that many excellent colleges are not listed here. Many are free-standing business schools. However, there is a lively international trade in information on business schools, in which QS is a significant player. Nobody wanting to know about top business schools will have troubling finding out about them (see **www.topmba.com** for detailed profiles of business schools around the world). Of course, most business schools do form part of a university. Those that do will have contributed to its overall position in our rankings.

Another group of colleges which sometimes fail the undergraduate teaching test are independent medical schools, including some of world standing such as the University of California at San Francisco, the London School of Hygiene and Tropical Medicine, and the Institute of Cancer Research in London. These are top-ranking institutions in their own fields, but it would be wrong to rank them alongside large general universities.

We also recognise that many users of this book will be interested in research, and not all research happens in universities. In some countries, such as the UK, most top researchers are based in universities, but in others they are not. Examples include France and Germany, where many researchers are employed by the Centre National de la Recherche Scientifique (CNRS) or the Max Planck Society respectively.

In the course of compiling the rankings, we have received many suggestions for alternative measures. Some of these fail a simple statistical test. One is the success of universities at winning Nobel Prizes. Only four of these are awarded per year in academic subjects, each to a maximum of three people. Even then, they are only available in a small range of subjects, namely physics, chemistry, economics and medicine. So even over a decade, only about 100 researchers win a Nobel Prize, and most excellent universities win none. This means that they cannot be used as a guide to university quality.

Other measures which might work well in a national context do not work on the world scale. One is alumni giving, regarded as a proxy in the US for how warmly graduates feel about their alma mater. Because no other country has the US charitable giving culture, this measure would not work internationally. In the same way, measures of different universities' library spending fail for the simple reason that a librarian in Oxford is bound to be paid more than one in Mumbai. Economists point out that some correction using purchasing power parities might cure this problem. But even if it did, there is still inconsistency in the way library spending is reported, such as whether it includes IT and staff costs.

Even in the modern globalised era, universities still exist in a national context. This too restricts the use of some quality measures. Entrance qualifications, for example, vary too much from country to country to be applied simply. The same goes for graduate employment. If one university finds that 10 per cent of its alumni are unemployed six months after graduating, while the figure for another university in another country is 20 per cent, we do not know that the second is a worse institution. It may just be in a country with a slower economy and higher unemployment.

Simplifications

A major university is both big and complex. These rankings attempt to encapsulate their quality by a few simple measures, but we recognise that this process involves simplification.

In particular, we have not attempted to look at the individual components of particular universities. Many universities have a number of campuses and centres, but it would be beyond our data-gathering capacity to distinguish between them. This applies especially to many US state universities. If we did analyse each component separately, fewer of them would appear in our rankings than we see today, and in lower positions.

We have taken a decision to attempt to match the units analysed in these rankings with universities as they exist in practice. For example, we itemise out the various colleges of the University of London, which have their own management structures and in some cases award their own degrees. We take the same approach to the University of California. So far we have regarded the Indian Institutes of Technology as a single body, but we may change this approach in future years.

Changes in the methodology

In their first three years, we have added one new criterion, employer opinion, to the rankings. We have also reduced from ten years to five the amount of citations data we use, to make the rankings more dynamic and less reflective of past glories. More importantly, we have improved our data gathering so that there are fewer gaps in our knowledge. We are always keen to receive suggestions for fresh forms of data which can be built into our calculations.

Reactions

In the three years of their existence, these rankings have brought in many thousands of responses. Most come from university managers. Students and their parents, academics, employers and policy-makers have also responded in numbers.

Some respondents reject the idea of quantifying university quality, or of using peer review to do so. As the existence of this book shows, we do not agree. Yet other respondents claim that "everyone knows" that some university we have rated highly is in fact no good. Our reply is simply that we have asked thousands of people their opinion, and have shown that "everyone" does not agree with whatever view is being expressed.

One encouraging factor is that in many cases, the various forms of data we collect all point in a surprisingly similar direction. Citations, academic opinion and employer opinion agree that there is a core group of about 200 universities in the world which produce most of the top research and most of the internationally sought-after graduates.

Indeed, some corroboration of our findings may be obtained by examining the other world ranking of universities, produced by Shanghai Jiao Tong University in China. It uses a quite different methodology from ours, concentrating on science research, but its ordering of the top institutions overlaps substantially with ours. In addition, the US universities in our ranking have much in common with those listed by US News and World Report, although its methodology is mainly based on considerations appropriate to potential undergraduates.

One issue with our rankings is the possibility of lag and bias amongst our academic and employer respondents. Some claim that universities which we rate highly were in fact excellent 30 years ago, but are now living on their reputation. Of course, if Harvard or Cambridge decided to do nothing for five years, they would still get votes in our peer review. But the first three years of our rankings show that academics are responsive to change in the system, as the movement in our tables shows. It may turn out that employers, who cannot be expected to track every university in the world, will be a more conservative influence on our rankings than academics. In addition, some observers have pointed out that both academics and employers are likely to be biased towards larger, older institutions with the name of a big city in their title.

We know that the rankings are of interest in policy circles on a national and international scale. Thus Lord Patten, who is leading the effort to set up the forthcoming European Research Council, has taken a lively interest in the rankings. Indeed, the ERC is being set up to address weaknesses in European research and innovation which our findings illuminate. Elsewhere, there has been wide interest at government level, especially in Asia.

Response to the rankings from university managers has accounted for most of the incoming emails. Because the major universities that appear in these pages are becoming more international, the world standing that these tables encapsulate will become increasingly important to their institutions' success.

In this spirit, many of the universities which contact us about these rankings ask one simple question, dressed up more or less subtly. It is: "How can we get a better position next year?"

The answer is a simple one and suggests itself to anyone who reads the column headings in our main table. A university which wants to be well placed here needs to ensure that it attracts staff and students from around the world, that it publishes in the most visible international journals, that its graduates are attractive to major employers, that its excellence is visible to academic colleagues globally, and that it has enough staff to teach its students. If these considerations are not part of the university's corporate plan, they probably should be.

Further research — dig deeper!

Finally, if you are after comparatively objective college data, many countries have bodies that collect it on a national scale. In the UK and the US respectively, there are the Higher Education Statistics Agency and the National Center for Education Statistics. In Japan, Australia, Hong Kong and elsewhere, such data tends to be gathered by government statistics agencies. In either case, a few hours online will yield basic numbers on topics such as course completion. The box, which is inevitably incomplete, suggests some starting points.

Higher education data sources

Australia	Department of Education, Science & Training www.dest.gov.au
	Government Education Portal www.education.gov.au
Canada	Canadian Education Statistics Council www.cesc.ca
China	National Bureau of Statistics www.stats.gov.cn/english/index.htm
Finland	Statistics Finland tilastokeskus.fi/index_en.html
France	Education Ministry www.education.gouv.fr
Germany	SBD http://www.destatis.de/e_home.htm
Greece	Ministry of National Education & Religious Affairs
	http://www.ypepth.gr/en_ec_home.htm
Hong Kong	Census and Statistics Department
	http://www.censtatd.gov.hk/hong_kong_statistics/index.jsp
Ireland	Department of Education and Science www.education.ie
Israel	Central Bureau of Statistics www.cbs.gov.il/engindex.htm
Japan	Statistics Bureau, Ministry of Internal Affairs ww.stat.go.jp/english/index.htm
	Ministry of Education http://www.mext.go.jp/english/
Malaysia	Department of Statistics Malaysia http://www.statistics.gov.my
Mexico	INEGI http://www.inegi.gob.mx/est/default.asp
Norway	Statistics Norway (education) http://www.ssb.no/english subjects 04/
Russia	Federal Service of State Statistics www.gks.ru/eng/
Singapore	Statistics Singapore www.singstat.gov.sg/
South Africa	Statistics South Africa www.statssa.gov.za/
Spain	Instituto Nacional de Estadistica www.ine.es/welcoing.htm
Sweden	Statistics Sweden (education) http://www.scb.se/templates Amnesomrade____3930.asp
Switzerland	Federal Statistical Office http://www.bfs.admin.ch/bfs/portal en/index.html
Turkey	Ministry of Education www.meb.gov.tr/english
Thailand	Ministry of Education www.moe.go.th
	Commission on Higher Education www.inter.mua.go.th
UK	Higher Education Statistics Agency www.hesa.co.uk
US	National Center for Education Statistics www.nces.ed.gov

Source: QS Quacquarelli Symonds

The world's top 200 universities

2006 rank	2005 rank	Name	Country	Peer review score 40%	Recruiter review 10%	Int'l faculty score 5%	Int'l students score 5%	Faculty/student score 20%	Citations/faculty score 20%	Overall score
1	1	Harvard University	United States	93	100	15	25	56	55	100.0
2	3	University of Cambridge	United Kingdom	100	79	58	43	64	17	96.8
3	4	University of Oxford	United Kingdom	97	76	54	39	61	15	92.7
4=	2	Massachusetts Institute of Technology	United States	81	93	11	39	42	54	89.2
4=	7	Yale University	United States	72	81	45	26	93	24	89.2
6	5	Stanford University	United States	82	85	9	34	32	55	85.4
7	8	California Institute of Technology	United States	53	21	24	40	67	100	83.8
8	6	University of California, Berkeley	United States	92	75	6	13	22	39	80.4
9	13	Imperial College London	United Kingdom	65	44	55	56	88	12	78.6
10	9	Princeton University	United States	68	61	21	29	53	34	74.2
11	17	University of Chicago	United States	57	67	19	30	73	17	69.8
12	20	Columbia University	United States	57	64	9	32	74	17	69.0
13	11	Duke University	United States	39	78	11	21	100	19	68.3
14	15	Peking University	China	70	55	5	11	69	2	67.9
15	14	Cornell University	United States	60	74	10	25	44	26	65.9
16	23	Australian National University	Australia	72	30	48	33	38	13	64.8
17	11	London School of Economics and Political Science	United Kingdom	42	85	89	100	53	1	63.9
18	24	Ecole Normale Supérieure	France	46	30	22	28	69	37	63.3
19=	22	National University of Singapore	Singapore	70	44	82	47	22	8	63.1
19=	16	University of Tokyo	Japan	72	29	8	10	35	27	63.1
21	24	McGill University	Canada	57	61	31	33	52	10	62.3

2006 rank	2005 rank	Name	Country	Peer review score 40%	Recruiter review 10%	Int'l faculty score 5%	Int'l students score 5%	Faculty/student score 20%	Citations/faculty score 20%	Overall score
22	19	University of Melbourne	Australia	72	44	51	36	25	7	61.6
23	27	Johns Hopkins University	United States	49	37	15	20	65	29	61.3
24	21	ETH Zurich	Switzerland	51	25	84	45	44	23	59.7
25	28	University College London	United Kingdom	46	28	39	47	70	12	58.7
26	32	University of Pennsylvania	United States	45	64	17	26	52	22	57.8
27	29	University of Toronto	Canada	63	51	37	17	15	25	57.7
28	62	Tsing Hua University	China	45	34	22	9	84	1	56.1
29=	31	Kyoto University	Japan	61	20	15	7	44	18	56.0
29=	36	University of Michigan	United States	50	61	15	19	46	15	56.0
31	37	University of California, Los Angeles	United States	58	42	2	12	34	25	55.9
32	26	University of Texas at Austin	United States	44	56	24	14	19	53	55.0
33=	30	University of Edinburgh	United Kingdom	54	42	28	29	42	11	54.8
33=	41	University of Hong Kong	Hong Kong	48	40	84	27	46	6	54.8
35=	44	Carnegie Mellon University	United States	44	64	28	40	48	11	54.6
35=	38	University of Sydney	Australia	65	26	56	31	23	8	54.6
37	10	École Polytechnique	France	37	40	18	40	64	17	53.0
38	33	Monash University	Australia	57	40	61	51	21	5	52.6
39	88	University of Geneva	Switzerland	26	13	69	58	81	7	49.9
40	35	University of Manchester	United Kingdom	44	50	42	29	38	6	49.0
41	40	University of New South Wales	Australia	56	36	23	37	20	7	48.2
42	46	Northwestern University	United States	32	71	12	20	44	19	47.9
43	56	New York University	United States	39	51	8	16	55	6	47.6
44	42	University of California, San Diego	United States	46	16	3	9	26	42	47.5
45	47	University of Queensland	Australia	52	26	51	31	18	12	47.2
46=	52	University of Auckland	New Zealand	51	17	44	21	38	2	46.8

46=	73	King's College London	United Kingdom	42	28	42	30	44	7	46.8
48=	73	University of Rochester	United States	21	26	8	23	91	12	46.7
48=	58	Washington University in St. Louis	United States	25	32	5	18	73	22	46.7
50=	38	University of British Colombia	Canada	51	38	23	15	19	16	46.4
50=	51	Chinese University of Hong Kong	Hong Kong	39	38	62	24	41	7	46.4
52	69	Sciences Po Paris	France	21	29	22	53	86	-	45.6
53	114	Vanderbilt University	United States	22	37	2	14	81	14	45.3
54=	71	Brown University	United States	32	32	34	20	50	18	45.0
54=	66	University of Copenhagen	Denmark	44	21	12	13	51	5	45.0
56	141	Emory University	United States	19	38	1	14	84	15	44.9
57	50	Indian Institute of Technology	India	45	34	0	1	27	24	44.5
58=	45	Ruprecht-Karls-Universität Heidelberg	Germany	43	28	17	28	36	11	44.3
58=	43	Hong Kong University of Science & Technology	Hong Kong	40	41	74	21	17	16	44.3
60	109	Case Western Reserve University	United States	19	34	3	24	77	19	44.2
61=	117	Dartmouth College	United States	22	56	13	17	59	16	43.7
61=	48	Nanyang Technological University	Singapore	40	37	77	56	21	3	43.7
63	93	Seoul National University	South Korea	43	13	2	7	57	4	43.6
64=	49	University of Bristol	United Kingdom	36	44	37	26	34	10	43.2
64=	34	Ecole Polytechnique Fédérale de Lausanne	Switzerland	28	13	70	66	47	11	43.2
66	54	Boston University	United States	35	38	9	21	47	10	42.9
67	70	Eindhoven University of Technology	Netherlands	19	18	21	11	92	3	42.1
68	84	Indian Institute of Management	India	31	46	0	10	60	2	41.6
69	58	University of Amsterdam	Netherlands	42	20	30	10	28	15	41.3
70=	103	School of Oriental and African Studies	United Kingdom	23	9	48	74	64	0	40.4
70=	105	Osaka University	Japan	39	0	4	9	45	17	40.4
72	92	Ecole Normale Supérieure Lyon	France	21	18	15	19	50	34	40.1
73	77	University of Warwick	United Kingdom	39	40	38	41	22	4	40.0
74	95	Universidad Nacional Autónoma de México	Mexico	29	36	3	1	65	0	39.8

2006 rank	2005 rank	Name	Country	Peer review score 40%	Recruiter review 10%	Int'l faculty score 5%	Int'l students score 5%	Faculty/ student score 20%	Citations/ faculty score 20%	Overall score
75	127	University of Basel	Switzerland	21	0	76	28	63	10	39.7
76	88	Catholic University of Louvain	Belgium	37	25	29	25	29	11	39.4
77	58	University of Illinois	United States	39	31	10	16	32	9	39.3
78	111	University of Dublin, Trinity College	Ireland	37	34	58	29	17	9	39.1
79=	186	University of Otago	New Zealand	26	17	94	20	45	3	38.5
79=	73	University of Wisconsin	United States	39	11	0	14	35	16	38.5
81	101	University of Glasgow	United Kingdom	35	33	17	16	35	9	38.4
82=	67	Macquarie University	Australia	32	40	100	51	10	5	38.3
82=	105	Technische Universität München	Germany	30	26	22	30	42	10	38.3
84	88	University of Washington	United States	31	23	13	10	38	20	38.2
85	97	University of Nottingham	United Kingdom	34	37	34	29	28	6	38.1
86	53	Delft University of Technology	Netherlands	34	13	52	18	37	7	38.0
87	65	University of Vienna	Austria	43	22	23	26	10	15	37.8
88	193	University of Pittsburgh	United States	22	19	20	10	62	11	37.6
89	133	University of Lausanne	Switzerland	20	21	54	33	53	9	37.3
90=	143	University of Birmingham	United Kingdom	34	27	34	29	28	9	37.2
90=	138	Leiden University	Netherlands	33	21	33	11	20	26	37.2
92	57	Erasmus University Rotterdam	Netherlands	22	49	24	31	11	38	37.1
93=	79	Lomonosov Moscow State University	Russia	42	28	1	7	30	3	37.0
93=	88	Université Pierre-et-Marie-Curie	France	31	0	29	35	49	6	37.0
95	120	Utrecht University	Netherlands	37	12	24	9	25	18	36.7
96	95	Catholic University of Leuven	Belgium	37	35	11	20	18	13	36.6
97	108	Wageningen University	Netherlands	16	9	16	45	61	17	36.5
98	55	Ludwig-Maximilians-Universität München	Germany	35	23	19	21	29	9	36.4
99=	112	Queen Mary, University of London	United Kingdom	26	9	44	40	47	4	36.3

99=	64	Pennsylvania State University	United States	33	43	7	8	31	6	36.3
101	124	University of Southern California	United States	27	28	7	28	45	9	36.2
102=	159	Georgetown University	United States	19	65	6	17	41	11	36.1
102=	150	Rice University	United States	20	31	12	23	50	15	36.1
102=	143	University of Sheffield	United Kingdom	31	22	32	28	33	8	36.1
105=	80	University of Adelaide	Australia	38	0	47	44	14	14	35.9
105=	112	Humboldt-Universität zu Berlin	Germany	32	15	18	18	43	5	35.9
105=	100	University of Sussex	United Kingdom	27	18	42	27	41	6	35.9
108	114	National Taiwan University	Taiwan	40	0	1	0	43	4	35.8
109=	136	University of St Andrews	United Kingdom	26	20	40	53	33	9	35.7
109=	85	University of Zurich	Switzerland	26	0	69	23	41	11	35.7
111=	133	University of Maryland	United States	27	33	16	15	35	14	35.6
111=	180	Uppsala University	Sweden	36	0	17	8	41	9	35.6
111=	199	Wake Forest University	United States	10	32	2	6	80	10	35.6
111=	80	University of Western Australia	Australia	34	11	61	28	19	13	35.6
115	217	University of Twente	Netherlands	23	15	29	16	59	3	35.5
116=	72	Fudan University	China	39	47	11	8	18	2	35.4
116=	62	University of Helsinki	Finland	38	20	7	5	16	20	35.4
118	99	Tokyo Institute of Technology	Japan	29	18	3	14	39	16	35.3
119	77	Hebrew University of Jerusalem	Israel	41	0	14	5	22	16	35.2
120	215	Keio University	Japan	28	25	18	4	48	2	35.1
121	103	University of Leeds	United Kingdom	32	33	28	25	25	7	35.0
122	180	Lund University	Sweden	35	0	26	9	36	10	34.8
123	143	University of North Carolina	United States	23	38	7	8	36	19	34.6
124=	68	University of Massachusetts, Amherst	United States	32	28	1	10	20	23	34.5
124=	109	University of York	United Kingdom	28	22	31	30	33	8	34.5
126	138	University of Aarhus	Denmark	30	15	38	13	33	9	34.4
127	61	Purdue University	United States	32	42	20	15	21	6	34.2

2006 rank	2005 rank	Name	Country	Peer review score 40%	Recruiter review 10%	Int'l faculty score 5%	Int'l students score 5%	Faculty/ student score 20%	Citations/ faculty score 20%	Overall score
128=	222	Kyushu University	Japan	21	17	8	8	59	7	34.1
128=	129	Nagoya University	Japan	29	11	4	9	41	13	34.1
130=	164	Tufts University	United States	17	31	12	17	42	22	33.9
130=	105	University of Virginia	United States	20	57	6	11	34	14	33.9
132	83	University of Durham	United Kingdom	25	41	43	25	23	10	33.8
133=	149	University of Alberta	Canada	32	11	40	21	17	18	33.6
133=	259	Vrije University Brussels	Belgium	16	15	21	17	72	-	33.6
133=	157	Hokkaido University	Japan	29	0	8	6	52	8	33.6
133=	168	University of Newcastle upon Tyne	United Kingdom	25	24	33	32	36	7	33.6
137	177	Radboud Universiteit Nijmegen	Netherlands	21	9	33	10	55	7	33.5
138	86	Vienna University of Technology	Austria	29	17	27	34	36	3	33.3
139	119	University of Liverpool	United Kingdom	26	26	32	21	32	8	33.2
140	234	Cranfield University	United Kingdom	14	26	31	62	52	2	33.0
141=	159	University of California, Santa Barbara	United States	31	11	7	8	22	24	32.9
141=	228	Cardiff University	United Kingdom	29	13	27	23	36	4	32.9
141=	219	University of Ghent	Belgium	29	9	20	10	43	4	32.9
141=	206	University of Southampton	United Kingdom	26	16	38	25	34	7	32.9
145	147	Georgia Institute of Technology	United States	30	36	2	27	19	13	32.8
146	82	RMIT University	Australia	34	26	31	65	9	1	32.5
147=	166	Chalmers University of Technology	Sweden	27	9	17	8	46	5	32.4
147=	188	Tel Aviv University	Israel	35	22	0	3	13	21	32.4
149	172	Freie Universität Berlin	Germany	37	0	27	17	25	6	32.3
150=	184	Korea University	South Korea	25	8	5	19	55	1	32.2
150=	125	Texas A&M University	United States	30	39	12	13	16	13	32.2
152	179	University of Notre Dame	United States	19	51	17	14	35	9	32.0

153	130	University of Bath	United Kingdom	21	36	34	35	32	5	31.8
154	178	City University of Hong Kong	Hong Kong	28	11	75	14	25	5	31.7
155	184	McMaster University	Canada	29	24	9	13	18	19	31.6
156=	101	Curtin University of Technology	Australia	28	18	71	70	12	-	31.5
156=	114	Georg-August-Universität Tübingen	Germany	32	0	17	17	31	8	31.5
158=	194	Technion - Israel Institute of Technology	Israel	31	17	6	6	23	16	31.4
158=	240	Universität Ulm	Germany	12	0	22	16	70	9	31.4
158=	202	Waseda University	Japan	27	24	11	6	42	1	31.4
161=	121	Chulalongkorn University	Thailand	33	18	9	1	33	0	31.2
161=	131	Université Louis Pasteur - Strasbourg I	France	25	15	22	34	28	12	31.2
163	121	Michigan State University	United States	28	39	10	12	21	9	31.1
164	219	Saint-Petersburg State University	Russia	26	18	1	9	47	1	30.7
165=	76	Université Libre de Bruxelles	Belgium	30	19	15	39	13	12	30.5
165=	93	University of Science and Technology of China	China	36	14	3	0	24	5	30.5
165=	175	State University of New York at Stony Brook	United States	26	16	6	15	30	14	30.5
168=	199	George Washington University	United States	24	46	3	13	30	5	30.4
168=	136	Tohoku University	Japan	26	0	8	7	31	21	30.4
170=	206	University of California, Davis	United States	30	0	2	8	30	17	30.3
170=	260	Eberhard Karls Universität Tübingen	Germany	21	21	21	19	37	9	30.3
172=	172	Rheinisch-Westfälische Technische Hochschule Aachen	Germany	23	37	24	24	28	4	30.2
172=	157	University of Maastricht	Netherlands	18	28	34	46	24	13	30.2
172=	196	Royal Institute of Technology	Sweden	24	11	17	12	43	4	30.2
172=	254	Yeshiva University	United States	7	0	9	6	70	20	30.2
176	261	Queen's University	Canada	21	36	38	8	28	7	30.0
177	138	University of Oslo	Norway	30	0	17	9	34	5	29.9
178	228	University of Bern	Switzerland	17	9	1	16	54	9	29.8
179	169	Shanghai Jiao Tong University	China	31	37	13	5	19	1	29.7
180	150	Nanjing University	China	35	20	24	2	16	3	29.6

2006 rank	2005 rank	Name	Country	Peer review score 40%	Recruiter review 10%	Int'l faculty score 5%	Int'l students score 5%	Faculty/ student score 20%	Citations/ faculty score 20%	Overall score
181=	172	Kobe University	Japan	25	17	8	7	38	5	29.4
181=	132	University of Montreal	Canada	25	25	48	11	13	14	29.4
183=	192	Jawaharlal Nehru University	India	32	14	2	6	27	4	29.3
183=	186	Free University of Amsterdam	Netherlands	25	9	19	8	36	8	29.3
185	289	Universiti Kebangsaan Malaysia	Malaysia	32	22	9	6	25	0	29.2
186	165	University of Innsbruck	Austria	23	0	30	48	32	6	29.1
187=	213	Brandeis University	United States	19	23	7	23	34	13	29.0
187=	142	Johann Wolfgang Goethe Universität Frankfurt	Germany	30	17	22	17	19	7	29.0
187=	150	University of Minnesota	United States	26	20	8	10	20	16	29.0
190=	240	University of Barcelona	Spain	31	16	2	11	26	4	28.9
190=	248	University of Reading	United Kingdom	21	19	32	25	30	6	28.9
192=	169	University of Malaya	Malaysia	33	14	10	7	24	1	28.6
192=	118	Queensland University of Technology	Australia	33	8	51	19	13	2	28.6
194	154	Technical University of Denmark	Denmark	25	0	19	19	25	17	28.5
195	267	University of Aberdeen	United Kingdom	20	9	37	25	33	7	28.3
196	308	University of Wollongong	Australia	23	8	69	64	15	3	28.2
197	125	Università degli Studi di Roma - La Sapienza	Italy	37	15	2	6	11	5	28.1
198=	254	University of California, Irvine	United States	24	16	2	10	19	21	28.0
198=	143	Korea Advanced Institute of Science & Technology	South Korea	24	11	14	6	29	12	28.0
200	305	Université Paris-Sorbonne (Paris IV)	France	32	29	6	29	13	0	27.9

The world's top universities by subject

On the pages that follow, we list the world's top universities in the five main areas of academic life — arts and humanities, life sciences and biomedicine, natural sciences, social sciences, and engineering and IT. We list the top 100 in the order in which academic staff in these subject areas voted for them in our peer review survey. We also list the impact of the papers each institution published in these different fields between 2001 and 2006, by giving the average number of citations in Thomson Scientific's Essential Science Indicators. We do not attempt to aggregate these columns and, as the following text explains, there is no valid citations data for the arts and humanities.

Top 100 in arts and humanities

Rank	Institution	Country	Score
1	University of Cambridge	United Kingdom	100.0
2	University of Oxford	United Kingdom	99.7
3	Harvard University	United States	92.3
4	University of California, Berkeley	United States	85.8
5	University of Sydney	Australia	83.6
6	Australian National University	Australia	81.9
7	University of Melbourne	Australia	79.9
8	Yale University	United States	79.7
9	Princeton University	United States	72.4
10	Peking University	China	68.2
11	University of Toronto	Canada	65.9
12	McGill University	Canada	65.8
13	University of Edinburgh	United Kingdom	64.2
14	Columbia University	United States	63.9
15	Stanford University	United States	62.9
16	Université Paris-Sorbonne (Paris IV)	France	62.5
17	University of Chicago	United States	61.0
18	University of New South Wales	Australia	60.6
19	London School of Economics	United Kingdom	59.9
20	University of California, Los Angeles	United States	59.4
21	Massachusetts Institute of Technology	United States	59.2
22	National University of Singapore	Singapore	58.6
23	King's College London	United Kingdom	57.7
24	University of Amsterdam	Netherlands	57.6
25	Ecole Normale Supérieure Paris	France	56.8
26	University of Copenhagen	Denmark	56.7
27	University of Tokyo	Japan	55.3
28	Monash University	Australia	54.7
29	University of Auckland	New Zealand	54.1
30	School of Oriental and African Studies	United Kingdom	53.9
31	University of Bologna	Italy	53.8
32	University of British Columbia	Canada	53.2
33=	Freie Universität Berlin	Germany	52.3
33=	University of Hong Kong	Hong Kong	52.3
35	University College London	United Kingdom	51.6
36	Kyoto University	Japan	51.2
37=	University of Vienna	Austria	50.4
37=	University of Warwick	United Kingdom	50.4

Rank	Institution	Country	Score
39=	University of Dublin, Trinity College	Ireland	50.2
39=	University of Michigan	United States	50.2
41	Cornell University	United States	50.0
42	University of Queensland	Australia	49.9
43	Hebrew University of Jerusalem	Israel	49.6
44	University of St Andrews	United Kingdom	48.2
45	University of Pennsylvania	United States	45.6
46	University of Texas at Austin	United States	45.4
47	New York University	United States	45.3
48=	Brown University	United States	44.9
48=	Johns Hopkins	United States	44.9
50	Macquarie University	Australia	44.8
51	University of Manchester	United Kingdom	44.0
52	Universität Heidelberg	Germany	43.8
53	Leiden University	Netherlands	43.1
54	La Trobe University	Australia	42.6
55=	University of Leeds	United Kingdom	42.2
55=	Università degli Studi di Roma - La Sapienza	Italy	42.2
57	University of Bristol	United Kingdom	42.1
58	Waseda University	Japan	41.9
59	RMIT University	Australia	41.6
60	Panthéon Sorbonne Universite Paris I	France	41.5
61	University of Helsinki	Finland	41.1
62	University of Sussex	United Kingdom	41.0
63	Utrecht University	Netherlands	40.7
64	University of York	United Kingdom	40.6
65	University of Oslo	Norway	40.4
66	University of Pittsburgh	United States	40.3
67	University of Birmingham	United Kingdom	39.6
68	University of Glasgow	United Kingdom	38.5
69	University of Tasmania	Australia	37.5
70	University of Gadjah Mada	Indonesia	37.3
71=	Duke University	United States	37.2
71=	Western Australia University	Australia	37.2
73=	University of Alberta	Canada	37.1
73=	Catholic University of Leuven (Flemish)	Belgium	37.1
75	University of Delhi	India	36.7
76=	Nanjing University	China	36.6
76=	University of Victoria	New Zealand	36.6
78	Tsing Hua University	China	36.5

Rank	Institution	Country	Score
79=	Catholic University of Louvain (French)	Belgium	36.2
79=	Queen Mary, University of London	United Kingdom	36.2
79=	Uppsala University	Sweden	36.2
82=	Fudan University	China	36.1
82=	Open University	United Kingdom	36.1
82=	University of Wisconsin	United States	36.1
85	Chinese University of Hong Kong	Hong Kong	35.8
86	Queensland University of Technology	Australia	35.4
87=	University of Geneva	Switzerland	35.1
87=	Tel Aviv University	Israel	35.1
89	Université Libre de Bruxelles	Belgium	34.4
90	University of Florence	Italy	34.3
91	Humboldt-Universität zu Berlin	Germany	33.8
92	Cardiff University	United Kingdom	33.7
93	Goldsmiths College	United Kingdom	33.5
94	University of Adelaide	Australia	33.1
95=	Universität Bielefeld	Germany	32.9
95=	University of California, Irvine	United States	32.9
95=	University of Newcastle	Australia	32.9
98	Dartmouth College	United States	32.8
99=	McMaster University	Canada	32.7
99=	University of Technology, Sydney	Australia	32.7

The world's top arts and humanities universities

The arts and humanities involve the study of human behaviour and creativity on an individual basis. In contrast to the social sciences, which study whole societies and often use statistical methods, the humanities involve the study of people and the things they make, especially the written record. History, art, languages and music are perhaps the canonical humanities subjects.

However, the arts and humanities are also of growing economic importance. Despite the rise of English, governments around the world are growing more aware of the need for language skills. International tourism has been driven by culture for centuries since people first flocked to see the Pyramids of Egypt and the temples of Rome and Athens. Today, art galleries, preferably from the drawing-board of a big-name architect, have replaced steel mills and car factories as the investment of choice for reviving a run-down inner city.

This expansion has meant a proliferation of courses in the arts and humanities. Museum curation and management, tourism and cultural studies might seem unusual to traditionalists, but they can lead to worthwhile careers. Almost by definition, they appeal to mobile and internationally minded students.

At the same time, older humanities subjects such as librarianship have been transformed by new technology. Even literature and history have shed their previously dusty image. History in particular has shown that it can produce best-selling books and well-watched TV programmes. And the ever-growing number of websites and TV channels means new opportunities for humanities graduates.

Many humanities subjects are among the more affordable to study at university. But the reason, in part, is that some of them lead to precarious and high-failure career paths such as becoming a novelist, musician or artist.

Unlike the others on these pages, this table does not include citations data. Many humanities subjects produce few refereed journal articles, as academics in these fields prefer to publish books and monographs. Even the articles that are published tend to appear in national rather than international journals. This table shows that it is the ancient universities of the UK and the US that dominate here, along with Australia and Canada. Despite their contributions to world culture, only two French universities make it to the top 30 and the first Italian institution comes behind one from New Zealand.

Popular subjects and courses

Popular arts and humanities subjects include American studies, archaeology, art and design, Asian studies, Celtic studies, classics, history in many forms from ancient to contemporary, Byzantine and modern Greek ctudies, drama, dance and performing arts, and English language and literature.

Art history has been a long-standing popular subject and is offered by just about all arts and humanities departments. Other favourites like drama may be offered less widely.

Career paths

The arts and humanities can provide its graduates with an exceptionally wide range of career options. But the humanities diploma is not known for being a prerequisite to wealth. The starving artist and novelist, however, are not the only options for humanities graduates, though they may be of aspiration for many.

Many arts and humanities graduates remain in the world of academia, or become school teachers, translators, or designers, to name just a few. One benefit of a humanities degree is the broad spectrum of career choices it can bring with it. For example, a major university such as London can offer a degree in virtually any language you might want to learn. This can take you anywhere, in this country or around the world, perhaps alongside qualifications in science or business.

In a category of their own are the performing arts. Although all professions are competitive, these are perhaps the arena in which the largest numbers of bright people strive to succeed relative to the work available to them, and where there is always more talent than there are outlets for it.

Even at times of full employment, there has never been a shortage of musicians or actors. Like sports people, their incomes follow what the statisticians term a power law rather than a bell curve. A few become world figures and earn millions, while most attract far more modest rewards or drop in favour of less glamorous but more definite employment.

Top 100 in life sciences and biomedicine

Rank	Institution	Country	Score	Citations per paper
1	University of Cambridge	United Kingdom	100.0	12.8
2	Harvard University	United States	99.1	14.0
3	University of Oxford	United Kingdom	95.1	13.0
4	Imperial College London	United Kingdom	83.7	9.5
5	Stanford University	United States	81.8	14.4
6	Johns Hopkins	United States	76.2	11.6
7	University of Melbourne	Australia	73.9	7.2
8	Peking University	China	70.8	–
9	National University of Singapore	Singapore	70.7	5.6
10	University of California, Berkeley	United States	69.6	15.0
11	Yale University	United States	68.1	12.5
12	University of Tokyo	Japan	67.5	9.0
13	Massachusetts Inst of Technology	United States	66.3	22.5
14=	University of California, San Diego	United States	63.6	12.9
14=	University of Edinburgh	United Kingdom	63.6	9.6
16	University College London	United Kingdom	60.1	9.7
17	Kyoto University	Japan	59.9	8.8
18	University of Toronto	Canada	59.7	8.9
19	Monash University	Australia	58.9	7.5
20	University of Sydney	Australia	58.1	6.5
21	McGill University	Canada	57.1	9.1
22	Cornell University	United States	56.4	10.8
23	University of Queensland	Australia	56.0	6.8
24	Australian National University	Australia	53.5	–
25	California Institute of Technology	United States	52.1	20.3
26=	University of Auckland	New Zealand	52.0	–
26=	University of California, Los Angeles	United States	52.0	10.8
28	Kings College London	United Kingdom	51.9	7.8
29	Columbia University	United States	50.7	10.8
30	Universität Heidelberg	Germany	50.3	7.5
31	University of Hong Kong	Hong Kong	48.7	6.5
32	British Columbia University	Canada	48.5	8.4
33	Duke University	United States	47.4	11.1
34	Seoul National University	South Korea	47.3	4.1
35	Swiss Federal Institute of Tech Zurich	Switzerland	47.1	11.5
36	University of Manchester	United Kingdom	46.5	8.2
37	Princeton University	United States	46.0	15.2

Rank	Institution	Country	Score	Citations per paper
38	Osaka University	Japan	45.3	9.4
39	University of Chicago	United States	44.9	10.9
40	Uppsala University	Sweden	44.2	7.7
41	University of Vienna	Austria	44.1	7.1
42	University of Helsinki	Finland	43.6	8.8
43	University of Adelaide	Australia	42.1	-
44	University of Copenhagen	Denmark	42.0	7.5
45	Université Louis Pasteur Strasbourg I	France	40.8	9.3
46	Washington University in St. Louis	United States	40.6	12.3
47	Fudan University	China	40.2	-
48	Chinese University of Hong Kong	Hong Kong	39.6	5.0
49	York University	United Kingdom	39.4	-
50	Boston University	United States	39.3	9.6
51	University of Nottingham	United Kingdom	39.1	6.7
52=	Lund University	Sweden	38.6	7.2
52=	University of New South Wales	Australia	38.6	6.0
54	Georg-August-Eberhard Karls Universität Tübingen	Germany	38.5	6.5
55	Michigan State University	United States	38.1	10.1
56=	Universiti Kebangsaan Malaysia	Malaysia	37.8	-
56=	Universität München	Germany	37.8	7.8
58	University of Pennsylvania	United States	37.5	10.7
59	National Taiwan University	Taiwan	37.0	-
60	University of Washington	United States	36.8	11.0
61	University of Hong Kong Sci & Tech	Hong Kong	36.5	-
62	Université Pierre-et-Marie-Curie	France	36.0	7.4
63=	Hebrew University of Jerusalem	Israel	35.9	7.8
63=	Tsing Hua University	China	35.9	-
65	University of Western Australia	Australia	35.8	6.9
66	Queensland University of Technology	Australia	35.7	-
67	Carnegie Mellon University	United States	35.5	-
68=	University of California, Davis	United States	34.8	8.0
68=	Vanderbilt University	United States	34.8	10.9
70=	University of Amsterdam	Netherlands	34.7	8.5
70=	Cardiff University	United Kingdom	34.7	7.2
70=	Indian Institute of Technology	India	34.7	-
73	University of Gadjah Mada	Indonesia	34.5	-
74	University of Otago	New Zealand	34.4	-
75=	University of Glasgow	United Kingdom	34.1	9.2

Rank	Institution	Country	Score	Citations per paper
75=	Lomonosov Moscow State University	Russia	34.1	-
77=	Ecole Normale Supérieure	France	34.0	-
77=	Eberhard Karls Universität Tübingen	Germany	34.0	7.3
79	Humboldt-Universität zu Berlin	Germany	33.9	8.5
80	Chulalongkorn University	Thailand	33.7	-
81	New York University	United States	33.6	9.6
82=	University of Bristol	United Kingdom	33.4	8.0
82=	Catholic University of Leuven	Belgium	33.4	8.4
84	Nanjing University	China	33.0	-
85	University of Dundee	United Kingdom	32.7	11.1
86=	University of Aarhus	Denmark	32.6	7.3
86=	University of Newcastle upon Tyne	United Kingdom	32.6	8.5
88	Freie Universität Berlin	Germany	32.5	8.3
89	University of Basel	Switzerland	31.9	9.2
90	Tohoku University	Japan	31.5	5.9
91=	Universität Frankfurt am Main	Germany	31.2	8.5
91=	Utrecht University	Netherlands	31.2	7.7
93	University of Dublin, Trinity College	Ireland	31.0	-
94	Nanyang Technological University	Singapore	30.9	-
95=	Hokkaido University	Japan	30.8	5.4
95=	University Sains Malaysia	Malaysia	30.8	-
97=	University of Alberta	Canada	30.7	7.2
97=	Texas A&M University	United States	30.7	6.7
99=	University of Bologna	Italy	30.4	5.8
99=	Jawaharlal Nehru University	India	30.4	-

The world's top life sciences and biomedicine universities

In every country in the world, university medical courses are a magnet for the brightest and most driven of applicants. As well as medicine, this applies to related topics such as dentistry and veterinary science, as well as nursing and other medical professions, which require university training in an increasing number of countries.

Qualifications in these subjects lead to a wide range of careers. Becoming a medical practitioner involves a medical degree, typically longer than other degree courses, along with experience in hospitals and clinics as well as specialist training. Practitioners are almost always certified by some official or professional body whose standards they are obliged to uphold.

In addition, these subject areas produce many scientists, normally qualified through the PhD route and often as medical practitioners as well. These people often have fascinating careers as academics, often in joint appointments in a university and a hospital. Some spend a lucrative part of their time in the pharmaceutical or healthcare industry, whether as employees or external consultants.

Students contemplating medical studies should be aware that they are setting out on a long and expensive process, and will need to think hard about finance. But they may also be lining themselves up for a career with unparalleled rewards, both psychic and spendable.

New breakthroughs in areas such as neuroscience and genetics mean that the power of modern biomedicine is growing apace. At the same time, new methods such as nanotechnology approaches to drug delivery are opening up novel therapeutic channels.

One effect of this rapid change is that medical research and associated areas of biology have a ferocious publishing and citation culture. The average biomedical paper from Massachusetts Institute of Technology is cited 22.5 times, while the excellent engineering and IT papers from the same institution have an average of 3.2 citations.

The table shows that the UK and the US are driving this field. Cambridge has eased ahead of Harvard into top slot, and UK and US universities fill 12 of the top 20 slots. Imperial College's decision to become a leading London medical college by acquiring teaching hospitals across west London has paid off with fourth place. However, this table omits high-powered medical colleges such as Rockefeller University which do not teach undergraduates. Some major US universities do not have a medical school but still carry out extensive medical research, as with Massachusetts Institute of Technology and Caltech, and teaching, as with Berkeley, which has a large public health school.

Popular subjects and courses

The citations and opinion data in this table cover medicine and related areas of the life sciences. Other areas of biology, including environmental sciences, botany, non-human genetics and agriculture, are regarded as part of the sciences. However, that still leaves a deep and wide series of disciplines under the remit of biomedicine, each with its own courses, professional structures and research communities. Popular courses include wide-ranging ones in the biological sciences overall, clinical and hospital laboratory sciences, neuroscience, branches of medicine such as cardiovascular medicine, oncology, infection and immunology, community-based clinical subjects, epidemiology, public health and health sciences, primary care, psychiatry, dentistry, pre-clinical studies, anatomy, physiology, pharmacology, pharmacy, nursing, psychology and veterinary science.

In the UK, the professions allied to medicine have emerged as a powerful group in their own right in recent years after new legislation entrenched their position. These professions include art and music therapy, chiropody, dietetics, occupational therapy, orthoptics, paramedicine, physiotherapy (perhaps the biggest), radiography, both therapeutic and investigative, and prosthetics.

Note that these professions are formally regulated in most countries. This may be all to the good for the patients. But it can mean that a qualification which is taken in one country is not always accepted in another, something to check out in advance if you are planning on studying abroad but coming home, or going to a third country, to work.

Medicine is inevitably a main focus for life science students in every country. Programmes vary but are always demanding, and admission is competitive. Students are usually required to take an entry exam such as UKCAT in the UK. Study time varies. In the UK, one studies medicine for five years, and some candidates, mainly those interested in research careers, obtain a BSc in biomedical science along the way. But it doesn't stop there. Qualified doctors have to climb the ranks from Junior House Officer to Senior House Officer before taking a registry exam.

The US system is different again, as the medical degree is a Master's, completed after the student has earned a Bachelor's degree. While many US medics have a first degree in some related topics such as biology or biochemistry, it is not unheard of to meet doctors whose original university education was in maths or history.

Life science students looking to go into psychiatry are required to earn a medical degree before opting to specialise and even then entry is highly competitive. Again, further study time varies from country to country, as do programmes, so it's essential that the candidate does their research before applying.

Nursing courses are significantly shorter, lasting approximately three years for a diploma course and three to four years for a degree course in the UK. Nurses can choose to specialise in areas such as adult, children's or mental health nursing, or can study to become midwives. In some countries, nursing has yet to become a graduate profession.

One area of the medical sciences which has been growing apace is sports medicine, in which there are lucrative careers plus a touch of glamour for those who get to work alongside Wimbledon champions or Olympic medal-winners. It tends to be taught as a Master's degree to biology graduates. Practitioners may have to worry about anything from the lung capacity of an athlete to their mental attitude to performance.

Because the life sciences are changing rapidly, new specialisms emerge continually. For example, neuroscience has appeared from the gaps between psychology, medicine and other parts of biology, and is set to grow as new techniques tell us more about the workings of the brain. New social and political concerns also affect medical priorities. At the moment, countries across the developed world are alarmed about their ageing populations. Both teaching and research in medicine are changing to reflect this new awareness.

Top 100 in natural sciences

Rank	Institution	Country	Score	Citations per paper
1	University of Cambridge	United Kingdom	100.0	7.6
2	University of Oxford	United Kingdom	95.0	7.5
3	University of California, Berkeley	United States	93.1	9.5
4	Harvard University	United States	88.9	11.1
5	Massachusetts Institute of Technology	United States	87.8	9.6
6	Princeton University	United States	80.1	11.6
7	Stanford University	United States	79.1	9.5
8	California Institute of Technology	United States	73.2	11.9
9	Imperial College London	United Kingdom	72.9	6.3
10	University of Tokyo	Japan	72.1	5.6
11	Swiss Federal Institute of Technology	Switzerland	71.6	6.8
12	Peking University	China	67.6	3.3
13	Kyoto University	Japan	66.6	4.9
14	Yale University	United States	65.7	9.5
15	Cornell University	United States	64.5	6.9
16	Australian National University	Australia	63.1	6.1
17	Ecole Normale Supérieure	France	60.8	6.0
18	University of Chicago	United States	60.4	11.6
19	Lomonosov Moscow State University	Russia	60.1	2.0
20	University of Toronto	Canada	54.9	6.0
21	University of California, Los Angeles	United States	53.1	8.2
22=	National University of Singapore	Singapore	52.4	3.5
22=	Université Pierre-et-Marie-Curie	France	52.4	4.8
24	École Polytechnique	France	52.3	4.9
25	Columbia University	United States	49.9	8.8
26	University of Texas at Austin	United States	49.2	6.6
27	University of Melbourne	Australia	48.6	5.0
28	Universität Heidelberg	Germany	48.0	6.7
29	University of Illinois	United States	47.5	6.0
30	Università degli Studi di Roma	Italy	46.4	4.6
31	University of California, Santa Barbara	United States	46.3	9.4
32	University of Science and Tech China	China	45.7	3.3
33	Indian Institute of Technology	India	45.1	-
34	Michigan State University	United States	45.0	7.1
35	University of Sydney	Australia	44.8	4.4
36	University of California, San Diego	United States	44.0	8.3
37=	Georg-August-Eberhard Karls Universität Tübingen	Germany	43.6	4.7

Rank	Institution	Country	Score	Citations per paper
37=	McGill University	Canada	43.6	5.0
39	Université Paris-Sud, Paris XI	France	43.5	5.5
40	Seoul National University	South Korea	43.3	4.2
41=	University of New South Wales	Australia	43.1	4.9
41=	Tsing Hua University	China	43.1	2.3
43	Universität München	Germany	43.0	5.9
44	Utrecht University	Netherlands	42.4	5.8
45	British Columbia University	Canada	41.3	6.4
46	University of Edinburgh	United Kingdom	40.6	7.8
47	University of Copenhagen	Denmark	40.2	4.8
48	Johns Hopkins University	United States	40.0	9.9
49	Osaka University	Japan	39.6	4.6
50	Technion Israel Institute of Technology	Israel	39.1	3.9
51	University of Wisconsin	United States	39.0	6.5
52	Hebrew University of Jerusalem	Israel	38.5	5.0
53	Rheinische Friedrich-Wilhelms-Universität Bonn	Germany	38.3	4.6
54	Monash University	Australia	37.9	-
55	University of Pennsylvania	United States	37.8	9.4
56=	Delft University of Technology	Netherlands	37.7	5.6
56=	Technical University of Berlin	Germany	37.7	-
58=	University of Auckland	New Zealand	37.5	-
58=	University of Queensland	Australia	37.5	4.3
58=	Tel Aviv University	Israel	37.5	5.4
61	National Taiwan University	Taiwan	37.4	3.4
62	Universiti Kebangsaan Malaysia	Malaysia	36.8	-
63	Fudan University	China	36.7	-
64	University of Aarhus	Denmark	36.6	6.4
65=	Tohoku University	Japan	36.2	4.6
65=	University of Warwick	United Kingdom	36.2	-
67=	Humboldt-Universität zu Berlin	Germany	36.1	5.3
67=	Tokyo Institute of Technology	Japan	36.1	-
69	Hong Kong University of Science & Technology	Hong Kong	35.8	-
70	Nanjing University	China	35.7	2.7
71	University of Hong Kong	Hong Kong	35.3	-
72	University of Helsinki	Finland	35.2	6.0
73=	Saint-Petersburg State University	Russia	35.1	-
73=	University of Vienna	Austria	35.1	4.7

Rank	Institution	Country	Score	Citations per paper
75	Technische Universität München	Germany	34.9	5.9
76	Georgia Institute of Technology	United States	34.2	5.8
77	Pennsylvania State University	United States	34.1	7.0
78	Leiden University	Netherlands	34.0	6.5
79	Lund University	Sweden	33.9	6.2
80	University of Adelaide	Australia	33.8	-
81	Rheinisch-Westfälische Technische Hochschule Aachen	Germany	33.6	4.9
82=	Korea Advanced Institute of Science and Technology	South Korea	32.9	-
82=	New York University	United States	32.9	-
84	Kings College London	United Kingdom	32.8	-
85	Nagoya University	Japan	32.7	5.4
86	University of Manchester	United Kingdom	32.5	5.0
87=	Nanyang Technological University	Singapore	32.4	-
87=	Vienna University of Technology	Austria	32.4	-
89	Carnegie Mellon University	United States	32.3	9.9
90=	Freie Universität Berlin	Germany	32.2	4.6
90=	University College London	United Kingdom	32.2	6.0
90=	SUNY	United States	32.2	7.5
93=	University of Bristol	United Kingdom	32.1	6.1
93=	University of Dublin, Trinity College	Ireland	32.1	-
95	University of Malaya	Malaysia	31.9	-
96	Chalmers University of Technology	Sweden	31.7	4.4
97=	University of Maryland	United States	31.5	7.2
97=	University of Waterloo	Canada	31.5	-
99	Brown University	United States	31.0	8.4
100=	Uppsala University	Sweden	30.7	5.3
100=	University of Washington	United States	30.7	8.9

The world's top natural sciences universities

Throughout the developed world, from Japan to the UK and from Germany to California, governments and employers wish that more people would opt for careers in the natural sciences. Science underpins everything from the internet to the weather forecast, they point out, and interesting and well-rewarded careers await anyone wishing to become a scientist.

Those opting to do so will typically go for a first degree followed by a PhD, perhaps with a Master's degree in their first postgraduate year. Some sciences have opted to imitate the kind of professional recognition long familiar in engineering, especially more applied subjects such as chemistry and geology, but others have not.

Potential students should bear in mind that in some sciences, such as chemistry, a PhD has virtually turned into the entry-level qualification for a career in science. PhDs have also changed a lot in science, with more emphasis on the formal learning of research methods as well as the pursuit of a narrowly defined research question intended to feed a final thesis.

Universities, companies and government research labs across the world are the career destination of many scientists. But others end up as consultants and government advisers and in a range of other occupations. The rise of the internet means that even sciences such as maths are now of industrial interest. There are also new sciences such as nanotechnology which are mainly fed by graduates from other disciplines, although courses and departments in nanotechnology are now emerging around the world.

This table of the top natural sciences universities displays less change from 2005 than any other in this book. It shows that Cambridge and Oxford are still regarded as the world's top science universities, with Harvard, Berkeley and Massachusetts Institute of Technology not far off the pace. A larger gap then follows before Princeton in sixth place. Evidence of any of these institutions is a plus for the scientist's CV.

This list is dominated by developed-world universities. By contrast with our ranking of engineering and IT, only Peking appears in the top 20 from outside, while the National University of Singapore is at 22. It is also made up largely by general universities, and has fewer specialist institutions near the top than our engineering and IT ranking. But some top institutions appear in both, such as Imperial College London.

Popular subjects and courses

The big natural sciences are physics, chemistry and mathematics. Also in this group are smaller but vital subjects such as agriculture and related topics such as forestry and aquaculture. It also covers the vital and fast-growing range of environmental sciences. These include environmental science itself, taught at a vast range of institutions, along with older but fast-changing sciences such as meteorology, oceanography and geology, which focus respectively on the airy, liquid and solid Earth. In recent years, the Earth sciences have been enhanced by our growing knowledge of other worlds, and anyone studying the Earth will find that Mars, Venus and other planets enter the course as well. Also in this group is astronomy, which can only be studied by applicants with good physics and maths skills.

The sciences as we define them here also include biology apart from those parts of it directly concerned with human life, which we regard as biomedicine. Here we find botany, zoology, biochemistry, microbiology, genetics and ecology, amongst others. In the past these were highly distinct disciplines. Now we are more aware that the basic processes underlying all life are identical, especially their reproduction via DNA, and they tend to be taught in a less category-based way.

Career paths

Scientists are always in demand. In recent years, countries such as Japan, the US and the UK have been trying to steer students towards science careers, with mixed success.

Career choices for science graduates vary from becoming a forensic scientist to being a science journalist. You could run a mining company, or become an environmental activist opposing the mining industry. Many scientists are highly dedicated to their research and would never consider a career change. But a science degree leaves open options such as teaching if the academic route palls or if the grants run out.

Many science courses are highly applied and lead directly into a career. An example is food science and technology. Studying for a degree here involves courses in topics such as microbiology, biochemistry and physiology. But it also means advanced courses in underlying topics such as biology, chemistry, maths and statistics, and physics. This means that graduates have a career lined up but can also use their basic science knowledge if they want to change their career or study path.

Many sciences have a substantial industry behind them in which graduates are likely to get jobs. Geologists work in oil, mining or water resources. Chemists have the chemical and pharmaceutical industry. People with agricultural qualifications may end up on the farm, but also have options in the food industry and with other related employers.

One common theme is that many of these subjects require postgraduate study. In chemistry, a PhD has become more or less the entry-level qualification. So applicants for undergraduate courses might want to prepare themselves for a longer-than-normal period of study before the first salary cheques come in. This also applies to career-change options such as science journalism, which may well involve taking a Master's degree.

However, scientists do have a better range of career options than most graduates. They can often manage to structure their jobs so that they work part-time in both industry and academia. If they have good ideas, they may be able to raise capital to start their own business to exploit it.

In addition, scientists are often in demand from unexpected directions. Financial organisations appreciate their numeracy and scepticism, as do a wide range of public-sector employers. This means that even courses in very specialist topics such as astronomy can lead to lucrative employment. And subjects that once seemed obscure can become important. For example, maths skills are in demand from the IT industry and mathematics that was once regarded as purely theoretical now underpins the security of the internet.

Top 100 in social sciences

Rank	Institution	Country	Score	Citations per paper
1	University of Oxford	United Kingdom	100.0	2.6
2	Harvard University	United States	98.5	4.0
3	London School of Economics	United Kingdom	94.9	-
4	University of Cambridge	United Kingdom	90.8	2.4
5	University of California, Berkeley	United States	89.2	3.1
6	Australian National University	Australia	85.0	1.6
7=	Stanford University	United States	81.2	3.2
7=	Yale University	United States	81.2	3.5
9	University of Chicago	United States	75.3	3.5
10	University of Melbourne	Australia	73.0	1.7
11	National University of Singapore	Singapore	72.2	1.5
12	Massachusetts Institute of Technology	United States	71.5	4.0
13	Princeton University	United States	69.2	3.4
14	Columbia University	United States	66.2	2.8
15	University of Tokyo	Japan	65.9	-
16	Monash University	Australia	64.9	1.2
17=	Peking University	China	62.6	-
17=	University of Toronto	Canada	62.6	2.0
19	University of Sydney	Australia	62.2	2.3
20	McGill University	Canada	58.6	1.9
21	University of New South Wales	Australia	58.4	2.0
22	Cornell University	United States	56.7	2.6
23	University of California, Los Angeles	United States	55.7	3.3
24	University of Pennsylvania	United States	55.3	3.5
25	British Columbia University	Canada	53.7	1.9
26	Indian Institute of Management	India	53.3	-
27	University of Queensland	Australia	52.1	1.6
28	Michigan State University	United States	51.1	3.3
29	New York University	United States	50.7	2.9
30=	University of Amsterdam	Netherlands	49.9	1.7
30=	University of Hong Kong	Hong Kong	49.9	1.5
30=	University of Warwick	United Kingdom	49.9	1.8
33	University of Auckland	New Zealand	49.5	1.5
34	University of Vienna	Austria	49.2	-
35	Carnegie Mellon University	United States	49.0	3.6
36	Kyoto University	Japan	48.0	-
37	Erasmus Univ Rotterdam	Netherlands	47.0	2.1

Rank	Institution	Country	Score	Citations per paper
38=	Catholic University of Louvain	Belgium	46.7	1.4
38=	University of Edinburgh	United Kingdom	46.7	1.8
40	University of Copenhagen	Denmark	45.2	-
41	Northwestern University	United States	45.0	3.0
42	Duke University	United States	44.1	3.1
43	Chinese University of Hong Kong	Hong Kong	43.9	1.4
44	Hebrew University of Jerusalem	Israel	43.4	1.8
45	University College London	United Kingdom	42.7	2.5
46	Massachusetts Institute of Technology University	Australia	42.4	-
47	University of Gadjah Mada	Indonesia	41.1	-
48	University of Wisconsin	United States	41.0	2.3
49	University of Malaya	Malaysia	40.6	-
50	Panthéon Sorbonne Université Paris I	France	40.5	-
51	Tel Aviv University	Israel	40.2	1.6
52	Hong Kong University of Science and Technology	Hong Kong	40.1	2.2
53=	City University of Hong Kong	Hong Kong	39.6	1.5
53=	Université Paris-Sorbonne (Paris IV)	France	39.6	-
53=	Stockholm School of Economics	Sweden	39.6	-
56	Seoul National University	South Korea	39.1	-
57	Jawaharlal Nehru University	India	38.7	-
58	National Taiwan University	Taiwan	38.3	-
59=	University of Bologna	Italy	38.2	-
59=	Fudan University	China	38.2	-
61=	Nanyang Technological University	Singapore	38.1	-
61=	University of Sussex	United Kingdom	38.1	1.9
63=	University of Helsinki	Finland	37.6	1.8
63=	University of Victoria	New Zealand	37.6	1.5
65	Imperial College London	United Kingdom	37.5	-
66=	Georgetown University	United States	37.4	2.2
66=	University of Manchester	United Kingdom	37.4	2.0
68=	Macquarie University	Australia	37.2	-
68=	University of Oslo	Norway	37.2	2.1
70	Universität Heidelberg	Germany	37.1	-
71	Catholic University of Leuven	Belgium	37.0	1.8
72	Boston University	United States	36.8	3.0
73	Chulalongkorn University	Thailand	36.6	-
74	Universität München	Germany	36.5	1.9
75	Keio University	Japan	36.3	-

Rank	Institution	Country	Score	Citations per paper
76=	University of Adelaide	Australia	36.1	-
76=	Freie Universität Berlin	Germany	36.1	-
76=	Utrecht University	Netherlands	36.1	2.2
79	Università degli Studi di Roma - La Sapienza	Italy	36.0	-
80	Kings College London	United Kingdom	35.6	2.2
81	University of Nottingham	United Kingdom	35.5	1.9
82	University of Maastricht	Netherlands	35.4	1.8
83	Pennsylvania State University	United States	35.3	2.4
84=	Rheinische Friedrich-Wilhelms- Universität Bonn	Germany	35.0	-
84=	Leiden University	Netherlands	35.0	2.1
86	University of Delhi	India	34.9	-
87	University of Illinois	United States	34.7	2.2
88	Kobe University	Japan	34.5	-
89	Johns Hopkins	United States	34.2	2.9
90	HEC Paris	France	33.9	-
91	University of Bristol	United Kingdom	33.8	2.8
92	Lancaster University	United Kingdom	33.7	2.2
93=	University of Dublin, Trinity College	Ireland	33.4	-
93=	University of Massachusetts, Amherst	United States	33.4	2.1
95	School of Oriental and African Studies	United Kingdom	33.3	-
96=	Bocconi	Italy	33.1	-
96=	University of Glasgow	United Kingdom	33.1	2.2
98=	La Trobe University	Australia	32.8	2.0
98=	University of Western Australia	Australia	32.8	2.2
100	University of Texas at Austin	United States	32.5	2.4

The world's top social sciences universities

The social sciences are a varied array of subjects which study human societies. Much the biggest social science is education, and teacher training is a mainstay of many universities around the world. Some social sciences, such as psychology and geography, overlap with the life and physical sciences. Others such as economics have a life of their own.

Definitions of the social sciences vary from country to country. In the UK and US funding systems, law is regarded as one of the humanities. But the European Science Foundation groups it with the social sciences and we follow that rule here.

The social sciences include the fast-growing area of business, and the reputation data and citations we give here include business schools which form part of universities. However, it does not cover institutions such as the London Business School which have no undergraduates.

The vast range of social science subjects means that it is hard to generalise about educational or career paths. Best established is the MBA, without doubt the most global of academic qualifications. People are willing to make substantial investments in MBAs, law degrees and other qualifications which can lead to high-earning careers. These courses often have fees, and entry standards, that reflect the earnings to which they can give access. Economists, too, can be in heavy demand from banks and other employers. But while teachers are always in demand, the financial rewards of their dedication are less and the difficulty of entering the profession reflects this.

Potential students with international ambitions should also recognise that qualifications in the social sciences vary in their portability. Economists can and do move from country to country easily. But a lawyer might face lengthy retraining to work in a different legal system from the one in which they trained.

The top institutions in this table all have world-renowned business schools. Oxford, in top slot, has one of the newest, the Said Business School, dating back to 1996. Harvard, in second position, also has perhaps the world's best-known law school, although many of these universities have been educating lawyers for centuries. The table shows that apart from Tokyo and Peking, the big mainland Asian institutions, English-speaking institutions in the UK, the US and Australia dominate the social sciences.

Popular subjects and courses

Popular subjects within the social science field include media studies, sociology, accounting, education, law and a wealth of courses with titles involving business studies and management. But the biggest social sciences are economics, geography and psychology. Both geography and psychology shade off into "hard" science. Geography has links to geology and the other Earth sciences. Psychology can be taught as one of the social sciences or in a manner more linked to biology and medicine. If you want to study either of these subjects, it is worth making sure that the course you apply for will approach the subject in a way that is appropriate to you.

You should also bear in mind that economics, psychology and sociology are closer than you might think to the laboratory sciences in their working methods. You will not be happy on courses in these subjects if you are not comfortable with mathematics, especially statistics. There are also maths-intensive elements to business courses including the MBA, and of course accounting.

The new media age has cultivated a new generation of students interested in learning both the conceptual and practical sides of the media industry. As a result, most social science faculties now have a media studies department to serve the needs of the millennials, the new university entrants born in the 1980s. While many media lecturers have PhDs in the subject, some have come from the field of sociology or cultural studies. There is also a growing variety of journalism courses, aiming to teach more specific skills than a media studies department would. They often offer very specific courses in areas such as magazine, newspaper, radio, TV or online journalism. Often these courses are taught by former practitioners who may well not have a PhD in the subject.

Law, along with medicine and religion, is perhaps the oldest profession taught in university. A Master's degree in the subject, such as an LLM or J.S.D., is normally required to practice as a lawyer. Leading law schools like those at Cornell or Stanford often have the competitive advantage of being top choices of global recruiters, willing to pay its graduates higher salaries than those from lower-calibre schools, and the same applies to their competitors around the world.

Business studies and accounting are often precursors to taking an MBA and are favoured by business-oriented students looking to climb the corporate ladder or start their own businesses. Most leading social science departments offer such degree programmes, as do free-standing business schools. There is also a trend for single elective classes in topics such as marketing to be offered to students of other disciplines.

Entry requirements

US school tend to value standardised tests like the SAT, whilst UK and Australian schools rely more on coursework performance or A-level and HSC results respectively.

Top US universities such as Harvard, Yale and Stanford do not have exact minimum SAT scores candidates must obtain to gain acceptance. But the majority of admitted students to such universities have obtained scores of 1400 and higher, on average, and have obtained perfect marks in all studied subjects in high school.

In the UK, top universities such as Oxford and Cambridge also use interviews in their selection process. For some courses, leading UK universities also examine essays the candidate has written for previous course assessment, and in some cases they will be asked to take a thinking skills assessment exam.

Career paths

Social science graduates have a dizzying array of options when it comes to career choices. Social worker, lawyer, politician, marketer and other forms of executive, economist and company director are only a few of the thousands of job titles social science graduates can aim for. Politics is not one of the social sciences, but top politicians have a strong tendency to have law degrees.

Top 100 in engineering and IT

Rank	Institution	Country	Score	Citations per paper
1	Massachusetts Institute of Technology	United States	100.0	3.2
2	University of California, Berkeley	United States	96.7	3.4
3	Indian Institute of Technology	India	87.1	-
4	Imperial College London	United Kingdom	83.5	2.3
5	Stanford University	United States	83.4	3.5
6	University of Cambridge	United Kingdom	81.8	2.3
7	University of Tokyo	Japan	79.3	1.8
8	National University of Singapore	Singapore	77.8	1.6
9	California Institute of Technology	United States	76.4	3.9
10	Carnegie Mellon University	United States	68.2	2.2
11	University of Oxford	United Kingdom	67.5	3.1
12	Swiss Federal Institute of Technology Zurich	Switzerland	67.4	2.4
13	Delft University of Technology	Netherlands	66.3	1.8
14	Tsing Hua University	China	66.0	1.1
15	Nanyang Technological University	Singapore	65.8	1.4
16	University of Melbourne	Australia	64.9	2.2
17	Hong Kong University of Science & Technology	Hong Kong	64.7	1.9
18	Tokyo Institute of Technology	Japan	64.2	-
19	University of New South Wales	Australia	63.4	1.6
20	Peking University	China	62.3	1.5
21	Kyoto University	Japan	62.0	1.8
22	Georgia Institute of Technology	United States	61.6	2.1
23	Harvard University	United States	58.9	3.8
24	Australian National University	Australia	57.7	1.8
25	University of Sydney	Australia	57.3	2.0
26	École Polytechnique	France	57.0	2.2
27	University of Toronto	Canada	56.4	2.0
28=	Cornell University	United States	54.7	3.0
28=	Monash University	Australia	54.7	1.4
30=	University of Illinois	United States	54.6	2.5
30=	Technion - Israel Institute of Technology	Israel	54.6	1.9
32	Technische Universität München	Germany	53.1	1.5
33	Princeton University	United States	52.6	3.4
34	University of California, Los Angeles	United States	52.2	3.3

Rank	Institution	Country	Score	Citations per paper
35	University of Texas at Austin	United States	51.8	2.1
36	Michigan State University	United States	51.7	2.4
37	Korea Advanced Institute of Science and Technology	South Korea	51.4	-
38	University of Queensland	Australia	50.4	1.7
39	Rheinisch-Westfälische Technische Hochschule Aachen	Germany	50.3	2.0
40	Purdue University	United States	49.6	2.0
41=	University of Science and Technology of China	China	48.8	2.0
41=	University of Manchester	United Kingdom	48.8	2.4
43=	University of Auckland	New Zealand	48.5	-
43=	National Taiwan University	Taiwan	48.5	1.5
45	Ecole Polytechnique Fédérale de Lausanne	Switzerland	47.5	2.3
46	Technical University of Denmark	Denmark	46.8	2.9
47	Vienna University of Technology	Austria	46.3	1.5
48=	University of California, San Diego	United States	45.4	3.3
48=	Shanghai Jiao Tong University	China	45.4	0.9
50	McGill University	Canada	45.2	2.1
51	British Columbia University	Canada	45.0	2.2
52	Seoul National University	South Korea	44.7	1.4
53=	Helsinki University of Technology	Finland	44.2	1.7
53=	Royal Institute of Technology	Sweden	44.2	-
55	Osaka University	Japan	43.8	1.5
56	Chalmers University of Technology	Sweden	43.6	1.7
57	Yale University	United States	43.4	3.7
58	Lomonosov Moscow State University	Russia	43.1	1.3
59	University of Waterloo	Canada	42.6	1.6
60	Texas A&M University	United States	42.5	1.9
61	University of Massachusetts, Amherst	United States	41.9	2.1
62	Technical University of Berlin	Germany	41.8	1.9
63=	Catholic University of Louvain	Belgium	41.4	2.3
63=	Politecnico di Milano	Italy	41.4	1.6
65	University of Wisconsin	United States	41.3	2.3
66	University of Edinburgh	United Kingdom	40.0	2.0
67	University of Hong Kong	Hong Kong	39.9	1.4
68	Indian Institute of Management	India	39.1	-
69	Eindhoven University of Technology	Netherlands	38.6	2.0
70	Queensland University of Technology	Australia	37.8	-

Rank	Institution	Country	Score	Citations per paper
71	Virginia Polytechnic Institute	United States	37.6	1.9
72	Chinese University of Hong Kong	Hong Kong	37.2	1.6
73	Universität Karlsruhe	Germany	36.9	1.7
74	University of Adelaide	Australia	36.8	-
75	Columbia University	United States	36.6	2.7
76	Universität Stuttgart	Germany	36.5	1.5
77=	Nagoya University	Japan	36.1	2.2
77=	Rensselaer Polytechnic Institute	United States	36.1	2.1
79=	Catholic University of Leuven	Belgium	36.0	2.0
79=	University of Twente	Netherlands	36.0	1.8
81	University of Pennsylvania	United States	35.9	3.1
82	University of Maryland	United States	35.6	2.2
83=	Ecole Normale Supérieure	France	35.4	2.5
83=	University of Technology, Sydney	Australia	35.4	-
85=	City University of Hong Kong	Hong Kong	34.8	1.7
85=	University of Melbourneersity	United States	34.8	3.0
87	Norwegian University of Science and Technology	Norway	34.6	1.8
88	RMIT University	Australia	34.3	-
89	University of Birmingham	United Kingdom	33.9	2.5
90=	Pennsylvania State University	United States	33.8	3.1
90=	Tohoku University	Japan	33.8	1.9
90=	University of Washington	United States	33.8	2.6
93	University of Sheffield	United Kingdom	33.7	1.6
94	University of California, Santa Barbara	United States	33.5	3.4
95=	Boston University	United States	33.3	2.9
95=	Chulalongkorn University	Thailand	33.3	-
97	Fudan University	China	33.1	-
98	Northwestern University	United States	32.9	2.8
99	Nanjing University	China	32.6	-
100	Université Pierre-et-Marie-Curie	France	32.5	2.3

The world's top engineering and IT universities

The existence of the World University Rankings is itself a tribute to technology. Without developments such as mass air travel and cheap communications, there would be far less interest in knowing where to study overseas, and fewer global employers wanting internationally oriented graduates.

Technology includes some of the longest-established topics in the university curriculum, such as civil engineering, along with newer entrants such as IT. Intending academics in these areas would regard a PhD as essential. But many courses in these areas are validated by professional organisations such as the engineering institutions in the US and UK.

A good degree is valuable in these subjects, but is often only one step in what the French term the "formation" of a professional engineer or technologist. Membership of a professional organisation is usually obtained by following academic study by structured work in industry. UK research on engineers at an early stage of their careers, carried out by Michael Eraut at the University of Sussex, shows that the support they receive then is vital to their professional success.

This table shows that internationally oriented institutions are top in technology. For example, Massachusetts Institute of Technology, in pole position here, has one of the most international student bodies of any US university. By contrast, technology is the area in which Harvard, usually near the top of all university rankings, is least impressive, in 23rd place.

It is no surprise to see Stanford and the University of California, Berkeley, the intellectual homes of Silicon Valley, doing well here in first and second places. Imperial College London, at number four, is definitively Europe's top technology university.

For anyone seeking a well-regarded qualification, technology is an area in which big, old, general universities are not necessarily the top choice. Specialist institutions such as Imperial, Swiss Federal Institute of Technology Zurich in Switzerland (the highest-rated institution in continental Europe), Cal Tech in the US, Tokyo Institute of Technology and the Hong Kong University of Science and Technology might all be worth a look instead.

Another message here is that emerging Asian nations are not planning to have a future as low-skill contractors to European, Japanese and US business. The Indian Institutes of Technology have placed well in these tables in all three years of their existence. They are joined here by universities in Singapore, China and Hong Kong.

Popular subjects and courses

Technology is a massive field that includes both new and long-established subjects. Older areas include mechanical and civil engineering, while the more contemporary subjects include areas of IT such as artificial intelligence and web programming.

Popular subjects in this field include chemical engineering, civil engineering, computer science and IT, electrical and electronic engineering, information systems, mechanical, aeronautical and manufacturing engineering, metallurgy and materials science, and mineral and mining engineering.

Competition for places in the IT and engineering departments of top universities is fierce, especially for the more contemporary subjects, which are attractive to the millennium generation. By contrast, many top-ranked universities are finding it difficult to recruit sufficient numbers of well-qualified candidates to the traditional subjects, even though these often yield similar career opportunities.

Career paths

IT and engineering graduates tend to have the chance of a wide selection of well-paying jobs after they graduate, depending on their specific subject of study.

Information systems and computer sciences are the fastest-growing subject areas in terms of employer demand. According to the US Bureau of Labour Statistics, close to 2.8 million people are currently employed in the broad category of "computer and mathematical" related professions in the US, with approximately 13,000 vacancies in the field being filled each month.

Dr. Edgar Whitley, Reader in Information Systems at the London School of Economics, backs up these figures. He says: "companies in industries ranging from consultancy, investment banking and electronics to energy and software will recruit students from information systems and computer science programmes to positions such as business analysts or information systems managers. This applies to organisations both large and small."

A Bachelors or Masters in engineering can lead people into technology positions in high-tech industries such as aerospace, automotive, computing, consumer electronics, defence, energy, mining, software manufacturing or telecommunications.

"The future growth of many companies today depends on getting the best out of engineering and research teams. Hiring smart engineers is always tough, but the best ones are always about 20 times better than the average ones. The best engineers and scientists can be company-makers," says David Nagel, CEO of Palm Source in Sunnyvale, California.

A Master's is often a necessary step for students who are serious about an advanced career in engineering, says Professor Peter Bryanston-Cross at the University of

Warwick. "You learn not about what works today, but what will work in three to five years. An MSc should empower students and transfer research skills, training them not just to design and fit components, but to create new products."

In the last four years, Bryanston-Cross has sought to make Warwick's MSc in advanced engineering more relevant and attractive for students from around the world. When students arrive at Warwick at the start of their MSc, they are asked to nominate research projects on which they will be expected to spend half their time. To support this work, modules in areas such as remote sensing, synthetic intelligence and internet engineering are then organised. Bryanston-Cross also insists that everyone is given a grounding in the skills required for research and for writing reports. He has seen too many postgraduates come unstuck for lack of guidance.

Once students have successfully completed their MScs, they can aim for jobs in industry paying £30-40,000 (US$40-75,000), which is about the same as a professor.

Technology courses can differ widely even when they have similar names. For example, aeronautics has largely given way to aerospace as a degree title. But it is worth checking whether a particular course with this title actually includes modules on space engineering, or has simply been rebadged to make a course about aeroplanes more enticing.

Even long-established engineering subjects are fast changing. For example, mechanical engineers are closely involved with biologists and chemists in the emerging science of nanotechnology. Only they know how to make machines that can move atoms one at a time.

Harvard University

Why this university?

Has Harvard lost its lustre? Hardly. For one thing, it has been top of our world rankings for all three years of their existence.

Sure, there was that unseemly spat in which the outraged faculty managed to oust their confrontational president, purportedly over his comments (largely taken out of context) about the ability of women to succeed in the sciences. There were two gossipy books about the university's internal travails. There was a leaked survey in which undergraduates criticised the quality of instruction and the inaccessibility of faculty, placing Harvard fifth from the bottom of 31 élite schools in student satisfaction. There were reports of grade inflation making academic success at Harvard an easy ride for anyone privileged enough to get in.

But America's oldest university continues to conduct ground-breaking research, largely in its affiliated hospitals, which are among the world's best. Beginning with the 19th-century introduction of anaesthesia, Harvard scientists were the first to synthesise chlorophyll and cholesterol, they invented the pacemaker, performed the first human kidney transplant, invented the defibrillator, learned how to decode the structure of genes, discovered nuclear magnetic resonance, developed the first transgenic mouse, and, along with peers from other institutions, located the gene for Huntington's disease. Harvard's faculty, which has produced more than 40 Nobel laureates, also developed the modern theory of magnetism based on quantum mechanics and proved that the universe will go on expanding forever.

So, evidently, will Harvard. It has begun a multibillion-dollar expansion of its campus

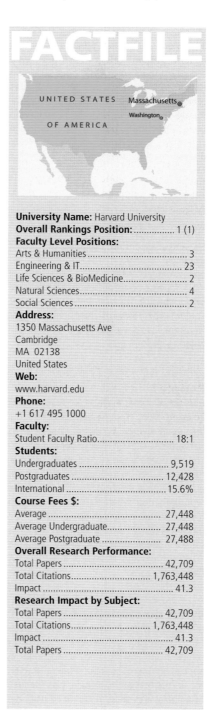

University Name: Harvard University
Overall Rankings Position: 1 (1)
Faculty Level Positions:
Arts & Humanities 3
Engineering & IT 23
Life Sciences & BioMedicine 2
Natural Sciences 4
Social Sciences 2
Address:
1350 Massachusetts Ave
Cambridge
MA 02138
United States
Web:
www.harvard.edu
Phone:
+1 617 495 1000
Faculty:
Student Faculty Ratio 18:1
Students:
Undergraduates 9,519
Postgraduates 12,428
International 15.6%
Course Fees $:
Average 27,448
Average Undergraduate 27,448
Average Postgraduate 27,488
Overall Research Performance:
Total Papers 42,709
Total Citations 1,763,448
Impact 41.3
Research Impact by Subject:
Total Papers 42,709
Total Citations 1,763,448
Impact 41.3
Total Papers 42,709

across the Charles River from its home in Cambridge to a vast swatch of land in Boston's Allston section that it purchased secretly through proxies. Though planning is still under way, the university has announced that it will build a 500,000-square-foot home in Allston for the Harvard Stem Cell Institute, the first noncommercial enterprise in the United States to create disease-specific stem-cell lines to develop treatments for now-incurable conditions. The institute is a direct affront to the Bush administration's effort to prevent stem-cell research by banning the use of government research money for it.

Harvard also continues to boast the largest academic library in the world and an endowment of nearly $26 billion, making it the richest nonprofit institution outside of the Vatican. This also allows it to admit students regardless of their ability to pay. Nine applicants vie for every seat in the entering class.

People?

Harvard's alumni have served as leaders in every field, from seven US presidents (including George W Bush, who went to Harvard Business School) to Benazir Bhutto and Al Gore. Some of the most famous, however, are the ones who dropped out, including Microsoft's Bill Gates (he reportedly quit when Harvard objected to his use of university computers for private business). Other Harvard dropouts: Polaroid founder Edwin Land, publishing magnate William Randolph Hearst, and actor Matt Damon.

What do students say?

It was the generous financial aid that made Harvard possible for Wojtek Kaszynski, a senior from Poland who is majoring in applied mathematics. But what attracted him in the first place, he said, was the idea of a liberal arts undergraduate education—

"this idea of going to school, yes to learn something, but more to just to go to school and figure things out."

Mr. Kaszynski doesn't dispute that students aren't always delighted with the teaching at Harvard. "The best researchers are not always the best teachers. And the faculty will not seek out actively to get in touch with you. It's on the side of the students to be proactive and meet the faculty.." But, he said, "my experience is that if I wanted to meet a particular professor, I certainly could. I've met a number of famous professors. I just emailed and set up an appointment."

Although students tend to be competitive, he has learned as much from his classmates as from faculty, Mr. Kaszynski said. "A friend of mine likes to say, 'Harvard may not do a great job teaching students. But it does a great job admitting them.' You can learn something from everyone here. You can sometimes learn more from your peers than from your professors. The people who are here are amazing. I've met very few people that I didn't want to get to know more."

As for the recent controversies, including the departure of President Lawrence Summers, Mr Kaszynski said they do not affect the lives of students. He illustrates this with an anecdote about a fellow mathematics major descended upon by journalists in the midst of the scandal. "They asked her, 'What do you think about the Larry Summers controversy?' And she said, 'Sorry, I don't have time. I have to go do my problem set.' She's in applied math. Why should she care what Larry Summers says?"

Good at?

Everything the human mind can cope with. Top four placings throughout except engineering & IT (23)

University of Cambridge

Why this university?

Only one university outperforms Cambridge in our ranking — and, importantly in the context of Britain's most enduring academic rivalry, it is not Oxford. The ancient universities are invariably bracketed together at the pinnacle of European higher education, but Cambridge has tended to score more highly in national assessments of teaching and research over recent years. Traditionally supreme in the sciences, where it has been ranked best in the world in successive years, Cambridge has also strengthened the arts and social sciences.

Cambridge is preparing to celebrate its 800th anniversary with a £1 billion fundraising campaign. There have been plenty of high-profile developments in the past decade — from attracting Microsoft's first research base outside the United States to securing £60 million from the government for an innovative link with the Massachusetts Institute of Technology — but overall funding levels have remained a concern. The campaign is intended to at least narrow the gap with the US Ivy League.

Twenty six per cent of the 21,290 students are from outside the European Union and the proportion may rise in the next few years. There are more than 9,000 postgraduates — more than half of whom are from overseas — and this is where any growth is likely to come.

The university dominates the small city of Cambridge, 50 miles north-east of London in East Anglia. All students belong to one of the 31 colleges which, with a handful of exceptions, are dotted around the city centre. Many boast historic buildings, several along the banks of the River Cam, where students and tourists go punting when the weather allows. Three

University Name: University of Cambridge
Overall Rankings Position..................2 (3)
Faculty Level Positions
Arts & Humanities...1
Engineering & IT...6
Life Sciences & BioMedicine..........................1
Natural Sciences...1
Social Sciences.. 4
Address:
Cambridge
CB2 1TN
United Kingdom
Web:
www.cam.ac.uk
Phone:
+44 1223 337733
Faculty:
Student Faculty Ratio:..........................18.9:1
Undergraduates:.................................11,855
Postgraduates:....................................9,435
International:......................................26.7%
Course Fees $:
Average:...18,559
Average Undergraduate:....................18,559
Average Postgraduate:.......................18,559
Overall Research Performance:
Total Papers:......................................20,339
Total Citations:.................................525,671
Impact:..25.8
Research Impact by Subject:
Engineering & IT:....................................2.3
Life Sciences & BioMedicine:..................12.8
Natural Sciences:....................................7.6
Social Sciences..1.4

121

colleges are for women only, while the rest are mixed.

Overseas students are guaranteed university-owned accommodation if they want it. A limited number of scholarships are available to overseas students and research students may be offered a small amount of teaching work.

People?

The 81 "affiliates" of the university who have won Nobel Prizes are divided among every category. They include Francis Crick and James Watson, who mastered the structure of DNA, and, more recently, Amartya Sen for his work in development economics and geneticist John Sulston. Stephen Hawking has become one of the world's best-known scientists, while the student drama company Footlights has produced a stream of stars for the cinema and theatre.

What do students say?

Denise Law, a second year engineering student from Hong Kong, applied to Cambridge because she felt it is one of the few UK universities that can compete with the US institutions. She has encountered a lot of positive aspects to studying at Cambridge: "It's a lovely city with great heritage and very nice and helpful people. Plus the education and facilities are first class."

However, she acknowledged that the workload involved took her by surprise: "You're expected to make the most of supervisions by asking questions and taking the initiative, as opposed to the "spoonfeeding" in the A Levels. The learning curve is steep."

But, reassuringly, she added: "I was told that no one was ever kicked out for finding the material difficult. You won't get into trouble unless you adopt a "can't be bothered" attitude or give up."

Good at?

Every academic area is in the top ten in our ranking. Cambridge is top in the natural sciences, biomedicine and the arts and humanities.

University of Oxford

Why this university?

Oxford is the oldest university in the English-speaking world, dating back nine centuries, and also probably the best known. Only two institutions rate more highly in our rankings, one of which is Cambridge. The two are practically inseparable in most respects, and Oxford comes out on top in some UK league tables.

The 39 Oxford colleges select their own students and are responsible for much of the teaching, especially in the arts and social sciences. The Vice-Chancellor, Dr John Hood, who arrived from Auckland University in 2004, has been pushing through reforms aimed at helping Oxford to compete not only with Cambridge but with the American Ivy League. The changes may include increasing the proportion of postgraduates and overseas students. At the moment, nearly two-thirds of the students are undergraduates and about a fifth are from outside the European Union. Some 130 nationalities are represented in the student body and among an increasingly cosmopolitan faculty.

Traditionally, Oxford's strengths have been in the arts and social sciences, which have provided most of the 25 UK prime ministers educated at the university. But the sciences have been growing in quality – a £60 million development houses the world's largest chemistry department, for example – and the Said Business School, established only in 1996, has already carved out a strong reputation.

Most of the colleges and other university buildings are in or close to the centre of the city of Oxford, which is within reach of some of England's most picturesque countryside but only an hour by train from London. Although best known for the

FACTFILE

UNITED KINGDOM

Oxford
● London

University Name: University of Oxford
Overall Rankings Position:................3 (4)
Faculty Level Positions:
Arts & Humanities.......................................2
Engineering & IT......................................11
Life Sciences & BioMedicine.......................3
Natural Sciences.......................................2
Social Science...1
Address:
Wellington Square
Oxford OX1 2JD
United Kingdom
Web:
www.ox.ac.uk
Phone:
+44 (0)1865 270000
Faculty:
Student Faculty Ratio...........................23.4:1
Students:
Undergraduates..................................15,495
Postgraduates.....................................7,145
International.......................................23.9%
Course Fees $:
Average................................. . 26,273
Average Undergraduate.................. 28,840
Average Postgraduate.................... 23,707
Percentage Graduates Employed:......82
Overall Research Performance:
Total Papers......................................17,711
Total Citations..............................487,496
Impact...27.5
Research Impact by Subject:
Engineering & IT 3.1
Life Sciences & BioMedicine...................13.0
Natural Sciences 7.5
Social Sciences..2.6

university, the city is large enough to have a life of its own.

Over seas students are guaranteed residential accommodation if they want it. Several hundred international students each year benefit from a range of scholarships and bursaries, the biggest of the schemes being the Rhodes Scholarships and the Clarendon Fund Scholarships. Details appear in the university's International Student Guide. Postgraduate fees for overseas students range from £8,800 in the social sciences to more than £30,000 for an Executive MBA, while Oxford puts average living costs at £8,700 a year.

People?
Among scores of famous alumni are Erasmus, the philosopher Thomas Hobbes, the playwright Oscar Wilde, the author JRR Tolkein and the chemist Dorothy Hodgkin, the only British woman to win a Nobel Prize. More recent alumni include President Bill Clinton and Tim Berners Lee, inventor of the World Wide Web.

What do students say?
Jenny Rigterink, a third-year English language and literature undergraduate: "The pros are the unparalleled teaching and resources at your fingertips, but the cons are a stagnant social scene that seems far too old for its audience."

She says "Oxford will transform your life."

"The majority of people seem willing to let Oxford change them, but Oxford is begging for a generation that will turn things upside down."

She suggests to potential overseas applicants: "If you're foreign, make contact with potential tutors before you apply."

Good at?
Only engineering and IT are outside the top ten in our rankings – and then only just. Oxford comes top in the social sciences and second in the arts and humanities and natural sciences.

124

Massachusetts Institute of Technology

Why this university?

Every January, the Massachusetts Institute of Technology runs an "Independent Activities Period" during which students can select such non-credit subjects as yoga, folk-dancing, chocolate sculpture-making, magic, palmistry, effective speaking, the symbolism of the Star Wars films, and how to make chain mail.

It is a whimsical break from the intensity of the demanding academics at a school whose students are required to take two semesters each of calculus and physics, one each of biology and chemistry, and various courses in the humanities, arts and social sciences.

What makes MIT so tough, beyond the pressure its high-achieving students famously put on themselves, is the concept of the "teaching laboratory", which was pioneered there, combining teaching with applied research. It also makes the university one of the leading research institutions in America, where 3,500 scientists and scholars in addition to the 1,000 faculty (and 2,500 graduate students employed as research assistants) work on more than $1 billion a year of research.

Just in the last few years, research teams at MIT, which is in the small city of Cambridge across the Charles River from Boston, have developed a single-electron transistor, invented a process similar to photosynthesis to produce hydrogen and invented a gas with super-high temperature fluidity. Undergraduates, too, work with faculty on research into fields including cancer treatment, solar power and molecular biology through the Undergraduate Research Opportunity Programme.

FACTFILE

UNITED STATES OF AMERICA — Massachusetts, Washington

University Name: Massachusetts Institute of Technology
Overall Rankings Position:..............4= (2)
Faculty Level:
Arts & Humanities 21
Engineering & IT.. 1
Life Sciences & BioMedicine...................... 13
Natural Sciences.. 5
Social Sciences 12
Address:
77 Massachusetts Avenue
Cambridge
MA 02139-4307
United States
Web:
web.mit.edu
Phone:
+1 617 253 1000
Faculty:
Student Faculty Ratio............................20.7:1
Students:
Undergraduates 4,136
Postgraduates 6,184
International 24.1%
Course Fees $:
Average 30,600
Average Undergraduate.................... 30,600
Average Postgraduate 30,600
Overall Research Performance:
Total Papers 16,496
Total Citations................................. 541,452
Impact 32.8
Research Impact by Subject:
Engineering & IT.. 3.2
Life Sciences & BioMedicine.................... 22.5
Natural Sciences.. 9.6
Social Sciences 4.0

The university has about 4,000 undergraduate and 6,000 graduate students, including 2,792 from other countries—the largest contingent from Asia. More than half the undergraduates who have declared a major are enrolled in engineering, the field in which MIT is indisputably pre-eminent.

This work is conducted in a collection of radically innovative buildings added in a just-completed building spree, including the Frank Gehry-designed Ray and Maria Stata Center for Computer, Informationand Intelligence Sciences and a huge new brain and cognitive sciences complex.

They are physical proof that the 140-year-old university is not resting on its laurels. Its new president, Susan Hockfield — a neuroscientist and the first woman to hold the post — has challenged MIT to find solutions to the world's energy crisis in a campaign involving all five of its schools—science,engineering,management, architecture and the humanities. The university is also the first to put all of the teaching materials used in its courses onto the Internet without charge, and has set up a biomedical institute in collaboration with nearby Harvard to specialise in genomic medicine.

In addition to its science disciplines, MIT has a top-flight business school, the Sloan School of Management, which attracts mostly mid-career managers. The average age of students in Sloan's MBA programme is 28, and the average age in its first-in-the-world university-based executive education programme is 38. Students in the Sloan School come from more than 60 countries.

People?

Sixty-one past and present MIT faculty and alumni have won the Nobel Prize, 31 have received the National Medal of Science, and four have been awarded the Kyoto Prize. MIT leads all universities in America in patents granted.

What do students say?

Even chocolate sculpture-making fails to completely lighten the mood at a place where the stakes are so high. "In the dorm that I live in, people tend to themselves. They're generally not outgoing. It's a little cold," said Dzikimaki Matara, a junior from Zimbabwe who is majoring in mechanical engineering. He, like many others, alleviates his stress by playing intramural sports (among other things, Matara takes part in an ice-hockey league for students who don't know how to skate). Some 65 per cent of all students play intramural sports, and among the university's many new facilities is a fitness centre with two swimming pools and international-scale squash courts.

"The workload is really much heavier than anywhere else," he said. "I talk to friends at other schools and when they're given homework, they can start it the day before it's due. You can't do that here. It took me a while to get used to that." Then again, he said, "After you graduate from MIT, because of all the pressure we have here, when you start working, it probably won't seem as hard."

Good at?

Engineering and IT, natural science, life science and biomedicine (1, 5 and 13 in the world) but not bad at social sciences (12) or arts and humanities (21)

Yale University

Why this university?

A university that numbers both George H.W. Bush and Bill Clinton, as well as both George W. Bush and John Kerry, among its graduates must be providing a broad education. In fact,Yale does have one of the broadest curricula in American higher education, requiring its undergraduates to take at least three classes in each of four groups—languages, culture, social sciencesand science and maths. All students are required to speak a foreign language and to submit a senior essay or project, unusual in American higher education.

The university also seeks to make itself affordable for the broadest possible range of students, easing the financial burden on long-squeezed middle-class families. Beginning in the 2005-06 school year, families with combined incomes below $45,000 a year were no longer required to pay any portion of the cost of their children's education at the school, a groundbreaking shift being watched closely by other universities. (International students are eligible for the same financial aid as US citizens.) There is also a loan-forgiveness programme for law school graduates who go into public service.

Many of the programmes at Yale centre around small classes; nearly a third of the classes enrol 10 fewer than 10 students, and three-quarters have fewer than 20. The law school, for example, has 115 full- and part-time faculty for its 650 students. Yale has around 10,000 students —about half of them undergraduates—and 3,333 faculty. Only one in 10 applicants is admitted, the lowest proportion in the country. Sixteen per cent of students there are international – top countries of origin are China, Canada, South Korea, India, the UK, Germany, Italy and Japan. Undergraduates are divided into 12 small residential colleges. The most popular undergraduate majors are history,

FACTFILE

University Name: Yale University
Overall Rankings Position: ....4= (7)
Faculty Level Positions:
Arts & Humanities 8
Engineering & IT.. 57
Life Sciences & BioMedicine...................... 11
Natural Sciences... 14
Social Sciences 7
Address:
United States
Web:
www.yale.edu
Phone:
+1 (203) 432-4771
Faculty:
Student Faculty Ratio:.......................... 34.3:1
Students:
Undergraduates 5,319
Postgraduates 4,877
International 15.9%
Course Fees $:
Average 27,575
Average Undergraduate.................... 29,820
Average Postgraduate 26,800
Percentage Graduates Employed:....... 87
Overall Research Performance:
Total Papers 16,728
Total Citations................................ 580,398
Impact 34.7
Research Impact by Subject:
Yale University.................................... 3.7
Life Sciences & BioMedicine.................. 12.5
Natural Sciences..................................... 9.5
Social Sciences 3.5

political science and economics.

Named for Elihu Yale, who gave the young school 417 books and a portrait of King George I in 1716, Yale is in New Haven, Connecticut, a small city plagued with problems of urban poverty. This economic decline appears to be slowly reversing,helped in part by the role of the university in attracting biomedical and pharmaceutical companies. Some $428 million a year in research is conducted at the university itself.

People?

Alumni include both president Bushes and President Clinton, but also presidents William Howard Taft and Gerald Ford and Mr Clinton's wife, Senator Hillary Rodham Clinton; actors Jodie Foster, Sigourney Weaver, Sam Waterston, and Meryl Streep; former and current CEOs of FedEx and Coca Cola; 12 Nobel laureates; and Samuel F.B. Morse, the inventor of the telegraph.

What do students say?

"The biggest advantage of Yale is that it represents a sort of bubble of ideas from different perspectives," said Komli-Kofi Atsina, a student from Ghana who just received his undergraduate degree in molecular biophysics and biochemistry and is going on to medical school at the University of Pittsburgh. "It is a place that is so representative of the wide diversity around the world, a melting pot for crazy ideas, genius ideas, different kinds of ideology. In that respect, it's a great place for learning."

Good at?

Only engineering and IT are outside the top 20 in our rankings. Yale is in the top ten for social sciences and the arts and humanities.

Stanford University

Why this university?

Stanford was once content to be known as the Harvard of the West. These days, people at Stanford like to call Harvard the Stanford of the East.

Stanford features the research and low-key, small-scale teaching that has spawned more than 350 cutting-edge companies, including Google, Yahoo!, Cisco Systems, ebay and Sun Microsystems.

Stanford, which opened in Palo Alto in 1891, is surrounded by one of the largest campuses in the US, more than 8,000 acres, given to the university by Californians Jane and Leland Stanford in memory of their only child who died at 15.

Small classes with individualised instruction is a strong selling point for Stanford. The business school's 750 MBA students are taught by 112 faculty. The law school has only 514 students, taught by 43 full-time and 48 part-time faculty. In all, there are 11,267 undergraduates and 6,555 graduate students at Stanford; nearly 70 per cent of classes have fewer than 20 students in them. First- and second-year students also can select from the Stanford Introductory Seminars, each focused on a narrow topic and none with more than 16 students.

The faculty includes 16 Nobel laureates. Research has led to such breakthroughs as the laser, the musical synthesiser, magnetic resonance imaging and global positioning systems. The two-mile-long Stanford Linear Accelerator Center, used in the study of particle physics, is run by the university under contract to the US Department of Energy. The Undergraduate Research Programme not only encourages students to work with faculty on research, it funds them to design their own research, projects, to the tune of more than $4 million a year.

FACTFILE

UNITED STATES OF AMERICA

Stanford •   Washington •

University Name: Stanford University
Overall Rankings Position: 6 (5)
Faculty Level Positions:
Arts & Humanities 15
Engineering & IT 5
Life Sciences & BioMedicine 5
Natural Sciences 7
Social Sciences 7
Address:
Old Union, Room 141, 520 Lasuen Mall
Stanford
CA 94305-3005
United States
Web:
www.stanford.edu
Faculty:
Student Faculty Ratio: 12.3:1
Students:
Undergraduates 6,555
Postgraduates 11,267
International 21.0%
Course Fees $:
Average 29,847
Average Undergraduate 29,847
Average Postgraduate 29,847
Overall Research Performance:
Total Papers 22,180
Total Citations 766,457
Impact 34.6
Research Impact by Subject:
Technology 3.5
BioMedicine 14.4
Science 9.5
Social Sciences 3.2

In all, about $1 billion a year in research is conducted at Stanford.

The medical school first synthesised DNA-like material, and it was where segments of DNA from two species were joined and made to replicate, leading to the creation of the biotechnology industry. A Stanford surgeon performed the first human heart transplant in the US and the world's first heart/lung transplant, and a Stanford researcher discovered the genetic mutation that causes narcolepsy. And it was a lab at Stanford that was the first to isolate stem cells. The Stanford Institute for Stem Cell Biology and Regenerative Medicine is today among the top such research centres in the world.

The National Research Council also ranks Stanford's programmes the best in America in computer science, electrical engineering and mechanical engineering, and rates it highly in aeronautics and astronautics and civil engineering. Among undergraduates, the most popular majors are biology, computer science, economics, English and psychology.

People?

Hewlett Foundation cofounders William Hewlett and David Packard; Nike CEO Philip Knight; former Israeli Prime Minister Ehud Barak, former Guatemalan President Jorge Serrano, Peruvian President Alejandro Toledo, Dolby Laboratories founder Ray Dolby, golfer Tiger Woods and Sally ride, the first American woman in space.

What do students say?

"Stanford has good resources, it has good libraries, it has good research, and the professors are very easy to approach," said Pumsaran Tongliemnak, a doctoral candidate from Thailand who is studying education economics. "They're world-class, but they're unassuming and students can approach them more easily than at other institutions."

As for the students, Mr Tongliemnak said: "They have the mentality of work, but they also, play hard, and they have a lot of creativity. They're just not the type that go to the library all the time. They have some fun.

Good at?

Every academic area is rated in the top 20 in the world. life sciences and biomedicine and engineering and IT are in the top five.

California Institute of Technology

Why this university?

The universe of astronomy has no centre, astronomer Martin Rees (now Lord Rees) once said, "but the universe of astronomers does." He placed that midpoint at Pasadena, California, just north of Los Angeles, home to the California Institute of Technology.

It was, in fact, an astronomer who first had the idea of transforming a sleepy polytechnic institute into Caltech in the early 1900s, but he did it by luring a physicist and a chemist west from the University of Chicago and MIT, respectively; wisecracking students call the founders "Tinker Thinker, and Stinker".

Caltech students boast the highest average scores in the nation on the SAT university entrance examination. Because there are so few of them, the student-faculty ratio is just three-to-one, and most work directly on research with their professors, 31 of whom are also Nobel laureates. Thirty per cent of classes have fewer than 10 students.

There are nearly two and a half times as many men as women enrolled. Students share an unusual honour code – it stipulates that "no member of the Caltech community shall take unfair advantage of any other member" – that encourages collaboration and leaves students to take tests without the supervision of proctors. And while it is possible to specialise in something other than science, students have to take a core curriculum that requires five terms of math and five terms of physics.

People?

Cal Tech has chalked up some of the most significant astronomical discoveries made since—including the first astronomical

FACTFILE

UNITED STATES OF AMERICA

Pasadena   Washington

University Name: California Institute of Technology
Overall Rankings Position:...................7 (8)
Faculty Level Positions:
Arts & Humanities ....212=
Engineering & IT.. 9
Life Sciences & BioMedicine...................... 25
Natural Sciences.. 8
Social Sciences ....169=
Address:
1200 East California Boulevard
Pasadena
Califania 91125
United States
Web:
www.caltech.edu
Phone:
+1 626 395 6811
Faculty:
Student Faculty Ratio:........................... 20.5:1
Students:
Undergraduates:.....................................896
Postgraduates 1,275
International 24.6%
Course Fees $:
Average 25,335
Average Undergraduate.................... 25,355
Average Postgraduate 25,355
Overall Research Performance:
Total Papers 9,863
Total Citations................................... 335,701
Impact 34.0
Research Impact by Subject:
Engineering & IT:....................................... 3.9
Life Sciences & BioMedicine:.................. 20.3
Natural Sciences:.................................... 11.9

131

survey of the entire sky visible from the Northern Hemisphere—but also breakthroughs in almost every other major scientific field, and the virtual invention of seismology. It was Caltech physicist Carl Anderson, for example, who discovered anti-matter, chemist Linus Pauling who showed how atoms link up to form molecules, psychobiologist Roger Sperry who devised the left brain-right brain theory, and geophysicist Charles Richter who invented the scale for measuring earthquakes. The university also operates the famous Jet Propulsion Laboratory for NASA.

Caltech's small size allows for plenty of peace and quiet to work on research like this. There are fewer than 900 undergraduates and 1,300 graduate students, who comprise a small, familiar community—including among the international contingent, which numbers barely 60. Their influence belies their small numbers; among Caltech's international alumni are former Israeli foreign and defence minister Moshe Arens and Steingrimur Hermannsson, the former prime minister of Iceland.

Alumni also include Chester Carlson, the inventor of photocopying, Intel chairman Gordon Moore, 15 Nobel Prize winners, and Frank Capra, director of film classic It's a Wonderful Life.

What do students say?

"Caltech classes are on a whole different level," said Todd Gingrich, a junior. "People all know each other, you're living with a group of your good friends, and people are always looking out for you in a way that doesn't happen in a bigger school. I have this amazing network of peers in every field of math and science and I use it all the time."

Many of these students live in small residential houses. "It's almost as if a bunch of nerds had taken over all the frats," said Mr Gingrich.

Unlike some other schools with reputations for academic rigor, Caltech is known for attracting students with a sense of humour. "The student body is pretty quirky. It's a very tight-knit group of students, and most of the people here have this mode they can switch into where they can relax."

There can be a downside to this, too. "It's a school that's highly focused on a very small subject and a very small area of study, so as a consequence you get a group of students who are all quite similar. Often times I love that, but there are times where people wish there were more people here, different types of people—like girls."

Like many Caltech students, Mr Gingrich jumped ahead to university courses while he was still in high school in his home state of Missouri. This left him wanting more of a challenge, which is what drew him to Caltech. "There's sort of this perception, which now that I'm here I can verify, that it's reasonably hardcore," he said.

Still, Caltech is less well-known than its much bigger peer institutions. "It's hidden away," Mr Gingrich said. "Not a lot of people know about it, and sometimes that's a good thing. But you can send us some kids who love math and science, that's okay."

Good at?

Technology, science and medicine: no surprises here.

University of California at Berkeley

Why this university?

Nestled in the hills near temperate San Francisco, the University of California at Berkeley is nothing if not well rounded. The National Research Council has ranked 35 of its 36 graduate programmes among the top 10 in their fields—best overall, in the cases of chemistry, English, German, mathematics and statistics. That is the best score in America. Berkeley is highly regarded in civil engineering, biological sciences, computer sciences, physics and intellectual property law. It produces more PhDs than any other US school. Its library is the fourth-largest at an American university.

Berkeley began as an outgrowth of the eastern higher education establishment. Its early classical curriculum was based on those of Harvard and Yale. Booming California and its wealthy civic leaders supported a grand building scheme on prime land with a view of San Francisco Bay. But the university soon turned toward the sciences, especially after the development of the first cyclotron by physicist Ernest O. Lawrence, whose work helped produce the atomic bomb.

The laboratory founded by Dr Lawrence, who also won the Nobel Prize, is now named for him, and is managed by the University of California on behalf of the Department of Energy. It has a budget of $500 million a year and 3,800 people work there, including more than 500 students, doing unclassified research in quantitative biology, nanoscience and other fields; the university also manages the government's Lawrence Livermore and Los Alamos nuclear science laboratories.

Faculty at Berkeley separately conduct an

University Name: University of California, Berkeley
Overall Rankings Position: 8 (6)
Faculty Level Positions:
Arts & Humanities 4
Engineering & IT.. 2
Life Sciences & BioMedicine...................... 10
Natural Sciences.. 3
Social Sciences 5
Address:
Berkeley
California CA 94720-4
United States
Web:
www.berkeley.edu
Phone:
(510) 642-6000
Faculty:
Student Faculty Ratio:.......................... 10.1:1
Students:
Undergraduates 22,880
Postgraduates 8,792
International 7.8%
Course Fees $:
Average 15,250
Average Undergraduate..................... 16,476
Average Postgraduate 14,694
Overall Research Performance:
Total Papers 22,171
Total Citations................................. 621,001
Impact 28.0
Research Impact by Subject:
Engineering & IT.. 3.4
Life Sciences & BioMedicine.................... 15.0
Natural Sciences.. 9.5
Social Sciences 3.1

additional half a billion dollars a year in research, though there have been cuts in services and scholarship money as higher education vies for a share of the perpetually overstretched California state budget.

Berkeley's 22,880 undergraduates (there are 8,792 graduate students and about 2,000 faculty) also benefit from this research. They can apply to take part in the Undergraduate Research Apprentice Programme and work side-by-side with faculty in any discipline.

People?

Nineteen Berkeley faculty have won the Nobel Prize, including physicist Charles Townes, whose work led to the invention of the laser; six current members of the faculty are Nobel laureates.

Alumni include former Pakistan President Zulfikar Ali Bhutto, Vietnam-era Defense Secretary Robert McNamara, economist John Kenneth Galbraith, California governor and onetime US presidential candidate Jerry Brown, actor Gregory Peck, Apple Computer cofounder Steve Wozniak, Intel CEO Andrew Grove, Twentieth Century Fox chairman Peter Chernin, Korean Airlines president Choon Kun Chom, The Gap CEO Don Fisher and Stephen Bechtel, founder of the controversial worldwide engineering firm that bears his name.

What do students say?

Arpita Roy, a doctoral student in cultural anthropology from India, said that in spite of the budget cuts: "What I find most remarkable about Berkeley is that it is a public university and yet it is doing so well academically, especially in a right-wing society like America. It just tells me that money is not everything, and that good research can be accomplished even under financial constraints."

Good at?

Every academic area is in the world's top ten, with second-placed engineering and IT the top performer.

Imperial College London

Why this university?

A staggering 39 per cent of Imperial College's students are from overseas — or 4,497 out of 11,490. Its specialisms of science, technology, medicine and engineering also make it the most male-dominated university institution in Britain. Female students, however, did double during the 1990s and are now up to a third.

Imperial is an academic powerhouse in its chosen fields and is considered to be a rival to Oxford and Cambridge. Its 2,904 academic and research staff include Nobel Prizewinners and 61 Fellows of the Royal Society. Three quarters of the academics entered in the latest research assessment exercise were in departments considered internationally outstanding — the highest proportion in any university — and almost all were in one of the top two categories.

Imperial's can claim the invention of penicillin and of magnetically-levitated trains among its successes. The college is also respected for its strong links with both industry and government. Many distinguished scientists and engineers make a significant contribution to the direction of UK business and policy.

Many eyes are on Imperial at present because it has announced that it is to leave the University of London in time for its centenary in 2007. What this will mean for students remains unclear, but the decision was made to trade on a reputation that puts the college in the top 20 universities in our world rankings.

Its headquarters could hardly be in a more glamorous part of London. South Kensington's cosmopolitan vibe and museums show off London at its best.

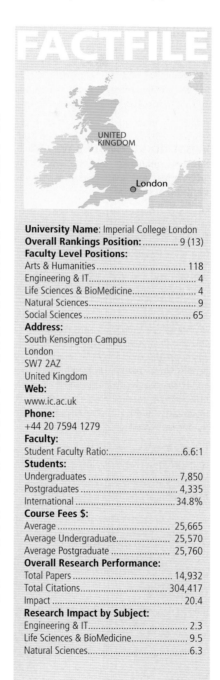

FACTFILE

UNITED KINGDOM

London

University Name: Imperial College London
Overall Rankings Position: 9 (13)
Faculty Level Positions:
Arts & Humanities 118
Engineering & IT 4
Life Sciences & BioMedicine 4
Natural Sciences 9
Social Sciences 65
Address:
South Kensington Campus
London
SW7 2AZ
United Kingdom
Web:
www.ic.ac.uk
Phone:
+44 20 7594 1279
Faculty:
Student Faculty Ratio: 6.6:1
Students:
Undergraduates 7,850
Postgraduates 4,335
International 34.8%
Course Fees $:
Average 25,665
Average Undergraduate 25,570
Average Postgraduate 25,760
Overall Research Performance:
Total Papers 14,932
Total Citations 304,417
Impact 20.4
Research Impact by Subject:
Engineering & IT 2.3
Life Sciences & BioMedicine 9.5
Natural Sciences 6.3

135

People?

Famous alumni include the four-minute miler and academic Sir Roger Bannister, politicians Rajiv Gandhi and Trevor Philips, the writers Simon Singh and HG Wells and pop star Brian May.

What do students say?

Natsuko graduated with an MSci in biochemistry in 2004 and is now studying for a PhD at Imperial.

She said: "I chose Imperial because of its worldwide reputation for teaching and research excellence. I also liked the fact that it is located in the centre of London.

"London was scary at first as I had never lived in such a large city before, but I soon got used to it and discovered that it is an exciting place to live as a student. There is an endless supply of entertainment, so you can always find things to do. It's very cosmopolitan and I got to meet lots of people from so many different countries and backgrounds! I spent most of my spare time with my friends. We often went out to restaurants, pubs and cinemas and visited the famous tourist spots.

"Imperial does work you hard, so you need to be committed and disciplined to be successful. But it really does pay off in the end. A lot of employers are interested in the graduates from Imperial College and you get a great network of people who can help you in your future career, whatever it is that you want to do."

Good at?

Imperial is ranked by other academics in the top ten in the world for natural sciences and in the top five for both biomedicine and engineering and IT.

Princeton University

Why this university?

Unlike other universities that have decried the high cost of a higher education, Princeton has put its money where its mouth is. Conscious that increasing tuition—and student indebtedness—was squeezing all-important middle-class families, it instituted a "no-loan" financial-aid policy, replacing loans with outright grants. Since then, no students receiving financial aid, including those from other countries, have been required to borrow money toward tuition.

Students have to be admitted before they can receive financial aid, and Princeton is among the most selective universities in America. Only one out of every 10 applicants gets in.

Its $11 billion endowment is the fourth-highest in the country (after Harvard's, Yale's and the University of Texas's).

There are around 4,700 undergraduate and 2,000 graduate students on the historic campus, which includes the building where the Continental Congress met during part of the Revolutionary War. The faculty numbers 700, including 10 Nobel laureates, and all of them teach as well as conduct research, supervising undergraduates who are required to submit a senior thesis (an obligation at Princeton that most other US universities make optional).

Undergraduates must also successfully complete two courses each in literature and the arts, science and technology, and social analysis, and one course each in epistemology and cognition, ethical thought and moral values, historical analysis, and quantitative reasoning. Even engineering students have to take at least seven humanities and social sciences courses.

FACTFILE

UNITED STATES OF AMERICA

New York
Washington

University Name: Princeton University
Overall Rankings Position:.............10 (9)
Faculty Level Positions:
Arts & Humanities.......................................9
Engineering & IT...33
Life Sciences & BioMedicine.....................37
Natural Sciences...6
Social Sciences..13
Address:
Princeton
NJ 08544
United States
Web:
www.princeton.edu
Phone:
(609) 258-3000
Faculty:
Student Faculty Ratio............................15.2:1
Students:
Undergraduates.....................................4,678
Postgraduates.......................................2,030
International...17.9%
Course Fees $:
Average 29,910
Average Undergraduate 29,910
Average Postgraduate 29,910
Overall Research Performance:
Total Papers...8,895
Total Citations...................................273,573
Impact...30.8
Research Impact by Subject:
Engineering & IT.......................................3.4
Life Sciences & BioMedicine....................15.2
Natural Sciences.....................................11.6
Social Sciences...3.4

137

Almost all the students live on campus; all are assigned to one of five residential colleges for their first two years. A sixth residential college is being added, allowing students—including undergraduates—to live in the same place all four years.

Its faculty conducts $148 million a year in research, excluding the Princeton Plasma Physics Laboratory, a $70 million-a-year partnership with the US Department of Energy for plasma and fusion studies. The university's Lewis-Sigler Institute for Integrative Genomics was set up to create interdisciplinary collaboration between biologists and scientists in physics, chemistry, chemical engineering, molecular biology and other fields; its endowment supports newly minted PhDs doing independent research.

The university's engineering school specialises in dissecting the connection between technology and economics, politics, the arts and other fields.

People?

Princeton has managed to lure top scholars away from other universities, too, including outspoken black studies professor Cornel West, who called it "the great center for humanistic studies".

Princeton alumni include US presidents James Madison and Woodrow Wilson, after whom the university named its Woodrow Wilson School of Public and International Affairs.

What do students say?

"It's a small university for the Ivy League, and there's a lot of focus on the undergraduates," said Ritu Kamal, a senior from India studying bioengineering. "The faculty are willing to take undergraduates into their labs and give them a lot of personal attention. In science departments, students do a lot of hands-on lab work alongside grad students who are doing research that will probably be published." Ms Kamal is doing hands-on work with stem cells. "It doesn't get much more cutting-edge than that," she said.

Good at?

Academics rate the natural sciences and arts and humanities in the top ten in the world, with the social sciences not far behind. Other areas are in the top 40.

University of Chicago

Why this university?

The columns that flank the Cobb Gate entrance to the University of Chicago campus are the backdrop to a sculpted melodrama. At the bottom are imposing-looking figures that purportedly represent the deans who decide whether students are admitted to the university or not. Those who do get past are depicted struggling to keep their footing on the steep ascent. At the pinnacle of the columns are the confident graduates.

Histrionics? Maybe. But not far off from the reality of what is considered one of the most intellectually serious universities in the United States. It was here that the first controlled, self-sustaining nuclear reaction was produced in 1942. So influential is the economics taught at the university by faculty including Nobel laureates Gary Becker, George Stigler, Merton Miller and Milton Friedman (also an alumnus) that it has given rise to an entire field of economics known as the Chicago School, combining basic theory with the psychology of what makes individuals and companies react the way they do.

Some 79 Nobel winners have been affiliated with the university, including America's first: Albert Michelson, who calculated the speed of light. Other Chicago faculty have demonstrated that cancer is genetic, verified black holes and the "big bang," developed the malaria pill, invented a way to preserve blood, discovered the jet stream, developed Carbon-14 dating and identified REM sleep. There are 2,160 faculty members in all.

This kind of heady stuff is taught in an imposing neo-Gothic setting in 10-week quarters that accelerate a learning process divided elsewhere into much longer semesters. The 4,550 undergraduates seem to be almost constantly sitting own

University Name: University of Chicago
Overall Rankings Position: 11 (17)
Faculty Level Positions:
Arts & Humanities:.......................................17
Engineering & IT:.................................... 132
Life Sciences & BioMedicine:..................... 39
Natural Sciences:..................................... 18
Social Sciences: 9
Address:
1101 E 58th Street
Chicargo
IL 60637
United States
Web:
www.uchicago.edu
Phone:
+1 773-702-8650
Faculty:
Student Faculty Ratio:............................ 8.5:1
Students:
Undergraduates:.................................... 4,550
Postgraduates: 8,262
International: 18.3%
Course Fees $:
Average: 31,435
Average Undergraduate:.................... 30,123
Average Postgraduate:....................... 31,680
Overall Research Performance:
Total Papers: 11,804
Total Citations:................................. 362,437
Impact: 30.7
Research Impact by Subject:
Engineering & IT:...................................... 4.0
Life Sciences & BioMedicine:................... 10.9
Natural Sciences:....................................11.6
Social Sciences: 3.5

to the comprehensive examinations on which they are graded. Updated in 1998, these requirements have been extended to include a foreign language and greater international and cross-cultural studies. The Graduate School of Business, second-oldest business school in the world (it opened in 1898) and consistently ranked among the best, has campuses in London and Singapore and a European studies programme that focuses on France is based in a new satellite centre in Paris that debuted in 2003. Nearer to home, the university also operates the Argonne National Laboratory, which conducts research in energy, physics and environmental sciences; a high-energy physics and particle astrophysics centre; and the Yerkes Observatory, home of the world's largest refracting telescope.

In all, the university conducts $375 million a year in research funding.

One thing in less supply here is fun. "Our un-fun-ness has been the subject of both mirth and pride," as a task force on the matter put it. "Although students take immense pride in the excellence of the academic programme here, many feel that this comes at a high price, citing excessive academic pressure, lack of time, and competitiveness, including student self-competitiveness, as the biggest difficulties they encounter." Some graduate students say it is the only school in America where the undergraduates are under more stress than the graduate students.

People?

Alumni include former US Attorney General John Ashcroft, authors Kurt Vonnegut Jr. and Philip Roth, astronomer Edwin Hubble, the Reverend Jesse Jackson, director Mike Nichols and economist Paul Samuelson.

What do students say?

It was Chicago's competitiveness that attracted Bonginkhosi Mzileni, a student from Swaziland now in his second year and majoring in chemistry. "It is tough," Mr Mzileni said. "I found it even harder than I expected. We do get a lot of work every week and the quarter system puts you under a lot of pressure." But in the end, he said, succeeding at a school known for being so competitive is likely to serve him well in his career.

The downside? "People are a bit too serious most of the time," Mr Mzileni said. "Even outside class people like to talk about mostly academics, about their homework, about how hard it is and how much work it is. You hear a lot of that."

Good at?

Strong overall, 9 in social sciences (all those economists)

Columbia University

Why this university?

When it opened in 1754 in lower Manhattan under a royal charter from King George II, what was then called King's College was confined to a small schoolhouse. Since renamed Columbia in a burst of Revolutionary War patriotism, it is again bursting at its seams, which has given rise to one of the most ambitious expansion schemes in the history of American higher education. One of the university's biggest selling points among prospective students is that it offers them a chance to attend an elite, Ivy League school near the heart of New York City. This draws so many applicants that Columbia takes only 13 per cent of them, one of the lowest acceptance rates of any university. The school is now seeking to expand into the neighboring Harlem section. Until now, Columbia has been largely confined to its fortress-like, Italian Renaissance-style Morningside Heights campus, built in 1897. It long ago ran out of room."Columbia is the quintessential great urban university and the most constrained for space," its president, Lee Bollinger, has said. "If college and university rankings were based on creativity per square foot, Columbia would surpass everyone." The expansion, which will take 30 years and cost $7.4 billion, will add five million square feet for research facilities, classrooms, offices, and housing, and 1.5 million square feet underground. Here will continue the work of the university's 3,282 faculty, who do nearly half a billion dollars a year in research and bring in more than $110 million in revenue annually through an aggressive licensing programme that has resulted in the awarding of some 90 patents a year. The modern science of anthropology was invented here, as was the field of modern genetics. Columbia physicists I.

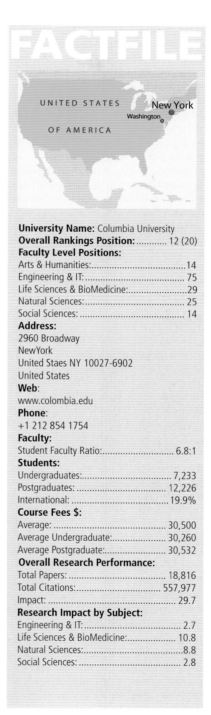

University Name: Columbia University
Overall Rankings Position: 12 (20)
Faculty Level Positions:
Arts & Humanities: 14
Engineering & IT: 75
Life Sciences & BioMedicine: 29
Natural Sciences: 25
Social Sciences: 14
Address:
2960 Broadway
NewYork
United Staes NY 10027-6902
United States
Web:
www.colombia.edu
Phone:
+1 212 854 1754
Faculty:
Student Faculty Ratio: 6.8:1
Students:
Undergraduates: 7,233
Postgraduates: 12,226
International: 19.9%
Course Fees $:
Average: 30,500
Average Undergraduate: 30,260
Average Postgraduate: 30,532
Overall Research Performance:
Total Papers: 18,816
Total Citations: 557,977
Impact: 29.7
Research Impact by Subject:
Engineering & IT: 2.7
Life Sciences & BioMedicine: 10.8
Natural Sciences: 8.8
Social Sciences: 2.8

141

I. Rabi, Enrico Fermi, and Polykarp Kusch conducted groundbreaking work into the atom. The School of International and Public Affairs, founded in the wake of World War II, is among the world's best, and the small, highly selective Graduate School of Journalism is considered the best in America.

Programmes such as these attract more than 5,200 international students, the fourth-largest proportion of any American university. Including scholars and their families, there are 8,547 non US residents at the school, most of them Asian and nearly 90 per cent of them attached to one of the 13 graduate and professional schools. Students from abroad most commonly enrol in engineering, public affairs, business and social sciences programmes.

People?

Columbia's prominent alumni may have made King George regret his royal charter. They include John Jay, the first chief justice of the United States; Alexander Hamilton, the first secretary of the treasury; Gouverneur Morris, the author of the final draft of the US constitution; and Robert Livingston, who helped draft the Declaration of Independence.

What do students say?

"Being in New York is one of its best features," said Stephanie Lew, a senior who said she "was always intrigued by the idea of going to school in New York City" from her small town in the suburbs of Boston.

"One of the best things about Columbia is the diversity," said Ms Lew. "It's an environment that's very accepting. Everyone expresses themselves and their cultures."

Ms Lew, who is majoring in neuroscience and behaviour and plans to become a physical therapist, found the pre-med classes she took to be comparatively large. "But the professors are always accessible.

They have office hours and they answer your emails right away." Though still an undergraduate, she is engaged in a clinical study at Columbia University Medical Center into spinal muscular atrophy.

"The only thing that's a negative here is housing," she said. "They just don't have the best housing. I guess that's New York City for you."

Good at?

Columbia is in the top 20 in our rankings for both social sciences and arts and humanities, and in the top 30 for natural sciences and life science and biomedicine.

Duke University

Why this university?

Anchoring the so-called Research Triangle in the Piedmont region of North Carolina (its other corners are North Carolina State University and the University of North Carolina), Duke is a southern centre of science whose graceful Gothic- and Georgian-style campus has sprouted cutting-edge facilities over the last few years to give the university a lead in fast-growing and emerging fields that is unusual for a school of its size.

The university has a $97 million Fitzpatrick Center for Interdisciplinary Engineering, which opened in 2004; a $41 million Institute for Genome Sciences and Policy, which opened in 2003; and the nearly completed $115 million French Sciences Building, which includes laboratories for biological chemistry, materials science, nanoscience, physical biology and bioinformatics. Its medical school is a leader in the science (and, as is inevitable in America, the politics) of stem-cell research.

Many of the students at Duke are pre-med, intending to go on to medical school; many of the rest are engineering majors. Undergraduates enroll in either the Trinity College of Arts and Sciences or the Pratt School of Engineering.

They also tend to leave the campus and its setting in the small city of Durham, at least for a while during their time enrolled there. Half of all undergraduates study abroad at some point, five times the U.S. average. A self-described "global gateway," Duke requires its students to take foreign language and international courses. One-fifth of its graduate and professional students (and five percent of its undergraduates) are international, and more than 400 international post-doctoral fellows do research at Duke. In all, the university has just under 1,600 faculty.

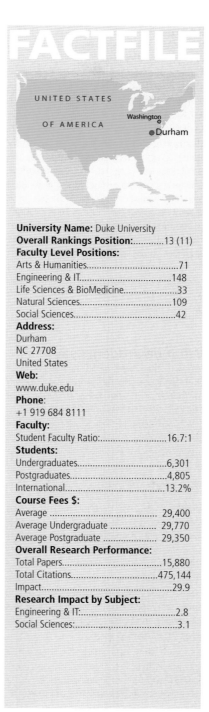

University Name: Duke University
Overall Rankings Position:............13 (11)
Faculty Level Positions:
Arts & Humanities......................................71
Engineering & IT......................................148
Life Sciences & BioMedicine....................33
Natural Sciences......................................109
Social Sciences..42
Address:
Durham
NC 27708
United States
Web:
www.duke.edu
Phone:
+1 919 684 8111
Faculty:
Student Faculty Ratio:...........................16.7:1
Students:
Undergraduates....................................6,301
Postgraduates.......................................4,805
International..13.2%
Course Fees $:
Average 29,400
Average Undergraduate 29,770
Average Postgraduate 29,350
Overall Research Performance:
Total Papers....................................15,880
Total Citations................................475,144
Impact..29.9
Research Impact by Subject:
Engineering & IT:.....................................2.8
Social Sciences:..3.1

People?

In the US, Duke is best known for its top-notch basketball team, the Blue Devils, named, peculiarly, for the French Chasseurs Alpins who were lauded for their courage in the Vosges Campaign in World War I. Athletics is the centre of a robust campus social scene that helps students blow off steam after long weeks of comparatively rigorous academics. It has also got the university into significant trouble of late after a black woman claimed she was raped by white members of the Duke lacrosse team at a party. The controversy "brought to glaring visibility underlying issues that have been of concern on this campus and in this town for some time." Duke President Richard Brodhed remarked. He was referring to the university's reputation as a place for wealthy white students (it's less than 10 per cent black).

What do students say?

"In just the three years I've been here, there has been so much expansion going on," said Shian Ling Keng, a senior from Malaysia who is majoring in biology. "It's still a growing university. My experience as an international student is that is was difficult for me to fit into the social environment here, maybe because of the cultural differences," Ms. Keng said. "Partying, drinking—people feel like that's the main way of social interaction, and I just don't party or do those things. But after a while I found that there are people who share my interests and I found my niche." Some good has also come out of the lacrosse team controversy, she said. "These issues have been underlying many campuses, maybe Duke especially, and this has really put them on the table where people can discuss them."

Good at?

Life sciences and biomedicine, 33 in world

144

Peking University

Why this university?

Founded in 1898, Peking University (Beijing Daxue, or Bei Da) is one of the oldest universities in China. Originally known as the Imperial Capital University, it was renamed the National Peking University in 1912, following the Xinhai Revolution. In 1919, students from the university formed the bulk of the protesters in the May Fourth Movement. In 1920, it became the second Chinese university to accept female students, after Nanjing University.

During the Second World War, the university moved to Kunming, where it formed the National Southwestern United University along with Tsinghua and Nankai. It returned to Beijing in 1946. After the founding of the People's Republic of China in 1949, it merged with Yenching University and dropped the "National" from its name, moving from central Beijing to the Yenching campus on the city's north-west outskirts. It remains there today, literally across the road from its rival Tsinghua.

Today, Peking is one of China's designated "national key universities" and competes with Tsinghua in the country's affections to be regarded as the best university in China. At present, Peking has over 46,000 students enrolled, of whom some 15,000 are undergraduates, 8,000 Master's students and 4,000 doctoral candidates, with the remainder on correspondence or night courses.

Peking University also has one of the largest intakes in China of international students, with almost 2,000 currently enrolled from 62 different countries. Approximately 40 per cent of the international students are from South Korea.

While offering a comprehensive range of study courses, Peking University is known mostly for arts and science, and is heavily geared towards scientific research. It has 216

FACTFILE

Beijing ○

C H I N A

University Name: Peking University
Overall Rankings Position:..............14 (15)
Faculty Level Positions:
Arts & Humanities:......................................10
Engineering & IT:...20
Life Sciences & BioMedicine:.........................8
Natural Sciences:.......................................12
Social Sciences:...17
Address:
Yiheyuan Road, Haidian District
Beijing
China 100871
China
Web:
www.pku.edu.cn
Phone:
+86-10-62752114
Faculty:
Student Faculty Ratio............................13.9:1
Students:
Undergraduates....................................14,240
Postgraduates.....................................12,732
% International...6.8
Course Fees $:
Average Undergraduate........................ 641
Overall Research Performance
Total Papers...8,154
Total Citations....................................64,942
Impact...8.0
Research Impact by Subject
Engineering & IT......................................1.5
Natural Sciences......................................3.3

145

research institutions at present, including two national engineering research centres, 81 key national disciplines and 12 national key laboratories.

Though Peking concentrates on research, in recent years it has committed to improving its teaching standards. The university's goal is to combine continued research with the training of the specialised personnel needed for China's skill-hungry workforce. Peking is a member of Universitas 21, an international collaboration network of research-intensive universities.

People?

Peking University has many famous alumni. Perhaps its most notable faculty member was Lu Xun, the godfather of modern Chinese literature, though early chancellor and May Fourth Movement leader Cai Yuanpei is a strong contender. Chinese Communist Party co-founders Chen Duxiu and Li Dazhao both worked there – the former was Dean of Letters, the latter head librarian.

A young Mao Zedong was a part-time student there while working as an assistant in the university library. Former full-time students include early Communist Party leader Zhang Guotao, the writer and journalist Mao Dun, and current Indian external affairs minister K. Natwar Singh.

Current academics of note at Peking University include the environmental scientist Tang Xiaoyan, who recently won the Vienna Convention Award for her contributions towards ozone layer protection; leading geoscientist Dong Shenbao; cellular biologist Zhai Zhonghe; and Xu Guangxian, head of the Applied Quantum Chemistry Group of the State Key Laboratory of Rare Earth Materials Chemistry and Applications.

What do students say?

He Qinzhou from Tianjin, China, who is studying computing, said: "The special thing about here is that it is a very comprehensive university. Almost anything you want to study, Peking University can provide it at a good level. For me, it was a great honour to be able to study here.

"However, like all Chinese universities at the moment, we are very undeveloped – there is a big disparity between China and the West. China definitely needs to keep improving. I believe that it will not be long before we can get the same level as the best universities in the world."

Good at?

Everything: 8 in life sciences and bio medicine

Cornell University

Why this university?

Cornell is a unique university in the US, where there is a broad division into public and private.

Cornell is the only one that is both. Partly private, it is also partly run and financially underwritten by the state of New York. It is also a member of the elite Ivy League. But its unusual status has given it something of an inferiority complex, one that has been aggravated by a recent slide in the pre-eminent American university rankings.

Now Cornell is fighting back. It is in the vanguard of universities that have adopted the tactics of consumer marketing to promote themselves. Its slogan, adopted from a favourite comment of 19th century founder Ezra Cornell: "Any person any study." Awkward, sure, but the idea is to emphasise that Cornell's large size makes it by far the Ivy League's most comprehensive, with 70 undergraduate specialities, or majors.

It is also one of the most international, despite being a distant five hours' drive northwest of New York City. Two thirds of the students are undergraduates while 15 per cent are from other countries. They are joined by 1,200 international academic staff. Though firmly landlocked, Cornell calls itself an international gateway, with 39 languages offered and more than 1,200 courses. An enormous amount of research is conducted at Cornell. Annual research expenditures there exceed half a billion dollars a year. The university's Center for Technology, Enterprise, and Commercialization helps to translate the results of this work into practical uses, filing more than 200 patent applications annually. Twenty nine Nobel laureates have been affiliated with Cornell, and there are

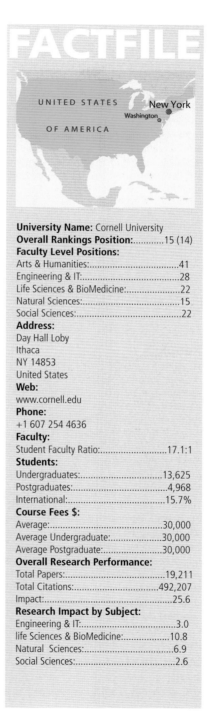

University Name: Cornell University
Overall Rankings Position:............15 (14)
Faculty Level Positions:
Arts & Humanities:....................................41
Engineering & IT:....................................28
Life Sciences & BioMedicine:....................22
Natural Sciences:....................................15
Social Sciences:....................................22
Address:
Day Hall Loby
Ithaca
NY 14853
United States
Web:
www.cornell.edu
Phone:
+1 607 254 4636
Faculty:
Student Faculty Ratio:..........................17.1:1
Students:
Undergraduates:..............................13,625
Postgraduates:....................................4,968
International:....................................15.7%
Course Fees $:
Average:....................................30,000
Average Undergraduate:..................30,000
Average Postgraduate:......................30,000
Overall Research Performance:
Total Papers:....................................19,211
Total Citations:..............................492,207
Impact:....................................25.6
Research Impact by Subject:
Engineering & IT:....................................3.0
life Sciences & BioMedicine:..................10.8
Natural Sciences:....................................6.9
Social Sciences:....................................2.6

three on the current faculty of 2,633.

Despite this, Cornell has taken its knocks in the American versions of university league tables, dropping from sixth to 14th-best university in America on the influential US News & World Report list. This led to a consensus on campus that it was not the reality, but the perception of the university that was the problem. An image-building campaign has begun to turn things around, and has Cornell rising up the rankings again.

"We are a very different beast," said Thomas Bruce, vice president for university communications, who was hired to accomplish this. "We really live at this intersection of the Ivy League and the state school. And there's nobody else there. Some of these rankings don't have the capacity to reflect how unique Cornell is."

People?

concerned with at least some aspect of international studies. Most noted specialities attest to Cornell's comprehensive nature—and its rural (and often very cold and snowy) setting. Its College of Agriculture and Life Sciences is the third largest in the United States, and usually rated the best. So is its School of Hotel Management, which has the largest faculty and curriculum of any programme of its kind and attracts a sizeable international enrolment representing, at last count, 28 countries. Its School of Industrial and Labor Relations offers the only four-year undergraduate degree in America devoted to workplace issues. And its College of Veterinary Medicine is the nation's most respected; among other things, it is where salmonella was discovered.

What do students say?

"I wanted a business degree, but I wanted the whole Ivy League experience," said

Arthur Chang, a senior from Hong Kong who is majoring in hotel management, plays violin in the university symphony, and has had internships at hotels in Vancouver and Hawaii. "It has exceeded my expectation. With the connections you gain from Cornell, you can really do anything you want. Definitely the weather is tough, but everybody survives it." And while Cornell is part of the Ivy League, he said, it's less stuffy than its smaller counterparts.

Good at?

Strong overall, 15 in natural sciences

The Australian National University

Why this university?

The Australian National University was the first to be created by an act of the federal parliament in 1946 and the first university founded in the national capital, Canberra.

One of Australia's Group of Eight research-intensive institutions, the ANU is a member of the International Alliance of Research Universities.

A recent independent quality review ranked the university among the world's best, with 77 per cent of external assessors placing the ANU as one of the top 50 universities. A rating of researchers who had made fundamental contributions to their disciplines over the last two decades identified 21 ANU academics among the 50 Australians mentioned.

The university campus spreads over 145 hectares adjacent to the city centre of Canberra but there are also smaller sites, including the astronomy observatories at Mt Stromlo west of Canberra and Siding Spring near Coonabarabran in western New South Wales.

The ANU's 1500 academics carry out research and teaching in seven colleges that cover the arts, Asian studies, economics and business, engineering and IT, science, medicine and health sciences, and law. Higher degrees are undertaken at the ANU's famed Institute of Advanced Studies which consists of 11 research schools and 15 centres, all dedicated solely to research and research training.

People

The ANU has four Nobel laureates among the many of its distinguished scholars who

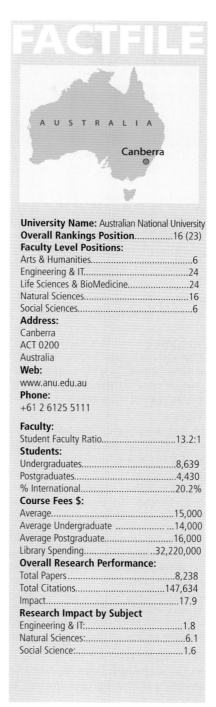

FACTFILE

AUSTRALIA

Canberra

University Name: Australian National University
Overall Rankings Position...............16 (23)
Faculty Level Positions:
Arts & Humanities...6
Engineering & IT...24
Life Sciences & BioMedicine......................24
Natural Sciences...16
Social Sciences...6
Address:
Canberra
ACT 0200
Australia
Web:
www.anu.edu.au
Phone:
+61 2 6125 5111

Faculty:
Student Faculty Ratio.............................13.2:1
Students:
Undergraduates......................................8,639
Postgraduates...4,430
% International......................................20.2%
Course Fees $:
Average...15,000
Average Undergraduate ....…14,000
Average Postgraduate...........................16,000
Library Spending.......................…..32,220,000
Overall Research Performance:
Total Papers...8,238
Total Citations....................................147,634
Impact..17.9
Research Impact by Subject
Engineering & IT:.......................................1.8
Natural Sciences:.......................................6.1
Social Science:...1.6

have achieved international recognition: John Eccles, John C Harsanyi and, joint-winners, Rolf Zinkernagel and Peter Doherty. It also has more Federation Fellows - lucrative fellowships awarded by the Australian Research Council - than any other Australian university. It also claims more members of the Royal Society on its staff than any of its counterparts in Australia.

What do students say?

Many of Australia's brightest young people apply to join students enrolled at the ANU. There are also 1,470 postgraduate international students and 1260 undergraduates who come from 100 other countries.

Malaysian Yew Kuen Tan , known as Kenny, who is completing his third year of a Bachelor of Medical Science degree. Mr Tan is president of the Malaysian Students Association and acts as a mentor for new students through a scheme linking first-years with those in later years to learn from their knowledge and experience of campus life.

He was awarded a full scholarship to the ANU but says one of main reasons he opted to study in Canberra was that it is quiet and good for study. He praises the university's student support services and says his course consists of a well-balanced system of assignments and examinations.

"I think the lecturers are fantastic," he says. "The ones I know are well aware that many international students have English as a second language so they speak slowly and are very approachable. They know that Asian students particularly tend not to question authority and do not speak out but, because they are so approachable, they help overcome that limitation."

Mr Tan is less happy with the Australian honours and PhD students who act as supervisors during laboratory classes. In contrast to the lecturers, he says they can be quite difficult to work with as some find it hard to understand international students and are not well trained in coping.

Good at?

Everything, especially social sciences and arts and humanities (6th in each category)

London School of Economics & Political Science

Why this university?

The London School of Economics describes itself as "the world's leading social science institution for teaching and research". An immodest claim perhaps, but when half its departments have been rated "internationally outstanding" and the school is near the top of the world rankings, who can blame them?

It is a top destination for future heads of state and Nobel prize winners.

An international feel on campus, therefore, comes as no surprise. The student population of 8,687 postgraduates and undergraduates spans 24 European Union countries and 113 non-EU countries.

Half the places go to non-Britons, which puts the school in second place after Manchester University for the most applications from overseas at undergraduate level.

The school is now planning 20 per cent more places, having acquired former government buildings near its Aldwych headquarters. A total of 44 per cent of the 768 full and part-time staff are from countries outside the UK, half of these are from the EU.

Despite its name, LSE is multidisciplinary. Law, management and history have received the top rating for teaching quality. Business, economics, psychology and mathematics have also produced good results.

Research specialisms include accounting, anthropology, economic history, international relations, maths, media and communications and social policy.

A pan-European survey showed LSE students to be more active in student associations, more entrepreneurial and

FACTFILE

UNITED KINGDOM

London

University Name: London School of Economics & Political Science
Overall Rankings Position: 17 (11)
Faculty Level Positions:
Arts & Humanities 19
Engineering & IT....................................... 276
Life Sciences & BioMedicine..................... 397
Natural Sciences....................................... 246
Social Sciences 3
Address:
Houghton Street
London
WC2A 2AE
United Kingdom
Web:
www.lse.ac.uk
Phone:
+44 20 7405 7686
Faculty:
Student Faculty Ratio:.............................21.1:1
Students:
Undergraduates 4,020
Postgraduates 4,795
International 61.8%
Course Fees $:
Average.. 23,692
Average Undergraduate 20,874
Average Postgraduate....................... 29,326
Overall Research Performance:
Total Papers...2,959
Total Citations.....................................13,065
Impact...4.4

more open to working abroad than those at other leading universities.

People?

Some 29 country leaders and 13 Nobel prize winners have studied there. Among them are Italian prime minister Romano Prodi, former Canadian prime minister Pierre Trudeau and Indian former president Shri KR Narayanan. The school was founded by socialist luminaries Sidney and Beatrice Webb and George Bernard Shaw. Labour Prime Minister Clement Atlee was a lecturer there. On a more modern note, the LSE is also the alma mater of Rolling Stone Mick Jagger.

What do students say?

Ali Dewji, from Toronto, is studying for a BSc in international relations and history. He describes the institution as an "urban and international academic powerhouse".

He said: "On any given day at LSE, I might find myself attending a public lecture given by a minister from Norway, meeting a friend for sushi and a chat about economic growth in Nigeria, practising my Spanish with some Peruvian postgraduates in an elevator on my way to a Debate Society meeting then heading back to my hall of residence to watch the latest episode of OC on tv.

"When I leave LSE, I will have spent three years studying alongside some of the brightest students in the world, whose lives and experiences are themselves part of an LSE education and part of what makes LSE such a unique place to study."

Good at?

The LSE is ranked third in the world for social sciences and in the top 20 for the arts and humanities.

Ecole Normale Supérieure

Why this university?

The Ecole Normale Supérieure in Paris is one of the great institutions of revolutionary France, a grande école created in 1794 to train university and lycée teachers for the agrégation, the competitive high-level teaching examination.

Today the school – also known as ENS, ENS-Paris, Normale Sup', ENS - Ulm is France's élite training ground not only for academics and researchers, but for those seeking careers in the upper echelons of the civil service, business or politics.

The present establishment, based in the Latin Quarter of Paris, is the result of a merger in the mid-1980s between the original school and the Ecole Normale Supérieure de Jeunes Filles in Sèvres, founded in 1880 to provide secondary education for young women.

Entry is generally by the traditional concours competitive exams preceded by two years' post-baccalauréat study in preparatory classes. Pupils selected by concours ("normaliens") have civil servant status and are paid about1,250 francs a month during their studies if they undertake to serve France for 10 years.

There are also alternative entry methods for students preparing for the ENS diploma, or for foreign applicants.

On its three Parisian sites ENS caters for a total of over 1,300 normaliens and other students up to doctorate level, with 224 teachers. As well as 150 school-employed researchers there are 1,004 associated researchers from other institutions such as the CNRS, the national scientific research centre, and Inserm, the national medical research institute.

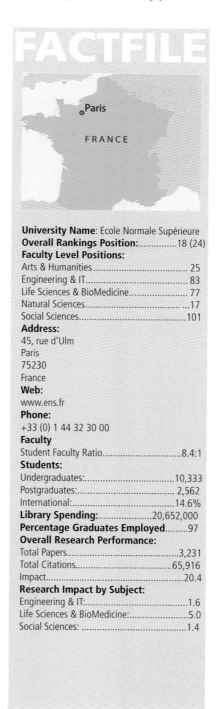

FACTFILE

Paris

FRANCE

University Name: Ecole Normale Supérieure
Overall Rankings Position:...............18 (24)
Faculty Level Positions:
Arts & Humanities 25
Engineering & IT... 83
Life Sciences & BioMedicine....................... 77
Natural Sciences..................................... ...17
Social Sciences...101
Address:
45, rue d'Ulm
Paris
75230
France
Web:
www.ens.fr
Phone:
+33 (0) 1 44 32 30 00
Faculty
Student Faculty Ratio................................8.4:1
Students:
Undergraduates:...................................10,333
Postgraduates:..................................... 2,562
International:..14.6%
Library Spending:....................20,652,000
Percentage Graduates Employed.........97
Overall Research Performance:
Total Papers..3,231
Total Citations....................................65,916
Impact...20.4
Research Impact by Subject:
Engineering & IT:......................................1.6
Life Sciences & BioMedicine:.......................5.0
Social Sciences: 1.4

ENS is the only grande école catering for both humanities and science students. Its watchwords are "interdisciplinarity" and "education through research". Courses and research are organised between 14 departments: biology, chemistry, cognitive studies, geography, history, computer sciences, literature and languages, history of art, pure and applied mathematics, philosophy, physics, sciences of antiquity, social sciences and earth-atmosphere-ocean.

Studies last for three or four years, leading to a licence (Bachelor's equivalent) and Master's, awarded jointly with another higher education establishment. Many pupils, including nearly all those following humanities courses, take the agrégation. ENS graduates might otherwise continue at other grande écoles to train as senior technocrats or follow careers in sought-after fields such as the media or publishing.

The school has agreements with about 60 universities worldwide through which it exchanges about 100 students each year. About 60 foreign academics visit annually for month-long visits; and nearly 300 international researchers stay for periods of up to two years.

The ENS International Division was created about five years ago for foreigners applying to study at the school. Candidates are rigorously tested by a panel of professors from French and foreign universities who evaluate their capacity for analysis, conceptualisation and synthesis, scientific and literary knowledge, intellectual curiosity and relevance of their chosen projects. About 20 foreigners were accepted for the 2006 session.

People?

Among ENS alumni (archicubes) are numerous eminent scientists, philosophers, writers, social scientists and politicians, including many winners of Nobel prizes and Fields medals.

Graduates include Louis Pasteur, Jean-Paul Sartre, Michel Foucault, Jacques Derrida, Simone Weil; Pierre Bourdieu; Romain Rolland, Charles Péguy; Jean Jaurès, Léon Blum and Georges Pompidou. Samuel Beckett taught here.

What do students say?

Klaus Speidel, 26, who was admitted to ENS in 2003 after studying philosophy for two years at Munich University, has just completed the second year of a Master's in philosophy. "At the ENS we are encouraged to choose courses in all kinds of subjects. Apart from my philosophy classes I studied literature, film studies and, especially, history of art."

He says interdisciplinarity and a close relationship with lecturers are the school's strong points. "The ENS has a system of personal tutors – you choose them at the beginning of your time there, and they sustain you in your choices, discuss and correct your work, and so on."

But he regrets that students are not encouraged more to talk during their studies. "Class participation is nearly impossible in France, and I miss it," he says. "It's clear people who attend the ENS are clever, but the teachers mainly give lectures even if the courses are called seminars. ENS's capital is really the students, but if you don't have the opportunity to hear what they have to say it's dead capital!"

Good at?

Most things: 17 in natural sciences

National University of Singapore

Why this university?

The National University of Singapore, founded in 1905, has forged a global reputation since independence from Malaysia in 1965 and now ranks in the top quartile of the world's universities. Set on a 1.5 square kilometre campus at Kent Ridge, scene in February 1942 of the heroic last stand by the Malay Regiment, NUS is a beacon for the huge investment in education at all levels made by the government of the Republic of Singapore. The law school is moving to a new site at Bukit Timah in the centre of the island.

Newly privatised on April 1 2006, the university continues to receive a government subsidy as the island-state seeks to maintain the highest all-round standards in education.

Current student enrolment is around 28,000, with more than 2,100 faculty.

Sellapan Ramanathan, Singapore's president, is the university's chancellor.

Student intake is from a wide spectrum of countries. In the Law School more than two dozen nationalities are represented, while student exchange programmes take Singaporean students to a number of countries including China, Canada, Australia and the US.

Active on an international level, NUS plays a leading role in the Association of Pacific Rim Universities (APRU), while consolidating its existing position at the forefront of the International Alliance of Research Universities. The university has five overseas colleges; Bio Valley (USA), Silicon Valley, Shanghai, Stockholm and Bangalore. A recent initiative has seen

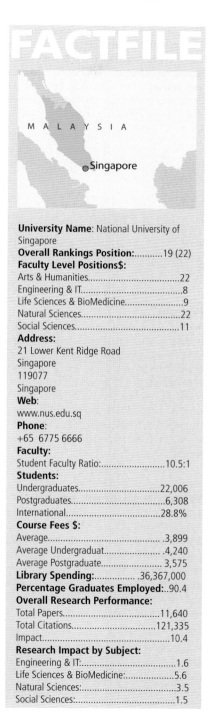

University Name: National University of Singapore
Overall Rankings Position:...........19 (22)
Faculty Level Positions$:
Arts & Humanities.....................................22
Engineering & IT...8
Life Sciences & BioMedicine......................9
Natural Sciences......................................22
Social Sciences...11
Address:
21 Lower Kent Ridge Road
Singapore
119077
Singapore
Web:
www.nus.edu.sq
Phone:
+65 6775 6666
Faculty:
Student Faculty Ratio:..........................10.5:1
Students:
Undergraduates................................22,006
Postgraduates....................................6,308
International......................................28.8%
Course Fees $:
Average...3,899
Average Undergraduat......................4,240
Average Postgraduate.......................3,575
Library Spending:................36,367,000
Percentage Graduates Employed:..90.4
Overall Research Performance:
Total Papers.....................................11,640
Total Citations................................121,335
Impact..10.4
Research Impact by Subject:
Engineering & IT:....................................1.6
Life Sciences & BioMedicine:...................5.6
Natural Sciences:....................................3.5
Social Sciences:......................................1.5

155

NUS enter the film-making world through the establishment of the NUS Hollywood Lab in co-operation with the University of Southern California School of Cinema and Television.

Facilities in Singapore are of the highest international standards and include six libraries and four museums, including the Raffles Museum of Biodiversity Research, which showcases over 500,000 specimens of flora and fauna.

Great all-round emphasis is placed on research at NUS. Current government reorientation of the republic's economy sets goals in new areas such as biotechnology and biomedicine, where NUS also plays a leading role.

People?

Among its leading graduates NUS can number Goh Chok Tong, former Prime Minister of Singapore, Kishore Mahbubani, dean of the Lee Kuan Yew School of Public Policy at NUS and Choo San Goh, prominent choreographer of the Washington Ballet. Of the current staff, Wong Lim Soon of the school of computing has established an international reputation in data base theories.

What do students say?

Reben Ng, who has recently graduated in psychology and intends to read for a Masters at NUS, exemplifies the university's international approach. He has qualified for an international award usually made to academics who have completed a PhD and five years' research on the basis of his undergraduate research paper.

Mr Ng wrote up his undergraduate internship with the Singapore police after only two years at NUS, becoming the first to qualify for the award from the International Council of Psychologists on the strength of his undergraduate work.

He says: "When I first stepped into NUS, I never expected that my university life would be so rich. In retrospect I realise I was given the opportunity to learn in three ways: from books, through travels and by interacting with people who were totally different from me.

"I now have friends from all over the world, and, more importantly, they are friends who are passionate about the same kinds of things."

Good at?

Academics rank NUS in the top ten for life sciences and biomedicine and engineering and IT. The social sciences are close behind and all areas rank in the top 25.

University of Tokyo

Why this university?

Tokyo University is the oldest in Japan and still stands out today as the most prestigious in the country. Perhaps it is in reflection of its unrivalled political status that the university received the biggest direct government grant of ¥95.7 billion (£445 million) in 2005, comprising just under 50 per cent of its total income of ¥193.3 billion that year. However, faced with a 1 per cent cut in the subsidies over the next five years, the university has set the target of raising ¥13 billion in endowment by next year.

The university that has five campuses – two in the heart of Tokyo – first started out in 1872 as a law school, largely for mandarin, before setting up science and liberal arts departments to be fully established as a tertiary education institution in 1877. The legacy of a mandarin training institution in a country of powerful bureaucracy persists to this day. Its law graduates dominate the top civil service posts. "The university provides training in law in the way civil servants should see it," says a law graduate.

However, in the country where Nobel Prize triumphs make huge newspaper headlines, Tokyo University's record has not been illustrious, with only a single winner in 2002 in physics by Professor Emeritus Masatoshi Koshiba.

President Hiroshi Komiyama is careful not to specify any particular area of strength, emphasizing instead the university's pursuit of excellence in all aspects of education and research. A university spokesman echoes this view: "It is not our policy to single out any specific areas."

As stated in its objectives, the university is striving to raise its international

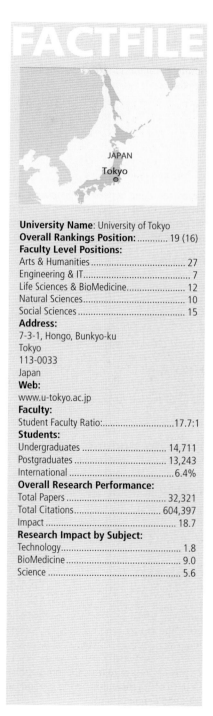

FACTFILE

JAPAN

Tokyo

University Name: University of Tokyo
Overall Rankings Position: 19 (16)
Faculty Level Positions:
Arts & Humanities 27
Engineering & IT 7
Life Sciences & BioMedicine 12
Natural Sciences 10
Social Sciences 15
Address:
7-3-1, Hongo, Bunkyo-ku
Tokyo
113-0033
Japan
Web:
www.u-tokyo.ac.jp
Faculty:
Student Faculty Ratio: 17.7:1
Students:
Undergraduates 14,711
Postgraduates 13,243
International 6.4%
Overall Research Performance:
Total Papers 32,321
Total Citations 604,397
Impact 18.7
Research Impact by Subject:
Technology 1.8
BioMedicine 9.0
Science 5.6

profile attracting overseas students and researchers, which in itself is the Educational Ministry's own objective. However, in 2005 only 1.6 per cent of all its 14,711 undergraduates and 11.7 per cent of its 13,243 post-graduates were foreign nationals. The foreign ratio' of faculty members is just as insignificant, with only 1.4 per cent. However, women's ratio is almost as small, representing only 9 per cent in the faculty. The university closest to Japan's power centre looks very much a Japanese male dominated institution. At the undergraduate level, women comprised 19 per cent and at postgraduate, 27 per cent in 2005.

People?

Faculty members include architect Tadao Ando, winner of the 1995 Pritzker Architecture Prize and Masatoshi Koshiba. Notable alumni include six prime ministers since 1946; mathematician Kunihiko Kodaira (Fields Medal winner); Nobel literature laureates Yasunari Kawabata and Kenzaburo Oe; writer Yukio Mishima; Nobel Physics laureates Leo Esaki and Masatoshi Koshiba; and industrialist Eiji Toyoda.

What do students say?

"International atmosphere is definitely lacking," says a 2nd - year student of literature. "I have yet to come across an undergraduate with a powerful personality – they all seem obedient, following the rules without a question."

Good at?

The natural sciences and engineering and technology are both in the top ten in our rankings. Social sciences and biomedicine are in the top 20.

McGill University

Why this university?

McGill University's big research pillars have traditionally been and remain medicine and law. Those two faculties have given the university a reputation in the fields of neurosciences, genomics, cancer, human rights and social policy.

Its engineering has spawned specialties in nanotechnology and biomedical engineering. It also has a dental school, a school of environmental sciences, a large music faculty and a full complement of arts and sciences.

In terms of those studying full time, last year, the Montreal university enrolled over 20,000 undergraduate and 7,000 graduate students, with more than 1,300 post-docs, residents and fellows.

Last autumn, over 2,000 of its international students came from the US, by far the most common nationality of its non-Canadian contingent. France and China were number two and three, respectively, for countries that McGill attracts. Last year, 119 UK students attended the university.

McGill counts 1,552 tenured or tenure-track professors, with a high proportion being new to both the university and the country. Since January 2000, McGill has hired 623 new faculty members, with 336 recruited from outside Canada, according to statistics gathered last December.

People?

In 1948, John Humphrey, a McGill graduate and law professor, authored the first draft of the Universal Declaration of Human Rights. Four McGill graduates have won Nobel Prizes: Andrew Victor Schally (Medicine, 1977), Val Fitch (Physics, 1980), David Hubel (Medicine, 1981) and Rudolph Marcus (Chemistry, 1992). Ernest

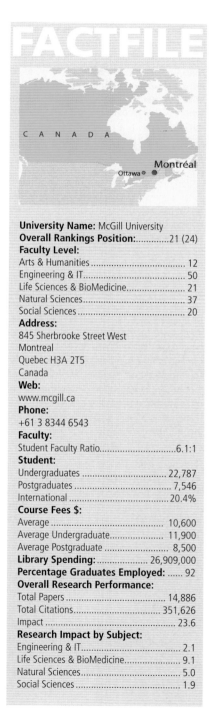

University Name: McGill University
Overall Rankings Position:............21 (24)
Faculty Level:
Arts & Humanities 12
Engineering & IT.. 50
Life Sciences & BioMedicine....................... 21
Natural Sciences.. 37
Social Sciences 20
Address:
845 Sherbrooke Street West
Montreal
Quebec H3A 2T5
Canada
Web:
www.mcgill.ca
Phone:
+61 3 8344 6543
Faculty:
Student Faculty Ratio...............................6.1:1
Student:
Undergraduates 22,787
Postgraduates 7,546
International 20.4%
Course Fees $:
Average 10,600
Average Undergraduate..................... 11,900
Average Postgraduate 8,500
Library Spending:................... 26,909,000
Percentage Graduates Employed: 92
Overall Research Performance:
Total Papers 14,886
Total Citations................................. 351,626
Impact 23.6
Research Impact by Subject:
Engineering & IT.. 2.1
Life Sciences & BioMedicine..................... 9.1
Natural Sciences.. 5.0
Social Sciences 1.9

Rutherford uncovered the alpha particle, which earned him the 1908 Nobel Prize in Chemistry, while on the staff of McGill; and Norman Bethune designed the world's first mobile medical unit and became a hero in China during the Second World War for training thousands of Chinese medics and doctors.

Other notable alumni include poet, miserabilist and literary icon Leonard Cohen; and William Shatner, best known as Captain James T. Kirk of Star Trek.

McGill is Canada's most research-intensive university, with the country's highest per-faculty research funding. Among some of its current crop, Jeffrey Mogil is conducting groundbreaking research on pain; Jody Heymann researches the relationship between global social and economic conditions and the health and development of children and families; Michael Meaney and Moshe Szyf are proving that maternal behaviour in rats can have a profound impact on the genetics of offspring; and Dan Levitin and Stephen McAdams have "conducted" innovative experiments to scientifically assess changes in emotional response to music among both musicians and audience members.

What do students say?

Astrophysics student Andrew McCann was attracted from Dublin by McGill's reputation and a very active and lively department. "Very few universities in the world research my particular area of study, and there are many talks and seminars of interest, as well as highly motivated students and teachers."

Mr McCann had been disappointed by what he believes was too little information provided on financial aid for international students. But he says that did not mar the academic excellence he saw at the university.

Good at?

Arts and humanities (12 in world), social sciences (20), life sciences and biomedicine (21)

University of Melbourne

Why this university?

Last year, Australia's second oldest university announced a bold new plan to transform itself along the lines of the Bologna model for European universities. Starting in 2008, students enrolling at the University of Melbourne will face a new set of broad undergraduate degrees leading to postgraduate professional programmes such as architecture, law and medicine.

The first intakes will begin distinctive "new generation" undergraduate and professional graduate courses. Initially, law, architecture, building and planning, as well as nursing, and some education courses will be offered only as graduate programmes with the final intakes in current courses in 2007. Thereafter other professional degrees will also become graduate-entry only, while undergraduates will be required to undertake a range of subjects in the liberal arts and sciences.

From its current numbers of 44,000 students, Melbourne expects to peak at around 50,000 but towards 2015 it will cut back to current levels or below. Some 20 per cent of these students will be in new graduate schools and a further 10-15 per cent engaged in postgraduate research.

Being large, venerable and of high prestige, Melbourne has huge financial, intellectual and locational assets. Its main crowded campus is a few minutes' tram ride from the central business district in the heart of cosmopolitan Carlton. A dozen other small campuses are dotted around Victoria, most the result of mergers with other institutions.

As with Australia's other older universities in the state capitals, Melbourne attracts a disproportionate number of students from socially advantaged homes and top private

FACTFILE

Canberra
Melbourne

University Name: University of Melbourne
Overall Rankings Position:............22 (19)
Faculty Level Positions:
Arts & Humanities 7
Engineering & IT....................................... 16
Life Sciences & BioMedicine........................ 7
Natural Sciences..................................... 27
Social Sciences 10
Address:
Admissions Office, Information Centre,
Richard Berry Building
Victoria
3010
Australia
Web:
www.unimelb.edu.au
Phone:
+61 3 8344 6543
Faculty:
Student Faculty Ratio.............................7.5:1
Students:
Undergraduates 30,081
Postgraduates 14,347
International 22.1%
Course Fees $:
Average 10,400
Average Undergraduate........................ 8,900
Average Postgraduate 13,200
Library Spending:....................19,705,000
Percentage Graduates Employed:.........84
Overall Research Performance:
Total Papers 10,538
Total Citations................................ 177,476
Impact 16.8
Research Impact by Subject:
Engineering & IT.. 2.2
Life Sciences & BioMedicine...................... 7.2
Natural Sciences....................................... 5.0

161

schools. But it claims to offer the nation's largest undergraduate scholarship scheme, although the main targets are highly able school students, and a special entry scheme aimed at those from less well-off backgrounds.

People?

Many of the 3,200 academics who teach Melbourne's students are among Australia's most accomplished, sought-after scholars and they account for 190 memberships of the four Australian learned academies. Melbourne has four Nobel Laureates on its staff — Peter Doherty, Clive Granger, Sir James Mirrlees and Bert Sakmann — while other staff and graduates have been winners of the Australia Prize, the Victoria Prize and the Nobel Prize.

What do students say?

The university enrols nearly 10,000 international students, of whom some 2700 are undertaking postgraduate studies. Nicklas Sandstrom travelled from Sweden to start as a first-year medical student at Melbourne this year after finishing school at home and then completing a year's military service.

"I wanted to try something different," Mr Sandstrom says. "I saw the problem-solving approach that Melbourne uses in its medical course and thought I'd like to try that form of learning."

The cost of a six-year medical degree at Melbourne amounts to more than A$200,000 ($82,000) but Mr Sandstrom says his tuition is paid for by the Swedish government although he must repay the loan after he graduates.

"I've learnt a lot more than I expected and have no complaints about the teaching so far," he says. "The problem-based approach and tutorials are different to the teaching back home where they don't have the small

discussion groups. You remember more and learn more while interacting with it, rather than looking at slides in a lecture."

Good at?

Very strong – 7 in the world for arts and humanities and for lifescience and biomedicine, 16 for engineering and IT, 10 for social sciences, 27 for social sciences

Johns Hopkins University

Why this university?

Johns Hopkins University has enjoyed more government research funding over the last few years than any other university in America, thanks largely to its top-ranked schools of medicine and public health. Its Bloomberg School of Public Health alone gets one-quarter of all federal research money awarded to the 28 US schools of public health.

No wonder such a disproportionate number of Johns Hopkins undergraduates are pre-med, planning for careers in medicine. The university's Whiting School of Engineering is also highly selective, and bioengineering is a popular major that spans both of the university's principal strengths. Its Applied Physics Laboratory, founded during World War II to improve the effectiveness of Allied anti-aircraft shells, today conducts research in fields including national security and space exploration, and has developed more than 100 biomedical devices in conjunction with Johns Hopkins' medical faculty and graduate students. In all, the university conducts more than $1 billion a year in research. Seventy per cent of engineering students and 50 per cent of other undergraduates work with faculty on primary research.

This tradition dates from Johns Hopkins' founding in 1876 as America's first university modelled after the European research institution. Today it's constructing the first academic building on its home campus dedicated to interdisciplinary research, the Computational Science and Engineering Building, where cross-departmental programmes in, among other subjects, robotics and computational medicine will be housed. Its renowned School of Advanced International Studies is named for Cold War architect Paul Nitze,

University Name: Johns Hopkins University
Overall Rankings Position: 23 (27)
Faculty Level Positions:
Arts & Humanities: 48
Engineering & IT: 85
Life Sciences & BioMedicine: 6
Natural Sciences: 48
Social Sciences: 89
Address:
1740 Massachusetts Avenue.N.W.
Washington
DC20036-1983
United States
Web:
www.jhu.edu
Phone:
+1 202 663 5700
Faculty:
Student Faculty Ratio: 7.8:1
Students:
Undergraduates 5,710
Postgraduates 12,435
International 12.3%
Course Fees $:
Average 30,140
Average Undergraduate 30,140
Average Postgraduate 30,140
Overall Research Performance:
Total Papers 23,797
Total Citations 803,654
Impact 33.8
Research Impact by Subject:
Engineering & IT 3.0
Life Sciences & BioMedicine 11.6
Natural Sciences 9.9
Social Sciences 2.9

who cofounded it in 1943. It is based in Washington, 45 minutes by train from the university's park-like, Georgian-style main campus in Baltimore.

But the medical school is the main reason for Johns Hopkins' fame. It was there that neurosurgery, urology, endocrinology, paediatrics, renal dialysis, and CPR were developed. Its doctors were the first to wear rubber gloves during surgery. The Nobel Prize-winning discovery of restriction enzymes, which can precisely cut double-stranded DNA, occurred there. The Bloomberg School of Public Health, oldest and largest of its kind in the world, has research under way in 40 countries and attracts students from 78 countries. The university has about 19,000 students in all—13 per cent of them international—and 3,100 faculty.

Johns Hopkins has been aggressive about extending its reach globally. Its Bologna campus houses the only full-time, resident American graduate school of international relations in Europe. It has a centre in Florence housing its Italian studies programme, another in Nanjing, and two in Singapore, one a collaboration between its Peabody Institute of Music and the National University of Singapore to establish a music conservatory.

People?

Horror film director Wes Craven (A Nightmare on Elm Street, Scream) is among the university's alumni. Other prominent graduates include New York Mayor Michael Bloomberg, pianist Andre Watts, Nobel economics winner Merton Miller, Nobel peace prize winner Jody Williams, IBM CEO Samuel Palmisano, and Hamilton Smith, the Nobel laureate who helped discover those restriction enzymes.

What do students say?

If you're interested in doing research, it's right there. You just have to ask," said Kristy Gangaram, a senior from Trinidad and Tobago who is majoring in public health. Ms. Gangaram undertook a research project to create a campus programme advertising health precautions and safe sex, she said, and "that experience helped me focus my career goals in terms of pubic health". Her friends are doing research into Alzheimer's disease. "As you walk along campus, you're able to look in the windows and see students working in the labs until well into the night."

Students grumble about the neighbourhood surrounding the main undergraduate campus. "Baltimore is the inner city so you have to be always cautious," said Ms Gangaram, who is president of a self-defence instruction group. "But we have a blue light system and when you feel unsafe, you press the button under a blue light and a security officer is there in 30 seconds." Lots of lighting has also been installed around the university, and escorts are available for travel at night.

A member of the Caribbean Student Association, Ms Gangaram said the network of fellow Caribbeans she has met "has made me feel at home at Hopkins".

Good at?

Medicine, 6 in world

ETH Zurich

Why this university?

The Eidgenössische Technische Hochschule (ETH Zurich) – Switzerland's largest and oldest federal university – was founded in 1854 as the "Eidgenössische Politechnische Schule". Then, its departments of architecture, civil engineering, mechanical engineering, chemistry, forestry, plus a department including mathematics, natural sciences, literature and social and political sciences were key players in the modernisation of Switzerland and in the brilliant engineering works, especially roads, railways, bridges and tunnels, which marked the late 19th and early 20th centuries.

Alfred Escher, the prominent Swiss politician, railway entrepreneur and founder of what is today Credit Suisse, was a co-founder of ETH. It was the Confederation's only federal higher education institution until 1969, when Lausanne's Ecole Polytechnique also acquired federal status.

The ETH focuses mainly on research and teaching in technical, mathematical and natural sciences. There are about 12,700 undergraduate and graduate students and 349 professors in 15 departments. Including technical and administrative staff, a total of 18,000 people from 80 nations work and study at ETH. It was among the first European universities to adopt the three-plus-two degree structure of the "Bologna Process," and the changeover from four and five year degrees appears to have been untraumatic. ETH claims its work in chemistry, physics and architecture is among the most advanced in the world, and that the Department of Biology is rapidly reaching the same level. A basic element of research policy is the creation of inter-disciplinary "platforms" for work on a specific field.

Entrance to ETH is open to all Swiss citizens who have passed the Matura school-leaving

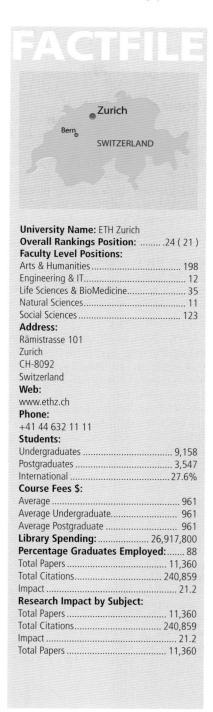

FACTFILE

Zurich

Bern

SWITZERLAND

University Name: ETH Zurich
Overall Rankings Position: .... .24 (21)
Faculty Level Positions:
Arts & Humanities 198
Engineering & IT 12
Life Sciences & BioMedicine 35
Natural Sciences 11
Social Sciences 123
Address:
Rämistrasse 101
Zurich
CH-8092
Switzerland
Web:
www.ethz.ch
Phone:
+41 44 632 11 11
Students:
Undergraduates 9,158
Postgraduates 3,547
International 27.6%
Course Fees $:
Average 961
Average Undergraduate......................... 961
Average Postgraduate 961
Library Spending: 26,917,800
Percentage Graduates Employed: 88
Total Papers 11,360
Total Citations................................. 240,859
Impact 21.2
Research Impact by Subject:
Total Papers 11,360
Total Citations................................. 240,859
Impact 21.2
Total Papers 11,360

exam, while foreign students have to sit an admission exam. For all, there is a rigorous selection after the first two semesters.

People?

ETH has an impressive list of 22 Nobel Prize winners. Albert Einstein, who studied there from 1896 to 1900, returned to teach physics from 1912 to 1916. Others include Wilhelm Conrad Röntgen (Physics 1901) and Felix Bloch (Physics 1952), while the most recent is ETH professor Kurt Wüthrich (Chemistry 2002).

What do students say?

Laila Houssain is a British PhD with a chemistry degree from Bristol University. At the ETH she is working in the department of chemistry and applied biosciences.

"The ETH is very multi-cultural, very inter-disciplinary. You meet and work with people from many different countries, and one's own research group often works with people from research groups in completely different fields. There are lots of lectures by key speakers from around the world. Not just on one's own subject, but on all kinds of themes.

"The atmosphere here is very focused, very professional. Everyone seems eager to help, but the standards are very high and they expect a great deal of effort and dedication."

Good at?

In a May 2006 ranking of German-speaking universities by the German CHE organisation, by "peer review" and "reputation" ETH came out on top in all natural, engineering and computer sciences. It is in this year's top 12 for natural sciences and for engineering and IT in our rankings.

University College London

Why this university?

University College London is a firm favourite with overseas students who make up almost a third of its student population. Of that third, 3,952 are from outside the European Union and 2,050 are from within it. The college expects these numbers to grow still further in the next few years.

Apart from its cosmopolitan feel, UCL shares many other similarities with Oxford and Cambridge. The college is committed to teaching in small groups, especially in the second and subsequent years of degree courses. This may well explain its high levels of achievement: almost three-quarters leave with a first or an upper second class degree. Its drop-out rate is also low: 6.6 per cent, according to the latest figures. This is well below the national average for the courses it offers and the entry grades it demands.

UCL has even overtaken Oxford and Cambridge in the past for the amount of research support it has been allocated by the British Government's funding council.

The university prides itself on excellence in biomedicine, Slavonic and East European Studies, among many other subjects. It pioneered degrees in architecture and law and has an excellent reputation for fine arts.

With 4,280 academic and research staff, UCL is comfortably the largest of London University's colleges. At the end of the 1990s it took in a number of specialist schools and institutes, most of which were medical or dental, adding to an already large medical school. The college has launched the biggest-ever fundraising effort at any UK university to support further developments.

University Name: University College London
Overall Rankings Position: 25 (28)
Faculty Level Positions:
Arts & Humanities 35
Engineering & IT 103
Life Sciences & BioMedicine 16
Natural Sciences 90
Social Sciences 45
Address:
Gower Street
London
WC1E 6BT
United Kingdom
Web:
www.ucl.ac.uk
Phone:
+44 (0)20 7679 2000
Faculty:
Student Faculty Ratio: 11.5:2
Students:
Undergraduates 12,085
Postgraduates 7,505
International 28.8%
Course Fees $:
Average 24,121
Average Undergraduate 23,051
Average Postgraduate 25,190
Overall Research Performance:
Total Papers 15,111
Total Citations 376,098
Impact 24.9
Research Impact by Subject:
Engineering & IT 2.5
Life Sciences & BioMedicine 9.7
Natural Sciences 6.0
Social Sciences 2.5

167

Although parts of UCL are in north London, such as the Royal Free Hospital, most of campus life is based in busy but beautiful Bloomsbury, in the centre of the city. Here the academic pace is frantic with its close proximity to the West End. Students have immediate access to London University's underused central students' union facilities. The main outdoor sports facilities are a coach ride away in leafy Hertfordshire.

People?

Former alumni include Indian leader Mahatma Gandhi (Law, 1889), TV presenter Jonathan Dimbleby (Philosophy, 1969), Japanese Prime Minister Junichiro Koizumi (Economics, 1969) and the inventor of the telephone Alexander Graham Bell (Phonetics, 1860s).

What do students say?

Erik Moore, from Australia is studying part-time for an MSc in environmental design and engineering. He said: "By offering the flexibility of working and studying at the same time I feel I've really got the most I could from my degree at UCL. It's been the right mix of academic work twinned with practical work – with loads of extra guest lectures for those that want to learn more. The standard of teaching has been exceptional and with a mix of international students from a range of different backgrounds, I've learnt a lot about how design works in different sectors."

Good at?

The medical school achieves the highest position in our rankings, finishing in the top 20 for biomedicine. UCL is also in the top 50 for social science and the arts and humanities.

University of Pennsylvania

Why this university?

America's original Renaissance man, Benjamin Franklin, is back in vogue, and so is the university he helped to found. The University of Pennsylvania follows Franklin's dictates of inventiveness, entrepreneurship and the idea that learning should not be limited to a single speciality.

The university has been aggressive about recruiting international students; It has the highest proportion in the Ivy League. It also boasts the highest proportion of American students studying abroad.

While, for example, Columbia benefits from its location as the Ivy campus near the heart of New York City, Penn suffers somewhat from its West Philadelphia setting. It is separated from the city's centre by an industrial wasteland to the east, which even a university task force described as "unattractive", saying it "contributes to a sense of disengagement of Penn from the city".

Urban blight afflicts the residential neighbourhood to the west. The university hopes to transform both with an ambitious expansion, starting with a new "East Campus."

People?

The university applies its academic firepower to international causes as well as in the US. Its Solomon Asch Center for the Study of Ethnopolitical Conflict advised the Kurdish delegation to Iraq's constitutional convention and has been helping the Sri Lankan government with post-tsunami planning. Medical school faculty and students are treating HIV-infected patients in Botswana. Penn's Graduate School of Education has teamed up with Beijing and

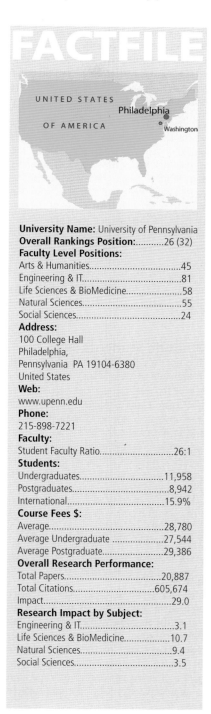

University Name: University of Pennsylvania
Overall Rankings Position:...........26 (32)
Faculty Level Positions:
Arts & Humanities.....................................45
Engineering & IT.......................................81
Life Sciences & BioMedicine.....................58
Natural Sciences.......................................55
Social Sciences...24
Address:
100 College Hall
Philadelphia,
Pennsylvania PA 19104-6380
United States
Web:
www.upenn.edu
Phone:
215-898-7221
Faculty:
Student Faculty Ratio.............................26:1
Students:
Undergraduates................................11,958
Postgraduates.....................................8,942
International......................................15.9%
Course Fees $:
Average...28,780
Average Undergraduate 27,544
Average Postgraduate.......................29,386
Overall Research Performance:
Total Papers.......................................20,887
Total Citations.................................605,674
Impact...29.0
Research Impact by Subject:
Engineering & IT.......................................3.1
Life Sciences & BioMedicine.................10.7
Natural Sciences......................................9.4
Social Sciences...3.5

East China Normal universities to offer the first education doctorates in China. The school has particularly close ties to India, and its Center for the Advanced Study of India is the only research institute of its kind in the United States.

Like Benjamin Franklin, a statue of whom sits at the centre of the campus, Penn is well-rounded. Its Wharton School, the world's first collegiate school of business and largest global business school, is consistently regarded among the top three in America. But its School of Nursing ranks in the top two and its School of Arts and Sciences and graduate schools of education, law, medicine and veterinary medicine are in the top 10. The university also has 174 research centres and institutes and its 4,200 faculty conduct more than $700 million a year in research.

What do students say?

"It is not the best feeling in the world to be at the edge of West Philly, but I sincerely believe that the campus has become a lot safer than it was a couple of years ago or when my sister came here," Schuchi Kothari, a senior business major from India (who also has a minor in psychology and has taken classes in subjects including photography and political science) said. "There have been a few incidents but everyone has come out safe. I do not feel unsafe walking around campus alone. There are security officers at every corner and street and the campus is well protected. The university does a great job of dealing with an area that most people would perceive as less than ideal."

She finds Penn a great place to meet and interact with people from all over the world. In some of her classes at the Wharton School of Business, she said, at least 40 per cent of the students come from other countries. "It's a great way to gain a different perspective of a question or argument, especially in classes where class discussion is stressed."

Good at?

Social sciences (24), perhaps mainly due to Wharton

University of Toronto

Why this university?

The University of Toronto aims high with its stated mission and purpose: "It is this human right to radical, critical teaching and research with which the university has a duty above all to be concerned; for there is no one else, no other institution and no other office in our modern liberal democracy, which is the custodian of this most precious and vulnerable right of the liberated human spirit."

That bold statement is an indication of the role the university has assumed. Canada's biggest university has almost 64,000 full-time students attending classes on its three campuses, with the majority at its 179-year-old downtown location. It employs over 11,000 faculty and staff and boasts 75 PhD programmes and 14 professional faculties, including medicine, law and management.

In its latest figures, it accumulated C$517 million (£251 million) in research grants and contract support and has spun off 95 companies. Its research library is one of the top four in North America and has more than 15 million holdings.

Research achievements have also been mammoth. It developed the first electronic heart pacemaker, artificial larynx, single-lung transplant, nerve transplant and artificial pancreas. It even created the infant cereal Pablum.

People?

Alumni include authors Margaret Atwood and Michael Ondaatje, film directors David Cronenberg and Norman Jewison, eBay's Jeff Skoll and former Canadian prime ministers Paul Martin and Lester B. Pearson.

University Name: University of Tronto
Overall Rankings Position: 27 (29)
Faculty Level Positions:
Arts & Humanities 11
Engineering & IT.................................... 27
Life Sciences & BioMedicine...................... 18
Natural Sciences 20
Social Sciences 17
Address:
S-304, 1265 Military Trail
Scarborough, Ontario
Canada M1C 1A4
Canada
Web:
www.utoronto.ca
Phone:
+1 416 978 2011
Faculty:
Student Faculty Ratio:............................15.6:1
Students:
Undergraduates 52,499
Postgraduates 11,430
International 10.4%
Course Fees $:
Average 4,700
Average Undergraduate...................... 2,840
Average Postgraduate 10,700
Library Spending: 55,461,000
Percentage Graduates Employed: 90
Overall Research Performance:
Total Papers 24,081
Total Citations............................... 552,938
Impact 23.0
Research Impact by Subject:
Technology.. 2.0
BioMedicine.. 8.9
Science 6.0
Social Sciences 2.0

Sir Frederick Banting and J.J.R. Macleod won the Nobel Prize in 1923 for their work with Charles Best in the discovery of the role of insulin in controlling diabetes. Communications guru Marshall McLuhan was a faculty member. John C. Polanyi won the 1986 Nobel Prize in Chemistry for pioneering work that led to the development of the laser. Geneticist Tak Mak was the first to clone a T-cell gene, a key part of the immune system. Medical biophysicist Lap-Chee Tsui led the team of researchers who discovered the cystic fibrosis gene.

What students think?

Audre Kapacinskas from Chicago is studying peace and conflict studies, psychology and economics. She appreciates the size and scope that she has seen in the institution. "I wanted a large university in a cosmopolitan city with a diverse student body." Kapacinskas says she also appreciated the variety of courses and found the flexibility attractive. She says requirements to complete credits in diverse academic areas like humanities and science meant she could try something different while focussing on what she was interested in. "It's a nice cross between European and US systems and allows you to combine different areas of study."

Weak points for her have been a frustrating student web service and a lack of student involvement in bolstering school spirit. But the university far exceeded her expectations: "I came for a fantastic city, nice campus and variety of courses. The people I've met and the professors I've had have made it an exceptionally positive experience. You develop a friendly, caring community around you, but you still have the resources of a large research institution at your disposal."

Good at?

Generally strong, with all areas ranked in the top 30.

Tsing Hua University

Why this university?

Established in 1911, with reparation money paid to the US after the Boxer Uprising, as a preparatory school for Chinese graduates pursuing further studies at American universities, Tsing Hua became a university in 1925, offering four-year undergraduate and postgraduate programmes.

The university's staff currently includes 2,877 teachers, of whom 1,069 are professors, 1,087 are associate professors and nearly 700 are doctoral advisers. Tsing Hua's faculty has 34 members of the Chinese Academy of Sciences and 28 members of the Chinese Academy of Engineering, more than any other college or university in China.

Tsing Hua has over 20,000 students, including nearly 14,000 undergraduates, 6,200 master's degrees candidates and 2,800 doctoral candidates. This includes just over 1,000 foreign students, about half of whom are Korean - the rest are from more than 50 different countries.

Within China, Tsing Hua is usually rated as one of the top two universities in the country. Located on the site of Qing dynasty royal gardens in the northwest of Beijing, it is usually considered the best university in China for engineering and business. Arts and languages are comparatively weak, being mostly a support system for science and engineering students to get through the government-mandated tests in various subjects outside their major, necessary to obtain their degrees. Tsing Hua is keen to remedy this situation. Last year, an independent art college was incorporated into the university and moved into a brand new on-campus building.

Tsing Hua also recently became the first Chinese university to offer a Master of Law

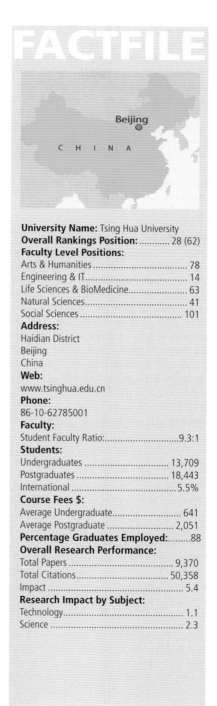

FACTFILE

Beijing

CHINA

University Name: Tsing Hua University
Overall Rankings Position: 28 (62)
Faculty Level Positions:
Arts & Humanities 78
Engineering & IT.. 14
Life Sciences & BioMedicine...................... 63
Natural Sciences....................................... 41
Social Sciences 101
Address:
Haidian District
Beijing
China
Web:
www.tsinghua.edu.cn
Phone:
86-10-62785001
Faculty:
Student Faculty Ratio:............................9.3:1
Students:
Undergraduates 13,709
Postgraduates 18,443
International 5.5%
Course Fees $:
Average Undergraduate........................... 641
Average Postgraduate 2,051
Percentage Graduates Employed:.........88
Overall Research Performance:
Total Papers 9,370
Total Citations.................................... 50,358
Impact 5.4
Research Impact by Subject:
Technology... 1.1
Science 2.3

programme in US law, and its law school now ranks as one of the best in China. While at the moment its appeal to overseas students and researchers is limited, Tsing Hua is keen to improve to the point where it can compete at the international level, turning national prestige into global recognition. However, while it is lauded for its innovative attitude towards improving its teaching methods and subject provision, the university has been criticised as hidebound and a poor climate for creative thought.

People?

Many of China's top scientists, engineers and politicians are Tsing Hua alumni. Among them are former premier Zhu Rongji, present Chinese President Hu Jintao and the Nobel Prize for Physics laureates Chen Ning Yang and Tsung-Dao Lee. The present faculty includes such luminaries as former Goldman Sachs president John L. Thornton and computer scientist Andrew Yao, who received the Turing Prize in 2000.

What do students say?

Indrayani Joe from Pernatang Siantar in Northern Sumatra, Indonesia, is studying graphic design.

"Tsing Hua is the most popular and famous university in China, which people say is the best. If we graduate from there, we can be very proud. It does have a very nice campus. But the school is not always honest with its students, both foreign and Chinese. The fees are four times more expensive for foreigners than for Chinese students, but the facilities and teaching we get are not as good as the Chinese students receive.

"Also, the teaching is not as good as I expected - it's a university but it is like going to high school. A lot of teachers dislike foreigners, which can make life difficult."

Good at?

Engineering and IT (14 in world), natural sciences (41)

174

Kyoto University

Why this university?

Kyoto University was founded in 1897 in the ancient capital of Japan, 10 years after the Tokyo University was established. Initially the university consisted of science and engineering, medicine and law, but it has since expanded to cover nearly all aspects of education and research including medicine and nuclear energy. The university's commitment to academic freedom has long been a hallmark of this institution – even in pre-war Japan under a military government. But the overseas composition of this prestigious university is limited. Language is a major barrier as nearly all lectures and seminars are in Japanese, as with Tokyo and other universities in the country. In 2005, only 1.2 per cent of 13,064 undergraduates and 6.5 per cent of 8,678 post-graduate students were from outside Japan. In post-graduate courses, many faculties accept theses in English. This is one of the reasons for the higher ratio of foreign students at the post-graduate level. As with Tokyo, competition for getting an undergraduate place is intense, awarded only to those who pass the national entrance exams as well as the university's own entrance exam, which are both set in Japanese, though there is now special selection process for foreign students and foreign educated Japanese. Kyoto, like Japan's 81 other former national universities, faces a one per cent subsidy cut starting next year for five years. In 2005, 54 per cent of its total income of ¥119.13 billion (£554 million) was government grant, which will automatically be cut by ¥640 million next year. Like Tokyo, Kyoto too has begun actively seeking endowment, for the first time in its over 100 year history.

The university has even lower ratio of foreign faculty members than Tokyo. In 2005, less than 1 per cent of 2,911 faculty members was a foreign national.

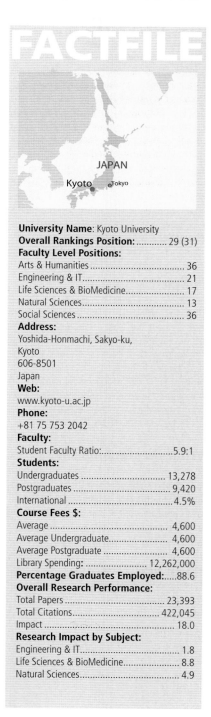

University Name: Kyoto University
Overall Rankings Position: 29 (31)
Faculty Level Positions:
Arts & Humanities 36
Engineering & IT.. 21
Life Sciences & BioMedicine...................... 17
Natural Sciences.. 13
Social Sciences 36
Address:
Yoshida-Honmachi, Sakyo-ku,
Kyoto
606-8501
Japan
Web:
www.kyoto-u.ac.jp
Phone:
+81 75 753 2042
Faculty:
Student Faculty Ratio:.............................5.9:1
Students:
Undergraduates 13,278
Postgraduates 9,420
International 4.5%
Course Fees $:
Average 4,600
Average Undergraduate....................... 4,600
Average Postgraduate 4,600
Library Spending: 12,262,000
Percentage Graduates Employed:.....88.6
Overall Research Performance:
Total Papers 23,393
Total Citations................................... 422,045
Impact 18.0
Research Impact by Subject:
Engineering & IT.. 1.8
Life Sciences & BioMedicine...................... 8.8
Natural Sciences.. 4.9

Subsidy cuts prompted by denationalisation in 2004 are forcing Kyoto, like all other Japanese universities, to rely on the private sector for research grants, which many academics fear could erode the university's autonomy. So far, the fact that Kyoto is more than 500 kilometres – or two hours' bullet train ride away – from the capital has somewhat shielded the university from political influences, academics say. Only a handful of Kyoto university lecturers and professors are on government advisory panels. However, young ambitious academics seeking media exposures are seeking positions at Tokyo-based universities – often of less prestige.

People

Perhaps it is because of its liberal tradition that the university has produced more Nobel and Field Medal winners than any of its Japanese rivals. In 1949 Physicist Hideki Yukawa, a Kyoto professor, was the first Japanese ever to win a Nobel prize. Since then, it has produced two winners in physics and science. In 1999, mathematician Shigefumi Mori won the Fields Medal.

What do students say?

"It's a liberal school," says a US PhD student, who completed a thesis on British-Japanese relations in late 19th century. "I think analysis approaches are not as strong as at American universities."

Good at?

Science (13 in world), medicine (17) and technology (21)

University of Michigan

Why this university?

The University of Michigan is the only university that claims an alumni chapter on the moon. The evidence is a little inaccessible - a plaque left on the lunar surface by the astronauts of Apollo 15, both of whom were Michigan graduates. But the record is there – and back on Earth, the public university flies pretty high, too, with top-rated programmes in business, education, engineering, law, library science, medicine, political science and sociology.

It also fields some of the most dominant sports teams in America, including an American football team that plays in the largest football-only stadium at any university in the world.

The first American university to use the seminar method of study, Michigan to this day offers more than 70 seminars for first-year students, each limited to a maximum of only 20. This despite the fact that there are 24,828 undergraduates and 12,184 graduate students. Those high numbers take a toll later on, when students find themselves in huge lecture classes or in courses taught by graduate students and not by one of the 5,000 faculty. But undergraduates do have a chance to work with faculty on research, and about 900 of them each year take advantage of the opportunity.

Michigan's leadership in research stems from Cold War and space race-era government grants for research and development and from the days when Detroit, about half an hour's drive away, was the world centre of the automotive industry. It still conducts nearly $800 million worth of research a year, more than almost any other US university. It was at Michigan that the polio vaccine and the

FACTFILE

UNITED STATES

OF AMERICA

Dearborn

Washington

University Name: University of Michigan
Overall Rankings Position: ....29= (36)
Faculty Level Positions:
Arts & Humanities 39
Engineering & IT.. 36
Life Sciences & BioMedicine...................... 55
Natural Sciences.. 34
Social Sciences 28
Address:
4901 Evergreen Road
Dearborn
Michigan 48128
United States
Web:
www.umich.edu
Phone:
+1 (313) 593-5000
Faculty:
Student Faculty Ratio:........................... 31.9:1
Students:
Undergraduates 24,828
Postgraduates 12,184
International 11.7%
Course Fees $:
Average 26,780
Average Undergraduate..................... 25,840
Average Postgraduate 27,124
Overall Research Performance:
Total Papers 24,517
Total Citations................................. 612,751
Impact 25.0
Research Impact by Subject:
Engineering & IT... 2.4
Life Sciences & BioMedicine.................... 10.1
Natural Sciences... 7.1
Social Sciences 3.3

EKG were developed.

One in five undergraduates specialises in engineering, which is also the pre-eminent graduate programme. The university's Phoenix Memorial Laboratory studies the peaceful uses of nuclear energy, and Michigan has top-flight laboratories for research into manufacturing engineering, manufacturing systems, an, not surprisingly, transportation. Its medical school is a partner with the University of Michigan Health System, one of the largest in the world.

The university attracts nearly 5,000 international students, a quarter of them undergraduates.

People?

In addition to astronauts, Michigan alumni include former President Gerald Ford, playwright Arthur Miller, actors James Earl Jones and Lucy Liu, Madonna, Iggy Pop, and Swedish Holocaust hero Raoul Wallenberg.

What do students say?

"The research facilities are sensational," said Simon Schenk, an Australian who just received his doctorate in kinesiology with articles published about his groundbreaking research into exercise, obesity, and diabetes in such high-profile journals. "That's one of the fortunate things at Michigan," Dr Schenk said. "Typically people might think of kinesiology as teaching physical education or something. But we were really at the cutting edge of basic science."

Good at?

Only biomedicine is outside the top 50 in our rankings – and that is 55th. Social science is the top-placed area, at 28th.

University of California, Los Angeles

Why this university?

Southern Californians joke that UCLA is actually short for "Under Construction in Los Angeles." That is because some $2 billion worth of new university buildings are rising from the Westwood hills.

They will complement the distinctive original red-brick buildings (many of them also under renovation to withstand the threat of earthquakes) built in the same gracious Mediterranean style - complete with rounded Roman arches - favoured by the Hollywood film stars who lived in nearby by Bel Air and Beverly Hills around the time when the university opened.

UCLA was established only in 1919, and moved to the current campus 10 years later. Since then it has sped into the ranks of schools hundreds of years older, especially in subjects such as film and television and in medicine and pubic health.

Considering UCLA's location in the entertainment capital of the world, it would be odd it its School of Theater, Film and Television was not to be among the best, and, in fact, its undergraduate component is usually ranked first in the nation. It encompasses the largest university-based film and television archive in the world and boasts an impressive roster of alumni who have worked in every aspect of the entertainment industry. The director, co-executive producer and actress who provides the voice of Bart Simpson on the animated television show The Simpsons all attended UCLA. Nearly 3,700 applicants compete annually for just 310 places in the entering class.

Just 50 years after admitting its first students, UCLA's David Geffen School of

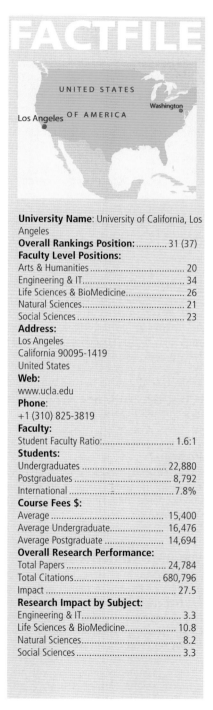

University Name: University of California, Los Angeles
Overall Rankings Position: 31 (37)
Faculty Level Positions:
Arts & Humanities 20
Engineering & IT... 34
Life Sciences & BioMedicine....................... 26
Natural Sciences.. 21
Social Sciences 23
Address:
Los Angeles
California 90095-1419
United States
Web:
www.ucla.edu
Phone:
+1 (310) 825-3819
Faculty:
Student Faculty Ratio:............................ 1.6:1
Students:
Undergraduates 22,880
Postgraduates 8,792
International 7.8%
Course Fees $:
Average 15,400
Average Undergraduate.................... 16,476
Average Postgraduate 14,694
Overall Research Performance:
Total Papers 24,784
Total Citations................................. 680,796
Impact 27.5
Research Impact by Subject:
Engineering & IT.. 3.3
Life Sciences & BioMedicine.................... 10.8
Natural Sciences.. 8.2
Social Sciences 3.3

Medicine (named for the record executive and Dreamworks cofounder who gave it $200 million in 2002) has rocketed to the top of the ranks of American medical schools. It is ninth in the country in research funding from the National Institutes of Health and third in research dollars from all sources (UCLA receives some $821 million a year in research funding across all disciplines). UCLA physicians reported the world's first AIDS cases.

The School of Public Health, opened in 1961, has also quickly risen to the top of its field and offers America's only doctoral programme in environmental science and engineering.

Innovative education also reaches undergraduates. The voluntary General Education Cluster Programme allows entering students to work on research with faculty on interdisciplinary topics by combining lecture classes with lab work and discussion sessions. Or they can take a Fiat Lux Freshman Seminar—an honours-style course meant to encourage intellectual discourse by investigating a specific question or topic, with no grades or homework, in groups of 20 or less.

People?
Film directors Francis Ford Coppola and Rob Reiner, actors James Dean and Tim Robbins and agent Mike Ovitz are among a host of famous alumni.

What do students say?
"Los Angeles is a place where strange encounters occur, something I happen to like without being able to say that you can be prepared for it in advance," said Stanislav "Stas" Shvabrin, a graduate student from Russia who was drawn to the university's highly regarded Slavic Studies department. "It's an inscrutable, impossible city that grows on you the way very few places do."

Good at?
All academic areas are placed in the top 40 worldwide, with the arts and humanities in the top 20.

University of Texas at Austin

Why this university?

Just like Texas, the University of Texas is vast, brash and ambitious. "We're Texas," the flagship public university stated in a stylish, high-concept marketing campaign that brought equal attention to the school's mascot (a longhorn steer named Bevo) and the 15th-century Gutenberg Bible in its library.

Narrated by legendary American broadcast journalist and alumnus Walter Cronkite, it intoned: "We don't claim to be able to change the world. We just change people. Then they change the world. We're Texas."

The advertising blitz was wildly successful. Burnt-orange T-shirts with the longhorn logo have become fashion statements and young Americans with no connection to the university flash the familiar "Hook 'em, Horns" hand signal.

But the university did not really need a catchy slogan to stand out. The largest university in America, UT boasts a correspondingly long list of distinctions. More than 37,000 undergraduate and 11,000 graduate students and 2,500 faculty populate its vast campus, whose most recognisable landmark is the 27-story UT Tower—six feet taller than the nearby Texas capitol building.

The College of Communication, the largest and most comprehensive of its kind, has 4,200 students and 120 faculty teaching advertising, communication studies, journalism, radio, television, and film. At the McCombs School of Business, more CEOs of companies ranked in the top 500 by the Standard & Poors bond-rating agency graduated than from any other business school.

The College of Engineering's graduate

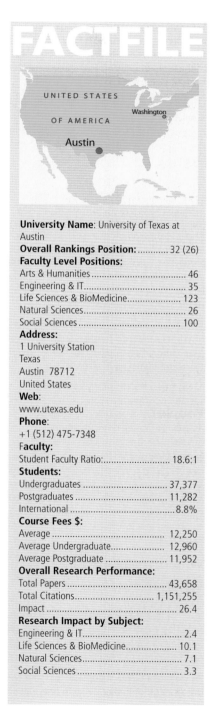

University Name: University of Texas at Austin
Overall Rankings Position: 32 (26)
Faculty Level Positions:
Arts & Humanities 46
Engineering & IT... 35
Life Sciences & BioMedicine..................... 123
Natural Sciences.. 26
Social Sciences 100
Address:
1 University Station
Texas
Austin 78712
United States
Web:
www.utexas.edu
Phone:
+1 (512) 475-7348
Faculty:
Student Faculty Ratio:............................ 18.6:1
Students:
Undergraduates 37,377
Postgraduates 11,282
International 8.8%
Course Fees $:
Average 12,250
Average Undergraduate.................... 12,960
Average Postgraduate 11,952
Overall Research Performance:
Total Papers 43,658
Total Citations..................... 1,151,255
Impact 26.4
Research Impact by Subject:
Engineering & IT.. 2.4
Life Sciences & BioMedicine................... 10.1
Natural Sciences.. 7.1
Social Sciences 3.3

programme in petroleum engineering is considered the best in America but it also has top-rated divisions of aerospace, chemical, civil, computer, electrical, environmental and mechanical engineering.

UT also has one of the biggest cultural archives in the world, while the new museum of art is, of course, the largest at any university in America and the academic library is the nation's fifth-largest.

Classes for undergraduates are large – introductory classes have as many as 400 students, with discussion sessions taught by graduate teaching assistants. And it is surprisingly diverse. Blacks, Asians and Hispanics make up one-third of the enrolment, and there are around 5,000 international students. The surrounding city of Austin, known for its innovative music scene, is a lively setting.

Athletics is a central, and successful, facet of UT. Its American football team has won four national championships, while all UT teams combined have taken 40.

People?

As well as Walter Cronkite, alumni include members of the Bush clan; J. M. Coetzee, Nobel Laureate for Literature; actors Farrah Fawcett, Jayne Mansfield, Tex Ritter and Renée Zellweger; rock singer Janis Joplin; Michael Dell, founder of the computer company Dell Inc; and Rex Tillerson, chairman and Chief Executive Officer of ExxonMobil.

What do students say?

Assem Nasr, a doctoral student in international communications from Beirut, said: "I've never seen that many students at one time. It's a huge university. I wondered, was I going to be lost in this place?

"Fortunately, I'm lucky to be in the department of radio, TV and film, where the professors get to know at least the graduate students on a personal basis, and what you're doing in terms of research and such."

He has found the faculty focused on the practical uses of his academic work, offering seminars about such things as how to look for a job. "They keep us on track and they're very motivating," he said.

Good at?

Natural sciences are the highest-placed area in our rankings, at 26th, but the arts and humanities and engineering and IT are not far behind.

University of Edinburgh

Why this university?

Edinburgh was founded in 1583 as the "Tounis (Town's) College," but its local roots are matched by an international outlook.

It is Scotland's most research-intensive university, with more than 96 per cent of its researchers in units carrying out work of international quality, according to the most recent Research Assessment Exercise. Its cutting edge research in medicine is set to be boosted by the opening this year of the £49 million Queen's Medical Research Institute. This brings together hundreds of elite researchers in inflammation research, cardiovascular medicine and reproductive biology, who will work together on conditions from diabetes and heart disease to cancer and menstrual disorders.

Edinburgh is also increasing its existing strength in informatics, a discipline covering computer science, artificial intelligence, cognitive science and linguistics, by bringing together researchers who are currently scattered across the city.

Commercialisation is seen as increasingly important. Edinburgh has pledged its commitment to boosting the Scottish economy, and in the wake of political devolution in 1999, has helped to create more than 50 companies.

The university recently restructured itself from nine faculties into three American-style colleges: humanities and social science, medicine and veterinary medicine, and science and engineering, which it believes will foster interdisciplinary work. It is also a prominent player in Scotland's pioneering "research pooling" ventures in physics, chemistry, geosciences, and engineering and mathematics. These ensure critical mass by letting researchers in different universities work together and

University Name: University of Edinburgh
Overall Rankings Position:............33 (30)
Faculty Level Positions:
Arts & Humanities:.....................................13
Engineering & IT:...66
Life Sciences & BioMedicine:.....................14
Natural Sciences:...46
Social Sciences:...38
Address:
South Bridge
Edinburgh
EH8 9YL
United Kingdom
Web:
www.ed.ac.uk
Phone:
+44(0)131 650 1000
Faculty:
Student Faculty Ratio:..........................4.1:1
Students:
Undergraduates:................................16,710
Postgraduates:....................................6,340
International:......................................18.2%
Course Fees $:
Average:... .. 19,819
Average Undergraduate:...................19,819
Average Postgraduate:.......................19,819
Overall Research Performance:
Total Papers:.......................................9,968
Total Citations:................................233,543
Impact:...23.4
Research Impact by Subject:
Engineering & IT:....................................2.0
life Sciences & BioMedicine:....................9.6
Natural Sciences:.....................................7.8
Social Sciences:.......................................1.6

share expensive equipment. And Edinburgh hopes it will also prove an attractive lure to international research stars.

It is also drawing on American experience to develop an ambitious £350 million fund - raising campaign. This will be launched this autumn and is to be headed by Young Dawkins III, previously vice-principal of development, and latterly president, of the University of New Hampshire Foundation. He says one of its top priorities will be scholarships and bursaries for both undergraduate and postgraduate students. Edinburgh is often stereotyped as Scotland's Oxbridge, attracting wealthy, privately educated English students. But it has been strenuously combating its elitist image with widening access schemes, and is already putting some £15 million into scholarships.

Edinburgh is Scotland's largest university, with around 4,000 academic and related staff and more than 22,000 students. There are roughly 17,000 undergraduates and 5,000 postgraduates, more than 4,000 of whom are international students from 130 different countries.

Edinburgh offers a blend of innovation and tradition: Old College, designed by alumnus Robert Adam, dates from the late 18th century and is in the centre of a World Heritage Site.

People?

Notable Edinburgh graduates include Charles Darwin, David Hume, James Hutton and writers Sir Walter Scott, Robert Louis Stevenson and Sir Arthur Conan Doyle.

Two of today's best known Scottish writers have Edinburgh connections: Ian Rankin, creator of detective John Rebus, is an Edinburgh graduate, while Alexander McCall Smith, author of the "No. 1 Ladies' Detective Agency" series, was professor of medical law until he retired last year to concentrate on writing.

What do students say?

Wen Hao Zou from China, in the final year of a business and accountancy degree, said: "My father runs a small business so I want to learn some new things. I realise here [the course] is more practical and I think it's very useful. I enjoy the course and the teachers are good. The first time I came to Edinburgh, I was carrying my bags and someone stopped in a car and gave me a lift. I could never imagine this happening in London. It's friendly. Edinburgh University has a lot of international students and we have a lot of fun."

Good at?

Life science and biomedicine, 13 in arts and humanities, good overall.

University of Hong Kong

Why this university?

The University of Hong Kong, Hong Kong's oldest university, was founded in 1911 and incorporated the Hong Kong College of Medicine, which was established in 1887. At the outset there were just three faculties in medicine, engineering and the arts. The university added a faculty of science in 1939 and six more faculties between 1967 and 2001: social sciences, dentistry, architecture, education, law and business and economics.

Its 10 faculties have a full-time student population of over 15,000, about 2,500 of them from overseas. Most – 59 per cent – are enrolled on undergraduate programmes, 29 per cent on taught Masters programmes, and 12 per cent on research degrees. The university has a teaching staff of 1,985; of which over half are international faculty. Its ethos of providing "outstanding teaching and world-class research" is signified by its Coat of Arms featuring two Chinese phrases from Confucius: "Illustrious Virtue" and "The investigation of things," combined with the Latin motto "Sapientia et Virtus" meaning "wisdom and virtue."

The faculty of medicine consolidated its international reputation when its influenza research team identified the coronavirus that triggered the 2003 SARS epidemic. While the faculty members and researchers worked behind the scenes to discover the origins of the virus and its mode of transmission, they also appeared in the local media to explain and educate the public about the virus.

The MBA programme offered by the faculty of business and economics also has a highly s regarded reputation, particularly in Asia. Its curriculum was further enhanced by recent partnerships that will allow students

FACTFILE

C H I N A

● Hong Kong

University Name: University of Hong Kong
Overall Rankings Position: 33 (41)
Faculty Level Positions:
Arts & Humanities 13
Engineering & IT... 67
Life Sciences & BioMedicine.......................31
Natural Sciences... 71
Social Sciences 30
Address:
Pok Fu Lam Road
Hong Kong
Hong Kong
Web:
www.hku.hk
Phone:
+852 2859 2111
Faculty:
Student Faculty Ratio:............................8.1:1
Students:
Undergraduates 8,842
Postgraduates 6,275
International 16.5%
Library Spending:........................22,100,000
Percentage Graduates Employed:........98
Overall Research Performance:
Total Papers 7,916
Total Citations..................................... 99,509
Impact 12.6
Research Impact by Subject:
Engineering & IT.. 1.4
Life Sciences & BioMedicine...................... 6.5
Social Sciences 1.5

to take classes at the London Business School and Columbia Business School.

The university's international outreach is further reflected in numerous joint initiatives and programmes with more than 150 overseas exchange partners involving over 1,200 students.

The university has big expansion plans as it approaches its centennial year in the form of a new Centennial Campus. Due to be completed in 2011 at the cost of over HK$2.4 billion (£170 million), the new 42,000 square-meter, state-of-the-art campus will allow the university to enhance its teaching and research facilities, as well as increase its student numbers by over 3,000 in preparation for the territory-wide introduction of a 4-year degree structure in 2012.

People?

As Hong Kong's pre-eminent research institution, the university receives the lion's share of government research grants. Its strength in scientific research is internationally recognised with members of the science faculty being offered an endowed lectureship by the Royal Society of Chemistry and many being elected as Fellows of the Royal Society; 13 are members of the prestigious Chinese Academy of Sciences and the Chinese Academy of Engineering; and 39 of its faculty were ranked by Thomson Scientific, source of the citations data used in this book, as being among the world's top one per cent of scientists based on the impact of their publications.

What do students say?

Alexander Schindler from Germany, who is in year three of his LLB at the faculty of law, was initially surprised by the diversity and competitiveness of his fellow students. He says: "The programme exceeded all my expectations. Scholars from all major jurisdictions offered a rich learning experience with special priority on business and financial law due to Hong Kong's position as an international trade centre."

Good at?

Arts and humanities, social sciences, and life science and biomedcine

Carnegie Mellon University

Why this university?

Unusual enough that a university most known for science and technology has a top drama programme. Carnegie Mellon takes this one step further by mixing up its 30 disparate academic fields in a culture of interdisciplinary research and teaching.

It has an Art Conservation Research Center, for example, that studies scientific methods of preserving paintings, books, and paper. Its Center for Arts Management and Technology develops information and communications technology specifically to manage arts and cultural organisations. Another programme combines engineering, social sciences, economics and the arts to help restore contaminated industrial spaces to productive use.

Its combination of technology and the humanities has helped propel the university, which is in the city of Pittsburgh, from a regional institution to one that is internationally known; applications for undergraduate admission have more than doubled in the last 10 years, and there is now a diverse blend of about 10,000 graduate and undergraduate students at Carnegie Mellon, a quarter of them from other countries.

But it's science that holds the edge at this university, which was founded in 1900 as a technical school by the industrialist Andrew Carnegie to train the children of Pittsburgh's working-class poor. Its School of Computer Science is one of the best in the world and includes the pre-eminent Robotics Institute, the largest at any US university, whose various robots are programmed to play football, help the elderly with chores and search for meteorites in Antarctica. Its Science and Technology Center for Light Microscope Imaging and Biotechnology is developing tools such as microscopy

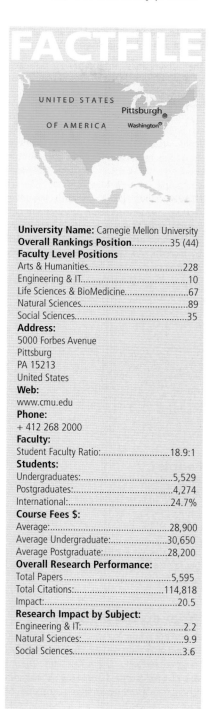

University Name: Carnegie Mellon University
Overall Rankings Position...............35 (44)
Faculty Level Positions
Arts & Humanities......................................228
Engineering & IT..10
Life Sciences & BioMedicine.........................67
Natural Sciences..89
Social Sciences..35
Address:
5000 Forbes Avenue
Pittsburg
PA 15213
United States
Web:
www.cmu.edu
Phone:
+ 412 268 2000
Faculty:
Student Faculty Ratio:..........................18.9:1
Students:
Undergraduates:....................................5,529
Postgraduates:......................................4,274
International:...24.7%
Course Fees $:
Average:..28,900
Average Undergraduate:......................30,650
Average Postgraduate:.........................28,200
Overall Research Performance:
Total Papers...5,595
Total Citations:...................................114,818
Impact:..20.5
Research Impact by Subject:
Engineering & IT:..2.2
Natural Sciences:..9.9
Social Sciences...3.6

workstations for biological research. It has 15 Nobel Laureates on its faculty of 1,421, and maintains a branch campus in California's Silicon Valley.

Even Carnegie Mellon's highly regarded business school is best known for information technology and operations management, among other programmes (including entrepreneurship). The university also practices what it preaches in computer science; its campus is among America's most wired. And Carnegie Mellon is the home to a 10-teraflop Cray XT3 computer called Big Ben, capable of 10 trillion calculations per second, or as much processing capacity as 30,000 PCs. Scientists have used it to model earthquake soil vibration, forecast severe thunderstorms, map blood flow in the heart in three dimensions, forecast Comet Shoemaker-Levy 9's impact with Jupiter and create a super-lightweight aluminum used in soda cans.

Concerned about public perceptions that universities with robust research programmes neglect undergraduate teaching, Carnegie Mellon was also one of the first universities in America to establish a centre aimed at helping faculty improve their classroom teaching.

People?

A concerted marketing and branding campaign has helped create a surge in the school's name recognition, as have the alumni of that conservatory-style drama programme, including the likes of George Peppard, Jack Klugman, Holly Hunter, Ted Danson, Blair Underwood, and producer Steven Bochco.

What do students say?

"When I told people I was going to Carnegie Mellon, they all thought that I was going to be an engineer. And when I told them I wasn't, they assumed I must be in the drama school," said Jen Johnson, a sophomore who describes herself as technologically unskilled and who is actually majoring in anthropology. "In fact, you get to know a lot of people outside of your field. We all feed off of each other's energies that way. You're surrounded by a wide array of different types of thinking."

Ms Johnson, who comes from a small town in Montana near the Canadian border, added: "A lot of the professors really do take a lot of interest in you as a person. Although they are obviously very bright and doing research of their own, they're able to bring that down into the classroom level. They're really accessible. I never feel that I'm being lectured to."

Its relatively small endowment of $837 million means the university has less money for scholarships than rival schools, however. "If there's a downside, it's that financial aid not as generous as students would like," Ms Johnson said.

Good at?

Engineering and IT – 10 in the world

University of Sydney

Why this university?

Australia's oldest university celebrated its 150th anniversary with the Sydney Olympics in 2000. As with other long-established inner-city universities, Sydney has a big reputation for research and its 2,500 academics are involved in hundreds of collaborative research projects with Australian governments and other organisations, and with colleagues overseas.

Founded in 1850 "to promote useful knowledge and to encourage the residents of New South Wales to pursue a regular course of liberal education", classes at the University of Sydney started two years later with 24 students enrolled in the faculty of arts. The course required three years study of Greek, Latin, mathematics and science.

The university began operating on its main campus on the edge of the Sydney Central Business District in 1860. Sweeping lawns and Gothic Revival sandstone architecture give the campus a sense of old world higher learning that continues within the grand quadrangle and the Great Tower, now a focal point.

As secondary education had hardly begun in the 1850s, it was 30 years before Sydney had attracted more than 100 students. Over the next century, numbers slowly, and then rapidly, increased so that by this year total enrolments exceeded 35,000, 19 per cent of which are international students.

Sydney is a member of Australia's Group of Eight research-intensive universities and has formal links with many of the world's leading research institutions. The global network of partners covers research collaboration, joint teaching projects as well as staff and student exchanges across 37 countries in Europe, North America and Asia.

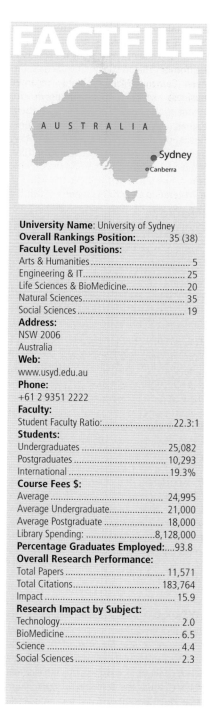

University Name: University of Sydney
Overall Rankings Position: 35 (38)
Faculty Level Positions:
Arts & Humanities 5
Engineering & IT 25
Life Sciences & BioMedicine 20
Natural Sciences 35
Social Sciences 19
Address:
NSW 2006
Australia
Web:
www.usyd.edu.au
Phone:
+61 2 9351 2222
Faculty:
Student Faculty Ratio: 22.3:1
Students:
Undergraduates 25,082
Postgraduates 10,293
International 19.3%
Course Fees $:
Average 24,995
Average Undergraduate 21,000
Average Postgraduate 18,000
Library Spending: 8,128,000
Percentage Graduates Employed: 93.8
Overall Research Performance:
Total Papers 11,571
Total Citations 183,764
Impact 15.9
Research Impact by Subject:
Technology 2.0
BioMedicine 6.5
Science 4.4
Social Sciences 2.3

The university is one of only two Australian institutions in the Association of the Pacific Rim Universities which comprises members from Asia, the United States and South America. Many of Sydney's research centres have an explicitly international focus, including the Asian Agribusiness Research Centre, the Institute for International Health, the Australian Centre for Innovation and International Competitiveness and the Research Institute for Asia and the Pacific.

Good at?

Most things – 5 in the world for arts and humanities, 19 for social sciences, 20 for life sciences and bio medicine, 25 for engieering and IT, 35 for natural sciences

People?

Graduates who have gained international recognition include Nobel laureates Professor Russell Robinson, Sir John Cornforth and Dr John Harsanyi, former president of the World Bank James Wolfensohn, academic and businesswoman Jill Ker Conway, film makers Phil Noyce, Jane Campion and Bruce Beresford, writers such as Germaine Greer and Clive James, and three prime ministers, including Australia's first - Andrew Barton - and current PM John Howard.

What do students say?

Diego Poveda from Bogota in Colombia initially hoped to study in America or Britain. The cost was more than his parents could afford so he opted for Australia. Mr Poveda is in the third year of a four-year Bachelor of chemical engineering course and finds it hard to think of anything to complain of about his lecturers, his studies or the university.

"When I saw the curriculum the University of Sydney had to offer, I realised that it had a balanced programme between theoretical classes and problem-based learning," he says. "I'd say that in large part it has met my expectations. The mix of theoretical subjects and problem based learning really put a smile on my face as I could see how learning about systems could be applied in a chemical plant."

Ecole Polytechnique

Why this university?

France's most prestigious engineering grande école, Ecole Polytechnique, has for over two centuries trained distinguished scientists, captains of industry, military chiefs and political leaders, as well as engineers.

Founded as the Ecole Centrale des Travaux Publics in 1794 by Lazare Carnot and Gaspard Monge, it was renamed a year later. In 1804 Napoleon established it as a military academy, with the motto "Pour la patrie, les sciences et la gloire" ("For the nation, sciences and glory").

The Defence Ministry is its supervisory authority. Students have military status and wear a distinctive uniform on special occasions. Women were first admitted in 1972. Entrance is through competitive exam after two years' studies in post-baccalauréat preparatory classes, though nowadays there is an alternative selection procedure for foreign students.

The school – nicknamed "X" - has an undergraduate programme, graduate school and many research laboratories mostly run in association with other institutions such as CNRS, the national centre for scientific research.

Polytechnique specialises in biology, chemistry, computer science, economics, pure and applied mathematics, mechanical engineering, physics and social sciences. But all students must study a broad range of subjects including two languages and general cultural courses, and follow several work placements.

Reforms in 2000 extended by a year the traditional three-year undergraduate engineering programme – one year each military service, common studies and specialisation – and introduced a civilian

---

FACTFILE

Paris
Palaiseau

FRANCE

University Name: Ecole Polytechniqe
Overall Rankings Position:............37 (10)
Faculty Level Positions:
Arts & Humanities:....................................198
Engineering & IT:...26
Life Sciences & BioMedicine:....................196
Natural Sciences:..24
Social Sciences:...203
Address:
rue de Saclay
Palaiseau
911228
France
Web:
www.polytechnique.fr
Phone:
+33(0)1 69 33 42 88
Faculty:
Student Faculty Ratio:...........................3.8:1
Students:
Undergraduates:.................................2,000
Postgraduates:.......................................600
International:.....................................24.6%
Course Fees $:
Average:..10,254
Average Undergraduate:.......................8,973
Average Postgraduate:........................12,818
Library Spending:............................961,350
Percentage Graduates Employed:......96
Overall Research Performance:
Total Papers:.......................................4,895
Total Citations:..................................64,586
Impact:...13.2
Research Impact by Subject:
Engineering & IT:.....................................2.2
Natural Sciences:.....................................4.9

service option. A year is spent at another university, possibly abroad.

Annual intake is 500, with foreigners of 40 nationalities representing a fifth of the 2,000 undergraduates. There are 150 Master's students, half from abroad, and 417 studying for doctorates, including 30 per cent international students. Twelve per cent of the school's 400 teachers are from abroad.

About 15 patents are registered annually. Areas of research include an asymmetric anti-noise wall; a proton-therapy laser for cancer treatments; an original procedure allowing easy access to compounds for cardiac therapies; a model for forecasting air quality.

Among Polytechnique-related high-technology projects are the TGV, France's high-speed train; Ariane rocket launchers; Airbus planes; and France's nuclear reactor system.

People?

Alumni include Presidents Sadi Carnot and Valéry Giscard d'Estaing, astronauts Jean-François Clervoy and Philippe Perrin, scientists André-Marie Ampère, Paul Lévy, Henri Poincaré and Nobel prize-winner for economics, Maurice Allais. Alfred Dreyfus and Generals Foch and Joffre are among military Polytechniciens. Numerous heads of industry, corporations and companies include André Citroën, Charles Bébéar, Jean-Marie Messier, Serge Dassault, Jacques Attali.

In 1976 the school moved from its historic site in Paris's Latin Quarter to its present campus at Palaiseau, south of the capital, where all students are housed.

What do students say?

British student Harry Robertson, 21, is halfway through the undergraduate programme. For his six-month stage de formation humaine – "roughly a leadership-

development work placement" he "worked as a full-time teacher for inmates at a Paris prison, which was an incredible experience." His final diploma will be equivalent to a French engineering degree and an MSc.

His "very high expectations of both the quality of the education and the student lifestyle" were "more than lived up to. I was pleasantly surprised at just how much freedom students have in picking their courses, and at how cosmopolitan the campus is." He spent a month this summer working in Beijing, after studying Chinese for a year.

He identifies the school's strengths as "the diversity and quality of its education, its budget per student – Polytechnique is very highly subsidised; and the student lifestyle – there's an incredible amount of clubs, activities and sport."

He says weaknesses are that "it is little known abroad, especially compared to the top British and American universities, and its relatively small size."

Good at?

Natural Sciences and engineering and IT

Monash University

Why this university?

The biggest university in Australia has more students, more staff and more campuses around the world than any other. Monash University was established by the Victorian parliament in 1958 and was the first university created in that state since the University of Melbourne 105 years earlier.

From an initial intake of 347 students in 1961, Monash grew rapidly in size and student numbers. The university also developed a wide range of courses in arts, commerce, engineering, education, law, medicine and science, and in 1990 began expanding, first around Melbourne, then outside the city and finally beyond Australia.

In 1998, the Malaysian Ministry of Education invited Monash to set up a campus near Kuala Lumpur jointly with the Sunway Group. The creation of Monash University Malaysia was followed by a second offshore in South Africa in 2001 while study centres were later established at Kings College in London and in Prato, Italy.

Monash is now a network of eight campuses and has partnerships with 110 institutions around the world. In 45 years, enrolments have grown from less than 400 to nearly 56,000 students from more than 100 countries. Almost 48,000 are studying on Monash campuses in Australia, including 11,500 from overseas, while another 6,500 are based either on the university's international campuses or with partner institutions.

The university has more than 1,900 beds on its campuses in Australia available for domestic and international students. The cost of accommodation ranges from A$106 to A$168 depending on the campus location and facilities provided. Monash

University Name: Monash University
Overall Rankings Position:............38 (33)
Faculty Level Positions:
Arts & Humanities.......................................28
Engineering & IT..28
Life Sciences & BioMedicine........................19
Natural Sciences..54
Social Sciences..16
Address:
Victoria
3800
Australia
Web:
www.monash.edu.au
Phone:
+61 3 9902 6000
Faculty:
Student Faculty Ratio..........................29.1:1
Students:
Undergraduates..................................39,073
Postgraduates....................................15,877
International.......................................31.2%
Course Fees $:
Average.. 15,800
Average Undergraduate 15,900
Average Postgraduate..................... 15,600
Library Spending: 11,414,000
Percentage Graduates Employed:.......77
Overall Research Performance:
Total Papers...7,574
Total Citations....................................119,060
Impact 15.7
Research Impact by Subject:
Engineering & IT.. 1.4
Life Sciences & BioMedicine...................... 7.5
Social Sciences 1.2

can also arrange homestay accommodation with local families for A$217 a week, which includes a room and three meals a day.

International students are encouraged to apply for scholarships, including International scholarships for excellence, which provide up to A$6,000 a year and Monash Global scholarships, which provide a A$6,000 one-off grant.

People?

Monash is one of the Group of Eight research-intensive universities and is home to 75 research centres. Three large projects have positioned the university at the epicentre of national and international science and technology breakthroughs: a A$300 million Science, Technology, Research and Innovation Precinct, a A$157 million synchrotron — the first to be built in Australia — and an Australian Stem Cell Centre which is one of the major tenants of the precinct.

What do students say?

Last year, Shyamala Nataraj came from India to complete a Masters degree in bioethics at Monash's main campus in Melbourne and is now doing a PhD in public health. Ms Nataraj has been nominated as one of the 1000 "Women for Nobel Peace Prize 2005" for her work on HIV/AIDS related issues. After learning about the Masters course, she thought it fitted exactly with the work she had been doing in the Tamil Nadu region over the past 18 years.

"Melbourne is such a lovely city to live in," she says. "I spent some time in the US and considered studying there but found I didn't want my son growing up in that country, so I brought him with me while my daughter is studying in America."

Ms Nataraj says the teaching at Monash varies between "good and very good": none of the lecturing is poor, she says, and most is good while some is excellent. The only limitation is that the content and context of the curriculum is "very western".

"That comes from the fact that I'm studying in an area that encompasses ethics and philosophy in the context of health. International students come from different cultures and many of us expect to go back and work in our own countries so the curriculum should look at what is produced in other places such as Asia where Australia has close ties."

Good at?

Social sciences (16 in world), life sciences and biomedicine (19)

University of Geneva

Why this university?

The University of Geneva, (Université de Genève), with its 14,000 students and 4,800 staff, is Switzerland's second largest university after Zurich's federal polytechnic.

It was founded in 1559 as the Académie de Genève, a seminary specialising in theology and the humanities.

Although law was also taught, theology remained its principal field of study until the late 17th century. During the Age of Enlightenment, interest broadened out to many aspects of "natural philosophy" and developed further in legal studies. This eventually led, in the mid-19th century, to its complete emancipation from the church and in 1873, with the opening of a medical school, to its re-definition as a university belonging to the Canton of Geneva.

The university reflects Geneva's character as an international capital and as Switzerland's second-largest city. Geneva hosts scores of international organisations such as the World Health Organisation and the Red Cross, and a number of international schools including the Ecole International de Genève.

The large number of foreign residents is one reason that over 30 per cent of the students are non-Swiss. Student numbers have been growing steadily, in particular in the faculties of law and of economic and social sciences. International exchanges for faculty and students are strongly encouraged and, since 1996, the number of students taking part in the European Union's Erasmus programme has increased five times. The university works on a number of networked projects with the University of Lausanne, Lausanne's EPFL and the University of Neuchatel.

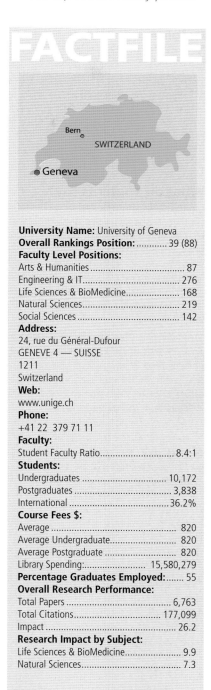

University Name: University of Geneva
Overall Rankings Position: 39 (88)
Faculty Level Positions:
Arts & Humanities 87
Engineering & IT...................................... 276
Life Sciences & BioMedicine..................... 168
Natural Sciences...................................... 219
Social Sciences 142
Address:
24, rue du Général-Dufour
GENEVE 4 — SUISSE
1211
Switzerland
Web:
www.unige.ch
Phone:
+41 22 379 71 11
Faculty:
Student Faculty Ratio............................. 8.4:1
Students:
Undergraduates 10,172
Postgraduates 3,838
International 36.2%
Course Fees $:
Average 820
Average Undergraduate.......................... 820
Average Postgraduate 820
Library Spending:...................... 15,580,279
Percentage Graduates Employed:....... 55
Overall Research Performance:
Total Papers 6,763
Total Citations................................. 177,099
Impact 26.2
Research Impact by Subject:
Life Sciences & BioMedicine..................... 9.9
Natural Sciences.. 7.3

People?

Theologian Jean Calvin was the religious and ideological driving force for its establishment, and Theodore de Beze, one of Calvin's closest disciples, was its first rector. Throughout the centuries, the university has been a refuge for religious and political exiles, who have both drawn from, and contributed to, the institution.

What do students say?

Andrea Puglisi, from Parma, Italy, a doctoral student in the department of molecular biology, says: "The level of research is very high, and financial resources are excellent, both for salaries and for the labs. In my field the environment is very international – we have people from Finland, Spain, Italy, India, the US, and only about 10 per cent are Swiss.

"Academically, the structure and schedule are such that there is a constant exchange of ideas. Also, Geneva is a very pleasant city that combines the efficiency and reliability of Swiss services with the enjoyability of a cosmopolitan capital."

Good at?

87 in arts and humanities, others more modest

University of Manchester

Why this university?

England's oldest civic university became Britain's first chartered university of the 21st century and the largest single-site institution in the country when Victoria University of Manchester merged with UMIST to form the University of Manchester in 2004.

Since the merger, Manchester has set its sights on becoming a world giant by 2015 in terms of academic achievement and reputation, bringing its size, significant human capital, impressive facilities, and half a billion pounds annual income to bear on the challenge.

It is already well on its way to achieving its globe-topping aims. In recognition of its achievements to date, Manchester was voted University of the Year in The Times Higher Education Supplement's annual awards. Its 4,500 academic and research staff notched up international-class rankings in 41 out of the university's 52 discipline areas in the last Research Assessment Exercise. Such impressive results have helped make Manchester the most popular among British students applying for places on undergraduate courses, and the UK's second most popular university among international students. The latter came from a total of 180 different countries.

There are more than 50 specialist research centres and groups at Manchester, each undertaking pioneering research into areas ranging from cancer treatments and genetic disorders to artificial intelligence and aeronautics. The university boasts the world-famous Jodrell Bank Observatory, the £35 million Manchester Interdisciplinary Biocentre, the Photon Science Institute, and the recently opened Integrative Centre for

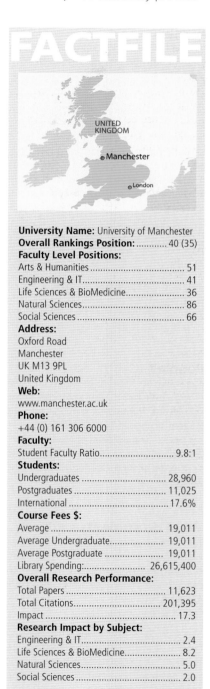

University Name: University of Manchester
Overall Rankings Position: 40 (35)
Faculty Level Positions:
Arts & Humanities 51
Engineering & IT.. 41
Life Sciences & BioMedicine...................... 36
Natural Sciences.. 86
Social Sciences 66
Address:
Oxford Road
Manchester
UK M13 9PL
United Kingdom
Web:
www.manchester.ac.uk
Phone:
+44 (0) 161 306 6000
Faculty:
Student Faculty Ratio.............................. 9.8:1
Students:
Undergraduates 28,960
Postgraduates 11,025
International 17.6%
Course Fees $:
Average 19,011
Average Undergraduate..................... 19,011
Average Postgraduate 19,011
Library Spending:........................ 26,615,400
Overall Research Performance:
Total Papers 11,623
Total Citations.................................... 201,395
Impact 17.3
Research Impact by Subject:
Engineering & IT.. 2.4
Life Sciences & BioMedicine...................... 8.2
Natural Sciences.. 5.0
Social Sciences 2.0

Molecular Cell Biology. Other new facilities include the Brooks World Poverty Institute and a new centre for cancer research.

Manchester is funding these developments with a £360 million capital investment programme – the largest ever seen in British higher education. As well as improving academic facilities, the money is being used to further enhance the university's city-centre campus. This it describes as a "mini-metropolis", with its own shops, accommodation, and social and sporting facilities.

Manchester guarantees university-managed accommodation, with more than 9,000 beds to choose from, throughout the duration of a course for all students paying overseas student fees. Manchester's students union, the biggest in the UK, provides additional student support along with societies and social events.

People?

More than 20 Nobel Prize winners include Ernest Rutherford, who split the atom. WS Jevons formulated the principles of modern economics, while AJP Taylor was the best-known historian of his generation. Tom Kilburn and Sir Freddie Williams were among the pioneers of computers in the 1940s.

What do students say?

Tomomi Kimura, a life sciences PhD student from Japan, said she felt the convenient, compact and comprehensive facilities on campus and in the city were among the university's greatest assets, along with its strong academic reputation.

She said: "It is easy to get whatever you need at Manchester, and the facilities are excellent. The student accommodation is very good and conveniently located, and arranged so that it is easy to make friends. Manchester itself is a convenient place from which to visit anywhere in England and to travel internationally from the airport. Sometimes the transport system is not very reliable, but other than that I have had no real disappointments."

Good at?

Biomedicine achieved the best position in our rankings, but all areas were in the top 100.

University of New South Wales

Why this university?

Although its origins can be traced back to the founding of the Sydney Mechanics Institute in 1843, it was not until 1949 that the institution which became the University of New South Wales was established.

The original Sydney institute had sought "the diffusion of scientific and special knowledge" and UNSW continues to apply those precepts today. Initially, the university's core focus was on teaching and research in science and technology but the courses also included humanities and commerce subjects and they are still a crucial component today, along with engineering, law and medicine.

UNSW is one of the heavyweights of Australian higher education. It enrols more than 40,000 students, nearly one in four of them from 125 countries overseas, employs 2,300 academics, offers 870 programmes in 75 schools to undergraduates and postgraduates, and has the biggest engineering course in Australia.

The university's main campus is in Kensington, an inner suburb of Sydney, but six others are scattered around the city. One of its most famous colleges, the Australian Defence Force Academy, is the nation's principal military training institute, based in Canberra.

Next year, the university will join Monash University in having its own campus in Asia. This followed an invitation by the Singapore government and UNSW Asia will be the first wholly foreign-owned research and teaching institution in the island state.

UNSW Asia plans to have an eventual enrolment of 15,000 students, with 10,000 expected to be drawn from other parts of the world. When completed by 2009, the $500

University Name: University of New South Wales
Overall Rankings Position:.............41 (40)
Faculty Level Positions:
Arts & Humanities......................................18
Engineering & IT..19
Life Sciences & BioMedicine......................52
Natural Sciences.......................................41
Social Sciences...21
Address:
Sydney
NSW 2052
Australia
Web:
www.unsw.edu.au
Phone:
+61 2 9385 1000
Faculty:
Student Faculty Ratio...............................9.8:1
Students:
Undergraduates...................................25,964
Postgraduates.....................................14,672
International...23.1%
Course Fees $:
Average 15,070
Average Undergraduate 14,920
Average Postgraduate.................. 15,330
Library Spending: 7,340,000
Overall Research Performance:
Total Papers..8,567
Total Citations...................................126,980
Impact...14.8
Research Impact by Subject:
Engineering & IT...1.6
Life Sciences & BioMedicine.....................6.0
Natural Sciences.......................................4.9
Social Science...2.0

million (£207 million) campus in Changi will incorporate a cluster-based teaching and research approach, underpinned by research centres.

The university says programmes offered at UNSW Asia will be of equal standing to those in Sydney and will go through the same approval, accreditation and quality assurance processes.

People?

As well as being a member of Australia's Group of Eight research-intensive universities, UNSW is also a founding member of Universitas 21, the international alliance of 20 leading universities in 11 countries. UNSW has more than 200 partnerships with overseas universities and academic linkages with leading institutions in Asia, Europe and North America.

What do students say?

Despite the establishment of UNSW Asia, most overseas students will still want to go to Australia to study, as is the case with Catharina Nawangpalupi.

Ms Nawangpalupi came with her four-year-old daughter and husband from the Indonesian island of Java last year, to undertake her PhD in the faculty of built evironment at UNSW after completing a Master's degree in engineering at the university in 2001.

"I initially decided on UNSW after comparing the ranking of its engineering course with others and it was one of the best," she says. "My supervisors and other staff give me a great deal of support and I find that excellent, although the library resources are not as good as when I did my Master's."

Ms Nawangpalupi says as well as receiving help with her studies, she also has the opportunity to tutor undergraduate students. She believes the experience in conducting her research and tutoring will be of great use when she returns to teach at a private university in Java in another three years' time.

Good at?

Arts and humanities (18 in world) , social sciences (21),engineering and IT (19)

Northwestern University

Why this university?

Its best-known alumni may be the graduates of its theatre programme – Charlton Heston, Warren Beatty, Cloris Leachman, Ann-Margret, Patricia Neal – but it's Northwestern's schools of management, law and journalism that have propelled it to prominence from origins as a regional university famous mainly for its losing football team.

Founded in 1850 in an office over a hardware store by Chicago civic leaders anxious to win respect for their gritty frontier town, Northwestern today has five doctoral programmes ranked in the top 10 per cent in America by the National Research Council and 10 others in the top 25 per cent. It likes to describe itself as "ambitious".

Many international students come to Northwestern to attend its top-rated Kellogg School of Business; about one-quarter of its 2,500 faculty was born in other countries and one-third of the business school's students are international, representing 50 countries. Like the university as a whole, the school has moved more nimbly than its peer institutions to incorporate such new programmes as internet marketing and entertainment management. More than 50 new courses in all have been introduced at Kellogg in the last 10 years. Its Global Initiatives in Management include two weeks of field study in such places as Central Europe, China, Russia and Vietnam.

Northwestern's School of Law is small (240 students) and unusually supportive, rather than competitive like many other US law schools. It includes a nine-month Master's programme for graduates of foreign law schools to learn American law and legal processes and a concentration in

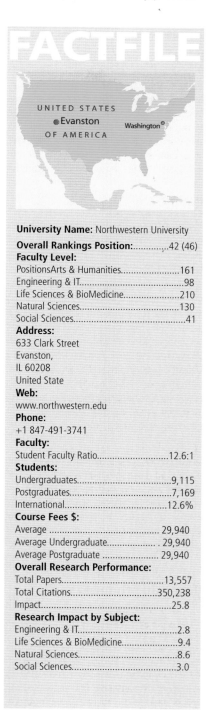

University Name: Northwestern University
Overall Rankings Position:...........,.42 (46)
Faculty Level:
PositionsArts & Humanities.......................161
Engineering & IT...98
Life Sciences & BioMedicine......................210
Natural Sciences...130
Social Sciences..41
Address:
633 Clark Street
Evanston,
IL 60208
United State
Web:
www.northwestern.edu
Phone:
+1 847-491-3741
Faculty:
Student Faculty Ratio.............................12.6:1
Students:
Undergraduates.....................................9,115
Postgraduates..7,169
International...12.6%
Course Fees $:
Average 29,940
Average Undergraduate................... . 29,940
Average Postgraduate 29,940
Overall Research Performance:
Total Papers...13,557
Total Citations..................................350,238
Impact..25.8
Research Impact by Subject:
Engineering & IT..2.8
Life Sciences & BioMedicine.......................9.4
Natural Sciences...8.6
Social Sciences...3.0

international human rights law.

People?

The university's Center for International Human Rights, headed by former US Ambassador at Large for War Crimes Issues David Scheffer, prepares students to argue before international criminal tribunals and does research into international law. It is adding a programme in corporate responsibility for human rights. And its Center for Wrongful Conviction, staffed largely by students from the law school with some involvement from the university's Medill School of Journalism, famously proved innocent nine inmates on Illinois's death row, causing the state's governor to declare a moratorium on executions.

The same real-world approach has made the McCormick School of Engineering among the top-ranked in America. It has a programme that gives first-year students the chance to work with real engineers on projects at partner companies including Abbott Laboratories, BP-Amoco, Ford, Motorola, and DuPont. The "Engineering First" idea, launched formally in 2000, stemmed from concern that engineering education previously emphasised scientific analysis at the expense of practical design.

The university's main campus is in Evanston, a city on Lake Michigan just north of Chicago that was named, in a switch, for one of the university's founders, John Evans. This gives Northwestern the feel of an urban university whose immediate surroundings are suburban.

What do students say?

"It's not inside the city, but if you need to go into the city, it takes maybe 30 minutes," Ruchit Duggal, a senior from India who is majoring in both economics and computer engineering, said. Without city distractions, he said, "you have close-knit communities, in spite of it being a big university. You run across new people every day, but you also make a lot of friends."

"You find people from all over the world, and they're definitely some of the smartest people to get in here," he said. Fewer than one in three applicants to the university are accepted to the ranks of its 16,000 undergraduate and graduate students; just over 12 percent are international. "It's a good mix of cultures," Mr Duggal said.

The major drawback, he said (at least now that the football team has ended its record streak of consecutive lost games): the relentless biting winds off the lake in the winter. "The only negative I've found is the weather in the winter, which gets you down a bit," Mr Duggal said.

Good at?

Social sciences (41 in world)

New York University

Why this university?

Like the city that surrounds it, New York University thinks big. It is regarded highly in not just one or two fields, but in many, including business, law, the sciences and the performing arts. It is the largest private university in the US, with more employees—16,000—than most universities have students. The members of its faculty remain active in the disciplines they teach, serving as advisors to government and industry, editors for publishing houses, and consultants to the global institutions with which they share the city of New York.

What NYU is best known for in America is the location of its central campus, which wraps around Washington Square in bohemian Greenwich Village, the very centre of Manhattan. The square, in turn, is a centre of political and cultural activism, random entertainment, and relatively constant, harmless urban lunacy.

It is a far cry from the seriousness of other schools that existed when NYU was founded in 1831 specifically to serve students other than those in the privileged classes. It still holds to that ideal. Among its students there are more than 5,000 from other countries, the fifth-highest proportion in the United States. (Despite NYU's huge enrolment, most classes are of a reasonable size; 82 per cent have fewer than 30 students.)

Its law school and Stern School of Business are among the nation's most distinguished. Its Courant Institute of Mathematical Sciences, founded by (and named for) pre-World War II exiles from the famous Mathematics Institute at the University of Göttingen, integrates mathematics and computational sciences as a unified field, applying maths and computation

University Name: New York University
Overall Rankings Position:............43 (56)
Faculty Level Positions:
Arts & Humanities.....................................47
Engineering & IT....................................209=
Life Sciences & BioMedicine.......................81
Natural Sciences...82=
Social Sciences..29
Address:
22 Washington Square North
New York
New York 10011
United States
Web:
www.nyu.edu
Phone:
+1 (212) 998-4500
Faculty:
Student FacultyRatio:............................17.5:1
Students:
Undergraduates...............................39,478
Postgraduates.....................................4,014
International.....................................13.0%
Course Fees $:
Average..24,400
Average Undergraduate....................28,328
Average Postgraduate......................23,304
Overall Research Performance:
Total Papers......................................11,119
Total Citations...............................293,633
Impact...26.4
Research Impact by Subject:
Life Sciences & BioMedicine....................2.7
Natural Sciences...9.6
Social Sciences..2.9

203

in groundbreaking ways to the biological, physical and economic sciences. Its Institute of Fine Arts specialises in not only the history of art and archaeology, but also the conservation and technology of works of art, collaborating with New York's superlative museums. And its Gallatin School of Individualised Study lets students design their own programme of study and create their own curriculum.

NYU's interest in international affairs goes beyond its significant enrolment in students from abroad. The undergraduate division of its business school requires— and pays for—all its students to go on an international business trip. The law school's "global faculty" includes leading legal thinkers from all over the world who come there for at least a term.

People?

Some of the best-known alumni attended the Tisch School of the Arts, one of the nation's leading centres of undergraduate and graduate study in the performing and cinematic arts (and the best film programme east of southern California). They include Spike Lee, Oliver Stone, Alec Baldwin, Amy Heckerling, Ang Lee, Tony Kushner, Marcia Gay Harden, and M. Night Shyamalan.

What do students say?

"It is all very well to read about globalisation but NYU is about living it," said Devyani Prabhat, a doctoral candidate in sociology from India, who was drawn to the law school's Global Public Service Law Project, which trains activist lawyers in human rights and social justice.

NYU, he said, "is always thinking ahead and not resting on its past glories. Like New York City, it is always two steps ahead of the rest. It is not scared to try new things and does not hide behind tradition." He applauds "a tremendous diversity of ideas

and forward thinkers from all over the planet who converge here.

"Greenwich Village is historical, artistic and global, so the university, which does not have a demarcated campus as such, merges with that and is steeped in its values."

Good at?

The social sciences are best-placed in our ranking, at 29th, with the arts and humanities also making the top 50.

University of California, San Diego

Why this university?

The president of the 10-campus University of California system, Robert Dynes, once called the University of California at San Diego "a start-up university".

However the former chancellor of UCSD did not mean that the school is less than 50 years old, but has risen up the ranks of better-known rivals that have been around for centuries. He meant that it has spun off more than 250 start-up companies, almost singlehandedly transforming the onetime US Navy port into a centre of biotechnology and telecommunications.

Some 63 biomedical start-ups alone have been founded by UCSD faculty, almost all of them within a three-mile radius of Torrey Pines Road, which borders the university campus and is where its first handful of spinoffs were spawned. The wireless company Qualcomm was founded by a UCSD professor. One biotech firm alone, Hybritech, was sold to Eli Lily for $345 million just seven years after it was established by two UCSD professors; they and their fellow scientists used the profits to form some 60 other companies.

The university aggressively promotes the commercialisation of technology developed from its research. An independent arm called UCSD Connect has been involved in starting some 900 companies, helping them raise more than $11 billion in venture capital and navigate the wilds of planning and regulation. And those companies have proven twice as likely to remain in business after five years than similar entrepreneurial concerns.

If that was not enough to attract ambitious students, the university's location right on

University Name: University of California, San Diego
Overall Rankings Position: 44 (42)
Faculty Level Positions:
Arts & Humanities 104
Engineering & IT.. 48
Life Sciences & BioMedicine........................ 14
Natural Sciences.. 36
Social Sciences 118
Address:
San Diego
California CA 92093
United States
Web:
www.ucsd.edu
Phone:
(858) 534-2230
Faculty:
Student Faculty Ratio:.......................... 20.2:1
Students:
Undergraduates 20,339
Postgraduates 3,743
International 5.5%
Course Fees $:
Average 15,400
Average Undergraduate.................... 16,476
Average Postgraduate 14,694
Overall Research Performance:
Total Papers 18,481
Total Citations................................... 609,277
Impact 33.0
Research Impact by Subject:
Engineering & IT.. 3.3
Life Sciences & BioMedicine.................... 12.9
Natural Sciences... 8.3
Social Sciences 3.2

the Pacific Ocean in La Jolla, in the prime surfing area just north of San Diego, probably would be.

UCSD is unapologetically looking toward the Pacific Rim. It is teaming up on science programmes with institutions in China, India and Singapore. The university ranks first nationally among major research schools in the number of its undergraduates and graduate students it sends abroad for at least a full academic year, and fourth in the number of international scholars.

UCSD's graduate and professional programmes include the Scripps Institution of Oceanography, ranked the best in the nation by the National Research Council. The research council also ranks UCSD's neurosciences programme America's best, and puts the university at 10th in the nation in overall quality of faculty and graduate programmes

UCSD is also is home to one of the government's two supercomputing centres. In all, nearly $730 million a year in research is conducted at UCSD, including more federally supported research than all but four other US schools; UCSD is the ninth-most-cited institution in the world, based on its published research in science and the social sciences from 1995 to 2005, according to the Institute for Scientific Information. The medical school alternates between first and second in the nation in research funding per faculty member. Eight members of the faculty have won Nobel Prizes, one a Fields Medal and one the Kyoto Prize.

UCSD's biomedical engineering programme, which launched so many spinoff companies, is also considered among the nation's best. And its California Institute for Telecommunications and Information Technology has made San Diego a centre for wireless technology.

Despite all of this entrepreneurship and the university's young age – it is

somewhat old-fashioned when it comes to undergraduates. Each is assigned to one of six undergraduate colleges, as at Princeton, and they study on a quarter system similar to the University of Chicago's, instead of the more typical semester scheme.

People?

Alumni include Mike Judge, writer/producer of Beavis and Butthead, professional poker player Paul Phillips, Susumu Tonegawa, Nobel Prize laureate for medicine and biologist Craig Venter.

What do students say?

"It's in a beautiful location, 10 minutes from the seaside," said Elizabeth Blackburn, a postdoctoral research in physics from Knaresborough, UK "It's a very pleasant place to be most of the time.

Within the University of California system, San Diego has a reputation as one of the harder schools. They seem to take their studies seriously and they work quite hard."

Good at?

Life sciences and biomedicine records the best finish in our rankings, at 14th, but the natural sciences and engineering and IT are also in the top 50.

University of Queensland

Why this university?

The University of Queensland is the oldest and most highly respected of the state's seven universities. It was founded in 1909 and its first lectures held two years later when 83 students, including 23 women, turned up for classes at Government House in the centre of the city.

Today, the main campus is located on a tranquil site on the bend of the Brisbane River seven kilometres from the central business district. But UQ also operates on some 50 locations across the state in hospitals, on tropical islands and it even has its own experimental mine.

With more than 2,100 academics researching and teaching in seven faculties, the university is large by Australian standards and is the biggest in Queensland. It is also the state's only provider for many disciplines, including dentistry, medicine, mining and minerals processing, pharmacy, space engineering, speech pathology and pharmacy.

Because it heads the academic and student status hierarchies in Queensland, UQ attracts the state's top school leavers, although this inevitably means that private school students are over-represented. Foreign students from 121 countries are also keen to study at the university.

People?

Around the world, UQ is probably best known for its many research institutes. Among the nine are institutes that specialise in molecular bioscience, bioengineering and nanotechnology, sustainable minerals, magnetic resonance capabilities and the Queensland Brain Institute.

The university is a member of Australia's Group of Eight research-intensive

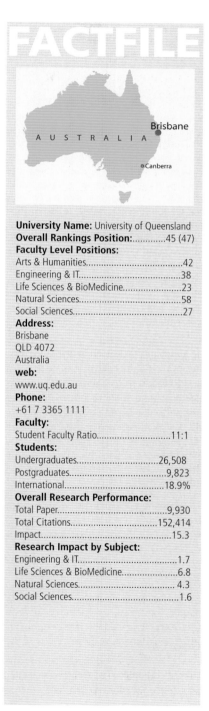

University Name: University of Queensland
Overall Rankings Position:............45 (47)
Faculty Level Positions:
Arts & Humanities.......................................42
Engineering & IT...38
Life Sciences & BioMedicine.......................23
Natural Sciences..58
Social Sciences...27
Address:
Brisbane
QLD 4072
Australia
web:
www.uq.edu.au
Phone:
+61 7 3365 1111
Faculty:
Student Faculty Ratio..............................11:1
Students:
Undergraduates................................26,508
Postgraduates....................................9,823
International.......................................18.9%
Overall Research Performance:
Total Paper..9,930
Total Citations................................152,414
Impact..15.3
Research Impact by Subject:
Engineering & IT.......................................1.7
Life Sciences & BioMedicine......................6.8
Natural Sciences......................................4.3
Social Sciences...1.6

universities and also of Universitas 21. With more than A$170 million (£70 million) in research grants last year, UQ accounts for 70 per cent of Queensland's research, as well as being one of the top three universities in this regard.

What do students say?

Asked how he was coping just before he completed his honours year in computer science at the University of Queensland last July, Chooi Guan Lim said his life was "pretty full on". It certainly was: not only was the Singaporean student concluding his studies, he was also working as a UQ tutor and research assistant while also running his own business, Skyjuice Software, and inventing computer programmes that included an "Ezy Grant Writer" that helps charity and community groups prepare applications for million of dollars in grants.

Mr Lim completed his honours degree after devising a system to enhance digital storytelling to children. The text-based programme is dispersed with pictures that tell changing stories as children read and interact with the plot. He says children use the keyboard to choose a different path in the story: the child controls the story by performing actions such as picking up objects, moving to different places and talking to friends.

Although he considers UQ a good place to study with excellent facilities, Mr Lim does not rate the lecturers highly as good teachers: "The truth is there is no incentive to teach at a university; the lecturers don't get paid more to teach whereas those who do the most research, publish the most papers, get the most money," he says.

Good at?

23 and 27 in the world for Life science and biomedicine and social sciences

University of Auckland

Why this university?

The ogee pinnacles and crockets that cap the University of Auckland's distinctive Clock Tower are now surrounded by functional multi-storey structures – an apt symbol of the university's concerted effort in recent years to assert a reputation based not on tradition, but the quality of its research.

Auckland describes itself as New Zealand's "pre-eminent research-led university". This bold statement is given credence by the university's lion's share of money awarded through the New Zealand's Performance-Based Research Fund.

The first PBRF assessment, carried out in 2003, reported that 'on virtually any measure, the University of Auckland is the country's leading research university'. Of the 41 subject areas assessed, Auckland gained first or second place in 26.

Engineering and medical research were particular areas of excellence, but anthropology, philosophy, music, geology, sociology and theology also scored well.

With six campuses situated throughout the greater Auckland region, Auckland is New Zealand's largest university. It employs nearly 2,000 academic staff and 2,300 support staff. About a third of the academic staff are from oveseas. In 2005, 41,209 students were enrolled in eight faculties: Business and Economics, Arts, and Science are the largest with more than 7,000 students apiece. Education has about 6,000, while there are 3,500 students enrolled in Medical and Health Sciences and a couple of thousand each in Engineering, and Creative Arts and Industries. Law is the smallest of the faculties with 1,500 students, and there is a small School of Theology.

FACTFILE

University Name: University of Auckland
Overall Rankings Position:..............46 (52)
Faculty Level Positions:
Arts & Humanities.......................................29
Engineering & IT.......................................43
Life Sciences & BioMedicine.....................26
Natural Sciences.......................................58
Social Sciences.......................................33
Address
Private Bag 92019
Auckland 1020
New Zealand
Web
www.auckland.ac.nz
Phone
+64 (9) 373-7999
Faculty
Student Faculty Ratio:.........................13.5:1
Students:
Undergraduates:.................................31,193
Postgraates:...8,074
Internatioal:..13.1%
Course Fees $:
Average:...12,600
Average Undergraduate:...................12,380
Average Postgraduate:......................13,830
Libary Spending:.........................19,146,000
Overall Research Performance:
Total Papers :...4,876
Average:..$12,600
Total Citations:...................................71,982
Impact:..14.8
Research Impact by Subject
Social Sciences..1.5

Just over 5,000 of Auckand's students are international, a substantial increase from 2002 when there were only about 1,000. China accounted for 2,700 of these students in 2005; the next largest source was the US with just 487 students. Overseas students account for 16 per cent of the postgraduate population.

People?

Notable Auckland alumni include New Zealand's incumbent Prime Minister Helen Clark and Chief Justice Sian Elias, as well as the novelist Maurice Gee and Tom Schnackenberg, design coordinator for New Zealand's America's Cup wins in 1995 and 2000. Sir Graham Liggins, who pioneered the treatment of babies in the womb, is remembered by the university's Liggins Institute, which carries out research on fetal and child health, and brain development and function. The institute works closely with the local biotechnology industry.

What do students say?

Heikki Hansen, a PhD candidate at the Yacht Research Unit in the Mechanical Engineering Department, says Auckland has taken great strides in its support for international students in the four years he has been there.

"The whole postgraduate experience wasn't perfect initially," he says. "But a lot has changed – the university is much more popular with international students now and the university has greatly improved its facilities and support."

Mr Hansen says locating external funding for research can be an issue compared with European universities, something he puts down to New Zealand's comparatively small size and lack of large businesses. But the quality of research does not suffer.

"I have been really impressed with the quality of research that is produced here, given the relative limitations of money and equipment," he says.

Mr Hansen attributes this to a "do it yourself" ethos of problem solving among the university's academic and technical support staff.

Good at?

Only the natural sciences are placed outside the top 50 in this year's rankings. Biomedicine and the arts and humanities both achieve top 30 finishes.

King's College London

Why this university?

At one time King's was known primarily for its science degrees, but it now also excels in Portuguese, Byzantine Greek, Law and War Studies. History, philosophy, psychiatry, developmental biology and dentistry have also been given the title "internationally outstanding" and a 5* grade in the latest research assessments.

These accolades, coupled with its prime location on London's Strand, are proving an obvious attraction for the high proportion of students from outside Britain who apply to King's. Of the college's 19,289 students, more than one in five are from overseas. Of this number, 8.2 per cent are from the European Union.

The outlook at King's is truly international. The college was among the first to follow the example of American universities by submitting to a credit rating, which took account of its academic and financial standing. It received an "AA minus" — better than that awarded to many big cities. Its achievements include discovering the structure of DNA, in collaboration with Cambridge and producing a string of high-powered alumni.

A £500 million redevelopment of the college's estate is nearly completed as if it is not enough to have three campuses close to the Thames.

So far this has funded the largest university building in London where 2,800 study health and life sciences.

Biomedical sciences, medicine and dentistry have also acquired new buildings.

Scientists dominate, but they are offered a wide range of interdisciplinary combinations. For example, alongside their degree, all students can take lectures on

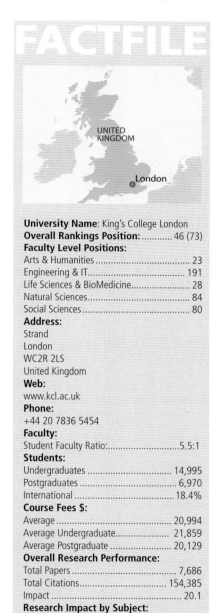

University Name: King's College London
Overall Rankings Position: 46 (73)
Faculty Level Positions:
Arts & Humanities 23
Engineering & IT 191
Life Sciences & BioMedicine 28
Natural Sciences 84
Social Sciences 80
Address:
Strand
London
WC2R 2LS
United Kingdom
Web:
www.kcl.ac.uk
Phone:
+44 20 7836 5454
Faculty:
Student Faculty Ratio: 5.5:1
Students:
Undergraduates 14,995
Postgraduates 6,970
International 18.4%
Course Fees $:
Average 20,994
Average Undergraduate 21,859
Average Postgraduate 20,129
Overall Research Performance:
Total Papers 7,686
Total Citations 154,385
Impact 20.1
Research Impact by Subject:
Life Sciences & BioMedicine 7.8
Social Sciences 2.2

211

ethics, philosophy, theology, biblical studies and Christian doctrine.

Research earnings top £100 million and the college's annual turnover of £365 million.

People?

Famous alumni include the Romantic poet John Keats, Archbishop Desmond Tutu, and John Eliot Gardiner. An array of distinguished staff is headed by Rosalind Franklin and Maurice Wilkins, the discoverers of DNA, Lord Lister, pioneer of antiseptic surgery, and Sir Edward Appleton, whose work on atmospheric layers paved the way for modern telecommunications. Florence Nightingale established the first professional school of nurse training at St Thomas's Hospital, now also part of the large medical school at King's.

What do students say?

Joanne Ooi, a Malaysian student studying medicine, said: "I'd chosen to study medicine at King's based on the strength of its international reputation, so naturally I started at university with very high hopes.

"Two years on, I'm delighted to say the King's experience has far exceeded my expectations. In a typical day I am fortunate enough to sample the best of all the worlds that college life could possibly offer. I attend lectures by world-class academics with students from diverse backgrounds in history-rich surroundings. I enjoy the excellent social and cultural opportunities of the capital by taking just a short walk down the Thames. I may have travelled halfway across the globe to get to King's, but I feel right at home here!"

Good at?

King's is in the top 30 in our rankings for both biomedicine and the arts and humanities. Only in engineering and IT is the college outside the top 100.

University of Rochester

Why this university?

The University of Rochester's innovative Rochester Curriculum has no required subjects, so its 4,500 undergraduates can study what they want.

Students pick a major in one of three divisions – humanities, social sciences or natural sciences and engineering – and take three or more related courses in the other two. The idea is to encourage an enduring enthusiasm for learning by letting students focus on subjects that are interesting to them.

It apparently pays off. Rochester ranks an impressive ninth out of 233 research and doctoral universities in the number of graduates who go on to earn PhDs, putting it in the same league as Harvard, Princeton, Yale and Chicago. It gives many of those students an early start, too, with a programme that allows the most motivated undergraduates to finish both their Bachelors and Masters degrees in any of 10 subjects within a total of five years.

The small, college-like campus (about 7,900 including graduate students) is on a bend in the Genesee River in upstate New York. The city of Rochester is home to Eastman Kodak, Bausch & Lomb and Xerox, ensuring the university is a centre of the study of optics and imaging. Its electronic imaging programmes and Institute of Optics, which dates from 1929, are considered among the nation's best.

Rochester's Eastman School of Music, named for Kodak founder and longtime university financial backer George Eastman, turns out musicians who perform with leading orchestras worldwide. Five Eastman-trained composers have received the Pulitzer Prize in music, while others have won Grammy, Tony and Emmy awards. The

FACTFILE

University Name: University of Rochester
Overall Rankings Position:............48 (73)
Faculty Level Positions:
Arts & Humanities.....................................276
Engineering & IT..173
Life Sciences & BioMedicine.....................258
Natural Sciences.......................................286
Social Sciences...139
Address:
Rochester,
NY 14627
United States
web:
www.rochester.edu
Faculty:
Student Faculty Ratio.............................7.5:1
Students:
Undergraduates.....................................4,535
Postgraduates..3,371
International...14.3%
Course Fees $:
Average 28,250
Average Undergraduate 28,250
Average Postgraduate.........................28,250
Overall Research Performance:
Total Papers...8,430
Total Citations...................................211,580
Impact..25.1
 Research Impact by Subject:
Engineering & IT..6.1
Life Sciences & BioMedicine......................9.4
Natural Sciences..6.8
Social Sciences..3.4

university's Laboratory for Laser Energetics is the home of Omega, the world's most powerful ultraviolet laser. Its Neurology Department is regarded as one of Americas top academic centres for research into neurological conditions, ranking third in the country in government-sponsored neurology research. In all, some $312 million a year in research is conducted at the University of Rochester, which ranks 12th among private universities in research productivity when the size of the schools is taken into account. Rochester faculty and alumni have earned eight Nobel prizes.

Rochester's medical school has a unique curriculum - the biopsychosocial model, which takes into account societal, psychological and interpersonal influences in the diagnosis and treatment of patients. The concurrent double-helix curriculum weaves together strands of basic research and clinical medicine throughout the four years of physician education.

The city has been through hard times, as Xerox moved its headquarters away and Eastman Kodak downsized. But the university, which now surpasses Kodak as the largest local employer, continues to grow.

People?

Prominent alumni include Broadway directors and composers, operatic soprano Renée Fleming, former Xerox CEO and US Deputy Education Secretary David Kearns, Pulitzer Prize-winning poet Galway Kinnell. and former US Treasury Secretary William Simon, for whom the business school is named.

What do students say?

Rochester still feels like a relatively small place, says Chinese-born Christy Lang, and is especially comfortable for its 1,400 international students. Ms Lang, who planned to major in economics but also loved to paint, was attracted by the Rochester Curriculum. "I still wanted to keep my hobby" she said – she has been able to combine her economics major with a minor in studio art.

"Here, I get to spread out all of my interests. They're really flexible. I have the opportunity to choose whatever I want."

When she wanted to study for a semester in Japan, Ms. Lang learned from a counsellor in the study-abroad office about a scholarship that would help her pay for it. The 1,253 faculty members she has met have been personable and supportive, she said.

Good at?

High point is 139 for the social sciences

214

Washington University in St Louis

Why this university?

Washington University may not have the name recognition of the best schools in America. It had to add the words "in St. Louis" to its name in 1976 just to avoid being confused with George Washington University in Washington, DC, the University of Washington, and the nearly 20 other US higher education institutions with "Washington" in their titles.

But while no one was looking, it has slowly crept into their top ranks. Wash U, as students call it, is sixth in the nation in doctoral degrees awarded, after Harvard, Stanford, Cornell, Yale and Northwestern.

It is fifth in federal research support, after Johns Hopkins, Harvard, Stanford and Duke, and its total sponsored research exceeds half a billion dollars annually. Its George Warren Brown School of Social Work is considered to be at the top of its field; so is its School of Law's clinical training programme. And its medical school is considered among the nation's best; many of the university's undergraduates are pre-med — so many that they are given their own separate orientation when they arrive.

While those many pre-med students find themselves crowded into huge lectures for their introductory science classes, the university's comparatively small size means that the faculty are otherwise usually accessible. Almost all are involved in research, and undergraduate and graduate students have the chance to work alongside them.

WUSTL also significant financial aid — about $53 million a year — including to international students. The school's endowment totals nearly $4.4 billion. Its

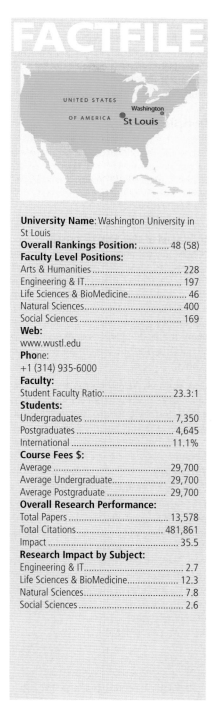

University Name: Washington University in St Louis
Overall Rankings Position: 48 (58)
Faculty Level Positions:
Arts & Humanities 228
Engineering & IT.. 197
Life Sciences & BioMedicine...................... 46
Natural Sciences....................................... 400
Social Sciences 169
Web:
www.wustl.edu
Phone:
+1 (314) 935-6000
Faculty:
Student Faculty Ratio:........................... 23.3:1
Students:
Undergraduates 7,350
Postgraduates 4,645
International 11.1%
Course Fees $:
Average 29,700
Average Undergraduate.................... 29,700
Average Postgraduate 29,700
Overall Research Performance:
Total Papers 13,578
Total Citations................................. 481,861
Impact 35.5
Research Impact by Subject:
Engineering & IT...................................... 2.7
Life Sciences & BioMedicine................... 12.3
Natural Sciences....................................... 7.8
Social Sciences 2.6

quiet, Gothic-style campus borders a large public park and some quiet suburbs of St. Louis - a city better known for barbecue than academics. The next-closest big city, Chicago, is about five hours away by car.

People?

The poet T.S. Eliot was the grandson of Washington's founder and took a diploma at the university. The most recent of 22 Nobel laureates was Aaron Ciechanover, who took the chemistry prize in 2004.

What do students say?

"Wash U has one of the best medical schools. It's known for that," said Patricia Cruz, a sophomore from El Salvador who is majoring in German and psychology with a minor concentration in Russian. "People outside of medicine don't really know much about it. But the students here realise that the quality is at the level of an Ivy League school."

One constant reminder for them is the university's rigorous curriculum; Wash U is known for being tough. "They really push you," Ms Cruz said. But it is also welcoming: "I can find myself hanging out with other Hispanic students or just with people who were in my orientation programme, who come from China, Japan, Malaysia."

Ms Cruz is doing research with a psychology professor whose introductory course she took. "It was a huge class and I didn't think he would remember me, but he did," she said. She has the chance to be listed as a co-author of the resulting study into the social psychology of prejudice, which could come in helpful when it is time to apply for graduate school.

Good at?

Biomedicine is by far the most highly rated area, at 46th in our ranking.

University of British Columbia

Why this university?

Out on Canada's west coast, the University of British Columbia offers a range of undergraduate, graduate and professional programmes in the arts, sciences, medicine, law, commerce and other faculties.

Over 30,000 full-time undergraduate students, 7,000 full-time graduate students and approximately 1,300 part-time students attend its main campus in Vancouver, while its small campus in the province's Okanagan valley counts just under 2,500 full- and part-time students. There are 5,567 international students from 138 countries at UBC.

As for those who teach and research at the university, UBC employs 2,359 faculty members, with quite an internationally educated contingent. Forty-three per cent of them earned their first degrees from institutions outside Canada

Neurosciences has become a leading discipline at the university, with UBC's Brain Research Centre bringing together 175 interdisciplinary investigators to form a powerhouse neuroscience research facility. Its physics and astronomy researchers are among the most cited in Canada.

In terms of research commercialisation, New Scientist in 2005 ranked it ninth in North America for life-science patents – the only Canadian university on the list. One of the products that had been developed in a UBC labortory was Visudyne, the leading treatment for age-related blindness.

The university also boasts a strong creative writing programme, and is particularly proud of the fact that its runs Canada's largest programme in Asian Studies and counts the largest Asian library collection in the country. Its Museum of Anthropology

University Name: University of British Columbia
Overall Rankings Position:............50 (38)
Faculty Level Positions:
Arts & Humanities.....................................32
Engineering & IT...51
Life Sciences & BioMedicine......................32
Natural Sciences..45
Social Sciences...25
Address:
2329 West Mall
Vancouver, B.C.
Canada V6T 1Z4
Canada
Phone:
+1 604 822 2211
Faculty:
Student Faculty Ratio:...........................13.8:1
Students:
Undergraduates.................................35,000
Postgraduates.....................................8,000
 International...9.3%
Overall Research Performance:
Total Papers.......................................14,672
Total Citations..................................302,389
Impact...20.6
Research Impact by Subject:
Engineering & IT:.......................................2.2
Life Sciences & BioMedicine:.....................8.4
Natural Sciences:.......................................6.4
Social Sciences:...1.9

is known internationally for a strong Pacific Northwest Collection.

Its mission it says is to "prepare students to become exceptional global citizens, promote the values of a civil and sustainable society, and conduct outstanding research to serve the people of British Columbia, Canada, and the world". It says its values are of excellence in research and teaching, global citizenship, sustainability and civil society.

People?

The late Michael Smith, a Nobel laureate in chemistry taught for decades at UBC, while physics researcher Carl Wieman, recently hired to spearhead reforms in the teaching of science, is their newest Nobel laureate. World famous opera singer Ben Heppner is a graduate of its School of Music, while former Canadian Prime Ministers Kim Campbell and John Turner also call UBC their alma mater.

What do students say?

Deniz Kuran, of Istanbul, Turkey, chose to pursue her studies at UBC primarily "because I knew it was one of the top universities in Canada and their business programme was one of the hardest to get into."

She also viewed its location as one of the school's strong points. "I had heard Vancouver was one of the best cities to live in the world." It also has some of the mildest weather in the country. Ms Kuran says her Bachelor of Commerce in Human Resources Management and International Business programme enjoys "strong company connections and good professors." While UBC met her expectations both academically and socially, she says the large population can pose problems: "(That kind of size) can be too much for some students and they might feel lost sometimes."

Good at?

Social sciences (25 in world), arts and humanities and life sciences and biomedicine (32 in world for each)

Chinese University of Hong Kong

Why this university?

The Chinese University of Hong Kong (CUHK) is a research university with philosophical foundations built on the traditions of bilingualism and biculturalism.

Established in 1963 through the amalgamation of three colleges, with the addition of a fourth college in 1986, the university is the only one in Hong Kong that follows a collegiate structure and a bilingual policy that places equal emphasis on English and Chinese.

The teaching faculty is organised around seven faculties: Arts, Business Administration, Education, Engineering, Medicine, Science and Social Science. A School of Law was established in 2005 and admitted its first intake in 2006. CUHK has a student population of around 10,000 in undergraduate programmes (80 per cent), publicly funded taught Masters programmes (6 per cent) and research postgraduate programmes including doctorates (8 per cent). There are also several thousand students in professional and continuing education leading to higher degrees. With the largest campus in Hong Kong (134 hectares) the university provides over 6,000 hostel places and its member colleges play important roles in fostering an intellectual community and providing pastoral care and support. Of the eight previous Rhodes Scholars from Hong Kong, six are from the university.

The university has an international mix, with 883 faculty from 24 countries, 87 per cent of them with overseas qualifications. Many of the academics have distinguished themselves with research in the medical and scientific fields, including the first successful cloning of the plant

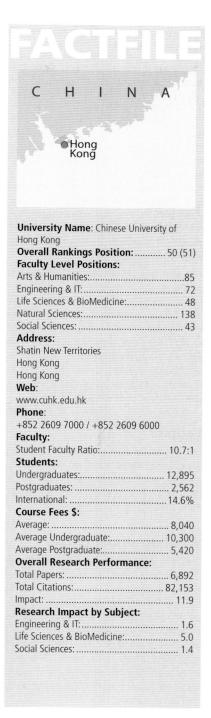

University Name: Chinese University of Hong Kong
Overall Rankings Position: 50 (51)
Faculty Level Positions:
Arts & Humanities: 85
Engineering & IT: 72
Life Sciences & BioMedicine: 48
Natural Sciences: 138
Social Sciences: 43
Address:
Shatin New Territories
Hong Kong
Hong Kong
Web:
www.cuhk.edu.hk
Phone:
+852 2609 7000 / +852 2609 6000
Faculty:
Student Faculty Ratio: 10.7:1
Students:
Undergraduates: 12,895
Postgraduates: 2,562
International: 14.6%
Course Fees $:
Average: 8,040
Average Undergraduate: 10,300
Average Postgraduate: 5,420
Overall Research Performance:
Total Papers: 6,892
Total Citations: 82,153
Impact: 11.9
Research Impact by Subject:
Engineering & IT: 1.6
Life Sciences & BioMedicine: 5.0
Social Sciences: 1.4

gene, the development of the world's smallest Bluetooth communications module and the formulation of network coding theory.

The university's MBA programmes are also highly regarded and have several notable firsts in Hong Kong: the first full-time MBA in 1966, the first part-time MBA in 1977, and the first EMBA in 1993. CUHK was also among those first in Hong Kong accredited by the AACSB in 1999. The faculty is highly regarded internationally in management and organisational research on Greater China and its international recognition is reflected in a student composition where more than 70 per cent are from Asia, Europe and North America.

Two new colleges will be built at the cost of £18 million in the next few years as the university aims to increase its student intake by 3,000 in preparation for Hong Kong's move towards a four-year degree structure in 2012. The university's bilingual education policy offers a unique advantage as it extends itself internationally to attract more overseas students and faculty, and to position itself as a university of choice in Asia.

People?

The university is the only one in Hong Kong to ever have Nobel Laureates among its staff, such as C. N. Yang, 1957 Nobel Laureate in Physics and Sir James Mirrlees, 1996 Nobel Laureate in Economics.

What do students say?

German MBA student Philipp Sayler studied and lived in several countries before arriving at CUHK. In addition to the quality of the programme, he was equally impressed by the dedication of the professors: "Every professor was always accessible, whether via email, instant messaging, phone, or in person. This level of close contact was extremely helpful and made the studies much more enjoyable as well as educational."

Good at?

The university's best positions in our rankings are in social sciences and life sciences and biomedicine, both of which enjoyed top 50 placings.

Sciences Po

Why this university?

The Institut d'Études Politiques de Paris (Sciences Po), aims to educate its students for decision-making and leadership in such fields as politics, law, finance, private and public management and administration and journalism. It was founded as the private École Libre des Sciences Politiques in 1872 by political scientist Emile Boutmy, who believed a multidisciplinary education was essential for excellence. Later it became a state institute and renamed, and today it has the status of a grand établissement, enjoying a large measure of freedom.

Its training remains intellectual, multidisciplinary and directed, it says, "towards action and responsibility in a globalised world where unpredictability is increasing, where repeating old formulas becomes more of a risk than an assurance, and where imagination, invention, innovation and ability to manage change have become essential".

Based in Saint-Germain-des-Prés, the political, cultural and economic area of Paris, Sciences Po also has four regional campuses at Dijon, Menton, Nancy and Poitiers, each specialising in a geographical and cultural area and catering for a high proportion of international students.

Altogether there are 6,910 students – 35 per cent undergraduates, 45 per cent studying for Masters and 20 per cent enrolled in the Doctoral School. They include 2,200 foreigners of over 40 nationalities, more than half from Europe and a quarter from North America. All students must spend a study period at one of IEP's 260 international partner universities.

Seventy tenured professors and lecturers are supplemented by 1,400 academics and professionals from the public and private sectors (among them WTO director-

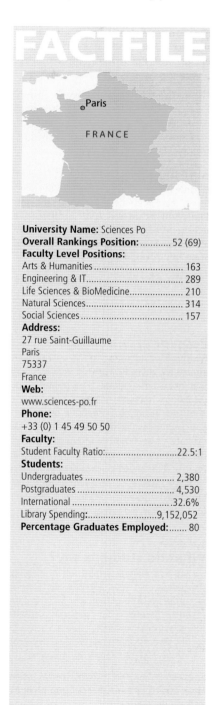

FACTFILE

Paris

FRANCE

University Name: Sciences Po
Overall Rankings Position: 52 (69)
Faculty Level Positions:
Arts & Humanities 163
Engineering & IT.. 289
Life Sciences & BioMedicine..................... 210
Natural Sciences.. 314
Social Sciences 157
Address:
27 rue Saint-Guillaume
Paris
75337
France
Web:
www.sciences-po.fr
Phone:
+33 (0) 1 45 49 50 50
Faculty:
Student Faculty Ratio:.............................22.5:1
Students:
Undergraduates 2,380
Postgraduates 4,530
International 32.6%
Library Spending:...........................9,152,052
Percentage Graduates Employed:....... 80

general Pascal Lamy and former finance minister Dominique Strauss-Kahn). Eighty visiting professors from abroad are invited annually.

There are nine research centres: international; political; European; sociology of organisations; sociology of change; economic situation; global economics; history; and socio-political data.

In 2001, director Richard Descoings introduced a reform to promote social equality - an alternative admission procedure for bright lycéens from poor areas, through interview instead of the traditional competitive exam. The scheme was controversial and contested, but Sciences Po has extended it and increasing numbers of grandes écoles are now following suit.

People?

Alumni include numerous politicians, diplomats, public and private sector leaders and managers. Three French presidents including Jacques Chirac, 13 prime ministers including Dominique de Villepin and Lionel Jospin, and 12 foreign heads of state or government attended Sciences Po, as did former UN secretary-general Boutros-Boutros Ghali, presidential hopeful Ségolène Royal, broadcasting journalist Christine Ockrent, fashion designer Christian Dior and writer Marcel Proust.

What do students say?

US student Juliana Galan, 23, is halfway through a two-year Masters specialising in European Union studies at Science Po's American Center. She was one of four Johns Hopkins University students selected for the two establishments' joint five-year BA/MA accelerated degree programme.

Sciences Po and her chosen specialisation have exceeded her expectations. "I began my first semester with almost no knowledge

of the European Union – yet now I am delving into such aspects as EU competition law." Her teachers were "knowledgeable, competent and very helpful". She found the Sciences Po method based on "exposé" – oral presentation – in which students lecture the class - allowed them to develop communication skills and explore a specific topic in greater depth.

Good at?

Social sciences are the main strength, although this is not fully recognised in the peer review of the area, which places Sciences Po outside the top 150.

Vanderbilt University

Why this university?

At many American universities, the promotional photograph of students lounging in the shade on the grass is an obligatory cliché. At Vanderbilt, it really is part of the attraction.

The campus is a nationally recognised arboretum, with more than 300 varieties of shrubs and trees, including stately magnolias framing buildings that date to 1873. This was when the university was founded with a (by some accounts, grudging) $1 million bequest from the ruthless railroad tycoon Cornelius Vanderbilt.

But the bucolic campus in the laid-back southern music capital of Nashville should not be mistaken for an academic backwater. Some $444 million a year in sponsored research is conducted there. Vanderbilt's PhD programme in pharmacology is one of the best in the nation, and its pharmacology faculty is the most cited in the world. The university is also highly rated in education and religion.

It has spent $762 million building and renovating facilities in the last 20 years, adding state-of-the-art space for psychology, chemistry and its noted music programme, and a new children's hospital. Its $61 million Center for Otolaryngology and Communications Sciences, completed in 2005, houses the nation's top audiology programme. The engineering school just moved into a new $28 million building with 50 teaching and research laboratories arrayed around a three-story atrium. The law school has undergone a $23.5 million renovation and expansion. The Owen Graduate School of Management is also considered one of the best at a US private university.

Vanderbilt's chancellor since 2000 has

University Name: Vanderbilt University
Overall Rankings Position: 53 (114)
Faculty Level Positions:
Arts & Humanities 266
Engineering & IT 463
Life Sciences & BioMedicine 68
Natural Sciences 219
Social Sciences 188
Address:
Nashville
Tennessee
37235
United States
Web:
www.vanderbilt.edu
Phone:
+1 (615) 322-7311
Faculty:
Student Faculty Ratio: 36.2:1
Students:
Undergraduates 6,272
Postgraduates 3,782
International 8.6%
Course Fees $:
Average 29,240
Average Undergraduate 29,240
Average Postgraduate 29,240
Overall Research Performance:
Total Papers 10,127
Total Citations 297,407
Impact 29.4
Research Impact by Subject:
Engineering & IT 3.0
Life Sciences & BioMedicine 10.9
Natural Sciences 6.9
Social Sciences 2.6

223

been Gordon Gee, former president of Brown university and a constant, energetic presence in his trademark bow tie. Most of Vanderbilt's 2,527 faculty are easily accessible to its undergraduate and graduate students – 80 per cent of classes have fewer than 30 students in them.

The university is trying to raise its profile internationally. It has aggressively recruited overseas and an increasing proportion of the students are from other countries.

What do students say?

"The park-like setting is one of the things that drew me to Vanderbilt," Ethel Neo, a senior from Singapore, said. "I'm a person who just loves to sit under a tree and read a book. And Vanderbilt is perfect for that kind of thing. People are always sitting on benches and on the grass relaxing.

"My professors have become mentors to me," Ms Neo said. "They've given me direction for my future."

Ms Neo is also a fan of Nashville, a small city of about 575,000 with a considerably slower pace of life than Singapore, New York or London. "It' s a small city and not crowded or crazy like New York or London. And for a college student, there are lots of cafés with great live music. Inevitably much of that music is of the genre for which the city is renowned – even country music is growing on me."

People?

Three former faculty have been awarded Nobel Prizes in physiology and medicine: Stanley Cohen (1986), Earl Sutherland (1971) and Max Delbruck (1969). Alumnus Stanford Moore was awarded the Nobel Prize for chemistry (1972).

Notable alumni include Al and Tipper Gore (Mr Gore attended but did not graduate from the law school); Muhammad Yunus,

economist and founder of the Grameen Bank Bangladesh; TV journalist David Brinkley; supermodel Molly Sims; and author James Patterson.

Good at?

Life sciences and biosciences at 68 in the rankings.

Brown University

Why this university?

It may be stressful to get into Brown – only slightly better than one in 10 applicants is accepted, making it one of the most selective US universities.

But after that, the pressure is off. Under Brown's so-called New Curriculum there are no distribution requirements and grades are optional, meaning students get to choose from any of 2,000 courses in 40 departments while forgoing the struggle for high grade-point averages that fuels ruthless competition at other Ivy League schools.

A student survey found it the happiest campus in America. More than 18,000 applicants apply for the 1,450 seats in each year's entering class.

Brown's comparatively small size means that it conducts itself less like a large research university than a liberal arts college, with close collaboration between students and the 630 faculty. With the proceeds of an ongoing $1.4 billion fund-raising campaign, Brown intends to add 100 more faculty, beef up undergraduate research, increase student financial aid, build new fitness and dining facilities, renovate residence halls, add a major library annex, and expand classroom and laboratory space for computer sciences, engineering, physics, English, creative writing, anthropology, and population studies.

Founded in 1764 on College Hill, overlooking the city of Providence, Rhode Island, Brown was the first US school to admit students of all religious persuasions. It has had a medical school since only 1975, and has 343 medical students – 58 per cent female and 44 per cent non-white.

Its undergraduate engineering programme is the oldest in the Ivy League; it has the only undergraduate Egyptology department

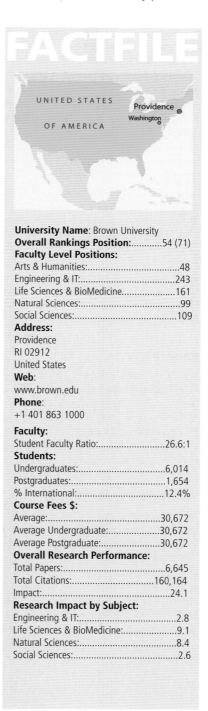

University Name: Brown University
Overall Rankings Position:............54 (71)
Faculty Level Positions:
Arts & Humanities:.....................................48
Engineering & IT:....................................243
Life Sciences & BioMedicine....................161
Natural Sciences:.......................................99
Social Sciences:.......................................109
Address:
Providence
RI 02912
United States
Web:
www.brown.edu
Phone:
+1 401 863 1000

Faculty:
Student Faculty Ratio:..........................26.6:1
Students:
Undergraduates:...................................6,014
Postgraduates:.....................................1,654
% International:...................................12.4%
Course Fees $:
Average:...30,672
Average Undergraduate:....................30,672
Average Postgraduate:.......................30,672
Overall Research Performance:
Total Papers:..6,645
Total Citations:................................160,164
Impact:..24.1
Research Impact by Subject:
Engineering & IT:.......................................2.8
Life Sciences & BioMedicine:......................9.1
Natural Sciences:.......................................8.4
Social Sciences:...2.6

in the Western Hemisphere and an undergraduate programme in the history of mathematics that was, until recently, the only one of its kind in the world.

Brown conducts a relatively modest $135 million in sponsored research but offers a big bang for the buck. One project, a collaboration with MIT, seeks to restore natural function to amputees with biohybrid limbs that allow an amputee to control a prosthesis with his own thoughts.

Brown's free-for-all curriculum, passion for diversity, and various social traditions make Brown a lightning rod for conservatives who decry political correctness. Feminist Camille Paglia has called Brown "that PC swamp."

Brown president Ruth Simmons – the first black and second female president of an Ivy League school – has voiced concern about her university's left-leaning reputation.

People?

Alumni include US Secretary of State and Chief Justice Charles Evans Hughes, First Daughter Amy Carter, Prince Faisal Ben Al Hussein of Jordan, Prince Nikolaos and Princess Theodora of Greece and Denmark, and Lady Gabriella Windsor, daughter of Prince Michael of Kent.

What do students say?

The students are competitive with themselves, not with other people, said Guy Bloembergen, a sophomore from the Netherlands. "I have friends who are very artsy people and aren't particularly good at science, but they can take a science course and not have to worry too much about the grade. They can focus on the class."

He was drawn by the openness of the curriculum. "That was probably the biggest pull for me."

Good at?

The arts and humanities provide Brown's best placing in the rankings, in the top 50, but it is also highly rated in natural sciences.

Copenhagen University

Why this university?

Situated in a number of impressive buildings scattered around "wonderful, wonderful Copenhagen", Denmark's top university has over 100 institutes, departments, laboratories and research centres.

The university has around 33,000 full-time students enrolled, 2,500 part-time students and approx. 57 per cent of students are women. The average age of students enrolling at the university is 24. In general, however, students starting medicine, science and the social sciences, tend to be younger. The number of international students has risen by 63 per cent since 2000 – there were 1,357 international students last year.

The university's engagement in research is evident in its commitment to both international and regional partners. The university is a member of IARU (International Alliance of Research Universities) – a new alliance of ten universities worldwide launched in Singapore in January 2006. The university is also a cornerstone of The Øresund University Partnership, which brings together 14 universities in eastern Denmark and southern Sweden the largest concentration of higher research and educational programmes in Scandinavia. The Øresund region comprising Copenhagen and Malmö is currently the fastest expanding area of Scandinavia and the university partnership provides researchers and students on both sides of the Sound with improved access to expertise in Denmark and Sweden.

The university's degree structure is divided into three levels. Three years of under graduate studies lead to a Bachelor's degree, and an additional two years to a Master's degree. Masters degrees can be extended with three more years of postgraduate work

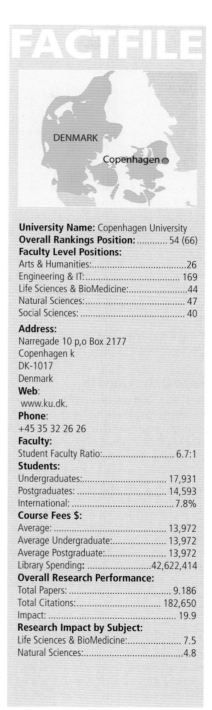

FACTFILE

DENMARK
Copenhagen

University Name: Copenhagen University
Overall Rankings Position: 54 (66)
Faculty Level Positions:
Arts & Humanities:......................................26
Engineering & IT:...................................... 169
Life Sciences & BioMedicine:........................44
Natural Sciences:....................................... 47
Social Sciences: 40
Address:
Narregade 10 p,o Box 2177
Copenhagen k
DK-1017
Denmark
Web:
 www.ku.dk.
Phone:
+45 35 32 26 26
Faculty:
Student Faculty Ratio:............................ 6.7:1
Students:
Undergraduates:................................. 17,931
Postgraduates: 14,593
International: 7.8%
Course Fees $:
Average: 13,972
Average Undergraduate:..................... 13,972
Average Postgraduate:........................ 13,972
Library Spending: 42,622,414
Overall Research Performance:
Total Papers: 9.186
Total Citations:.............................. 182,650
Impact: 19.9
Research Impact by Subject:
Life Sciences & BioMedicine:..................... 7.5
Natural Sciences:.......................................4.8

227

leading to a PhD degree.

Students take on average 4.3 years to complete their Bachelors, and 7.7 to complete their Masters.

Together, the university's six faculties offer approximately 200 study programmes in the humanities, health sciences, social sciences, law, science and theology. The university's ethos is to prepare students for a broad range of jobs in the private and public sectors. All degree programmes promote the learning and application of specific skills as well as academic knowledge.

To appeal to an international audience, the university offers a significant number of courses in English each semester across all faculties and disciplines. However, all degree courses require Danish proficiency.

According to a new university law in Denmark tuition fees will be charged from students from non-EU/EØS countries starting with the academic year 2006/07. At present, the tuition fees have not been set.

Research strength

The university's research profile is focused on what it calls four major interdisciplinary research priority areas until 2007: Religion in the 21st Century, Body and Mind, BioCampus (biotechnology) and Europe in Transition. The spirit of this research is perhaps best illustrated by ground-breaking research into breast cancer. A project run by the university's Institute of Molecular Biology and the Finsen Laboratory at Copenhagen University Hospital has shown that one particular enzyme — uPA (urokinase-type plasminogen activator) — causes breast cancer to spread throughout the body.

What do students say?

Fabrizio Loce-Mandes from Perugia in Italy studied anthropology at the University of Copenhagen as a student on the Socrates/Erasmus exchange programme last year.

"Conditions for international students in Copenhagen are very unique. We are very close, and there are great opportunities for experiencing things and meeting new people, because everything is close by.

"I have become enchanted in that I, like the Danes, enjoy being able to walk safely down the street at night."

Good at?

Fair overall, 26 in arts and humanities, no-show for engineering and IT

Emory University

Why this university?

Emory University, founded by Methodists in a rural town named after Oxford, runs on Coke.

It moved to Atlanta, Georgia, in 1914 thanks to a gift of $1 million and a swathe of land from Coca-Cola founder Asa Candler, whose brother was the university's president. But it remained a little-known regional school until, in 1979, Coke chairman Robert Woodruff and his brother gave it $105 million worth of the Atlanta-based company's stock, then the largest gift ever to any American higher education institution.

Of the $350 million a year in research conducted at the university, $320 million is in the health sciences, focusing on research areas including, among others, cancer, the neurosciences, immunity, cardiovascular and epithelial biology and global health.

Emory has added more than 300,000 square metres of space in the last seven years for teaching, research, and healthcare, including medical science and neuroscience research buildings, a paediatrics building a cancer institute, a vaccine research building, and a mathematics and science centre. A new medical education building is also under construction. The university plans to beef up its faculty of 2,500 by another 100 and significantly increase financial aid to lure top students.

Already, the student body of about 10,000 includes representatives of some 100 countries. Forbidden by Georgia law from admitting blacks until it successfully sued in 1962 to reverse that policy, Emory now claims to be the most ethnically and religiously diverse of America's top research universities.

The university's comparatively small enrolment and the breadth of its

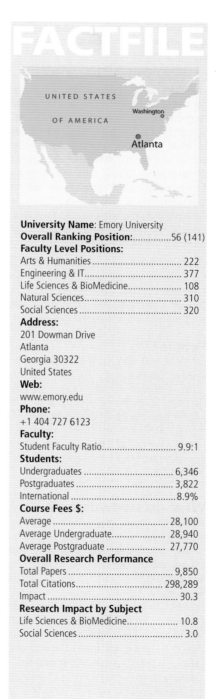

University Name: Emory University
Overall Ranking Position:...............56 (141)
Faculty Level Positions:
Arts & Humanities 222
Engineering & IT....................................... 377
Life Sciences & BioMedicine..................... 108
Natural Sciences....................................... 310
Social Sciences 320
Address:
201 Dowman Drive
Atlanta
Georgia 30322
United States
Web:
www.emory.edu
Phone:
+1 404 727 6123
Faculty:
Student Faculty Ratio.............................. 9.9:1
Students:
Undergraduates 6,346
Postgraduates 3,822
International 8.9%
Course Fees $:
Average 28,100
Average Undergraduate.................... 28,940
Average Postgraduate 27,770
Overall Research Performance
Total Papers 9,850
Total Citations.................................. 298,289
Impact 30.3
Research Impact by Subject
Life Sciences & BioMedicine.................... 10.8
Social Sciences 3.0

programmes combine to give students a lot of choice, but also a low student-faculty ratio of seven to one.

At graduate level, Emory's research-intensive medical school received more than 60 applicants for every seat in one recent entering class. Its highly ranked School of Law is known for its specialities in child advocacy, human rights law, and environmental law, and encourages its graduates to go into lower-paying public service jobs through a tuition loan forgiveness programme. And its Goizueta Business School is also top-rated, particularly for its undergraduate and executive MBA programmes.

Unusually among US universities, Emory has never in its 170-year history had an American football team – a president thought intercollegiate sports were evil (and, more to the point, too expensive).

People?
Emory is next door to the US Center for Disease Control, runs the cutting-edge Yerkes National Primate Center for the National Institutes of Health, and is a partner with the Carter Center, founded by former President Jimmy Carter – a local, and former governor of Georgia — to promote human rights around the world.

What do students say?
Yong Lee, a senior who is from Indonesia, picked Emory over a smaller liberal arts school. Specialising in economics and international studies, he is considering going into public health. "There's a lot of versatility in terms of the vast range of courses you can take. I had no idea what I wanted to study. I knew it was going to be business or the social sciences, but I was still up in the air, and Emory has both the liberal arts and the business programmes."

Good at?
108 in life sciences and biomedicine

Indian Institutes of Technology

Why this university?

At a 50th anniversary reunion of alumni of the Indian Institutes of Technology in Silicon Valley in 2003, Microsoft chairman Bill Gates hailed them as an "incredible institution with worldwide impact".

The IIT community is used to praise, but such a plaudit from the international guru of technology was something special.

"It was a recognition that IITs have finally arrived on the international scene," said one former student of IIT Delhi who was present at the event.

In India, the IITs have always been regarded as the best advertisement for the country's higher education. A government committee described them as "centres of excellence in a sea of mediocrity" saying that they should become a model for other Indian universities. Most IIT faculty said they had succeeded because they had "three basic freedoms—the freedom to choose whom to teach, what to teach and who will teach".

The first IIT was set up in 1950 and there are now seven: Delhi, Kanpur and Roorkee in the north; Mumbai in the west; Chennai in the south; Kharagpur in the east; and Guwahati in the north-east.

They enjoy an unparalleled degree of autonomy, in contrast to other universities in the country — and that is where their strength — and , indeed, the key to their success lies. They have the freedom to develop their own programmes, set their own admission norms and hire the best academic minds. The emphasis is on quality rather than quantity and therefore the student intake is kept low to ensure a healthy student-teacher ratio. Of the thousands of candidates who sit for the nationwide competitive joint entrance

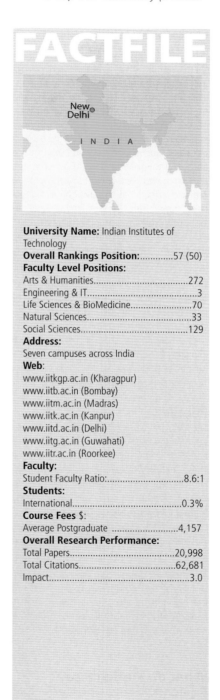

University Name: Indian Institutes of Technology
Overall Rankings Position:.............57 (50)
Faculty Level Positions:
Arts & Humanities.......................................272
Engineering & IT..3
Life Sciences & BioMedicine........................70
Natural Sciences...33
Social Sciences..129
Address:
Seven campuses across India
Web:
www.iitkgp.ac.in (Kharagpur)
www.iitb.ac.in (Bombay)
www.iitm.ac.in (Madras)
www.iitk.ac.in (Kanpur)
www.iitd.ac.in (Delhi)
www.iitg.ac.in (Guwahati)
www.iitr.ac.in (Roorkee)
Faculty:
Student Faculty Ratio:..............................8.6:1
Students:
International..0.3%
Course Fees $:
Average Postgraduate 4,157
Overall Research Performance:
Total Papers..20,998
Total Citations...62,681
Impact...3.0

examination only a few hundred get in.

Inspired by the vision of Jawaharlal Nehru, India's first prime minister after independence who called them "temples of learning", IITs were set up on the lines of the Massachusetts Institute of Technology in the US. Their brief was to produce engineering graduates who "would be on a par with those from first class institutions abroad". Though funded by the government, they were promised complete autonomy—a promise which successive governments have kept. The IITs are encouraged to engage in industry related research, form ties with foreign institutions and develop their own programmes without seeking government approval.

The government is under pressure to set up more IITs in response to the failure of mainstream universities to provide world-class technical education. But experts say that "massification" of IITs would lead to a decline in standards and destroy the very idea behind them.

People?

The IITs are widely cited in international forums and many of their graduates have made a huge mark in the IT industry. These include Nandan Nilekani of Infosys; NR Narayanamurthy, founder of Infosys; Kanwal Rekhi founder of Exclan; 2002 Magsasay award winner Sandeep Pandey; Gururaj Deshpande, founder of Sycamore Networks; and Arun Bose, founder of Bose Systems.

A study by Anna Lee Saxewan of the University of California found that 10 per cent of all start-ups in Silicon Valley between 1995 and 1998 were by Indians, most of whom had come from IITs.

What do students say?

The IITs in Delhi, Mumbai and Chennai stand out from the other four. In the academic year 2005-06, IIT Bombay admitted 41 overseas students. This year students have applied to study there from countries as diverse as Bangladesh, Sweden, the US France, Germany, Singapore, Norway and Switzerland. Pradipta Banerji, dean for alumni and international relations at IIT (Mumbai) says: "The expectations of these students are to study and research in one of the premier institutions in the world."

Good at?

Technology (3 in world) and science (33)

Ruprecht-Karls-Universität Heidelberg

Why this university?

Eight Nobel Prize winners and over 60 other famous academics have helped the University of Heidelberg ensure it remains Germany's best-known university.

A member of the League of European Research Universities (LERU) that includes just 19 others, the Ruprecht Karl University of Heidelberg, as it is known in full, has proved itself a leader in forward thinking as well as research and development since its founding in 1386.

Set up by Ruprecht I, Count Palatine of the Rhine, the university initially acted as an ecclesiastical centre for theologians and law experts from throughout the Holy Roman Empire. However it quickly established itself into a hub for philosophers and independent thinkers and developed into a stronghold of humanism in the 15th century.

Its refusal to submit to a set doctrine whether from the Catholic or later the Evangelical Church, as well as its ability to balance religious and scientific teachings, ensured its reputation as a haven for open-mindedness and innovation.

However the university suffered during the Thirty Years' War of 1618-1648 and its decline of intellectual and financial wealth was not curbed for almost two centuries when Grand Duke Karl-Friedrich of Baden turned it into a state-owned institution in 1803. By the end of the 19th century it was once again celebrated as a centre of liberal thinking thanks to German sociologist Max Weber.

The Third Reich saw the second dark period in Heidelberg University's history when Hitler's anti-Semitic policies saw many

GERMANY
Berlin
Heidelberg

University Name: Ruprecht-Karls-Universität Heidelberg
Overall Rankings Position:..............58 (45)
Faculty Level Positions:
Arts & Humanities.......................................52
Engineering & IT..173
Life Sciences & BioMedicine.......................30
Natural Sciences...28
Social Sciences...70
Address:
Heidelberg
D-69117
Germany
Web:
www.uni-heidelberg.de
Phone:
+49 (0) 62 21/54 0
Faculty:
Student Faculty Ratio...........................12.6:1
Students:
Undergraduates..................................22,995
Postgraduates......................................2,005
International..17.2%
Lbrary Spending:............................7,690,800
Overall Research Performance:
Total Papers.......................................10,859
Total Citations...............................226,155
Impact...20.8
Research Impact by Subject:
Total Papers.......................................10,859
Total Citations...............................226,155
Impact...20.8
Total Papers.......................................10,859
Research Impact by Subject:
Life Sciences & BioMedicine.....................7.5
Natural Sciences...6.7

notable professors expelled from its ranks. Turbulence arose once again in the 1960s and 1970s when links were forged between students and the left-wing terrorist organisation Red Army Faction.

Today its roots are firmly planted in the sciences, but it has still managed to keep its metaphysical traditions with large theology and philosophy faculties all of which help attract students and professors from around the globe.

International Affairs professor Angelos Chaniotis added: "International students are attracted to the university not only because of its organisation, infrastructure, manpower and research facilities, but also because of its tradition as a leader in innovation.

"We also have some of the best scientific institutes in Europe on our doorstep, which makes us very much research orientated – another reason for our success."

Included among the numerous institutes are the European Laboratory for Molecular Biology, the German Cancer Research Centre and a number of Max Planck institutes.

These collaborate with the university's 12 faculties and eight of its own research institutes.

People?

Weber is just one of over 70 illustrious names who studied or taught at the university. They include eight Nobel Prize winners. Among them are Philipp Lenard, who won the Nobel Prize for Physics for his groundbreaking work on cathode rays, Hans Jensen, who also won the Physics prize for helping to develop the shell nuclear model and Georg Wittig, who won the Nobel Prize for Chemistry in 1979. Other notables include the founder of the German Bank, Georg von Siemens, chemist Robert Bunsen, after whom the Bunsen burner was named and former German chancellor Helmut

Kohl. Nazi Minister for Propaganda, Joseph Goebbels, also attained his degree from the university in 1921.

What do students say?

Oksana Jurevic is just one of over 5,000 international students enrolled at the university which has a student body of around 25,000 and some 400 professors.

The 28-year-old economics student from Lithuania has just completed her first year at Heidelberg. She said: "I was attracted to Heidelberg University because of its history and reputation and so far haven't been disappointed. International students must have some degree of German in order to study here, and even though I am not completely fluent, I get a lot of support from the university and its staff.

"We are also given plenty of opportunity for one-to-one tutorials that you just do not get at other universities, and the standard of teaching is excellent. The city itself also provides a safe and positive environment for international students."

Good at?

Heidelberg's best scores in our rankings come in the natural sciences and biomedicine, both of which are in the top 30. The arts and humanities are also highly rated, just missing the top 50.

Hong Kong University of Science and Technology (HKUST)

Why this university?

Established in 1991, Hong Kong University of Science and Technology (HKUST) is a young, dynamic research-intensive university, conceived originally with the goal of propelling Hong Kong towards a knowledge-based economy.

But the university has won a global reputation and presence in a relatively short space of time.

The teaching faculty is organised around four schools: science, engineering, business and management and humanities and social science. It has a student population of about 9,000, with 64 per cent on undergraduate courses, 23 per cent on taught Masters programmes and 13 per cent in post-graduate research. About 13 per cent are non-local students. Every year a few hundred undergraduates participate in exchange programmes with over 100 institutions overseas.

The university's 3,000 postgraduates work in either research-postgraduate programmes leading to MPhil and PhD degrees, or in taught postgraduate programmes. HKUST's EMBA programme, run jointly with the Kellogg School of Management, is consistently ranked among the best in the world. Its reputation is reflected in its international makeup of students: over 40 per cent "fly in" to Hong Kong to take classes.

The university has an international faculty mix, with 450 faculty members from 24 countries. More than half of the faculty

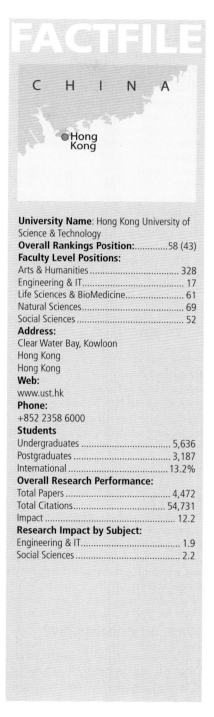

FACTFILE

C H I N A

● Hong Kong

University Name: Hong Kong University of Science & Technology
Overall Rankings Position:............58 (43)
Faculty Level Positions:
Arts & Humanities 328
Engineering & IT.. 17
Life Sciences & BioMedicine....................... 61
Natural Sciences.. 69
Social Sciences 52
Address:
Clear Water Bay, Kowloon
Hong Kong
Hong Kong
Web:
www.ust.hk
Phone:
+852 2358 6000
Students
Undergraduates 5,636
Postgraduates 3,187
International 13.2%
Overall Research Performance:
Total Papers 4,472
Total Citations..................................... 54,731
Impact 12.2
Research Impact by Subject:
Engineering & IT...................................... 1.9
Social Sciences 2.2

members (52 per cent) are from outside Hong Kong and Mainland China, and about one-third are from North America.

HKUST laboratories have made many groundbreaking discoveries, including production of the world's smallest carbon nanotubes, genetic associations in schizophrenia, anti-aging drug development, and fast motion estimation algorithms for the MPEG4 standard. Two departments at the engineering school are ranked among world's top leaders in the number of papers published in international journals.

The university has close links to business and industry, and is active in the commercialisation of research outcomes. It operates both research and commercialisation bases in southern China, capitalising on the region's dynamic growth and emerging opportunities for technology and knowledge transfer.

People?

HKUST is too new to have produced prime ministers or Nobel prize winners. In 2006 the Institute for Advanced Study was inaugurated at HKUST, with a mission to further scientific advancement by inviting the world's foremost scientists to work in partnership with local academics in the fields of nanotechnology and nanoscience, biotechnology and bioscience, information technology, the environment and sustainable development. The 13-member international advisory board consists of nine Nobel Laureates. Its inaugural lecture was delivered by Stephen Hawking in June 2006.

What do students say?

Gesche Haas, from Bonn, was heavily influenced by HKUST's proximity to China when she chose to join a BBA in Global Business programme in 2005 over other offers in Germany and the UK. But even she was surprised by the quality of the university and the study and living environment.

"All professors at HKUST received their PhDs and other qualifications from prestigious universities all over the world," she says. "They also have a lot of working experience and are well connected to many companies."

She added that the university still has a lot to do to make itself better known to an international audience, saying that "HKUST's real potential does not seem to be fully realised by the entire world".

Good at?

17 in engineering and IT, good overall bar arts and humanities

Case Western Reserve University

Why this university?

Created by the merger of two adjacent universities 40 years ago, Case Western Reserve has seemed determined to rise into the ranks of America's top schools.

One way of doing that has been a branding campaign that shortened the university's name to the simpler Case. Another: to spend $181 million improving the campus and undergraduate education, with a gleaming new signature building by the architect Frank Gehry, among other things. Case occupies a large part of the 550-acre University Circle parkland on the eastern edge of Cleveland, Ohio.

The university has also built up its faculty, expanding it by 20 per cent in five years, to 2,523. And while walls have gone up apace on campus, the walls between departments have been falling, allowing robust interdisciplinary cooperation.

All of this has not been without pain. Alumni, stung by the name change, have withheld their support. So has the billionaire philanthropist who paid for the Gehry building (meant, ironically, to house the school of management) which went hugely over budget. Having failed to raise the money needed for his ambitious master plan, the president was forced to resign when the beefed-up faculty voted no confidence in him.

But the changes have taken on their own momentum, spurred on by the perception (as at many large US research universities) that undergraduates at Case were being shortchanged. Nearly one in ten first-year students there fail to return for a second year, noticeably more than at comparable schools, so much of the construction on the campus has or soon will provide those

University Name: Case Western Reserve University
Overall Rankings Position:...........60 (109)
Faculty Level Positions:
Arts & Humanities:....................................398
Engineering & IT:....................................173
Life Sciences & BioMedicine:.....................121
Natural Sciences:....................................365
Social Sciences:...305
Address:
10900 Euclid Ave
Clevland
Ohio 44106-7027
United States
Web:
www.cwru.edu
Phone:
+1 216 368 4390
Faculty:
Student Faculty Ratio:...........................12.1:1
Students:
Undergraduates:....................................3,516
Postgraduates:.......................................4,019
International:...14.6%
Course Fees $:
Average:..25,600
Average Undergraduate:.....................26,500
Average Postgraduate:.........................25,400
Overall Research Performance:
Total Papers:..9,329
Total Citations:....................................255,154
Impact:..27.4
Research Impact by Subject:
Engineering & IT:..2.8
Life Sciences & BioMedicine:..................10.9
Social Sciences:...2.4

undergraduates with new residence halls, a $60 million student centre, and other amenities.

Half the undergraduates at Case specialise in engineering and the sciences, and three-quarters go on to earn advanced degrees. Its new $110 million Wolstein Research Building houses 700 people studying cancer, genetic epidemiology, and other subjects. Another building is planned to accommodate work in fuel-cell technology and structural biology. And there is a proposal for an academic and commercial research park dedicated to biomedical science.

People?

Faculty and alumni have received 14 Nobel Prizes, including the first ever to an American physicist (Albert Michelson in 1907). Case ranks 12th among private universities in government funding for research, receiving a combined $376 million annually from the government and other sources.

A diverse alumni include the first female rear admiral in the US Navy, Craigslist founder Craig Newmark, Ecuadorian President Alfredo Palacio, several congressmen, and physicist Lawrence Krauss, author of the book The Physics of Star Trek.

What do students say?

Case feels dynamic and energetic, said Sumitha Nair, a doctoral candidate from India studying biomedical engineering. "We have new faculty and there has been a lot of construction, with much better space now than we had when I first got here in the summer of 2000. The programme is very good here at Case, and very broad."

One downside is Cleveland's climate. "I guess I have come to like it more now than when I first came here, but I'm from the southernmost state in India, with a tropical climate. I had never seen snow before in my life. I have seen a lot now."

Good at?

Case prides itself on its engineering and science. Its best performance in the peer review of different faculties was in life sciences and biomedicine, where it was just outside the top 100.

Dartmouth College

Why this university?

Dartmouth College's motto, Vox clamantis in deserto, roughly translates as "a voice crying in the wilderness". And it is in the forested wilderness of northern New England that the university's campus – one of America's most beautiful – is located, at the centre of the picture-postcard small New Hampshire town of Hanover.

Dartmouth is the smallest school in the élite Ivy League, with 4,000 undergraduates and 1,300 graduate students, taught by 633 faculty, including the Ivy League's largest percentage of tenured women faculty (about a third of the total). And while they are just as smart – barely 15 per cent of applicants are accepted – its students are far less ruthless than their counterparts at other Ivies where its common to hear that classmates refuse to study together for fear of giving each other an advantage. There are 1,050 international students, faculty and scholars.

Much of the extracurricular discussion at Dartmouth is about politics. Ever since the launch of a conservative student newspaper bankrolled by leading American conservatives, it has been a lightning rod for debate about free speech and political correctness. Founded by a Congregational minister to educate native Americans, Dartmouth today has an enrolment that is 33 per cent non-white, up from 20 per cent in just five years.

The graduate programmes are just as competitive, if not more so. Dartmouth Medical School, the fourth-oldest in America and considered among the best, receives a staggering 5,000 applications annually to fill just 82 places in its entering class. Its Thayer School of Engineering, founded in 1867, was the first professional

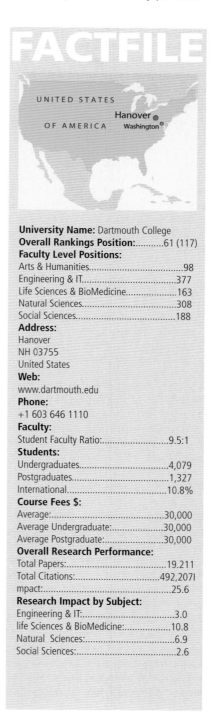

University Name: Dartmouth College
Overall Rankings Position:...........61 (117)
Faculty Level Positions:
Arts & Humanities......................................98
Engineering & IT.....................................377
Life Sciences & BioMedicine....................163
Natural Sciences.....................................308
Social Sciences..188
Address:
Hanover
NH 03755
United States
Web:
www.dartmouth.edu
Phone:
+1 603 646 1110
Faculty:
Student Faculty Ratio:.........................9.5:1
Students:
Undergraduates....................................4,079
Postgraduates......................................1,327
International......................................10.8%
Course Fees $:
Average:...30,000
Average Undergraduate:....................30,000
Average Postgraduate:.......................30,000
Overall Research Performance:
Total Papers:.......................................19.211
Total Citations:................................492,207I
mpact:..25.6
Research Impact by Subject:
Engineering & IT:......................................3.0
life Sciences & BioMedicine:..................10.8
Natural Sciences:......................................6.9
Social Sciences:..2.6

239

school of engineering in America and the Tuck School of Business, routinely ranked among the nation's best, was the first graduate school of management in the world, established in 1900.

To stay in the top ranks, Dartmouth has launched a $1.3 billion fund-raising campaign. Half the money will go into recruiting and keeping top faculty to push class sizes down, and to adding studios, laboratories, and other academic space. Another $187 million is for new dining and athletic facilities and residence halls to relieve a chronic housing crunch. And much of the rest will go into financial aid for students who need it.

People?

Notable alumni include senator and statesman Daniel Webster, poet Robert Frost, and former Surgeon General C. Everett Koop. Chris Miller III, one of the script writers for National Lampoon's Animal House movie starring John Belushi, drew on his time as a member of the Alpha Delta Phi fraternity at Dartmouth. The storm generated by that association has died down, and the university has resigned itself in its mission statement to encouraging political and social activism, which tends strongly towards the liberal.

What do students say?

The academic work is demanding, says Mitalee Patil, a junior from India majoring in business with chemistry. "This is the hardest I've ever worked to get good grades. It is good preparation for dealing with the pressures of a job later on when you have deadlines and you're expected to meet them...

"Anytime I looked lost and confused, someone would come over without my having to say anything and ask me if I needed help. There are always people

tossing a Frisbee on the green. It has a very carefree atmosphere."

Dartmouth boasts close student contact with faculty. Although about a fifth of its courses have more than 30 students, and 10 per cent of them more than 50, Ms Patil said faculty remain approachable.

Good at?

98 in arts and humanities, 163 in medicine

Nanyang Technological University, Singapore

Why this university?

Nanyang Technological University (NTU) was founded in the last phase of colonial times in 1955 as Nanyang University. Like the National University of Singapore it went private on April 1 2006 but continues to receive government funding. Setting its goals very high, NTU aims, according to The Straits Times, to become "the MIT of the East".

The university occupies the Yunnan Garden campus designed by renowned Japanese architect Kenzo Tage close to the world-famous Jurong Bird Park in the west of the island. The 2-kilometre square setting is well served by the republic's reliable and extensive public transport system with both bus and Mass Rapid Transit links. Housing 13 schools and departments, including the incorporated National Institute of Education (NIE) and the Nanyang Business School, NTU can claim to have facilities of the highest physical quality right across the board, among them excellent libraries and laboratories.

Nanyang's leading role in technological innovation is widely known. For example, it was the first higher education institution in southeast Asia to open a virtual reality theatre with its NTU Reality facility, which is a collaboration with SGI in the United States that highlights, amongst other things, research in biological and medical science, a field in which NTU prides itself. The university's Centre for Advanced Media Technology pursues leading-edge work in computer graphics and scientific visualization along with simulation and animation. The Reality Theatre is available

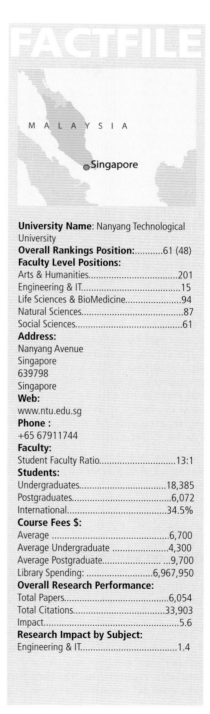

University Name: Nanyang Technological University
Overall Rankings Position:............61 (48)
Faculty Level Positions:
Arts & Humanities.....................................201
Engineering & IT..15
Life Sciences & BioMedicine......................94
Natural Sciences...87
Social Sciences..61
Address:
Nanyang Avenue
Singapore
639798
Singapore
Web:
www.ntu.edu.sg
Phone :
+65 67911744
Faculty:
Student Faculty Ratio..............................13:1
Students:
Undergraduates...................................18,385
Postgraduates.......................................6,072
International...34.5%
Course Fees $:
Average 6,700
Average Undergraduate 4,300
Average Postgraduate...................... ...9,700
Library Spending: 6,967,950
Overall Research Performance:
Total Papers...6,054
Total Citations....................................33,903
Impact..5.6
Research Impact by Subject:
Engineering & IT..1.4

to all NTU departments for teaching and research.

The Centre has been involved in a number of highly innovative projects that include the Augmented Reality Chinese Character Learning system, an example of next-generation technology. The university also plans to open a School of International Relations named after a prominent Singaporean Indian, S. Rajaratnam.

Amongst the 2006 graduates are pioneer batches in the biological sciences, a field in which NTU has invested heavily. Students, who include now a large contingent from other Asian countries, among them Vietnam, are housed in comfortable, unstressed facilities and have ample leisure and recreational facilities on offer.

People?

Among the outstanding graduates of NTU is Adrian Yeo of the 2002 first class honours pass from the School of Civil and Environmental Engineering who, on his own initiative, has been delivering potable water to villagers of the tsunami-stricken Indonesian province of Aceh through Water Initiative for Securing Health (WISH).

Indonesian Ardian Kristanto Poernomo, another alumnus, was the 2006 winner of the Google India Code Jam in Bangalore, India; this annual competition attracts over 14,000 contestants.

What do students say?

Nguyen Minh An, son of Vietnamese president Nguyen Minh Triet, joined the business school's Nanyang Fellows programme, run in collaboration with MIT's Sloan School.

"It was great making friends with people from different cultures. That was a very meaningful experience for me. I attended classes and did research with experienced and devoted professors...and I was able to learn more about effective management skills."

Good at?

NTU is ranked in the top 20 for engineering and IT, and is well placed in the sciences.

Seoul National University

Why this university?

Few universities have their own on-campus cobbler. But the staff and students at Seoul National University have enjoyed the benefits of their own shoe-repairer for 45 of its 60 years of history.

Ha Yong Jin (74) is now the oldest person still working on the campus of Korea's first national university, founded in 1946.

Seoul National now has 19,810 undergraduate and 10,310 graduate students enrolled in 16 colleges with 84 departments, one graduate school with 98 departments and six professional schools, staffed by 4,292 faculty.

Just 4 per cent of students are from overseas. They come from 33 different countries but more than half are from China. Only a small proportion of courses are offered in English. The overwhelming majority of its 56 foreign professors are from the US, while 67 of its own professors are teaching and researching overseas.

The number of foreign universities with which SNU has developed academic exchanges rose from 46 four years ago to 98 in 2005. It has academic exchange agreements with Yale, Princeton, Vienna, Tokyo and Toronto and has plans for a joint doctoral degree with Paris-Sud University.

SNU claims to have contributed significantly to the country's spectacular economic progress, while spearheading democratisation efforts on the peninsula. The proportion of high-ranking government officials with SNU degrees has declined from 81.7 per cent to a still-remarkable 68.8 per cent.

SNU has 28 dormitory buildings with 2,600 rooms accommodating 4,500 students.

University Name: Seoul National University
Overall Rankings Position: 63 (93)
Faculty Level Positions:
Arts & Humanities 131
Engineering & IT 52
Life Sciences & BioMedicine 34
Natural Sciences 40
Social Sciences 56
Address:
San 56-1, Sillim-dong, Gwanak-gu
Seoul
151742
South Korea
Web:
www.snu.ac.kr
Phone:
+82 2 8805114
Faculty:
Student Faculty Ratio: 17.9:1
Students:
Undergraduates 19,810
Postgraduates 10,310
International 4.3%
Library Spending: 7,529,600
Percentage Graduates Employed: 55
Overall Research Performance:
Total Papers 12,971
Total Citations 141,009
Impact 10.9
Research Impact by Subject:
Engineering & IT 1.4
Life Sciences & BioMedicine 4.1
Natural Sciences 4.2

People?

Among its alumni, diplomat and former international relations student Ban Ki-moon has been tipped as a front runner to replace Kofi Annan as UN secretary-general. Its philosophy department produced Kim Young-sam, president of South Korea from 1993 to 1998.

The university was required to weather an international storm last year when one of its top research sicentists, Hwang Woo-suk, was dismissed after claims that his team had produced the first stem cells from human cloned embryos were shown to have been fabricated. Hwang, currently on trial for misappropriating state and private research funds worth an estimated US$3.2 million, is reported to be opening a private research laboratory focusing on cross-species organ transplants.

What do students say?

Wei-yi Sun, from Qingdao, China, is reading for a Masters in Korean language education after majoring in Korean language education with Chinese literature.

"SNU is the one of the most prestigious universities in Korea, especially when it comes to Korean language education. Plus, the campus is really beautiful.

But the process of being accepted and coming to SNU was long and painful. In 1999, SNU didn't receive applications through the internet, so everything had to be done through airmail, which is quite expensive and very time consuming. I even had to take the English and Korean test the school had requested on the phone, due to visa problems. Even though these experiences were really strenuous, I got to appreciate my life in Korea and at SNU even more thanks to them.

"The biggest problem is that SNU has only one Korean class for foreign students. So after attending the language education institute, there are no alternative classes foreigners can take to improve their Korean skills."

Good at?

Ranked in the top 50 for life sciences and biomedicines and natural sciences.Just outside the top 50 for engineering and IT and social sciences.

University of Bristol

Why this university?

With an average of 11 applicants for every undergraduate place, Bristol University is one of the UK's most popular universities. In total the institution has only 15,000 full-time undergraduates, and nearly 8,000 postgraduate students - including 2,000 international students from 100 countries. Bristol has 5,500 staff: of these 1,728 are university-funded academics and 1,183 are externally funded academics.

Bristol is an old, city-based institution. A prominent member of the Russell group of research-intensive universities, the university has a strong research reputation across a wide variety of traditional disciplines. In the last research assessment exercise in 2001, 36 departments received the top 5 or 5* ratings. This means that just over three-quarters of all academic staff work in departments rated world class or internationally excellent for research. Areas of particular strength include mathematics, chemistry, biological sciences, civil engineering, drama, geography, clinical dentistry, veterinary science, law, classics and modern languages.

The university is pushing hard on knowledge transfer: to date 21 companies have spun out from university research, and 20 patents have been filed. Bristol was awarded the highest level of confidence in the last institutional audit by the Quality Assurance Agency for Higher Education.

The university owns 400 hectares of land and 370 buildings. Between 1996 and 2005 it has invested around £160 million in new facilities. It plans to spend another £300 million over the next six years on infrastructure and staff. Major investments are planned in physics, mathematics, biological sciences, library and IT facilities, as well as on new premises for the students'

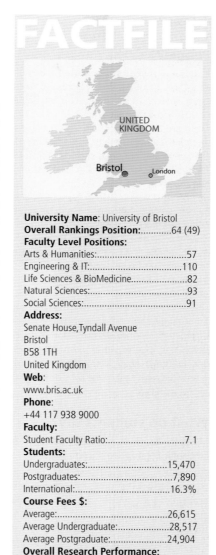

University Name: University of Bristol
Overall Rankings Position:............64 (49)
Faculty Level Positions:
Arts & Humanities:....................................57
Engineering & IT:....................................110
Life Sciences & BioMedicine.....................82
Natural Sciences:....................................93
Social Sciences:......................................91
Address:
Senate House, Tyndall Avenue
Bristol
B58 1TH
United Kingdom
Web:
www.bris.ac.uk
Phone:
+44 117 938 9000
Faculty:
Student Faculty Ratio:...............................7.1
Students:
Undergraduates:.............................15,470
Postgraduates:.................................7,890
International:...................................16.3%
Course Fees $:
Average:...26,615
Average Undergraduate:...................28,517
Average Postgraduate:.....................24,904
Overall Research Performance:
Total Papers:....................................9,471
Total Citations:..............................189,023
Impact:..20.0
Research Impact by Subject:
Engineering & IT:....................................2.6
Life Sciences & BioMedicine:...................8.0
Natural Sciences:....................................6.1
Social Sciences:.....................................2.8

union and student support services.

People?

Four Nobel Laureates have worked at Bristol: Paul Dirac (1933), a Bristol graduate; Cecil Frank Powell (1950); Hans Albrecht Bethe (1967); and Sir Neville Francis Mott (1977). There are 30 fellows of the Royal Society and nine fellows of the British Academy on the active and emeritus staff. Sir Winston Churchill became Chancellor in 1929 and continued in the role for more than a quarter of a century. Other famous Bristol alumni include: Sir Liam Donaldson, chief medical officer of England; Will Hutton, Chief Executive of The Work Foundation. Author of The State We're In and The State to Come; Sue Lawley, television and radio presenter; (Owen) Josh Lewsey, the rugby union international; and Lembit Opik, Liberal Democrat Member of Parliament for Montgomeryshire. Distinguished faculty members now include Professor Michael Berry, one of the world's top physicists, and Professor Peter Fleming, whose work is credited with saving the lives of 100,000 babies worldwide.

What do students say?

Matthew Seow, a 4th Year Electrical & Electronic Engineering student said:

"The university's biggest strength is that it's managed to get that tricky balance between academic achievement, activities outside academia and social life close to perfection. It's quite hard to think of weaknesses but I guess it could do a bit more to integrate international students into the general student body and vice-versa.

Studying at Bristol University was the best thing that's ever happened to me, and the whole experience has definitely exceeded my expectations."

Good at?

Bristol's best finish in this year's rankings was for arts and humanities, where it finished 57th, but the university was in the top 100 for all but engineering and IT.

Ecole Polytechnique Federale de Lausanne

Why this university?

The Ecole Polytechnique Federale de Lausanne is, with Zurich's ETH, one of the twin pinnacles of Switzerland's higher education and research. The two are the only two federal rather than cantonal institutions and have a common national supervisory system.

It has a strongly international vision, since 32 per cent of its students and 46 per cent of its teaching, research, technical and administrative staff is foreign. There are now 6,500 students, including doctoral students, and 250 professors, more than half of whom are non-Swiss. Many are from neighbouring Germany and France, but others come from all over the world. In addition to the professors, there are about 2,000 "scientific collaborators", a category covering various types of researchers and technicians who in many cases also do some teaching.

EPFL can trace back its history for over 500 years, with the foundation in 1537 of the Schola Lausannensis, a religious institution for educating the young and training adults as ministers of the church. But it was only in the 19th century that it developed into a modern university, or rather as the engineering and technology "wing" of the University of Lausanne, under Cantonal control. Emancipation came in 1969, when the Ecole Polytechnique de l'Universite' de Lausanne (EPUL) became an autonomous federal institution as the EPFL.

Today EPFL has an agreement with the Cantonal universities of both Lausanne and Geneva to distribute sectors of research among the three institutions, striving for

FACTFILE

Bern
SWITZERLAND
Lausanne

University Name: Ecole Polytechnique Federale de Lausanne
Overall Rankings Position: 64 (34)
Faculty Level Positions:
Arts & Humanities 277
Engineering & IT 45
Life Sciences & BioMedicine 154
Natural Sciences 115
Social Sciences 372
Address:
EPFL
1015 Lausanne
Switzerland
Web:
www.epfl.ch
Phone:
+41 21 693 11 11
Faculty:
Student Faculty Ratio:............................17.2:1
Students:
Undergraduates 4,868
Postgraduates 1,581
International 40.8%
Course Fees $:
Average 1,038
Average Undergraduate...................... 1,038
Average Postgraduate 20,073
Library Spending:................... 5,925,441
Percentage Graduates Employed:.......87
Overall Research Performance:
Total Papers 5,472
Total Citations.................................... 78,448
Impact 14.3
Research Impact by Subject:
Engineering & IT...................................... 2.3
Natural Sciences.. 5.3

a "critical mass" on any given project, and to encourage networked, interdisciplinary programmes.

EPFL has seven departments: architecture, civil and environmental engineering; computer and communication sciences; basic sciences; engineering sciences and techniques; life sciences; humanities; management and technology.

People?

The accent is on applied, inter-disciplinary science and technology. One of EPFL's flagship projects is ongoing research and development regarding the Alinghi yacht that took the America's Cup for Switzerland in 2002 and is this year's defender. Another is "Solar Impulse", the development and construction of a solar-powered aircraft to fly round the world which will be piloted by Bertrand Picard. Among EPFL's alumni is Daniel Borel, one of the founders of Logitech.

What do students say?

Abhijit Patil is an Indian graduate student in electrical engineering. "EPFL is a truly global university, with students from over 80 countries," he says. "The university has state-of-the-art facilities and eminent professors, and in fields like material science is working on cutting-edge technology. Researchers are encouraged to commercialise their innovations; there is a separate incubation centre at the scientific park on campus.

"Students have excellent living standards and PhD students are paid very well. The negative side is that there is still reluctance in many departments to speak English, which can force foreigners to learn French. Also, in some labs where the Swiss are paid high salaries, the foreigners are paid a little bit less. But leaving aside these negative aspects, I believe EPFL is a very good place

to pursue advanced studies, and EPFL graduates are recognised even in the best American universities."

Good at?

Engineering and IT, 45 in world

Boston University

Why this university?

The newest landmark on the sprawling urban campus of Boston University is its "student village" of high-rise residence halls, a sparkling fitness centre, and an arena for its top-ranked ice hockey team. But rather than a beloved professor or a generous alumnus, it is named for a corporate sponsor that shelled out $20 million for the privilege, making it a symbol of the university's reputation for both hard-headedness and entrepreneurship.

Personified by a long-time president who made plenty of enemies along the way, that hard-headedness indisputably has elevated BU from gritty commuter school to the upper ranks of American universities. (In size alone, it ranks fourth among private universities, with nearly 32,000 students, a disproportionate 59 per cent of them women.) And its entrepreneurship has not only helped to make it rich — its venture-capital arm, almost unheard-of among American universities, built a $4 million investment into a $30 million payoff — it has helped make BU's School of Management one of the top draws for the 4,541 international students who make up almost a sixth of the university's enrolment.

Housed in a gleaming new building complete with its own Starbucks, the business school offers an unusual combined MS-MBA degree rooted in the connection between information technology and business management in an equally unique team-learning approach.

The other programme in which BU is pre-eminent is engineering, within which the most popular speciality is the emerging discipline of biomedical engineering. It is also where much of the nearly half-billion dollars' worth of research at the university is now under way, including groundbreaking, largely government-

University Name: Boston University
Overall Rankings Position:............66 (54)
Faculty Level Positions:
Arts & Humanities:...................................139
Engineering & IT:..95
Life Sciences & BioMedicine....................…50
Natural Sciences:....................................110
Social Sciences:...72
Address:
One Sherborn Street
Boston
MA 02215
United States
Web:
www.bu.edu
Phone:
+617 353 2000
Faculty:
Studen FacultRatio:.............................27.3:1
Students:
Undergraduates:...............................17,740
Postgraduates:.....................................9,811
International:.......................................13.0%
Course Fees $:
Average:...29,988
Average Undergraduate:.....................29,988
Average Postgraduate:........................29,988
Overall Research Performance:
Total Papers:.......................................10,470
Total Citations:..................................285,276
Impact:..27.2
Research Impact by Subject:
Engineering & IT:.......................................2.9
Life Sciences & BioMedicine:....................9.6
Natural Sciences:......................................9.3
Social Sciences:..3.0

supported work in photonics for commercial and military applications.

People?

BU has also enlisted top names in its climb to the top. Its nearly 4,000 faculty include Nobel Prize winners Derek Walcott and Elie Wiesel. Long concerned with social justice — and once called Berkeley East for its students' activism — it's where Martin Luther King Jr. received his doctorate, and, in 1872, became the first American university to open all of its divisions to women. Its School of Education took over the management of a nearby failed public school system in an attempt to turn it around, and its medical school merged with a city hospital that largely serves urban, low-income patients.

What do students say?

As for the students, they are largely drawn from middle- and upper-class families (the largest number come from New York). Some of their social activism these days is directed against the university's tough grading system, an anomaly in an era of so-called "grade inflation." This puts undergraduates at a perceived disadvantage when competing with students from other, less demanding schools.. There are also old-fashioned regulations that require visitors to student dormitories to request permission in advance and register in writing.

Despite its size, students say BU offers personal attention. "It has a 'community' feeling," says Masayo Nishida, a student from Japan who is working toward her doctorate in sociology. "In general, the professors are very approachable."

She has the same thing to say about the university's location. "Boston is especially attractive because it is not a huge city but also not a typical college town in the middle of nowhere so that I can concentrate on my studies and also enjoy cultural life from time to time," Ms Nishida said. "The concentration of academic institutes is also a plus."

Good at?

No real high points, no-show in arts and humanities

Eindhoven University of Technology

Why this university?

Eindhoven is a high-technology city in the south of the Netherlands, long associated with the electronics company Philips and still home to its research laboratories and technology campus. So it is no surprise to find that Eindhoven University is also focused on technology.

Established in 1956 as a technical college, the Technische Universiteit Eindhoven sees its main task as training engineers at Master level, and the 11 regular Bachelor courses on offer are intended to lead students directly into the Masters programmes. There are 16 of these in core engineering disciplines, plus another nine in specialist subjects such as broadband telecommunications technologies and nano-engineering. There are also Masters programmes for science teachers, plus various post-doctoral and professional programmes.

In 2005 Eindhoven had around 240 professors, 7,200 students at Bachelor and Master level, and 600 PhD students. Only 3 per cent of Bachelor students are from outside the Netherlands, rising to 22 per cent of Masters students and 41 per cent of PhD students.

Even more popular with international students are the university's eight post-doctoral programmes for technological designers, which aim to meet industry's demand for engineers able to design and develop new products and processes in complex, multidisciplinary environments. Some 250 students were following these courses in 2005, more than half from abroad.

In research the university prefers to focus on areas in which it considers it can make an impression at the international level.

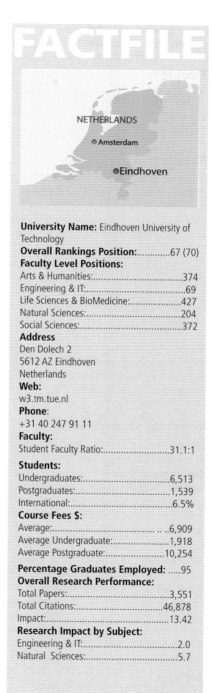

FACTFILE

NETHERLANDS

⊙ Amsterdam

⊙Eindhoven

University Name: Eindhoven University of Technology
Overall Rankings Position:............67 (70)
Faculty Level Positions:
Arts & Humanities:....................................374
Engineering & IT:....................................69
Life Sciences & BioMedicine:....................427
Natural Sciences:....................................204
Social Sciences:....................................372
Address
Den Dolech 2
5612 AZ Eindhoven
Netherlands
Web:
w3.tm.tue.nl
Phone:
+31 40 247 91 11
Faculty:
Student Faculty Ratio:..........................31.1:1
Students:
Undergraduates:..................................6,513
Postgraduates:..................................1,539
International:..................................6.5%
Course Fees $:
Average:.............................. ...6,909
Average Undergraduate:....................1,918
Average Postgraduate:....................10,254
Percentage Graduates Employed: 95
Overall Research Performance:
Total Papers:..................................3,551
Total Citations:..................................46,878
Impact:..................................13.42
Research Impact by Subject:
Engineering & IT:..................................2.0
Natural Sciences:..................................5.7

Current research strengths are biomedical engineering sciences, broadband telecommunications technologies, catalysis and process engineering, mechanics and control, nano-engineering of functional materials and devices, polymer sciences and technology, and the science and engineering of embedded systems

People?

Philips' current chief executive, Gerard Kleisterlee, studied electronic engineering at the university, as did Kees Schouhamer Immink, who went on to play a significant role developing digital recording technology for the company.

Computer programmeming pioneer Edsger Dijkstra was on the university staff, from 1962 to 1984, as was noted mathematician Nicolaas Govert de Bruijn. However, it is in chemistry that the university has picked up plaudits in recent years, with Bert Meijer and Rutger van Santen receiving the highest Dutch award for science, the Spinoza, for work in organic chemistry and inorganic catalysis respectively.

What do students say?

Masters student Alex Gomperts was attracted to Eindhoven from his home near Boston in the USA. "I've been very happy with it, especially with the opportunity to work closely with companies, and with Philips in particular. There have also been quite a few surprises," he says of the experience.

Among these has been the course's emphasis on theory rather than the project-based approach Alex was used to in the US. "There has been lots of mathematics, lots of fundamentals, and building on those fundamentals in a way that we didn't do back home. But the way they use mathematics is very interesting, because it allowed me to learn a broader variety of things in a more standardised fashion."

Good at?

Engineering and IT, not surprisingly, are by far the highest-ranked areas, making the top 70 in our ranking.

Indian Institutes of Management

Why this university?

The Indian Institutes of Management (IIMs) are one of the biggest success stories of Indian higher education.

The six IIMs — located in Ahmedabad, Bangalore, Khozikhode, Calcutta, Indore and Lucknow — are to management studies what the Indian Institutes of Technology are to engineering. Like the IITs, they have achieved international status and are regarded as being among the best B-schools in the world. .

A brainchild of Independent India's visionary first Prime Minister, Pandit Jawahar Lal Nehru, the IIMs were set up between 1961 and 1998 — most of them after his death.

The first opened in 1961 in Calcutta, followed by Ahmedabad, which has led the way in excellence.

According to a 2005 survey by the Economist Intelligence Unit, IIM-A (as IIM Ahmedabad is known) is one of the toughest business schools in the world to get into.

The six IIMs, though wholly state-funded, are completely autonomous and because they have been so successful they are able to withstand government pressures. It is widely recognised that the key to their excellence lies in the degree of academic and administrative freedom they enjoy from central and state governments. They have the freedom to devise their own curricula, make faculty appointments, decide on expansion plans and enter into bilateral tie-ups with other international business schools.

Candidates sit a written nationwide Common Admission Test (CAT) and those who pass are then put through a stringent group discussion programme and personal

University Name: Indian Institutes of Management
Overall Rankings Position: 68 (84)
Faculty Level Positions:
Arts & Humanities 293
Engineering & IT.. 68
Life Sciences & BioMedicine.................... 204
Natural Sciences..................................... 260
Social Sciences 26
Address:
Six campuses across India
Web:
www.iiml.ac.in (Lucknow)
www.iimahd.ernet.in (Ahmedebad)
www.iimb.ernet.in (Bangalore)
www.iimcal.ac.in (Calcutta)
www.iimidr.ac.in (Indore)
www.iimk.ac.in (Kozikode)
Phone:
+91 522 2734101
Faculty:
Student Faculty Ratio:............................10.7:2
Overall Research Performance:
Total Papers..344
Total Citations..667
Impact...1.9

interviews. In 2005, 150,000 students applied for fewer than 1,200 places at the six IIMs. For every place available, 532 candidates applied. The overall acceptance rate ranges from 0.15-0.4 per cent, making them tougher to get into than some of the best-known business schools in the US.

The IIMs offer a two-year postgraduate programme in management. There are also shorter management training programmes. They have links with the best B-schools internationally including Harvard, Wharton, and Kellogg.

Apart from student and faculty exchange programmes, IIMs constantly update their teaching techniques, making their MBA programmes more relevant to the job market. Candidates are flooded with the best job offers internationally even before they leave campus

People?

The list of IIM alumni reads like a "Who's Who" of the corporate world and includes Indira Nooyi, president of Pepsico US, Jerry Rao, chairman and CEO of Mphasis, C.K. Prahlad, Professor of Business Administration and Professor of Corporate Strategy and International Business at the University of Michigan Business School, and Ajay Banga, Chairman and Chief Executive Officer of Citigroup's Global Consumer Group international businesses.

Most students feel that the gruelling pace at IIM prepares them to face any eventuality and have said that the pace of work makes everything else seem "simple".

The government's plan to introduce compulsory quotas for students from disadvantaged castes is seen by the IIMs as a threat to their autonomy. They fear that caste-based admissions, without regard to strict merit, would affect standards and damage the IIMs' reputation as world-class institutions.

A recent proposal from the IIM Bangalore to set up a campus in Singapore has been put on the back burner by the government. If it eventually does so, it would become the third business school from the Wall Street Journal's top 100 to set up an offshore campus.

Fees for overseas students are R512,000 (£5,800), inclusive of tuition, course materials, and board and lodging. Scholarships are awarded to foreign students as well as Indian nationals.

What do students say?

Dhaval Saikar, who took the postgraduate programme in management at IIM — Indore in 2004-05, said: "I believe this education will help me grow in the corporate world and realise my dreams."

Good at?

26 in the world at social sciences, the area that encompasses management, and 68 at technology

Amsterdam University

Why this university?

The Universiteit van Amsterdam prides itself on its ancient roots, which stretch back to the Athenaeum Illustré founded in 1632 to educate students in trade and philosophy.

This became a university in 1877, and has since spread through the city, taking over old buildings and putting up its own modern structures along the canals and courtyards that make Amsterdam famous.

The university emphasises its comprehensive approach, taking in every discipline except technology, and offering a classical education that, it boasts, does not just cram students for the job market. It has seven faculties, from the humanities and social and behavioural sciences, to economics and business, medicine and dentistry, and science.

In 2005 the university had 24,844 students enrolled, 1,518 of whom were from outside the Netherlands. It offers 62 Bachelor programmes taught in Dutch and over 100 international study programmes taught in English. It has a total of 2,587 academic staff (including PhD students), of whom 262 are associate professors and 522 full professors. Twenty two associates and 57 professors are from outside the Netherlands.

People

The golden age of science at the university was between 1901 and 1910, when three of its professors won Nobel prizes: Jacobus van 't Hoff in chemistry, and Pieter Zeeman and Johannes van der Waals in physics. Now the university's strengths are very much on the mathematical side and where maths touches on physics and astronomy. In recent years it has picked up several

FACTFILE

NETHERLANDS
• Amsterdam
• Rotterdam

University Name: Amsterdam University
Overall Rankings Position:..............69 (58)
Faculty Level Positions:
Arts & Humanities:......................................24
Engineering & IT:.....................................128
Life Sciences & BioMedicine:...................... 70
Natural Sciences: 102
Social Sciences: 30

Address:
Spul 21
1012 WX Amsterdam
Netherlands
Web:
www.uva.nl
Phone:
+31 20 525 9111

Faculty:
Student Faculty Ratio:..........................16.1:1
Students:
Undergraduates:................................ 14,821
Postgraduates: 10,023
International: 6.1%
Overall Research Performance:
Total Papers: 10,961
Total Citations:................................ 236,808
Impact: 21.6
Research Impact by Subject:
Engineering & IT:..................................... 2.2
Life Sciences & BioMedicine:...................... 8.5
Natural Sciences:..................................... 7.1
Social Sciences: 1.7

Spinoza awards — the Dutch Nobels -- for work in these disciplines. Particularly distinguished is Edward van den Heuvel, of the university's Anton Pannekoek Astrophysical Institute, who also led an international team researching the origins of gamma-ray bursts, which won an EU Déscartes award in 2002.

The university can also claim Spinoza awards for Daan Frenkel, in macromolecular simulations, and Ronald Plasterk in molecular biology. Meanwhile Willem Saris, of the social and behavioural science faculty, was part of the team that won a Dscartes award in 2005 for cross-national social surveys.

In the arts and humanities, Amsterdam is particularly strong in European studies, philosophy, film and television studies, linguistics and several areas of language and literature. Among the noted faculty are John Neubauer, specialist in comparative literature, Latin scholar Harm Pinkster, and Mieke Bal, professor of theory of literature and a founding director of the Amsterdam School for Cultural Analysis.

Unlike the rest of the university, the laboratories and research institutes of the medical faculty have been extracted from the city and united with three hospitals under the single roof of the Academic Medical Centre. In 2005 a graduate school for the medical sciences was created to raise the profile of this part of the medical centre's work. It has over 100 PhD graduations per year, divided over seven research institutes and 80 individual science programmes, ranging from genetic factors in cancer biology to public health screening projects.

The AMC has the largest permanently exhibited collection of post-war Dutch visual art in the world. Intensive collecting, with government support, began in the early 1980s, and the collection now includes some 5,000 paintings, works on paper, graphic art and photography, with a generous selection of work from the CoBrA, Mixed-Media Art, Zero Art and New Figuration movements.

Good at?

Arts and humanities, life sciences and biomedicine, social sciences

School of Oriental and African Studies

Why this university?

Established in 1916, the School of Oriental and African Studies (SOAS) is the UK's national centre for the study of Asia, Africa and the Middle East.

As well as departments dedicated to international studies, development and non-European languages, SOAS also offers courses in familiar subjects such as economics, history and law, though with a slightly different emphasis. Part of the University of London, SOAS is made up of around 4,455 students and 200 members of academic staff.

The original SOAS campus is located in Bloomsbury, close to the British Museum and British Library, and in 2001 the school opened a second campus at Vernon Square, Islington.

Although more than 80 per cent of undergraduates are British, the real diversity of the school's student body can be seen among the postgraduate population: the current group of postgraduates come from over 100 countries. Around a third of all SOAS students come from outside the EU.

In recent years, an increased demand for postgraduate study has been driven by an impressive research record, with ten of the school's 15 departments placed in the top two categories in the most recent assessments. History was rated as internationally outstanding.

One distinguishing feature of SOAS is the sheer breadth of language learning opportunities available to its students: 40 non-European languages are currently taught and the school has been chosen as the home of a national teaching centre for

University Name: School of Oriental and African Studies
Overall Rankings Position: 70 (103)
Faculty Level Positions:
Arts & Humanities 13
Technology...390
Sciences 40
Social Sciences...95
Address:
Thornhaugh Street Russell Square
London
WC1H 0XG
United Kingdom
Web:
www.soas.co.uk
Phone:
+44 (0)20 7637 2388
Faculty:
Student Faculty Ratio:............................11.4:1
Students:
Undergraduates 2,250
Postgraduates 2,205
International 45.6%
Course Fees $:
Average 19,011
Average Undergraduate...................... 19,011
Average Postgraduate 19,011
Library Spending:......................... 5,205,003
Percentage Graduates Employed:....... 96
Overall Research Performance:
Total Papers...106
Total Citations... 207
Impact 2.5

languages.

The diverse student population (including people destined for influential roles in developing countries) means that political debate within the school is always lively. Although this inevitably leads to tensions at times, the atmosphere is typically a friendly one, and many students welcome the opportunity to learn and debate about world issues outside the lecture theatre.

People?

Alumni include Luisa Diogo, the current Prime Minister of Mozambique; Sir Michael Jay, Permanent Secretary at the Foreign and Commonwealth Office; David Lammy, Labour MP for Tottenham and Minister for Culture; British politician Enoch Powell; singer Paul Robeson; comedian Dom Joly; and Jemima Khan.

What do students say?

Gopika Bashi is a third-year social anthropology and development studies student, who travelled from India to study at SOAS. She feels that one of the school's main strengths is the broad portfolio of courses it offers: "The courses are so diverse and regionally specific and that really sets it apart from any other university in the UK. Its really small, so the atmosphere is really personal and comfortable, which is great." She admits that she initially found it difficult to settle in: "It is a bit hard as an international student at first, because its difficult coming to grips with London as a whole, and SOAS is kind of like a microcosm of the world so you really get thrown in!" Despite this, Gopika says she would recommend the SOAS student experience to others, adding: "Its really inspiring to be in a place where everyone, in a sense, wants to change the world!"

Good at?

The arts and humanities, not surprisingly, produced SOAS's best score, finishing in the top 20 in the world.

Osaka University

Why this university?

The sixth-oldest national university in Japan, Osaka University was established in 1931 in the heart of one the commercial centres of Japan, 500 kilometres south west of Tokyo. Its roots lie in a local medical college founded in 1869.

At the outset the university consisted only of medical and science faculties. Today, medicine and science studies are considered the backbone of the university, which operates its own hospital. However, all undergraduates take liberal arts programmes for the first three semesters.

Osaka University currently has 12,500 undergraduates, only 1.6 per cent foreign nationals, of which 82 per cent are Asian. Of the overwhelming Japanese students, around 80 per cent are from the south west Japan. About half of all foreign students receive grants through the university, including some from the Japanese government.

Among the teaching staff, only 2.2 per cent are from overseas and just 8.3 per cent women. The university has the motto "Live locally, grow globally", underlining the international ambitions which have been at the heart of its activities since the "semi-privatisation" of Japanese universities two years ago. Plans are afoot to send more Japanese students abroad with the aim of giving a third of the university's undergraduates overseas exposure. Osaka already has exchange programmes with numerous European and American institutions, including Nottingham University and University College London.

In October 2007 the university is scheduled to take over the Osaka University of Foreign Studies, which specialises in studies of more than 20 modern languages, including Urdu and Swahili, making it the largest national

FACTFILE

University Name: Osaka University
Overall Rankings Position...........70 (105)
Faculty Level Positions
Arts & Humanities..................................126
Engineering & IT.....................................55
Life Sciences & BioMedicine....................38
Natural Sciences.....................................49
Social Sciences.....................................140
Address:
1-4 Machikaneyama, Toyonaka
Osaka
560-0043
Japan
Web:
www.osaka-u.ac.jp
Phone:
+81 6 6879 7103
Faculty:
Student Faculty Ratio..........................14.8:1
Students:
Undergraduates.................................12,527
Postgraduates....................................8,273
International...5.5%
Course Fees $:
Average..4,670
Average Undergraduate 4,670
Average Postgraduate........................4.670
Librar Spending:...........................8,623,000
Percentage Graduates Employed:......96
Overall Research Performance:
Total Papers.....................................20,443
Total Citations.................................375,789
Impact...18.4
Research Impact by Subject:
Engineering & IT....................................1.5
Life Sciences & BioMedicine....................9.4
Natural Sciences....................................4.6

university in Japan, with a total of more than 25,000 students.

People?

Among the university's most cited scientists is Shizuo Akira, 54, winner of the 2004 Robert Koch Prize for his discovery of the "toll-like receptor" that activates immune system cells upon recognition of pathogenic organisms. He was also recently named "the hottest researcher" by Thomson Scientific for outnumbering his peers in citation. Professor Akira currently leads a government-funded project that seeks to combine microbiology with immunology at the university's Research Institute of Microbial Disease. "We have great facilities for medical research that is backed by our long tradition. We also get a lot of bright students in our department," says Profesor Akira, who also cites robotic engineering as an area of strength for the university.

Alumni include Manga author Osamu Tezuka, Sony founder Akio Morita, and Nobel physics laureate Hideki Yukawa.

What do students say?

"The university provides an excellent atmosphere for research," says Ngan Chew Yee, a Malaysian student currently researching into anticancer drug mechanisms. "The graduate school of medicine provides an almost unlimited source of information and excellent student guidance by the 'sensei' (professors),"

Good at?

Academics rank both biomedicine and the natural sciences in the top 50 in the world, with engineering and IT close behind at 55th.

Ecole Normale Supérieure Lyon

Why this university?

The Ecole Normale Supérieure de Lyon opened in the mid-1980s after reorganisation of the ENS group of grandes écoles, which were established to train university and lycée teachers for the competitive agrégation examination. Also known as ENS-Lyon, Normale Sup' Lyon and ENSL, the school is devoted to science.

Its 10 laboratories specialise in physics; chemistry; molecular and cell biology; plant reproduction and development; human virology; astronomy; pure and applied mathematics; earth sciences; computer science applied to parallelism, and one which is interdisciplinary. These work closely with researchers from the CNRS (the national scientific research centre), Inserm (medical and health research institute) and INRA, the agricultural research institute.

As well as training for the agrégation, the school offers courses from undergraduate to PhD level. Student numbers total 868, of whom 101 are from abroad – 60 per cent European, 15 per cent from Africa and the Maghreb, 15 per cent Asian (mostly

Chinese) and 10 per cent from the Americas. A quarter of PhD students are international, compared with 12 per cent of the total student roll.

Over three-quarters of its graduates enter careers in teaching or public research.

The school employs about 270 permanent and part-time academic and research staff, of whom 17 per cent of tenured lecturers and researchers and 24 per cent of tenured professors are from abroad, most of them from European Union countries.

Under the EU Socrates/Erasmus programme ENS-Lyon has exchange partnerships with about 20 other universities, as well as other

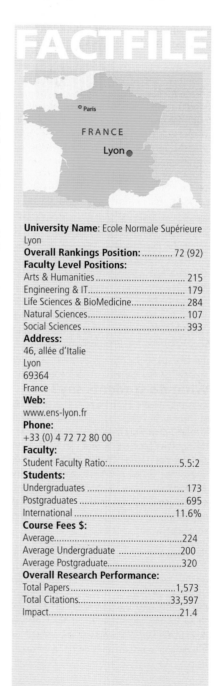

University Name: Ecole Normale Supérieure Lyon
Overall Rankings Position: 72 (92)
Faculty Level Positions:
Arts & Humanities 215
Engineering & IT.. 179
Life Sciences & BioMedicine.................... 284
Natural Sciences....................................... 107
Social Sciences 393
Address:
46, allée d'Italie
Lyon
69364
France
Web:
www.ens-lyon.fr
Phone:
+33 (0) 4 72 72 80 00
Faculty:
Student Faculty Ratio:...........................5.5:2
Students:
Undergraduates 173
Postgraduates 695
International 11.6%
Course Fees $:
Average...224
Average Undergraduate 200
Average Postgraduate............................320
Overall Research Performance:
Total Papers...1,573
Total Citations...................................33,597
Impact..21.4

links which include East Europe, China, Brazil and Canada.

ENS-Lyon research has led to spin-off companies specialising in such products as an electrically operated optic lens; animal models for therapeutic purposes; scientific and technical instrumentation in the field of micro-structuration of surfaces; and libraries of new analogue chemicals of natural products.

People?

Faculty includes a number of members and award-winners of France's prestigious Académie des Sciences. Francis Albarède, professor in the Earth Sciences laboratory, has been awarded the European Union of Geosciences' Arthur Holmes medal; and Patrick Flandrin, CNRS research director of the Physics laboratory, is holder of the Wavelet Pioneer Award of the International Society for Optical Engineering (SPIE).

What do students say?

Johannes-Geert Hagmann, 24, is starting a three-year ENS-Lyon PhD specialising in non-linear and statistical physics, after taking two Masters degrees at ENS-Lyon and at the University of Karlsruhe. He first chose ENS-Lyon "in particular for its outstanding course in theoretical physics, and more generally for its excellent reputation in fundamental research and education".

He rates the school's "excellent academic staff and important scientific output relative to its size". "Classes are small, and the level of courses usually demanding." But a difficulty for international students "may be the fact that most courses are held in French. A working knowledge of the language on arrival is certainly of great help."

Good at?

The natural sciences are highest-placed in the World University Rankings, just outside the top 100.

University of Warwick

Why this university?

Warwick has carved out a place among the élite of British higher education institutions, with excellent ratings in both teaching and research and a reputation as being in the top drawer of Britain's universities after Oxford and Cambridge.

With "entrepreneurial, research-based, innovative" promoted as its watchwords, its unglamorous location near Coventry does not prevent it attracting a substantial layer of top undergraduate and graduate students.

The university is divided into four faculties that give it genuine breadth of academic influence. The Faculty of Arts teaches everything from classics to film and television studies, while the science faculty teaches the key disciplines in their core forms, avoiding the trend for academic dilution. The university also has faculties of social studies and medicine, the latter only founded in 2000 after many years when Warwick concentrated on its well-established links with industry and commerce.

Warwick is one of Britain's top research universities. Six subjects were rated internationally outstanding for research – business, economics, applied mathematics and statistics, English and theatre studies – and ninety per cent of academics entered for the research assessment exercise were rated in the two highest categories. Warwick is a member of the 1994 Group of research-intensive institutions, as well as the Russell Group of elite universities. Warwick's teaching standards are also excellent, with seven maximum scores in assessments.

The university attracts students from 102 different countries. The proportion of state

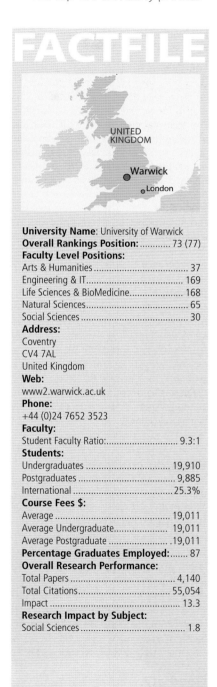

University Name: University of Warwick
Overall Rankings Position: 73 (77)
Faculty Level Positions:
Arts & Humanities 37
Engineering & IT 169
Life Sciences & BioMedicine 168
Natural Sciences 65
Social Sciences 30
Address:
Coventry
CV4 7AL
United Kingdom
Web:
www2.warwick.ac.uk
Phone:
+44 (0)24 7652 3523
Faculty:
Student Faculty Ratio: 9.3:1
Students:
Undergraduates 19,910
Postgraduates 9,885
International 25.3%
Course Fees $:
Average 19,011
Average Undergraduate 19,011
Average Postgraduate 19,011
Percentage Graduates Employed: 87
Overall Research Performance:
Total Papers 4,140
Total Citations 55,054
Impact 13.3
Research Impact by Subject:
Social Sciences 1.8

263

school students is smaller than at many other leading universities, standing at less than a quarter, but the representation of working class students is also below the national average for Warwick's subjects and academic standards.

The student union is well organised and active, leading a boycott of a nationwide student satisfaction survey, meaning that no results were calculated for the university. Union facilities have been refurbished, one of many improvements to the estate enabled by £335 million of investment. The Arts Centre, the second largest in the country, was refurbished with a £33 million lottery grant.

People?

Leading academics at Warwick include Lord Bhattacharyya, Director of Warwick Manufacturing Group, economics professor Andrew Oswald and Lord Skidelsky, who recently retired as Professor of Political Economy. Famous alumni include leading politicians Baroness Amos and David Davis, and Tony Wheeler, co-founder of the Lonely Planet travel guides.

What do students say?

Damian King, a physics PhD student at Warwick, said: "Academically Warwick is a very strong university and in physics I have always found that staff contact time is readily available, particularly from my PhD supervisor, although other departments can differ greatly. Being a campus university Warwick won't suit all people, as many will find it isolated. However, with a strong campus life, living in Coventry in your second year and easy links to Birmingham, it's far from boring."

Good at?

The social sciences and the arts and humanities are in the top 40 in our rankings, and the natural sciences are also well-placed.

Universidad Nacional Autonoma de Mexico

Why this university?

The Universidad Nacional Autonoma de Mexico (UNAM) is the nation's most prestigious academic institution, the foremost in Latin America and probably the largest in the world. It originated as the Royal and Pontifical University of Mexico established in 1551. It was re-founded in 1910 as UNAM has pioneered research in fields such as genomics, ecology, philosophy of science and Mexican regional studies.

Today UNAM has some 177,000 students, and 33,000 teachers in 22 faculties. Its 20,500 postgraduate students represent 20 per cent of the nation's total. One of every two doctorates awarded in Mexico is from UNAM.

The university is made up of 30 institutes and research centres and employs 3,780 full-time researchers and technicians. It generates 50 per cent of all research in Mexico and has more than 30 per cent of Mexico's researchers with a publication rate of 12,500 science articles a year. The university publishes an average of three books a day.

Additionally UNAM is heavily engaged in cultural activities. Annually it presents some 8,000 music, theatre, dance and cinema productions. The university runs 13 museums and 18 historical sites with 152 murals, 50 stained-glass windows, 800 sculptures and 86,000 paintings and drawings.

Its Universum science museum receives five million visitors annually and more than 300,000 people per year visit the university's Cultural Centre. UNAM's 143

University Name: Universidad Nacional Autonoma de Mexico
Overall Rankings Position: 74 (95)
Faculty Level Positions:
Arts & Humanities 110
Engineering & IT....................................... 139
Life Sciences & BioMedicine..................... 109
Natural Sciences...................................... 137
Social Sciences 176
Address:
Ciudad Universitaria, s/n
Ciudad de Mexico
Distrito Federal 04510
Mexico
Web:
www.unam.mx
Phone:
52(55) 5622-3686
Faculty:
Student Faculty Ratio:.......................... 15.9:1
Students:
Undergraduates 156,434
Postgraduates 20,747
International 0.7%
Course Fees $:
Average 870
Average Undergraduate......................... 450
Average Postgraduate 1,000
Library Spending:..........................20,056,000
Overall Research Performance:
Total Papers 9,772
Total Citations.................................. 96,171
Impact 9.8
Research Impact by Subject:
Natural Sciences.......................................2.9

libraries represent 20 per cent of the nation's total.

Public services provided by UNAM include: 20 earthquake-monitoring centres, the National Astronomy Observatory, the National Botanic Garden, the National Library, the National Newspaper Archive, 22 stations in the National Marine Network, the National Herbarium, four ecological reserves and monitoring of Popacatepetl volcano.

The university's installations are spread throughout Mexico and abroad — 23 in Mexico City and 21 in the rest of Mexico, the United States and Canada — and comprise 5,500 hectares containing 1,525 buildings totalling two million cubic metres connected by 1610 kilometres of fibre optic cable.

Despite the general leftist orientation of UNAM students and professors, some right - wing organisations have also drawn on the university's members. The university confers a degree of political awareness not present among the population at large and political unrest is not uncommon.

People?
Among its alumni are Nobel prizewinners Alfonso Garcia Robles, who won the Peace Prize in 1982, Octavio Paz (Literature 1990) and Mario Molina (Chemistry 1995). The university has educated five past Mexican presidents and former presidents of Costa Rica and Guatemala; political economist William F Buckley; and writer Carlos Fuentes.

What do students say?
Jan Bouda from the Czech Republic says: "Foreign students at UNAM are treated excellently. Mexican students and teachers are always interested in exchanging opinions with the foreigners. I enjoyed my studies at the UNAM. There I met a lot of people and learned a great deal. The teachers are well prepared — generally they are specialised and have Masters degrees or doctorates in their fields. At UNAM one meets all kinds of people from all over Mexico . This gives one the chance to learn about the customs and culture of Mexico."

Good at?
Life sciences and biomedicine and the arts and humanities are the university's most highly rated areas, both just outside the top 100 in this year's rankings.

University of Basel

Why this university?

The University of Basel (Basel Universitat) is the oldest in Switzerland and among the oldest in Europe.

It was founded in 1460 by the Council of Basel with the patronage of Pope Pius II, initially for the study of divinity, law and medicine.

Philippus Paracelsus (1493-1541), considered the father of modern medicine and among the first to advocate the use of scientific experimentation, the study of anatomy and the use of specific drugs, lectured at Basel during 1527-1528, but was sacked when his patron died.

Five hundred years later, the life sciences are still the university's main area of excellence. Basel has for many decades had one of Europe's most important institutes for tropical diseases, and in recent years work on the most modern aspects of medical research, biology, nano-technologies and allied fields has emerged strongly. Basel acts as leader of the Swiss network for research and teaching in nano-technologies.

Basel's interest in medical research is fostered by the fact that a number of multinational pharmaceutical companies are located in and around the city.

With fewer than 10,000 undergraduate and graduate students. The university is still substantial in size by Swiss standards.

It is the only Swiss university to offer African studies, Jewish studies, environmental sciences and nursing sciences. Many of its facilities are housed in medieval buildings in the old centre of the city, resulting in a "university town" atmosphere.

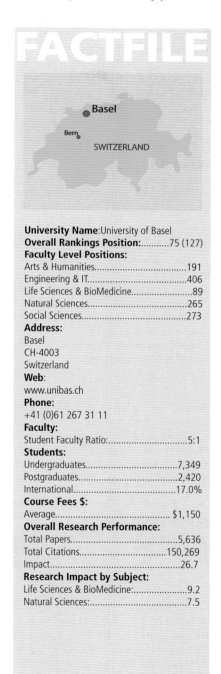

FACTFILE

University Name:University of Basel
Overall Rankings Position:...........75 (127)
Faculty Level Positions:
Arts & Humanities.....................................191
Engineering & IT.......................................406
Life Sciences & BioMedicine.........................89
Natural Sciences.......................................265
Social Sciences...273
Address:
Basel
CH-4003
Switzerland
Web:
www.unibas.ch
Phone:
+41 (0)61 267 31 11
Faculty:
Student Faculty Ratio:................................5:1
Students:
Undergraduates....................................7,349
Postgraduates......................................2,420
International...17.0%
Course Fees $:
Average... $1,150
Overall Research Performance:
Total Papers..5,636
Total Citations..................................150,269
Impact...26.7
Research Impact by Subject:
Life Sciences & BioMedicine:.....................9.2
Natural Sciences:......................................7.5

People?

In addition to Paracelsus, Basel's role of honour includes art historian Jacob Burckhardt, philosopher Friedrich Nietzsche, theologian Karl Barth, and two Nobel laureates for medicine Tadeus Reichstein in 1950 and Werner Arber in 1978.

What do students say?

Enrico Gnecco, a graduate of the University of Genoa in northern Italy, was a doctoral student at Basel and is now a researcher, specialising in nano-mechanics. "The organisation of work, for both students and researchers, is excellent," he says. "There is a good combination of friendliness and high motivation, and each individual feels strongly appreciated. Also, the life-sciences departments have a high proportion of foreign students, and here, much more than in other parts of the university, the environment is very international, with English as the lingua franca.

"The only negative side is that outside the university one finds oneself in a medium-sized town in German-speaking Switzerland, and establishing friendships with its inhabitants is heavier going than it might be in Italy, France or the UK. But this is a minor quibble, and only a little patience is required."

Good at?

Life sciences and biomedicine – 89 in the world, in three figures for everything else

Université Catholique de Louvain

Why this university?

It is Louvain in French, and Leuven in Dutch, a small town 30 kilometres east of Brussels in a region of Belgium whose population is mainly Dutch-speaking. The town has had a university since 1425, with French the main academic language. However, from the late 19th Century parallel courses in Dutch were gradually introduced, until complete bilingualism was established in 1911.

Following student unrest in the late 1960s around claims of language discrimination, it was decided to create a new campus – indeed a whole new town – to accommodate a separate francophone institution, the Université Catholique de Louvain. The move to Louvain-la-Neuve, in French speaking Brabant to the south of Brussels, was completed in 1979. The medical faculty, meanwhile, moved to Brussels to be close to a large teaching hospital.

In 2004-05 UCL had 21,248 students, 6,520 in the first cycle and 9,247 in the second or teacher training. Some 1,369 were studying for doctorates. Within this student population, 3,770 were from outside Belgium, the large majority from elsewhere in Europe. The university has an academic staff of 1,334, among whom are 23 foreign academics, appointed over the past five years.

UCL is a generalist university offering courses and carrying out research across all disciplines. Its work in the life sciences has long been a strength. UCL also has strong centres in disciplines such as systems engineering, nanotechnology, operations research, and the computational treatment of languages.

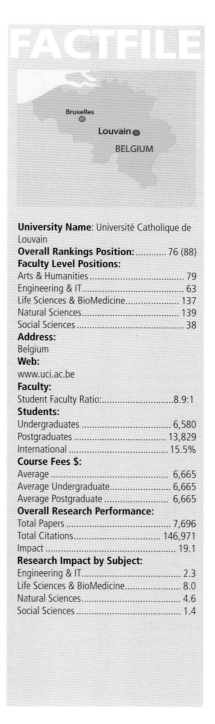

University Name: Université Catholique de Louvain
Overall Rankings Position: 76 (88)
Faculty Level Positions:
Arts & Humanities 79
Engineering & IT 63
Life Sciences & BioMedicine 137
Natural Sciences 139
Social Sciences 38
Address:
Belgium
Web:
www.uci.ac.be
Faculty:
Student Faculty Ratio: 8.9:1
Students:
Undergraduates 6,580
Postgraduates 13,829
International 15.5%
Course Fees $:
Average 6,665
Average Undergraduate 6,665
Average Postgraduate 6,665
Overall Research Performance:
Total Papers 7,696
Total Citations 146,971
Impact 19.1
Research Impact by Subject:
Engineering & IT 2.3
Life Sciences & BioMedicine 8.0
Natural Sciences 4.6
Social Sciences 1.4

269

People?

Christian de Duve, who founded the university's Institute for Cellular Pathology, won the Nobel prize in medicine in 1974 for his work on the structure of cells. André Goffeau headed the European project uniting some 100 laboratories which successfully decoded the yeast genome.

Alumni inlcude Georges Lemaître (who proposed the Big Bang theory), Geza Vermes, translator into English of the Dead Sea Scrolls, and Gustavo Gutierrez, Peruvian theologian and founder of Liberation Theology

What do students say?

While the creation of Louvain-la-Neuve is a source of considerable pride for the university, it is a mixed blessing for international students. Outside of term time, and often at weekends, the town is somewhat lifeless. Fabio Waltenberg Domingues, originally from Brazil and studying for a PhD in economics, has solved the problem by moving to Brussels, 25 kilometres away. "Now I manage to have a normal city life, but still be near the campus to work."

The university offers its PhD students excellent infrastructure and support, he says, but also the flexibility to build a programme out of courses available at other Belgian universities if it does not have the required specialisms. Fabio's area of interest is poverty and development, and he has been able to compose his own programme from courses at Namur, Brussels and even at the Dutch-speaking university in Leuven.

Good at?

The social sciences achieve by far the best position in our rankings, with a place in the top 40. The arts and humanities and engineering and IT are also comfortably inside the top 100.

University of Illinois

Why this university

The University of Illinois at Champaign-Urbana university is a world leader in supercomputing design and applications. It was here, for example, that the hypermedia browser Mosaic – precursor to Internet Explorer – was invented.

Its Integrated Systems Laboratory specialises in human-computer intelligent interaction, using the largest virtual reality chamber in the world. Its Beckman Institute for Advanced Science and Technology bypasses the traditional university hierarchy with interdisciplinary research into such things as biological intelligence and molecular and electronic nanostructures. More students go on to work for software megalith Microsoft than graduates of any other university.

In its Coordinated Science Laboratory, more than 450 researchers work on the development of infrastructure for information technology, including computing, communications, signal processing and wireless transmission for applications ranging from home entertainment to disaster response.

The Illinois Center for Cryptography and Information Protection is one of only four university-based cryptography centres in the world. The university also has one of the most highly regarded semiconductor and nanotechnology research facilities in the United States, the Micro and Nanotechnology Laboratory. And its National Center for Supercomputing Applications is a partner in the National Science Foundation's TeraGrid project to build the world's largest, fastest integrated scientific database.

The university of Illinois covers a vast, flat stretch of land in rural southern Illinois,

FACTFILE

University Name: University of Illinois
Overall Rankings Position: 77 (58)
Faculty Level Positions:
Arts & Humanities 218
Engineering & IT.. 30
Life Sciences & BioMedicine..................... 153
Natural Sciences.. 29
Social Sciences 87
Address:
Box 5220
Chicago
Illinois 60680-5220
United States
Web:
www.uillinois.edu
Phone:
+1 (312) 996-4350
Faculty:
Student Faculty Ratio:........................... 14.1:1
Students:
Undergraduates 47,601
Postgraduates 19,067
International 9.8%
Course Fees $:
Average 15,400
Average Undergraduate..................... 16,476
Average Postgraduate 14,694
Overall Research Performance:
Total Papers 24,825
Total Citations.................................. 460,725
Impact 18.6
Research Impact by Subject:
Engineering & IT... 2.5
Life Sciences & BioMedicine..................... 7.7
Natural Sciences.. 6.0
Social Sciences 2.2

surrounded by farms - many of them run under the auspices of its College of Agriculture, Consumer and Environmental Science. The university has the largest Greek system in the world — some 65 fraternities and sororities, to which 20 per cent of the students belong.

In addition to accounting, the university is highly ranked in civil, environmental, mechanical, electrical and computer engineering; materials science; analytical science; kinesiology; and library and information sciences, including the new field of digital librarianship. Its 2,047 tenured professors include 11 Nobel laureates. It has the largest library collection of any public university in the world, and the largest engineering library in the United States.

But the university has also established a niche for itself in areas like the simulation of solid-propellant rockets in its Center for the Simulation of Advanced Rockets, set up in 1997. Its Food and Brand Lab, launched in 1992, studies why consumers buy what they buy and eat what they eat. And its new Soybean Free Air Gas Concentration Enrichment programme is studying the effects of atmospheric change on agriculture.

People
Alumni include Playboy magazine founder Hugh Hefner; actor Gene Hackman; director Ang Lee; and the Reverend Jesse Jackson, who attended for a year but was expelled.

What students say
Hlaing Hlaing Win, a Malaysian undergraduate reading actuarial science, was drawn to the school after her older brother went there to study in the university's top-ranked accounting programme. The location is the only down side, she said. Ms Win regularly travels the three-hour bus trip to Chicago (there is a train service, too, and an airport owned by the university, which is served by three commercial airlines), where her brother now lives and works. Also, she said, "the weather is too cold".

Good at?
The natural sciences and engineering and IT both appear in the top 30 of this year's rankings. Illinois is also in the top 100 for social sciences.

University of Dublin, Trinity College

Why this university?

Trinity College Dublin is Ireland's oldest university: it was established in 1592 and is the sole constituent college of the University of Dublin.

Most of college's activities are based on the 47-acre city centre campus which contains much of Dublin's finest architecture. The west end of the campus is laid out in five quadrangles with buildings from the eighteenth century, including the old library which houses the priceless Book of Kells, written in the ninth century. The magnificent legal deposit library is also an invaluable resource to scholars.

The construction of a new building for nanoscience which will house Ireland's first science gallery is underway. At the heart of Trinity's strategy to meet the goal of a world reference point in key themes is a focus on interdisciplinarity. Its flagship interdiscipinary institutes are in areas such as nanostructures/nanodevices; molecular medicine; neuroscience; and international integration studies.

The Irish government is pouring money into science and research and wants to double the number of PhD students within the next few years. The college was well poised to tap some of the additional funds and now over a third of students in Trinity is studying at postgraduate level.

However, funding at undergraduate level is a problem and the average student:staff ratio is quite is high by international standards. Trinity plans to hold its undergraduate student population to no more than 11,500. It is fortunate that more than half of its Irish students have at least 500 out of a maximum of 600 points in the Irish

University Name: University of Dublin, Trinity College
Overall Rankings Position: 78 (111)
Faculty Level Positions:
Arts & Humanities 39
Engineering & IT.. 109
Life Sciences & BioMedicine........................ 93
Natural Sciences.. 93
Social Sciences 93
Address:
College Green
Dublin 2
Ireland
Web:
www.tcd
Phone:
(+353) 01 608 1000
Faculty:
Student Faculty Ratio:.............................15:1
Students:
Undergraduates 10,966
Postgraduates 4,298
International 17.7%
Course Fees $:
Average 1,795
Average Undergraduate..................... 19,515
Average Postgraduate 14,472
Library Spending:......:................. 17,945,200
Percentage Graduates Employed: 93
Overall Research Performance:
Total Papers 2,791
Total Citations.................................... 55,552
Impact 19.9

schools' Leaving Certificate. However, it has also met its target of 15 per cent intake of non-traditional learners. At present 17 per cent of its student base is from overseas – of these around 40 per cent come from outside the European Union.

People?

One of its first students, James Ussher, was a notable religious scholar and since then many of its alumni have helped shape the history of Ireland and of the English-speaking world. They include George Berkeley, Jonathan Swift, Edmund Burke, Theobald Wolfe Tone, Edward Carson, Oscar Wilde, Oliver Goldsmith and William Rowan Hamilton.

Two alumni have won Nobel prizes - Ernest Walton for physics in 1951 and Samuel Beckett for literature in 1968.

Both Mary Robinson, the former President of Ireland, and Mary McAleese, the current President, were on the staff of its law school.

What do students say?

The grandparents of Meghan Brown from Buffalo, New York, came from Schull, Co Cork. But it was not just sentimental attachment to Ireland that prompted her to study sociology and Spanish in Dublin. "The only way to be successful in a globalised world is to have a world-recognised degree – Trinity offers that" she says.

Good at?

The arts and humanities are Trinity's top performers, with a place in the top 40 of this year's rankings. The social sciences, biomedicine and the natural sciences are all in the top 100.

University of Otago

Why this university?

The University of Otago is New Zealand's oldest, founded by Scottish settlers in 1869 just 20 years after their arrival. The Scots' emphasis on education is a tradition the university remains proud of, but today it prefers to emphasise the international reputation it has gained as a result of the quality of its teaching and research.

Much of this research effort is concentrated in medicine and related sciences, but the university's second place ranking in New Zealand's Performance-Based Research Fund also demonstrated excellence in fields as diverse as anthropology, history, philosophy, psychology and zoology.

Otago has a presence in each of New Zealand's three major cities, but the small southern city of Dunedin is home to the great majority of its students, and Otago has successfully parlayed this relative isolation to its advantage. Nearly three quarters of Otago's first-year students arrive from outside its local catchment. Of the city's 120,000 residents, a fifth are students at the university and its neighbouring institutions. Dunedin is now a true university town and its northern district, spanning the Water of Leith, enjoys a thriving, sometimes boisterous student culture.

The university consists of four academic divisions of approximately equal size: the School of Business, and the Divisions of Health Sciences, Humanities, and Sciences. Postgraduate students made up nearly 19 per cent of the total student roll.

International student numbers have increased rapidly in recent years, from 1,200 in 2001 to over 2,700 in 2005. They now make up 12 per cent of equivalent full-time numbers, which is the limit set by

University Name: University of Otago
Overall Rankings Position:..........79 (186)
Faculty Level Positions:
Arts & Humanities...................................107
Engineering & IT...................................377
Life Sciences & BioMedicine....................74
Natural Sciences...................................224
Social Science...................................142
Address:
PO Box 56
Dunedin
New Zealand
Web:
www.otago.ac.nz
Phone:
64 3 479 1100
Faculty:
Student Faculty Ratio...........................5.7:1
Students:
Undergraduates...............................15,083
Postgraduates....................................2,656
International.......................................12.4%
Course Fees $:
Average.............................. . .9,839
Average Undergraduate 9,740
Average Postgraduate.................. ..10,400
Library Spending:............... 15,830,000
Percentage Graduates Employed:...... 82
Overall Research Performance:
Total Papers...3,675
Total Citations....................................57,058
Impact...15.5
Research Impact by Subject:
Social Sciences.....................................1.9

the university. Most come from China, the US, Malaysia and Germany.

Otago can boast a cosmopolitan academic make-up. Almost two-thirds of its 1600 academic and research staff are drawn from overseas. A further 1600 support staff are employed at the university.

People?

Otago claims one of the most widely scattered alumni populations in the world; fewer than a fifth live locally and the rest are based in more than 120 other countries.

Distinguished alumni include Dame Judith Mayhew Jonas, now Provost of King's College, Cambridge; Murray Brennan, who chairs the department of surgery at the Memorial Sloan-Kettering Cancer Center in New York; and Sir Kamisese Mara, the Fijian politician.

What do students say?

Catheryn Khoo is now enrolled as a PhD candidate in the university's Department of Marketing, after completing a Masters degree in Malaysia. She says Otago's location is a very real strength. While the campus environment is peaceful and quiet, a regular stream of visiting academics and robust communication networks negate any suggestion of isolation.

"A real strength of the university is the level of support that's available from staff and the department," she says. "Staff treat students with respect, allowing them the rights to question and to seek help. It feels possible to think independently and courageously." However, Khoo says she is surprised that Otago does not have better networks established with business and industry.

Good at?

Life sciences and biomedicine is Otago's top ranked field, at 74th. The arts and humanities are only just outside the top 100.

University of Wisconsin

Why this university?

On autumn Saturdays in Madison, the capital of the Midwestern state of Wisconsin, everything turns red – the official colour of the University of Wisconsin - which dominates the city, and red is worn by everyone when the school's football team plays.

During the rest of the week the university and its 38,000 students get back to business. Particularly highly ranked in the sciences, with an emphasis on agricultural and life sciences (it is also extremely well-regarded for its sociology and education programmes), Wisconsin hosts $714 million a year in sponsored research, putting it third in the nation in research expenditures and fifth in non-federally funded research. It is second among all US universities in the number of doctorates conferred. Its faculty have won 17 Nobel prizes since the 1940s.

While some large US research universities have begun dividing themselves up into smaller units to give students the feeling that they are at small colleges, Wisconsin revels in its bigness, touting the size of its library holdings (7.2 million volumes), the number of areas of study it offers (136 undergraduate majors, 155 Master's and 110 doctoral degree programmes), the variety of living arrangements on the campus, and the hundreds of student organisations.

Supported by financial contributions from its exceptionally loyal alumni, the university has recently completed a new health-sciences building, a genetics and biotechnology building, an engineering lab and office centre, a pharmaceutical studies building, a chemistry research tower, an addition to its biochemistry

FACTFILE

Madison

UNITED STATES

Washington

OF AMERICA

University Name: University of Wisconsin
Overall Rankings Position:............79 (73)
Faculty Level Positions:
Arts & Humanities 82
Engineering & IT.. 65
Life Sciences & BioMedicine.................... 123
Natural Sciences... 51
Social Sciences... 48
Web:
www.wisc.edu
Phone:
+1 (608)-263-2400
Faculty:
Student Faculty Ratio:.......................... 10.4:1
Students:
Undergraduates 29,078
Postgraduates 8,928
International 8.5%
Course Fees $:
Average 21,700
Average Undergraduate.................... 19,254
Average Postgraduate 22,978
Overall Research Performance:
Total Papers 23,347
Total Citations.................................. 501,059
Impact 21.5
Research Impact by Subject:
Engineering & IT...................................... 2.3
Life Sciences & BioMedicine..................... 9.3
Natural Sciences...................................... 6.5
Social Sciences 2.3

building and a $22 million renovation of its physics building.

Restricted by state law in the number of students it can accept from outside traditionally agricultural Wisconsin, the university is 90 per cent white; international students make up 8.5per cent of the enrolment.

The university is also known for what it calls "the Wisconsin Idea," first advanced in 1904, when the then-chancellor encouraged it to use its influence for public service. This is something that is taken seriously still. Wisconsin is first among all US universities in the number of graduates who join the Peace Corps, for example.

People?

Prominent alumni have included Charles Lindbergh, architect Frank Lloyd Wright, astronaut Jim Lovell, movie producers Jerry and David Zucker and Vice President Dick Cheney.

What do students say?

Fan Yang, a sophomore from China majoring in actuarial science in the business school, says: "If you're in a general course, there could be more than 100 students in a class, though I have been in more specialised courses with as few as 10." But even in large classes, the faculty "are very patient and very quick to answer questions."

"I think this campus is very friendly, but I do talk with other international students about the distance between us and the American students. Sometimes there is trouble communicating," said Ms Yang.

Good at?

Social sciences (48 in the world), also 51 in natural sciences and 65 in engineering and IT, 82 in arts and humanities, not placed in life sciences and biomedicine

University of Glasgow

Why this university?

Glasgow, founded in 1451, has one of the largest research bases in the UK, with more than 3,400 researchers across nine faculties. The money they raise in new research grants and contracts now passes the £100 million a year mark.

The most recent Research Assessment Exercise reported that 96 per cent of staff worked in subject areas producing international quality research. Glasgow won elite 5* ratings for English language and literature, European studies, psychology, sport-related subjects, and the infection and immunity grouping in clinical laboratory sciences, and the top research quality rating for 24 subjects, including history, physics and religious studies.

Glasgow is involved in Scotland's research pooling initiatives to bring together researchers from different universities, but for almost a decade it has had a "Synergy" partnership with neighbouring Strathclyde University. This has created some 200 active collaborations, including a full merger of Strathclyde's department of ship and marine technology and Glasgow's department of naval architecture and ocean engineering, which Glasgow calculates has raised more than £20 million of extra funding.

The university currently has approaching 6,000 staff, almost 300 of whom are from overseas. By 2010, it aims to have a "truly diverse student community," with an increasing proportion of both international and postgraduate students.

It has always attracted a high proportion of undergraduates from the surrounding area, and was the first of Scotland's four ancient universities to start widening access. Some 20 years ago, it launched a scheme to bring in pupils from deprived areas with non-

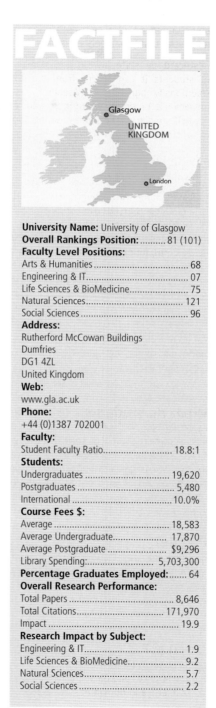

University Name: University of Glasgow
Overall Rankings Position: 81 (101)
Faculty Level Positions:
Arts & Humanities 68
Engineering & IT.. 07
Life Sciences & BioMedicine....................... 75
Natural Sciences....................................... 121
Social Sciences 96
Address:
Rutherford McCowan Buildings
Dumfries
DG1 4ZL
United Kingdom
Web:
www.gla.ac.uk
Phone:
+44 (0)1387 702001
Faculty:
Student Faculty Ratio............................ 18.8:1
Students:
Undergraduates 19,620
Postgraduates 5,480
International 10.0%
Course Fees $:
Average 18,583
Average Undergraduate.................... 17,870
Average Postgraduate $9,296
Library Spending:......................... 5,703,300
Percentage Graduates Employed:....... 64
Overall Research Performance:
Total Papers 8,646
Total Citations.................................... 171,970
Impact 19.9
Research Impact by Subject:
Engineering & IT.. 1.9
Life Sciences & BioMedicine....................... 9.2
Natural Sciences....................................... 5.7
Social Sciences 2.2

traditional entrance qualifications. It is now a key player in the GOALS project for 10-18 year olds, which targets schools in the west of Scotland with low rates of higher education participation.

In 2004, the university won the grading of Broad Confidence, the highest expression of satisfaction, for its teaching. Its medical faculty has been a pioneer of new teaching methods, establishing an undergraduate curriculum round problem-based learning. This introduces all medical students to clinical work from the very beginning of their education.

In 1999, Glasgow faculty of veterinary medicine became only the third European school to win approved status from the American Veterinary Medical Association. It is currently raising funds for a £10 million small animal hospital, not only improving care, but creating innovative teaching and learning techniques.

The city's skyline is dominated by the university's neo-Gothic main building, but it spends around £30 million annually on building projects, and is commited to cutting energy costs and environmental pollution in the process. Its four newest buildings, a biological field station at Loch Lomond, a cancer research facility, a computing science building and a biomedical and cardiovascular building are at the forefront of sustainable construction.

People?

Glasgow has a distinguished roll of scholars, including physicist Lord Kelvin and economist Adam Smith, who were both students and professors. James Watt conducted some of his early experiments with steam power while working at the university, and John Logie Baird, a pioneer of television, was a student when the First World War intervened.

What do students say?

Zhaofeng Zhou, from China, is doing a PhD in competition law. He says: "There are several reasons why I chose to come to Glasgow. First, it has a very long history. It is the fourth-oldest university in the English speaking world. Second, many famous people are associated with Glasgow university, such as Adam Smith and Lord Kelvin. Third, it has a great reputation in regard to helping international students. For example, the university runs some subsidised trips for international students. Fourth, there are some of the best staff in my research areas within the law school. This is important for research students. Fifth, it provides excellent social events for students. It is the only British university that has two student unions. Sixth, it provides me with an excellent chance to improve my English because I work as a senior resident at Murrano street student village where most of the residents are first-year British students. Last,but certainly not the least, the campus it very impressive. Particularly the main building is absolutely gorgeous. The least thing I like about the university is the summer holiday because most students are at home and the university is too quiet."

Good at?

Mid-ranking in life sciences and biomedicine, social sciences and arts and humanities

Macquarie University

Why this university?

Macquarie University was established in 1964 as a radical experiment intended to break with the traditions established by the venerable University of Sydney. It enrolled its first students in 1967 just as protests against the Vietnam War erupted and a wave of social change hit Australian society.

Today, the university is still influenced by the education reform movements of the 1960s and most of its courses offer the 31,000 students a degree of freedom to design their own programmes and to combine studies across disciplines. Part-timers are welcome and many courses can be undertaken online and via distance education.

Located 18 kilometres from the Sydney central business district, adjacent to a high-tech industrial precinct and research park, Macquarie has high entry standards for many of its degrees. The demand among students for places is a result of its reputation and its 14 national research centres, several university and divisional centres and nine centres of research excellence.

Because it has partnerships with more than 250 institutions in 60 countries worldwide, Macquarie's reputation draws foreign students in large numbers. But the university also sends more of its students on international study exchanges than any other in the country.

In 2005, 30 per cent of the university's graduates had travelled overseas as part of their studies and its exchange programme is supported by a A$2 million (£822,260) travel scholarship scheme — the most generous in Australia.

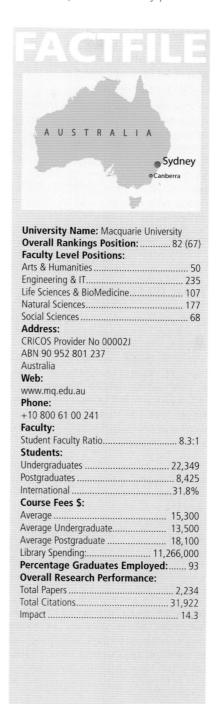

University Name: Macquarie University
Overall Rankings Position: 82 (67)
Faculty Level Positions:
Arts & Humanities 50
Engineering & IT....................................... 235
Life Sciences & BioMedicine..................... 107
Natural Sciences.. 177
Social Sciences 68
Address:
CRICOS Provider No 00002J
ABN 90 952 801 237
Australia
Web:
www.mq.edu.au
Phone:
+10 800 61 00 241
Faculty:
Student Faculty Ratio............................. 8.3:1
Students:
Undergraduates 22,349
Postgraduates 8,425
International 31.8%
Course Fees $:
Average 15,300
Average Undergraduate..................... 13,500
Average Postgraduate 18,100
Library Spending:........................ 11,266,000
Percentage Graduates Employed:....... 93
Overall Research Performance:
Total Papers 2,234
Total Citations..................................... 31,922
Impact 14.3

People?

As a research-oriented university, Macquarie has many of Australia's top academic researchers. They include four internationally known Federation Fellows as well as Paul Davies, the renowned author, physicist, cosmologist and science communicator, and Naguib Kanawati, a professor of ancient history and Australia's foremost Egyptologist. In teaching, too, Macquarie is well known. Its Master of applied finance (offered through its Applied Finance Centre) is the largest of its type in the world, teaching almost 900 students in Sydney, Melbourne, Brisbane, Singapore, Tokyo and Beijing.

What do students say?

British student Olivia Wilson is undertaking a degree programme at Macquarie. After completing school in Canterbury, Ms Wilson began investigating marine science courses in Britain and America but finally opted for Macquarie. Arriving in Sydney in 2005, she won a three-year full tuition scholarship and says she has been able to engage in ventures such as whale watching with research students she could never have done at home.

Although she has complaints about the low level of federal government funding for universities and new legislation that she says limits student bargaining power, she speaks highly of Macquarie's lecturers. She says the university's courses are "incredibly flexible" and the option to undertake subjects outside of marine science has allowed her to take units ranging from anthropology to world cinema.

Ms Wilson is one of those to have gone abroad and last year she spent two months at the University of the South Pacific, one of Macquarie's exchange partners, in Fiji.

"That was really something," she says. "Those sorts of opportunities were very much part of the appeal of the marine science course. The Macquarie travel grants are amazing."

Scholarships

In 2006, more than A$12 million (£4.9 million) is available in scholarships to support internationalisation, including full and partial scholarships and academic prizes for outstanding students to cover international tuition fees for undergraduate or postgraduate coursework degrees. There are also sports scholarships for international students, giving access to high-level coaching programmes.

Accommodation for international students includes free airport pick-up, temporary accommodation booking, on-campus accommodation ranging from A$100 to A$220 per week.

Good at?

Arts and humanities (50 in world) and social sciences (68)

Technical University Munich

Why this university?

The Technical University Munich (TUM) began life in 1868 as a "polytechnic school". Transformed into a university in 1970, the institute grabbed its new title with both hands and has built upon the prestige of its new name ever since - becoming one of the leading technical universities in the world.

Together with the Ludwig-Maximilians University, the TUM has helped make the Bavarian capital one of the most appealing cities for students and researchers and is one of the nine largest technical universities in Germany.

The institute prides itself on its international standing, claiming that its graduates go on to conduct careers in all corners of the globe, while its professors are diverse in origin.

At present, at least 4,100 international students are enrolled at the university which is also home to 37 foreign professors and 490 international scientists.

Part of the TUM's success is believed to be down to its continuity in leadership. Chemistry professor Wolfgang A. Herrmann, renowned in Germany for reforming higher education, has been president of the university since 1995 after being re-elected twice. It was under his initiative that fundamental structural reforms at the TUM were made, which were then followed by universities in other states as well as in neighbouring Austria.

Unlike the majority of technical universities across Europe, the TUM has also successfully managed to establish strong links with the life sciences, offering degree programmes in a variety of areas including nutrition and

FACTFILE

GERMANY

Berlin

Munich

University Name: Technical University Munich
Overall Rankings Position: 82 (105)
Faculty Level Positions:
Arts & Humanities 311
Engineering & IT 32
Life Sciences & BioMedicine 137
Natural Sciences 75
Social Sciences 411
Address:
Germany
Web:
www.tu-munchen.de
Faculty:
Student Faculty Ratio: 11:1
Students
Total Students 19,887
International 18.3%
Overall Research Performance:
Total Papers 9,637
Total Citations 187,018
Impact 19.4
Research Impact by Subject:
Technology 1.5
BioMedicine 8.9
Science 5.9

food, biotechnology, bioinformatics and medicine.

Much of its innovative research and teaching has emerged from collaborations between the disciplines of its 12 faculties as well as a number of research centres.

The TUM prides itself on allowing scientists freedom to experiment and in 2005 set up the 'TUM Institute for Advanced Study' that claims to add "entrepreneurial spirit" to the academic world.

Projects carried out at the university range in diversity from researching innovative medicines to furthering nanoelectronic technologies and to creating ice that does not melt.

The university is also heavily involved in EU projects and is actively involved in helping the bloc create a European Research Area (ERA) to promote co-operation and mobility between universities across the continent.

Female students and academics are also actively encouraged at the TUM. Of the 20,500 students currently enrolled more than 6, 400 are female. It is the institute's goal to become the most attractive technical university for women in the country and a number of unconventional measures have been taken to create courses and work places that match the requirements of women as well as those with young families.

People?

Alumni include Rudolf Diesel, who invented the engine that bears his name, and the aeroplane designer Willy Messerschmitt. The TUM can count six Nobel Laureates. Of these four won the prize for chemistry, including Professor Robert Huber who was awarded a Nobel in 1988 for his work on protein structure. Other laureates at the university include Professor Heinrich Otto Wieland, Nobel Prize for Chemistry 1927, Professor Rudolf L Moessbauer, Nobel Prize

for Physics 1961 and Professor Klaus von Klitzing who was also awarded the physics prize in 1985.

Good at?

The university is best known for engineering and IT, where it ranks 32nd in the world. It is also in the top 100 for natural sciences.

University of Washington

Why This University?

The University of Washington, the largest university in that part of the US that is home to economic powerhouses Microsoft and Boeing, is inextricably linked to the entrepreneurship of the Pacific Northwest.

It benefits from the philanthropy of the people it has made rich. Microsoft cofounder Bill Gates' parents were alumni and regents (Gates himself flunked out of Harvard). His partner Paul Allen's father was a longtime librarian of the university. Both men have made substantial contributions, Allen to a new library and the state-of-the-art Center for Computer Science and Engineering, Gates to a new law school and to scholarships to recruit outstanding students and underwrite student research, among other things.

Among the graduates of the university's top-rated Department of Aeronautics and Astronautics were the designers of Boeing's B-52, 707, 727, 747 and other planes. The manufacturer still uses its wind tunnel to test new models and seven-times Tour de France winner Lance Armstrong used it to try out a new line of cycling kit by Nike, which is based in nearby Oregon.

The university conducts almost $1 billion a year in sponsored research, receiving more federal government research funding than any other public university, second only to Johns Hopkins among all US universities. Its 4,100 faculty have won six Nobel prizes. Graduate students often receive not only waivers of tuition, but also stipends and health insurance.

The university's medical centre is home to one of America's top-ranked medical schools for training primary-care physicians. The departments of bioengineering and computer science and its School of Social

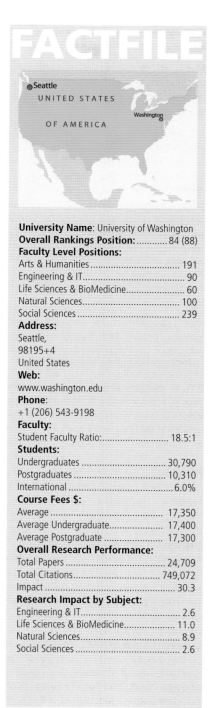

University Name: University of Washington
Overall Rankings Position: 84 (88)
Faculty Level Positions:
Arts & Humanities 191
Engineering & IT.. 90
Life Sciences & BioMedicine...................... 60
Natural Sciences....................................... 100
Social Sciences 239
Address:
Seattle,
98195+4
United States
Web:
www.washington.edu
Phone:
+1 (206) 543-9198
Faculty:
Student Faculty Ratio:.......................... 18.5:1
Students:
Undergraduates 30,790
Postgraduates 10,310
International 6.0%
Course Fees $:
Average 17,350
Average Undergraduate.................... 17,400
Average Postgraduate 17,300
Overall Research Performance:
Total Papers 24,709
Total Citations................................. 749,072
Impact 30.3
Research Impact by Subject:
Engineering & IT.. 2.6
Life Sciences & BioMedicine................... 11.0
Natural Sciences.. 8.9
Social Sciences 2.6

Work are at the top of their fields, and the law and business schools are highly regarded nationally; among other innovative courses of study, the business school has launched a technology management MBA programme for working professionals in the high-tech industry.

Already home to the Cesar Pelli-designed physics and astronomy building, which includes 20 physics labs built underground to provide the most stable possible environment, the campus has also added the $74 million William H. Gates Hall at the law school, a $90 million medical school surgery pavilion, the aforementioned $72 million Paul Allen Center for Computer Science and Engineering, and the $150 million William H. Foege Bioengineering and Genome Sciences Building, dedicated by Bill Gates.

It is also known for its colleges of forestry, ocean and fisheries sciences and urban planning, which specialises in environmental issues and sustainability.

The sprawling campus in Seattle was originally laid out for the 1909 world's fair, and continues to incorporate some of the original buildings.

People?

In addition to the substantial Boeing fraternity, prominent alumni include the first man to fly faster than Mach 2, the men who directed the lunar orbiter programme and Rockwell Internationals Apollo work, the head of the space shuttle programme, and five shuttle astronauts, including Michael Anderson, who died in the Columbia disaster.

What do students say?

Famously rainy Seattle is overcast 60 per cent of the time but Mathieu Fregeau, a Canadian doctoral student working on plasma generation and propulsion for space flight, does not mind the weather. "For me it's like paradise," he said, comparing the city with his native Montreal. "People are very laid back. I enjoy just walking on the campus and meeting everyone."

Good at?

60 in life sciences and biomedicine, 90 for engineeering and IT, 100 for natural sciences

University of Nottingham

Why this university?

Nottingham University is a campus-based, research-led institution with a strong international presence and reputation. Traditionally one of the most popular universities among British students seeking places on undergraduate courses, the university also attracts a high volume of applications from overseas.

Three attractive campuses set in parkland with award-winning buildings are all within easy reach of Nottingham city centre. The main 330-acre University Park campus is set around a lake with extensive greenery, and is regarded as one of the most attractive in the country. This campus is the focus of university life for most students, and includes 12 halls of residence, a conference and exhibition centre, sports facilities and an arts centre. Adjacent to University Park is Nottingham's medical school.

Jubilee campus, opened in 1999, houses the schools of education, computer science and information technology, and Nottingham's business school. A new research and innovation park is being built here. Most biosciences students are based at Sutton Bonington campus, which is also home to the university's new School of Veterinary Medicine and Science.

Nottingham offers overseas students a guarantee of university accommodation for the first two years of study, with over 6,000 rooms to choose from on or close to one of the university's campuses. Support for international students includes a foundation programme, offered both in Nottingham and at the university's two overseas campuses in China and Malaysia. English language tuition is provided on campus and online by a Centre for English Language Education. Meanwhile

University Name: University of Nottingham
Overall Rankings Position:............85 (97)
Faculty Level:
PositionsArts & Humanities.....................141
Engineering & IT.....................................116
Life Sciences & BioMedicine.....................51
Natural Sciences....................................120
Social Sciences..81
Address:
Nottingham
NG7 2RD
United Kingdom
Web:
www.nottingham.ac.uk
Phone:
+44 (0) 115 951 5151
Faculty:
Student Faculty Ratio.............................6.3:1
Students:
Undergraduates.................................24,865
Postgraduates.....................................7,755
International...18.0%
Course Fees $:
Average.. 19,334
Average Undergraduate.................. 19,334
Average Postgraduate..................... 19,334
Overall Research Performance:
Total Papers..8,096
Total Citations................................134,652
Impact..16.6
Research Impact by Subject:
Engineering & IT.....................................1.6
Life Sciences & BioMedicine...................6.7
Natural Sciences.....................................4.9
Social Sciences.......................................1.9

Nottingham's students' union, one of the largest in the UK, helps enrich campus social life with over 70 sports clubs and 130 societies.

Nottingham has 1,237 academic staff, including 432 professors. Its impressive academic track record, particularly in research, plays an equally important part in maintaining its international reputation. In the last Research Assessment Exercise, 26 of its departments were awarded world-class ratings, placing Nottingham in the top ten of UK institutions for research. In both teaching and research, the University is considered particularly excellent in healthcare, nanotechnology, molecular biosciences, the built environment, transport engineering, philosophy, international relations and cultural studies.

People?

Distinguished faculty include Nobel Prize winners Sir Peter Mansfield in the field of cognitive behaviour and scanning and economist Sir Clive Granger. The novelist DH Lawrence is the most famous alumnus, but table-tennis champion Deng Yaping enjoys superstar status in her native China, while Dato Seri Najib Razak became deputy prime minister of Malaysia in 2004.

What do students say?

It was Nottingham's "tranquil" environment that first attracted and has impressed Julie Walabyeki, a Commonwealth Shared Scholarship Scheme scholar from Uganda, who is taking a Master's in public health at the university.

She said: "The university and its environment has lived up to my hopes and expectations. My course has been very intensive, but so good that I now want to do a PhD here. As a mature student, I have found the social scene at Nottingham very inclusive."

Good at?

Biomedicine is the best-placed area in our rankings, just missing the top 50. The social sciences also do well.

Delft University of Technology

Why this university?

Delft University of Technology has chosen Prometheus' flame as its symbol, and like Prometheus the university sees itself as bringing technical knowledge to the aid of humanity.

A relatively new creation, gaining university status in 1986, TU Delft is inheritor of a tradition of engineering education in the town that dates back to 1842.

Delft is a small city between Den Haag and Rotterdam, greatly influenced by the university's presence. Ten percent of its 100,000 inhabitants are students and the university has attracted a large number of technology-oriented companies.

Four of the university's eight faculties cover engineering disciplines, the remainder taking on related subjects such as architecture, information technology, applied sciences and technology policy and management. It offers 16 Bachelor courses, almost all taught in Dutch, and 29 Masters courses, all taught in English. In 2005 there were a total of 13,563 students at the university, roughly half on Bachelor courses, half on Masters. Of these, 1,418 were from outside the Netherlands.

At the same time there were 2,428 scientific staff, of which 161 were full professors and 854 PhD students. Just under half of the scientific staff are from outside the Netherlands, including a substantial number of PhD students.

People?

The university is particularly strong in nanoscience, and in 2004 attracted substantial funding from the Kavli Foundation in the US to establish a research institute that now has a staff of

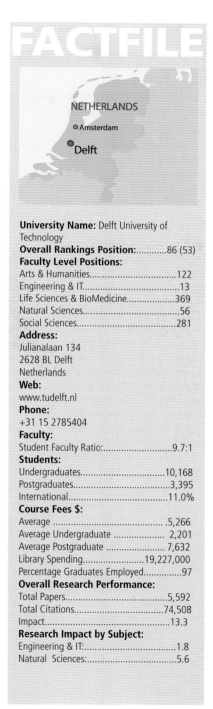

FACTFILE

NETHERLANDS

⊚ Amsterdam

● Delft

University Name: Delft University of Technology
Overall Rankings Position:............86 (53)
Faculty Level Positions:
Arts & Humanities...................................122
Engineering & IT.......................................13
Life Sciences & BioMedicine...................369
Natural Sciences.......................................56
Social Sciences..281
Address:
Julianalaan 134
2628 BL Delft
Netherlands
Web:
www.tudelft.nl
Phone:
+31 15 2785404
Faculty:
Student Faculty Ratio:............................9.7:1
Students:
Undergraduates................................10,168
Postgraduates....................................3,395
International.......................................11.0%
Course Fees $:
Average 5,266
Average Undergraduate 2,201
Average Postgraduate 7,632
Library Spending.......................19,227,000
Percentage Graduates Employed..............97
Overall Research Performance:
Total Papers...5,592
Total Citations...................................74,508
Impact...13.3
Research Impact by Subject:
Engineering & IT:....................................1.8
Natural Sciences:....................................5.6

16 professors and over 90 PhD students and postdocs. This is home to two of the university's most noted faculty, Hans Mooij, who works on quantum computing, and Cees Dekker, who received a Spinoza award (the highest Dutch honour for science) in 2003 for his work on carbon nanotubes.

The university's other Spinoza winner is René de Borst, who works in the equally strong aerospace engineering faculty. This is also home to Adriaan Beukers, who in 2006 was named the Netherlands' most entrepreneurial scientist.

What do students say?

The commercial relevance of Delft's courses was one of the things that attracted Nitesh Bharosa to the university from his home in Suriname, although being able to study in Dutch was also a draw. He completed his Bachelor degree at Delft and is currently finishing a Masters in systems engineering and policy analysis, with a focus on information and communication technologies. "Other programmes mainly consist of ICT courses or programmeming alone, but Delft offered a lot more company-specific courses, like the economics of ICT, human skills, and the management of ICT systems. That attracted me a lot," he explains.

Delft has lived up to its promise, and even compared well to UCLA, where Nitesh followed a summer course in 2005. "The teaching methods here are more advanced, they use a lot more technology, including internet resources to provide information. Class material and so on is all on line, and that is much appreciated. Also the topics taught are really novel. When I was at UCLA, for example, they were teaching programmeming languages that aren't popular any more, while at Delft they teach the languages that are in demand from companies."

The one down side is that Delft does not provide much support for international students. "The university only has one small office that offers you aid in a lot of bureaucratic issues, such as housing and banking. Other universities have a much better focus on international students." However, on balance Nitesh is very pleased with the experience of studying in Delft.

Good at?

Engineering and IT – 13 in world

University of Vienna

Why this university?

Sited on the Austrian capital's Imperial Ringstrasse, the University of Vienna blends in with majestic surroundings that include the 19th century Town Hall and the Austrian Parliament.

But although the main building was built at around the same time – 1877-1884 – the university's history goes back much further.

Founded in 1365 by Duke Rudolf IV, the university is the oldest in the German-speaking world and the second oldest university in central Europe after Prague.

At the time it was founded, religion was one of the main subjects taught around Europe but, unlike other universities, Vienna did not have a theology faculty. This changed in 1384 when a theology faculty was set up to join the institute's other three faculties of law, medicine and philosophy.

The university now offers more than 130 degree programmes in 17 different faculties. It's medical faculty became so popular and expanded its capacity so much that in 2004 a separate Medical University Vienna was created, which still co-operates with Vienna University's other scientific faculties and centres today.

At the moment 5,414 academics make up the university's scientific staff, including 2,738 women. It has a strong tradition of international relations and has established Erasmus partnerships with 311 universities, attracting thousands of international students each year from 130 different countries. It is also viewed as a gateway between east and west Europe and has been instrumental in strengthening ties with institutes and governments in south east Europe. At the moment 16 per cent of

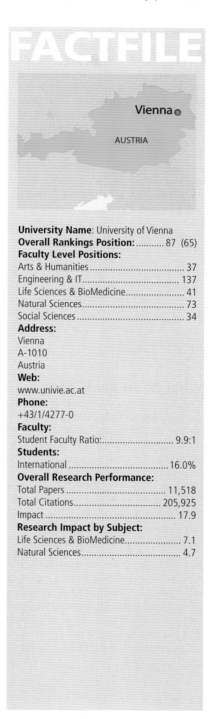

University Name: University of Vienna
Overall Rankings Position: 87 (65)
Faculty Level Positions:
Arts & Humanities 37
Engineering & IT 137
Life Sciences & BioMedicine 41
Natural Sciences 73
Social Sciences 34
Address:
Vienna
A-1010
Austria
Web:
www.univie.ac.at
Phone:
+43/1/4277-0
Faculty:
Student Faculty Ratio: 9.9:1
Students:
International 16.0%
Overall Research Performance:
Total Papers 11,518
Total Citations 205,925
Impact 17.9
Research Impact by Subject:
Life Sciences & BioMedicine 7.1
Natural Sciences 4.7

students are from abroad.

People?

The university has a long history of attracting the best professors from around the world after Duke Albrecht III took advantage of problems within the Sorbonne and brought a number of Paris's top professors to the Austrian capital. Since then some of the best scientific minds have taught at the university, including nine Nobel Prize winners, among them psychiatrist Julius Wagner-Jauregg, chemist Hans Fischer, immunologist Karl Landsteiner, physicist Erwin Schroedinger and biologist Konrad Lorenz.

The university has also educated a number of other prominent people, the father of psychoanalysis, Sigmund Freud, being the most notable, but others include Pope Pius III, former UN Secretary General Kurt Waldheim and current Austrian Chancellor Wolfgang Schuessel.

What do students say?

English Literature student Tanja Maleska, 25, from Macedonia says the opportunities for her at Vienna are far better than in her homeland. "More money is invested in universities in Austria and a degree from the University of Vienna is more recognisable than one from the University of Skopje. There has also been a great improvement in the courses on offer over the four years I have been studying here and we have many guest professors from other countries."

But she added there were problems with the university's popularity. "There are simply too many students enrolled, which means courses are quickly filled and lecture halls overcrowded. And you often get the feeling that you are on your own as professors do not have enough time for each individual."

Good at?

Social sciences (34 in world), arts and humanities (37), life sciences and medicine (41)

University of Pittsburgh

Why this university?

Money has been pouring into the University of Pittsburgh, in the heart of the resurgent onetime steel town in south west Pennsylvania.

Founded in 1797 in a log cabin on what was then the American frontier (most of the rest of the city would catch up to it later), the university has often pushed boundaries. The polio vaccine was developed there. A Pitt chemistry professor was the first to identify the chemical structure of vitamin C. It was at Pitt that the world's first double transplant operation was performed and surgeons there continue to carry out more organ transplants than at any other institution. And the university's supercomputing centre operates one of the fastest non-military supercomputers in the world.

A $500 million fund-raising campaign has proven so successful that administrators doubled the goal to $1 billion and then doubled it again to $2 billion, which will be used to add faculty and increase student financial aid, among other things. Already, the university has doubled the amount of sponsored research it conducts to $600 million annually in such trendy fields as nanotechnology, ageing, biotechnology and computer modelling. It was quick to carve out a particular niche for itself after the September 11 2001 terrorist attacks by making global security a research priority. And it has added more than 200,000 square metres of space to its urban campus in just 10 years, including a new state-of-the-art American football stadium that it shares with the Pittsburgh Steelers pro team.

The number of applicants for admission has doubled in just six years, sending the quality of incoming freshmen at the university soaring.

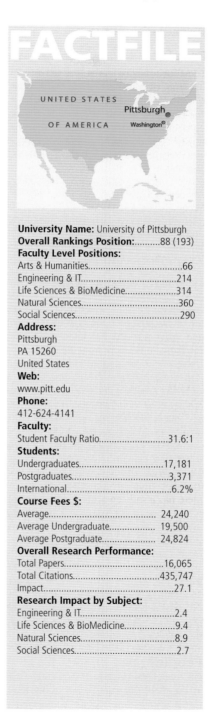

University Name: University of Pittsburgh
Overall Rankings Position:..........88 (193)
Faculty Level Positions:
Arts & Humanities.....................................66
Engineering & IT.......................................214
Life Sciences & BioMedicine....................314
Natural Sciences.....................................360
Social Sciences...290
Address:
Pittsburgh
PA 15260
United States
Web:
www.pitt.edu
Phone:
412-624-4141
Faculty:
Student Faculty Ratio............................31.6:1
Students:
Undergraduates.................................17,181
Postgraduates.......................................3,371
International...6.2%
Course Fees $:
Average.. 24,240
Average Undergraduate................. 19,500
Average Postgraduate..................... 24,824
Overall Research Performance:
Total Papers.......................................16,065
Total Citations................................435,747
Impact..27.1
Research Impact by Subject:
Engineering & IT.....................................2.4
Life Sciences & BioMedicine....................9.4
Natural Sciences.....................................8.9
Social Sciences...2.7

293

Highly regarded for drug discovery, Pitt is creating a chemical library, one of two in the country, where an inventory of chemical compounds will be stored that can be used in drug development. Like many other universities, it has added a programme in the emerging field of nanoscience. And, in collaboration with neighbouring Carnegie Mellon University, it is investing $600 million to boost Pittsburgh's biotechnology industry.

Pitt is aggressively undertaking academic research in the hottest topic of all – security – at its Center for National Preparedness and Matthew B. Ridgway Center for International Security, named for a Korean War-era American general.

Faculty and students specialising in public and international affairs, public health, law, medicine and information sciences are researching such topics as bioterrorism and cyber security. Pitt lured the Center for Biosecurity away from Johns Hopkins University to be part of this effort. And Pitt researchers are already developing a system to provide quick detection of disease outbreaks by sounding an alert when there are spikes in hospital emergency visits related to a specific complaint. Within minutes of the terrorist attacks on New York and Washington, a law professor was keeping track online of the legal implications of the changed world order, and continues to monitor the balance between public security and personal rights, not only in the US but in other countries.

More than two-thirds of Pitt's students are undergraduates (1,618 in all come from other countries, mainly China, India, South Korea, Taiwan, and Turkey), and they can take advantage of the breadth of the programme and the research under way there. There are 4,696 faculty.

People?
Pitt runner John Woodruff won 800m Gold at the 1936 Olympics – and is the black medal-winner from Berlin whose name you don't remember. But you have heard of alumnus Gene Kelly (Singin' in the Rain). Charles Glen King determined the structure of vitamin C here in 1927, and Jonas Salk produced the polio vaccine in 1955.

What do students say?
Justin Chalker, who just graduated from Pitt and is off to Oxford to study organic chemistry on a Rhodes scholarship, chose Pitt because, he said, "they give you the freedom to pursue any interest you might have."

He added: "If you're a motivated undergraduate, you're treated like a graduate student. Yet while I was focused on science for my degree, I was also able to take a lot of excellent liberal arts courses."

Good at?
Arts and humanities – 66 in the world

University of Lausanne

Why Lausanne?

The University of Lausanne shares with its near neighbour, the Ecole Polytechnique Federale de Lausanne, a history dating back to its foundation in 1537 as a school of theology. It became a university in 1890, with the final separation from the Ecole Polytechnique in 1969. However, today one can think in terms of the Lausanne area as a large campus including both the University and the Polytechnique, with a certain amount of sharing of facilities and exchanges.

The University has three main sites, the largest of which, on the shores of Lake Geneva, inspired Peter Breughel the elder's masterpiece, "The Harvesters." The medical and biology school is in central Lausanne near major hospitals, while the third, focusing on biochemistry, is located north of Lausanne close to the Swiss Institute for Research on Cancer.

The University has some 10,000 students. Of these, about 1,500 are from overseas.

There are seven faculties (theology, law, arts, social and political science, economics and business administration, geo-science and environment, biology and medicine), with about 2,200 researchers, 500 of them professors.

The School of Lausanne, a neoclassical school of economics founded at the university by Léon Walras and Vilfredo Pareto, is associated with the development of general equilibrium theory.

There are more than 130 teaching and research units at the University of Lausanne covering such widely disparate fields as Greek numismatics, cybermarketing and developmental biology.

A three-way cooperation with the

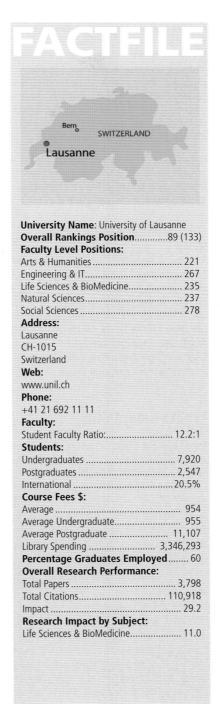

FACTFILE

SWITZERLAND
Bern
Lausanne

University Name: University of Lausanne
Overall Rankings Position.............89 (133)
Faculty Level Positions:
Arts & Humanities 221
Engineering & IT....................................... 267
Life Sciences & BioMedicine..................... 235
Natural Sciences...................................... 237
Social Sciences 278
Address:
Lausanne
CH-1015
Switzerland
Web:
www.unil.ch
Phone:
+41 21 692 11 11
Faculty:
Student Faculty Ratio:.......................... 12.2:1
Students:
Undergraduates 7,920
Postgraduates 2,547
International 20.5%
Course Fees $:
Average 954
Average Undergraduate.......................... 955
Average Postgraduate 11,107
Library Spending 3,346,293
Percentage Graduates Employed........ 60
Overall Research Performance:
Total Papers 3,798
Total Citations.................................. 110,918
Impact 29.2
Research Impact by Subject:
Life Sciences & BioMedicine................... 11.0

universities of Geneva and Neuchâtel is known as the "Azure Triangle". In 2001 the universities of Geneva and Lausanne and the Federal Polytechnic School of Lausanne signed the Science, Life, and Society Convention (SVS) aimed at creating dynamic scientific interaction through the exploration of new fields of inter-disciplinary research and teaching.

Tuition fees are around £247 (CHF 580) a semester and the university suggests that total study costs including accommodation and food will be £765 a month.

Who?

At least one head of state, Bhumibol Adulyadej, king of Thailand, was a student at Lausanne, as was the late Prince Bernhard of the Netherlands. So were at least two former prime ministers - Semsettin Günaltay (Turkey) and Muhammad Sa'ed (Iran). Other alumni include Joseph 'Sepp' Blatter, current president of FIFA, the world football authority, himself Swiss.

What students say

Karen Dickson , of the University of York, spent a year studying languages at Lausanne under the Erasmus student mobility programme. "I took a number of courses and found the overall teaching quality varied enormously. By far and away the best teacher was the linguistics professor, who brought an inspiring amount of enthusiasm, research and wit into his classes. I wanted to change my major!

"It was frequently difficult to find situations where I could speak French since many people in Switzerland are already fluent in English and enjoy the opportunities to practise it with a native speaker. I found it quite off putting to be responded to in English when speaking French and actually found I spoke French most frequently with the many German speakers who were also

in Lausanne to learn French."

Good at

Below 200 in all our faculty-level analyses but scores well in being international and having a good staff/student ratio

University of Birmingham

Why this university?

Birmingham takes immense pride in its self-proclaimed standing as the 'Oxbridge of the Midlands', and with good reason. The university can boast two thirds of its departments as nationally or internationally outstanding, with research, especially in languages, winning the university twelve 5* ratings in the Research Assessment Exercise. Teaching also scores well, with top marks in assessments going to mathematics, biological sciences, physiotherapy and electrical and electronic engineering. It therefore comes as little surprise that eight applicants contest every student place.

The university's prestigious medical school has recently seen the largest expansion in the country with a new £11.8 million student facilities building. The engineering department has also been bolstered in recent years, now offering interdisciplinary courses combining technology with subjects as diverse as modern languages and flood management.

The Birmingham Business School, the oldest in England, has also won a high level of respect, being one of only 13 UK business schools in the Financial Times global top 100 for MBA rankings, with The Economist magazine giving the school top ranking in the UK for 2004-05.

Like the city itself, the university is a melting pot of cultures and nationalities. Echoing the 26.4 per cent of Birmingham residents who self-defined as 'non-white' in the 2001 census, the university claims 4,500 international students from 150 countries. The city, around three miles from campus, has a growing reputation amongst students, but many opt to use the plethora of bars, shops and restaurants around the college itself.

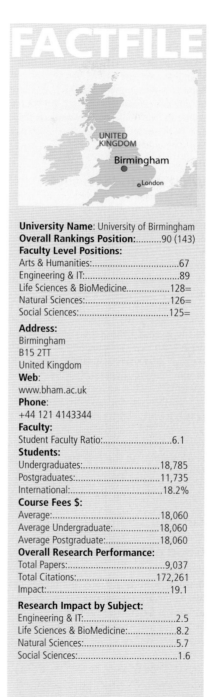

University Name: University of Birmingham
Overall Rankings Position:..........90 (143)
Faculty Level Positions:
Arts & Humanities:....................................67
Engineering & IT:.....................................89
Life Sciences & BioMedicine.................128=
Natural Sciences:..................................126=
Social Sciences:....................................125=

Address:
Birmingham
B15 2TT
United Kingdom
Web:
www.bham.ac.uk
Phone:
+44 121 4143344
Faculty:
Student Faculty Ratio:............................6.1
Students:
Undergraduates:..............................18,785
Postgraduates:.................................11,735
International:......................................18.2%
Course Fees $:
Average:...18,060
Average Undergraduate:..................18,060
Average Postgraduate:.....................18,060
Overall Research Performance:
Total Papers:......................................9,037
Total Citations:...............................172,261
Impact:...19.1

Research Impact by Subject:
Engineering & IT:...................................2.5
Life Sciences & BioMedicine:...................8.2
Natural Sciences:....................................5.7
Social Sciences:......................................1.6

People?

With a list of alumni featuring four Nobel Prize winners as well as the Mayor of Shanghai and the Prime Minister of the Bahamas, Birmingham has had its share of prestigious students. Actor Tim Curry, politician Ann Widdecombe, and zoologist and TV presenter Desmond Morris also hail from the university.

What do students say?

Irene Michael, a student who came from Cyprus three years ago to study physiotherapy, praised the level of support given by the university to international students. "I think it's great. The university provides a very good induction, with a student union really enabling students to develop."

Irene chose Birmingham largely due to the level of help given to her to get a place on the course in the first place. While other institutions at the time gave little or no financial support to international students wishing to get on her chosen course, Birmingham gave her funding to match the NHS bursary available for home students. "The university also gives free English courses as well as advice on visas and jobs for both students and employers," she adds. "The community here is good, but it could do better with engaging students throughout the year. The Union is playing a big part in strengthening the community."

Good at?

Birmingham is in the top 100 in our rankings both for the arts and humanities and for engineering and IT.

University of Leiden

Why this university?

Legend has it that in 1575 William of Orange offered the people of Leiden a choice of rewards for withstanding a Spanish siege: they could be excused paying certain taxes, or he would establish a university in the town.

They chose the university, thinking it would last longer than a tax cut. Whether or not the story is true, the university has endured. It is the oldest in the Netherlands, and gives a venerable academic air to a modestly sized city, part way between Amsterdam and The Hague.

Leiden has a broad range of academic interests, from archaeology and the arts to mathematics and natural sciences. In 2004-05 it had approximately 17,250 students, of which 1,424 were from outside the Netherlands. The university gives a strong international push to its students, with all research masters and PhD students obliged to take a placement abroad as part of their courses.

The nine faculties offer some 50 bachelor and 70 master degree programmes (most of the masters in English), while post-academic training is provided in education and environmental science. A separate campus in The Hague specialises in post-academic training in the field of law and political science.

Going into 2005 the university had 4,000 members of staff (not including those in the medical faculty who are employed by the University Medical Centre). Of these, 220 were full professors and 555 PhD students. The previous year 240 doctoral dissertations were completed and 1,829 master degrees were awarded.

University Name: Leiden University
Overall Rankings Position: 90 (138)
Faculty Level Positions:
Arts & Humanities 53
Engineering & IT 336
Life Sciences & BioMedicine 104
Natural Sciences 78
Social Sciences 84
Address:
P.O. Box 9500
2300 RA Leide
Netherlands
Web:
www.leiden.edu
Phone:
31 (0)71 527 27 27
Faculty:
Student Faculty Ratio: 10.5:1

Students:
Undergraduates 14,063
Postgraduates 4,390
International 6.8%
Course Fees $:
FeesAverage 8,844
Average Undergraduate 1,923
Average Postgraduate 14,100
Library Spending: 11,664,380
Percentage Graduates Employed: 91
Overall Research Performance:
Total Papers 5,472
Total Citations 78,448
Impact 14.3
Research Impact by Subject:
Life Sciences & BioMedicine 8.2
Natural Sciences 6.5
Social Sciences 2.1

People?

Leiden has an impressive record in the Spinoza awards, the highest Dutch academic award, with 10 winners from fields as different as clinical epidemiology and educational psychology. Strength in languages and linguistics is marked by two awards, while four have touched on mathematics and physics. This builds on a tradition that includes two Nobel prizes in physics, for Heike Kamerlingh Onnes and Hendrik Antoon Lorentz, and associations with figures such as Einstein, John Quincey Adams, ethologist Nikolaas Tinbergen and Paul Ehrenfest.

More recently Leiden has been the place of study for members of the Dutch royal family, and noted alumni include former European commissioner Frits Bolkestein and film director Paul Verhoeven.

What do students say?

Roosje Pertz came to Leiden from the Dutch speaking part of Belgium to take the 'book and byte' masters, a course taught in English covering book publishing and digital media. "It's very specialised, and not the sort of thing they would offer in Belgium," says Roosje, who heard of the course during an internship with a publishing house.

It lived up to her expectations, with the small size of the class and the flexibility of tutors particularly positive. "They treat you as an adult, and you can organise your own work," she explains. "At other universities, or where you are on bigger programmes, you are just a number." On the other hand, this freedom was sometimes hard to deal with. "There is structure, but not a firm hand that says you have to do this or that. That is good, but it can also be a bit weird when you come from a more authoritarian university."

Good at?

Leiden makes the top 100 in three areas: the arts and humanities (53rd), natural sciences (78th) and social sciences (84th).

Erasmus University Rotterdam

Why this university?

Appropriately for a university in one of the world's largest sea ports, Rotterdam's university has its roots in commerce.

In 1913, the city's leading merchants founded the Netherlands School of Commerce to train academics who could contribute to Rotterdam's economic development.

Later known as the Netherlands School of Economics, it merged in 1973 with the city's teaching hospital to form Erasmus University Rotterdam.

Later years saw the development of law, culture and society as complementary areas of study.

In 2004-05 the university enrolled 15,500 undergraduate students, of whom 2,890 were from outside the Netherlands, and 1,780 Masters students, of whom 520 were from abroad. There were 586 academics on the faculty, 91 of whom were from outside the Netherlands. This total does not including PhD students, who are generally treated as employees of the university under the Dutch system. Some 645 PhD students were employed in 2004-05, around 65 of them from abroad.

Economics and management remain among the university's strongest areas, both as academic disciplines and through the "post-experience" Masters programmes that the university has developed with industry, professional bodies and government. Around 4,000 students, most of them graduates with several years of working experience, participate in these programmes each year. In addition to the inevitable MBA, these include subjects such as global transport and logistics, maritime

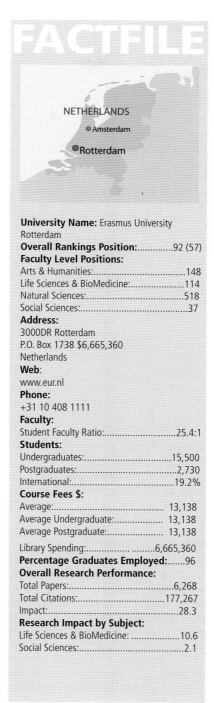

FACTFILE

NETHERLANDS
⊚ Amsterdam
● Rotterdam

University Name: Erasmus University Rotterdam
Overall Rankings Position:..............92 (57)
Faculty Level Positions:
Arts & Humanities:....................................148
Life Sciences & BioMedicine:....................114
Natural Sciences:.....................................518
Social Sciences:..37
Address:
3000DR Rotterdam
P.O. Box 1738 $6,665,360
Netherlands
Web:
www.eur.nl
Phone:
+31 10 408 1111
Faculty:
Student Faculty Ratio:............................25.4:1
Students:
Undergraduates:...................................15,500
Postgraduates:......................................2,730
International:...19.2%
Course Fees $:
Average:.. 13,138
Average Undergraduate:................... 13,138
Average Postgraduate:..................... 13,138

Library Spending:................. 6,665,360
Percentage Graduates Employed:.......96
Overall Research Performance:
Total Papers:...6,268
Total Citations:..................................177,267
Impact:..28.3
Research Impact by Subject:
Life Sciences & BioMedicine: 10.6
Social Sciences:..2.1

management and housing and urban studies.

People?

Erasmus University's most famous academic was Jan Tinbergen, the first Nobel laureate in economics. The econometrics institute that he helped establish celebrates its 50th anniversary in 2006, and will mark the occasion by giving a chair to Nobel prize winner Sir Clive Granger. The institute's current director, Philip Hans Franses, has a growing international reputation and will soon take over as dean of the Erasmus School of Economics.

Meanwhile, Barbara Krug is among the stars of the Rotterdam School of Management. An expert on governance, entrepreneurship and comparative business environments, her research has focused on the Chinese economy.

The university's other strength is in medicine and health, and in 2002 its medical faculty merged with the University Hospital Rotterdam to form the Erasmus Medical Center. With 47 research departments, it is particularly strong in cardiovascular diseases, cell biology and genetics, and molecular medicine. Its virology department, led by celebrated virus hunter Albert Osterhaus, acts as a World Health Organization reference laboratory for influenza and exotic viruses such as Ebola and Lassa.

What do students say?

German PhD student Christiane Reitz came to the Erasmus MC via Columbia University in New York. It was there that she started to collaborate with her current PhD supervisor, the neuro-epidemiologist Monique Breteler, and her project remains a joint project between the two institutions. "Erasmus MC has very good classes with excellent international teachers," she explains. "There is a high standard of education, which is comparable with that of Columbia University."

Johan Beijers, meanwhile, is a Dutch student completing his second Masters degree at the School of Management. His first was in marketing, the current one in business administration. "Erasmus is well known as one of the best, if not the best, for business administration in the Netherlands. So, if you are serious about your choice of study and specific topics like marketing, then most ambitious people end up at Erasmus." The university has lived up to his expectations. "If I mention Erasmus in London or in China, it is internationally well known."

However, the university's high reputation can be a disadvantage. "Sometimes the Bachelor part of the studies is maybe a bit too large," he says. "Sometimes you are in rooms with 600 to 1000 people. If it was on a little bit smaller scale that would be better, but in general the education and the professors are very good."

Good at?

Social sciences (37)

Lomonosov Moscow State University

Why this university?

Russia's oldest university, Moscow State University, was founded in 1755 by Mikhail Lomonosov, a native of St Petersburg who as a young man in pursuit of education set out on foot for Moscow.

His passion for obtaining the best education then available took him to the University of Marburg in Hesse, Germany – then one of Europe's top colleges – before he returned to Russia to teach in St Petersburg, eventually founding Moscow University on St Tatiana's Day, January 12 (now January 25), which to this day is celebrated across Russia as a holiday for students

Although commonly known the world over by its Soviet-era name, Moscow State University (or by its Russian initials MGU – Moskovskii Gosudarstvenniye Universitet), is now Lomonosov Moscow State University. As Russia's leading university, MSU has an international reputation for scientific achievement, particularly in physics, counting a number of Nobel laureates for physics among its graduates and professors. It is also noted for its research excellence in mechanics, nuclear physics, lasers, astronomy, molecular biology, biorganic chemistry, anthropology, materials science, ecology and the humanities.

More than 45,000 students are enrolled full or part-time at the university, which occupies a green and leafy campus covering 205 hectares, with commanding views of Moscow from the Lenin Hills. Over 5,000 foreign students from more than 80 countries study for a wide range of undergraduate and postgraduate courses, mostly taught in Russian. The university has a complement of 9,000 tutors, more

FACTFILE

RUSSIAN FEDERATION

Moscow (Mockba)

University Name: Lomonosov Moscow State University
Overall Rankings Position:............93 (79)
Faculty Level Positions:
Arts & Humanities...................................118
Engineering & IT.....................................58
Life Sciences & BioMedicine......................75
Natural Sciences.....................................19
Social Sciences......................................119
Address:
GSP-2, Leninskie Gory,
Moscow
119992
Russia
Web:
www.msu.ru
Phone:
(095) 939-10-00
Faculty:
Student Faculty Ratio:...........................12:1
Students:
Undergraduates.............................40,000
Postgraduates..................................7,000
International...4.3%
Overall Research Performance:
Total Papers....................................14,881
Total Citations.................................89,942
Impact...6.0
Research Impact by Subject:
Engineering & IT:...................................1.3
Natural Sciences:...................................2.0

than 7,000 of whom hold higher degrees.

All courses offered through MSU's 27 faculties are open to foreign students, subject to proficiency in Russian and annual fees (2006/2007) range from R1223,000 (£2,455) for undergraduate courses to R257,000 (£5,122) for highly specialised post-doctoral degrees.

People?

Nobel laureates include Aleksandr Prokhorov, who won the 1964 Nobel prize for physics for his work in quantum electronics, just two years after Lev Landau — a professor of theoretical physics — was recognised for his pioneering theories on condensed matter, particularly liquid helium. In 1958 Igor Tamm was one of a group of three Russian physicists awarded the Nobel prize for their discovering and interpretation of the 'Cherenkov effect'. Tamm, who graduated from MSU in 1918 and taught there 1924-37 went on to head a department at the Lebedev Institute of Physics, founded by another famous MSU graduate, Pyotr Nikolaevich Lebedev. Other notable alumni include former Soviet leader Mikhail Gorbachev, physicist and dissident Andrei Sakharov, Anton Chekov and abstract painter Wassily Kandinsky.

What do students say?

American student Judy Voratanitkitkul, 26, who studied Russian language at Moscow State's philology faculty 2005-2006, said: "You get what you put into it, plus the opportunity to meet people from all over the world."

Good at?

Natural sciences is by far MSU's strongest area, placed in the top 20 in this year's ranking. However, the university is also in the top 100 for biomedicine and engineering and IT.

Université Pierre-et-Marie-Curie

Why this university?

The University of Paris-6, Pierre-et-Marie-Curie (UPMC), is recognised as one of the leading higher education institutions in France – and Europe – specialising in science and medicine.

It was created in 1971 following the major post-1968 reorganisation of higher education that split the five faculties of the Sorbonne into 13 separate universities. Paris-6 took over most of the functions of the former Faculty of Sciences, and the new university was officially named Pierre-et-Marie-Curie in 1974, after its two famous alumni, professors and Nobel prize-winners.

The biggest scientific and medical complex in France, UPMC is based at the Jussieu campus, in the Latin Quarter of Paris, with a number of sites in and around the capital. Its faculties of medicine train 10,000 medical students who enrol each year. Among its other operations, it runs three marine research stations.

The university caters for around 29,000 students, including 6,500 students from 120 diffrent countries. It employs 4,000 teaching and research personnel, with many foreign academics and researchers participating in international exchanges. UPMC undertakes 550 joint research projects and partnerships with more than 330 institutions based in 87 countries worldwide. It has partnerships with over 100 universities in the European SOCRATES programme; and more than 160 European research contracts under the EU's framework research programme. It has six educational centres of excellence selected under the European Commission's research and development programme.

Recent restructuring has reorganised the

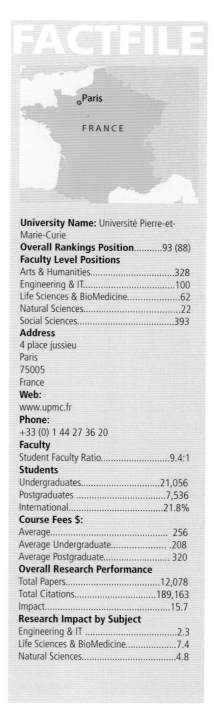

University Name: Université Pierre-et-Marie-Curie
Overall Rankings Position............93 (88)
Faculty Level Positions
Arts & Humanities.................................328
Engineering & IT.................................100
Life Sciences & BioMedicine...................62
Natural Sciences.....................................22
Social Sciences..393
Address
4 place jussieu
Paris
75005
France
Web:
www.upmc.fr
Phone:
+33 (0) 1 44 27 36 20
Faculty
Student Faculty Ratio..........................9.4:1
Students
Undergraduates...............................21,056
Postgraduates 7,536
International......................................21.8%
Course Fees $:
Average.. 256
Average Undergraduate.....................208
Average Postgraduate......................... 320
Overall Research Performance
Total Papers.....................................12,078
Total Citations...............................189,163
Impact..15.7
Research Impact by Subject
Engineering & IT 2.3
Life Sciences & BioMedicine...................7.4
Natural Sciences....................................4.8

university's main areas of research into four multidisciplinary sections: Modelling and engineering; Matter and new materials; Space, environment and ecology; and Genomics, cellular communication systems and new therapeutic approaches. They cover all the university's major disciplines of biology, chemistry, electronics, information technology, mathematics, mechanics, oceanology, physics, earth sciences and medicine.

UPMC is a member of the Alliance Paris Universitas with other Paris-based establishments including ENS-Paris and EHESS (École des Hautes Études en Sciences Sociales), and is developing close links with engineering schools such as Polytechnique.

People?

As well as the Curies, other distinguished alumni and/or faculty include Nobel prizewinners Claude Cohen-Tannoudji and Pierre-Gilles De Gennes; Fields Medal holders Laurent Schwartz, Jean-Pierre Serre, Alain Connes, Pierre-Louis Lions and 2006 winner Wendelin Werner; Hubert Curien, scientist, former minister and first president of the European Space Agency; mathematician Jacques-Louis Lions; materials scientist Marie-Paule Pileni; and AIDS researchers Willy Rosenbaum and Michel Kazatchkine.

What do students say?

Nicolas Troussard, 22, is about mid-way through a five-year engineering degree, studying material science. He chose UMPC "mainly because it's the best scientific university in France, but also because it offers a real engineering course, challenging the grandes écoles.

"Also, the course I chose is selective, meaning there's a limited number of students." His degree will open the way "to continue with an MBA, for example, or a PhD." He is considering taking an MBA in the US.

He identifies the strengths of UPMC as "the facilities, quality of teaching and high level of studies." On the downside "bureaucracy is a really tough problem, and there is asbestos on part of the campus."

Good at?

The natural sciences are the university's top scorer by far in this year's ranking, placed 22nd. Biomedicine also does well at 62nd.

Utrecht University

Why this university?

Utrecht University mixes ancient and modern, boasting a heritage that goes back to the 7th Century plus an ultra-modern campus with buildings by Rem Koolhaas. It can also claim to be the largest Dutch university in terms of student numbers - around 28,000 in 2006, of which 2,000 were from outside the Netherlands. They are spread over 47 Bachelor programmes, across all disciplines, 175 Master programmes, and 18 teacher-training programmes. Excluding medicine, there are 640 professors and 275 professors by special appointment. Some 400 PhDs were granted in 2006.

The university has recently taken steps to further improve the quality of its intake of Bachelor students, including quotas and selection processes. Once admitted, students can choose a minor subject from any of the programmes offered by the university, while honours programmes cater for the needs of outstanding students. International degrees are offered through University College Utrecht, an international Bachelor programme in economics, and almost 90 international Master programmes.

Graduate research programmes are clustered within six schools, each covering related research Masters and PhDs, the aim being to stimulate interactions between the various research areas. There are also 'prestige' Master programmes linked to research areas in which Utrecht holds a leading position worldwide. Students participating in these programmes are closely involved in the international activities of these research groups and spend part of their programme abroad.

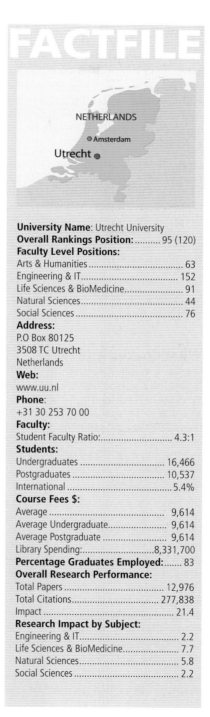

University Name: Utrecht University
Overall Rankings Position: 95 (120)
Faculty Level Positions:
Arts & Humanities 63
Engineering & IT 152
Life Sciences & BioMedicine 91
Natural Sciences 44
Social Sciences 76
Address:
P.O Box 80125
3508 TC Utrecht
Netherlands
Web:
www.uu.nl
Phone:
+31 30 253 70 00
Faculty:
Student Faculty Ratio: 4.3:1
Students:
Undergraduates 16,466
Postgraduates 10,537
International 5.4%
Course Fees $:
Average 9,614
Average Undergraduate 9,614
Average Postgraduate 9,614
Library Spending: 8,331,700
Percentage Graduates Employed: 83
Overall Research Performance:
Total Papers 12,976
Total Citations 277,838
Impact 21.4
Research Impact by Subject:
Engineering & IT 2.2
Life Sciences & BioMedicine 7.7
Natural Sciences 5.8
Social Sciences 2.2

People?

Utrecht is one of the few Dutch universities that can claim a living Nobel laureate, in the form of Gerard 't Hooft. He shared the 1999 physics prize with Martinus Veltman (his former supervisor at Utrecht, who later went to the University of Michigan) for their work on the weak force, and he still works at Utrecht.

Other Nobel Laureates are Nicolaas Bloembergen (physics), Peter Debye (physics), Christiaan Eijkman (physics), Willem Einthoven (physician and physicist), Tjalling Charles Koopmans (mathematician, physicist, economist), Wilhelm Röntgen (physics), Lavoslav Ruzicka (chemistry) and Martinus J.G. Veltman (physics).

English statesman Charles Spencer, 3rd Earl of Sunderland (1674-1722) studied at Utrecht.

What do students say?

One of the "prestige students" is Leila Kushan, from Los Angeles, who was attracted to the Masters in neuroscience and cognition because of the length of the programme and the opportunity of doing an internship abroad. A further factor was that the university accepts US federal student loans.

"I've been very satisfied with the programme," she says. "It's research based, rather than theoretical, so I've learned many new skills and techniques. The co-ordinators are very helpful and there is a sense of community within the programme." This has the effect of greater-than-expected involvement with the programme. "Since the programme is relatively small (only about 40 new students a year) the co-ordinators encourage student involvement both for arranging social gatherings and organising academic events like symposia and special courses."

Bureaucracy has been the main negative aspect of her experience, both in terms of coming to study abroad and the administrative problems of joining a newly established Masters programme.

Good at?

Utrecht makes the top 50 for natural sciences. It is in the top 100 for all other areas except engineering and IT.

Katholieke Universiteit Leuven

Why this university?

A Catholic university has existed in Leuven since 1425, although for much of its history the academic discourse in French was at odds with the Dutch spoken in the town. Dutch courses began to be given in the late Nineteenth Century, with complete bilingualism established in 1911.

However, the language divide continued to produce tensions, and following student unrest in 1968 it was decided to split the university in two. The French speakers set up a new campus, and a new town, at Louvain-la-Neuve, while the Dutch speakers remained in Leuven.

The Katholieke Universiteit Leuven is now the largest of Belgium's Flemish universities, with more than 31,000 students, around 12 per cent of whom are international. The academic staff is 5,287 strong, spread over 14 faculties. KU Leuven also supports five hospitals, three affiliated hospitals, and a campus at Kortrijk in West Flanders which caries out bachelor and master programmes in Dutch only, plus some research.

As well as exchange programmes the university has set up a number of international academic programmes aimed both at Belgian and international students, which are taught in English. Most are masters programmes, although full bachelor degree programmes are also offered in English for theology and philosophy students. The international masters are closely linked to the leading research areas at KU Leuven, but span the whole range of disciplines, from theology and philosophy, to law and economics, pharmaceutical science and bio-engineering.

FACTFILE

Bruxelles

Leuvin

BELGIUM

University Name: Katholieke Universiteit Leuven
Overall Rankings Position: 96 (95)
Faculty Level Positions:
Arts & Humanities 73
Engineering & IT.. 79
Life Sciences & BioMedicine........................ 82
Natural Sciences..................................... 102
Social Sciences 71
Address:
Naamsestraat 22
3000 Leuven
Belgium
Web:
www.kuleuven.ac.be
Phone:
+32 16 32 42 71
Faculty:
Student Faculty Ratio:.............................11.2:1
Students:
Undergraduates 11,560
Postgraduates 18,380
International 12.5%
Course Fees $:
Average 6,409
Average Undergraduate........................ 6,409
Average Postgraduate 6,409
Library Spending: 16,347,052
Percentage Graduates Employed:........90
Overall Research Performance:
Total Papers 10,000
Total Citations.................................. 169,821
Impact 17.0
Research Impact by Subject:
Engineering & IT.. 2.0
Life Sciences & BioMedicine...................... 8.4
Natural Sciences 3.9
Social Sciences 1.8

People?

Leuven tempted back Catherine Verfaillie, a pioneer of work with adult stem cells, from Minnesota this year to lead a new stem cell institute. The university also has an international reputation in cryptography, and was home to Vincent Rijmen and Joan Daemen, the two researchers who developed the Rijndael advanced encryption standard adopted by the US Government.

In the 2005 round of 'Flemish Nobels', awarded every five years, Leuven faculty picked up three of the five awards. They went to Bart De Strooper (human genetics), Victor Moshchalkov (solid state physics and magnetism) and Frans Van de Werf (cardiology).

Alumni include Frank Vandenbroucke, the present education minister in Belgium's Flemish government, humanist and theologian Desiderius Erasmus, Dr A. Q. Khan, the founder of Pakistan's Nuclear Programme and cartographer Gerard Mercator.

What do students say?

British post-doc Simon Reeve was attracted to Leuven by the prospect of joining a research group in neurobiology being set up by an American investigator who had been persuaded to move to the university. "With him establishing a lab here, and the lab being a new place, I figured that the support, the funding, the interest would all be at a maximum." The experience has lived up to his expectations, and he has no regrets at choosing Leuven over a position in the USA. "It's a very dynamic environment," he says. "People suggest things and they go ahead." His only regret is that, in the university's English-speaking environment, there is no incentive to learn Dutch and so engage more with the local community. "From one perspective it's an advantage, but from another it's not."

Good at?

Only the natural sciences are outside the top 100 in our rankings – and only by two places. The social sciences are best-placed, at 71st.

Wageningen University

Why this university?

The area around Wageningen is marketed as Food Valley, so great is the concentration of agriculture, food and other related businesses. The university and its research centres play an important part in this project, providing both future employees and expertise to solve the food industry's problems.

Agricultural education in Wageningen dates back to 1876, with the university following after World War One. Over time it has developed a broad range of expertise in the life sciences and natural resource management, adding social sciences and economics to the more traditional plant and animal sciences.

The university currently offers 18 Bachelor and 30 Master programmes, which in 2004-05 included 4,808 students, 1,140 from outside the Netherlands. This is double the number of foreign students attending in 1999-2000. Bachelor courses are taught in either a mix of Dutch and English, or entirely in English, while all Master courses are in English. There is also an emphasis on professional experience, with all Master courses including a six-month internship.

There are 205 professors on the academic staff, and research at the university is organised into five departments: agrotechnology and food sciences; animal sciences; environmental sciences; plant sciences; and social sciences. Staff from across these departments also participate in the seven graduate schools that provide Wageningen's PhD programmes. These cover topics such as plant health, food and nutrition, or environment and climate change research. Approximately 200 PhD students graduate annually from Wageningen, following a four-year,

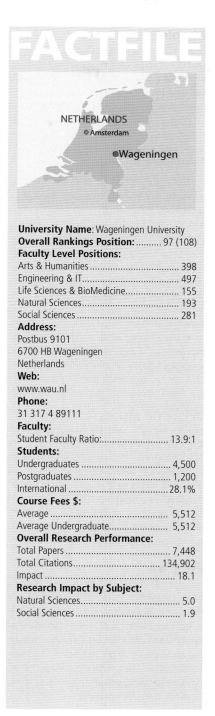

University Name: Wageningen University
Overall Rankings Position: 97 (108)
Faculty Level Positions:
Arts & Humanities 398
Engineering & IT...................................... 497
Life Sciences & BioMedicine.................... 155
Natural Sciences....................................... 193
Social Sciences 281
Address:
Postbus 9101
6700 HB Wageningen
Netherlands
Web:
www.wau.nl
Phone:
31 317 4 89111
Faculty:
Student Faculty Ratio:........................... 13.9:1
Students:
Undergraduates 4,500
Postgraduates 1,200
International 28.1%
Course Fees $:
Average 5,512
Average Undergraduate...................... 5,512
Overall Research Performance:
Total Papers 7,448
Total Citations................................. 134,902
Impact 18.1
Research Impact by Subject:
Natural Sciences....................................... 5.0
Social Sciences 1.9

research-based programme.

One of the university's key collaborations is the Wageningen Research Centre, established in 1997, which brings together the university, the Van Hall Larenstein School of Higher Professional Education and the former research institutes of the Dutch Ministry of Agriculture. The centre pools resources to address scientific, social and commercial problems in the life sciences and natural resource management.

Wageningen has been particularly successful in building links with Asia. While non-Dutch Europeans make up the largest proportion of international students, nearly as many come in from East Asia, particularly China. Meanwhile, almost all of the university's science groups are active in this region, in one way or another. The most significant links include contacts with China Agricultural University for the BSc students, with the Chinese Academy of Agricultural Sciences for a potato genome sequencing project, and with Tsinghua University for an MSc course on environmental policy. There are also intensive contacts with Malaysia, Indonesia and India.

Within Europe, the university has been quick to implement the Bologna reforms, becoming the first Dutch university to introduce the Bachelor-Master system, in 2002, and three years later the first to receive the label for implementing the European Credit Transfer and Accumulation System across its entire education programme.

People?
Notable alumni include Louise Fresco, former assistant director general of the Food and Agriculture Organisation; Rudy Rabbinge, advisor to UN secretary-general Kofi Annan on food security and agricultural productivity in Africa; Dongyu Qu, vice-president of the Chinese Academy of Agricultural Sciences and Karel Vuursteen, former CEO of Heineken NV.

What do students say?
Alina Amador from Costa Rica, who is doing an MSc International Development Programme, chose Wageningen for its track record in programmes related to development.

"Wageningen has a lot of projects directed towards development in countries in Latin America as well as Africa and other developing areas of the world ... and has shown it was interested in applying initiatives and research in developing countries, not only in giving lectures and making recommendations."

Although only at the beginning of her studies, she has found the lecturers well prepared, with up-to-date information.

"The diversity of students and the variety of nationalities that attend this university greatly enriches the experience. For me, for my academic and my professional future, I consider Wageningen to be a very good choice."

Good at?
Life sciences and biomedicine and the natural sciences are the highest-ranked areas, but neither makes the top 100.

Technical University Munich

Why this university?

The Technical University Munich (TUM) began life in 1868 as a "polytechnic school". Transformed into a university in 1970, the institute grabbed its new title with both hands and has built upon the prestige of its new name ever since - becoming one of the leading technical universities in the world.

Together with the Ludwig-Maximilians University, the TUM has helped make the Bavarian capital one of the most appealing cities for students and researchers and is one of the nine largest technical universities in Germany.

The institute prides itself on its international standing claiming that its graduates go on to conduct careers in all corners of the globe while its professors are diverse in origin.

At present, at least 4,100 international students are enrolled at the university which is also home to 37 foreign professors and 490 international scientists.

Part of the TUM's success is believed to be down to its continuity in leadership. Chemistry professor Wolfgang A. Herrmann, renowned in Germany for reforming higher education, has been president of the university since 1995 after being re-elected twice. It was under his initiative that fundamental structural reforms at the TUM were made, which were then followed by universities in other states as well as in neighbouring Austria.

Unlike the majority of technical universities across Europe, the TUM has also successfully managed to establish strong links with the life sciences, offering degree programmes in a variety of areas including nutrition and

University Name: Technical University Munich
Overall Rankings Position.............98 (55)
Faculty Level Positions
Arts & Humanities ....191=
Engineering & IT.................................145=
Life Sciences & BioMedicine....................56=
Natural Sciences.. 43
Social Sciences 74
Address
ZVS, Sonnenstrasse 171
Dortmund
44128
Germany
Web
www.uni-muenchen.de
Phone
0231/1081-0
Faculty
Student Faculty Ratio 17.5:1
Students
Undergraduates 39,478
Postgraduates 4,014
International 13.0%
Course Fees
Average 1,025
Average Undergraduate........................ 1,521
Average Postgraduate 1,025
Library Spending 7,306,260
Overall Research Performance
Total Papers 13,556
Total Citations................................... 268,762
Impact 19.8
Research Impact by Subject
Life Sciences & BioMedicine.................... 7.8
Natural Sciences..................................... 5.9
Social Sciences 1.9

food, biotechnology, bioinformatics and medicine.

Much of its innovative research and teaching has emerged from collaborations between the disciplines of its 12 faculties as well as a number of research centres.

The TUM prides itself on allowing scientists freedom to experiment and in 2005 set up the 'TUM Institute for Advanced Study' that claims to add "entrepreneurial spirit" to the academic world.

Projects carried out at the university range in diversity from researching innovative medicines to furthering nanoelectronic technologies and to creating ice that does not melt.

The university is also heavily involved in EU projects and is actively involved in helping the bloc create a European Research Area (ERA) to promote co-operation and mobility between universities across the continent..

Female students and academics are also actively encouraged at the TUM. Of the 20,500 students currently enrolled more than 6, 400 are female. It is the institute's goal to become the most attractive technical university for women in the country and a number of unconventional measures have been taken to create courses and work places that match the requirements of women as well as those with young families.

People?

Alumni include Rudolf Diesel, who invented the engine that bears his name, and the aeroplane designer Willy Messerschmitt. The TUM can count six Nobel Laureates. Of these four won the prize for chemistry, including Professor Robert Huber who was awarded a Nobel in 1988 for his work on protein structure. Other laureates at the university include Professor Heinrich Otto Wieland, Nobel Prize for Chemistry 1927, Professor Rudolf L Moessbauer, Nobel Prize for Physics 1961 and Professor Klaus von Klitzing who was also awarded the physics

Good at?

The university is best-known for engineering and IT, where it ranks 32nd in the world. It is also in the top 100 for natural sciences.

Queen Mary, University of London

Why this university?

Queen Mary is currently the fourth largest college of the University of London, with around 11,000 students and over 1000 academic staff. In recent years, the university has spent more than £160 million on new buildings and refurbishments, including London's largest fully integrated campus at its Mile End site.

Because of this campus-based arrangement, Queen Mary prides itself on providing a relatively peaceful work and study environment in spite of its size and location in the capital.

The oldest building on campus is the Queens' Building built in 1887; originally known as The People's Palace, it provided entertainment and cultural opportunities for the local population. It was admitted to the University of London in 1915.

Around four-fifths of the students are undergraduates and almost half of these are from within the Greater London area. The college attracts a diverse intake: around a third of students are of non-white ethnic origin and 24 per cent of the total student population comes from outside the UK. Overseas students at Queen Mary can benefit from the presence of a unit specialising in English as a foreign language.

In the most recent assessments of research quality, Iberian and Latin American languages and commercial law and linguistics were rated as internationally outstanding and 60 per cent of departments across the college were awarded one of the top two ratings. In terms of teaching, the most highly rated subjects were dentistry, politics and modern languages.

FACTFILE

UNITED KINGDOM

London

University Name: Queen Mary, University of London
Overall Rankings Position:...........99 (112)
Faculty Level Positions:
Arts & Humanities.....................................79
Engineering & IT......................................276
Life Sciences & BioMedicine....................186
Natural Sciences.....................................237
Social Sciences.......................................115
Address:
Mile End Road
London
E1 4NS
United Kingdom
web:
www.qmw.ac.uk
Phone:
+44 20 7882 5555
Faculty:
Student Faculty Ratio...............................5:1
Students:
Undergraduates....................................8,225
Postgraduates......................................2,785
International...24.6%
Overall Research Performance
Average 18,232
Average Undergraduate 18,232
Average Postgraduate 18,232

A major part of the recent investment has been on a new home for Barts and The London, Queen Mary's School of Medicine and Dentistry. This incorporates six institutes and is home to the first university-based Cancer Research UK Clinical Centre, which is advertised as taking an innovative 'molecules to patient' approach to research.

People?

Notable Alumni include philanthropist Dr Thomas Barnardo, novelist Sir Malcolm Bradbury, politicians Baroness Falkender and Peter Hain, Nobel laureate Sir Peter Mansfield, historian Sir Roy Strong and rock musicians Bruce Dickinson (Iron Maiden) and Pete Doherty.

What do students say?

Leslie Pomplun transferred from the University of Minnesota to Queen Mary to complete a degree in Marine and Freshwater Biology. "I chose to study at Queen Mary because it offers classes that are not available at any other university in London, as well as the opportunity to study classes within and outside of your area of study" she says.

Location was also very important. "Queen Mary is a great place to study because it is a nice, clean, centrally located campus in a culturally diverse area, and it is easy to find your way around". She feels that being based on campus helped her adjust to life in London, adding: "Settling in is quite easy, as long as you are adaptable and open-minded. Living in a dorm on campus makes it easier because you can get familiar with the area quickly and build up your confidence."

Good at?

The arts and humanities are Queen Mary's greatest strength. Academics place them 79th in the world.

Pennsylvania State University

Why this university?

The impact of athletics at many large US universities cannot be overstated, and nowhere has athletics had as great an impact as at Pennsylvania State University.

The university's long-serving, Ivy League-educated American football coach has used his extraordinary popularity (and the generous salary he receives) not only to require that his players answer questions from the media in grammatical sentences, but to push the school itself to raise its academic standards. The coach, Joe Paterno—the most successful in the history of university football—has personally given $4 million to Penn State to endow faculty and scholarships and the university library, a wing of which is named for him.

The high-profile success of his team has generated enormous name recognition for the university and attracts student attention. A survey found Penn State to be the 12th-most popular university in the US and almost 30,000 a year apply for admission.

All of this has helped propel the school from a tiny agricultural college to a multi-campus university with 63,500 undergraduate and 10,000 graduate students, 3,500 of them international, who come for top-ranked programmes in disciplines such as engineering and meteorology and, still, in agriculture. One in 50 professionally licensed engineers in the US, and one in four meteorologists, is a Penn State graduate. Some $640 million a year of research is conducted on the campus, in the rural centre of Pennsylvania, about three and a half hours from Philadelphia and five hours from New York City. Penn State is third in the nation in industry- (as opposed to government-) sponsored research.

University Name: Pennsylvania State University
Overall Rankings Position 99 (64)
Faculty Level Positions
Arts & Humanities.....................................153
Engineering & IT..90
Life Sciences & BioMedicine....................128
Natural Sciences..77
Social Sciences..83
Address
201 Shields Building, Box 3000 ,University Park
PA 16804-3000
United States
Web:
www.psu.edu
Phone:
(814) 865-5471
Faculty
Student Faculty Ratio..........................16.5:1
Students
Undergraduates..................................63,833
Postgraduates.....................................10,310
International.....................................4.7%
Course Fees $:
Average...20,500
Average Undergraduate.................. ..29,910
Average Postgraduate 16,654
Overall Research Performance
Total Papers...8,895
Total Citations..................................273,573
Impact..30.8
Research Impact by Subject
Engineering & IT...3.4
Life Sciences & BioMedicine....................15.2
Natural Sciences......................................11.6
Social Sciences...3.4

Penn State's business and engineering schools are at the top of their games in supply chain management and logistics and industrial and manufacturing engineering and materials, respectively; the university is first in the nation in the number of citations by its materials science faculty. The Design Futures Council rates its architecture programme highly, and it is also well regarded in landscape architecture and nuclear engineering and for its doctoral programmes in geology, hydrology and geochemistry.

Class sizes are generally large; nearly 40 per cent of courses have 30 or more students in them. There are 2,200 faculty. But there is also an honours college with smaller classes and extracurricular activities tailored to the most academically talented students; applicants often choose the honours college over admission to Ivy League schools, lured in part by guaranteed scholarships for everyone who enrols.

People?

Faculty have included authors John Barth and Joseph Heller, and philosopher Ivan Illich. Alumni include 1980 Nobel chemistry laureate Paul Berg, Eugene O'Kelly, chairman emeritus and former CEO of KPMG and William Schreyer, chairman emeritus and former CEO of Merrill Lynch.

What do students say?

"The research that's going on here is top notch and the faculty are great at both the teaching and the research," said Xiaole Mao a doctoral candidate from China who is studying bioengineering. "The professors are very engaged in teaching, even though they're all quite busy with their own research projects." An aspiring teacher, Mr Mao said the university "pays a lot of attention to helping students developing teaching skills.0"

Good at?

Natural sciences, social sciences and engineering and IT are all in the top 100 in the world.

The top ten countries

Six countries host 67 per cent of the world's foreign or mobile students — 23 per cent in the United States, followed by the United Kingdom (12 per cent), Germany (11 per cent), France (10 per cent), Australia (7 per cent) and Japan (5 per cent). Each of these countries is featured in this chapter, along with Singapore, Canada, the Netherlands and the Nordic countries (treated as a whole).

According to the Institute for International Education, the twenty five countries which supply the most students to study overseas are: China, India, Korea, Japan, Greece, Germany, France, Turkey, Morocco, Italy, Taiwan, Malaysia, Canada, USA, Indonesia, Spain, Hong Kong, UK, Kazakhstan, Russia, Thailand, Singapore, Poland, Brazil and Ireland.

Students of different nationalities have different needs, be it language preparation, social networks or adapting to teaching styles. It is impossible to address all these issues, but we hope the information contained in this book will help you narrow down the relative suitability and feasibility of one country as a study destination, relative to others.

We review the ten most popular country study destinations, with a focus on the types of institutions, their recognition internationally, the type of accreditation and quality control locally, the prevailing attitudes towards international students and services available.

We try to capture some of the non-quantitative differences, like the teaching styles in each country. For example, the style of teaching in UK institutions is different from many other systems of education. Bachelors degrees are taught by a mix of lectures, tutorials and self-study - very little of this structure is compulsory, as the emphasis of learning in the UK system is the individual student's responsibility, with grades based primarily in "finals" exams. By contrast, the US grade point average system is a cumulative total of each individual course grade, requiring attendance at lectures and consistent performance throughout your university career.

Where possible, we also comment on lifestyle, accommodation and availability of employment opportunities for international students. We also provide further insight into government grants and subsidies for overseas students.

Study in Australia

Things to consider

+ Clear framework of qualifications
+ Reasonable cost of tuition and living costs
+ Ability to work and study
+ Good international reputation for the quality of degrees

- Ease of gaining an entry visa
- High numbers of international students on some programmes

Types of institution

With 13 institutions in the top 200 of the rankings, six of which are in the top 50, Australian universities have a deserved reputation for high international quality. Australia's education system benefits from a very simple and open series of qualifications, encapsulated in the Australian Qualifications Framework (AQF). This structure enables students of all types to move from one institution to another, even though they may be of very different types.

There are 41 universities, 38 of which are publicly funded by the Australian Government and three private, located over the entire country. The highest concentration of universities is in New South Wales, in the south east of Australia, Victoria, in the south, and Queensland, in the north east. The leading set of universities in Australia is known as the Group of Eight and covers the major research institutions of the University of Adelaide, Australian National University, University of Melbourne, Monash University, University of New South Wales, University of Queensland, University of Sydney and the University of Western Australia.

All universities offer Bachelors, Masters and research programmes. Like all qualifications governed by the AQF, the Bachelors qualification throughout the country subscribes to defined learning outcomes and overall structure, ensuring that students are aware of exactly what their programme should consist of and result in.

Additionally, government-funded technical and further education institutions (TAFE) offer more vocationally orientated courses intended for those with more specific hands-on career goals. These institutions offer a range of qualifications from certificates, diplomas to advanced diplomas, all of which can act as alternatives ways to access degree level education. These qualifications vary in length, but tend to last between one and two years.

There is certainly a distinctive academic style in Australian institutions, where interaction with academic members of staff and fellow students is encouraged

Experience
Excellence

e University of Newcastle is a
ogressive, comprehensive university
th an international focus and
esearch reputation which
ecognised globally.

r student population is just under 26,000,
luding some 4,000 international students
m more than 80 countries studying both on
d off-shore in business, engineering, medicine,
rsing, science, teaching and technology.

e achievements of our graduates demonstrate
e professional relevance of our degrees. When you
oose to study at the University of Newcastle, you
e choosing a university that demands high standards,
suring that your degree is respected and valued
oughout the world.

e University of Newcastle is ranked in the top:

10 research universities in Australia

100 Asian Pacific universities

200 universities in the world

st importantly, our students are our
mber one priority. You will become part
a community that provides educational
port and an overall memorable experience.

University of Newcastle is the perfect
ce in which to grow academically,
fessionally and personally.

it our website for more information:
w.international.newcastle.edu.au

COS Provider Code No. 00109J

The UNIVERSITY
of NEWCASTLE
AUSTRALIA

as an important part of the learning process. Like the UK system, most degree programmes are based around lectures for basic instruction with smaller, follow-up classes to tackle certain themes or issues. Each course will have a set number of texts to review and term papers to submit as part of your assessment. Students are encouraged to work around their lecture subjects and develop close working relationships with other students and academic staff, where relevant.

Quality and recognition of qualifications

Australian undergraduate qualifications are regarded as being amongst the leaders in the world. A robust system of quality control ensures that degrees and other qualifications all reach minimum standards that are equal to international systems of quality assurance. As with other countries, the quality and recognition of qualifications from Australia forms one of the key reasons why so many international students choose to study in the country.

Unlike most other countries, Australian quality assurance is enacted through parliamentary legislation and includes four key measures: establishment of a university only through state or federal act, the AQF; the Educational Services for Overseas Students (ESOS) Act, which guarantees basic consumer rights to international studies following Australian qualifications; and the Australian Universities Quality Assurance (AUQA), an independent organisation that audits universities every five years.

Fees, finance and cost of living

Australia offers excellent value for money in terms of both the cost of tuition and living. Tuition fees are set by individual universities and vary by faculty and individual programme. On average, fees vary from AUD$14,000 per year for an arts degree at a smaller university to AUD$50,000 per year for a medicine degree at one of the country's most prestigious institutions. However, degree programmes in the most popular fields for international students, such as business, law and engineering, tend to range between AUD$18,000 and AUD$25,000 per year.

Though there are regional variations and differences between certain cities, the cost of living in Australia is lower than in countries such as the UK and the USA. On average you will require approximately AUD$12,000 per year to pay for your books, accommodation, food, utility bills and entertainment.

Scholarships

Similar to the situation in the UK: very few scholarships are offered at the undergraduate level to international students. Possible sources for this kind of funding are the Australian Government, whose awards are often administered by IDP Education Australia, individual universities and private organisations. Those

THE TIMES, they are a'changing

Excellence is being re-defined at Australia's five-star university

★★★★★ Positive graduate outcomes
★★★★★ Getting a job
★★★★★ Graduate starting salary
★★★★★ Educational experience: overall satisfaction
★★★★★ Educational experience: generic skills
★★★★ Educational experience: overall experience
★★★★ Staff qualifications

ngs from the 2007 Australian Good Universities Guide.

ww.uow.edu.au

iversity of Wollongong

that are available tend to be highly competitive and therefore difficult to obtain. Details are available online at **http://students.idp.com/english/study/article33.asp** and the websites of individual universities.

Entry requirements

All Australian institutions set their own entry requirements but for most university programmes 12 years of education is the minimum standard required. Additionally, if your education has not been conducted in English then you will also need to submit a recognised language qualification, the level of which will be set by the institution you are interested in. For those without appropriate qualifications, bridging qualifications are also offered by Australian institutions to enable students to qualify for degree level programmes.

Applications at the undergraduate level for Australian institutions are made either direct to the institution in question or via the Universities Admissions Centre (UAC), the latter representing 16 universities throughout the country. Details of the application process through UAC are available at **www.uac.edu.au**.

Living and working

Australia is regarded as one of the most welcoming and friendly places in which to live, work and study in the world today. It is a country that has distinct seasons, magnificent natural scenery, beautiful and well-planned cities and a diverse population. From the cultural centres of Sydney and Melbourne to the coastal areas and rainforests of Queensland and the preserved wilderness of Tasmania, visitors enjoy many different aspects of life in Australia.

Life in Australia tends to be very informal and is built on a very tolerant view of the world. A quarter of Australia's 20 million population was born overseas and the country boasts a varied ethnic mix. Immigration has been central to the development of modern Australia and the resulting diversity, often concentrated in the urban areas, stands as a contrast to the ancient and indigenous culture.

The country is very large and distances between major urban centres can be very great indeed. Travel is often best undertaken by airplane, though long distance bus and rail routes can often be cheaper. Within individual states and cities, a range of transport options are available, the costs of which are very reasonable and often even more economical with a student discount.

Medical care is not free in Australia. All students are expected to maintain an Overseas Student Health Cover (OSHC), an insurance policy that allows them to claim back the cost of their medical treatment from your health fund. Many academic institutions have medical care on campus or at least can recommend a local doctor or hospital.

As a full-time international student you are permitted to work a maximum of 20 hours a week during term time and full time in vacations. Before applying for work, however, you will need to have applied and obtained a work permit at the local Department of Immigration, Multicultural & Indigenous Affairs (DIMIA) office. Students are encouraged to seek employment in a field that is relevant or at least complimentary to their field of study, though in reality many seek casual employment in the popular entertainment, catering and retails sectors.

Student life

At every level of education in Australia you will find a welcoming and supporting student infrastructure to make your period of study as fulfilling as possible. Sports, social, cultural and academic clubs are all organised on or near to campus and provide an excellent way to meet other students and get to know a little more about the Australian way of life. As with other countries, these clubs tend to be organised and managed by the institution's students' union which subsidises a great number of student activities.

Social life in Australian institutions takes many forms and is often made more dynamic by the friendly and open manner with which many Australians welcome visitors. As a student you will benefit from discounts at restaurants, cinemas, pubs and clubs leaving you with a choice of things to do throughout the year. Additionally, should you need it, support is on hand from both academic and personal advisers to ensure that your student life is as trouble free as possible.

Study in Canada

Things to consider

+ Good choice of institutions and programmes
+ Reasonable tuition and living fees
+ Opportunities to stay after graduating
+ Well-regarded quality of education

- Smaller number of world-famous universities
- Differences in the structure of degree programmes between the provinces

Types of institution

Seven of Canada's 89 universities appear in the top 200 of the rankings, demonstrating the good level of quality and reputation in the country's higher education system. At present the majority of Canada's institutions are publicly funded and are located across ten provinces. Additionally, Canada boasts a range of other post-secondary school education institutions, known as colleges, university colleges, institutes of technology and advanced learning, community colleges and colleges of applied arts and technology. Many of these institutions are able to grant degree level qualifications, though many of the community colleges offer diplomas, certificates and associate degrees.

Canada's leading universities are known as the Group of Thirteen. These institutions are amongst the most research active in the country and specialise in offering joint research programmes. The member institutions are the Universities of Alberta, British Columbia, Calgary, Dalhousie, Laval, McGill, McMaster, Montréal, Ottawa, Queen's, Toronto, Waterloo and Western Ontario. A range of other Canadian universities are equally well known and offer taught and research programmes across a broad range of academic subject areas.

There are over 200 universities and colleges that are currently permitted to grant undergraduate degrees in Canada. The majority of these programmes are structured around three or four years of teaching, depending on the province and whether the degree is general or specialised. Honours degrees – or a baccalaureate programme – indicate a higher level of academic achievement within the Canadian system, concentrating in the major subject area. At some universities, the honours degree stream may take an additional year to complete. There are, however, small differences between institutions and provinces within the Canadian post-secondary school education system and so each individual university is the best source of information for exact specifications and requirements.

Like many other systems of higher education, the teaching and learning experience at a Canadian university is centred on a blend of teaching methods. Large lectures are common in the early stages of an undergraduate degree, with as many as 500 students in some of the common, core subjects. However, as the programme becomes more specialised or you enter your senior years, the lectures invariably get smaller. As Canadian universities offer a range of core components, students are often able to have a great deal of flexibility in their choice of subjects and so can design their own timetable to suit their tastes. Smaller classes follow up the larger lectures and enable a student to develop their own ideas based on the work undertaken outside of class.

Because most Canadian universities follow a semesterised system, there are three sessions – fall, winter/spring and summer – the latter being optional for many students. Individual courses making up a programme can last one semester or the entire academic year, the level of credit earned being adjusted accordingly. Assessment is based on a combination of mid-term examinations, term papers and class presentations.

Quality and recognition of qualifications

As one of the largest systems of higher education in the world, Canada has an extremely robust quality assurance and accreditation process ensuring that degree level studies are recognised internationally. Most Canadian institutions subscribe to the Association of Universities and Colleges of Canada principles of institutional quality assurance. Adherence to these principles is renewed every five years. Further details are available at **www.aucc.ca/qa/principles/index_e.html**.

Within the Canadian structure, universities have to also be in compliance with provincial or regional authorities for quality assurance, thus creating a double guarantee for students. All institutions and programmes subscribe to a regular cycle of reviews by the appropriate authority. These tend to be peer led and involve an element of self-evaluation and external review by subject experts, the results of which are made public for the sake of transparency.

Fees, finance and cost of living

Tuition fees are set by each individual institution and vary between private and public institutions and also by subject areas. Undergraduate programmes range from CA$11,000 to CA$19,000 per year depending on what and where you choose to study.

As in the USA, Canada has a moderate cost of living, allowing students to stretch their budgets as far as possible. Accommodation is very often provided at a reasonable cost by universities in at least the first year of your programme and in subsequent years many students seek private housing off-campus. Costs depend on the part of the country you are studying in but students are able to live reasonably well on between CA$8,500 and CA$10,500 a year.

Scholarships

Scholarships are available to offset some of the costs of studying in Canada. The best source of funds tends to be individual universities and colleges, many of whom offer a range of different scholarships types that cover tuition costs or living expenses and sometimes both. Many awards are based solely on academic merit and therefore financial aid is not taken into account through the application process.

The Canadian Government also offers a range of awards for undergraduate students as do a large number of individual universities. A free service coordinates most scholarships and is available at **www.scholarshipscanada.com**. A number of scholarships that offer funds to cover tuition fees and living expenses are administered by the Association of Universities and Colleges of Canada, details of which can be found at **www.aucc.ca/scholarships/open_e.html**.

Entry requirements

Canadian universities have long enjoyed educating students from all over the world and are therefore very familiar with a range of high school qualifications. The minimum entry requirements are those that lead to university entrance in your own country, though most students will have completed 12 years of formal school education before their undergraduate degree. Students apply directly to the university in which they are interested for admission, using the institutions application materials, most of which are to be found online.

Each individual university sets its entry standards and these tend to vary according to the subject you are applying for. If you have not been educated in English then you will be expected to demonstrate your language ability through either an IELTS or TOEFL result. All Canadian institutions operate deadlines unique to their own requirements, but most undergraduate applications should be submitted between January and March in the year when you wish to commence your studies.

Living and working

Put simply, Canada is a vast country that offers international students a vast array of possibilities during their period of study. From the multicultural, world cities of Vancouver and Toronto to the smaller cities of Montréal and Ottawa, Canada boasts a proud and unique history that blends both British and French cultures — the country is officially bilingual — with significant minorities from Germany, Holland, Greece, Poland, China, Ireland and the Ukraine.

Transport links are excellent, though the journey between some cities can take a surprising length of time. The size of the country is something that few visitors ever quite understand, but this sense of scale and openness is an important facet in Canadian life and character. There are six time zones in the country and overall Canada is the same size as the entire continent of Europe! The outdoor life is something that attracts many international students, with unparalleled opportunities for skiing and camping throughout the country.

As an international student you are allowed to work in Canada, though you must first obtain a social insurance number before seeking employment. Full-time students are permitted to work on campus without a work permit if they are enrolled at an appropriately recognised institution. Off-campus work is also available, to a maximum of 20 hours per week in term time and full time in vacations, if certain requirements are fulfilled. These include being a full-time student for six of the preceding 12 months, having a good academic record and paying the work permit application fee.

Access to medical care is dependent on the province that you are studying in. Alberta, British Columbia and Saskatchewan cover international students under their provincial healthcare plans. All other provinces require students to make their own arrangements and have sufficient private healthcare cover for the length of their studies.

Student life

Student life tends to be centred on events and clubs organised by on-campus groups in Canada, though the social scene in towns and cities around the country is equally inviting. Most students spend between 15 and 20 hours a week in formal classes, allowing a lot of free time for other activities. Larger universities organise many activities for their students and encourage active participation in the life of the university community.

Student societies and campus groups offer a myriad of possibilities for the new student and it is not uncommon to be faced with a choice of 200 different associations to become involved with. Sports, academic, cultural, religious and the purely social clubs are all available on-campus and make life rich with possibilities.

Study in France

Things to consider

+ Large number of highly reputable universities
+ Many government grants for international students
+ Many bilingual French – English language-based Masters
+ Reasonable employment opportunities for students
+ Moderate tuition fees

- Most undergraduate courses in French only
- Moderate acceptance rate for international students
- Difficult post-study visa situation for employment
- Many private colleges of dubious quality

France is one of the world's leading destinations for foreign students: more than 245,000 choose France every year. As Juliette Linares of EduFrance points out, France has many attractions for foreign students: "France is one of the world's top tourist venues, renowned for its art and culture. France is a first-class centre for scientific and technological innovation, in such fields as aerospace, transportation, electronics, telecommunications, chemistry, biotechnology and health."

Types of institution

The traditionally high quality of French degrees is rooted in a network of internationally renowned research centres and institutions of higher education, of which there are more than 3,000, including 87 universities, 240 engineering schools and 230 business schools, plus 2,000 other establishments devoted to such fields as art, fashion, design, architecture and paramedical training.

The Universities. France's 87 public universities are spread throughout the country, from the Sorbonne in Paris (founded in 1179) to the high-tech campus of Nice-Sophia-Antipolis, and cover the entire range of academic disciplines. Every level is represented in the awarding of national diplomas, including the Licence, Master's degree and Doctorat (PhD).

Research activities are an integral part of the universities: 315 doctoral schools train 4,000 doctoral candidates in connection with more than 1,200 research laboratories (affiliated to both the universities and research organizations). French doctoral schools have always been very open to international students. The university system also stays in step with today's world, offering technological specialisations and professional degrees, including:

- University engineering diplomas
- Professional qualification training via the Institutes Universitaires de Technologie (IUT) (a 2-year studies programme after the baccalaureat), offering more than 25 specialties
- A complete professional curriculum
- Management training through the Instituts d'Administration des Entreprises (IAE)
- Political science and economics degrees through the Instituts d'Études Politiques (IEP)
- Journalism and communications, with the Institut Français de Presse (IFP) and the École des hautes études en sciences de l'information et de la communication (CELSA) or the Centre de formation des Journalistes (CCFJ)

Studies of medicine, pharmacology and dentistry are connected with the universities in partnership with university hospitals and have their own organization and courses of study.

The Grandes Écoles. The Grandes Écoles are uniquely French institutions. Created in the early 19th century in parallel to the university system, they are extremely selective and offer education at a very high standard. Students are recruited either just after the baccalaureat, or at various levels depending on their academic background. Once they get the Grande Ecole Diploma, they can pursue doctorate studies upon specific conditions. Grandes Écoles offer diplomas at the baccalaureat plus five years level, Master's degrees. Graduates can follow up this degree with a specialisation, such as a specialised engineering degree or a Master of Business Administration (MBA). There are also roughly 240 engineering schools, which share common characteristics; this guarantees the quality of the engineering degree, which is at Masters level and covers all areas of engineering science. Grandes Écoles also exist for business and management; the business schools (about 230 of them) offer specialisations and training adapted to the changing economic environment and new management practices. Instruction is often structured around internships and international exchanges.

Specialised Schools. So-called specialised schools offer higher-level training in specific areas such as art, design, fashion, tourism, paramedical services, social services, and so on. There are three types of art schools: the Écoles nationales supérieures d'art (Grandes Écoles for art), which offer a national diploma after four or five years of study; the schools for applied art, which are supervised by the Ministry of National Education; and the schools of fine art by the Ministry of Culture, offering diplomas after three or five years of study. All have selective admission policies. Additionally, there are 20 architecture schools, overseen by the Ministry of Culture, offering the DPLG (Diplôme Par Le Gouvernement) architectural diploma, the only qualification in the field recognised for those working as architects in France. Studies last for six years in three cycles of two years each.

Fees, finance and cost of living

As mentioned previously, international students pay the same fees as domestic students. In national universities, the state pays a very large part of each student's study expenses (about 10,000 per year), keeping admission fees relatively low.

As with all EU countries, since the introduction of the Euro the costs of basic items like food and rent have risen significantly. Cost of living indices suggest that Paris is about 15 per cent less expensive than London. Other French cities are significantly less expensive than Paris. The availability of student accommodation is generally very high, though the quality tends to be somewhat shabby on most campuses – offering plenty of opportunity to appreciate the artistic merits of graffiti.

Entry requirements and admissions procedures

No distinction is made in France between French and foreign students: the entrance requirements and admission fees are the same, and the degrees are identical.

French higher education is based on a common architecture (LMD) – recognised at the European level — that counts the number of years of validated study following the baccalaureat (French secondary school matriculation examination). The table below outlines the structure of the French system. As long as he or she meets the entrance requirements, any foreign student in an institution of higher education in his or her home country may request admission to a comparable French institution.

+9 years	• Diplôme d'État de docteur en Médecine	**DOCTORAT**
+8 years	• Doctorat	
+6 years	• Diplôme d'État de docteur en Chirurgie dentaire	
	• Diplôme d'État de docteur en Pharmacie	
+5 years	• Master recherche - Diplôme d'Études Approfondies (DEA)	**MASTER**
300 ECTS	• Master professionnel - Diplôme d'Études Supérieures Spécialisées (DESS)	
	• Diplôme d'ingénieur	
	• Diplômes des Écoles de Commerce et de Gestion	
+4 years	• Maitrise	
+ 3 years	• Licence	**LICENCE**
180 ECTS	• Licence professionnelle	
+2 years	• Diplôme d'Études Universitaires Générales (DEUG)	
	• Diplôme Universitaire de Technologie (DUT)	
	• Brevet de Technicien Supérieur (BTS)	
	• Diplôme d'Études Universitaires Scientifiques et Techniques (DEUST)	

End of secondary studies + baccalaureat = admission to higher education system

The "N+i" Network. Designed for students already having a Bachelors degree in their own country, it brings together 60 Grandes Écoles and engineering training programmes and delivers, after two years, the national engineering diploma (Masters degree).

N+i covers virtually all engineering fields. For more information, visit **www. nplusi.com**. The advantages of this shared network are numerous:

- a single online registration and common application deadline
- shared selection of students with collective access to the student's file and common selection committee meetings
- a shared semester of training in language and study methods for all students enrolled.

Living and working

For food and sports aficionados, France is a wonderful place to live and work. It is a racy, sexy country which embraces modernism while retaining a strong sense of history and culture. Young people are allowed to be vocal and opinionated. For international students willing to learn the language, this can be a great experience.

Like all big cities, Paris can be a bit daunting for people, especially if they do not speak the language. It will take time to get to know local people and to break out of the international student community. Many campuses are also quite rural in their settings, which can also result in a sense of isolation. For those willing to embrace the culture, it can be a life changing experience, which is why many foreign students choose to settle in France after their studies, work permits allowing.

Unlike the UK, though, there is no easy route to working visas after a course has finished. Internships are generally available, but with 20 per cent youth unemployment, there is a great deal of local competition for graduate jobs. It is not wise to be reliant on a career in France to help pay for studies.

Student life

Sports facilities at most French universities are excellent. The French government has invested heavily in providing excellent track, field and stadia for sports in all except the inner city universities.

Student services tend not to differentiate between local and foreign students and with many students living at home, these services can be limited in scope. Generally international students form their own groups. Political activism is common on French campuses, providing an interesting, if opinionated network. Cinema and cultural networks are also very common — great for lovers of art and theatre.

Study in Germany

Things to consider
+   No or low tuition fees
+   Excellent academic reputation
+   Familiarity of international students

−   Ease of admission
−   Lack of English language taught programmes

Types of institution

With more than 300 institutions of higher education throughout the country, Germany offers one of the largest university systems in Europe. Ten German universities appear in the top 200 rankings, underlining the quality of both teaching and research in these institutions. German universities are well regarded internationally and over the centuries they have been responsible for great discoveries across the entire range of academic disciplines.

There are seven main types of institutions in Germany, all offering different types of higher education. The two main categories are universities and universities of applied sciences (Fachhochschule). Universities offer programmes where research and study are very closely aligned, with the result that graduates have a firm grasp of the theoretical nature of the subject they have studied. Universities of applied sciences offer students the opportunity to combine a basic level of academic knowledge with a more practical application relevant to the work environment. Because these institutions are orientated towards the development of students for a range of careers, members of teaching staff tend to be experienced professionals able to guide the curriculum to support their students in meeting their career goals.

Other categories of institution include art and music colleges, Church-sponsored universities, vocational universities in certain German states and private colleges. The latter institutions are currently very popular in the German system, though not all of them are officially recognised. About 50 recognised colleges currently exist and offer a range of qualifications, including degree level study, for those students willing to pay their tuition fees.

German universities offer different types of degrees, many of which are unique to the German system. The "Diplom", "Magister Artium" and "Staatsexamen" all represent qualifications that are currently available in many subject areas. Most degrees should be completed in four years, or eight semesters, though the availability of courses and the volume of work often result in degrees taking a much longer period of time. However, in line with the Bologna Declaration reforms, the German system of degrees is being overhauled so that Bachelors programmes last three and four years and Masters degree a further one or two years. This process has already resulted in more than 2,000 Bachelors programmes being offered in 2006.

German university programmes offer two strands of education — one general, the other specialised. General education offers students the opportunity to gain essential analytical and scientific skills relevant to their chosen area of study. On completion of an intermediate examination, students then move on to a period of study that is much more focused on their particular subject, developing an in-depth knowledge and understanding of their specialisation.

Like other systems of European education, German universities feature a blend of teaching methods that includes lectures, classes and seminars. Much of the work involved in attaining a German degree occurs outside of the classroom, with self-directed study, background reading and the preparation of assignments and class material contributing to a successful study experience. Tutorials and seminars are a student's opportunity to present their own ideas and tackle particular problems or discussions.

Quality and recognition of qualifications

German qualifications at all levels are regarded as being of the highest quality, based on a system of education that blends thorough theoretical knowledge with cutting-edge research, informed by contemporary technology and discoveries. The need for quality assurance amongst German qualifications is well recognised and is the ultimate responsibility of the Standing Conference of Ministers for Cultural Affairs (KMK), which has now implemented a number of measures to ensure adherence to agreed quality standards.

An Accreditation Council now implements standard procedures for all institutions of higher education that wish to have government recognition and uses additional agencies to support and enforce this process. Additionally, with many German universities moving towards the Bologna system, quality standards that match with the rest of Europe ensure that German degree programmes are internationally recognised.

Fees, finance and cost of living

One of the major attractions of studying in Germany is the almost universal support of all students by the state governments, meaning that there are no or very low tuition fees for international students. Though there are currently plans to introduce annual fees of 1,000, it is likely that the cost of tuition will continue to remain very low in the years to come.

In common with many European destinations, the cost of living in Germany is relatively high, though students are able to live economically on a budget of between 600 and 800 a month. Student discounts reduce the cost associated with many things such as train travel, museum entry and some clubs and bars.

Scholarships

Because tuition fees are not levied in most cases, the need for financial aid and scholarships is greatly reduced. However, a range of awards exist that support students' living and study expenses in Germany. Many of these awards are offered by individual German states and are specific to the country of origin of the student applying for the award. A comprehensive database that covers all German awards and is administered by the DAAD is available at **www.daad. de/deutschland/foerderung/stipendiendatenbank/00462.en.html**.

Entry requirements

A major advantage of applying to study at a German university is that the application procedure is relatively straightforward. The minimum requirement is for students to have completed their country's equivalent of the German Abitur, the local high school qualification, taken after 13 years of education. However, students may also be required to take an admission assessment test (Feststellungsprüfung) that varies according to the type of institution that they are interested in. Most often, this test requires the completion of a preparatory course known as a Studienkollegs that lasts as long as two semesters.

Students also have to demonstrate a knowledge of German if the programme of study they wish to pursue is taught in the local language. This is done through successful completion of the Deutsche Sprachprüfung für den Hochschulzugang (DSH) or the Test Deutsch als Fremdsprache (TestDaF) examinations. The latter examination can often be taken abroad at your local Goethe Institute. An increasing number of international programmes are now being offered at German institutions. These use English as the language of instruction and you do not need to demonstrate your ability in German.

Applications are generally made direct to the university you are interested in using forms supplied by either DAAD or the institution itself. However, more than 50 German universities now use the "uni-assist procedure", that allows international students to apply to a number of institutions with the same documents. Full details are available at **www.uni-assist.de**.

Living and working

As one of the largest countries in Europe, Germany offers something for everyone. With a vibrant culture and rich history, students find Germany to be a fascinating yet welcoming country in which to live and study. Though Germans have a reputation for being very serious and punctual, contemporary Germany is relaxed, open, welcoming to strangers, exciting and above all diverse. With large immigrant communities all over the country, culture and cuisine are now international yet proud of their strong German traditions.

The country itself is large, but excellent transport links — probably the best in all of Europe — allow trips of discovery whenever you have a spare weekend. From the mountains of the south, where cross-country skiing and trekking are popular, to the ports of the north, each state has a slightly different character and charm. Additionally, with its central location, Germany is a good base to explore the rest of Europe and has excellent air links to the rest of the world.

Though many people do speak English, knowledge of the German language is a definite advantage. Daily life will certainly be easier if you are comfortable with the basics of the language. The standard of healthcare is excellent in Germany and all international students are required to have public health insurance before they are permitted to register for their classes. This insurance covers all medical expenses and costs less than 50 a month. Students over the age of 30, however, are not eligible for this cover and must obtain private health insurance.

All students are allowed to work while they study in Germany without a work permit, though students from outside the EEA are limited to a fixed period of time of 90 days or 180 half-days throughout the year. Some local states may operate slightly different rules, but the local employment office will be able to offer the best advice. Students tend to be very popular employees in Germany, since employers are required to only pay a small element of their social welfare contributions for part-time workers.

Student life

Like other university systems, German universities offer a range of activities for their students. Sports and social clubs are commonplace and offer an excellent way to make friends and enjoy some of the local life. Additionally, many German university academic departments have a representative body that co-ordinates student activities and represents your interests, particularly regarding your academic life.

Though many German universities offer large campuses few have large halls of residence, so finding accommodation and a centre for your social life can be different than in other countries. There are, however, many attractions available to you, irrespective of the size of town or city you are studying in, all of which are open to you as a student. Bars and restaurants are very popular student destinations and the friendly nature of German social life makes for an exciting social scene.

Study in Japan

Things to consider

+ Excellent reputation for academic excellence throughout Asia
+ Large number of scholarships for international students
+ Excellent support from universities for international students

– High cost of tuition and living expenses
– Limited number of programmes taught in English
– Lack of global reputation for undergraduate degrees

Types of institution

Japan is the powerhouse of higher education in Asia, with 11 universities in the top 200 of the rankings and three in the top 100 — University of Tokyo (23rd), Kyoto University (32nd) and Osaka University (74th). Higher education is split into a number of clearly defined sections and students can enter any one of five types of institutions. These are Colleges of Technology, Professional Training Colleges (senmom gakko), Junior Colleges, Colleges and Universities and Graduate Schools. All of these institutions fall into a further three categories, depending on their administrative status, of national, local public and private.

There are over 700 universities in Japan, the majority of which are private. The 87 national and 73 local public universities derive the majority of their funding from the government and teach across the entire range of academic subjects at undergraduate and postgraduate levels. Junior colleges offer two-year diplomas, generally vocational in emphasis, where the education is centred on developing skills for the workplace. At present, few of these programmes are offered in English. Professional training colleges also provide for more vocational education, offering courses lasting anywhere between one and four years.

Undergraduate programmes at universities and colleges tend to take four years to complete across most subject areas. There are some six-year programmes in the fields of dentistry, medicine and veterinary science. Almost all instruction is conducted in Japanese and there are very few Bachelor degrees offered in English, though some short-term programmes are available. A searchable database is available at **www.jasso.go.jp/cgi-bin/user/univ_search.cgi**.

The style of instruction in most undergraduate programmes in the Japanese system is a split between formal lectures, laboratories (where relevant) and classes. Work is monitored through examinations and each course usually requires a number of class papers to be submitted every semester. Each student is assigned a tutor from the academic staff and international students are often also provided with a student tutor to enable them to adapt to the different learning culture.

Quality and recognition of qualifications

Though the Japanese Government has been deregulating higher education over the last ten years, the Ministry of Education retains the right to approve new institutions and major new academic programmes. An established list of criteria is used to judge the quality of individual programmes, including proposed curriculum, expected enrolments, staff/student ratio and facilities. This process ensures that Japanese higher education qualifications will conform to international standards and therefore be recognised outside of the country.

Since 2004 all public and private institutions are required to be accredited by a national organisation under the management of the Ministry of Education so that the quality of all programmes and institutions is assured. As the new accreditation system is only two years old, not all institutions have undergone a visit under the regime and it is likely to take a further four years before the entire higher education sector has been audited.

Fees, finance and cost of living

Japan is regarded as one of the most expensive countries in the world. The tuition fees for most institutions of higher education, however, are very competitively priced. Universities, language institutes, junior colleges and professional training colleges all have different fees as well as different levels of fee depending on the subject in question.

National universities charge in the region of YEN834,800 ($7,900) per year; local public universities YEN950,000 ($9,000) per year; private universities between YEN1,118,000 ($11,500) and YEN5,000,000 ($48,000) per year, depending on subject area. Junior colleges range between YEN580,000 ($5,700) and YEN1,300,000 ($12,500) per year, depending on whether an institution is national, local or private. In all cases the first year of a programme's tuition fee is approximately 30 per cent higher than in subsequent years, as there is an admission fee.

Living expenses vary according to where you choose to study. Kanto and Tokyo tend to be the most expensive cities in the country, though other cities are also quite costly. On average students spend YEN130,800 ($1,300) per month on living expenses, including all housing, study and entertainment costs. The majority of this expenditure goes towards accommodation costs, whether in university halls of residence or private apartments.

Scholarships

Scholarships are available for many of the different types of higher education institutions in Japan for international students, though they are less common in professional training colleges and language institutes. Scholarships are administered through the individual institutions where the application and selection of the award is administered.

The majority of these scholarships do not cover all expenses, rather they meet some or all of the tuition fee amount, plus an amount in respect of living costs. Students applying for these awards can either be resident in Japan or another country at the time of application, though they should ensure that they meet all other requirements at the point of application.

Japanese Government or Monbukagakusho Scholarships provide for up to YEN135,000 ($1,500) a month for potential undergraduate students and are tenable for the entire period of study. Additionally funding is available from JASSO, local government, individual educational institutions, corporate bodies and private foundations.

Entry requirements

When applying for an undergraduate degree, students must have completed 12 years of education and demonstrate their ability to this level through a recognised high school qualification. Where students have completed only 11 years of schooling, university preparatory courses are offered by some institutions to help bridge the academic gap. For international students there is a further requirement that they are 18 years of age.

Each university has its own application procedure and requirements for supporting documentation. Generally an application form, a letter of reference, high school transcript and medical certificate will be required. Application schedules are announced in June for programmes beginning in April the following year, though some universities also announce a September or October admissions procedure. Not all universities accept direct applications from international students, though approximately 100 do. Full details are available at **www.jasso.go.jp**.

Students must also sit and pass an entrance examination for Japanese universities. The Examination for Japanese University Admission for International Students (EJU) is administered by the Japan Student Services Organisation (JASSO) and each university sets their own timetable for when this examination is offered. At present the exam is most commonly offered twice yearly in June and November. Additionally some universities require non-native Japanese applicants to complete the Japanese Language Proficiency Test before admission is granted.

Living and working
Living in Japan allows a student to experience one of the most modern, dynamic and individual cultures in the world today. Ancient traditions stand side-by-side with modern technology and architecture, making Japan a feast for all. As a country, Japan enjoys a varied geographical character with four distinct seasons, all integral to the development of local art and culture. High mountains, hot springs, modern metropolises and a varied coastline contribute to a fascinating country.

Culturally, there is no other country quite like Japan. Rich in festivals and folk art, contemporary cinema and traditional poetry, as well as deeply traditional ceremonies and unique sports, Japan also celebrates its distinctive cuisine as a central part of life. As an international student you will have the choice of living in university or private accommodation at the heart of such a culture, though close to 75 per cent of students live in the latter. However, because of both the cost and availability of housing in Japan, students can encounter some difficulty in finding a place to live. University service centres and private accommodation bureaux can help in most cases.

International students are free to work part-time once they have formal permission from their university and the local immigration bureau; without the necessary documentation you are likely to be deported. You are allowed to work a maximum of 28 hours per week during term-time and a maximum of eight hours a day in vacations, though there are certain restrictions on the kinds of work

Nagoya University

A Liberal and creative atmosphere that cultivated a Nobel Laureate

A leading national university located in the heart of Japan

oyoda Auditorium, donated by Toyota Motor Corporation

Research Excellence

- Globally renowned award-winning faculty including a Nobel Laureate, and winners of the Fields Medal, the King Faisal International Prize, and other awards
- Recipient of one of the largest numbers of "the 21st Century Center of Excellence" research grants allocated by the Japanese government
- Highly ranked in ISI Essential Science Indicators
- Active in research collaborations, especially with Asian countries

Quality in Education

- Nine schools and 13 graduate schools covering a wide range of disciplines, such as medicine, natural science, liberal arts, social science, engineering
- 10,000 undergraduate and 6,000 graduate students, 7% of whom are internationals
- Various study abroad/field study opportunities

Internationalization

- More than 200 overseas partner institutions
- Founder of the Academic Consortium 21 (AC21), consisting of institutional members from all over the world
- Professional services provided for international students and scholars
- More than 20 overseas liaison offices and research labs

International Affairs Division, Nagoya University
Furo-cho, Chikusa-ku, Nagoya 464-8601 JAPAN
+81-52-789-2044
intl@post.jimu.nagoya-u.ac.jp   http://www.nagoya-u.ac.jp/en/

you can engage in. Most students obtain employment through their university careers office or private agencies.

Healthcare is offered through the National Health Insurance system, which all students must enrol in. Payments are made monthly under the scheme and vary according to where you live, though students tend to pay a lower premium than others. Under the scheme, students pay only 30 per cent of their medical expenses for treatment covered by the insurance.

More international students are now considering staying in Japan after graduation to work. The procedure is similar to that undertaken by local students and requires a rigorous job search through your local careers office, applications, interviews, a testing phase and final confirmation. Once employment has been secured an international student can then apply for a change in their immigration status through the nearest immigration bureau. This process is normally very efficient and successful if the skills of the student and their residence record match that of the job in question.

Student life

Because of the nature of Japanese culture and society, student life can be very interesting and diverse. All institutions support their students through excellent facilities and the opportunities to meet other international and local students alike. However, student life can be daunting if there is a language barrier and so campus support networks, such as student organisations, can play a vital role in making you feel at home.

Much of your student social life will be enjoyed on campus, where many of the activities and services are subsidised. For a low annual fee, you will have access to sports, entertainment, social and arts facilities where you can meet other students on a more informal level. Some institutions offer classes in sports and languages, outside of the normal curriculum, if you have a particular skill you would like to improve.

Additionally, institutions often offer a cooperative society (CO-OP) on campus for students to buy essential supplies. A membership organisation, the CO-OP serves a similar role as a students' union in many other countries and allows you to use important services such as a travel agency, a housing association, a bookshop, food stores and restaurants.

Study in the Netherlands

Things to consider

+ Excellent value for money with moderate tuition fees
+ Unique problem-based learning tradition
+ Location in Europe
+ English language teaching

– Ease of gaining an entry visa
– Lack of knowledge of Dutch degrees internationally

Types of institution

The higher education system in the Netherlands consists of two distinct types of institution – universities (universiteiten) and universities of professional education (hogescholen); the former focus on research and teaching from an academic point of view, while the latter aims to prepare students more directly for the workplace. There are also a small number of International Education Institutes intended to provide specific programmes for international students. Most programmes of study are offered in English throughout the Netherlands, making it a very accessible system of education for all international students.

There are 200,000 students currently attending the 14 government-approved universities in the Netherlands, three of which specialise in engineering. All offer undergraduate and postgraduate programmes and are fully integrated with the Bologna system of qualifications and credit transfer. It is in these institutions where the majority of research is undertaken in the Netherlands across a full range of subjects, informing both the academic and the professional communities in the country. Of these institutions, 11 are in the top 200 rankings in 2006, making university education in the Netherlands one of the highest performing in the world today.

There are a further 42 government-approved universities of professional-education, offering career-orientated education to more than 350,000 students a year. These institutions offer a range of qualifications, most commonly in one of seven areas – agriculture, engineering and technology, economics and business administration, healthcare, fine and performing arts, education (teacher training) and social welfare. In addition to lectures and classes, students are expected to complete a period of work placement as part of their period of study. Eleven International Education Institutes offer advanced courses taught exclusively in English. These focus on development-related subjects taught in small groups comprising a range of nationalities.

Three-year Bachelors degrees are arranged around lectures and tutorials — and laboratories for the more technical degrees. Learning is encouraged through a mix of theoretical, conceptual and practical approaches, all of which seek to educate students to be able to think individually about and solve problems. Larger lectures are followed up with much smaller tutorial groups, led by an academic member of staff whom leads you through specific issues and discussions. A student's performance is measured at the end of each year, either by written or oral examination depending on the programme of study. The overall style of education in Dutch universities is known as problem-based learning and is regarded as one of the best approaches to higher education in the world today.

Quality and recognition of qualifications

Dutch higher education programmes have rightly secured a reputation for high quality and well-organised content. The Ministry of Education, Culture and Science has responsibility for ensuring that programmes meet the required international standards through a rigorous timetable of regulation, audit and accreditation. All Dutch programmes are compelled to publish the status of their accreditation, making it easy for students to determine the quality. In some cases it is possible for Dutch programmes to be accredited by another country's national accreditation organisation.

Degree level study has to be accredited under the 2002 Government Act, The Accreditation of Higher Education. All programmes are checked against an established list of criteria to ensure consistent standards. Because of this rigorous system, Dutch degree programmes are widely recognised around the world for their academic level and intellectual rigour.

Fees, finance and cost of living

Tuition fees at Dutch institutions are subsidised by the national government and so represent good value for money for the standard and quality of the education provision. At the undergraduate degree level, fees vary according to the subject with the more popular areas such as business, economics, law and management being more expensive than literature and history, with fees anywhere between 2,000 and 8,000 a year being common.

The cost of living in Holland is relatively expensive, though there are slight differences across the country. Many students live on between 700 and 900 a month throughout the year, with accommodation costs either in university or private residences accounting for between 300 and 450 of that budget. Student discounts and subsidised food costs at institutions can offset some of the expenses of being a student in the Netherlands.

Scholarships

There are few nationally organised undergraduate scholarships available for studying in the Netherlands, though a number of major schemes exist for postgraduate taught and research programmes. Some undergraduate scholarships exist for specific countries around the world and these tend to be administered by local Netherlands Education Support Offices. One way of locating scholarships in the Netherlands is by using the online search facility offered by Grantfinder at **www.grantfinder.nl**.

Some individual universities do offer scholarships to incoming international students, but these are organised, funded and awarded through the specific university.

Entry requirements

Entry requirements in the Netherlands tend to be dependent on three elements — your educational qualifications, your language skills and any specific requirements of the academic field of study you would like to pursue. As a minimum, a student will have to have the equivalent of a Dutch VWO Diploma, awarded after 13 years of education. In systems of education where only 12 years are provided for, bridging courses are available for those students wishing to study in a Dutch institution. As many programmes are available in English, you will not need to demonstrate any ability in the Dutch language, though you will be expected to show competence in English through an IELTS or TOEFL examination result. The procedure for applying to universities is straightforward. Each institution requires you to complete their application materials and submit your details before the appropriate deadlines in April or May in the year you would like to commence your period of study.

Living and working

With over 16 million citizens, the Netherlands is one of the most crowded countries in the world yet it retains a relaxed and easygoing nature that most students thoroughly enjoy. Located at the point where the cultures of Britain, France and Germany meet, the Netherlands is diverse and essentially multicultural. Because of the position of the country in Europe, the Netherlands is internationally open and this is often expressed in a willingness to accept new ideas and the famous Dutch aptitude for speaking many languages.

The Netherlands is often known best for its capital city, Amsterdam. With its famous canals and traditional architecture, Amsterdam offers something for everyone with the enormous Rijksmuseum, Anne Frank's house, diamond factories and even the Heineken brewery. But away from the capital, towns such as Leiden, Utrecht, Tilburg and Maastricht all show another side of Dutch life no less interesting and welcoming than the big city.

As a student in the Netherlands you will enjoy the compact nature of the country and excellent infrastructure and travel links. In cities and towns, many people use a bicycle to get around, though cars, buses and trams are also plentiful. For longer journeys trains, buses and planes provide reasonably priced fares all over the Netherlands and further afield. Again, because of its location, the Netherlands is an ideal base from which to explore the rest of Europe — by ferry to the UK, by plane to southern Europe, or bus or train to Belgium, France and Germany.

All international students are required to obtain health insurance before they arrive in the Netherlands and this is needed in order to obtain an entry visa for the country. If a student is under the age of 30, working part-time or staying longer than three years, then the situation regarding health cover alters. Full details are available from the institution you wish to study in.

Students from outside of the European Economic Area are allowed to work while they study, though they require a work permit to do so. Students have two options to pursue, either on a seasonal basis in June, July and August full-time, or part-time throughout the year, working no more than ten hours per week. Students must choose one working method. The best way of finding a job is through an employment agency or your institution.

Student life

Being a student in the Netherlands is a little different than in other countries. Most universities and other institutions do not offer a campus environment so student life is often mixed with the life of the surrounding town or city. However, student clubs and societies are still very important and popular as a way of meeting other students. Many institutions also offer well-equipped sports facilities where you can play the sport of your choice either competitively or socially.

Student discounts allow you to travel cheaply and receive reduced admissions at museums and art galleries throughout the country. These schemes are both local to your institution and nationally available, offsetting some of your costs everywhere you go.

Social life in the Netherlands can be very varied and includes the theatre and cinema, in addition to cafés, clubs and bars. Many students enjoy the liberal atmosphere of the Netherlands and most Dutch towns offer a mix of restaurants and a range of different foods, a legacy of the Netherlands being such an international country.

Study in the Nordic countries
Denmark, Finland, Iceland, Norway and Sweden

Things to consider

+ Free or low cost tuition
+ High academic quality, strictly enforced and maintained
+ Active social and cultural life

- High cost of living
- Limited numbers of programmes taught in English in some of the countries
- Some difficulty with residence permits

Types of institution

Given the size of the respective populations and the limited number of universities in each of the five countries, the Nordic region performs remarkably well in the top 200 rankings. Nine universities appear in the top 200, with the University of Copenhagen (Denmark) the region's best performing institution, listed at 54. Four institutions from Sweden, three from Denmark, one from each of Finland and Norway all reach the top 200, underlining both the quality of teaching and research in the respective country systems.

The higher education systems in all five Nordic countries are organised around a very similar structure and therefore have much in common. All of the systems have adopted the Bologna structure and therefore offer three or four year Bachelors degrees and one or two years Masters programmes. The five systems are all largely state dominated, offering public institutions with little or no private sector available. Universities tend to offer degree level teaching while university colleges and vocational colleges offer diplomas and certificates in the more vocational subject areas.

The smallest of the five systems is that of Iceland, where ten institutions of higher education offer degree and vocational education programmes to 12,000 students, mostly in Icelandic. The other four countries offer much larger systems of higher education, where universities and colleges teach larger numbers of students from all over the world in either English or the local language. Norway has the most private investment in higher education, with 29 institutions holding either programme or institutional accreditation from the government. Finland boasts the largest number of English language programmes in Europe taught outside of the UK, within their parallel binary system of universities (offering more academic programmes) and polytechnics (where the more vocational and technical subjects are taught). Sweden and Denmark offer diverse systems of higher education, where vocational and academic programmes are both readily available.

The teaching style in all of the Nordic countries is dominated by the Northern European approach of larger lectures followed up by smaller classes. What is taught in the classroom or the laboratory is just the tip of the iceberg in the educational process and much of the emphasis of the Nordic system is on the individual student working alone or in small groups reading around the subjects at hand and developing their own approach to and opinion on the issues. Methods of assessment vary, but continuing written work through the course of the academic year augments traditional semester and yearly examinations.

Quality and recognition of qualifications

All five systems of the Nordic countries offer fully accredited programmes that subscribe to international standards in the quality assessment of higher education. Each of the five countries operates a fully autonomous quality assurance agency that visits individual universities and colleges to ensure the maintenance of agreed standards. Sweden's National Agency of Higher Education evaluates all courses offered by universities and university colleges every six years using a number of assessment methods, including a student satisfaction survey of more than 15,000 currently enrolled students. Failure to meet the required standards results in the power to award qualifications being removed from the institution in question.

In Finland, all institutions offer a Diploma Supplement according to the Bologna reforms, thus making the contents of the qualifications transportable and immediately recognisable throughout the EU and further afield. In Iceland, the Ministry of Education, Science and Culture ensures the quality of all institutions and their programmes under their direction through regular and comprehensive visits based in institutions internally assessing themselves.

The qualifications offered from Denmark and Norway institutions are similarly strictly quality controlled by national agencies through a combination of self-assessment and external visits. The resulting standards are extremely high and recognised the world over, irrespective of the individual subject offered.

Fees, finance and cost of living

One of the great advantages of higher education in the Nordic countries is that tuition fees are either very low or non-existent. At present only Denmark charges market-rate tuition fees and even these are on the more modest scale. Each individual university or college may charge a small administrative fee for every semester, but these amounts are nothing like the tuition fees of other European countries.

However, almost without exception, the cost of living in all of the five countries making up the Nordic region is very high, though students have plenty of methods to reduce the costs as much as possible. University or private accommodation tend to be the largest single expenditure, though other aspects of living can be as cheap as any other European country. Socialising and eating out can still be accommodated even on the tightest budget with some careful planning, as can travel and playing sports.

Scholarships

Scholarships are available for a number of the Nordic countries. Denmark, for example, offers a number of government schemes and additionally supports a range of EU mobility programmes. Norway, similarly administers a range of awards and scholarships through the Norwegian Centre for International Cooperation in Higher Education (SIU). A quota scheme also exists for 1,100 students every year from developing countries, Eastern Europe and Central Asia. Sweden and Iceland both offer scholarships to cover living costs through their national agencies and in all countries, individual universities and colleges may also offer specific awards for either certain countries or academic subject areas and details can be found at individual institution's websites.

Entry requirements

The five Nordic countries share a very similar structure in their education systems and therefore have a certain amount of common entry requirements. At the first degree level, secondary school education consisting of a minimum of 12 years of education is the lowest requirement needed for successful applications. In the case of Denmark, Finland and Norway it is more common to award a high school diploma after 13 years of education and so this should be considered the minimum requirement for university entry. Where your qualification is not sufficient to meet the required entry levels it may be possible for you to complete a year's university preparatory course first.

Each individual university in each of the five country systems establishes its own application process and deadlines exist for almost all programmes. Application materials are available between six and nine months ahead of registration and it is increasingly popular to apply online to the institution you are interested in.

Living and working

Each of the five Nordic countries has very different characteristics and unique aspects to offer the student wishing to live in one of them. Sweden is a particularly diverse country that promotes equality amongst both the sexes and the different ethnic groups that make up the country, while Finland and Iceland offer completely unique natural environments that boast lakes, glaciers and hot geysers amongst their wonderful natural attractions. Denmark is known for the equally unique aspect of the Danish character, hygge: the quality many Danes enjoy of socialising with friends or family over a drink or around a table, dining and laughing. Norway, on the other hand, is famous for its crystal clear fjords and its mountains.

All of the five countries have, however, many things in common. The weather is something that the populations of each of the countries talk about. Expect long hard winters, with little and sometimes no light and plenty of snow; and then beautiful summers, with long, light filled days where people try to spend as much time as possible outside. Each of the countries offers some of the most vibrant capital cities to be found anywhere in the world — Copenhagen (Denmark), Helsinki (Finland), Reykjavik (Iceland), Oslo (Norway) and Stockholm (Sweden) — with eclectic cultural and social scenes, known for their contemporary fashion, art and design.

Each of the countries has an excellent transport network that allows you to explore not only your place of study but also the other Nordic countries located close by. Trains, long distance buses and an increasing number of budget airlines cater for students through various discounts and a number of ferry companies enable you to enjoy very cheap travel between Finland and Sweden in particular.

Another element of life in the Nordic countries that is common to all is the excellent welfare state, offering care protection for all in society. As a student from the European Economic Area (EEA) you are covered for all medical care, including emergencies, by your own medical system. Other international students are covered by the local system in Denmark (after a period of six weeks), Finland (if you are a member of the students' union), Iceland (if your programme of study is full time), Norway and Sweden (if your programme of study is longer than a year in length).

As an international student you are permitted to work in all of the Nordic countries, though each of the five have specific conditions that need to be satisfied in order for you to work legally. In most cases you are allowed to work 20 hours in term time and full time during the vacation periods, subject to the status of your study visa or residence permit.

Student life

Your social life as a student in the Nordic countries very much depends on where you are located. Universities and colleges in the big cities benefit from far more facilities than those in the more rural areas. Common to all institutions is the customary range of academic, social and sporting clubs organised on or near campus by students for their fellow students. Students' unions and guilds are primarily political organisations, but they also offer useful resources for students in terms of discounts and various kinds of advice. Other institutions often offer social committees that organise a range of activities for all students and their varied interests. University and college halls of residence also offer great platforms for student social life.

Coffee bars, cafés and bars are all common destinations for students living in the Nordic countries. It is common for evenings to start late and continue well into the following morning, with a variety of options on offer. One of the common factors between all of the five countries is an interest in the more social side of life, making strangers feel welcome in any way possible.

Study in Singapore

Things to consider

+ Increasing international reputation
+ Reasonably priced tuition fees
+ Ability to work after graduation
+ Links to Asia

– Lack of global visibility for Singaporean qualifications
– Vast array of private colleges with unclear reputations
– Limited numbers of students from all over the world

Types of institution

The Singaporean post-secondary school education scene is particularly dynamic. Three publicly funded universities exist, two of which are included in the top 100 of the rankings and attract many more applications from local as well as international students than there are places available. The National University of Singapore, Nanyang Technological University and Singapore Management University teach the entire range of academic areas and all offer undergraduate degree qualifications, in addition to postgraduate and research programmes. Singapore also has five polytechnics, offering two and three year diplomas in many different subject areas. These institutions tend to educate students in a more vocational way, developing skills relevant to the workplace.

Additionally, Singapore plays host to both an increasingly diverse private education scene and a growing number of offshore campuses. Private institutions, which are tightly regulated by the Singaporean Ministry of Education, offer undergraduate and diploma programmes that attract local and international students alike. A number of these institutions also offer qualifications with completely

A global university of excellence

Established in 1955, Nanyang Technological University (NTU) is a research-intensive tertiary institution in Singapore with strengths in science and technology. Our world-class standing is supported by international rankings.

- Strong international relationships and collaboration programmes are a hallmark of NTU.

- We prepare students for global leadership through a strong, multi-disciplinary and broad academic foundation.

- Our illustrious and entrepreneurial faculty has received international recognition and awards.

- Our cosmopolitan and vibrant environment nurtures talent, advocates self-discovery and hones leadership skills.

www.ntu.edu.sg

internationa curricula such as those for the Chartered Institute of Marketing and the Association of Chartered Certified Accountants. Moreover, others offer international undergraduate programmes from universities in countries such as Australia, Finland, New Zealand, the UK and the US.

Sixteen universities from Asia, Europe and the US have established significant interests in Singapore, including the opening of campuses, offering a range of programmes including those at the undergraduate level. Institutions such as the German Institute of Science and Technology offer internationalised curricula taught by local and international staff at a fraction of the cost if a student were to travel overseas for the same programme. A number of international programmes are also taught in Singapore through three overseas universities.

Most undergraduate programmes are taught through a mix of lectures and smaller seminars, with engineering, technology and science courses requiring additional laboratory classes. A student's workload is dependent on their course of study, but is generally high, as degree level study is demanding across all subject areas. In some cases, it is possible to take more than one subject for your degree. These programmes are known as double degree programmes (DPP) and are popular in the fields of business, economics, engineering and law.

Quality and recognition of qualifications

Though not all of Singapore's institutions are internationally known, the effect of having two universities in the top 100 rankings raises the profile of the entire higher education sector. The Ministry of Education directly accredits the three publicly funded universities in the country and ensures that teaching and research activities are all of an appropriate standard.

The increasing numbers of private education providers, including those which offer international partnerships, subscribe to an Education Excellent Framework. This scheme promotes excellence in academic affairs, through an accreditation programme, organisational issues and student welfare and protection. The Education Services Accreditation Council provides private education providers with guidelines to meet in these three areas and reviews each institution on a regular basis.

Additionally, the international universities teaching in Singapore generally meet the standards required of their own national systems of quality assurance, thus making their qualifications particularly well recognised around the world.

Fees, finance and cost of living

Individual institutions set tuition fees at the undergraduate level. Fees at the three local universities tend to vary by academic subject but generally vary between SIN$20,000 and SIN$24,000. Exceptional programmes, such as those in the medical field, are priced at a much higher level and students can expect to pay anything up to SIN$80,000 a year for tuition fees. Singapore's five polytechnics offer programmes at a lower fee rate for their diploma programmes, with annual costs of SIN$12,160.

Cost of living in Singapore is very reasonable. Though there are some variations in the costs of accommodation, depending on whether you live in university or polytechnic halls of residence or elsewhere, students should budget between SIN$750 and SIN$1,500 a month. This estimate would cover all costs including transport, entertainment, health insurance and books.

Scholarships

Though not strictly a form of financial aid, all national and international students are free to apply to the Singaporean Ministry of Education for a tuition grant once they have been admitted to their programme of choice. This scheme allows for a grant of between SIN$14,000 and SIN$16,000 for most programmes to be paid against tuition fees, thus reducing the amount considerably. For programmes such as medicine and music, the grant can be as much as SIN$65,500 a year. However, international students are required to sign a bond in order to obtain a tuition grant, committing them to working in Singapore for three years after the completion of their university or polytechnic programme.

Scholarships and bursaries are also available from either the Ministry of Education or individual universities. Such schemes include the ASEAN Undergraduate Scholarships that provide for tuition costs, SIN$3,500 annual living allowance and return travel between the scholar's country and Singapore, and the Singapore Technologies International Scholarships. Further details can be found at **www.moe.gov.sg**.

Entry requirements

Admission to both universities and polytechnics is dependent on individual programme requirements. At both the university and polytechnic levels, it is expected that a student should have completed at least 12 years of secondary education in his or her respective education system. As Singaporean institutions are used to receiving applications from international students, admissions staff are familiar with a range of high school or equivalent qualifications. For those wishing to study medicine or dentistry, an application requires grades to be presented rather than predicted, as is the case with many other subjects.

Depending on the programme you are interested in, application deadlines are either at the end of December in the year before you wish to commence your period of study, or at the end of February in the year of study. Applications are made directly to the institution, usually through their own online system with supporting documents sent separately. As with many countries, the more popular a programme is the more competition there is for admission.

Living and working

It would certainly be true to say that there is nowhere quite like Singapore. It is a small island state, covering an area of just over 600 square kilometres, yet boasts a population of four million people. Known as one of the great financial and trade centres of the world, Singapore has long attracted a variety of visitors and this leads to a fusion of races and cultures ideal for a unique student experience. Chinese, Malay, Indian and European cultures collide to form an exciting environment in almost every aspect.

With an excellent transport system, superb infrastructure and reputation for safety, Singapore is one of the world's favoured destinations. It offers a great variety of culinary, cultural and shopping experiences — enough to suit most tastes in an entire lifetime, let alone a period of study. From the world famous zoo to the tropical island of Sentosa, Singapore also offers an environment of natural diversity. It is also one of the most technologically advanced countries in the world today.

Singapore's location also makes it a travel hub. As a student you will have access to reduced travel costs that allow you to explore different countries in the region, including Australia, Cambodia, Indonesia, Malaysia and Thailand.

As a student you have access to both university and private accommodation. The former is regarded as the best option for international students as it provides a good introduction to the society and allows you to make friends very quickly and also tends to be the most economical. Those wishing to seek housing through private apartment rentals will find Singapore to be expensive. In terms of healthcare, international students are recommended to have medical insurance for the duration of their period of study.

Full-time students attending either polytechnic, university or other approved education institutions are free to seek part-time employment during their period of study. Students may work a maximum of 16 hours a week during term time and full time during the vacations. In some cases the immigration status of a student prevents them from legally seeking employment. The latest information is available at the Ministry of Manpower's website at **www.mom.gov.sg**.

After graduation, those students who have accepted the Ministry of Education's tuition grant to fund their period of studies will be required to work in Singapore for three years. Other graduates are also free to apply for employment in Singapore, though their success is dependent on their qualification and the type of employment that they are seeking.

Student life

Singapore is an exciting place to be a student, not only because of the quality of the institutions, but because of the rich cultural mix. All institutions support their international student population though an office most commonly called international student services. Through this office activities such as student orientations, cultural programmes and introductions to host families are made, all adding to your student experience.

Many different kinds of student activities outside of the classroom are encouraged and are organised both on- and off-campus. Sporting and social clubs make up the majority of student interest groups, though various clubs representing cultural and academic interests also exist. Facilities tend to be of the highest order in Singapore and students are free to use them for a small fee.

Since the end of 2005, there has also been an Overseas Students' Association that supports all international students over the age of 16 in their social, intellectual and pastoral needs. More details can be found at **www.osa.org.sg**.

Study in the UK

Things to consider

+ World-class reputation for quality undergraduate degrees
+ English language teaching
+ Familiarity of institutions with international students
+ Varied history and links to Europe

- High cost of tuition and living expenses
- High numbers of international students on some programmes

Types of Institution

UK universities are regarded as amongst the finest in the world. The top 200 rankings include no less than 29 UK institutions, seven of which appear in the top 50. World famous names such as Cambridge, Imperial College and Oxford, synonymous internationally with education and learning, underline the quality of the UK higher education system. There are more than 130 institutions in the UK that are able to grant undergraduate degrees to students, in addition to a further 500 colleges that are able to offer educational programmes of differing kinds.

UK universities and colleges are comprehensive and multifaculty, offering the full range of academic subject areas from accountancy to zoology. No separate institutions exist for subjects such as business, law and medicine at the undergraduate level, these programmes being offered within larger universities. Some institutions do, however, offer specific subject specialisations such as the London School of Economics (social sciences), the School of Pharmacy (pharmaceutical sciences) and the Institute of Education (teaching training and education).

Almost all universities in the UK are state financed, with the exception of the University of Buckingham and a small number of private colleges, though tuition fees are still payable. Until 1992 there were two types of degree awarding institutions in the UK, the polytechnics − newer institutions that offered Bachelor qualifications in technical and more vocational areas − and the universities − traditional, research-led institutions anywhere between 30 and 1,000 years old, offering Bachelor qualifications across the full spectrum of subject areas. Now this division has been abandoned and all UK institutions are regarded as operating in a system of open competition for teaching students and research grants from various organisations.

Universities and colleges offer five broad types of qualifications to incoming students. Colleges tend to teach for the Higher National Certificate (HNC), Higher National Diploma (HND), Foundation Degree and Diploma of Higher Education, all lasting between one and two years and are the equivalent of the early stages of a Bachelors degree in a range of subjects such as art and design, engineering, media, social studies and technology. Universities tend to teach three or four year undergraduate degree programmes that are more academic in nature and lead to a Bachelor's qualification. Degree programmes that are four years in length tend to include a period in industry or commerce, or a period of study abroad, such as on an exchange scheme in Europe or the US.

The style of teaching in UK institutions is different from many other systems of education. Bachelors degrees are taught by a mix of lectures, tutorials, laboratories (if relevant), seminars and self-directed study. Usually, very little of this structure is compulsory, as the emphasis of learning in the UK system is the individual student's responsibility. Lectures form the basis of most degrees, allowing you to gain an overall outline of a particular subject that is then detailed and discussed in seminars and tutorials. A UK lecturer will rarely tell you that an answer is right or wrong, rather they will want to seek an understanding of the structure and basis of your argument. Much of the work associated with a UK degree is conducted on your own or in small groups, developing your own ideas, point of view and appreciation of the subject matter. Regular assessment takes place through class and term papers and end of year examinations.

Quality and recognition of qualifications

UK undergraduate qualifications are regarded as being amongst the highest quality and most internationally recognised the world over. Various UK agencies, independent from the universities and colleges themselves, govern the quality of

World Class Education
in a World Class City

ndon is the world's knowledge capital and home to a unique cluster of world class universities, ecialist collections, museums, galleries and libraries. Whether it is a professional or specialist alification, London's vast choice of undergraduate and postgraduate courses will equip with the skills you need for a successful career.

cts on London

80,000 students study in London and come from over 200 countries

0,000 courses are taught ranging from Anatomy to Zoology

lore international students study in London than in New York or Sydney

ondon is the most multi-culturally diverse city in the world

learn more visit www.studylondon.ac.uk and wnload the free Study London brochure and ndon study map.

teaching and research in all UK institutions to ensure the highest standards are being maintained. Most individual programmes are subject to external assessment at least every three years, in addition to the internal processes institutions impose upon themselves.

The Quality Assurance Agency (**www.qaa.ac.uk**) safeguards the standard of education provision at all universities through collaborative audit and academic review across all subject disciplines. Additionally, the quality of teaching and research are monitored by a range of audit exercises, the results of which appear on the Teaching Quality Information website (**www.tqi.ac.uk**) and in the Research Assessment Exercise (**www.hero.ac.uk/sites/hero/rae**). In almost all cases the reports from assessment visits to individual universities and colleges are published on the web.

Fees, finance and cost of living

The UK Government allows universities and colleges to set their own tuition fee level. At most universities in England, students from the UK and the European Union have to pay £3,000 a year for tuition, while international students pay somewhere between £6,500 and £13,000 a year, depending on whether a programme is classroom or laboratory based. Tuition fee levels also vary according to the prestige of the university you are applying to.

The UK is a relatively expensive country in which to study. Costs such as accommodation, utilities and books are generally high, though there are regional differences. As a very general rule, London and the southeast of the UK has a higher cost of living than other parts of the country. However, as a student you will have access to discounts of all sorts that will reduce some of your expenditure. Students can expect to pay anywhere between £5,500 and £7,500 (outside of London and the southeast) a year on living costs.

Scholarships

At the undergraduate level, scholarships are very difficult to obtain in the UK. There are no schemes administered by UK Government organisations and only partial funding offered by individual universities and colleges. Information is available from universities on their international office or undergraduate admissions webpages. Most schemes require you to hold an offer of admission before seeking an application for financial aid.

Entry requirements

Because UK universities and colleges are used to receiving applications from international students from all over the world, a wide range of qualifications are acceptable. Generally, students must have completed 13 years of education prior to coming to the UK and offering their local high school qualification equivalent to the UK A-levels. Acceptable entry grades are entirely dependent on the university or college you are applying to, all of which publish explicit entry standards on their websites or in their prospectuses. Students without 13 years of education are able to apply to UK universities and colleges that offer foundation or bridging programmes. These courses enable to students to upgrade their existing qualifications and reach the required standard for entry into the undergraduate system.

Applications are generally made through a central system administered by the Universities and Colleges Admissions Service (UCAS). Students are able to apply for up to six institutions on one form and UCAS collate all correspondence and decisions between the student and the institution concerned. Full details are available at **www.ucas.ac.uk**, including information on the application process and deadlines.

Living and working

As with studying abroad in any country, coming to the UK is both an exciting and challenging experience. The UK is known as a friendly, open and well-mannered society that is amongst the most multiracial in the world. When you first arrive there will be many differences between what you are used to and what the UK offers, but you will soon get used to these. The country is well known for its traditions and colourful history, much of which is celebrated through exciting museums. As well as castles, palaces and monuments, the UK is energised with a dynamic contemporary culture of clubs, fashion and a vibrant music scene.

Because the UK is relatively small, the transport system is well developed and moderately priced for students. Train, bus and flight networks cover the entire country and allow you to travel very easily and quickly. Additionally, as a student, you will have access to free medical care if your programme of study is over six months in length. You can register with a doctor close to your institution that will allow you to seek general and hospital care. Other care, such as optical and dental, will require you to pay some fees.

The opportunities for working for international students are very varied. Students from the European Economic Area (EEA) can work freely in the UK. Most other students on programmes longer than six months in duration will be given a sticker in their passport on entry that allows them to work part time alongside their course. You will be allowed to work a maximum of 20 hours a week in term time and full time during the vacations. It is also possible that your spouse or partner may also be able to seek work if they accompany you to the UK. Full details are available at **www.dfes.gov.uk/international-students/wituk.shtml** and **www.ukcosa.org.uk**.

The types of employment you may find as a student will vary. Often temporary

student living

want to live London your way?

Nido is a stylish home in the heart of London designed for modern life. This great space includes everything you need for hassle free living, and all just five tubes stops away from London's major universities.

- A community of 950 students
- Central zone 1 location near King's Cross
- Café, fitness centre and movie screening room
- Free internet access and VOIP system
- Student services support team and resident's intranet
- 24/7 security

Opening September 2007

to find out more visit:
www.nidolondon.com

Nido
LONDON

jobs in the retail and service sector are most common, such as waiting tables and serving in shops. However, some postgraduate students may secure employment relevant to their degree studies.

Student life

All UK universities and colleges offer a range of services for students to enjoy, such as restaurants, bars, clubs, sports facilities and special interest societies. As a student in the UK you will be eligible to join the National Union of Students, an organisation that campaigns for the rights of all students and offers discounts across a wide range of services such as transport, entertainment and some retail outlets.

Universities and colleges organise cultural and sporting activities for all students. Whether you wish to compete at a college or national level, most sports will be catered for with first rate facilities and coaching staff. Other organisations offer networks for those with shared ideas and interests. Such activities can vary from the academic, debating and political societies being two examples, to the cultural, such as clubs offering a glimpse of life in places like China and Mauritius.

Restaurants and pubs are also central to student life in the UK. Both tend to be informal in nature and atmosphere and provide a great opportunity to meet other students and local residents alike.

Study in the US

Things to consider

+ Large number of highly reputable universities
+ Well-resourced private and public universities
+ Streamlined online admissions processes
+ Generally high quality campus support services for international students
+ English language based
+ Strong employment opportunities
+ Many scholarships and financial aid for international students

- High tuition fees
- Low acceptance rate for international students
- Tough student visa requirements
- Difficult post-study visa situation for employment

Types of institution

The US has seven of the world's top ten universities within the World University Rankings in 2006 — Harvard, MIT, Yale, Stanford, CalTech, Berkeley and Princeton. Only Oxford and Cambridge universities and Imperial College in the UK have challenged the supremacy of US universities this year.

However, the US's dominance of world higher education may be not as clear cut as many of their own academics would like to think. The US has 53 universities in the top 200, while Europe has 85, and this despite the fact that most citation data utilised in the rankings is based on English language papers, which disadvantage many European universities.

Harvard and MIT, as well as being neighbours on the Charles River in Boston, are also both independent and funded entirely by income from student fees, research awards and fundraising. This structure is also shared by Stanford, Yale, Princeton, Duke, Cornell, Chicago and Columbia, all of which appear among the top 20 universities worldwide. The remainder of the Ivy League — Pennsylvania, Brown and Dartmouth — are also private, as are 75 per cent of US universities.

State funded universities, although only 25 per cent of the total, have 75 per cent of US students. The University of California, which is well funded, has five campuses within the top 200 institutions. More orthodox state universities are generally less well funded than their private rivals, especially under the current Republican administration, which has systematically diverted resources away from education. These state universities have fewer high profile research groups, but this is offset by the fact that they charge lower fees.

Our rankings do not feature many of the private liberal arts colleges, which tend to produce fewer research papers and have a lower profile internationally. Nevertheless, domestically, schools like Williams and Swarthmore attract high calibre students who seek a broad based education, rather than a more vocational or subject focused programme. A growing number of US universities now offer liberal arts degrees, which also allow this flexible, broad learning experience, which remains almost exclusive to the US. The credit system also means that it is much easier for a student who starts out as, say a history major, to transfer to a different subject, after a year or two, without losing any time. This credit system even makes transfers between universities relatively straightforward.

Medical studies in the US differ from the rest of the world. There are no undergraduate medical degrees (Northwestern University being almost the only exception). Would-be medics take another subject in their first degree, while at the same time preparing for their MCAT — nine hours of multiple choice testing — to gain entry to medical school.

Law studies in the US are similar to medical studies, in that there are no undergraduate degrees. Students take a liberal arts degree, while having to pass the LSAT test to gain entry to law school.

Business education is different. In addition to having many of the world's best MBA programmes, the US also has many of the world's best undergraduate business programmes. The University of Pennsylvania's Wharton School is a good example of both a pre-eminent MBA and undergraduate business degree, attracting many international students. Harvard, Stanford and Yale feature very prominently in our social sciences subject rankings, and have very strong undergraduate business departments.

Quality and recognition of qualifications

All the universities featured in our guide are accredited. If you need to look beyond our elite group, The Council for Higher Education in Washington DC produces the definitive list of government approved US universities at undergraduate level. For business schools, there is the AACSB (American Association of Collegiate Schools of Business) which accredits about 400 institutions.

The Ivy League — Brown, Columbia, Cornell, Dartmouth, Harvard, Penn, Princeton and Yale — are amongst the best known but, as we show in this book, no longer dominate the rankings. The grouping actually began as a sports league. Their reputations and attractive East Coast locations and historic campuses ensure that application ratios are amongst the most competitive in the world.

All students complete their degree with a grade point average (GPA). This grade point average is a cumulative total of each individual course grade multiplied by the course credit. Students tend to be fanatical about their GPA because this is influential in the employment marketplace. To achieve high grades requires regular attendance at lectures and consistent performance.

Fees, finance and cost of living

The elite US universities are the most expensive in the world. At the same time they can be a gateway to the most attractive employment market in the world, as well as providing value for money in terms of class time and access to professors. There is a great emphasis on tuition and access to professors.

An added attraction for international students are the huge number of scholarships and financial aid packages available at many well-funded private universities, making them open to even the most disadvantaged but bright students.

Many US universities' financial aid departments ask for a statement of your family's financial situation. If they decide that your family can only contribute $1,000 per year that is all you will have to pay — if they want you. Alternatively they may have international student loan schemes. For those whose families can afford the bills, be prepared for tuition and fees varying between $3,500 and $60,000 per academic year. As a guideline, the average is about $16,000 per year, which is usually based on a nine month academic year from September to May.

Books, travel and living costs need to be added in. Costs vary by city, with New York, Boston and San Francisco amongst the most expensive. A budget of $3,000-8,000 will be necessary.

Entry requirements and admissions procedures

All US universities publish general criteria on their websites. Generally speaking admissions offices will be familiar with grading systems in different countries. If you achieve top 10 per cent grades in your country, the chances are you can gain entry to the top 10 per cent of US universities, but there will be some exceptions. Some country high school qualifications are considered more advanced than US equivalents. For example, UK A-level grades can count towards credit for many US degrees, potentially taking as much as 12 months off the length of the degree. Domestic applicants have to take the SAT exam. If SAT results are a long way short of the average, it is generally not worth applying.

Living and working

American universities encourage their students to work alongside their course. There are often "employment offices" which offer paid work on campus, for which an international student visa will suffice. You will need to apply for a social security number, at which point you can take any campus job — as a teaching assistant, sports attendant, etc.

As part of an international visa, an international student is allowed one year of optional practical training (OPT), enabling them to work anywhere in the US, in consulting, banking, engineering or any other field. The year can be used in batches during summer internships, or in full after your degree. There is also curricular practical training, which allows a student to find paid work as long as it relates to the subject being studied. This is most applicable for students in sciences and technology. Professors are generally amenable and there is no time limit or impact on the OPT allowance.

Student life

Fraternities and sororities still form a fundamental part of student life on many US campuses. These college groups offer a private building where you can party, or relax in smaller cohesive groups. It is a good way to get to know people and often offers alternative accommodation to university dorms. Special interest clubs and sports clubs also play a major part in the social scene at many universities. If you are good at a sport or a musical instrument, you are guaranteed a like-minded social set and lots of activities. If drinking is your only hobby, there are lots of Irish pubs in most cities which gather a regular crowd of graduate students, but you need to check out the legal drinking age in each state which can vary from 18 to 21.

ARGENTINA

Austral University

CONTACT DETAILS

Address
Avda. Juan de Garay 125
Ciudad de Buenos Aires
C1063ABB
Argentina
Web http://www.austral.edu.ar/
Phone +54(11) 5921-8000

INSTITUTION STATS

Undergraduates	2,265
Postgraduates	1,132
International Students	7.3%
Student Faculty Ratio	12.9:1
Avg UG Fees	5,000
Avg PG Fees	5,000

RANKINGS PERFORMANCE

Faculty Level Positions
Engineering & IT   436=

University of Belgrano

CONTACT DETAILS

Address
Zabala 1837
Buenos Aires
1428
Argentina

Web www.ub.edu.ar
Phone +54(11)4788-5400

INSTITUTION STATS

Student Faculty Ratio   6.4:1

RANKINGS PERFORMANCE

Faculty Level Positions
Natural Sciences   509=

University of Buenos Aires

CONTACT DETAILS

Address
Viamonte 430
Buenos Aires
1053
Argentina

Web www.uba.ar
Phone +54(11) 4510 1253

INSTITUTION STATS

Total Students	279,306
International Students	7.1%
Total Citations	60,649

RANKINGS PERFORMANCE

Faculty Level Positions
Arts & Humanities   328=
Engineering & IT   303=
Life Sciences & BioMedicine 258=
Natural Sciences   335=
Social Sciences   269=

Universidad Torcuato di Tella

CONTACT DETAILS

Address
Miñones 2177
Buenos Aires
1428
Argentina

Web www.utdt.edu
Phone +54 (11) 4784- 0080

INSTITUTION STATS

Undergraduates	1,178
Postgraduates	819
International Students	6.9%
Student Faculty Ratio	30.1:1
Avg UG Fees	4,000
Avg PG Fees	4,350

RANKINGS PERFORMANCE

Faculty Level Positions
Engineering & IT   482=
Social Sciences   251=

AUSTRALIA

University of Adelaide

CONTACT DETAILS

Address
The University of Adelaide
Adelaide
SA 5005
Australia

Web www.adelaide.edu.au
Phone +61 8 8303 4455

INSTITUTION STATS

Undergraduates	11,268
Postgraduates	5,736
International Students	26.9%
Student Faculty Ratio	18.1:1
Total Citations	78,486
Avg UG Fees	13,700
Avg PG Fees	13,500

RANKINGS PERFORMANCE

Overall Rankings Position	105=
Faculty Level Positions	
Arts & Humanities	94
Engineering & IT	74
Life Sciences & BioMedicine	43
Natural Sciences	80
Social Sciences	76=

Australian National University

CONTACT DETAILS

Address
Canberra
ACT 0200
Australia

Web www.anu.edu.au
Phone +61 2 6125 5111

INSTITUTION STATS

Undergraduates	8,639
Postgraduates	4,430
International Students	20.2%
Student Faculty Ratio	13.2:1
Total Citations	147,634
Avg UG Fees	14,000
Avg PG Fees	16,000

RANKINGS PERFORMANCE

Overall Rankings Position	16
Faculty Level Positions	
Arts & Humanities	6
Engineering & IT	24
Life Sciences & BioMedicine	24
Natural Sciences	16
Social Sciences	6

Curtin University of Technology

CONTACT DETAILS

Address
GPO Box U1987
Perth
WA 6845
Australia

Web www.curtin.edu.au
Phone +61 8 9266 9266

INSTITUTION STATS

Undergraduates	28,680
Postgraduates	12,247
International Students	43.1%
Student Faculty Ratio	13.3:1

RANKINGS PERFORMANCE

Overall Rankings Position	156=
Faculty Level Positions	
Arts & Humanities	113=
Engineering & IT	132=
Life Sciences & BioMedicine	148=
Natural Sciences	217=
Social Sciences	105=

La Trobe University

CONTACT DETAILS

Address
Victoria
3086
Australia

Web www.latrobe.edu.au
Phone +61 3 9479 1111

INSTITUTION STATS

Undergraduates	19,705
Postgraduates	6,874
International Students	17.1%
Student Faculty Ratio	6.5:1
Total Citation	31,337
Avg UG Fees	11,400
Avg PG Fees	11,000

RANKINGS PERFORMANCE

Faculty Level Positions	
Arts & Humanities	54
Engineering & IT	267=
Life Sciences & BioMedicine	135=
Natural Sciences	175=
Social Sciences	98=

AUSTRALIA

Macquarie University

CONTACT DETAILS		INSTITUTION STATS		RANKINGS PERFORMANCE	
Web	www.mq.edu.au	**Undergraduates**	22,349	**Overall Rankings Position**	82=
Phone	10 800 61 00 241	**Postgraduates**	8,425	**Faculty Level Positions**	
		International Students	31.8%	Arts & Humanities	50
		Student Faculty Ratio	8.3:1	Engineering & IT	235=
		Total Citations	31,922	Life Sciences & BioMedicine	107
		Avg UG Fees	13,500	Natural Sciences	177=
		Avg PG Fees	18,100	Social Sciences	68=

University of Melbourne

CONTACT DETAILS		INSTITUTION STATS		RANKINGS PERFORMANCE	
Address		**Undergraduates**	30,081	**Overall Rankings Position**	22
Admissions Office, Information		**Postgraduates**	14,347	**Faculty Level Positions**	
Centre, Richard Berry Building		**International Students**	22.1%	Arts & Humanities	7
Victoria		**Student Faculty Ratio**	7.5:1	Engineering & IT	16
3010		**Total Citations**	177,476	Life Sciences & BioMedicine	7
Australia		**Avg UG Fees**	8,900	Natural Sciences	27
		Avg PG Fees	13,200	Social Sciences	10
Web	www.unimelb.edu.au				
Phone	+61 (3) 8344 6543				

Monash University

CONTACT DETAILS		INSTITUTION STATS		RANKINGS PERFORMANCE	
Address		**Undergraduates**	39,073	**Overall Rankings Position**	38
Victoria		**Postgraduates**	15,877	**Faculty Level Positions**	
3800		**International Students**	31.2%	Arts & Humanities	28
Australia		**Student Faculty Ratio**	29.1:1	Engineering & IT	28=
		Total Citations	119,060	Life Sciences & BioMedicine	19
Web	www.monash.edu.au	**Avg UG Fees**	15,900	Natural Sciences	54
Phone	+61 3 9902 6000	**Avg PG Fees**	15,600	Social Sciences	16

University of New South Wales

CONTACT DETAILS		INSTITUTION STATS		RANKINGS PERFORMANCE	
Address		**Undergraduates**	25,964	**Overall Rankings Position**	41
SYDNEY		**Postgraduates**	14,672	**Faculty Level Positions**	
NSW 2052		**International Students**	23.1%	Arts & Humanities	18
Australia		**Student Faculty Ratio**	9.8:1	Engineering & IT	19
		Total Citations	126,980	Life Sciences & BioMedicine	52=
Web	www.unsw.edu.au	**Avg UG Fees**	14,920	Natural Sciences	41=
Phone	+61 2 9385 1000	**Avg PG Fees**	15,330	Social Sciences	21

AUSTRALIA

University of Newcastle

CONTACT DETAILS

Address
Callaghan
NSW 2308
Australia

Web www.newcastle.edu.au
Phone +61(02) 4921 5000

INSTITUTION STATS

Undergraduates	19,380
Postgraduates	6,162
% International Students	18.3%
Student Faculty Ratio	6.3:1
Total Citations	41,054
Avg UG Fees	12,300
Avg PG Fees	12,300

RANKINGS PERFORMANCE

Faculty Level Positions	
Arts & Humanities	95=
Engineering & IT	147
Life Sciences & BioMedicine	103
Natural Sciences	246=
Social Sciences	128

University of Queensland

CONTACT DETAILS

Address
Brisbane
QLD 4072
Australia

Web www.uq.edu.au
Phone +61 7 3365 1111

INSTITUTION STATS

Undergraduates	26,508
Postgraduates	9,823
International Students	18.9%
Student Faculty Ratio	11:1
Total Citations	152,414

RANKINGS PERFORMANCE

Overall Rankings Position	45
Faculty Level Positions	
Arts & Humanities	42
Engineering & IT	38
Life Sciences & BioMedicine	23
Natural Sciences	58=
Social Sciences	27

Queensland University of Technology

CONTACT DETAILS

Address
2 George St
Brisbane
QLD 4001
Australia

Web www.qut.edu.au
Phone +61 7 3864 2111

INSTITUTION STATS

Undergraduates	29,818
Postgraduates	8,021
International Students	12.0%
Student Faculty Ratio	7.1:1
Total Citations	18,285
Avg UG Fees	12,400
Avg PG Fees	13,200

RANKINGS PERFORMANCE

Overall Rankings Position	192=
Faculty Level Positions	
Arts & Humanities	86
Engineering & IT	70
Life Sciences & BioMedicine	66
Natural Sciences	234=
Social Sciences	134

RMIT University

CONTACT DETAILS

Address
Melbourne
Victoria 3001
Australia

Web www.rmit.edu.au
Phone +61 3 9925 2000

INSTITUTION STATS

Undergraduates	28,656
Postgraduates	10,320
International Students	40.2%
Student Faculty Ratio	53.7:1
Total Citations	5,515
Avg UG Fees	12,800
Avg PG Fees	13,700

RANKINGS PERFORMANCE

Overall Rankings Position	146
Faculty Level Positions	
Arts & Humanities	59
Engineering & IT	88
Life Sciences & BioMedicine	160
Natural Sciences	210=
Social Sciences	46

AUSTRALIA

University of South Australia

CONTACT DETAILS

Address
GPO Box 2471
Adelaide,
South Australia 5001
Australia

Web www.unisa.edu.au
Phone +61 8 8302 6611

INSTITUTION STATS

Undergraduates	23,723
Postgraduates	8,484
International Students	13.0%
Student Faculty Ratio	7.8:1
Total Citations	10,369
Avg UG Fees	12,000
Avg PG Fees	9,800

RANKINGS PERFORMANCE

Faculty Level Positions
Arts & Humanities	146=
Engineering & IT	235=
Life Sciences & BioMedicine	151=
Natural Sciences	225
Social Sciences	203=

University of Technology ,Sydney

CONTACT DETAILS

Address
PO Box 123
Broadway
NSW 2007
Australia

Web www.uts.edu.au
Phone +61 2 9514 2000

INSTITUTION STATS

Undergraduates	19,403
Postgraduates	12,199
International Students	25.9%
Student Faculty Ratio	25.4:1
Total Citations	9,854
Avg UG Fees	13,000
Avg PG Fees	13,000

RANKINGS PERFORMANCE

Faculty Level Positions
Arts & Humanities	99=
Engineering & IT	83=
Life Sciences & BioMedicine	148=
Natural Sciences	244=
Social Sciences	132=

University of Sydney

CONTACT DETAILS

Address
NSW 2006
Australia

Web www.usyd.edu.au
Phone +61 2 9351 2222

INSTITUTION STATS

Undergraduates	25,082
Postgraduates	10,293
International Students	19.3%
Student Faculty Ratio	22.3:1
Total Citations	183.764
Avg UG Fees	21,000
Avg PG Fees	18,000

RANKINGS PERFORMANCE

Overall Rankings Position 35=
Faculty Level Positions
Arts & Humanities	5
Engineering & IT	25
Life Sciences & BioMedicine	20
Natural Sciences	35
Social Sciences	19

University of Tasmania

CONTACT DETAILS

Address
P.O. Box 986
LAUNCESTON
TAS 7250
Australia

Web www.utas.edu.au
Phone (03) 6335 4711

INSTITUTION STATS

Undergraduates	11,341
Postgraduates	2808
International Students	11.2%
Student Faculty Ratio	13.7:1
Total Citations	32.244

RANKINGS PERFORMANCE

Faculty Level Positions
Arts & Humanities	69
Engineering & IT	219=
Life Sciences & BioMedicine	302=
Natural Sciences	204=
Social Science	155=

AUSTRALIA

University of Western Australia

CONTACT DETAILS		INSTITUTION STATS		RANKINGS PERFORMANCE	
Address		**Undergraduates**	13,392	**Overall Rankings Position**	111=
35 Stirling Highway		**Postgraduates**	3,955	**Faculty Level Positions**	
CRAWLEY		**International Students**	17.6%	Arts & Humanities	71=
WA 6009		**Student Faculty Ratio**	23:1	Engineering & IT	126=
Australia		**Total Citations**	96,827	Life Sciences & BioMedicine	65
		Avg UG Fees	15,700	Natural Sciences	132=
Web	www.uwa.edu.au	**Avg PG Fees**	13,800	Social Sciences	98=
Phone	+61 8 6488 2889				

University of Wollongong

CONTACT DETAILS		INSTITUTION STATS		RANKINGS PERFORMANCE	
Address		**Undergraduates**	14,948	**Overall Rankings Position**	196
NSW, 2522		**Postgraduates**	7,312	**Faculty Level Positions**	
Australia		**International Students**	39.8%	Arts & Humanities	204=
		Student Faculty Ratio	3.7:1	Engineering & IT	157=
		Total Citations	21,417	Life Sciences & BioMedicine	191
Web	www.uow.edu.au	**Avg UG Fees**	13,000	Natural Sciences	335=
Phone	1300 367 869	**Avg PG Fees**	16,700	Social Sciences	157=

AUSTRIA

Karl-Franzens-University Graz

CONTACT DETAILS		INSTITUTION STATS		RANKINGS PERFORMANCE	
Address		**Total Students**	23,544	**Faculty Level Positions**	
Universitätsplatz 3		**Total Citations**	35,446	Arts & Humanities	132=
Graz				Engineering & IT	122
A - 8010				Life Sciences & BioMedicine	122
Austria				Natural Sciences	177=
				Social Sciences	346=
Web	www.kfunigraz.ac.at				
Phone	+43 316 380-0				

University of Innsbruck

CONTACT DETAILS		INSTITUTION STATS		RANKINGS PERFORMANCE	
Address		**Undergraduates**	18,666	**Overall Rankings Position**	186
Christoph-Probst-Platz		**Postgraduates**	1,943	**Faculty Level Positions**	
Innrain 52		**International Students**	29.5%	Arts & Humanities	254
6020		**Student Faculty Ratio**	9.7:1	Engineering & IT	267=
Austria		**Total Citations**	86,273	Life Sciences & BioMedicine	132
		Avg UG Fees	897	Natural Sciences	118
		Avg PG Fees	897	Social Sciences	273=
Web	www.uibk.ac.at				
Phone	+43(0)512/507-0				

AUSTRIA

Johannes Kepler University Linz

CONTACT DETAILS

Address
Universitätsplatz 3
Graz
A - 8010
Austria

Web www.uni-linz.ac.at
Phone +43 732 / 2468

INSTITUTION STATS

Undergraduates	10,818
Postgraduates	756
International Students	11.3%
Student Faculty Ratio	18.4:1

RANKINGS PERFORMANCE

Faculty Level Positions
Arts & Humanities	398=
Engineering & IT	349=
Life Sciences & BioMedicine	427=
Natural Sciences	368=
Social Sciences	359=

University of Vienna

CONTACT DETAILS

Address
Vienna
A-1010
Austria

Web www.univie.ac.at
Phone +43/1/4277-0

INSTITUTION STATS

Total Students	63,000
International Students	16.0%
Student Faculty Ratio	9.9:1
Total Citations	205,925

RANKINGS PERFORMANCE

Overall Rankings Position	87
Faculty Level Positions	
Arts & Humanities	37=
Engineering & IT	137
Life Sciences & BioMedicine	41
Natural Sciences	73=
Social Sciences	34

Vienna University of Technology

CONTACT DETAILS

Address
Karlsplatz 13
Wien
A-1040
Austria

Web www.tuwien.ac.at
Phone +43/(0)1/58801-0

INSTITUTION STATS

Undergraduates	7,116
Postgraduates	9,105
International Students	20.9%
Student Faculty Ratio	10.3:1
Total Citations	36,944
Avg UG Fees	1,461
Avg PG Fees	1,461

RANKINGS PERFORMANCE

Overall Rankings Position	138
Faculty Level Positions	
Arts & Humanities	215=
Engineering & IT	47
Life Sciences & BioMedicine	215=
Natural Sciences	87=
Social Sciences	305=

BANGLADESH

University of Dhaka

CONTACT DETAILS

Address
Ramna
Dhaka
1000
Bangladesh

Web www.univdhaka.edu
Phone +880 2 9661900 19

INSTITUTION STATS

Total Students	30,000
International Students	0.1%
Student Faculty Ratio	15.1:1
Total Citations	1,907

RANKINGS PERFORMANCE

Faculty Level Positions
Arts & Humanities	191=
Engineering & IT	183=
Life Sciences & BioMedicine	204=
Natural Sciences	286=
Social Sciences	229=

BELGIUM

University of Antwerp

CONTACT DETAILS

Address
Antwerpen
B-2020
Belgium

Web www.ua.ac.be
Phone +32 3 265 35 77

INSTITUTION STATS

Undergraduates	7,772
Postgraduates	2,188
International Students	10.7%
Student Faculty Ratio	24.3:1
Total Citations	49,320
Avg UG Fees	647
Avg PG Fees	8,552

RANKING PERFORMANCE

Faculty Level Positions
Arts & Humanities	115=
Engineering & IT	322=
Life Sciences & BioMedicine	193=
Natural Sciences	318=
Social Sciences	229=

Vrije University Brussels

CONTACT DETAILS

Address
Pleinlaan 2
Elsene
B-1050
Belgium

Web www.vub.ac.be
Phone +32 (0)2 629.21.11

INSTITUTION STATS

Undergraduates	3,676
Postgraduates	4,237
International Students	10.6%
Student Faculty Ratio	11.4:1
Avg UG Fees	647
Avg PG Fees	1,288

RANKINGS PERFORMANCE

Overall Rankings Position	133=
Faculty Level Positions	
Arts & Humanities	233=
Engineering & IT	406=
Life Sciences & BioMedicine	225=
Natural Sciences	409=
Social Sciences	305=

Université Libre de Bruxelles

CONTACT DETAILS

Address
avenue F.D. Roosevelt 50
1050 Bruxelles
Belgium

Web www.ulb.ac.be

INSTITUTION STATS

Undergraduates	19,389
Postgraduates	19,455
International Students	24.2%
Student Faculty Ratio	22.2:1
Total Citations	139,345
Avg UG Fees	8,011
Avg PG Fees	8,011

RANKINGS PERFORMANCE

Overall Rankings Position	165=
Faculty Level Positions	
Arts & Humanities	89
Engineering & IT	179=
Life Sciences & BioMedicine	113
Natural Sciences	104=
Social Sciences	142=

Catholic University of Leuven

CONTACT DETAILS

Address
Naamsestraat 22
3000 Leuven
Belgium

Web www.kuleuven.ac.be
Phone +32 16 32 42 71

INSTITUTION STATS

Undergraduates	11,560
Postgraduates	18,380
International Students	12.5%
Student Faculty Ratio	11.2:1
Total Citations	169,821
Avg UG Fees	6,409
Avg PG Fees	6,409

RANKINGS PERFORMANCE

Overall Rankings Position	96
Faculty Level Positions	
Arts & Humanities	73=
Engineering & IT	79=
Life Sciences & BioMedicine	82=
Natural Sciences	102=
Social Sciences	71

BELGIUM

Catholic University of Louvain

CONTACT DETAILS

Web www.ucl.ac.be

INSTITUTION STATS

Undergraduates	6,580
Postgraduates	13,829
International Students	15.5%
Student Faculty Ratio	8.9:1
Total Citations	146,971
Avg UG Fees	6,665
Avg PG Fees	6,665

RANKINGS PERFORMANCE

Overall Rankings Position	76
Faculty Level Positions	
Arts & Humanities	79=
Engineering & IT	63=
Life Sciences & BioMedicine	137=
Natural Sciences	139=
Social Sciences	38=

University of Ghent

CONTACT DETAILS

Address
Sint-Pietersnieuwstraat 25
Ghent
B - 9000
Belgium

Web www.ugent.be
Phone +32 9 264 70 00

INSTITUTION STATS

Undergraduates	11,893
Postgraduates	15,823
International Students	6.1%
Student Faculty Ratio	10:1
Total Citations	120,831
Avg UG Fees	647
Avg PG Fees	647

RANKINGS PERFORMANCE

Overall Rankings Position	141=
Faculty Level Positions	
Arts & Humanities	115=
Engineering & IT	128=
Life Sciences & BioMedicine	128=
Natural Sciences	115=
Social Sciences	192

University of Liege

CONTACT DETAILS

Address
place du 20-Août, 9
Liège
B- 4000
Belgium

Web www.ulg.ac.be
Phone +32 4 366 21 11

INSTITUTION STATS

Undergraduates	16,760
Postgraduates	3,391
% International Students	22.4%
Student Faculty Ratio	27.1:1
Total Citations	70,122
Avg Fees	973

RANKINGS PERFORMANCE

Faculty Level Positions	
Arts & Humanities	244=
Engineering & IT	178
Life Sciences & BioMedicine	369=
Natural Sciences	226=
Social Sciences	225=

BRAZIL

State University of Campinas

CONTACT DETAILS

Address
Cidade Universitária Zeferino Vaz
Campinas
São Paulo 13083-970
Brazil

Web www.unicamp.br
Phone +55 (19) 3788 2121

INSTITUTION STATS

Undergraduates	12,476
Postgraduates	1,471
International Students	1.5%
Student Faculty Ratio	9.6:1
Total Citations	52,850

RANKINGS PERFORMANCE

Faculty Level Positions	
Engineering & IT	183=
Life Sciences & BioMedicine	284=
Natural Sciences	300=
Social Sciences	359=

BRAZIL

Dom Cabral Foundation

CONTACT DETAILS	INSTITUTION STATS		RANKINGS PERFORMANCE	
Address	**Student Faculty Ratio**	23.1:1	**Faculty Level Positions**	
Avenida Princesa Diana, 760			Social Sciences	426=
Nova Lima				
MG 34000-000				
Brazil				

Web www.fdc.org.br
Phone +55 (31) 3589 7200

Fundacao Getulio Vargas

CONTACT DETAILS	INSTITUTION STATS		RANKINGS PERFORMANCE	
Address	**Student Faculty Ratio**	12.8:1	**Faculty Level Positions**	
Praia de Botafogo, 190			Engineering & IT	398=
Rio de Janeiro			Life Sciences & BioMedicine	497=
22250-900			Natural Sciences	514=
Brazil			Social Sciences	213=

Web www.fgv.br
Phone +55 (21) 2559-6087

State University of Paulista

CONTACT DETAILS	INSTITUTION STATS		RANKINGS PERFORMANCE	
Address	**Undergraduates**	30,000	**Faculty Level Positions**	
Alameda Santos, 647	**Postgraduates**	9,100	Engineering & IT	438=
São Paulo	**International Students**	0.6%	Life Sciences & BioMedicine	421=
01419-901	**Student Faculty Ratio**	6.7:1	Natural Sciences	429=
Brazil			Social Sciences	426=

Web www.unesp.br
Phone +55 (11) 3252-0233

Federal University of Rio de Janeiro

CONTACT DETAILS	INSTITUTION STATS		RANKINGS PERFORMANCE	
Address	**Undergraduates**	36,714	**Faculty Level Positions**	
Avenida Brigadeiro Trompowski,	**Postgraduates**	7,650	Arts & Humanities	398=
s/nº	**International Students**	0.6%	Engineering & IT	209=
Rio de Janeiro	**Student Faculty Ratio**	36.8:1	Life Sciences & BioMedicine	284=
21941-590	**Total Citations**	48,380	Natural Sciences	297=
Brazil			Social Sciences	359=

Web www.ufrj.br
Phone +55(11) 2598-1727

BRAZIL

Pontifícia Universidade Católica do Rio de Janeiro

CONTACT DETAILS

Address
Rua Marquês de São Vicente, 225
Rio de Janeiro
22453-900
Brazil

Web www.puc-rio.br
Phone +55 (21) 3114-1001

INSTITUTION STATS

Undergraduates	273
Postgraduates	36
International Students	3.8%
Student Faculty Ratio	3.8:1
Avg UG Fees	6,940
Avg PG Fees	8,580

RANKINGS PERFORMANCE

Faculty Level Positions
Arts & Humanities	398=
Engineering & IT	368=
Life Sciences & BioMedicine	397=
Natural Sciences	434=
Social Sciences	281=

University of São Paulo

CONTACT DETAILS

Address
Caixa Postal 66281
São Paulo
05311-970
Brazil

Web www.usp.br
Phone +55 (11) 3091-6119

INSTITUTION STATS

Undergraduates	48,530
Postgraduates	25,007
International Students	1.8%
Student Faculty Ratio	16:1
Total Citations	133,901

RANKINGS PERFORMANCE

Faculty Level Positions
Arts & Humanities	238=
Engineering & IT	250=
Life Sciences & BioMedicine	155=
Natural Sciences	230=
Social Sciences	213=

CANADA

University of Alberta

CONTACT DETAILS

Address
114 St. - 89 Ave
Edmonton
Alberta T6G 2E1
Canada
Web www.ualberta.ca
Phone +1 780 492-3111

INSTITUTION STATS

Undergraduates	26,369
Postgraduates	5,219
International Students	12.9%
Student Faculty Ratio	13.1:1
Total Citations	216,432
Avg UG Fees	13,800
Avg PG Fees	5,900

RANKINGS PERFORMANCE

Overall Rankings Position	133=
Faculty Level Positions	
Arts & Humanities	73=
Engineering & IT	118
Life Sciences & BioMedicine	97=
Natural Sciences	126=
Social Sciences	135=

University of British Columbia

CONTACT DETAILS

Address
2329 West Mall
Vancouver, B.C.
V6T 1Z4
Canada

Web www.ubc.ca
Phone +1 604 822 2211

INSTITUTION STATS

Undergraduates	35,000
Postgraduates	8,000
International Students	9.3%
Student Faculty Ratio	13.8:1
Total Citations	302,389

RANKINGS PERFORMANCE

Overall Rankings Position	50=
Faculty Level Positions	
Arts & Humanities	32
Engineering & IT	51
Life Sciences & BioMedicine	32
Natural Sciences	45
Social Sciences	25

CANADA

University of Calgary

CONTACT DETAILS	INSTITUTION STATS		RANKINGS PERFORMANCE	
Address	**Undergraduates**	22,445	**Faculty Level Positions**	
2500 University Drive NW	**Postgraduates**	4,046	Arts & Humanities	222=
Calgary, Alberta	**International Students**	6.9%	Engineering & IT	132=
T2N 1N4	**Student Faculty Ratio**	17.9:1	Life Sciences & BioMedicine	390=
Canada	**Total Citations**	131,815	Natural Sciences	258=
Web www.ucalgary.ca	**Avg UG Fees**	13,700	Social Sciences	319
Phone +1 403 220-6645	**Avg PG Fees**	9,500		

Carleton University

CONTACT DETAILS	INSTITUTION STATS		RANKINGS PERFORMANCE	
Address	**Undergraduates**	20,907	**Faculty Level Positions**	
1125 Colonel By Drive	**Postgraduates**	2,932	Arts & Humanities	305=
Ottawa	**International Students**	9.9%	Engineering & IT	336=
K1S 5B6	**Student Faculty Ratio**	27.6:1	Life Sciences & BioMedicine	338=
Canada	**Total Citations**	36,266	Natural Sciences	343=
Web www.carleton.ca	**Avg UG Fees**	10,200	Social Sciences	251=
Phone +1 613 5207400	**Avg PG Fees**	7,690		

Concordia University

CONTACT DETAILS	INSTITUTION STATS		RANKINGS PERFORMANCE	
Address	**Undergraduates**	26,136	**Faculty Level Positions**	
1455 de Maisonneuve Blvd	**Postgraduates**	4,794	Arts & Humanities	163=
Montreal	**International Students**	11.4%	Engineering & IT	303=
H3G 1M8	**Student Faculty Ratio**	20.2:1	Life Sciences & BioMedicine	385=
Canada	**Total Citations**	21.099	Social Sciences	200=
Web www.concordia.ca				
Phone +1 514 8482424				

Dalhousie University

CONTACT DETAILS	INSTITUTION STATS		RANKINGS PERFORMANCE	
Address	**Total Students**	15,800	**Faculty Level Positions**	
Halifax	**International Students**	7.6%	Arts & Humanities	291
Nova Scotia B3H 3J5	**Student Faculty Ratio**	18.2:1	Engineering & IT	267=
Canada"	**Total Citations**	87,262	Life Sciences & BioMedicine	258=
			Natural Sciences	214=
Web www.dal.ca			Social Sciences	268
Phone +1 (902) 494-2211				

CANADA

Laval University

CONTACT DETAILS

Web   www.ulaval.ca

INSTITUTION STATS

Undergraduates	28,651
Postgraduates	9,043
International Students	9.3%
Student Faculty Ratio	17.6:1
Total Citations	119,837

RANKINGS PERFORMANCE

Faculty Level Positions

Arts & Humanities	369=
Engineering & IT	303=
Life Sciences & BioMedicine	363=
Natural Sciences	394=
Social Sciences	350

University of Manitoba

CONTACT DETAILS

Address
Winnipeg, MB
R3T 2N2
Canada

Web   www.umanitoba.ca
Phone   +1 204 474 8880

INSTITUTION STATS

Undergraduates	23,935
Postgraduates	3,696
International Students	8.1%
Student Faculty Ratio	9.8:1
Total Citations	80,245

RANKINGS PERFORMANCE

Faculty Level Positions

Engineering & IT	349=
Life Sciences & BioMedicine	363=
Natural Sciences	310=
Social Sciences	426=

McGill University

CONTACT DETAILS

Address
845 Sherbrooke Street West
Montreal
Quebec H3A 2T5
Canada
Web   www.mcgill.ca
Phone   +1 514 398 4455

INSTITUTION STATS

Undergraduates	22,787
Postgraduates	7,546
International Students	20.4%
Student Faculty Ratio	6.1:1
Total Citations	351,626
Avg UG Fees	11,900
Avg PG Fees	8,500

RANKINGS PERFORMANCE

Overall Rankings Position	21
Faculty Level Positions	
Arts & Humanities	12
Engineering & IT	50
Life Sciences & BioMedicine	21
Natural Sciences	37=
Social Sciences	20

McMaster University

CONTACT DETAILS

Address
1280 Main St W
Hamilton, ON
L8S 4M1
Canada
Web   www.mcmaster.ca
Phone   +1 (905) 525-9140

INSTITUTION STATS

Undergraduates	19,691
Postgraduates	2,801
International Students	7.8%
Student Faculty Ratio	16.8:1
Total Citations	180,677
Avg UG Fees	9,600
Avg PG Fees	10,600

RANKINGS PERFORMANCE

Overall Rankings Position	155
Faculty Level Positions	
Arts & Humanities	99=
Engineering & IT	119=
Life Sciences & BioMedicine	137=
Natural Sciences	122
Social Sciences	196

CANADA

University of Montreal

CONTACT DETAILS

Address
PO Box 6128, Station Centre-ville
Montréal QC
H3C 3J7
Canada
Web   www.umontreal.ca
Phone   +1 (514) 343-6111

INSTITUTION STATS

Total Students	37,705
International Students	6.7%
Student Faculty Ratio	12:1
Total Citations	160,599

RANKINGS PERFORMANCE

Overall Rankings Position	181=
Faculty Level Positions	
Arts & Humanities	135=
Engineering & IT	152=
Life Sciences & BioMedicine	173=
Natural Sciences	204=
Social Sciences	186=

Ottawa University

CONTACT DETAILS

Address
75 Laurier Ave. E.
Ottawa, Ontario
K1N 6N5
Canada
Web   www.uottawa.ca
Phone   +1 613 562 5700

INSTITUTION STATS

Undergraduates	29,567
Postgraduates	4,009
International Students	6.1%
Student Faculty Ratio	28.8:1
Total Citations	101,839

RANKINGS PERFORMANCE

Faculty Level Positions	
Arts & Humanities	238=
Engineering & IT	197=
Life Sciences & BioMedicine	338=
Natural Sciences	295=
Social Sciences	351=

University of Quebec

CONTACT DETAILS

Address
475 Rue e l'Eglise
Québec
Canada

Web   www.uquebec.ca

INSTITUTION STATS

Undergraduates	69,742
Postgraduates	14,999
International Students	9.3%
Student Faculty Ratio	18.9:1

RANKINGS PERFORMANCE

Faculty Level Positions	
Engineering & IT	289=
Life Sciences & BioMedicine	225=
Natural Sciences	291=
Social Sciences	254=

Queen's University

CONTACT DETAILS

Address
99 University Avenue
Kingston
K7L 3N6
Canada
Web   www.queensu.ca
Phone   +1 613 533 2000

INSTITUTION STATS

Undergraduates	15,258
Postgraduates	2,492
International Students	4.7%
Student Faculty Ratio	27.2:1
Total Citations	88,679
Avg UG Fees	13,775
Avg PG Fees	10,185

RANKINGS PERFORMANCE

Overall Rankings Position	176
Faculty Level Positions	
Arts & Humanities	167=
Engineering & IT	250=
Life Sciences & BioMedicine	242=
Natural Sciences	338
Social Sciences	148=

CANADA

Simon Fraser University

CONTACT DETAILS

Address
8888 University Drive
Burnaby, B.C.
V5A 1S6
Canada
Web   www.sfu.ca
Phone   +1 604 2913111

INSTITUTION STATS

Undergraduates	19,979
Postgraduates	3,558
International Students	10.1%
Student Faculty Ratio	35:1
Total Citations	40,648
Avg UG Fees	12,800
Avg PG Fees	2,600

RANKINGS PERFORMANCE

Faculty Level Positions

Arts & Humanities	203
Engineering & IT	276=
Life Sciences & BioMedicine	225=
Natural Sciences	263=
Social Sciences	148=

University of Toronto

CONTACT DETAILS

Address
S-304, 1265 Military Trail
Scarborough, Ontario
Canada M1C 1A4
tion is really fucked at the mot
Web   www.utoronto.ca
Phone   +1 416 978 2011

INSTITUTION STATS

Undergraduates	52,499
Postgraduates	11,430
International Students	10.4%
Student Faculty Ratio	15.6:1
Total Citations	552,938
Avg UG Fees	2,840
Avg PG Fees	10,700

RANKINGS PERFORMANCE

Overall Rankings Position	27
Faculty Level Positions	
Arts & Humanities	11
Engineering & IT	27
Life Sciences & BioMedicine	18
Natural Sciences	20
Social Sciences	17=

University of Victoria

CONTACT DETAILS

Address
3800 Finnerty Road
Victoria
BC V8P 5C2
Canada
Web   www.uvic.ca
Phone   +1 250 721 7211

INSTITUTION STATS

Undergraduates	18,930
Postgraduates	2,423
International Students	11.1%
Student Faculty Ratio	10.5:1
Total Citations	49,659
Avg UG Fees	1,200
Avg PG Fees	5,000

RANKINGS PERFORMANCE

Faculty Level Positions

Arts & Humanities	305=
Engineering & IT	250=
Life Sciences & BioMedicine	385=
Natural Sciences	423=
Social Sciences	299=

University of Waterloo

CONTACT DETAILS

Address
200 University Avenue West
Waterloo
Ontario N2L 3G1
Canada
Web   www.uwaterloo.ca
Phone   +1 519 888 4567

INSTITUTION STATS

Undergraduates	23,235
Postgraduates	2,891
International Students	8.6%
Student Faculty Ratio	10.1:1
Total Citations	71,109
Avg UG Fees	7,650
Avg PG Fees	4,500

RANKINGS PERFORMANCE

Faculty Level Positions

Arts & Humanities	328
Engineering & IT	59
Life Sciences & BioMedicine	221=
Natural Sciences	97=
Social Sciences	224

CANADA

University of Western Ontario

CONTACT DETAILS

INSTITUTION STATS

RANKINGS PERFORMANCE

Address
1151 Richmond Street, Suite 2
London, Ontario
N6A 5B8
Canada
Web www.uwo.ca
Phone +1 519 661 2111

Undergraduates	20,777
Postgraduates	3,428
International Students	9.3%
Student Faculty Ratio	23:1
Total Citations	129,484

Faculty Level Positions
Arts & Humanities	238=
Engineering & IT	287=
Life Sciences & BioMedicine	209
Natural Sciences	423=
Social Sciences	351=

York University

CONTACT DETAILS

INSTITUTION STATS

RANKINGS PERFORMANCE

Address
4700 Keele Street
Toronto, Ontario
M3J 1P3
Canada
Web www.yorku.ca
Phone +1 416 736 5000

Undergraduates	45,895
Postgraduates	4,796
International Students	1.2%
Student Faculty Ratio	8.6:1
Total Citations	37,900

Faculty Level Positions
Arts & Humanities	162
Engineering & IT	438=
Natural Sciences	388=
Social Sciences	109=

CHILE

Adolfo Ibanez University

CONTACT DETAILS

INSTITUTION STATS

RANKINGS PERFORMANCE

Address
Avenida Presidente Errázuriz
Las Condes
3425
Chile
Web www.uai.cl
Phone +56 (32) 369-3609

Undergraduates	5,214
Postgraduates	1,750
International Students	7.8%
Student Faculty Ratio	20.5:1
Avg UG Fees	5,556
Avg PG Fees	29,000

Faculty Level Positions
Engineering & IT	438=

Pontificia Universidad Católica de Chile

CONTACT DETAILS

INSTITUTION STATS

RANKINGS PERFORMANCE

Address
Avenida Libertador Bernardo
O'Higgins 340
Santiago
4860
Chile
Web www.puc.cl
Phone +56 (2) 354 2810

Undergraduates	17,334
Postgraduates	5,337
International Students	8.8%
Student Faculty Ratio	7.6:1
Total Citations	4,091
Avg UG Fees	4,448
Avg PG Fees	5,309

Faculty Level Positions
Arts & Humanities	277=
Engineering & IT	276=
Natural Sciences	297=
Social Sciences	318

CHILE

Universidad de Chile

CONTACT DETAILS

Address
Diagonal Paraguay 265
Santiago
833-0015
Chile
Web   www.uchile.cl
Phone   +562 978-2000

INSTITUTION STATS

Undergraduates	24,502
Postgraduates	5,611
International Students	6.8%
Student Faculty Ratio	8.2:1
Total Citations	40,050
Avg UG Fees	3,340
Avg PG Fees	15,800

RANKINGS PERFORMANCE

Faculty Level Positions

Arts & Humanities	321=
Engineering & IT	406=
Life Sciences & BioMedicine	421=
Natural Sciences	394=
Social Sciences	305=

Universidad de Santiago De Chile

CONTACT DETAILS

Web   www.usach.cl
Phone   +562 681 1100

INSTITUTION STATS

Student Faculty Ratio	13.4:1

RANKINGS PERFORMANCE

Faculty Level Positions

Engineering & IT	315=
Natural Sciences	461=
Social Sciences	426=

CHINA

Fudan University

CONTACT DETAILS

Address
220 Handan Road
Shanghai
200433
China
Web   www.fudan.edu.cn
Phone   +86 21 65642222

INSTITUTION STATS

Undergraduates	15,700
Postgraduates	11,000
International Students	5.0%
Student Faculty Ratio	4.3:1
Total Citations	35,583
Avg UG Fees	641
Avg PG Fees	1,282

RANKINGS PERFORMANCE

Overall Rankings Position	116=

Faculty Level Positions

Arts & Humanities	82=
Engineering & IT	97
Life Sciences & BioMedicine	47
Natural Sciences	63
Social Sciences	59=

University of Science and Technology of China

CONTACT DETAILS

Address
Jinzhai Road
Hefei
230026
China
Web   www.ustc.edu.cn
Phone   +86-551-3602949

INSTITUTION STATS

Undergraduates	7,490
Postgraduates	8,796
International Students	0.2%
Student Faculty Ratio	22.7:1
Total Citations	47,837
Avg UG Fees	2,500
Avg PG Fees	3,800

RANKINGS PERFORMANCE

Overall Rankings Position	165=

Faculty Level Positions

Arts & Humanities	268
Engineering & IT	41=
Life Sciences & BioMedicine	116=
Natural Sciences	32
Social Sciences	140=

CHINA

University of Jilin

CONTACT DETAILS

Web www.en.jlu.edu.cn

INSTITUTION STATS

Total Students	59,000
International Students	1.1%
Student Faculty Ratio	9.7:1
Total Citations	21,878

RANKINGS PERFORMANCE

Faculty Level Positions

Engineering & IT	328=
Life Sciences & BioMedicine	302=
Natural Sciences	360=
Social Sciences	313=

Nanjing University

CONTACT DETAILS

Address
Hankou Road 22#
Nanjing
China

Web www.nju.edu.cn
Phone +86-25-83592700

INSTITUTION STATS

Undergraduates	12,202
Postgraduates	9,964
International Students	1.5%
Student Faculty Ratio	12.6:1
Total Citations	45,866
Avg UG Fees	590
Avg PG Fees	897

RANKINGS PERFORMANCE

Overall Rankings Position	180

Faculty Level Positions

Arts & Humanities	76=
Engineering & IT	99
Life Sciences & BioMedicine	84
Natural Sciences	70
Social Sciences	152=

Peking University

CONTACT DETAILS

Address
Yiheyuan Road, Haidian District
Beijing
China 100871
China
Web www.pku.edu.cn
Phone +86-10-62752114

INSTITUTION STATS

Undergraduates	14,240
Postgraduates	12,732
International Students	6.8%
Student Faculty Ratio	13.9:1
Total Citations	64,942

RANKINGS PERFORMANCE

Overall Rankings Position	14

Faculty Level Positions

Arts & Humanities	10
Engineering & IT	20
Life Sciences & BioMedicine	8
Natural Sciences	12
Social Sciences	17=

Shandong University

CONTACT DETAILS

Address
Shanda South Road 27#
Jinan
Shandong Province
China

Web www.sdu.edu.cn
Phone +86-531-88395114

INSTITUTION STATS

Undergraduates	40,978
Postgraduates	10,755
International Students	4.8%
Student Faculty Ratio	10.3:1
Total Citations	17,859

RANKINGS PERFORMANCE

Faculty Level Positions

Engineering & IT	227
Life Sciences & BioMedicine	207=
Natural Sciences	295=
Social Sciences	372=

CHINA

Shanghai Jiao Tong University

CONTACT DETAILS

INSTITUTION STATS

RANKINGS PERFORMANCE

Address
1954 Huashan Road
Shanghai
200030
China
Web   www.sjtu.edu.cn
Phone +86 21 62932214 ext.8015

Undergraduates	14,665
Postgraduates	9,649
International Students	2.9%
Student Faculty Ratio	24.4:1
Total Citations	18,700
Avg UG Fees	641
Avg PG Fees	1,400

Overall Rankings Position	179
Faculty Level Positions	
Arts & Humanities	170=
Engineering & IT	48=
Life Sciences & BioMedicine	116=
Natural Sciences	170=
Social Sciences	159

Southeast University

CONTACT DETAILS

INSTITUTION STATS

RANKINGS PERFORMANCE

Web   www.seu.edu.cn

Undergraduates	17,000
Postgraduates	9,000
International Students	1.3%
Student Faculty Ratio	12.4:1
Total Citations	4,058

Faculty Level Positions	
Arts & Humanities	381=
Engineering & IT	315=
Life Sciences & BioMedicine	275=
Natural Sciences	401=
Social Sciences	330=

Tianjin University

CONTACT DETAILS

INSTITUTION STATS

RANKINGS PERFORMANCE

Address
92 Weijin Road
Tianjin
300072
China
Web   www.tju.edu.cn
Phone   +86 22 27404167

Undergraduates	15,507
Postgraduates	9,700
International Students	3.0%
Student Faculty Ratio	8.9:1
Total Citations	7,984
Avg UG Fees	538
Avg PG Fees	1,282

Faculty Level Positions	
Arts & Humanities	381=
Engineering & IT	328=
Life Sciences & BioMedicine	300
Natural Sciences	417=
Social Sciences	254=

Tongji University

CONTACT DETAILS

INSTITUTION STATS

RANKINGS PERFORMANCE

Address
Siping Road 1239#,
Shanghai
China

Web   www.tongji.edu.cn
Phone   + 86-21-65982200

Undergraduates	22,574
Postgraduates	15,418
International Students	2.8%
Student Faculty Ratio	30.4:1

Faculty Level Positions	
Arts & Humanities	272=
Engineering & IT	219=
Life Sciences & BioMedicine	275=
Natural Sciences	331=

CHINA

Tsing Hua University

CONTACT DETAILS

Address
Haidian District
Beijing
China
Web www.tsinghua.edu.cn
Phone +86-10-62785001

INSTITUTION STATS

Undergraduates	13,709
Postgraduates	18,443
International Students	5.5%
Student Faculty Ratio	9.3:1
Total Citations	50,358
Avg UG Fees	641
Avg PG Fees	2,051

RANKINGS PERFORMANCE

Overall Rankings Position	28
Faculty Level Positions	
Arts & Humanities	78
Engineering & IT	14
Life Sciences & BioMedicine	63=
Natural Sciences	41=
Social Sciences	101=

Xi'an Jiaotong University

CONTACT DETAILS

Address
Xianyang west road
Xi'an
710049
China
Web www.xjtu.edu.cn
Phone +86-29-82668234

INSTITUTION STATS

Undergraduates	18,971
Postgraduates	12,735
International Students	1.8%
Student Faculty Ratio	12.2:1
Total Citations	9,504
Avg UG Fees	766
Avg PG Fees	1,154

RANKINGS PERFORMANCE

Faculty Level Positions	
Engineering & IT	152=
Life Sciences & BioMedicine	242=
Natural Sciences	381=
Social Sciences	471=

Zhejiang University

CONTACT DETAILS

Address
Hangzhou
China
Web www.zju.edu.cn
Phone +86-571-87951111

INSTITUTION STATS

Undergraduates	25,000
Postgraduates	17,900
International Students	2.8%
Total Citations	36,595

RANKINGS PERFORMANCE

Faculty Level Positions	
Arts & Humanities	328=
Engineering & IT	141=
Life Sciences & BioMedicine	143
Natural Sciences	198=
Social Sciences	223

COLOMBIA

Universidad de Los Andes

CONTACT DETAILS

Address
Carrera 1 N° 18A 10
Bogota
00001
Colombia
Web ingles.uniandes.edu.co
Phone +57(1) 339 9999

INSTITUTION STATS

Undergraduates	10,959
Postgraduates	1,601
International Students	0.4%
Student Faculty Ratio	13.7:1
Avg UG Fees	6,000
Avg PG Fees	4,680

RANKINGS PERFORMANCE

Faculty Level Positions	
Engineering & IT	297=
Natural Sciences	476=
Social Sciences	281=

CZECH REPUBLIC

Brno University of Technology

CONTACT DETAILS

Address
Antonínská 548/1
Brno
CZ 601 90
Czech Republic
Web www.vutbr.cz
Phone +420 54114 1111

INSTITUTION STATS

Undergraduates	8,451
Postgraduates	10,172
International Students	5.1%
Studen Faculty Ratio	4.9:1

RANKINGS PERFORMANCE

Faculty Level Positions

Arts & Humanities	255=
Engineering & IT	403
Life Sciences & BioMedicine	409=
Natural Sciences	433
Social Sciences	426=

Charles University

CONTACT DETAILS

Address
Thákurova 3
Prague 6
160 00
Czech Republic
Web www.cuni.cz
Phone +420 220 181 384

INSTITUTION STATS

Total Students	44,391
International Students	11.2%
Student Faculty Ratio	4.8:1
Total Citations	53,426

RANKINGS PERFORMANCE

Faculty Level Positions

Arts & Humanities	102
Engineering & IT	322=
Life Sciences & BioMedicine	171
Natural Sciences	148=
Social Sciences	178=

DENMARK

University of Aarhus

CONTACT DETAILS

Address
Nordre Ringgade 1
Aarhus C
DK-8000
Denmark
Web www.au.dk
Phone +45 8942 1111

INSTITUTION STATS

Undergraduates	9,886
Postgraduates	10,852
International Students	8.1%
Student Faculty Ratio	24:1
Total Citations	150,707
Avg UG Fees	15,638
Avg PG Fees	15,638

RANKINGS PERFORMANCE

Overall Rankings Position	126
Faculty Level Positions	
Arts & Humanities	271
Engineering & IT	179=
Life Sciences & BioMedicine	86=
Natural Sciences	64
Social Sciences	105=

University of Copenhagen

CONTACT DETAILS

Address
Nørregade 10, P.O. Box 2177
Copenhagen K
DK-1017
Denmark
Web www.ku.dk
Phone +45 35 32 26 26

INSTITUTION STATS

Undergraduates	17,931
Postgraduates	14,593
International Students	7.8%
Student Faculty Ratio	6.7:1
Total Citations	182,650
Avg UG Fees	13,972
Avg PG Fees	13,972

RANKINGS PERFORMANCE

Overall Rankings Position	54=
Faculty Level Positions	
Arts & Humanities	26
Engineering & IT	169=
Life Sciences & BioMedicine	44
Natural Sciences	47
Social Sciences	40

DENMARK

University of Southern Denmark

CONTACT DETAILS	INSTITUTION STATS		RANKINGS PERFORMANCE	
Address	**Undergraduates**	6,545	**Faculty Level Positions**	
Campusvej 55	**Postgraduates**	5,331	Arts & Humanities	293=
Odense M	**International Students**	13.5%	Engineering & IT	406=
DK-5230	**Student Faculty Ratio**	12.4:1	Life Sciences & BioMedicine	284=
Denmark	**Total Citations**	53,644	Natural Sciences	291=
Web www.sdu.dk	**Avg UG Fees**	13,074	Social Sciences	393=
Phone +45 6550 1000	**Avg PG Fees**	13,177		

Technical University of Denmark

CONTACT DETAILS	INSTITUTION STATS		RANKINGS PERFORMANCE	
Address	**Undergraduates**	3,388	**Overall Rankings Position**	194
Anker Engelundsvej 1	**Postgraduates**	3,559	**Faculty Level Positions**	
Kgs. Lyngby	**International Students**	11.8%	Arts & Humanities	430=
DK-2800	**Student Faculty Ratio**	14.8:1	Engineering & IT	46
Denmark	**Total Citations**	70,955	Life Sciences & BioMedicine	141
Web www.dtu.dk			Natural Sciences	167=
Phone +45 45 25 25 25			Social Sciences	359=

EGYPT

Cairo University

CONTACT DETAILS	INSTITUTION STATS		RANKINGS PERFORMANCE	
Address	**Total Students**	155,000	**Faculty Level Positions**	
Gamaa Street	**International Students**	1.1%	Arts & Humanities	148=
Giza	**Student Faculty Ratio**	16.1:1	Engineering & IT	228=
Egypt	**Total Citations**	12,677	Life Sciences & BioMedicine	314=
Web www.cu.edu.eg			Natural Sciences	326=
			Social Sciences	178=

FINLAND

Helsinki University of Technology

CONTACT DETAILS	INSTITUTION STATS		RANKINGS PERFORMANCE	
Address	**Undergraduates**	32,821	**Overall Rankings Position**	116=
P.O. Box 33	**Postgraduates**	5,482	**Faculty Level Positions**	
FI-00014	**International Students**	3.1%	Arts & Humanities	61
Finland	**Student Faculty Ratio**	14.7:1	Engineering & IT	164
	Total Citations	292,604	Life Sciences & BioMedicine	42
Web www.helsinki.fi			Natural Sciences	72
			Social Sciences	63=

FINLAND

Helsinki University of Technology

CONTACT DETAILS

INSTITUTION STATS

RANKINGS PERFORMANCE

Address
P.O.Box 1000
Helsinki
FI-02015
Finland"
Web   www.tkk.fi
Phone   +358 9 4511

Undergraduates	12,049
Postgraduates	2,954
International Students	4.6%
Student Faculty Ratio	6.7:1
Total Citations	37,787

Faculty Level Positions

Arts & Humanities	176=
Engineering & IT	53=
Life Sciences & BioMedicine	369=
Natural Sciences	113=
Social Sciences	313=

University of Jyväskylä

CONTACT DETAILS

INSTITUTION STATS

RANKINGS PERFORMANCE

Address
P.O.Box 35
FI-40014
Finland

Web   www.jyu.fi
Phone   + 358 14 260 1211

Undergraduates	12,340
Postgraduates	1,608
International Students	2.3%
Student Faculty Ratio	12.1:1
Total Citations	27,853

Faculty Level Positions

Arts & Humanities	324=
Engineering & IT	382=
Life Sciences & BioMedicine	292=
Natural Sciences	260=
Social Sciences	269=

Kuopio University

CONTACT DETAILS

INSTITUTION STATS

RANKINGS PERFORMANCE

Address
P.O. Box 1627
Kuopio
FI-70211
Finland
Web   www.uku.fi
Phone   +358 17 162 211

Undergraduates	5,379
Postgraduates	1,454
International Students	2.0%
Student Faculty Ratio	30:1
Total Citations	79,742

Faculty Level Positions

Engineering & IT	438=
Life Sciences & BioMedicine	292=
Natural Sciences	426=
Social Sciences	372=

University of Oulu

CONTACT DETAILS

INSTITUTION STATS

RANKINGS PERFORMANCE

Address
Pentti Kaiteran katu 1,
OULUN YLIOPISTO
90014
Finland
Web   www.oulu.fi
Phone   +358 (08) 553 1011

Undergraduates	14,233
Postgraduates	1,843
International Students	1.7%
Student Faculty Ratio	4:1
Total Citations	70,685

Faculty Level Positions

Engineering & IT	241=
Life Sciences & BioMedicine	239=
Natural Sciences	455=
Social Sciences	426=

FINLAND

University of Tampere

CONTACT DETAILS

INSTITUTION STATS

RANKINGS PERFORMANCE

Address
Tampereen yliopisto
33014
Finland

Web www.uta.fi
Phone +358 (03) 355 111

Undergraduates	13,543
Postgraduates	1,834
International Students	2.4%
Student Faculty Ratio	20.3:1
Total Citations	54,255

Faculty Level Positions
Arts & Humanities	263=
Engineering & IT	219=
Life Sciences & BioMedicine	369=
Natural Sciences	408
Social Sciences	209=

University of Turku

CONTACT DETAILS

INSTITUTION STATS

RANKINGS PERFORMANCE

Address
TURUN YLIOPISTO
FI-20014
Finland

Web www.utu.fi
Phone +358-2-333 51

Undergraduates	13,830
Postgraduates	2,067
International Students	1.5%
Student Faculty Ratio	9.6:1
Total Citations	98,507

Faculty Level Positions 369=
Arts & Humanities	274=
Engineering & IT	173=
Life Sciences & BioMedicine	260=
Natural Sciences	193=
Social Sciences	

FRANCE

Universite de Caen Basse-Normandie

CONTACT DETAILS

INSTITUTION STATS

RANKINGS PERFORMANCE

Address
Esplanade de la Paix
Caen
14032
France

Web www.unicaen.fr
Phone +33 (0) 2 31 56 55 00

Total Students	24,712
International Students	11.8%
Student Faculty Ratio	17.1:1
Total Citations	23,404

Faculty Level Positions
Arts & Humanities	412=
Engineering & IT	406=
Natural Sciences	348=
Social Sciences	426=

Ecole Normale Supérieure Lyon

CONTACT DETAILS

INSTITUTION STATS

RANKINGS PERFORMANCE

Address
46, allée d'Italie
Lyon
69364
France

Web www.ens-lyon.fr
Phone + 33 (0) 4 72 72 80 00

Undergraduates	173
Postgraduates	695
International Students	11.6%
Student Faculty Ratio	5.5:1
Total Citations	33,597
Avg UG Fees	200
Avg PG Fees	320

Overall Rankings Position 72
Faculty Level Positions
Arts & Humanities	215=
Engineering & IT	179=
Life Sciences & BioMedicine	284=
Natural Sciences	107=
Social Sciences	393=

FRANCE

Ecole Normale Supérieure

CONTACT DETAILS

Address
45, rue d'Ulm
Paris
75230
France

Web www.ens.fr
Phone + 33 (0) 1 44 32 30 00

INSTITUTION STATS

Undergraduates	244
Postgraduates	888
International Students	17.5%
Student Faculty Ratio	8.4:1
Total Citations	65,916

RANKINGS PERFORMANCE

Overall Rankings Position	18
Faculty Level Positions	
Arts & Humanities	25
Engineering & IT	83=
Life Sciences & BioMedicine	77=
Natural Sciences	17
Social Sciences	101=

École Polytechnique

CONTACT DETAILS

Address
rue de Saclay
Palaiseau
911228
France
Web www.polytechnique.fr
Phone +33 (0)1 69 33 42 88

INSTITUTION STATS

Undergraduates	2,000
Postgraduates	600
International Students	24.6%
Student Faculty Ratio	3.8:1
Total Citations	64,586
Avg UG Fees	8,973
Avg PG Fees	12,818

RANKINGS PERFORMANCE

Overall Rankings Position	37
Faculty Level Positions	
Arts & Humanities	198=
Engineering & IT	26
Life Sciences & BioMedicine	196=
Natural Sciences	24
Social Sciences	203=

The ENPC School of International Management

CONTACT DETAILS

Address
28, rue des Saints-Pères
Paris
75343
France
Web http://www.enpcmbaparis.com
Phone + 33 (0)1 49 23 20 00

INSTITUTION STATS

Undergraduates	48
Postgraduates	50
International Students	31.9%
Avg UG Fees	5,127
Avg PG Fees	18,586

RANKINGS PERFORMANCE

Faculty Level Positions	
Engineering & IT	245=
Life Sciences & BioMedicine	397=
Natural Sciences	368=
Social Sciences	484=

ESCP-EAP European School of Management

CONTACT DETAILS

Address
79 avenue de la République
Paris
75011
France
Web www.escp-eap.net
Phone + 33 (0)1 49 23 20 00

INSTITUTION STATS

Total Students	3,276
International Students	41.2%
Student Faculty Ratio	8:1
Avg Fees	24,867

RANKINGS PERFORMANCE

Faculty Level Positions	
Engineering & IT	349=
Natural Sciences	476=
Social Sciences	330=

FRANCE

ESSEC Business School, Paris

CONTACT DETAILS

Address
CNIT - BP230
Paris
92 053
France
Web   www.essec.edu
Phone   +33 (0) 1 46 92 49 00

INSTITUTION STATS

Undergraduates	1,212
Postgraduates	2,425
International Students	14.0%
Student Faculty Ratio	12.9:1
Avg UG Fees	9,101
Avg PG Fees	24,482

RANKINGS PERFORMANCE

Faculty Level Positions

Arts & Humanities	412=
Engineering & IT	497=
Natural Sciences	500=
Social Sciences	271=

Université Joseph-Fourier, Grenoble I

CONTACT DETAILS

Address
17 avenue des Martyrs
Grenoble
38054
France
Web   www.ujf-grenoble.fr
Phone   + 33 (0)4 38 78 91 02

INSTITUTION STATS

Undergraduates	10,812
Postgraduates	6,745
International Students	12.8%
Student Faculty Ratio	21.9:1
Total Citations	78,260
Avg UG Fees	159
Avg PG Fees	295

RANKINGS PERFORMANCE

Faculty Level Positions

Arts & Humanities	277=
Engineering & IT	151
Life Sciences & BioMedicine	268=
Natural Sciences	113=
Social Sciences	299=

Universite Pierre Mendes, Grenoble 2

CONTACT DETAILS

Address
151, rue des universités
Saint-Martin d'Hères
38400
France
Web   www.upmf-grenoble.fr
Phone   +33 (0) 4 76 82 54 00

INSTITUTION STATS

Total Students	19,531
International Students	7.5%
Student Faculty Ratio	5.5:1
Avg UG Fees	237
Avg PG Fees	440

RANKINGS PERFORMANCE

Faculty Level Positions

Engineering & IT	438=
Natural Sciences	420=
Social Sciences	464=

Université Stendhal Grenoble III

CONTACT DETAILS

Address
1180 avenue Centrale Domaine
Universitaire
Grenoble
38400
France
Web   http://www.u-grenoble3.
fr/stendhal/index.html
Phone   + 33 (0) 476 82 43 00

INSTITUTION STATS

Student Faculty Ratio	9:1

RANKINGS PERFORMANCE

Faculty Level Positions

Arts & Humanities	374=
Natural Sciences	461=
Social Sciences	464=

FRANCE

HEC School of Management

CONTACT DETAILS	INSTITUTION STATS		RANKINGS PERFORMANCE	
Address	**Undergraduates**	356	**Faculty Level Positions**	
1, rue de la Libération	**Postgraduates**	2,789	Arts & Humanities	328=
Paris	**International Students**	20.5%	Engineering & IT	463=
78351	**Student Faculty Ratio**	29.9:1	Natural Sciences	489=
France	**Avg UG Fees**	10,126	Social Sciences	90
Web www.hec.fr	**Avg PG Fees**	21,150		
Phone + 33 (0) 1 39 67 70 00				

Universite des Sciences et Technologies de Lille

CONTACT DETAILS	INSTITUTION STATS		RANKINGS PERFORMANCE	
Address	**Undergraduates**	8,115	**Faculty Level Positions**	
Cité Scientifique	**Postgraduates**	5,795	Engineering & IT	494=
Villeneuve d'Ascq	**International Students**	22.4%	Life Sciences & BioMedicine	427=
59655	**Student Faculty Ratio**	28:1	Natural Sciences	343=
France	**Avg UG Fees**	465		
Web www.univ-lille1.fr	**Avg PG Fees**	588		
Phone + 33 (0) 3 20 43 43 43				

University of Lille 2

CONTACT DETAILS	INSTITUTION STATS		RANKINGS PERFORMANCE	
Address	**Undergraduates**	7,232	**Faculty Level Positions**	
42, rue Paul Duez	**Postgraduates**	4,123	Social Sciences	447=
Lille	**International Students**	10.7%		
59800	**Student Faculty Ratio**	10.2:1		
France	**Avg UG Fees**	231		
Web www.univ-lille2.fr	**Avg PG Fees**	354		
Phone +33 0 3 20 96 43 43				

University of Lille 3 - Charles de Gaulle

CONTACT DETAILS	INSTITUTION STATS		RANKINGS PERFORMANCE	
Address	**Undergraduates**	16,562	**Faculty Level Positions**	
rue du Barreau	**Postgraduates**	4,891	Arts & Humanities	255=
Villeneuve d'Ascq	**International Students**	4.5%	Life Sciences & BioMedicine	409=
60149	**Student Faculty Ratio**	20.9:1	Natural Sciences	476=
France				
Web www.univ-lille3.fr				
Phone + 33 (0)3 20 41 61 61				

393

FRANCE

Universite Claude Bernard- Lyon 1

CONTACT DETAILS

Address
43 boulevard du 11 Novembre 1918
Villeurbanne
69622
France
Web   www.univ-lyon1.fr
Phone   +33 (0)4 72 44 80 00

INSTITUTION STATS

Undergraduates	15,449
Postgraduates	13,684
International Students	12.0%
Student Faculty Ratio	14.3:1
Avg UG Fees	82,545
Avg PG Fees	295

RANKINGS PERFORMANCE

Faculty Level Positions

Engineering & IT	258=
Life Science & BioMedicine	201=
Natural Sciences	268
Social Sciences	372=

University Lumiere Lyon 2

CONTACT DETAILS

Address
86 rue Pasteur
Lyon
69007
France
Web   www.univ-lyon2.fr
Phone   +33 (0) 4 78 69 70 00

INSTITUTION STATS

Undergraduates	16,223
Postgraduates	8,713
International Students	16.7%
Student Faculty Ratio	35.8:1
Avg UG Fees	253
Avg PG Fees	308

RANKINGS PERFORMANCE

Faculty Level Positions

Arts & Humanities	277=
Natural Sciences	500=
Social Sciences	411=

University of Lyon 3 - Jean Moulin

CONTACT DETAILS

Address
1, rue de l'Université
Lyon
69007
France
Web   www.univ-lyon3.fr
Phone   + 33 (0) 4 72 72 20 20

INSTITUTION STATS

Total Students	22,109
International Students	15.3%
Student Faculty Ratio	12:1

RANKINGS PERFORMANCE

Faculty Level Positions

Arts & Humanities	430=
Natural Sciences	500=
Social Sciences	458=

University of Montpellier 1

CONTACT DETAILS

Address
5 bd Henri IV
Montpellier
34967
France
Web   www.univ-montp1.fr
Phone   33 (0) 4 67 41 75 15

INSTITUTION STATS

Undergraduates	11,002
Postgraduates	10,547
International Students	9.5%
Student Faculty Ratio	26:1
Total Citations	7,967

RANKINGS PERFORMANCE

Faculty Level Positions

Arts & Humanities	305=
Engineering & IT	162
Life Sciences & BioMedicine	127
Natural Sciences	331=
Social Sciences	313=

FRANCE

University of Montpellier 2 Sciences and Techniques

CONTACT DETAILS

Address
Place Eugene Bataillon
Montpellier
34095
France
Web www.univ-montp2.fr
Phone +33(0)4 67 14 30 30

INSTITUTION STATS

Undergraduates	6,447
Postgraduates	5,486
International Students	7.6%
Student Faculty Ratio	11.8:1
Total Citations	69,172

RANKINGS PERFORMANCE

Faculty Level Positions

Engineering & IT	438=
Life Sciences & BioMedicine	225=
Natural Sciences	500=
Social Sciences	426=

University of Montpellier 3 - Paul Valery

CONTACT DETAILS

Address
17, rue Abbé de l'Épée
Montpellier
34090
France
Web www.univ-montp3.fr
Phone + 33 (0) 4 67 14 23 42

INSTITUTION STATS

Undergraduates	13,370
Postgraduates	5,213
International Students	17.6%

RANKINGS PERFORMANCE

Faculty Level Positions

Arts & Humanities	430=
Natural Sciences	500=
Social Sciences	393=

University of Nancy 1 - Henri Poincare

CONTACT DETAILS

Address
24-30, rue Lionnois
Nancy
54003
France
Web www.uhp-nancy.fr
Phone +33 (0) 3 83 68 20 27

INSTITUTION STATS

Undergraduates	6,165
Postgraduates	10,628
International Students	12.6%
Student Faculty Ratio	16.6:1
Total Citations	23,486

RANKINGS PERFORMANCE

Faculty Level Positions

Arts & Humanities	311=
Engineering & IT	241=
Life Sciences & BioMedicine	369=
Natural Sciences	237=

University of Nancy 2

CONTACT DETAILS

Address
25, Rue Baron Louis
Nancy
54001
France
Web www.univ-nancy2.fr
Phone +33 03 83 95 76 00

INSTITUTION STATS

Undergraduates	12,723
Postgraduates	5,259
International Students	12.5%
Student Faculty Ratio	27.6:1

RANKINGS PERFORMANCE

Faculty Level Positions

Natural Sciences	500=

FRANCE

Sciences Po Paris

CONTACT DETAILS

Address
27 rue Saint-Guillaume
Paris
75337
France
Web www.sciences-po.fr
Phone + 33 (0) 1 45 49 50 50

INSTITUTION STATS

Undergraduates	2,380
Postgraduates	4,530
International Students	32.6%
Student Faculty Ratio	22.5:1
Avg UG Fees	1,170
Avg PG Fees	641

RANKINGS PERFORMANCE

Overall Rankings Position	52
Faculty Level Positions	
Arts & Humanities	163=
Engineering & IT	289=
Life Sciences & BioMedicine	210=
Natural Sciences	314=
Social Sciences	157=

Panthéon Sorbonne Universite Paris I

CONTACT DETAILS

Address
12, Place du Panthéon
Paris
75005
France
Web www.univ-paris1.fr
Phone +33 (0) 1 44 07 80 00

INSTITUTION STATS

Undergraduates	20,062
Postgraduates	15,447
International Students	19.4%
Student Faculty Ratio	16.7:1
Total Citations	19
Avg UG Fees	214
Avg PG Fees	277

RANKINGS PERFORMANCE

Faculty Level Positions	
Arts & Humanities	60
Engineering & IT	197=
Life Sciences & BioMedicine	196=
Natural Sciences	191=
Social Sciences	50

Universite Paris-Sorbonne (Paris IV)

CONTACT DETAILS

Address
1, rue Victor Cousin
Paris
75005
France
Web www.paris4.sorbonne.fr
Phone +33 (0) 1 40 46 22 11

INSTITUTION STATS

Undergraduates	10,034
Postgraduates	15,249
International Students	17.8%
Student Faculty Ratio	7.1:1
Total Citations	337

RANKINGS PERFORMANCE

Faculty Level Positions	
Arts & Humanities	16
Engineering & IT	245=
Life Sciences & BioMedicine	380=
Natural Sciences	253=
Social Sciences	53=

University Paris Dauphine

CONTACT DETAILS

Address
Place du Maréchal de Lattre de
Tassigny
Paris
75775
France
Web www.dauphine.fr
Phone +33 (0) 1 44 05 44 05

INSTITUTION STATS

Total Students	9,000
International Students	23.0%
Student Faculty Ratio	14.4:1
Total Citations	3,094

RANKINGS PERFORMANCE

Faculty Level Positions	
Engineering & IT	463=
Natural Sciences	256=
Social Sciences	346=

FRANCE

University of Paris 5 - Rene Descartes

CONTACT DETAILS

INSTITUTION STATS

RANKINGS PERFORMANCE

Address
12, rue de l'Ecole de médecine
Paris
75270
France
Web   www.univ-paris5.fr
Phone   +33 (0) 1 40 46 16 16

Undergraduates	32,000
International Students	17.6%
Total Citations	61,255

Faculty Level Positions
Arts & Humanities	328=
Life Sciences & BioMedicine	409=
Natural Sciences	329=
Social Sciences	426=

Université Pierre-et-Marie-Curie

CONTACT DETAILS

INSTITUTION STATS

RANKINGS PERFORMANCE

Address
4 place jussieu
Paris
75005
France
Web   www.upmc.fr
Phone   +33 (0) 1 44 27 36 20

Undergraduates	21,056
Postgraduates	7,536
International Students	21.8%
Student Faculty Ratio	9.4:1
Total Citations	189,163
Avg UG Fees	208
Avg PG Fees	320

Overall Rankings Position	93=
Faculty Level Positions	
Arts & Humanities	328=
Engineering & IT	100
Life Sciences & BioMedicine	62
Natural Sciences	22=
Social Sciences	393=

University of Paris 7 - Denis Diderot

CONTACT DETAILS

INSTITUTION STATS

RANKINGS PERFORMANCE

Address
2 place Jussieu
Paris
75251
France

Web   www.univ-paris7.fr
Phone   + 33 (0) 1 44 27 44 27

Toatal Students	26,000
International Students	17.6%
Student Faculty Ratio	11:1
Total Citations	85,885

Faculty Level Positions
Arts & Humanities	398=
Engineering & IT	438=
Natural Sciences	123=
Social Sciences	305=

Universite Paris X Nanterre

CONTACT DETAILS

INSTITUTION STATS

RANKINGS PERFORMANCE

Address
200 Avenue de la Republique
Paris
92001
France
Web   http://www.u-paris10.fr
Phone   +33 (0) 1 40 97 74 61

Student Faculty Ratio	12.2:1

Faculty Level Positions
Arts & Humanaties	250=
Life Sciences & BioMedicine	473
Natural Sciences	261=

FRANCE

Université Paris-Sud, Paris XI

CONTACT DETAILS	INSTITUTION STATS		RANKINGS PERFORMANCE	
Address	Undergraduates	13,161	**Faculty Level Positions**	
15, rue Georges Clémenceau	**Postgraduates**	13,187	Engineering & IT	214=
Orsay	**International Students**	17.0%	Life Sciences & BioMedicine	314=
91405	**Student Faculty Ratio**	15:1	Natural Sciences	39
France	**Total Citations**	161,307		
Web www.u-psud.fr	**Avg UG Fees**	295		
Phone +33(0) 1 69 15 67 50	**Avg PG Fees**	340		

University of Rennes

CONTACT DETAILS	INSTITUTION STATS		RANKINGS PERFORMANCE	
Address	Undergraduates	6,435	**Faculty Level Positions**	
2, rue du Thabor	**Postgraduates**	5,595	Engineering & IT	368=
Rennes	**International Students**	11.4%	Life Sciences & BioMedicine	397=
35065	**Student Faculty Ratio**	14.1:1	Natural Sciences	351=
France	**Total Citations**	37,645		
Web www.univ-rennes1.fr	**Avg UG Fees**	217		
Phone +33 (0) 2 23 23 35 35	**Avg PG Fees**	297		

Université Louis Pasteur - Strasbourg I

CONTACT DETAILS	INSTITUTION STATS		RANKINGS PERFORMANCE	
Address	Undergraduates	7,459	**Overall Rankings Position**	161=
4, rue Blaise Pascal	**Postgraduates**	10,669	**Faculty Level Positions**	
Strasbourg	**International Students**	21.2%	Arts & Humanities	374=
67070	**Student Faculty Ratio**	20.8:1	Engineering & IT	232=
France	**Total Citations**	143,453	Life Sciences & BioMedicine	45
Web www-ulp.u-strasbg.fr			Natural Sciences	132=
Phone + 33 (0) 3 90 24 50 00			Social Sciences	271=

University of Toulouse 1 Sciences Sociales

CONTACT DETAILS	INSTITUTION STATS		RANKINGS PERFORMANCE	
Address	Undergraduates	9,813	**Faculty Level Positions**	
Place Anatole France	**Postgraduates**	6,819	Engineering & IT	347=
Toulouse	**International Students**	22.0%	Life Sciences & BioMedicine	248=
31042	**Student Faculty Ratio**	32.7:1	Natural Sciences	351=
France	**Total Citations**	1,157	Social Sciences	129=
Web www.univ-tlse1.fr	**Avg UG Fees**	191		
Phone +33 (0) 5 61 63 35 00	**Avg PG Fees**	287		

FRANCE

University of Toulouse 2 - Le Mirail

CONTACT DETAILS

Address
5, allées Antonio Machado
Toulouse
31106
France
Web www.univ-tlse2.fr
Phone + 33 (0) 5 61 50 40 57

INSTITUTION STATS

Total Students	26,507
International Students	12.9%
Student Faculty Ratio	29:1

RANKINGS PERFORMANCE

Faculty Level Positions	
Arts & Humanities	412=

University of Toulouse 3 - Paul Sabatier

CONTACT DETAILS

Address
118, Route de Narbonne
Toulouse
31062
France
Web www.ups-tlse.fr
Phone + 33 (0) 5 61 55 66 11

INSTITUTION STATS

Total Students	28,000
International Students	17.6%
Student Faculty Ratio	10.2:1
Total Citations	55,529

RANKINGS PERFORMANCE

Faculty Level Positions	
Engineering & IT	232=
Life Sciences & BioMedicine	231=
Natural Sciences	278=

GERMANY

Rheinisch-Westfälische Technische Hochschule Aachen

CONTACT DETAILS

Adress
Pressesprecher/Abteilungsleiter
Germany
Web www.rwth-aachen.de
Phone +490 0228/73 7647

INSTITUTION STATS

Undergraduates	24,564
Postgraduates	5,034
International Students	14.9%
Student Faculty Ratio	14.7:1
Total Citations	72,458
Avg UG Fees	1,282
Avg PG Fees	1,282

RANKINGS PERFORMANCE

Overall Rankings Position	172=
Faculty Level Positions	
Engineering & IT	39
Life Sciences & BioMedicine	284=
Natural Sciences	81
Social Sciences	458=

Universität Bayreuth

CONTACT DETAILS

Web www.uni-bayreuth.de

INSTITUTION STATS

Undergraduates	9,100
Postgraduates	400
International Students	6.9%
Student Faculty Ratio	13.3:1
Total Citations	49,936

RANKINGS PERFORMANCE

Faculty Level Positions	
Arts & Humanities	398=
Life Sciences & BioMedicine	369=
Natural Sciences	242

GERMANY

Universität Bielefeld

CONTACT DETAILS

INSTITUTION STATS

RANKINGS PERFORMANCE

Address
Postfach 10 01 31
D 33501 Bielefeld
Germany

Web www.uni-bielefeld.de
Phone +49 (0) 521 106-4075

Undergraduates	15,239
Postgraduates	2,021
International Students	6.2%
Student Faculty Ratio	18.4:1
Total Citations	38,052

Faculty Level Positions

Arts & Humanities	95=
Engineering & IT	433=
Life Sciences & BioMedicine	273
Natural Sciences	152
Social Sciences	242=

Rheinische Friedrich-Wilhelms-Universität Bonn

CONTACT DETAILS

INSTITUTION STATS

RANKINGS PERFORMANCE

Address
RWTH Aachen University
Aachen
52056 Germany

Web www.uni-bonn.de
Phone +49 241 801

Total Students	37,059
International Students	10.0%
Student Faculty Ratio	10.4:1
Total Citations	131,770

Faculty Level Positions

Arts & Humanities	263=
Engineering & IT	212=
Life Sciences & BioMedicine	196=
Natural Sciences	53
Social Sciences	84=

Universität Bremen

CONTACT DETAILS

INSTITUTION STATS

RANKINGS PERFORMANCE

Address
Bibliothekstraße 1
Bremen
D-28359
Germany
Web www.uni-bremen.de
Phone +49 421 218-1

Undergraduates	17,670
Postgraduates	9,188
International Students	10.3%
Student Faculty Ratio	18.4:1
Total Citations	32,475

Faculty Level Positions

Arts & Humanities	241=
Engineering & IT	205=
Life Sciences & BioMedicine	302=
Natural Sciences	339
Social Sciences	242=

Universität Dortmund

CONTACT DETAILS

INSTITUTION STATS

RANKINGS PERFORMANCE

Web www.uni-dortmund.de
Phone +49 (0231) 755-3720

Undergraduates	20,944
Postgraduates	1,419
International Students	9.8%
Student Faculty Ratio	17.1:1
Total Citations	29,489
Avg UG Fees	391
Avg PG Fees	391

Faculty Level Positions

Engineering & IT	322=
Life Sciences & BioMedicine	338=
Natural Sciences	263=
Social Sciences	372=

GERMANY

Universität Düsseldorf

CONTACT DETAILS

INSTITUTION STATS

RANKINGS PERFORMANCE

Address
Heinrich-Heine-Universität,
Universitätsstr.1,
40225 Düsseldorf
Germany
Web www.uni-duesseldorf.de

Undergraduates	14,499
Postgraduates	1,780
International Students	7.9%
Student Faculty Ratio	7.4:1
Total Citations	122,104
Avg UG Fees	1,282
Avg PG Fees	1,282

Faculty Level Positions

Engineering & IT	258=
Life Sciences & BioMedicine	201=
Natural Sciences	273=
Social Sciences	484=

Universität Erlangen-Nürnberg

CONTACT DETAILS

INSTITUTION STATS

RANKINGS PERFORMANCE

Address
91023 ERLANGEN,
Germany

Web www.uni-erlangen.de
Phone +49 9131 85 -0

Undergraduates	13,312
Postgraduates	12,382
International Students	10.1%
Student Faculty Ratio	32.2:1
Total Citations	140,454
Avg UG Fees	1,282
Avg PG Fees	1,282

Faculty Level Positions

Arts & Humanities	311=
Engineering & IT	302
Life Sciences & BioMedicine	231=
Natural Sciences	210=
Social Sciences	458=

Universität Duisburg-Essen

CONTACT DETAILS

INSTITUTION STATS

RANKINGS PERFORMANCE

Web http://www.uni-duisburg-essen.de/
Phone +49-(0)201-183-2229

Total Students	23,161
International Students	10.1%
Student Faculty Ratio	13.4:1

Faculty Level Positions

Engineering & IT	406=
Life Sciences & BioMedicine	278=
Natural Sciences	307
Social Sciences	419=

European Business School

CONTACT DETAILS

INSTITUTION STATS

RANKINGS PERFORMANCE

Address
International University Schloß
Reichartshausen
Oestrich-Winkel
65375
Germany
Web www.ebs.de
Phone +49 6723 69-0

Total Students	1,068
International Students	5.3%

Faculty Level Positions

Arts & Humanities	328=
Engineering & IT	463=
Social Sciences	209=

GERMANY

Universität Frankfurt am Main

CONTACT DETAILS	INSTITUTION STATS		RANKINGS PERFORMANCE	
	Total Students	42,420	**Overall Rankings Position**	187=
Web www.uni-frankfurt.de	**International Students**	10.3%	**Faculty Level Positions**	
	Student Faculty Ratio	7.5:1	Arts & Humanities	122=
	Total Citations	124,889	Engineering & IT	191=
			Life Sciences & BioMedicine	91=
			Natural Sciences	111
			Social Sciences	120=

Freie Universität Berlin

CONTACT DETAILS	INSTITUTION STATS		RANKINGS PERFORMANCE	
Address	**Undergraduates**	18,589	**Overall Rankings Position**	149
Str. 16-18	**Postgraduates**	4,406	**Faculty Level Positions**	
Berlin	**International Students**	10.5%	Arts & Humanities	33=
14195	**Student Faculty Ratio**	19.3:1	Engineering & IT	191=
Germany	**Total Citations**	135,988	Life Sciences & BioMedicine	88
Web www.fu-berlin.de			Natural Sciences	90=
Phone +49 30 838-1			Social Sciences	76=

Universität Freiburg

CONTACT DETAILS	INSTITUTION STATS		RANKINGS PERFORMANCE	
Address	**Undergraduates**	20,534	**Faculty Level Positions**	
Fahnenbergplatz	**Postgraduates**	1,634	Arts & Humanities	108
Freiburg	**International Students**	16.2%	Engineering & IT	322=
79085	**Student Faculty Ratio**	18.2:1	Life Sciences & BioMedicine	274
Germany	**Total Citations**	158,000	Natural Sciences	214=
Web www.uni-freiburg.de			Social Sciences	183=
Phone +49 0761 / 203 - 0				

JLU Gießen

CONTACT DETAILS	INSTITUTION STATS		RANKINGS PERFORMANCE	
Address	**Undergraduates**	21,600	**Faculty Level Positions**	
Justus-Liebig-Universität Giessen	**Postgraduates**	1,180	Arts & Humanities	328=
Gutenberg	**International Students**	4.9%	Engineering & IT	463=
strasse 6,	**Student Faculty Ratio**	11.7:1	Life Sciences & BioMedicine	369=
D-35390 Giessen	**Total Citations**	73,119	Natural Sciences	273=
Germany	**Avg UG Fees**	513	Social Sciences	447=
	Avg PG Fees	513		
Web www.uni-giessen.de				

GERMANY

Universität Göttingen

CONTACT DETAILS		INSTITUTION STATS		RANKINGS PERFORMANCE	
Web	www.uni-goettingen.de	Undergraduates	21,566	Overall Ranking Position	156=
Phone	+49 (0)551 / 39-4558	Postgraduates	3,041	Faculty Level Positions	
		International Students	10.6%	Arts & Humanities	141=
		Student Faculty Ratio	11.9:1	Engineering & IT	186=
		Total Citations	127,099	Life Sciences & BioMedicine	54
		Avg UG Fees	1,730	Natural Sciences	37=
		Avg PG Fees	1,730	Social Sciences	217=

University Halle-Wittenberg

CONTACT DETAILS	INSTITUTION STATS		RANKINGS PERFORMANCE	
Address	Total Students	17,355	Faculty Level Positions	
Martin-Luther-Universität Halle-	International Students	5.5%	Arts & Humanities	430=
Wittenberg	Student Faculty Ratio	18.1:1	Engineering & IT	406=
Halle			Life Sciences & BioMedicine	409=
06099			Natural Sciences	440=
Germany			Social Sciences	426=
Web www.uni-halle.de				

Universität Hamburg

CONTACT DETAILS		INSTITUTION STATS		RANKINGS PERFORMANCE	
Web	www.uni-hamburg.de	Undergraduates	25,649	Faculty Level Positions	
Phone	+49 40 428 38 4709	Postgraduates	12,633	Arts & Humanities	130
		International Students	4.6%	Engineering & IT	141=
		Student Faculty Ratio	6.2:1	Life Sciences & BioMedicine	196=
		Total Citations	150,926	Natural Sciences	123=
		Avg UG Fees	608	Social Sciences	242=
		Avg PG Fees	10,254		

Universität Hannover

CONTACT DETAILS		INSTITUTION STATS		RANKINGS PERFORMANCE	
Address		Undergraduates	20,914	Faculty Level Positions	
Welfengarten 1		Postgraduates	3,211	Arts & Humanities	423=
Hannover		International Students	13.8%	Engineering & IT	258=
D-30167		Student Faculty Ratio	8:1	Life Sciences & BioMedicine	258=
Germany		Total Citations	34,194	Natural Sciences	275
Web	www.uni-hannover.de	Avg UG Fees	1,282	Social Sciences	354=
Phone	+49 511.762-0	Avg PG Fees	1,179		

GERMANY

Universität Heidelberg

CONTACT DETAILS		INSTITUTION STATS		RANKINGS PERFORMANCE	
Address		**Undergraduates**	22,995	**Overall Rankings Position**	58=
Heidelberg		**Postgraduates**	2,005	**Faculty Level Positions**	
D-69117		**International Students**	17.2%	Arts & Humanities	52
Germany		**Student Faculty Ratio**	12.6:1	Engineering & IT	173=
		Total Citations	226,155	Life Sciences & BioMedicine	30
Web	www.uni-heidelberg.de			Natural Sciences	28
Phone	+49 (0) 62 21/54 - 0			Social Sciences	70

Humboldt-Universität zu Berlin

CONTACT DETAILS		INSTITUTION STATS		RANKINGS PERFORMANCE	
Address		**Undergraduates**	38,960	**Overall Rankings Position**	105=
Unter den Linden 6		**Postgraduates**	3,480	**Faculty Level Positions**	
Berlin		**International Students**	11.2%	Arts & Humanities	91
10099		**Student Faculty Ratio**	10.8:1	Engineering & IT	289=
Germany		**Total Citations**	181,653	Life Sciences & BioMedicine	79
Web	www.hu-berlin.de			Natural Sciences	67=
Phone	+49 30 20930			Social Sciences	112=

Universität Jena

CONTACT DETAILS		INSTITUTION STATS		RANKINGS PERFORMANCE	
Web	www.uni-jena.de	**Undergraduates**	17,945	**Faculty Level Positions**	
Phone	+49(03641) 9-41000	**Postgraduates**	1,082	Arts & Humanities	293=
		International Students	4.1%	Engineering & IT	438=
		Student Faculty Ratio	17.8:1	Life Sciences & BioMedicine	281=
		Total Citations	69,494	Natural Sciences	334
				Social Sciences	458=

Universität Karlsruhe

CONTACT DETAILS		INSTITUTION STATS		RANKINGS PERFORMANCE	
Address		**Undergraduates**	17,112	**Faculty Level Positions**	
Kaiserstraße 12		**Postgraduates**	1,230	Arts & Humanities	311=
Karlsruhe		**International Students**	16.7%	Engineering & IT	73
76131		**Student Faculty Ratio**	16.5:1	Natural Sciences	106
Germany		**Total Citations**	73,521	Social Sciences	484=
Web	www.uni-karlsruhe.de				
Phone	+49(0)721/608-0				

GERMANY

Universität zu Kiel

CONTACT DETAILS	INSTITUTION STATS		RANKINGS PERFORMANCE	
Address	**Total Students**	20,193	**Faculty Level Positions**	
Christian-Albrechts-Universität	**International Students**	8.6%	Arts & Humanities	246=
zu Kiel	**Student Faculty Ratio**	27.5:1	Engineering & IT	463=
Kiel 24098	**Total Citations**	98,117	Life Sciences & BioMedicine	281=
Germany			Natural Sciences	360=
Web www.uni-kiel.de			Social Sciences	295=
Phone +49 (0431) 880-00				

WHU - Wissenschaftliche Hochschule für

CONTACT DETAILS	INSTITUTION STATS		RANKINGS PERFORMANCE	
Web www.whu.edu	**Undergraduates**	338	**Faculty Level Positions**	
Phone +49 (0261) 65 09-150	**Postgraduates**	142	Engineering & IT	497=
	International Students	6.3%	Social Sciences	426=
	Student Faculty Ratio	12:1		
	Aug UGfees	12,818		
	Avg PG Fees	35,089		

Universität zu Köln

CONTACT DETAILS	INSTITUTION STATS		RANKINGS PERFORMANCE	
Address	**Undergraduates**	42,601	**Faculty Level Positions**	
University of Cologne Albertus-	**Postgraduates**	5,115	Arts & Humanities	204=
Magnus-Platz D	**International Students**	6.6%	Engineering & IT	382=
Cologne	**Student Faculty Ratio**	6.4:1	Life Sciences & BioMedicine	225=
50923	**Total Citations**	110,455	Natural Sciences	221=
Germany			Social Sciences	185
Web www.uni-koeln.de				

Universität Konstanz

CONTACT DETAILS	INSTITUTION STATS		RANKINGS PERFORMANCE	
Address	**Undergraduates**	9,731	**Faculty Level Positions**	
Universität Konstanz	**Postgraduates**	653	Arts & Humanities	181=
Konstanz	**International Students**	11.8%	Engineering & IT	423=
78457	**Student Faculty Ratio**	5:1	Life Sciences & BioMedicine	427=
Germany			Natural Sciences	351=
Web www.uni-konstanz.de			Social Sciences	330=
Phone +49 (0)7531 / 88 - 0				

GERMANY

Universität Leipzig

CONTACT DETAILS

INSTITUTION STATS

RANKINGS PERFORMANCE

Address
Airport Leipzig/Halle
Germany

Web www.uni-leipzig.de
Phone +49 0341 2241155

Undergraduates	31,173
Postgraduates	4,529
International Students	6.9%
Student Faculty Ratio	10.8:1
Total Citations	72,872

Faculty Level Positions

Arts & Humanities	246=
Engineering & IT	297=
Life Sciences & BioMedicine	179=
Natural Sciences	265=
Social Sciences	290=

Universität Mainz

CONTACT DETAILS

INSTITUTION STATS

RANKINGS PERFORMANCE

Address
Postfach
Mainz
D 55099
Germany
Web www.uni-mainz.de

Undergraduates	19,826
Postgraduates	1,514
International Students	10.8%
Student Faculty Ratio	15.2:1
Total Citations	152,938

Faculty Level Positions

Arts & Humanities	324=
Engineering & IT	438=
Natural Sciences	163
Social Sciences	484=

Universität Mannheim

CONTACT DETAILS

INSTITUTION STATS

RANKINGS PERFORMANCE

Address
Universität Mannheim
Mannheim
68131
Germany
Web www.uni-mannheim.de

Undergraduates	6,304
Postgraduates	6,194
International Students	11.5%
Student Faculty Ratio	17.4:1
Avg UG Fees	1,282
Avg PG Fees	1,282

Faculty Level Positions

Engineering & IT	463=
Natural Sciences	518=
Social Sciences	254=

Universität Marburg

CONTACT DETAILS

INSTITUTION STATS

RANKINGS PERFORMANCE

Web www.uni-marburg.de

Total Students	19,332
International Students	9.3%
Student Faculty Ratio	13.2:1
Total Citations	102,502

Faculty Level Positions

Arts & Humanities	430=
Engineering & IT	497=
Life Sciences & BioMedicine	292=
Natural Sciences	461=
Social Sciences	393=

GERMANY

Universität München

CONTACT DETAILS

Address
ZVS, Sonnenstrasse 171
Dortmund
44128
Germany
Web www.uni-muenchen.de
Phone +49 0231/1081-0

INSTITUTION STATS

Undergraduates	39,478
Postgraduates	4,014
International Students	13.0%
Student Faculty Ratio	17.5:1
Total Citations	268,762
Avg UG Fees	1,521
Avg PG Fees	1,025

RANKINGS PERFORMANCE

Overall Ranking Postion	98
Faculty Level Positions	
Arts & Humanities	191=
Engineering & IT	145=
Life Sciences & BioMedicine	56=
Natural Sciences	43
Social Sciences	74

University of Münster

CONTACT DETAILS

Web www.uni-muenster.de

INSTITUTION STATS

Toatl Students	42,490
International Students	6.2%
Student Faculty Ratio	9.7:1
Total Citations	133,258

RANKINGS PERFORMANCE

Faculty Level Positions	
Arts & Humanities	191=
Engineering & IT	482=
Life Sciences & BioMedicine	397=
Natural Sciences	329=
Social Sciences	417=

Universität Regensburg

CONTACT DETAILS

Address
University of Regensburg
Regensburg 93040
Germany

Web www.uni-regensburg.de
Phone +49 94194301

INSTITUTION STATS

Undergraduates	16,462
Postgraduates	1,279
International Students	7.0%
Student Faculty Ratio	7:1
Total Citations	73,694

RANKINGS PERFORMANCE

Faculty Level Positions	
Arts & Humanities	430=
Engineering & IT	406=
Life Sciences & BioMedicine	284=
Natural Sciences	341=
Social Sciences	393=

Ruhr-Universität Bochum

CONTACT DETAILS

Address
Post-office box Postfach 10 21 48
Bochum 44721
Germany

Web www.ruhr-uni-bochum.de

INSTITUTION STATS

Undergraduates	28,578
Postgraduates	4,177
International Students	7.9%
Student Faculty Ratio	23.4:1
Total Citations	92,528

RANKINGS PERFORMANCE

Faculty Level Positions	
Arts & Humanities	412=
Engineering & IT	258=
Life Sciences & BioMedicine	338=
Natural Sciences	297=
Social Sciences	447=

GERMANY

Saarland University

CONTACT DETAILS | **INSTITUTION STATS** | **RANKINGS PERFORMANCE**

Address
Saarbrücken
66041
Germany

Web www.uni-saarland.de

Undergraduates	12,085
Postgraduates	1,662
International Students	13.7%
Student Faculty Ratio	8.6:1
Total Citations	48,364

Faculty Level Positions
Arts & Humanities	365=
Engineering & IT	358=
Natural Sciences	386
Social Sciences	372=

Universität Stuttgart

CONTACT DETAILS | **INSTITUTION STATS** | **RANKINGS PERFORMANCE**

Address
Postfach 10 60 37
Stuttgart
70049
Germany
Web www.uni-stuttgart.de
Phone +49-711-685 - 0

Total Students	19,452
International Students	22.1%
Student Faculty Ratio	15.2:1
Total Citations	59,330

Faculty Level Positions
Arts & Humanities	184=
Engineering & IT	76
Life Sciences & BioMedicine	427=
Natural Sciences	126=
Social Sciences	393=

Technical University of Berlin

CONTACT DETAILS | **INSTITUTION STATS** | **RANKINGS PERFORMANCE**

Address
Strasse des 17. Juni 135
Berlin
10623
Germany
Web www.tu-berlin.de
Phone +49-30-314-0

Total Students	30,548
International Students	15.4%
Student Faculty Ratio	18.3:1
Total Citations	53,441

Faculty Level Positions
Arts & Humanities	115=
Engineering & IT	62
Life Sciences & BioMedicine	314=
Natural Sciences	56=
Social Sciences	372=

Technische Universität Braunschweig

CONTACT DETAILS | **INSTITUTION STATS** | **RANKINGS PERFORMANCE**

Address
TU Braunschweig
Braunschweig
38092
Germany
Web www.tu-braunschweig.de

Undergraduates	1,253
Postgraduates	10,372
International Students	11.1%
Student Faculty Ratio	8.3:1
Avg UG Fees	1,795
Avg PG Fees	1,795

Faculty Level Positions
Arts & Humanities	328=
Engineering & IT	289=
Life Sciences & BioMedicine	397=
Natural Sciences	378=
Social Sciences	419=

GERMANY

Technische Universität Dresden

CONTACT DETAILS		INSTITUTION STATS		RANKINGS PERFORMANCE	
Address		**Undergraduates**	18,200	**Faculty Level Positions**	
Helmholtzstr. 10		**Postgraduates**	3,006	Arts & Humanities	328=
Dresden		**International Students**	8.0%	Engineering & IT	186=
01069		**Student Faculty Ratio**	26.1:1	Life Sciences & BioMedicine	314=
Germany		**Avg UG Fees**	352	Natural Sciences	277
Web	www.tu-dresden.de	**Avg PG Fees**	3,845		

Technische Universität München

CONTACT DETAILS		INSTITUTION STATS		RANKINGS PERFORMANCE	
Web	www.tu-muenchen.de	**Total Students**	19,887	**Overall Rankings Position**	82=
		International Students	18.3%	**Faculty Level Positions**	
		Student Faculty Ratio	11:1	Arts & Humanities	311=
		Total Citations	187,018	Engineering & IT	32
				Life Sciences & BioMedicine	137=
				Natural Sciences	75
				Social Sciences	411=

TU Darmstadt

CONTACT DETAILS		INSTITUTION STATS		RANKINGS PERFORMANCE	
Web	www.tu-darmstadt.de	**Total Students**	20,588	**Faculty Level Positions**	
		Postgraduates	14.1%	Arts & Humanities	233=
		International Students	8.5:1	Engineering & IT	107=
		Student Faculty Ratio	34,712	Natural Sciences	272
				Social Sciences	390=

Universität Tübingen

CONTACT DETAILS		INSTITUTION STATS		RANKINGS PERFORMANCE	
Address		**Undergraduates**	24,000	**Overall Rankings Position**	170=
Eberhard Karls Universität Tübingen		**Postgraduates**	13,570	**Faculty Level Positions**	
Wilhelmstr. 7		**International Students**	11.5%	Arts & Humanities	110=
Tübingen		**Student Faculty Ratio**	21.8:1	Engineering & IT	368=
72074		**Total Citations**	166,925	Life Sciences & BioMedicine	77=
Germany		**Avg UG Fees**	1,282	Natural Sciences	204=
Web	www.uni-tuebingen.de	**Avg PG Fees**	1,282		
Phone	+49 (0)7071 29-0				

GERMANY

Universität Ulm

CONTACT DETAILS

INSTITUTION STATS

RANKINGS PERFORMANCE

Address
Universität Ulm
Ulm
89069
Germany
Web www.uni-ulm.de

Total Students	6,767
Student Fauulty Ratio	9.8%
International Students	8.9:1
Total Citations	100,753

Overall Rankings Position	158=
Faculty Level Positions	
Engineering & IT	328=
Life Sciences & BioMedicine	363=
Natural Sciences	209
Social Sciences	419=

Universität Würzburg

CONTACT DETAILS

INSTITUTION STATS

RANKINGS PERFORMANCE

Address
Sanderring 2
Würzburg 97070
Germany

Web www.uni-wuerzburg.de

Undergraduates	18,183
International Students	8.2%
Student Faculty Ratio	5:1
Total Citations	149,145

Faculty Level Positions	
Arts & Humanities	423=
Engineering & IT	406=
Life Sciences & BioMedicine	268=
Natural Sciences	237=
Social Sciences	458=

GREECE

Aristotelian University of Thessaloniki

CONTACT DETAILS

INSTITUTION STATS

RANKINGS PERFORMANCE

Address
GR 541 24 Thessaloniki
Greece

Web www.authgr
Phone +30 2310 99
06771

Total Students	101,136
International Students	6.2%
Student Faculty Ratio	15.4:1

Faculty Level Positions	
Arts & Humanities	423=
Engineering & IT	258=
Natural Sciences	368=
Social Sciences	372=

National Technical University of Athens

CONTACT DETAILS

INSTITUTION STATS

RANKINGS PERFORMANCE

Address
Iroon Polytexneiou 9,
Zografou
15780
Greece
Web www.ntua.gr

Total Students	10,000
International Students	3.6%
Student Faculty Ratio	9.2:1

Faculty Level Positions	
Engineering & IT	124=
Natural Sciences	351=

GREECE

University of Athens

CONTACT DETAILS

Address
7, Palaion Patron Germanou str
10561 Athens (7th floor)
Greece

Web   www.uoa.gr

INSTITUTION STATS

Student Faculty Ratio	5.1:1
Total Citations	54,671

RANKINGS PERFORMANCE

Faculty Level Positions
Arts & Humanities	159=
Engineering & IT	267=
Life Sciences & BioMedicine	338=
Natural Sciences	246=
Social Sciences	229=

Athens University of Economy and Business

CONTACT DETAILS

Address
76, Patission Str.
Athens 104 34
Greece

Web   www.aueb.gr
Phone   30210 8203250

INSTITUTION STATS

Undergraduates	8,000
Postgraduates	1,650
International Students	1.1%
Student Faculty Ratio	9.1:1
Avg UG Fees	513
Avg PG Fees	11,536

RANKINGS PERFORMANCE

Faculty Level Positions
Natural Sciences	461=
Social Sciences	265=

University of Crete

CONTACT DETAILS

Address
74 100 Rethymnon,
Crete
Greece

Web   www.uoc.gr
Phone   + 30 831 77000

INSTITUTION STATS

Undergraduates	11,011
Postgraduates	2,130
International Students	0.5%
Student Faculty Ratio	30:1

RANKINGS PERFORMANCE

Faculty Level Positions
Engineering & IT	274=
Life Sciences & BioMedicine	427=
Natural Sciences	321=
Social Sciences	417=

University of Patras

CONTACT DETAILS

Address
Rio, 26500 Patras
Greece

Web   www.upatras.gr
Phone   +30 2610 991822

INSTITUTION STATS

Undergraduates	10,815
Postgraduates	7,045
International Students	6.7%
Student Faculty Ratio	11.2:1
Avg UG Fees	4,630
Avg PG Fees	4,630

RANKINGS PERFORMANCE

Faculty Level Positions
Engineering & IT	219=
Natural Sciences	348=

411

香港城市大學
**City University
of Hong Kong**

Study at CityU

*An energetic and rapidly
ascending university*

*An internationally
renowned institution*

*A leading education provider
in Asia-Pacific region*

*A cradle to nurture
future professionals*

*A place where East meets West
and Modernity meets Tradition*

A gateway to mainland China

*Ranked for three consecutive years
among Top 200 Universities
in the world by THES*

*Ranked for four consecutive years
among Top Ten Universities
in Greater China
by Shanghai Jiao Tong University*

TODAY, CITYU HAS:

- 25,506 students
- 952 academics from 32 countries
- 376 collaborative agreements
  with 240 partners from 30 countries
- more than 150 programmes at
  undergraduate and postgraduate
  levels

FACULTIES AND SCHOOLS

Faculty of Business

Faculty of Humanities and Social Sciences

Faculty of Science and Engineering

School of Creative Media

School of Law

▶ CONTACTS

General Enquiry
**External Liaison and
Cooperation Office**
Telephone hotline: (852) 2788 7373
Fax: (852) 2788 7445
Email: overseas@cityu.edu.hk

Admissions Enquiry
Admissions Office
Telephone hotline: (852) 2788 9094
Fax: (852) 2788 9086
Email: asadmit@cityu.edu.hk

Postgraduate Enquiry
School of Graduate Studies
Telephone hotline: (852) 2788 9076
Fax: (852) 2788 9940
Email: sg@cityu.edu.hk

▶ APPLICATION

- **University Website**
  http://www.cityu.edu.hk
- **Undergraduate Programmes**
  http://www6.cityu.edu.hk/puo/ProspectusProd/ProgrammeList/ba-proglist.aspx
- **Taught Postgraduate Programmes**
  http://www6.cityu.edu.hk/puo/ProspectusProd/ProgrammeList/pg-proglist.aspx
- **MPhil, PhD and Professional Doctorate Programmes**
  http://www.cityu.edu.hk/sgs/

HONG KONG

Chinese University of Hong Kong

CONTACT DETAILS		INSTITUTION STATS		RANKINGS PERFORMANCE	
Address		**Undergraduates**	10,333	**Overall Rankings Position**	50=
Shatin, New Territories		**Postgraduates**	2,562	**Faculty Level Positions**	
Hong Kong		**International Students**	14.6%	Arts & Humanities	85
Hong Kong		**Student Faculty Ratio**	10.7:1	Engineering & IT	72
		Total Citations	82,153	Life Sciences & BioMedicine	48
Web	www.cuhk.edu.hk	**Avg UG Fees**	10,300	Natural Sciences	138
Phone	+852 2609 7000 / +852	**Avg PG Fees**	5,420	Social Sciences	43
2609 6000					

City University of Hong Kong

CONTACT DETAILS		INSTITUTION STATS		RANKINGS PERFORMANCE	
Address		**Undergraduates**	9,881	**Overall Rankings Position**	154
Tat Chee Avenue, Kowloon		**Postgraduates**	3,432	**Faculty Level Positions**	
Hong Kong SAR		**International Students**	8.6%	Arts & Humanities	209=
Hong Kong		**Student Faculty Ratio**	35.2:1	Engineering & IT	85=
		Total Citations	35,059	Life Sciences & BioMedicine	302=
Web	www.cityu.edu.hk	**Avg UG Fees**	7,725	Natural Sciences	200=
Phone	+852 2788 7654	**Avg PG Fees**	10,815	Social Sciences	53=

University of Hong Kong

CONTACT DETAILS		INSTITUTION STATS		RANKINGS PERFORMANCE	
Address		**Undergraduates**	8,842	**Overall Rankings Position**	33=
Pok Fu Lam Road		**Postgraduates**	6,275	**Faculty Level Positions**	
Hong Kong		**International Students**	16.5%	Arts & Humanities	33=
Hong Kong		**Student Faculty Ratio**	8.1:1	Engineering & IT	67
		Total Citations	99,509	Life Sciences & BioMedicine	31
Web	www.hku.edu.hk	**Avg UG Fees**	9,000	Natural Sciences	71
Phone	+852 2859 2111	**Avg PG Fees**	16,300	Social Sciences	30=

Hong Kong University of Science & Technology

CONTACT DETAILS		INSTITUTION STATS		RANKINGS PERFORMANCE	
Address		**Undergraduates**	5,636	**Overall Rankings Position**	58=
Clear Water Bay, Kowloon		**Postgraduates**	3,187	**Faculty Level Positions**	
Hong Kong		**International Students**	13.2%	Arts & Humanities	328=
Hong Kong		**Student Faculty Ratio**	15.1:1	Engineering & IT	17
		Total Citations	54,731	Life Sciences & BioMedicine	61
Web	www.ust.hk			Natural Sciences	69
Phone	+852 2358 6000			Social Sciences	52

HUNGARY

Eötvös Loránd University

CONTACT DETAILS	INSTITUTION STATS	RANKINGS PERFORMANCE

Web   www.elte.hu

Toatal Students	38,000	
International Students	3.3%	
Student Faculty Ratio	14.6:1	

Faculty Level Positions

Arts & Humanities	215=
Engineering & IT	438=
Life Sciences & BioMedicine	427=
Natural Sciences	135
Social Sciences	359=

University of Szeged

CONTACT DETAILS	INSTITUTION STATS	RANKINGS PERFORMANCE

Address
Feketesas u. 28., Szeged
6720-Hungary
Hungary

Web   www.u-szeged.hu
Phone   + 36 62 / 54 41 35

Total Students	30,000	
International Students	3.9%	
Student Faculty Ratio	18.7:1	

Faculty Level Positions

Engineering & IT	433=
Life Sciences & BioMedicine	328=
Natural Sciences	230=
Social Sciences	372=

INDIA

University of Calcutta

CONTACT DETAILS	INSTITUTION STATS	RANKINGS PERFORMANCE

Address
Senate House, 87 /1 College Street
Kolkata
West Bengal 700 073
India
Web   www.caluniv.ac.in
Phone   +91 33 2241 0071

Student Faculty Ratio	11.8:1	
Total Citations	4,709	

Faculty Level Positions

Arts & Humanities	174
Engineering & IT	176=
Life Sciences & BioMedicine	217=
Natural Sciences	162
Social Sciences	221=

University of Delhi

CONTACT DETAILS	INSTITUTION STATS	RANKINGS PERFORMANCE

Address
University Road
Delhi
110 007
India
Web   www.du.ac.in
Phone   +91 11 27667725

Undergraduates	315,188	
Postgraduates	20,194	
International Students	0.3%	
Student Faculty Ratio	23.4:1	
Total Citations	12,574	

Faculty Level Positions

Arts & Humanities	75
Engineering & IT	126=
Life Sciences & BioMedicine	147
Natural Sciences	161
Social Sciences	86

415

INDIA

Indian Institute of Management

CONTACT DETAILS	INSTITUTION STATS		RANKINGS PERFORMANCE	
Address	**Total students**	319	**Overall Rankings Position**	68
Prabandh Nagar, Off Sitapur Road	**International Students**	6.3%	**Faculty Level Positions**	
Lucknow	**Student Faculty Ratio**	10.7:1	Arts & Humanities	293=
226013	**Total Citations**	667	Engineering & IT	68
India			Life Sciences & BioMedicine	204=
Web www.iiml.ac.in (Lucknow			Natural Sciences	260=
campus)			Social Sciences	26
Phone +91 522 2734101				

Indian Institute of Technology

CONTACT DETAILS	INSTITUTION STATS		RANKINGS PERFORMANCE	
Address	**TotalStudents**	4,201	**Overall Rankings Position**	57
Hauz Khas	**International Students**	0.3%	**Faculty Level Positions**	
New Delhi	**Student Faculty Ratio**	8.6:1	Arts & Humanities	272
110 016	**Total Citations**	62,681	Engineering & IT	3
India			Life Sciences & BioMedicine	70=
Web www.iitd.ernet.in			Natural Sciences	33
Phone +91 011 2658 2027			Social Sciences	129=

Jawaharlal Nehru University

CONTACT DETAILS	INSTITUTION STATS		RANKINGS PERFORMANCE	
Address	**Total Students**	5,151	**Overall Rankings Position**	183=
New Mehrauli Road	**International Students**	4.0%	**Faculty Level Positions**	
New Delhi	**Student Faculty Ratio**	5.4:1	Arts & Humanities	105=
110067	**Total Citations**	11,797	Engineering & IT	138
India			Life Sciences & BioMedicine	99=
Web www.jnu.ac.in			Natural Sciences	150=
Phone +91 11 26717676			Social Sciences	57

University of Mumbai

CONTACT DETAILS	INSTITUTION STATS		RANKINGS PERFORMANCE	
Address	**Student Faculty Ratio**	15.1:1	**Faculty Level Positions**	
Fort	**Total Citations**	2,274	Arts & Humanities	304
Mumbai			Engineering & IT	163
400 032			Life Sciences & BioMedicine	176
India			Natural Sciences	167=
Web www.mu.ac.in			Social Sciences	172=
Phone +91 22652819 / 22652825				

INDIA

University of Pune

CONTACT DETAILS

Address
Ganeshkhind Road
Pune
Maharashtra 411007
India
Web www.unipune.ernet.in
Phone +91 20 25691162

INSTITUTION STATS

Total Students	170,000
International Students	0.3%
Student Faculty Ratio	37:1
Total Citations	2,105

RANKINGS PERFORMANCE

Faculty Level Positions
Arts & Humanities	188=
Engineering & IT	156
Life Sciences & BioMedicine	159
Natural Sciences	186
Social Sciences	229=

INDONESIA

Airlangga University

CONTACT DETAILS

Address
Moestopo 47
Surabaya
Indonesia

Web www.unair.ac.id
Phone +62 31 5030255

INSTITUTION STATS

Undergraduates	15,381
Postgraduates	1,431
International Students	0.7%
Student Faculty Ratio	12.3:1

RANKINGS PERFORMANCE

Faculty Level Positions
Social Sciences	330=

Bandung Institute of Technology

CONTACT DETAILS

Address
Jl, Tamansari 64
Bandung
40116
Indonesia
Web www.itb.ac.id
Phone +62 22 2500935

INSTITUTION STATS

Undergraduates	11,321
Postgraduates	3,456
International Students	0.3%
Student Faculty Ratio	13.2:1
Total Citations	455

RANKINGS PERFORMANCE

Faculty Level Positions
Arts & Humanities	320
Engineering & IT	111=
Life Sciences & BioMedicine	179=
Natural Sciences	154
Social Sciences	217=

Diponegoro University

CONTACT DETAILS

Address
Semarang
Jawa Tengah
50147
Indonesia
Web www.undip.ac.id
Phone +62 24 7460057

INSTITUTION STATS

Undergraduates	3,720
Postgraduates	233
International Students	0.5%
Student Faculty Ratio	10:1
Avg UG Fees	150
Avg PG Fees	2,700

RANKINGS PERFORMANCE

Faculty Level Positions
Engineering & IT	482=
Natural Sciences	440=
Social Sciences	471=

INDONESIA

University of Gadjah Mada

CONTACT DETAILS

Web	www.ugm.ac.id
Phone	+62(274)6491833

INSTITUTION STATS

Undergraduates	30,776
Postgraduates	10,214
International Students	0.5%
Student Faculty Ratio	23.6:1
Total Citations	1,033
Avg UG Fees	6,000
Avg PG Fees	2,000

RANKINGS PERFORMANCE

Faculty Level Positions

Arts & Humanities	70
Engineering & IT	243=
Life Sciences & BioMedicine	73
Natural Sciences	150=
Social Sciences	47

University of Indonesia

CONTACT DETAILS

Address
Depok
16424
Indonesia

Web	www.ui.ac.id
Phone	+62 21 78849060

INSTITUTION STATS

Undergraduates	14,460
Postgraduates	10,979
International Students	0.6%
Student Faculty Ratio	11.8:1
Total Citations	2,777
Avg UG Fees	290
Avg PG Fees	1,580

RANKINGS PERFORMANCE

Faculty Level Positions

Arts & Humanities	145
Engineering & IT	315=
Life Sciences & BioMedicine	278=
Natural Sciences	406=
Social Sciences	163=

IRELAND

University College Cork

CONTACT DETAILS

Address
Cork
Ireland

Web	www.ucc.ie
Phone	+353 21 490 3000

INSTITUTION STATS

Undergraduates	12,853
Postgraduates	2,931
International Students	11.9%
Student Faculty Ratio	18.6:1
Total Citations	35,201
Avg UG Fees	20,637
Avg PG Fees	10,716

RANKINGS PERFORMANCE

Faculty Level Positions

Arts & Humanities	170=
Engineering & IT	219=
Life Sciences & BioMedicine	427=
Natural Sciences	401=
Social Sciences	346=

Dublin City University

CONTACT DETAILS

Address
Dublin 9
Ireland

Web	www.dcu.ie
Phone	+353-1-7005566

INSTITUTION STATS

Undergraduates	6,072
Postgraduates	2,340
International Students	15.9%
Student Faculty Ratio	20.5:1
Total Citations	9,650
Avg UG Fees	14,873
Avg PG Fees	13,687

RANKINGS PERFORMANCE

Faculty Level Positions

Engineering & IT	382=
Life Sciences & BioMedicine	427=
Natural Sciences	476=
Social Sciences	447=

IRELAND

Dublin Institute of Technology

CONTACT DETAILS		INSTITUTION STATS		RANKINGS PERFORMANCE	
Address		**Undergraduates**	14,334	**Faculty Level Positions**	
30 Upper Pembroke Street		**Postgraduates**	1,594	Arts & Humanities	374=
Dublin 2		**International Students**	4.8%	Engineering & IT	297=
Ireland		**Student Faculty Ratio**	3.5:1	Natural Sciences	447=
		Total Citations	3,861		
Web	www.dit.ie	**Avg UG Fees**	12,818		
Phone	+353 1 402 3000	**Avg PG Fees**	12,818		

University College Dublin

CONTACT DETAILS		INSTITUTION STATS		RANKINGS PERFORMANCE	
Address		**Undergraduates**	13,582	**Faculty Level Positions**	
Belfield		**Postgraduates**	5,882	Arts & Humanities	207=
Dublin 4		**International Students**	9.1%	Engineering & IT	205=
Ireland		**Student Faculty Ratio**	13.5:1	Life Sciences & BioMedicine	163=
		Total Citations	36,418	Natural Sciences	313
Web	www.ucd.ie	**Avg UG Fees**	18,266	Social Sciences	167=
Phone	+ 353-1-7167777	**Avg PG Fees**	9,614		

Trinity College Dublin

CONTACT DETAILS		INSTITUTION STATS		RANKINGS PERFORMANCE	
Address		**Undergraduates**	10,966	**Overall Rankings Position**	78
College Green		**Postgraduates**	4,298	**Faculty Level Positions**	
Dublin 2		**International Students**	17.7%	Arts & Humanities	39=
Ireland		**Student Faculty Ratio**	15:1	Engineering & IT	109
		Total Citations	55,552	Life Sciences & BioMedicine	93
Web	www.tcd.ie	**Avg UG Fees**	19,515	Natural Sciences	93=
Phone	+353 01 608 1000	**Avg PG Fees**	14,472	Social Sciences	93=

National University of Ireland, Galway

CONTACT DETAILS		INSTITUTION STATS		RANKINGS PERFORMANCE	
Address		**Undergraduates**	9,795	**Faculty Level Positions**	
University Road		**Postgraduates**	2,929	Arts & Humanities	398=
Galway		**International Students**	14.1%	Engineering & IT	347=
Ireland Ireland		**Student Faculty Ratio**	11.7:1	Natural Sciences	439
		Total Citations	8,975	Social Sciences	254=
Web	www.nuigalway.ie	**Avg UG Fees**	15,702		
Phone	+353 91 524411	**Avg PG Fees**	13,138		

IRELAND

University of Limerick

CONTACT DETAILS		INSTITUTION STATS		RANKINGS PERFORMANCE	
Address		**Undergraduates**	10,399	**Faculty Level Positions**	
Limerick		**Postgraduates**	2,299	Engineering & IT	358=
Ireland		**International Students**	3.8%	Natural Sciences	461=
		Student Faculty Ratio	11:1	Social Sciences	330=
		Total Citations	4,627		
Web	www.ul.ie	**Avg UG Fees**	16,282		
Phone	+353 (0) 61-202700	**Avg PG Fees**	1,458		

ISRAEL

Ben Gurion University of the Negev

CONTACT DETAILS		INSTITUTION STATS		RANKINGS PERFORMANCE	
Address		**Undergraduates**	11,500	**Faculty Level Positions**	
P.O. Box 653		**Postgraduates**	5,106	Arts & Humanities	159=
Beer-Sheva 84105		**International Students**	1.2%	Engineering & IT	179=
Israel		**Student Faculty Ratio**	22.4:1	Life Sciences & BioMedicine	186=
		Total Citations	56,170	Natural Sciences	278=
Web	www.bgu.ac.il	**Avg UG Fees**	182	Social Sciences	426=
Phone	+972-8-646-1111	**Avg PG Fees**	480		

Hebrew University of Jerusalem

CONTACT DETAILS		INSTITUTION STATS		RANKINGS PERFORMANCE	
Address		**Undergraduates**	11,800	**Overall Rankings Position**	119
Mount Scopus		**Postgraduates**	10,105	**Faculty Level Positions**	
Jerusalem		**International Students**	2.8%	Arts & Humanities	43
91905		**Student Faculty Ratio**	21.4:1	Engineering & IT	124=
Israel		**Total Citations**	181,441	Life Sciences & BioMedicine	63=
Web	www.huji.ac.il	**Avg UG Fees**	2,275	Natural Sciences	52
Phone	+972 02-5882811	**Avg PG Fees**	2,275	Social Sciences	44

Technion - Israel Institute of Technology

CONTACT DETAILS		INSTITUTION STATS		RANKINGS PERFORMANCE	
Address		**Undergraduates**	8,690	**Overall Rankings Position**	158=
Technion City		**Postgraduates**	3,500	**Faculty Level Positions**	
Haifa 32000		**International Students**	3.9%	Arts & Humanities	212=
Israel		**Student Faculty Ratio**	13.4:1	Engineering & IT	30=
		Total Citations	103,609	Life Sciences & BioMedicine	186=
Web	www.technion.ac.il	**Avg UG Fees**	2,363	Natural Sciences	50
Phone	+972-4829 2111	**Avg PG Fees**	3,070	Social Sciences	447=

ISRAEL

Tel Aviv University

CONTACT DETAILS

Address
P.O. Box 39040
Tel Aviv 69978
Israel

Web www.tau.ac.il
Phone + 972-(0)3-640-8111

INSTITUTION STATS

Undergraduates	15,723
Postgraduates	12,267
International Students	1.9%
Student Faculty Ratio	18.5:1
Total Citations	178,516
Avg UG Fees	1,880
Avg PG Fees	2,550

RANKINGS PERFORMANCE

Overall Rankings Position	147=
Faculty Level Positions	
Arts & Humanities	87=
Engineering & IT	176=
Life Sciences & BioMedicine	112
Natural Sciences	58=
Social Sciences	51

ITALY

University of Bari

CONTACT DETAILS

Address
Piazza Umberto I,1
Bari
70121
Italy
Web www.uniba.it
Phone +39 (0)80 5714488

INSTITUTION STATS

Total Students	69,365
International Students	1.5%
Student Faculty Ratio	13.3:1
Total Citations	58,128

RANKINGS PERFORMANCE

Faculty Level Positions	
Arts & Humanities	412=
Engineering & IT	494=
Natural Sciences	447=

University of Bocconi

CONTACT DETAILS

Address
Via Sarfatti, 25
Milan
20136
Italy
Web www.uni-bocconi.it
Phone +39 (0)2 5836 5820

INSTITUTION STATS

Undergraduates	12,817
Postgraduates	801
International Students	11.6%
Student Faculty Ratio	7.5:1
Avg Fees	8,204

RANKINGS PERFORMANCE

Faculty Level Positions	
Arts & Humanities	412=
Life Sciences & BioMedicine	427=
Natural Sciences	476=
Social Sciences	96=

University of Bologna

CONTACT DETAILS

Address
Via Zamboni, 33
Bologna
40126
Italy
Web www.unibo.it
Phone +39 (0) 51209 4516

INSTITUTION STATS

Undergraduates	83,878
Postgraduates	12,281
International Students	4.3%
Student Faculty Ratio	13.2:1
Total Citations	140,384

RANKINGS PERFORMANCE

Faculty Level Positions	
Arts & Humanities	31
Engineering & IT	113
Life Sciences & BioMedicine	99=
Natural Sciences	139=
Social Sciences	59=

ITALY

Catania University

CONTACT DETAILS

Address
Piazza Università, 2
Catania
95124
Italy
Web   www.unict.it
Phone   +39 (0)95 7307111

INSTITUTION STATS

Total Students	49,713
International Students	4.0%
Student Faculty Ratio	8.9:1
Total Citations	36,139

RANKINGS PERFORMANCE

Faculty Level Positions

Arts & Humanities	430=
Engineering & IT	276=
Natural Sciences	506=
Social Sciences	359=

University of Florence

CONTACT DETAILS

Address
P.zza S.Marco, 4
Florence
50121
Italy
Web   www.unifi.it
Phone   +39(0)55 2756209

INSTITUTION STATS

Undergraduates	59,322
Postgraduates	9,035
International Students	3.2%
Student Faculty Ratio	18.1:1
Total Citations	114,040

RANKINGS PERFORMANCE

Faculty Level Positions

Arts & Humanities	90
Engineering & IT	358=
Life Sciences & BioMedicine	145=
Natural Sciences	183=
Social Sciences	163=

University of Genoa

CONTACT DETAILS

Address
Via Balbi, 5
Genoa
16126
Italy
Web   www.unige.it
Phone   +39(0)10 20991

INSTITUTION STATS

Total Students	40,363
International Students	2.6%
Student Faculty Ratio	18.2:1
Total Citations	82,595

RANKINGS PERFORMANCE

Faculty Level Positions

Arts & Humanities	328=
Engineering & IT	311=
Life Sciences & BioMedicine	338=
Natural Sciences	429=
Social Sciences	419=

Catholic University of the Sacred Heart - Milan Campus

CONTACT DETAILS

Address
Largo A. Gemelli, 1
Milan
20123
Italy
Web   www.unicatt.it
Phone   +39(0)2 7234 2254

INSTITUTION STATS

Total Students	41,964
International Students	3.9%
Student Faculty Ratio	7.2:1

RANKINGS PERFORMANCE

Faculty Level Positions

Arts & Humanities	293=
Engineering & IT	497=
Life Sciences & BioMedicine	338=
Natural Sciences	314=
Social Sciences	458=

ITALY

Politecnico di Milano

CONTACT DETAILS

Address
Piazza Leonardo Da Vinci, 32
Milan
20133
Italy
Web www.polimi.it
Phone + 39(0)0223991

INSTITUTION STATS

Undergraduates	28,946
Postgraduates	11,947
International Students	2.1%
Student Faculty Ratio	8.2:1
Total Citations	26,750

RANKINGS PERFORMANCE

Faculty Level Positions
Arts & Humanities	156=
Engineering & IT	63=
Life Sciences & BioMedicine	328=
Natural Sciences	187
Social Sciences	411=

University of Modena

CONTACT DETAILS

Address
Via Università, 4
Modena
41100
Italy
Web www.unimo.it
Phone +39(0)59 2056511

INSTITUTION STATS

Undergraduates	13,822
Postgraduates	4,174
International Students	4.7%
Student Faculty Ratio	18.1:1
Avg UG Fees	1,365
Avg PG Fees	1,500

RANKINGS PERFORMANCE

Faculty Level Positions
Engineering & IT	390=
Natural Sciences	491=

University of Naples 2 - Federico

CONTACT DETAILS

Address
Piazzale V. Tecchio
Naples
80125
Italy
Web www.unina.it
Phone +39(0) 81 768 2232

INSTITUTION STATS

Total Students	20,700
International Students	3.3%
Student Faculty Ratio	11.8:1
Total Citations	98,511

RANKINGS PERFORMANCE

Faculty Level Positions
Arts & Humanities	201=
Engineering & IT	358=
Life Sciences & BioMedicine	380=
Natural Sciences	455=
Social Sciences	163=

The University of Padua

CONTACT DETAILS

Address
via 8 Febbraio, 2
Padova
35122
Italy
Web www.unipd.it
Phone +39 (0) 49 827 5111

INSTITUTION STATS

Toatal Students	63,109
International Students	3.5%
Student Faculty Ratio	26.4:1
Total Citations	153,434

RANKINGS PERFORMANCE

Faculty Level Positions
Arts & Humanities	269
Engineering & IT	297=
Life Sciences & BioMedicine	181=
Natural Sciences	141=
Social Sciences	225=

423

ITALY

Università degli Studi di Pavia

CONTACT DETAILS		INSTITUTION STATS		RANKINGS PERFORMANCE	
Address		**Undergraduates**	21,495	**Faculty Level Positions**	
Strada Nuova, 65		**Postgraduates**	3,773	Arts & Humanities	374=
Pavia		**International Students**	3.4%	Engineering & IT	258=
27100		**Student Faculty Ratio**	24.9:1	Life Sciences & BioMedicine	427=
Italy		**Total Citations**	78,814	Natural Sciences	414
Web	www.unipv.it	**Avg UG Fees**	1,410	Social Sciences	330=
Phone	+39(0)38 2984529	**Avg PG Fees**	1,666		

Perugia University

CONTACT DETAILS		INSTITUTION STATS		RANKINGS PERFORMANCE	
Address		**Undergraduates**	20,600	**Faculty Level Positions**	
Piazza dell'Università, 1		**Postgraduates**	12,440	Engineering & IT	438=
Perugia		**International Students**	4.6%	Life Sciences & BioMedicine	427=
06100		**Student Faculty Ratio**	5.6:1	Natural Sciences	518=
Italy		**Total Citations**	60,805	Social Sciences	426=
Web	www.unipg.it				
Phone	+39(0) 0755851				

University of Pisa

CONTACT DETAILS		INSTITUTION STATS		RANKINGS PERFORMANCE	
Address		**Total Students**	49,394	**Faculty Level Positions**	
Lungarno Pacinotti, 43		**International Students**	1.7%	Arts & Humanities	109
Pisa		**Student Faculty Ratio**	10.3:1	Engineering & IT	205=
56126		**Total Citations**	95,980	Life Sciences & BioMedicine	145=
Italy				Natural Sciences	112
Web	www.unipi.it			Social Sciences	242=
Phone	+ 39(0)50 2212111				

Università degli Studi di Roma - La Sapienza

CONTACT DETAILS		INSTITUTION STATS		RANKINGS PERFORMANCE	
Address		**Undergraduates**	142,743	**Overall Rankings Position**	197
P.le Aldo Moro,5		**Postgraduates**	8,294	**Faculty Level Positions**	
Rome		**International Students**	3.6%	Arts & Humanities	55=
00185		**Student Faculty Ratio**	8.1:1	Engineering & IT	116=
Italy		**Total Citations**	190,621	Life Sciences & BioMedicine	158
Web	www.uniroma1.it	**Avg UG Fees**	974	Natural Sciences	30
Phone	+ 39(0)649911	**Avg PG Fees**	923	Social Sciences	79

ITALY

Universita Degli Studi di Roma Tor Vergata

CONTACT DETAILS	INSTITUTION STATS		RANKINGS PERFORMANCE	
Address	**Undergraduates**	35,500	**Faculty Level Positions**	
Via Orazio Raimondo, 18	**Postgraduates**	6,153	Arts & Humanities	137=
Rome	**International Students**	2.2%	Engineering & IT	358=
00173	**Student Faculty Ratio**	23.4:1	Life Sciences & BioMedicine	369=
Italy	**Total Citations**	77,423	Natural Sciences	204=
Web http://web.uniroma2.it/	**Avg UG Fees**	1,282	Social Sciences	295=
Phone +39(0) 672592017	**Avg PG Fees**	3,845		

University of Siena

CONTACT DETAILS	INSTITUTION STATS		RANKINGS PERFORMANCE	
Address	**Undergraduates**	21,083	**Faculty Level Positions**	
Via Banchi di Sotto, 55	**Postgraduates**	3,116	Arts & Humanities	292
Siena	**International Students**	5.3%	Engineering & IT	482=
53100	**Student Faculty Ratio**	27.9:1	Life Sciences & BioMedicine	314=
Italy	**Total Citations**	41,591	Natural Sciences	461=
Web www.unisi.it	**Avg UG Fees**	1,215	Social Sciences	246=
Phone + 39(0)577 232111	**Avg PG Fees**	1,918		

University of Trento

CONTACT DETAILS	INSTITUTION STATS		RANKINGS PERFORMANCE	
Address	**Undergraduates**	14,190	**Faculty Level Positions**	
via Belenzani, 12	**Postgraduates**	2,725	Arts & Humanities	412=
Trento	**International Students**	4.6%	Engineering & IT	258=
38100	**Student Faculty Ratio**	4.1:1	Natural Sciences	340
Italy	**Avg UG Fees**	878	Social Sciences	330=
Web www.unitn.it	**Avg PG Fees**	942		
Phone + 39(0)461 881111				

University of Trieste

CONTACT DETAILS	INSTITUTION STATS		RANKINGS PERFORMANCE	
Address	**Undergraduates**	21,228	**Faculty Level Positions**	
Piazzale Europa, 1	**Postgraduates**	3,379	Arts & Humanities	412=
Trieste	**International Students**	6.6%	Engineering & IT	250=
34127	**Student Faculty Ratio**	9.5:1	Life Sciences & BioMedicine	390=
Italy	**Total Citations**	53,613	Natural Sciences	160
Web www.univ.trieste.it	**Avg UG Fees**	949	Social Sciences	426=
Phone +39(0)11 6706111	**Avg PG Fees**	1,090		

ITALY

University of Turin

CONTACT DETAILS		INSTITUTION STATS		RANKINGS PERFORMANCE	
Address		**Total Students**	66,841	**Faculty Level Positions**	
Via Verdi, 8		**International Students**	2.1%	Arts & Humanities	231=
Turin		**Student Faculty Ratio**	5.9:1	Engineering & IT	228=
10124		**Total Citations**	113,685	Natural Sciences	246=
Italy				Social Sciences	161=
Web	www.unito.it				
Phone	+ 39(0)11 6706111				

Politecnico di Torino

CONTACT DETAILS		INSTITUTION STATS		RANKINGS PERFORMANCE	
Address		**Undergraduates**	16,882	**Faculty Level Positions**	
Corso Duca degli Abruzzi, 24		**Postgraduates**	5,032	Arts & Humanities	
Turin		**International Students**	3.1%	Engineering & IT	365=
10129		**Student Faculty Ratio**	5:1	Life Sciences & BioMedicine	165=
Italy		**Avg UG Fees**	486	Natural Sciences	427=
Web	www.polito.it	**Avg PG Fees**	197	Social Sciences	378=
Phone	+ 39 (0)11564 6666				393=

JAPAN

Aoyama Gakuin University

CONTACT DETAILS		INSTITUTION STATS		RANKINGS PERFORMANCE	
Address		**Undergraduates**	18,774	**Faculty Level Positions**	
6-16-1, Chitosedai		**Postgraduates**	1,361	Arts & Humanities	250=
Satagayaku Tokyo		**International Students**	1.0%	Engineering & IT	497=
157-8572		**Student Faculty Ratio**	13.6:1	Life Sciences & BioMedicine	413=
Japan				Natural Sciences	458=
Web	www.aoyama.ac.jp			Social Sciences	273=
Phone	+81 3 3309 6633				

Chiba University

CONTACT DETAILS		INSTITUTION STATS		RANKINGS PERFORMANCE	
Address		**Undergraduates**	11,012	**Faculty Level Positions**	
1-33, Yayoi-cho, Inage-ku		**Postgraduates**	3,528	Arts & Humanities	381=
Chiba		**International Students**	3.1%	Engineering & IT	303=
263-8522		**Student Faculty Ratio**	14.4:1	Life Sciences & BioMedicine	118
Japan		**Total Citations**	84,156	Natural Sciences	291=
Web	http://www.chiba-u.ac.jp/			Social Sciences	359=
Phone	+81 43 251 1111				

JAPAN

Doshisha University

CONTACT DETAILS

INSTITUTION STATS

RANKINGS PERFORMANCE

Address
Kyoto
602-8580
Japan

Web www.doshisha.ac.jp
Phone +81 75 251 3930

Undergraduates	23,029
Postgraduates	2,342
International Students	1.2%
Student Faculty Ratio	8.6:1
Avg UG Fees	11,260
Avg PG Fees	8,767

Faculty Level Positions

Arts & Humanities	381=
Engineering & IT	349=
Life Sciences & BioMedicine	413=
Natural Sciences	310=
Social Sciences	447=

Gifu University

CONTACT DETAILS

INSTITUTION STATS

RANKINGS PERFORMANCE

Address
Yanagido 1-1
Gifu
501-1193
Japan
Web www.gifu-u.ac.jp
Phone +81 58 293 2142

Undergraduates	5,988
Postgraduates	1,602
International Students	4.2%
Student Faculty Ratio	11.1:1
Total Citations	40,676

Faculty Level Positions

Engineering & IT	390=
Life Sciences & BioMedicine	217=
Natural Sciences	350
Social Sciences	471=

Gunma University

CONTACT DETAILS

INSTITUTION STATS

RANKINGS PERFORMANCE

Address
4-2 Aramaki-machi
Maebashi
Gunma 371-8510
Japan
Web www.gunma-u.ac.jp

Undergraduates	5,667
Postgraduates	1,375
International Students	3.3%
Student Faculty Ratio	18:1
Total Citations	42,387

Faculty Level Positions

Engineering & IT	336=
Life Sciences & BioMedicine	302=
Natural Sciences	412=
Social Sciences	471=

Hiroshima University

CONTACT DETAILS

INSTITUTION STATS

RANKINGS PERFORMANCE

Address
3-2, Kagamiyama 1 chome
Higashi-Hiroshima
739-8511
Japan
Web www.hiroshima-u.ac.jp
Phone +81 082-422-7111

Undergraduates	10,946
Postgraduates	4,314
International Students	3.9%
Student Faculty Ratio	7.6:1
Total Citations	88,321

Faculty Level Positions

Arts & Humanities	188=
Engineering & IT	188=
Life Sciences & BioMedicine	144
Natural Sciences	155=
Social Sciences	203=

JAPAN

Hitotsubashi University

CONTACT DETAILS		INSTITUTION STATS		RANKINGS PERFORMANCE	
Web	www.hit-u.ac.jp	Undergraduates	4,562	**Faculty Level Positions**	
Phone	+81 42 580 8000	Postgraduates	1,978	Arts & Humanities	163=
		International Students	7.8%	Engineering & IT	349=
		Student Faculty Ratio	20.4:1	Life Sciences & BioMedicine	338=
		Total Citations	1,012	Natural Sciences	412=
		Avg UG Fees	4,670	Social Sciences	112=
		Avg PG Fees	4,670		

Hokkaido University

CONTACT DETAILS		INSTITUTION STATS		RANKINGS PERFORMANCE	
Address		Undergraduates	11,153	**Overall Rankings Position**	133=
Kita 17 Nishi 8, Kita-ku		Postgraduates	6,041	**Faculty Level Positions**	
Hokkaido		International Students	3.7%	Arts & Humanities	126=
060-0817		Student Faculty Ratio	27.1:1	Engineering & IT	139=
Japan		Total Citations	157,324	Life Sciences & BioMedicine	95=
Web	www.htokai.ac.jp			Natural Sciences	164=
				Social Sciences	172=

Kagoshima University

CONTACT DETAILS		INSTITUTION STATS		RANKINGS PERFORMANCE	
Address		Undergraduates	9,426	**Faculty Level Positions**	
8-35-1, Sakuragaoka		Postgraduates	1,819	Arts & Humanities	381=
Kagoshima		International Students	2.5%	Engineering & IT	463=
890-8544		Student Faculty Ratio	14:1	Natural Sciences	356=
Japan		Total Citations	32,262	Social Sciences	471=
Web	www.kagoshima-u.ac.jp				
Phone	+81 099 285 8515				

Kanazawa University

CONTACT DETAILS		INSTITUTION STATS		RANKINGS PERFORMANCE	
Address		Undergraduates	8,217	**Faculty Level Positions**	
Kanazawa		Postgraduates	2,539	Arts & Humanities	381=
920-1192		International Students	2.7%	Engineering & IT	390=
Japan		Student Faculty Ratio	4.7:1	Life Sciences & BioMedicine	221=
		Total Citations	65,087	Natural Sciences	426=
Web	www.kanazawa-u.ac.jp			Social Sciences	471=
Phone	+81 76 264 6063				

JAPAN

Keio University

CONTACT DETAILS	INSTITUTION STATS		RANKINGS PERFORMANCE	
Address	**Undergraduates**	28,012	**Overall Rankings Position**	120
2-15-45 Mita, Minato-ku	**Postgraduates**	4,300	**Faculty Level Positions**	
Tokyo	**International Students**	2.6%	Arts & Humanities	188=
108-8345	**Student Faculty Ratio**	9:1	Engineering & IT	132=
Japan	**Total Citations**	84,547	Life Sciences & BioMedicine	101=
Web www.keio.ac.jp	**Avg UG Fees**	9,000	Natural Sciences	285
Phone +81 3 3453 4511	**Avg PG Fees**	6,700	Social Sciences	75

Kobe University

CONTACT DETAILS	INSTITUTION STATS		RANKINGS PERFORMANCE	
Address	**Undergraduates**	12,829	**Overall Rankings Position**	181=
Kobe	**Postgraduates**	4,728	**Faculty Level Positions**	
Hyogo 657-8501	**International Students**	4.3%	Arts & Humanities	272=
Japan	**Student Faculty Ratio**	16.2:1	Engineering & IT	188=
	Total Citations	70,326	Life Sciences & BioMedicine	192
Web www.kobe-u.ac.jp			Natural Sciences	164=
Phone +81 0 78 360 4946			Social Sciences	88

Kumamoto University

CONTACT DETAILS	INSTITUTION STATS		RANKINGS PERFORMANCE	
Address	**Undergraduates**	8,002	**Faculty Level Positions**	
39-1,Kurokami 2-chome	**Postgraduates**	2,096	Engineering & IT	438=
Kumamoto	**International Students**	3.0%	Life Sciences & BioMedicine	413=
860-8555	**Student Faculty Ratio**	10:1	Natural Sciences	405
Japan	**Total Citations**	65,411	Social Sciences	359=
Web www.kumamoto-u.ac.jp	**Avg UG Fees**	4,600		
Phone +81 96 344 2111	**Avg PG Fees**	4,600		

Kyoto University

CONTACT DETAILS	INSTITUTION STATS		RANKINGS PERFORMANCE	
Address	**Undergraduates**	13,278	**Overall Rankings Position**	29=
Yoshida-Honmachi, Sakyo-ku,	**Postgraduates**	9,420	**Faculty Level Positions**	
Kyoto	**International Students**	4.5%	Arts & Humanities	36
606-8501	**Student Faculty Ratio**	5.9:1	Engineering & IT	21
Japan	**Total Citations**	422,045	Life Sciences & BioMedicine	17
Web www.kyoto-u.ac.jp	**Avg UG Fees**	4,600	Natural Sciences	13
Phone +81 75 753 2042	**Avg PG Fees**	4,600	Social Sciences	36

JAPAN

Kyushu University

CONTACT DETAILS

Address
6-10-1 Hakozaki, Higashi-ku
Fukuoka
812-8581
Japan
Web www.kyushu-u.ac.jp
Phone +81 92 6422 1133

INSTITUTION STATS

Undergraduates	11,763
Postgraduates	6,376
International Students	4.7%
Student Faculty Ratio	13.3:1
Total Citations	178,270

RANKINGS PERFORMANCE

Overall Rankings Position	128=
Faculty Level Positions	
Arts & Humanities	250=
Engineering & IT	167=
Life Sciences & BioMedicine	203
Natural Sciences	181=
Social Sciences	295=

Mie University

CONTACT DETAILS

Address
1577 Kurimamachiya-cho
Tsu-city
Mie-Pref Japan
Web www.mie-u.ac.jp
Phone +81 59 232 1211

INSTITUTION STATS

Undergraduates	6,229
Postgraduates	1,204
International Students	2.9%
Student Faculty Ratio	17.3:1
Total Citations	34,846

RANKINGS PERFORMANCE

Faculty Level Positions	
Natural Sciences	422
Social Sciences	372=

Nagasaki University

CONTACT DETAILS

Address
1-14 Bunkyo-machi
Nagasaki-shi
852-8521
Japan
Web www.nagasaki-u.ac.jp
Phone +81 95 819 2043

INSTITUTION STATS

Undergraduates	7,712
Postgraduates	1,409
International Students	2.9%
Student Faculty Ratio	24.9:1
Total Citations	42,807

RANKINGS PERFORMANCE

Faculty Level Positions	
Engineering & IT	349=
Life Sciences & BioMedicine	220
Natural Sciences	368=
Social Sciences	261=

Nagoya University

CONTACT DETAILS

Address
Furo-cho, Chikusa-ku
Nagoya
464-8601
Japan
Web www.nagoya-u.ac.jp
Phone +81 52 789 2044

INSTITUTION STATS

Undergraduates	9,791
Postgraduates	6,103
International Students	5.7%
Student Faculty Ratio	21.2:1
Total Citations	199,215
Avg UG Fees	4,600
Avg PG Fees	4,600

RANKINGS PERFORMANCE

Overall Rankings Position	128=
Faculty Level Positions	
Arts & Humanities	255=
Engineering & IT	77=
Life Sciences & BioMedicine	148=
Natural Sciences	85
Social Sciences	172=

JAPAN

Niigata University

CONTACT DETAILS

Address
8050 Ikarashi 2-no-cho
Niigata City
950-2181
Japan
Web www.niigata-u.ac.jp
Phone +81 25 262 7000

INSTITUTION STATS

Undergraduates	10,818
Postgraduates	2,421
International Students	2.4%
Student Faculty Ratio	7.9:1
Total Citations	63,237

RANKINGS PERFORMANCE

Faculty Level Positions
Engineering & IT	438=
Life Sciences & BioMedicine	278=
Natural Sciences	434=

Ochanomizu Inversity

CONTACT DETAILS

Web www.ocha.ac.jp
Illel

INSTITUTION STATS

Undergraduates	2,184
Postgraduates	1,097
International Students	5.3%
Student Faculty Ratio	9.8:1

RANKINGS PERFORMANCE

Faculty Level Positions
Arts & Humanities	420=
Engineering & IT	497=
Natural Sciences	476=

Okayama University

CONTACT DETAILS

Address
1-1, Tsushima Naka, 1-Chome
Okayama
700-8530
Japan
Web www.okayama-u.ac.jp
Phone +81 86 251 7211

INSTITUTION STATS

Undergraduates	10,795
Postgraduates	3,365
International Students	3.2%
Student Faculty Ratio	13.2:1
Total Citations	69,667
Avg UG Fees	4,600
Avg PG Fees	4,600

RANKINGS PERFORMANCE

Faculty Level Positions
Engineering & IT	423=
Natural Sciences	368=

Osaka City University

CONTACT DETAILS

Address
3-3-138, Sugimoto,Sumiyoshi-ku,
Sugimoto
Osaka
558-8585
Japan
Web www.osaka-cu.ac.jp
Phone +81 6 6605 2244

INSTITUTION STATS

Undergraduates	7,044
Postgraduates	2,036
International Students	2.7%
Student Faculty Ratio	7.7:1
Total Citations	55,592

RANKINGS PERFORMANCE

Faculty Level Positions
Engineering & IT	228=
Life Sciences & BioMedicine	338=
Natural Sciences	217=
Social Sciences	330=

JAPAN

Osaka University

CONTACT DETAILS

Address
1-4 Machikaneyama, Toyonaka
Osaka
560-0043
Japan
Web   www.osaka-u.ac.jp
Phone   +81 6 6879 7103

INSTITUTION STATS

Undergraduates	12,527
Postgraduates	8,273
International Students	5.5%
Student Faculty Ratio	14.8:1
Total Citations	375,789
Avg UG Fees	4,670
Avg PG Fees	4,670

RANKINGS PERFORMANCE

Overall Rankings Position	70=
Faculty Level Positions	
Arts & Humanities	126=
Engineering & IT	55
Life Sciences & BioMedicine	38
Natural Sciences	49
Social Sciences	140=

Ritsumeikan University

CONTACT DETAILS

Address
56-1 Toji-in Kitamachi, Kita-ku
Kyoto
525-8577
Japan
Web   www.ritsumei.ac.jp
Phone   +8175 465 1111

INSTITUTION STATS

Undergraduates	31,372
Postgraduates	3,051
International Students	2.0%
Student Faculty Ratio	31.7:1

RANKINGS PERFORMANCE

Faculty Level Positions	
Engineering & IT	404=
Natural Sciences	458=
Social Sciences	254=

Saitama University

CONTACT DETAILS

Address
255 Shimo-Okubo, Sakura-ku
Saitama City
338-8570
Japan
Web   www.saitama-u.ac.jp
Phone   +81 48 858 3044

INSTITUTION STATS

Undergraduates	7,651
Postgraduates	1,082
International Students	4.7%

RANKINGS PERFORMANCE

Faculty Level Positions	
Engineering & IT	368=
Life Sciences & BioMedicine	413=
Natural Sciences	434=

Science University Tokyo

CONTACT DETAILS

Address
1-3 Kagurazaka, Shinjyuku-ku
Tokyo
162-8601
Japan
Web   www.sut.ac.jp
Phone   +81 3 5228 8107

INSTITUTION STATS

Undergraduates	17,180
Postgraduates	2,975
International Students	0.4%
Student Faculty Ratio	14.5:1
Total Citations	43,084

RANKINGS PERFORMANCE

Faculty Level Positions	
Engineering & IT	217=
Life Sciences & BioMedicine	413=
Natural Sciences	226=

JAPAN

Showa University

CONTACT DETAILS

Address
-5-8 Hatanodai, Shinagawa-ku
Tokyo
142-8555
Japan
Web www.showa-u.ac.jp
Phone +81-3-3784-8000

INSTITUTION STATS

Undergraduates	2,845
Postgraduates	427
International Students	0.7%
Student Faculty Ratio	7.8:1
Total Citations	33,292
Avg UG Fees	15,253
Avg PG Fees	4,125

RANKINGS PERFORMANCE

Faculty Level Positions	
Engineering & IT	423=
Life Sciences & BioMedicine	302=
Natural Sciences	476=

Tohoku University

CONTACT DETAILS

Address
Sendai-shi
980-8577
Japan

Web www.tohoku.ac.jp

INSTITUTION STATS

Undergraduates	10,791
Postgraduates	6,374
International Students	4.1%
Student Faculty Ratio	17:1
Total Citations	263,056

RANKINGS PERFORMANCE

Overall Rankings Position	168=
Faculty Level Positions	
Arts & Humanities	293=
Engineering & IT	90=
Life Sciences & BioMedicine	90
Natural Sciences	65=
Social Sciences	471=

Tokai University

CONTACT DETAILS

Address
Hiratsuka, Kanagawa Japan
Kitakaname
1117
Japan
Web http://www.u-tokai.ac.jp/
english/
Phone +8146 358 1211

INSTITUTION STATS

Undergraduates	27,531
Postgraduates	1,363
International Students	1.3%
Student Faculty Ratio	9.9:1
Total Citations	43,013

RANKINGS PERFORMANCE

Faculty Level Positions	
Arts & Humanities	381=
Engineering & IT	132=
Life Sciences & BioMedicine	302=
Natural Sciences	300=
Social Sciences	225=

Tokyo Institute of Technology

CONTACT DETAILS

Address
2-12-1 Ookayama
Tokyo
152-8550
Japan
Web www.titech.ac.jp
Phone +8135 734 3827

INSTITUTION STATS

Undergraduates	5,001
Postgraduates	5,080
International Students	8.9%
Student Faculty Ratio	5.7:1
Total Citations	145,314
Avg UG Fees	4,670
Avg PG Fees	4,670

RANKINGS PERFORMANCE

Overall Rankings Position	118
Faculty Level Positions	
Engineering & IT	18
Life Sciences & BioMedicine	151=
Natural Sciences	67=
Social Sciences	392

JAPAN

Tokyo Metropolitan University

CONTACT DETAILS

Address
1-1 Minami-Osawa, Hachioji-shi
Tokyo
Japan
192-0397
Web   www.metro-u.ac.jp

INSTITUTION STATS

Undergraduates	6,992
Postgraduates	1,975
International Students	2.8%
Student Faculty Ratio	22.3:1
Total Citations	41,364

RANKINGS PERFORMANCE

Faculty Level Positions	
Arts & Humanities	328=
Engineering & IT	390=
Life Sciences & BioMedicine	242=
Natural Sciences	183=
Social Sciences	330=

University of Tokyo

CONTACT DETAILS

Address
7-3-1, Hongo, Bunkyo-ku
Tokyo
113-0033
Japan
Web   www.u-tokyo.ac.jp

INSTITUTION STATS

Undergraduates	14,711
Postgraduates	13,243
International Students	6.4%
Student Faculty Ratio	17.7:1
Total Citations	604,397

RANKINGS PERFORMANCE

Overall Rankings Position	19=
Faculty Level Positions	
Arts & Humanities	27
Engineering & IT	7
Life Sciences & BioMedicine	12
Natural Sciences	10
Social Sciences	15

University of Tsukuba

CONTACT DETAILS

Address
1-1-1 Tennodai
Tsukuba-shi Ibaraki-ken
305-8577
Japan

Web   www.tsukuba.ac.jp
Phone   +81-29-853-2111

INSTITUTION STATS

Undergraduates	10,171
Postgraduates	5,810
International Students	7.2%
Student Faculty Ratio	8.3:1
Total Citations	113,284

RANKINGS PERFORMANCE

Faculty Level Positions	
Arts & Humanities	327
Engineering & IT	188=
Life Sciences & BioMedicine	385=
Natural Sciences	136
Social Sciences	359=

Waseda University

CONTACT DETAILS

Address
1-104 Totsukamachi
Tokyo
169-8050
Japan
Web   www.waseda.ac.jp
Phone   +81-3-3203-4141

INSTITUTION STATS

Undergraduates	46,034
Postgraduates	8,460
International Students	3.6%
Student Faculty Ratio	4.7:1
Total Citations	33,948
Avg UG Fees	8,800
Avg PG Fees	7,900

RANKINGS PERFORMANCE

Overall Rankings Position	158=
Faculty Level Positions	
Arts & Humanities	58
Engineering & IT	105
Life Sciences & BioMedicine	334=
Natural Sciences	321=
Social Sciences	152=

JAPAN

Yokohama City University

CONTACT DETAILS	INSTITUTION STATS		RANKINGS PERFORMANCE	
Web www.yokohama-cu.a	Undergraduates	3,729	**Faculty Level Positions**	
Phone +81 045-787-2311	Postgraduates	703	Engineering & IT	197=
	International Students	2.7%	Life Sciences & BioMedicine	221=
	Student Faculty Ratio	35.8:1	Natural Sciences	474=
	Total Citations	37,897	Social Sciences	411=

MALAYSIA

University of Malaya

CONTACT DETAILS	INSTITUTION STATS		RANKINGS PERFORMANCE	
Address	Undergraduates	18,151	**Overall Rankings Position**	192=
Pusat Teknologi Maklumat	Postgraduates	8,293	**Faculty Level Positions**	
Kuala Lumpur	International Students	4.3%	Arts & Humanities	113=
50603	Student Faculty Ratio	18.7:1	Engineering & IT	157=
Malaysia	Total Citations	8,212	Life Sciences & BioMedicine	101=
Web www.um.edu.my	Avg UG Fees	874	Natural Sciences	95
Phone +60 3 7567561	Avg PG Fees	2,488	Social Sciences	49

Universiti Kebangsaan Malaysia

CONTACT DETAILS	INSTITUTION STATS		RANKINGS PERFORMANCE	
Address	Undergraduates	19,468	**Overall Rankings Position**	185
43600 UKM, Bangi	Postgraduates	8,403	**Faculty Level Positions**	
Selangor Darul Ehsan	International Students	3.7%	Arts & Humanities	220
Malaysia	Student Faculty Ratio	9.3:1	Engineering & IT	150
	Total Citations	388	Life Sciences & BioMedicine	56=
Web www.ukm.my			Natural Sciences	62
Phone +60 3 89254599/89215039			Social Sciences	115=

University Putra Malaysia

CONTACT DETAILS	INSTITUTION STATS		RANKINGS PERFORMANCE	
Address	Undergraduates	22,146	**Faculty Level Positions**	
43400 Serdang	Postgraduates	5,188	Arts & Humanities	241=
Selangor Darul Ehsan	International Students	3.6%	Engineering & IT	197=
Malaysia	Student Faculty Ratio	24.8:1	Life Sciences & BioMedicine	161=
	Total Citations	2,241	Natural Sciences	170=
	Avg UG Fees	3,100	Social Sciences	203=
Web www.upm.edu.my	Avg PG Fees	2,300		
Phone +60 3 7567561				

MALAYSIA

University Sains Malaysia

CONTACT DETAILS

Address
11800 Minden
Penang
Malaysia
Web www.usm.my
Phone +60 4 6533888

INSTITUTION STATS

Undergraduates	23,189
Postgraduates	6,545
International Students	4.6%
Student Faculty Ratio	22.9:1
Total Citations	7,119

RANKINGS PERFORMANCE

Faculty Level Positions

Arts & Humanities	326
Engineering & IT	167=
Life Sciences & BioMedicine	95=
Natural Sciences	132=
Social Sciences	178=

MEXICO

Iberoamericana University

CONTACT DETAILS

Address
Prolongación Paseo de la Reforma 880
Ciudad de México
01210
Mexico
Web www.uia.mx
Phone + 52 (55) 5950-4000

INSTITUTION STATS

Undergraduates	10,071
Postgraduates	829
International Students	1.8%
Student Faculty Ratio	5.8:1
Avg UG Fees	10,000
Avg PG Fees	8,000

RANKINGS PERFORMANCE

Faculty Level Positions

Arts & Humanities	398=
Engineering & IT	406=
Life Sciences & BioMedicine	397=
Natural Sciences	514=

Universidad Nacional Autónoma de México

CONTACT DETAILS

Address
Ciudad Universitaria, s/n
Ciudad de Mexico
Distrito Federal 04510
Mexico
Web www.unam.mx
Phone +52(55) 5622-3686

INSTITUTION STATS

Undergraduates	156,434
Postgraduates	20,747
International Students	0.7%
Student Faculty Ratio	15.9:1
Total Citations	96,171
Avg UG Fees	450
Avg PG Fees	1,000

RANKINGS PERFORMANCE

Overall Rankings Position	74

Faculty Level Positions

Arts & Humanities	110=
Engineering & IT	139=
Life Sciences & BioMedicine	109=
Natural Sciences	137
Social Sciences	176=

Tecnológico de Monterrey

CONTACT DETAILS

Address
Carretera Lago de Guadalupe
Atizapán de Zaragoza
Estado de México 52926
Mexico
Web www.itesm.mx
Phone +52 (55) 5864 5555

INSTITUTION STATS

Total Students	95,000
International Students	3.7%
Student Faculty Ratio	13.7:1

RANKINGS PERFORMANCE

Faculty Level Positions

Arts & Humanities	328=
Engineering & IT	267=
Natural Sciences	488
Social Sciences	351=

NETHERLANDS

University of Amsterdam

CONTACT DETAILS

Address
Spui 21
1012 WX Amsterdam
Netherlands

Web www.uva.nl
Phone + 31 20 525 9111

INSTITUTION STATS

Undergraduates	14,821
Postgraduates	10,023
International Students	6.1%
Student Faculty Ratio	16.1:1
Total Citations	236,808

RANKINGS PERFORMANCE

Overall Rankings Position	69
Faculty Level Positions	
Arts & Humanities	24
Engineering & IT	128=
Life Sciences & BioMedicine	70=
Natural Sciences	102=
Social Sciences	30=

Delft University of Technology

CONTACT DETAILS

Address
Julianalaan 134
2628 BL Delft
Netherlands

Web www.tudelft.nl
Phone +31 15 2785404

INSTITUTION STATS

Undergraduates	10,168
Postgraduates	3,395
International Students	11.0%
Student Faculty Ratio	9.7:1
Total Citations	74,508
Avg UG Fees	2,201
Avg PG Fees	7,632

RANKINGS PERFORMANCE

Overall Rankings Position	86
Faculty Level Positions	
Arts & Humanities	122=
Engineering & IT	13
Life Sciences & BioMedicine	369=
Natural Sciences	56=
Social Sciences	281=

Eindhoven University of Technology

CONTACT DETAILS

Address
Den Dolech 2
5612 AZ Eindhoven
Netherlands

Web w3.tm.tue.nl
Phone +31 40 247 91 11

INSTITUTION STATS

Undergraduates	6,513
Postgraduates	1,539
International Students	6.5%
Student Faculty Ratio	31.1:1
Total Citations	46,878
Avg UG Fees	1,918
Avg PG Fees	10,254

RANKINGS PERFORMANCE

Overall Rankings Position	67
Faculty Level Positions	
Arts & Humanities	374=
Engineering & IT	69
Life Sciences & BioMedicine	427=
Natural Sciences	204=
Social Sciences	372=

Erasmus University Rotterdam

CONTACT DETAILS

Address
3000 DR Rotterdam
P.O. Box 1738
Netherlands

Web www.eur.nl
Phone + 31 10 408 1111

INSTITUTION STATS

Undergraduates	15,500
Postgraduates	2,730
International Students	19.2%
Student Faculty Ratio	25.4:1
Total Citations	177,267
Avg UG Fees	13,138
Avg PG Fees	13,138

RANKINGS PERFORMANCE

Overall Rankings Position	92
Faculty Level Positions	
Arts & Humanities	148=
Life Sciences & BioMedicine	114=
Natural Sciences	518=
Social Sciences	37

NETHERLANDS

University of Groningen

CONTACT DETAILS		INSTITUTION STATS		RANKINGS PERFORMANCE	
Address		**Undergraduates**	17,894	**Faculty Level Positions**	
P.O. Box 72		**Postgraduates**	8,778	Arts & Humanities	124=
9700 AB Groningen		**International Students**	8.1%	Engineering & IT	276=
Netherlands		**Student Faculty Ratio**	12.1:1	Life Sciences & BioMedicine	299
		Total Citations	187,808	Natural Sciences	226=
Web	www.rug.nl	**Avg UG Fees**	3,076	Social Sciences	235=
Phone	+ 31 50 363 9111	**Avg PG Fees**	10,767		

Leiden University

CONTACT DETAILS		INSTITUTION STATS		RANKINGS PERFORMANCE	
Address		**Undergraduates**	14,063	**Overall Rankings Position**	90=
P.O. Box 9500		**Postgraduates**	4,390	**Faculty Level Positions**	
2300 RA Leide		**International Students**	6.8%	Arts & Humanities	53
Netherlands		**Student Faculty Ratio**	10.5:1	Engineering & IT	336=
		Total Citations	221,020	Life Sciences & BioMedicine	104=
Web	www.leiden.edu	**Avg UG Fees**	1,923	Natural Sciences	78
Phone	+ 31 (0)71 527 27 27	**Avg PG Fees**	14,100	Social Sciences	84=

University of Maastricht

CONTACT DETAILS		INSTITUTION STATS		RANKINGS PERFORMANCE	
Address		**Undergraduates**	11,961	**Overall Rankings Position**	172=
PO Box 616		**Postgraduates**	1,693	**Faculty Level Positions**	
6200 MD Maastricht		**International Students**	28.6%	Arts & Humanities	374=
Netherlands		**Student Faculty Ratio**	14.3:1	Engineering & IT	382=
		Total Citations	98,585	Life Sciences & BioMedicine	239=
		Avg UG Fees	7,691	Natural Sciences	429=
Web	www.unimaas.nl	**Avg PG Fees**	10,254	Social Sciences	82
Phone	+31 043-3882222				

Radboud Universiteit Nijmegen

CONTACT DETAILS		INSTITUTION STATS		RANKINGS PERFORMANCE	
Address		**Undergraduates**	11,644	**Overall Rankings Position**	137
P.O. Box 9102		**Postgraduates**	5,575	**Faculty Level Positions**	
6500 HC Nijmegen		**International Students**	6.1%	Arts & Humanities	263=
Netherlands		**Student Faculty Ratio**	14.7:1	Engineering & IT	349=
		Total Citations	143,379	Life Sciences & BioMedicine	128=
Web	www.ru.nl	**Avg UG Fees**	3,365	Natural Sciences	193=
Phone	+ 31-24-3616161	**Avg PG Fees**	8,716	Social Sciences	221=

NETHERLANDS

University of Twente

CONTACT DETAILS

Address
P.O. Box 217
7500 AE Enschede
Netherlands

Web www.utwente.nl
Phone +31-53-489 9111

INSTITUTION STATS

Undergraduates	4,882
Postgraduates	3,420
International Students	9.6%
Student Faculty Ratio	8.6:1
Total Citations	39,155
Avg UG Fees	5,640
Avg PG Fees	9,357

RANKINGS PERFORMANCE

Overall Rankings Position	115
Faculty Level Positions	
Arts & Humanities	277
Engineering & IT	79=
Life Sciences & BioMedicine	369=
Natural Sciences	189
Social Sciences	235=

Utrecht University

CONTACT DETAILS

Address
P.O Box 80125
3508 TC Utrecht
Netherlands

Web www.uu.nl
Phone +31 30 253 70 00

INSTITUTION STATS

Undergraduates	16,466
Postgraduates	10,537
International Students	5.4%
Student Faculty Ratio	4.3:1
Total Citations	277,838
Avg UG Fees	9,614
Avg PG Fees	9,614

RANKINGS PERFORMANCE

Overall Rankings Position	95
Faculty Level Positions	
Arts & Humanities	63
Engineering & IT	152=
Life Sciences & BioMedicine	91=
Natural Sciences	44
Social Sciences	76=

Free University of Amsterdam

CONTACT DETAILS

Address
De Boelelaan 1083,
NL 1081 HV Amsterdam
Netherlands

Web www.cs.vu.nl
Phone +31 (0)20 598 7513

INSTITUTION STATS

Undergraduates	14,544
Postgraduates	3,255
International Students	5.2%
Student Faculty Ratio	4.4:1
Total Citations	111,915
Avg UG Fees	2,350
Avg PG Fees	10,575

RANKINGS PERFORMANCE

Overall Rankings Position	183=
Faculty Level Positions	
Arts & Humanities	209=
Engineering & IT	235=
Life Sciences & BioMedicine	196=
Natural Sciences	166
Social Sciences	104

Wageningen University

CONTACT DETAILS

Address
Postbus 9101
6700 HB Wageningen
Netherlands

Web www.wau.nl
Phone +31 317 4 89111

INSTITUTION STATS

Undergraduates	4,500
Postgraduates	1,200
International Students	28.1%
Student Faculty Ratio	13.9:1
Total Citations	134,902
Avg Fees	5,512

RANKINGS PERFORMANCE

Overall Rankings Position	97
Faculty Level Positions	
Arts & Humanities	398=
Engineering & IT	497=
Life Sciences & BioMedicine	155=
Natural Sciences	193=
Social Sciences	281=

NEW ZEALAND

University of Auckland

CONTACT DETAILS	INSTITUTION STATS		RANKINGS PERFORMANCE	
Address	**Undergraduates**	31,193	**Overall Rankings Position**	46=
Private Bag 92019	**Postgraduates**	8,074	**Faculty Level Positions**	
Auckland 1020	**International Students**	13.1%	Arts & Humanities	29
New Zealand	**Student Faculty Ratio**	13.5:1	Engineering & IT	43=
	Total Citations	71,982	Life Sciences & BioMedicine	26=
Web www.auckland.ac.nz	**Avg UG Fees**	12,380	Natural Sciences	58=
Phone +64 (9) 373-7999	**Avg PG Fees**	13,830	Social Sciences	33

University of Canterbury

CONTACT DETAILS	INSTITUTION STATS		RANKINGS PERFORMANCE	
Address	**Total Students**	13,430	**Faculty Level Positions**	
Christchurch	**International Students**	16.4%	Arts & Humanities	241=
Private Bag 4800	**Student Faculty Ratio**	30.8:1	Engineering & IT	141=
New Zealand	**Total Citations**	20,158	Life Sciences & BioMedicine	338=
			Natural Sciences	190
Web www.canterbury.ac.nz			Social Sciences	203=
Phone +64 33 64 22 04				

Massey University

CONTACT DETAILS	INSTITUTION STATS		RANKINGS PERFORMANCE	
Address	**Undergraduates**	16,149	**Faculty Level Positions**	
Palmerston North	**Postgraduates**	4,699	Arts & Humanities	186
Private Bag 11 222	**International Students**	19.3%	Engineering & IT	235=
New Zealand	**Student Faculty Ratio**	13.8:1	Life Sciences & BioMedicine	133=
	Total Citations	23,696	Natural Sciences	221=
	Avg UG Fees	12,077	Social Sciences	193=
Web www.massey.ac.nz	**Avg PG Fees**	11,286		
Phone +64 6 356 9099				

University of Otago

CONTACT DETAILS	INSTITUTION STATS		RANKINGS PERFORMANCE	
Address	**Undergraduates**	15,083	**Overall Rankings Position**	79=
PO Box 56	**Postgraduates**	2,656	**Faculty Level Positions**	
Dunedin	**International Students**	12.4%	Arts & Humanities	107
New Zealand	**Student Faculty Ratio**	5.7:1	Engineering & IT	377=
	Total Citations	57,058	Life Sciences & BioMedicine	74
Web www.otago.ac.nz	**Avg UG Fees**	9,740	Natural Sciences	224
Phone +64 3 479 1100	**Avg PG Fees**	10,400	Social Sciences	142=

NEW ZELAND

Victoria University of Wellington

CONTACT DETAILS

Address
PO Box 600
Wellington 6001
New Zealand

Web www.vuw.ac.nz
Phone +64-4-472 1000

INSTITUTION STATS

Undergraduates	15,711
Postgraduates	4,669
International Students	16.7%
Student Faculty Ratio	9.8:1
Total Citations	49,659
Avg UG Fees	9,370
Avg PG Fees	11,000

RANKINGS PERFORMANCE

Faculty Level Positions
Arts & Humanities	76=
Engineering & IT	315=
Life Sciences & BioMedicine	333
Natural Sciences	291=
Social Sciences	63=

University of Waikato

CONTACT DETAILS

Address
Gate 1 Knighton Road
Private Bag 3105
New Zealand

Web www.waikato.ac.nz
Phone +64 7 856 2889

INSTITUTION STATS

Undergraduates	9,402
Postgraduates	3,071
International Students	29.7%
Student Faculty Ratio	20.3:1
Total Citations	9,776
Avg UG Fees	12,469
Avg PG Fees	14,621

RANKINGS PERFORMANCE

Faculty Level Positions
Arts & Humanities	287=
Engineering & IT	289=
Natural Sciences	351=
Social Sciences	193=

NIGERIA

University of Ibadan

CONTACT DETAILS

Web www.ui.edu.ng

INSTITUTION STATS

Total Students	17,304
Postgraduates	0.4%
International Students	13:1

RANKINGS PERFORMANCE

Faculty Level Positions
Arts & Humanities	328=
Engineering & IT	438=
Life Sciences & BioMedicine	427=
Natural Sciences	447=
Social Sciences	290=

NORWAY

University of Bergen

CONTACT DETAILS

Address
Post box 7800
Bergen
N- 5020
Norway
Web www.uib.no
Phone +47 55 58 00 00

INSTITUTION STATS

Undergraduates	9,920
Postgraduates	5,530
International Students	10.9%
Student Faculty Ratio	11.7:1
Total Citations	68,975

RANKINGS PERFORMANCE

Faculty Level Positions
Arts & Humanities	207=
Engineering & IT	423=
Life Sciences & BioMedicine	292=
Natural Sciences	341=
Social Sciences	160

NORWAY

Norwegian University of Science and Technology

CONTACT DETAILS	INSTITUTION STATS		RANKINGS PERFORMANCE	
Address	**Undergraduates**	12,496	**Faculty Level Positions**	
NO-7491	**Postgraduates**	8,971	Arts & Humanities	311=
Trondheim	**International Students**	7.7%	Engineering & IT	87
Norway	**Student Faculty Ratio**	9.6:1	Life Sciences & BioMedicine	338=
	Total Citations	51,476	Natural Sciences	244=
Web www.ntnu.no	**Avg UG Fees**	64	Social Sciences	313=
Phone +47 73 59 50 00	**Avg PG Fees**	64		

University of Oslo

CONTACT DETAILS	INSTITUTION STATS		RANKINGS PERFORMANCE	
Address	**Undergraduates**	16,494	**Overall Rankings Position**	177
Boks 1072 Blindern	**Postgraduates**	13,753	**Faculty Level Positions**	
OSLO	**International Students**	5.3%	Arts & Humanities	65
NO-0316	**Student Faculty Ratio**	18.8:1	Engineering & IT	245=
Norway	**Total Citations**	127,206	Life Sciences & BioMedicine	190
			Natural Sciences	141=
Web www.uio.no			Social Sciences	68=
Phone +47 22 85 50 50				

University of Tromso

CONTACT DETAILS	INSTITUTION STATS		RANKINGS PERFORMANCE	
Address	**Total Students**	20,963	**Faculty Level Positions**	
Universitetet i Tromsø	**International Students**	6.5%	Arts & Humanities	244=
Tromsø	**Student Faculty Ratio**	12.3:1	Natural Sciences	392=
9037	**Total Citations**	32,996	Social Sciences	359=
Norway				
Web www.uit.no				
Phone + 47 77 64 40 00				

PAKISTAN

University of Lahore

CONTACT DETAILS	INSTITUTION STATS		RANKINGS PERFORMANCE	
Address	**Student Faculty Ratio**	25.6:1	**Faculty Level Positions**	
1 KM Raiwind Road	**Total Citations**	6	Arts & Humanities	191=
Lahore			Engineering & IT	250=
Pakistan			Life Sciences & BioMedicine	172
			Natural Sciences	250=
Web www.uolcc.com			Social Sciences	137
Phone +92 42 5411901-905				

PERU

Pontificia Universidad Católica del Perú

CONTACT DETAILS

INSTITUTION STATS

RANKINGS PERFORMANCE

Address
Avenida Universitaria Cdra. 18
Lima
1761
Peru

Total Students	17,000
Student Faculty Ratio	1.8%
International Students	11.7:1

Faculty Level Positions

Arts & Humanities	328=
Engineering & IT	482=
Natural Sciences	360=
Social Sciences	464=

Web   www.pucp.edu.pe
Phone   (511)626-2000

PHILIPPINES

Ateneo de Manila University

CONTACT DETAILS

INSTITUTION STATS

RANKINGS PERFORMANCE

Address
Katipunan Avenue, Loyola Heights
Quezon City
1108
Philippines

Undergraduates	7,161
Postgraduates	3,827
International Students	3.9%
Student Faculty Ratio	31.1:1

Faculty Level Positions

Engineering & IT	497=
Natural Sciences	476=
Social Sciences	471=

Web   www.ateneo.net
Phone   +632 4266001

De La Salle University

CONTACT DETAILS

INSTITUTION STATS

RANKINGS PERFORMANCE

Address
2401 Taft Avenue
Manila
1004
Philippines
Web   www.dlsu.edu.ph
Phone   +63 2 5234230

Total Students	10,000
International Students	0.3%
Student Faculty Ratio	319.4:1

Faculty Level Positions

Arts & Humanities	293=
Engineering & IT	438=
Natural Sciences	476=
Social Sciences	254=

University of the Philippines

CONTACT DETAILS

INSTITUTION STATS

RANKINGS PERFORMANCE

Address
Diliman
Quezon City
1101
Philippines

Total Students	13,753
International Students	0.4%
Student Faculty Ratio	12.4:1
Total Citations	5,492

Faculty Level Positions

Arts & Humanities	293=
Engineering & IT	296
Life Sciences & BioMedicine	242=
Natural Sciences	214=
Social Sciences	200=

Web   www.upd.edu.ph
Phone   +63 9818500

443

PHILIPPINES

University of Santo Tomas

CONTACT DETAILS

Address
España St.
Manila
1008
Philippines
Web www.ust.edu.ph
Phone +63 2 7313101

INSTITUTION STATS

Total Students	11,764
International Students	0.4%
Student Faculty Ratio	6.1:1

RANKINGS PERFORMANCE

Faculty Level Positions
Arts & Humanities	328=
Engineering & IT	497=
Natural Sciences	440=

POLAND

Jagiellonian University

CONTACT DETAILS

Address
ul. Golebia 24
Krakow
31-007
Poland
Web www.uj.edu.pl
Phone +48 12 422-10-33

INSTITUTION STATS

Undergraduates	8,023
Postgraduates	39,503
International Students	2.1%
Student Faculty Ratio	10.4:1
Total Citations	46,537
Avg UG Fees	5,127
Avg PG Fees	6,409

RANKINGS PERFORMANCE

Faculty Level Positions
Arts & Humanities	141=
Engineering & IT	276=
Life Sciences & BioMedicine	268=
Natural Sciences	172
Social Sciences	273=

Lodz University

CONTACT DETAILS

Address
ul. Narutowicza 65
90-131
Poland
Web www.uni.lodz.pl
Phone +48 (042) 635 40 00

INSTITUTION STATS

Undergraduates	38,839
Postgraduates	1,918
International Students	0.4%
Student Faculty Ratio	7.9:1
Avg UG Fees	3,845
Avg PG Fees	4,486

RANKINGS PERFORMANCE

Faculty Level Positions
Arts & Humanities	277=
Engineering & IT	423=
Life Sciences & BioMedicine	338=
Natural Sciences	409=
Social Sciences	464=

Warsaw University of Technology

CONTACT DETAILS

Address
Pl. Politechniki 1
Warsaw
00-661
Poland
Web www.pw.edu.pl
Phone +48-22 6607211

INSTITUTION STATS

Undergraduates	30,521
Postgraduates	3,022
International Students	0.5%
Student Faculty Ratio	8.2:1
Total Citations	13,277
Avg UG Fees	3,845
Avg PG Fees	6,794

RANKINGS PERFORMANCE

Faculty Level Positions
Arts & Humanities	233=
Engineering & IT	114
Life Sciences & BioMedicine	427=
Natural Sciences	234=

POLAND

Warsaw University

CONTACT DETAILS

Address
Krakowskie Przedmiescie 26/28
Warszawa
00-927
Poland

Web www.uw.edu.pl
Phone +48 22 552 00 00

INSTITUTION STATS

Undergraduates	44,805
Postgraduates	20,180
International Students	1.6%
Student Faculty Ratio	11.4:1
Total Citations	53,665
Avg UG Fees	5,127
Avg PG Fees	6,409

RANKINGS PERFORMANCE

Faculty Level Positions
Arts & Humanities	222=
Engineering & IT	276=
Life Sciences & BioMedicine	284=
Natural Sciences	141=
Social Sciences	273=

PORTUGAL

Universidade Catolica Portuguesa, Lisboa

CONTACT DETAILS

Address
Palma de Cima
Lisbon
1649-023
Portugal
Web www.ucp.pt
Phone +351(0) 21 726 58 38

INSTITUTION STATS

Undergraduates	8,366
Postgraduates	2,838
International Students	5.6%
Student Faculty Ratio	13.3:1

RANKINGS PERFORMANCE

Faculty Level Positions
Arts & Humanities	277=
Engineering & IT	463=
Natural Sciences	489=
Social Sciences	330=

University of Coimbra

CONTACT DETAILS

Address
Paço das Escolas
Coimbra
3004-531
Portugal

Web www.uc.pt
Phone +351(0) 239 859 993

INSTITUTION STATS

Undergraduates	9,986
International Students	6.0%
Student Faculty Ratio	18.7:1
Total Citations	20,546

RANKINGS PERFORMANCE

Faculty Level Positions
Arts & Humanities	170=
Engineering & IT	358=
Life Sciences & BioMedicine	235=
Natural Sciences	388=
Social Sciences	295=

Universidade Nova de Lisboa

CONTACT DETAILS

Address
Campolide Campus
Lisbon
1099-085
Portugal

Web www.unl.pt
Phone +351(0) 21 371 56 00

INSTITUTION STATS

Undergraduates	12,531
Postgraduates	1,468
International Students	7.3%
Student Faculty Ratio	10.1:1
Total Citations	17,218
Avg UG Fees	890
Avg PG Fees	12,818

RANKINGS PERFORMANCE

Faculty Level Positions
Arts & Humanities	311=
Engineering & IT	368=
Life Sciences & BioMedicine	328=
Natural Sciences	506=
Social Sciences	178=

ROMANIA

University of Bucharest

CONTACT DETAILS

Address
36-46, M. Koglniceanu Bd, Sector 5
Bucharest
70709
Romania
Web   www.unibuc.ro
Phone   +40-21-307 73 00

INSTITUTION STATS

Total Students	31,737
International Students	0.3%
Student Faculty Ratio	49.1:1

RANKINGS PERFORMANCE

Faculty Level Positions

Arts & Humanities	277=
Engineering & IT	336=
Life Sciences & BioMedicine	427=
Natural Sciences	447=
Social Sciences	330=

RUSSIA

Kazan State University

CONTACT DETAILS

Address
18 Kremlyovskaya St
Kazan
420008
Russia
Web   www.ksu.ru
Phone   +7 (843) 2927600

INSTITUTION STATS

Undergraduates	17,126
Postgraduates	567
International Students	1.6%
Student Faculty Ratio	10.8:1
Avg UG Fees	2,000
Avg PG Fees	3,000

RANKINGS PERFORMANCE

Faculty Level Positions

Arts & Humanities	381=
Engineering & IT	497=
Natural Sciences	258=
Social Sciences	393=

Lomonosov Moscow State University

CONTACT DETAILS

Address
GSP-2, Leninskie Gory,
Moscow
119992
Russia

Web   www.msu.ru
Phone   (095) 939-10-00

INSTITUTION STATS

Undergraduates	40,000
Postgraduates	7,000
International Students	4.3%
Student Faculty Ratio	12:1
Total Citations	89,942

RANKINGS PERFORMANCE

Overall Rankings Position	93=
Faculty Level Positions	
Arts & Humanities	118=
Engineering & IT	58
Life Sciences & BioMedicine	75=
Natural Sciences	19
Social Sciences	119

Novosibirsk State University

CONTACT DETAILS

Web   www.nsu.ru
Phone   +7(383) 339 73 78

INSTITUTION STATS

Undergraduates	6,411
Postgraduates	259
International Students	4.8%
Student Faculty Ratio	13.6:1
Total Citations	5,135
Avg UG Fees	3,500
Avg PG Fees	4,100

RANKINGS PERFORMANCE

Faculty Level Positions

Arts & Humanities	233=
Engineering & IT	358=
Life Sciences & BioMedicine	427=
Natural Sciences	107=
Social Sciences	393=

RUSSIA

Saint-Petersburg State University

CONTACT DETAILS

Address
7-9, universitefskay nab
St.Petersburg
199034
Russia

Web www.spbu.ru
Phone +7-812-2382000

INSTITUTION STATS

Total Students	37,900
International Students	5.5%
Student Faculty Ratio	11.1:1
Total Citations	26,400

RANKINGS PERFORMANCE

Overall Rankings Position	164
Faculty Level Positions	
Arts & Humanities	167=
Engineering & IT	115
Life Sciences & BioMedicine	292=
Natural Sciences	73=
Social Sciences	290=

Tomsk State University

CONTACT DETAILS

Address
36 Lenin Prospek
Tomsk
634050
Russia

Web www.tsu.ru
Phone +7-3822-52-98-52

INSTITUTION STATS

Undergraduates	22,000
Postgraduates	680
International Students	0.1%
Student Faculty Ratio	23.5:1
Avg UG Fees	2,500
Avg PG Fees	4,000

RANKINGS PERFORMANCE

Faculty Level Positions	
Arts & Humanities	381=
Life Sciences & BioMedicine	427=
Natural Sciences	381=

SINGAPORE

Nanyang Technological University

CONTACT DETAILS

Address
Nanyang Avenue
Singapore
639798
Singapore
Web www.ntu.edu.sg
Phone +65 67911744

INSTITUTION STATS

Undergraduates	18,385
Postgraduates	6,072
International Students	34.5%
Student Faculty Ratio	13:1
Total Citations	33,903
Avg UG Fees	4,200
Avg PG Fees	9,700

RANKINGS PERFORMANCE

Overall Rankings Position	61=
Faculty Level Positions	
Arts & Humanities	201=
Engineering & IT	15
Life Sciences & BioMedicine	94
Natural Sciences	87=
Social Sciences	61=

National University of Singapore

CONTACT DETAILS

Address
21 Lower Kent Ridge Road
Singapore
119077
Singapore

Web www.nus.edu.sg
Phone +65 6775 6666

INSTITUTION STATS

Undergraduates	22,006
Postgraduates	6,308
International Students	28.8%
Student Faculty Ratio	10.5:1
Total Citations	121,335
Avg UG Fees	4,240
Avg PG Fees	3,575

RANKINGS PERFORMANCE

Overall Rankings Position	19=
Faculty Level Positions	
Arts & Humanities	22
Engineering & IT	8
Life Sciences & BioMedicine	9
Natural Sciences	22=
Social Sciences	11

SLOVENIA

University of Ljubljana

CONTACT DETAILS		INSTITUTION STATS		RANKINGS PERFORMANCE	
Address		**Undergraduates**	45,970	**Faculty Level Positions**	
Kongresni trg 12		**Postgraduates**	4,845	Arts & Humanities	198=
Ljubljana		**International Students**	3.4%	Engineering & IT	358=
SI – 1000		**Student Faculty Ratio**	3.9:1	Life Sciences & BioMedicine	380=
Slovenia		**Total Citations**	33,936	Natural Sciences	304=
Web	www.uni-lj.si	**Avg UG Fees**	1,914	Social Sciences	330=
Phone	+386 1 241 85 00	**Avg PG Fees**	3,520		

SOUTH AFRICA

University of Cape Town

CONTACT DETAILS		INSTITUTION STATS		RANKINGS PERFORMANCE	
Address		**Undergraduates**	14,491	**Faculty Level Positions**	
Private Bag		**Postgraduates**	1,182	Arts & Humanities	246=
Rondebosch		**International Students**	12.9%	Engineering & IT	303=
7701		**Student Faculty Ratio**	7.2:1	Life Sciences & BioMedicine	268=
South Africa		**Total Citations**	45,246	Natural Sciences	255
Web	www.uct.ac.za	**Avg UG Fees**	6,300	Social Sciences	142=
Phone	+27 21 650 2696	**Avg PG Fees**	5,300		

University of KwaZulu-Natal

CONTACT DETAILS		INSTITUTION STATS		RANKINGS PERFORMANCE	
Address		**Undergraduates**	28,724	**Faculty Level Positions**	
Cnr. Richmond & Marianhill Rd		**Postgraduates**	9,466	Engineering & IT	389
Pinetown		**International Students**	5.8%	Natural Sciences	497
3605		**Student Faculty Ratio**	18.8:1	Social Sciences	330=
South Africa					
Web	www.ukzn.ac.za				

University of Pretoria

CONTACT DETAILS		INSTITUTION STATS		RANKINGS PERFORMANCE	
Address		**Undergraduates**	27,515	**Faculty Level Positions**	
Lynnwood road		**Postgraduates**	14,279	Arts & Humanities	369=
Hillcrest		**International Students**	5.3%	Engineering & IT	382=
0002		**Student Faculty Ratio**	590.3:1	Natural Sciences	381=
South Africa		**Avg UG Fees**	4,800	Social Sciences	203=
		Avg PG Fees	2,850		
Web	www.up.ac.za				
Phone	+27 12 420 4111				

SOUTH AFRICA

University of the Witwatersrand

CONTACT DETAILS

Address
Private Bag 3, WITS
Johannesburg
2050
South Africa

Web www.wits.ac.za
Phone +27 (0)11 717 1000

INSTITUTION STATS

Undergraduates	16,126
Postgraduates	7,106
International Students	8.9%
Student Faculty Ratio	15.2:1
Total Citations	32,502

RANKINGS PERFORMANCE

Faculty Level Positions

Arts & Humanities	233=
Engineering & IT	267=
Life Sciences & BioMedicine	310=
Natural Sciences	394=
Social Sciences	123

SOUTH KOREA

Chonbuk National University

CONTACT DETAILS

Address
664-14 1GR Duck-Dong Duckjin-gu
Jeonju
JEONBUK
561156
South Korea
Web www.chonbuk.ac.kr
Phone +81 86 251 7902

INSTITUTION STATS

Undergraduates	7,685
Postgraduates	879
International Students	3.8%
Student Faculty Ratio	20.8:1
Avg UG Fees	4,300
Avg PG Fees	6,000

RANKINGS PERFORMANCE

Faculty Level Positions

Engineering & IT	404=
Natural Sciences	509=
Social Sciences	393=

Chonnam National University

CONTACT DETAILS

Address
300 Yongbong-dong, Buk-gu
Gwangju
500757
South Korea

Web www.chonnam.ac.kr/en
Phone +82 62 5303114

INSTITUTION STATS

Undergraduates	25,904
Postgraduates	5,264
International Students	0.8%
Student Faculty Ratio	13.5:1

RANKINGS PERFORMANCE

Faculty Level Positions

Arts & Humanities	328=
Engineering & IT	438=
Natural Sciences	491=

Chungnam National University

CONTACT DETAILS

Address
220 Gung-dong, Yuseong-gu
Daejeon
305764
South Korea
Web http://plus.cnu.ac.kr/eng/
Phone +82 42 821 5013

INSTITUTION STATS

Undergraduates	18,056
Postgraduates	4,681
International Students	1.9%
Student Faculty Ratio	9.8:1

RANKINGS PERFORMANCE

Faculty Level Positions

Engineering & IT	497=
Life Sciences & BioMedicine	413=
Natural Sciences	514=

449

SOUTH KOREA

Ehwa Womans University

CONTACT DETAILS

INSTITUTION STATS

Address
11-1 Daehyun-dong
Seodaemun-gu
Seoul
120-750
South Korea
Web   www.ewha.ac.kr
Phone   +82 2 32772011

Undergraduates	16,124
Postgraduates	4,935
International Students	0.6%
Student Faculty Ratio	9.7:1

Hanyang University

CONTACT DETAILS

INSTITUTION STATS

RANKINGS PERFORMANCE

Address
17 Haengdang-dong
Seongdong-gu
Seoul
133-791
South Korea

Web   www.hanyang.ac.kr
Phone   +82 2 22900296

Undergraduates	25,010
Postgraduates	11,065
International Students	1.3%
Student Faculty Ratio	15.6:1
Total Citations	26,069

Faculty Level Positions

Arts & Humanities	293=
Engineering & IT	406=
Natural Sciences	434=
Social Sciences	447=

Korea Advanced Institute of Science & Technology

CONTACT DETAILS

INSTITUTION STATS

RANKINGS PERFORMANCE

Address
373-1 Guseong-dong, Yuseong-gu
Daejeon
305701
South Korea

Web   www.kaist.edu
Phone   +82 42 8692114

Undergraduates	3,115
Postgraduates	4,376
International Students	3.5%
Student Faculty Ratio	16.7:1
Total Citations	60,698
Avg UG Fees	5,600
Avg PG Fees	7,200

Overall Rankings Position	198=
Faculty Level Positions	
Engineering & IT	37
Life Sciences & BioMedicine	242=
Natural Sciences	82=
Social Sciences	372=

Korea University

CONTACT DETAILS

INSTITUTION STATS

RANKINGS PERFORMANCE

Address
Anam-dong Seongbuk-Gu
Seoul
136701
South Korea

Web   www.korea.ac.kr
Phone   +82 2 32901152

Undergraduates	19,522
Postgraduates	8,520
International Students	11.6%
Student Faculty Ratio	7.9:1
Total Citations	38,502
Avg UG Fees	7,178
Avg PG Fees	8,698

Overall Rankings Position	150=
Faculty Level Positions	
Arts & Humanities	170
Engineering & IT	204
Life Sciences & BioMedicine	204=
Natural Sciences	200=
Social Sciences	120=

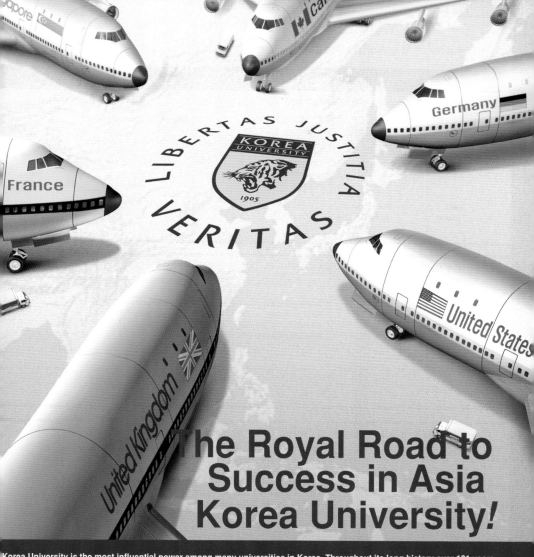

The Royal Road to Success in Asia Korea University!

Korea University is the most influential power among many universities in Korea. Throughout its long history over 101 years, many KU alumni are playing essential role in many societies, economic fields and political parties of Korea.(congressman 18%, lawyer 20%, listed enterprise CEO 20%, major journalist 21%, CPA 16%) And, there is no doubt the power of these many respectable alumni is a huge benefit to your step into your future in Korea after your graduation in KU.

Korea University's globalized system is the known as the best not only in Korea, but throughout Asia also. KU has established student oriented system in both class and administration for those who can speak English. If you can speak English, you will never have any difficulty in studies and campus life. A number of excellent foreign faculties and the proportion of lecture in English is increasing constantly. At present, the proportion of lectures proceeded in English is near 35%, and it will be reaching to 60% in the year of 2010. Also, KU is famous of Summer Classes with all classes in English lecture in its huge scale.

Especially, Korea University welcomes to the foreign students who came from outside of Korea. You have many opportunities to get various types of scholarship based on abundant amount of financial supports. The doctor/master's course in KU provides you a chance to get reduction of tuition in maximum of 75%, and most engineering and science major students can get chance of 100% of scholarship. Students who came from all over the world studying in Korea University can enjoy world best quality of facilities and classes, and also they stay at nice dormitory rooms like hotel.

In you choose the Korea University, you are insured to have a chance to succeed in Korea and Asia.

For more information about the university, please contact us
The Office of International Affairs, Korea University
http://www.korea.edu   Phone: +82-2-3290-1150~9
Fax: +82-2-922-5820   E-mail: studyabroad@korea.ac.kr

KOREA UNIVERSITY

SOUTH KOREA

Kyung Hee University

CONTACT DETAILS

Address
130-701, 1, Hoegi-dong,
Dongdaemun-gu
Seoul
South Korea

Web www.kyunghee.ac.kr
Phone +82 2 5458101

INSTITUTION STATS

Undergraduates	20,470
Postgraduates	2,530
International Students	0.2%
Student Faculty Ratio	25.2:1

RANKINGS PERFORMANCE

Faculty Level Positions
Engineering & IT	497=
Natural Sciences	491=

Kyungpook National University

CONTACT DETAILS

Address
Daegu
702-701
South Korea

Web www.kyungpook.ac.kr
Phone +82 53 9506091

INSTITUTION STATS

Undergraduates	17,299
Postgraduates	5,398
International Students	1.6%
Student Faculty Ratio	0:1

RANKINGS PERFORMANCE

Faculty Level Positions
Engineering & IT	436=
Natural Sciences	476=

Pohang University of Science and Technology

CONTACT DETAILS

Address
San 31, Hyoja-dong, Num gu,
Pohang
Gyungbuk
790-784
South Korea

Web www.postech.ac.kr
Phone +82 54 2790114

INSTITUTION STATS

Undergraduates	1,376
Postgraduates	1,522
International Students	2.0%
Student Faculty Ratio	15.2:1
Total Citations	42,365
Avg UG Fees	4,658
Avg PG Fees	5,669

RANKINGS PERFORMANCE

Faculty Level Positions
Engineering & IT	172
Life Sciences & BioMedicine	217=
Natural Sciences	153
Social Sciences	471=

Pusan National University

CONTACT DETAILS

Address
Geumjeong-gu
Busan
609-735
South Korea

Web www.pusan.ac.kr
Phone +82 51 5101105

INSTITUTION STATS

Undergraduates	17,644
Postgraduates	6,005
International Students	0.8%
Student Faculty Ratio	17.2:1

RANKINGS PERFORMANCE

Faculty Level Positions
Engineering & IT	235=
Life Sciences & BioMedicine	252=
Natural Sciences	343=

Seoul National University

SEOUL NATIONAL UNIVERSITY

DATA

University contact
Office of International Affairs (OIA)

Address
Office of International Affairs, Seoul National University,
San 56-1 Sillim-dong, Gwanak-gu, Seoul, 151-742, Korea

Telephone +82 2 880 8633~8
Fax +82 2 880 8632
Email snuoia@snu.ac.kr
Website http://www.snu.ac.kr
      http://oia.snu.ac.kr

University's main claims to international academic or non-academic excellence
The leading institution for higher education in Korea, globally recognized for its excellence and commitment to teaching and research

University's international achievements in innovation
World-class research university, ranked 30th worldwide in 2005 based on the number of academic papers published in journals certified by the Scientific Citation Index (SCI)

Total number of students
18,400 undergraduates and 9,800 graduates

Range of tuition fees
Undergraduate:
US $2,100~$4,500 (per semester)
Graduate:
US $2,000~$7,600 (per semester)

Language support
The Faculty of Liberal Education, the College of Humanities and the Language Education Institute offer courses in Korean, Chinese, English, French, German, Japanese, Russian and Spanish.

Accommodation
A wide range of on-campus accommodation is available at affordable rates for students and families.

Price range
Dormitories: US $530~$600 (per semester)
Family Accommodation: US $290~$320 (per month)

Modes of study
Full time

Levels of study & research
Undergraduate
Masters
Doctorate
Postdoctorate

PROFILE

A TRADITION OF EXCELLENCE
Since its foundation in 1946, Seoul National University has been the undisputed leader of higher education in Korea and has established a global reputation. Its graduates have long served as leaders in Korean society and in the international community.

WORLD-CLASS EDUCATION
SNU honors the ideals of liberal education and aims to teach students a lifelong love of learning. It is also committed to preparing students to work and live in an increasingly competitive global environment.

SNU trains the most outstanding students in Korea in a wide array of areas in the undergraduate, masters and doctorate programs. Its freshmen belong to the top 2.5% of those who take the National University Entrance Examination. Faculty members at SNU are also highly qualified, with a talent for scholarship and a dedication to teaching. Of all faculty members, 95.6% have doctoral degrees, most of which have been earned from prestigious universities around the world.

CUTTING-EDGE RESEARCH
SNU is committed to fostering productive research environments. As a result, many of its departments and research institutes, especially in the field of Engineering and Natural Sciences, are now globally recognized for their cutting-edge research.

The number of academic papers published in international journals certified by the Scientific Citation Index (SCI) was 3,946 as of 2005 — ranked 30th in the world — and that figure continues to increase sharply. A Quality Index of Research Capacity, based on the citation number of scientific papers, shows that SNU is comparable with the top 10~30 universities in the United States.

DIVERSITY AND GLOBALIZATION
On its 60th anniversary, SNU is embracing diversity and globalization more than ever. It continues to promote international collaborations and has academic exchange agreements with around 350 universities and research institutes worldwide. It also offers a number of dual degree programs in conjunction with prestigious universities. *Sejong* International Summer School, to be held in 2007, will be of unprecedented depth and scale.

Currently there are more than 1,000 students and visiting scholars from over 50 countries on campus. To assist its international students, SNU has an Office of International Affairs. It also provides various scholarships to international students and is set to increase its financial support in the near future.

Over 250 classes at SNU are taught in English and the number is rapidly increasing. For example, International Studies, Korean Studies, Mechanical and Aerospace Engineering, and Business Administration are mostly taught in English.

VIBRANT CAMPUS LIFE
SNU offers a wealth of invaluable academic and cultural resources. Public lectures and forums are daily events and visits from renowned international speakers are common. It also has two nationally acclaimed museums, both of which add to the cultural vibrancy of the campus.

Facilities like a medical center, a counselling service and recreational and sporting centers add to the convenience and quality of life on campus. In addition, SNU is famous as a high technology campus, with its wireless networks, a high-speed gigabyte backbone network for general operations, and a Super Computer Facility for research that requires higher performance computing services.

Seoul National University is the ideal choice for international students who want to be leaders in the global community. Talented students from all over the world are more than welcome.

SUBJECTS OFFERED AT UNDERGRADUATE AND GRADUATE LEVELS
Humanities, Social Sciences, Natural Sciences, Agriculture and Life Sciences, Business Administration, Dentistry, Education, Engineering, Fine Arts, Human Ecology, Law, Medicine, Music, Nursing, Pharmacy, Veterinary Medicine

SUBJECTS OFFERED AT PROFESSIONAL SCHOOLS
Business, Dentistry, Environmental Studies, International Studies, Public Administration, Public Health

SOUTH KOREA

Seoul National University

CONTACT DETAILS

Address
San 56-1, Sillim-dong, Gwanak-gu
Seoul
151742
South Korea
Web   www.snu.ac.kr
Phone   +82 2 8805114

INSTITUTION STATS

Undergraduates	19,810
Postgraduates	10,310
International Students	4.3%
Student Faculty Ratio	17.9:1
Total Citations	141,009
Avg UG Fees	2,734
Avg PG Fees	3,269

RANKINGS PERFORMANCE

Overall Rankings Position	63
Faculty Level Positions	
Arts & Humanities	131
Engineering & IT	52
Life Sciences & BioMedicine	34
Natural Sciences	40
Social Sciences	56

Sogang University

CONTACT DETAILS

Address
C.P.O. Box 1142
Seoul
100-611
South Korea

Web   www.sogang.ac.kr
Phone   +82 2 7058621

INSTITUTION STATS

Undergraduates	7,762
Postgraduates	1,281
International Students	0.9%
Student Faculty Ratio	14.4:1

RANKINGS PERFORMANCE

Faculty Level Positions	
Natural Sciences	434=

Sungkyunkwan University

CONTACT DETAILS

Address
53 Myeongnyun-dong 3-ga,
Jongno-gu
Seoul
110-745
South Korea
Web   www.skku.ac.kr
Phone   +82 2 7600114

INSTITUTION STATS

Undergraduates	16,726
Postgraduates	5,677
International Students	0.6%
Student Faculty Ratio	8.4:1

RANKINGS PERFORMANCE

Faculty Level Positions	
Arts & Humanities	420=
Engineering & IT	482=
Life Sciences & BioMedicine	413=
Natural Sciences	426=

Yonsei University

CONTACT DETAILS

Address
134 Sinchon-dong, Seodaemun-gu
Seoul
120-749
South Korea

Web   www.yonsei.ac.kr
Phone   +82 2 22270114

INSTITUTION STATS

Undergraduates	36,115
Postgraduates	12,286
International Students	2.2%
Student Faculty Ratio	11.4:1
Total Citations	60,247

RANKINGS PERFORMANCE

Faculty Level Positions	
Arts & Humanities	293=
Engineering & IT	406=
Life Sciences & BioMedicine	413=
Natural Sciences	324=
Social Sciences	313=

SPAIN

University of Barcelona

CONTACT DETAILS | **INSTITUTION STATS** | **RANKINGS PERFORMANCE**

Address	**Undergraduates**	51,446	**Overall Rankings Position**	190=
Gran Via Corts Catalanes, 585	**Postgraduates**	8,484	**Faculty Level Positions**	
Barcelona	**International Students**	6.6%	Arts & Humanities	118=
08007	**Student Faculty Ratio**	5.5:1	Engineering & IT	149
Spain	**Total Citations**	154,251	Life Sciences & BioMedicine	106
	Avg UG Fees	913	Natural Sciences	126=
Web www.ub.edu	**Avg PG Fees**	2,692	Social Sciences	101=
Phone +34 (0) 93 402 11 00				

Universidad Autònoma de Barcelona

CONTACT DETAILS | **INSTITUTION STATS** | **RANKINGS PERFORMANCE**

Address	**Undergraduates**	39,026	**Faculty Level Positions**	
Edificio C	**Postgraduates**	3,301	Arts & Humanities	250=
Barcelona	**International Students**	5.1%	Engineering & IT	228=
08193	**Student Faculty Ratio**	11:1	Life Sciences & BioMedicine	157
Spain	**Total Citations**	67,794	Natural Sciences	196=
			Social Sciences	132=
Web www.uab.es				
Phone +34 (0) 3 5811310				

Escuela Superior de Administración Y Dirección de Madrid

CONTACT DETAILS | **INSTITUTION STATS** | **RANKINGS PERFORMANCE**

Address	**Student Faculty Ratio**	10.8:1	**Faculty Level Positions**	
Mateo Inurria 27			Arts & Humanities	381=
Madrid			Engineering & IT	438=
28036			Social Sciences	225=
Spain				
Web www.esade.edu				
Phone +34(0) 913 597 714				

University of Granada

CONTACT DETAILS | **INSTITUTION STATS** | **RANKINGS PERFORMANCE**

Address	**Undergraduates**	56,693	**Faculty Level Positions**	
Cuesta del Hospicio, s/n	**Postgraduates**	9,234	Arts & Humanities	381=
Granada	**International Students**	8.9%	Engineering & IT	390=
18071	**Student Faculty Ratio**	27.2:1	Life Sciences & BioMedicine	369=
Spain	**Avg UG Fees**	865	Natural Sciences	417=
	Avg PG Fees	1,730	Social Sciences	359=
Web www.ugr.es				
Phone +34 (0) 958 243025				

455

SPAIN

Universidad Autónoma de Madrid

CONTACT DETAILS

Address
Ciudad Universitaria de
Cantoblanco
Madrid
28049
Spain
Web www.uam.es
Phone +34(0) 91 497 50 00

INSTITUTION STATS

Undergraduates	25,275
Postgraduates	3,426
International Students	5.6%
Student Faculty Ratio	25:1
Total Citations	103,005

RANKINGS PERFORMANCE

Faculty Level Positions

Arts & Humanities	156=
Engineering & IT	276=
Life Sciences & BioMedicine	215=
Natural Sciences	173=
Social Sciences	290=

University Complutense Madrid

CONTACT DETAILS

Address
Ciudad Universitaria
Madrid
28040
Spain

Web www.ucm.es/info/ucmp/index.php
Phone +34(0) 914520400

INSTITUTION STATS

Total Students	88,636
International Students	5.6%
Student Faculty Ratio	14.4:1
Total Citations	91,624

RANKINGS PERFORMANCE

Faculty Level Positions

Arts & Humanities	132=
Engineering & IT	212=
Life Sciences & BioMedicine	210=
Natural Sciences	179
Social Sciences	246=

The University of Murcia

CONTACT DETAILS

Address
Avenida Teniente Flomesta, 5
Murcia
30003
Spain

Web www.um.es
Phone +34(0) 968 363000

INSTITUTION STATS

Undergraduates	27,795
Postgraduates	1,266
International Students	2.2%
Student Faculty Ratio	5.4:1

RANKINGS PERFORMANCE

Faculty Level Positions

Arts & Humanities	365=
Engineering & IT	438=
Natural Sciences	461=
Social Sciences	484=

University of Navarra

CONTACT DETAILS

Address
Campus Universitario
Navarra
31080
Spain

Web www.unav.es
Phone + 34(0) 948 42 56 00

INSTITUTION STATS

Undergraduates	9,773
Postgraduates	3,900
International Students	11.8%
Student Faculty Ratio	6.3:1
Total Citations	20,250
Avg UG Fees	9,357
Avg PG Fees	12,946

RANKINGS PERFORMANCE

Faculty Level Positions

Arts & Humanities	381=
Life Science	268=
Natural Sciences	447=
Social Sciences	330=

SPAIN

Universitat Pompeu Fabra

CONTACT DETAILS	INSTITUTION STATS		RANKINGS PERFORMANCE	
Address	**Undergraduates**	8,428	**Faculty Level Positions**	
Plaça de la Mercè, 10-12	**Postgraduates**	962	Arts & Humanities	311=
Barcelona	**International Students**	6.7%	Life Sciences & BioMedicine	390=
08002	**Student Faculty Ratio**	6.6:1	Natural Sciences	518=
Spain	**Total Citations**	17,707	Social Sciences	147

Web www.upf.es
Phone + 34(0) 93 542 20 00

University of Salamanca

CONTACT DETAILS	INSTITUTION STATS		RANKINGS PERFORMANCE	
Address	**Undergraduates**	26,971	**Faculty Level Positions**	
Patio de Escuelas, 1	**Postgraduates**	2,218	Arts & Humanities	181=
Salamanca	**International Students**	5.6%	Life Sciences & BioMedicine	369=
37008	**Student Faculty Ratio**	22.5:1	Natural Sciences	314=
Spain				

Web www.usal.es
Phone +34(0) 923 294 400

Universidade de Santiago de Compostela

CONTACT DETAILS	INSTITUTION STATS		RANKINGS PERFORMANCE	
Address	**Undergraduates**	31,730	**Faculty Level Positions**	
Praza do Obradoiro, s/n	**Postgraduates**	4,942	Arts & Humanities	381=
Santiago de Compostela	**International Students**	5.6%	Engineering & IT	406=
15782	**Student Faculty Ratio**	14.1:1	Natural Sciences	420=
Spain			Social Sciences	372=

Web www.usc.es
Phone +34(0) 981 56 31 00

Universidad de Sevilla

CONTACT DETAILS	INSTITUTION STATS		RANKINGS PERFORMANCE	
Address	**Undergraduates**	61,345	**Faculty Level Positions**	
Po. de las Delicias, s/n	**Postgraduates**	3,506	Arts & Humanities	381=
Sevilla	**International Students**	2.6%	Engineering & IT	336=
41013	**Student Faculty Ratio**	10.4:1	Life Sciences & BioMedicine	292=
Spain			Natural Sciences	461=
			Social Sciences	305=

Web www.us.es
Phone +34(0) 954 48 12 55

SPAIN

Universitat de Valencia

CONTACT DETAILS

Address
Avenida Blasco Ibáñez, 13
Valencia
46010
Spain

Web www.uv.es
Phone +34 (0) 963 86 41 00

INSTITUTION STATS

Undergraduates	45,682
Postgraduates	2,084
International Students	5.8%
Student Faculty Ratio	12.4:1
Total Citations	82,737

RANKINGS PERFORMANCE

Faculty Level Positions
Arts & Humanities	287=
Engineering & IT	368=
Life Sciences & BioMedicine	292=
Natural Sciences	335=
Social Sciences	299=

Universidad Politecnica de Valencia

CONTACT DETAILS

Address
Camino de Vera, s/n
Valencia
46022
Spain

Web www.upv.es
Phone + 34(0) 963 87 70 07

INSTITUTION STATS

Undergraduates	38,000
Postgraduates	28,933
International Students	2.7%
Student Faculty Ratio	28.9:1
Avg Fees	940

RANKINGS PERFORMANCE

Faculty Level Positions
Arts & Humanities	365=
Engineering & IT	286
Natural Sciences	455=
Social Sciences	484=

Universidad de Zaragoza

CONTACT DETAILS

Address
Pedro Cerbuna, 12
Zaragoza
50009
Spain

Web www.unizar.es
Phone +34 (0) 976 761001

INSTITUTION STATS

Undergraduates	33,546
Postgraduates	2,048
International Students	3.3%
Avg UG Fees	1,971
Avg PG Fees	1,114

RANKINGS PERFORMANCE

Faculty Level Positions
Arts & Humanities	287=
Engineering & IT	482=
Natural Sciences	378=
Social Sciences	393=

SRI LANKA

University of Colombo

CONTACT DETAILS

Address
94, Cumaratunga Munidasa
Mawatha
Colombo 3
Sri Lanka

Web www.cmb.ac.lk
Phone +941 581835

INSTITUTION STATS

Undergraduates	8,246
Postgraduates	7,178
International Students	0.2%
Student Faculty Ratio	4.7:1
Avg UG Fees	7,500
Avg PG Fees	7,500

RANKINGS PERFORMANCE

Faculty Level Positions
Arts & Humanities	293=
Engineering & IT	336=
Natural Sciences	401=
Social Sciences	411=

SWEDEN

Chalmers University of Technology

CONTACT DETAILS

Address
GÖTEBORG
SE-412 96
Sweden

Web www.chalmers.se
Phone +46 (0)31-772 1000

INSTITUTION STATS

Undergraduates	9,280
Postgraduates	1,012
International Students	5.0%
Student Faculty Ratio	11.1:1
Total Citations	54,974

RANKINGS PERFORMANCE

Overall Rankings Position	147=
Faculty Level Positions	
Arts & Humanities	287=
Engineering & IT	56
Life Sciences & BioMedicine	314=
Natural Sciences	96
Social Sciences	209=

Gothenburg University

CONTACT DETAILS

Address
GÖTEBORG
405 30 Göteborg
Sweden

Web www.gu.se
Phone +46 31 773 1000

INSTITUTION STATS

Undergraduates	30,043
Postgraduates	1,987
International Students	2.3%
Student Faculty Ratio	18.6:1
Total Citations	140,578

RANKINGS PERFORMANCE

Faculty Level Positions	
Arts & Humanities	146=
Engineering & IT	336=
Life Sciences & BioMedicine	123=
Natural Sciences	461=
Social Sciences	125=

Linköping University

CONTACT DETAILS

Address
LINKÖPING
581 83
Sweden

Web www.liu.se
Phone +46 13-28 10 00

INSTITUTION STATS

Undergraduates	26,700
Postgraduates	1,400
International Students	4.5%
Student Faculty Ratio	11.8:1
Total Citations	71,919

RANKINGS PERFORMANCE

Faculty Level Positions	
Arts & Humanities	398=
Engineering & IT	214=
Life Sciences & BioMedicine	397=
Natural Sciences	445
Social Sciences	229

Lund University

CONTACT DETAILS

Address
Lund
S-221 00
Sweden

Web www.lu.se
Phone +46 46-222 00 00

INSTITUTION STATS

Undergraduates	24,100
Postgraduates	9,980
International Students	5.3%
Student Faculty Ratio	8.8:1
Total Citations	259,372

RANKINGS PERFORMANCE

Overall Rankings Position	122
Faculty Level Positions	
Arts & Humanities	105=
Engineering & IT	104
Life Sciences & BioMedicine	52=
Natural Sciences	79
Social Sciences	129=

SWEDEN

Royal Institute of Technology

CONTACT DETAILS	INSTITUTION STATS		RANKINGS PERFORMANCE	
Address	Undergraduates	13,963	**Overall Rankings Position**	172=
Stockholm	**Postgraduates**	1,590	**Faculty Level Positions**	
SE-100 44	**International Students**	7.3%	Arts & Humanities	321=
Sweden	**Student Faculty Ratio**	19.5:1	Engineering & IT	53=
	Total Citations	55,325	Life Sciences & BioMedicine	328=
			Natural Sciences	148=
Web www.kth.se			Social Sciences	305=
Phone +46 8 790 60 00				

Stockholm School of Economics

CONTACT DETAILS	INSTITUTION STATS		RANKINGS PERFORMANCE	
Address	Undergraduates	1,350	**Faculty Level Positions**	
P.O. Box 6501	**Postgraduates**	632	Engineering & IT	463=
Stockholm	**International Students**	9.2%	Natural Sciences	491=
SE-113 83	**Student Faculty Ratio**	19:1	Social Sciences	53=
Sweden				
Web www.hhs.se				
Phone +46-8-736 90 00				

Stockholm University

CONTACT DETAILS	INSTITUTION STATS		RANKINGS PERFORMANCE	
Address	Undergraduates	24,652	**Faculty Level Positions**	
Stockholm	**Postgraduates**	1,821	Arts & Humanities	246=
SE-106 91	**International Students**	3.0%	Engineering & IT	303=
Sweden	**Student Faculty Ratio**	14.2:1	Life Sciences & BioMedicine	210=
	Total Citations	99,877	Natural Sciences	196=
Web www.su.se			Social Sciences	114
Phone +46 08-16 20 00				

Umeå University

CONTACT DETAILS	INSTITUTION STATS		RANKINGS PERFORMANCE	
Address	Undergraduates	27,664	**Faculty Level Positions**	
Umeå	**Postgraduates**	1,359	Arts & Humanities	423=
SE-901 87	**International Students**	3.0%	Engineering & IT	390=
Sweden	**Student Faculty Ratio**	14.2:1	Life Sciences & BioMedicine	314=
	Total Citations	100,115	Natural Sciences	406=
			Social Sciences	346=
Web www.umu.se				
Phone +46 (0)90-786 50 00				

460

SWEDEN

Uppsala University

CONTACT DETAILS

Address
Uppsala
SE-751 05
Sweden

Web www.uu.se
Phone +46 18 471 00 00

INSTITUTION STATS

Undergraduates	24,820
Postgraduates	2,186
International Students	4.8%
Student Faculty Ratio	13.4:1
Total Citations	223,190

RANKINGS PERFORMANCE

Overall Rankings Position	111=
Faculty Level Positions	
Arts & Humanities	79=
Engineering & IT	145=
Life Sciences & BioMedicine	40
Natural Sciences	100=
Social Sciences	105=

SWITZERLAND

University of Basel

CONTACT DETAILS

Address
Basel
CH-4003
Switzerland

Web www.unibas.ch
Phone +41 (0)61 267 31 11

INSTITUTION STATS

Undergraduates	7,349
Postgraduates	2,420
International Students	17.0%
Student Faculty Ratio	5:1
Total Citations	150,269
Avg Fees	1,150

RANKINGS PERFORMANCE

Overall Rankings Position	75
Faculty Level Positions	
Arts & Humanities	191=
Engineering & IT	406=
Life Sciences & BioMedicine	89
Natural Sciences	265=
Social Sciences	273=

University of Bern

CONTACT DETAILS

Web www.unibe.ch

INSTITUTION STATS

Undergraduates	6,048
Postgraduates	6,008
International Students	9.7%
Student Faculty Ratio	12.5:1
Total Citations	140,358
Avg UG Fees	1,077
Avg PG Fees	327

RANKINGS PERFORMANCE

Overall Rankings Position	178
Faculty Level Positions	
Arts & Humanities	231=
Engineering & IT	423=
Life Sciences & BioMedicine	235=
Natural Sciences	321=
Social Sciences	254=

Ecole Polytechnique Fédérale de Lausanne

CONTACT DETAILS

Address
EPFL
1015 Lausanne
Switzerland

Web www.epfl.ch
Phone +41 21 693 11 11

INSTITUTION STATS

Undergraduates	4,868
Postgraduates	1,581
International Students	40.8%
Student Faculty Ratio	17.2:1
Total Citations	78,448
Avg UG Fees	1,038
Avg PG Fees	20,073

RANKINGS PERFORMANCE

Overall Rankings Position	64=
Faculty Level Positions	
Arts & Humanities	277=
Engineering & IT	45
Life Sciences & BioMedicine	154
Natural Sciences	115=
Social Sciences	372=

SWEDEN

ETH Zurich

CONTACT DETAILS	INSTITUTION STATS		RANKINGS PERFORMANCE	
Address	**Undergraduates**	9,158	**Overall Rankings Position**	24
Rämistrasse 101	**Postgraduates**	3,547	**Faculty Level Positions**	
Zurich	**International Students**	27.6%	Arts & Humanities	198=
CH-8092	**Total Citations**	240,859	Engineering & IT	12
Switzerland	**Avg UG Fees**	961	Life Sciences & BioMedicine	35
	Avg PG Fees	961	Natural Sciences	11
Web www.ethz.ch			Social Sciences	123
Phone +41 44 632 11 11				

University of Geneva

CONTACT DETAILS	INSTITUTION STATS		RANKINGS PERFORMANCE	
Address	**Undergraduates**	10,172	**Overall Rankings Position**	39
24, rue du Général-Dufour	**Postgraduates**	3,838	**Faculty Level Positions**	
GENEVE 4 - SUISSE	**International Students**	36.2%	Arts & Humanities	87=
1211	**Student Faculty Ratio**	8.4:1	Engineering & IT	276=
Switzerland	**Total Citations**	177,099	Life Sciences & BioMedicine	168=
	Avg UG Fees	820	Natural Sciences	219=
Web www.unige.ch	**Avg PG Fees**	820	Social Sciences	142=
Phone +41 22 - 379 71 11				

University of Lausanne

CONTACT DETAILS	INSTITUTION STATS		RANKINGS PERFORMANCE	
Address	**Undergraduates**	7,920	**Overall Rankings Position**	89
Lausanne	**Postgraduates**	2,547	**Faculty Level Positions**	
CH-1015	**International Students**	20.5%	Arts & Humanities	221
Switzerland	**Student Faculty Ratio**	12.2:1	Engineering & IT	267=
	Total Citations	110,918	Life Sciences & BioMedicine	235=
	Avg UG Fees	955	Natural Sciences	237=
Web www.unil.ch	**Avg PG Fees**	11,107	Social Sciences	278=
Phone +41 21 692 11 11				

University of St Gallen

CONTACT DETAILS	INSTITUTION STATS		RANKINGS PERFORMANCE	
Address	**Total Students**	4,508	**Faculty Level Positions**	
Dufourstrasse 50	**International Students**	25.0%	Arts & Humanities	328=
St.Gallen	**Student Faculty Ratio**	6.7:1	Engineering & IT	463=
CH-9000	**Total Citations**	1,149	Life Sciences & BioMedicine	338=
Switzerland	**Avg Fees**	1,759	Social Sciences	152=
Web www.unisg.ch				
Phone +41 (0)71 224 2111				

SWEDEN

University of Zurich

CONTACT DETAILS

Address
Theologischen Fakultät
Kirchgasse 9
CH-8001 Zürich
Switzerland

Web www.unizh.ch
Phone +41 44 634 47 21

INSTITUTION STATS

Undergraduates	17,189
Postgraduates	3,260
International Students	14.1%
Total Citations	240,421
Avg UG Fees	1,298
Avg PG Fees	475

RANKINGS PERFORMANCE

Overall Rankings Position	109=
Faculty Level Positions	
Arts & Humanities	152
Engineering & IT	245=
Life Sciences & BioMedicine	104=
Natural Sciences	213
Social Sciences	120=

TAIWAN

Fu Jen Catholic University

CONTACT DETAILS

Web www.fju.edu.tw

INSTITUTION STATS

Total Students	44,882
International Students	3.9%
Student Faculty Ratio	17.8:1

RANKINGS PERFORMANCE

Faculty Level Positions	
Arts & Humanities	420=
Engineering & IT	497=
Social Sciences	447=

National Central University

CONTACT DETAILS

Address
No.300, Jhongda Rd
Jhongli
Taoyuan County 32001
Taiwan

Web www.ncu.edu.tw
Phone +886 3 4227151

INSTITUTION STATS

Undergraduates	5,437
Postgraduates	3,134
International Students	3.6%
Student Faculty Ratio	12:1

RANKINGS PERFORMANCE

Faculty Level Positions	
Engineering & IT	406=
Natural Sciences	281=
Social Sciences	359=

National Cheng Kung University

CONTACT DETAILS

Address
No.1, Ta-Hsueh Road
Tainan
701
Taiwan

Web www.ncku.edu.tw
Phone +8866-275-7575

INSTITUTION STATS

Total Students	19,153
International Students	0.4%
Student Faculty Ratio	19.8:1
Total Citations	49,793

RANKINGS PERFORMANCE

Faculty Level Positions	
Arts & Humanities	328=
Engineering & IT	141=
Life Sciences & BioMedicine	242=
Natural Sciences	343=

TAIWAN

National Chengchi University

CONTACT DETAILS

INSTITUTION STATS

RANKINGS PERFORMANCE

Address
NO.64 Sec.2 ZhiNan Rd Wenshan
Distric
Taipei City
11605
Taiwan

Undergraduates	9,220
Postgraduates	3,898
International Students	2.7%
Student Faculty Ratio	20.2:1
Avg UG Fees	33
Avg PG Fees	205

Faculty Level Positions
Engineering & IT	303=
Natural Sciences	509=
Social Sciences	197=

Web www.nccu.edu.tw
Phone +886-2-29393091

National Chiao Tung University

CONTACT DETAILS

INSTITUTION STATS

RANKINGS PERFORMANCE

Address
1001 Ta Hsueh Road
Hsinchu
300
Taiwan

Toatal Students	12,005
International Students	0.7%
Student Faculty Ratio	9.5:1
Total Citations	24,844

Faculty Level Positions
Engineering & IT	183=
Natural Sciences	276
Social Sciences	320=

Web www.nctu.edu.tw
Phone +886-3-571-2121

National Chung Hsing University

CONTACT DETAILS

INSTITUTION STATS

RANKINGS PERFORMANCE

Address
Kuo Kuang Road
Taichung
250
Taiwan

Undergraduates	7,815
Postgraduates	5,552
International Students	0.3%
Student Faculty Ratio	8.1:1
Avg UG Fees	1,625
Avg PG Fees	1,324

Faculty Level Positions
Natural Sciences	474=

Web www.nchu.edu.tw
Phone +886-4-22873181

National Sun Yat-sen University

CONTACT DETAILS

INSTITUTION STATS

RANKINGS PERFORMANCE

Address
70 Lien-hai Rd.
Kaohsiung
804
Taiwan

Total Students	9,500
International Students	0.2%
Student Faculty Ratio	17:1

Faculty Level Positions
Engineering & IT	482=
Life Sciences & BioMedicine	383=
Natural Sciences	394=
Social Sciences	411=

Web www.nsysu.edu.tw
Phone +886-7-525-2633

TAIWAN

National Taiwan Normal University

CONTACT DETAILS

Address
No.162, Sec.1, Heping East Road,
Taipei,
106
Taiwan

Web www.ntnu.edu.tw
Phone + 886-2-2362-5101

INSTITUTION STATS

Undergraduates	6,942
Postgraduates	4,113
International Students	13.6%
Student Faculty Ratio	15.7:1
Avg UG Fees	535
Avg PG Fees	377

RANKINGS PERFORMANCE

Faculty Level Positions
Engineering & IT	423=
Life Sciences & BioMedicine	383=
Natural Sciences	509=
Social Sciences	471=

National Taiwan University

CONTACT DETAILS

Address
No.1, Sec. 4, Roosevelt Road,
Taipei,
Taiwan 106
Taiwan

Web www.ntu.edu.tw
Phone + 886-2-33663366

INSTITUTION STATS

Undergraduates	17,724
Postgraduates	12,853
International Students	0.2%
Student Faculty Ratio	8.1:1
Total Citations	112,353
Avg UG Fees	915
Avg PG Fees	1,046

RANKINGS PERFORMANCE

Overall Rankings Position	108

Faculty Level Positions
Arts & Humanities	124=
Engineering & IT	43=
Life Sciences & BioMedicine	59
Natural Sciences	61
Social Sciences	58

National Tsing Hua University

CONTACT DETAILS

Address
101, Section 2 Kuang Fu Road
Hsinchu, Taiwan
30013
Taiwan

Web www.nthu.edu.tw
Phone +886-3-5715131

INSTITUTION STATS

Undergraduates	4,700
Postgraduates	4,800
International Students	1.2%
Student Faculty Ratio	8.1:1
Total Citations	36,756
Avg UG Fees	853
Avg PG Fees	6,730

RANKINGS PERFORMANCE

Faculty Level Positions
Arts & Humanities	293=
Engineering & IT	101=
Life Sciences & BioMedicine	338=
Natural Sciences	175=
Social Sciences	372=

National Yang Ming University

CONTACT DETAILS

Address
No. 155, Sec. 2, Linong St
Beitou District, Taipei City 112,
(R.O.C.) Taiwan

Web http://www.ym.edu.tw/
Phone +886-2-28267000

INSTITUTION STATS

Undergraduates	1,973
Postgraduates	1,842
International Students	0.0%
Student Faculty Ratio	17.4:1
Total Citations	36,387
Avg UG Fees	1,097
Avg PG Fees	19,309

RANKINGS PERFORMANCE

Faculty Level Positions
Engineering & IT	482=
Life Sciences & BioMedicine	302=
Natural Sciences	491=

TAIWAN

Taiwan University of Science and Technology

CONTACT DETAILS	INSTITUTION STATS		RANKINGS PERFORMANCE	
Address	**Undergraduates**	4,635	**Faculty Level Positions**	
#43,Sec.4,Keelung	**Postgraduates**	3,515	Arts & Humanities	328=
Rd.,Taipei,106,Taiwan	**International Students**	0.3%	Engineering & IT	152=
	Student Faculty Ratio	12.5:1	Life Sciences & BioMedicine	275=
	Total Citations	6,812	Natural Sciences	243
Web www.ntust.edu.tw	**Avg UG Fees**	4,909	Social Sciences	372=
Phone +886 2733-3141	**Avg PG Fees**	30,390		

THAILAND

Chiang Mai University

CONTACT DETAILS	INSTITUTION STATS		RANKINGS PERFORMANCE	
Address	**Undergraduates**	19,442	**Faculty Level Positions**	
239 Huay Keaw Road, Suthep,	**Postgraduates**	7,384	Arts & Humanities	380
Muang	**International Students**	0.7%	Engineering & IT	297=
Chiang Mai	**Student Faculty Ratio**	8.5:1	Life Sciences & BioMedicine	301
50200	**Total Citations**	5,971	Natural Sciences	230=
Thailand			Social Sciences	447=
Web www.chiangmai.ac.th				
Phone +66 68221699				

Chulalongkorn University

CONTACT DETAILS	INSTITUTION STATS		RANKINGS PERFORMANCE	
Address	**Undergraduates**	21,457	**Overall Rankings Position**	161=
254 Phyathai Road, Patumwan	**Postgraduates**	12,595	**Faculty Level Positions**	
Bangkok	**International Students**	0.8%	Arts & Humanities	121
Thailand	**Student Faculty Ratio**	13.8:1	Engineering & IT	95=
	Total Citations	10,082	Life Sciences & BioMedicine	80
	Avg UG Fees	8,145	Natural Sciences	157=
Web www.chula.ac.th	**Avg PG Fees**	9,402	Social Sciences	73
Phone +66 2 21508713				

Kasetsart University

CONTACT DETAILS	INSTITUTION STATS		RANKINGS PERFORMANCE	
Address	**Undergraduates**	37,718	**Faculty Level Positions**	
50 Phahonyothin Road	**Postgraduates**	11,134	Arts & Humanities	328=
Lat Yao Subdistrict	**International Students**	0.6%	Engineering & IT	336=
Bangkok	**Student Faculty Ratio**	10.6:1	Life Sciences & BioMedicine	177=
10900	**Total Citations**	2,709	Natural Sciences	226=
Thailand			Social Sciences	330=
Web www.ku.ac.th				
Phone +66 2 9428500-11				

THAILAND

Khon Kaen University

CONTACT DETAILS

Address
Mittraphab Road
Khon Kaen
40002
Thailand

Web www.kku.ac.th
Phone +66 43 202222-4

INSTITUTION STATS

Undergraduates	15,300
Postgraduates	1,700
International Students	0.4%
Student Faculty Ratio	7.3:1

RANKINGS PERFORMANCE

Faculty Level Positions

Life Sciences & BioMedicine	248=
Natural Sciences	331=
Social Sciences	447=

Mahidol University

CONTACT DETAILS

Address
Mahidol University
25/25 Moo 3,
Phuttamonthon 4 Road
Salaya, Phuttamonthon District
Nakhon Pathom 73170

Web www.mahidol.ac.th
Phone + 66 2 849-6231-3

INSTITUTION STATS

Undergraduates	14,604
Postgraduates	9,197
International Students	2.8%
Student Faculty Ratio	13.8:1
Avg UG Fees	6,493
Avg PG Fees	4,153

RANKINGS PERFORMANCE

Faculty Level Positions

Engineering & IT	377=
Life Sciences & BioMedicine	133=
Natural Sciences	281=
Social Sciences	330=

Prince of Songkla University

CONTACT DETAILS

Address
Ko Hong
Songkla
90112
Thailand

Web www.psu.ac.th
Phone +66 74 287897

INSTITUTION STATS

Undergraduates	19,823
Postgraduates	3,950
International Students	0.6%
Student Faculty Ratio	16.4:1
Total Citations	3,217

RANKINGS PERFORMANCE

Faculty Level Positions

Arts & Humanities	328=
Engineering & IT	438=
Life Sciences & BioMedicine	248=
Natural Sciences	326=
Social Sciences	471=

Thammasat University

CONTACT DETAILS

Address
99 Mhu 18, Paholyothin Rd.,
12121
Thailand

Web www.tu.ac.th
Phone +66 2 564 4440

INSTITUTION STATS

Total Students	20,667
International Students	0.6%
Student Faculty Ratio	10.8:1
Total Citations	797

RANKINGS PERFORMANCE

Faculty Level Positions

Arts & Humanities	226
Engineering & IT	406=
Life Sciences & BioMedicine	334=
Natural Sciences	509=
Social Sciences	163=

TURKEY

Bilkent University

CONTACT DETAILS

Address
06800 Bilkent Ankara
Turkey

Web www.bilkent.edu.tr
Phone +90 312 290 4000

INSTITUTION STATS

Total Students	11,000
International Students	1.0%
Student Faculty Ratio	51.7:1

RANKINGS PERFORMANCE

Faculty Level Positions

Arts & Humanities	328=
Engineering & IT	390=
Natural Sciences	308=
Social Sciences	393=

Cukurova University

CONTACT DETAILS

Web www.cukurova.edu.tr

INSTITUTION STATS

Total Students	32,700
International Students	0.1%
Student Faculty Ratio	15.9:1

RANKINGS PERFORMANCE

Faculty Level Positions

Engineering & IT	463=
Life Sciences & BioMedicine	314=
Natural Sciences	461=

Istanbul Technical University

CONTACT DETAILS

Address
Kampüsü
Maslak-Istunbal
80626
Turkey"

Web www.itu.edu.tr
Phone +90212 285 66 11

INSTITUTION STATS

Toatal Students	18,638
International Students	2.7%
Student Faculty Ratio	12.8:1
Total Citations	11,850

RANKINGS PERFORMANCE

Faculty Level Positions

Engineering & IT	219=
Life Sciences & BioMedicine	338=
Natural Sciences	401=
Social Sciences	393=

Istanbul University

CONTACT DETAILS

Address
Orhanli - Tuzla,
Istanbul
34956
Turkey

Web www.istanbul.edu.tr
Phone +90 0216 483 9000

INSTITUTION STATS

Total Students	53,105
International Students	3.3%
Student Faculty Ratio	9.5:1
Total Citations	20,679

RANKINGS PERFORMANCE

Faculty Level Positions

Arts & Humanities	328=
Engineering & IT	358=
Life Sciences & BioMedicine	123=
Natural Sciences	368=
Social Sciences	372=

TURKEY

Sabanci University

CONTACT DETAILS

Web   www.sabanciuniv.edu

INSTITUTION STATS

Undergraduates	2,441
Postgraduates	439
International Students	0.8%
Student Faculty Ratio	16.3:1
Avg UG Fees	13,000
Avg PG Fees	8,700

RANKINGS PERFORMANCE

Faculty Level Positions

Engineering & IT	463=
Natural Sciences	447=
Social Sciences	471=

UNITED KINGDOM

University of Aberdeen

CONTACT DETAILS

Address
Aberdeen
AB24 3FX
United Kingdom

Web   www.abdn.ac.uk/
Phone   +44 (0)1224-272000

INSTITUTION STATS

Undergraduates	10,220
Postgraduates	3,720
International Students	15.7%
Student Faculty Ratio	14.8:1
Total Citations	78,827
Avg UG Fees	18,330
Avg PG Fees	18,330

RANKINGS PERFORMANCE

Overall Rankings Position	195
Faculty Level Positions	
Arts & Humanities	227
Engineering & IT	311=
Life Sciences & BioMedicine	142
Natural Sciences	368=
Social Sciences	237=

University of Wales, Aberystwyth

CONTACT DETAILS

Address
Gwynedd
LL57 2DG
United Kingdom

Web   www.aber.ac.uk
Phone   +44(01248) 351151

INSTITUTION STATS

Undergraduates	8,380
Postgraduates	2,305
International Students	12.3%
Student Faculty Ratio	15.1:1

RANKINGS PERFORMANCE

Faculty Level Positions

Arts & Humanities	258=
Life Sciences & BioMedicine	397=
Natural Sciences	387
Social Sciences	281=

University of Wales, Bangor

CONTACT DETAILS

Address
Gwynedd
LL57 2DG
United Kingdom

Web   www.bangor.ac.uk
Phone   +44 (01248) 351151

INSTITUTION STATS

Undergraduates	7,685
Postgraduates	1,815
International Students	8.6%
Student Faculty Ratio	29.5:1

RANKINGS PERFORMANCE

Faculty Level Positions

Arts & Humanities	430=
Engineering & IT	494=
Natural Sciences	416

UNITED KINGDOM

University of Bath

CONTACT DETAILS		INSTITUTION STATS		RANKINGS PERFORMANCE	
Address		**Undergraduates**	9,775	**Overall Rankings Position**	153
Bath		**Postgraduates**	4,790	**Faculty Level Positions**	
BA2 7AY		**International Students**	21.5%	Arts & Humanities	258=
United Kingdom		**Total Citations**	48,995	Engineering & IT	258=
		Avg UG Fees	19,011	Life Sciences & BioMedicine	137=
		Avg PG Fees	19,011	Natural Sciences	233
Web	www.bath.ac.uk			Social Sciences	278=
Phone	+44 (0) 1225 388388				

University of Birmingham

CONTACT DETAILS		INSTITUTION STATS		RANKINGS PERFORMANCE	
Address		**Undergraduates**	18,785	**Overall Rankings Position**	90=
Birmingham		**Postgraduates**	11,735	**Faculty Level Positions**	
B15 2TT		**International Students**	18.2%	Arts & Humanities	67
United Kingdom		**Student Faculty Ratio**	16:1	Engineering & IT	89
		Total Citations	172,261	Life Sciences & BioMedicine	128=
		Avg UG Fees	18,060	Natural Sciences	126=
Web	www.bham.ac.uk	**Avg PG Fees**	18,060	Social Sciences	125=
Phone	+44 (0)121 414 3344				

University of Bradford

CONTACT DETAILS		INSTITUTION STATS		RANKINGS PERFORMANCE	
Address		**Undergraduates**	8,545	**Faculty Level Positions**	
West Yorkshire		**Postgraduates**	4,110	Arts & Humanities	311=
Bradford		**International Students**	27.6%	Engineering & IT	368=
BD7 1DP		**Student Faculty Ratio**	26.3:1	Life Sciences & BioMedicine	235=
United Kingdom		**Total Citations**	14,466	Natural Sciences	447=
				Social Sciences	217=
Web	www.bradford.ac.uk				
Phone	+44 (0) 1274 232323				

Bristol University

CONTACT DETAILS		INSTITUTION STATS		RANKINGS PERFORMANCE	
Address		**Undergraduates**	15,470	**Overall Rankings Position**	64=
Senate House, Tyndall Avenue		**Postgraduates**	7,890	**Faculty Level Positions**	
Bristol		**International Students**	16.3%	Arts & Humanities	57
BS8 1TH		**Student Faculty Ratio**	7:1	Engineering & IT	110
United Kingdom		**Total Citations**	189,023	Life Sciences & BioMedicine	82=
		Avg UG Fees	28,517	Natural Sciences	93=
Web	www.bris.ac.uk	**Avg PG Fees**	24,904	Social Sciences	91
Phone	+441179289000				

UNITED KINGDOM

Brunel University

CONTACT DETAILS	INSTITUTION STATS		RANKINGS PERFORMANCE	
Address	**Undergraduates**	10,190	**Faculty Level Positions**	
Borough Road	**Postgraduates**	5,260	Arts & Humanities	381=
Isleworth	**International Students**	20.5%	Engineering & IT	336=
Middlesex TW7 5DU	**Student Faculty Ratio**	21.2:1	Life Sciences & BioMedicine	338=
United Kingdom	**Total Citations**	25,404	Natural Sciences	506=
			Social Sciences	393=
Web www.brunel.ac.uk				
Phone +44 208 891 0121				

University of Cambridge

CONTACT DETAILS	INSTITUTION STATS		RANKINGS PERFORMANCE	
Address	**Undergraduates**	11,855	**Overall Rankings Position**	2
Cambridge	**Postgraduates**	9,435	**Faculty Level Positions**	
CB2 1TN,	**International Students**	26.7%	Arts & Humanities	1
United Kingdom	**Student Faculty Ratio**	18.9:1	Engineering & IT	6
	Total Citations	525,671	Life Sciences & BioMedicine	1
Web www.cam.ac.uk	**Avg UG Fees**	18,559	Natural Sciences	1
Phone +44 1223 337733	**Avg PG Fees**	18,559	Social Sciences	4

Cardiff University

CONTACT DETAILS	INSTITUTION STATS		RANKINGS PERFORMANCE	
Address	**Undergraduates**	21,600	**Overall Rankings Position**	141=
Wales	**Postgraduates**	7,070	**Faculty Level Positions**	
CF10 3XQ	**International Students**	14.0%	Arts & Humanities	92
United Kingdom	**Student Faculty Ratio**	4.5:1	Engineering & IT	169=
	Total Citations	106,649	Life Sciences & BioMedicine	70=
Web www.cf.ac.uk	**Avg UG Fees**	17,937	Natural Sciences	253=
Phone +44 (0)29 2087 4000	**Avg PG Fees**	17,937	Social Sciences	155=

Cranfield University

CONTACT DETAILS	INSTITUTION STATS		RANKINGS PERFORMANCE	
Address	**Undergraduates**	215	**Overall Rankings Position**	140
Cranfield	**Postgraduates**	4,390	**Faculty Level Positions**	
Bedfordshire	**International Students**	38.2%	Engineering & IT	295
MK43 0AL	**Student Faculty Ratio**	15.3:1	Life Sciences & BioMedicine	252=
United Kingdom	**Total Citations**	11,336	Natural Sciences	461=
			Social Sciences	178=
Web www.cranfield.ac.uk				
Phone +44 1234 754171				

UNITED KINGDOM

University of Dundee

CONTACT DETAILS

Address
DUNDEE
DD1 4HN
United Kingdom

Web www.dundee.ac.uk
Phone +44(0)1382344000

INSTITUTION STATS

Undergraduates	13,590
Postgraduates	4,670
International Students	16.2%
Student Faculty Ratio	6.9:1
Total Citations	108,899

RANKINGS PERFORMANCE

Faculty Level Positions

Arts & Humanities	430=
Engineering & IT	311=
Life Sciences & BioMedicine	85
Natural Sciences	278=
Social Sciences	372=

University of Durham

CONTACT DETAILS

Address
Old Elvet
Durham
DH1 3HP
United Kingdom

Web www.dur.ac.uk
Phone +44 (0)191 334 6328

INSTITUTION STATS

Undergraduates	11,700
Postgraduates	5,280
International Students	15.8%
Student Faculty Ratio	5.1:1
Total Citations	90,480
Avg UG Fees	18,735
Avg PG Fees	18,735

RANKINGS PERFORMANCE

Overall Rankings Position	132
Faculty Level Positions	
Arts & Humanities	101
Engineering & IT	335
Life Sciences & BioMedicine	210=
Natural Sciences	155=
Social Sciences	138

University of Edinburgh

CONTACT DETAILS

Address
South Bridge
Edinburgh
EH8 9YL
United Kingdom

Web www.ed.ac.uk
Phone +44 (0)131 650 1000

INSTITUTION STATS

Undergraduates	16,710
Postgraduates	6,340
International Students	18.2%
Student Faculty Ratio	4.1:1
Total Citations	233,543
Avg UG Fees	19,819
Avg PG Fees	19,819

RANKINGS PERFORMANCE

Overall Rankings Position	33=
Faculty Level Positions	
Arts & Humanities	13
Engineering & IT	66
Life Sciences & BioMedicine	14=
Natural Sciences	46
Social Sciences	38=

University of Exeter

CONTACT DETAILS

Address
Exeter
EX4 4QJ
United Kingdom

Web www.ex.ac.uk
Phone +44 1392 661000

INSTITUTION STATS

Undergraduates	10,020
Postgraduates	4,550
International Students	15.0%
Student Faculty Ratio	28.7:1
Total Citations	41,182

RANKINGS PERFORMANCE

Faculty Level Positions

Arts & Humanities	270
Engineering & IT	322=
Life Sciences & BioMedicine	225=
Natural Sciences	360=
Social Sciences	261=

UNITED KINGDOM

University of Glasgow

CONTACT DETAILS

Address
Rutherford McCowan Buildings
Dumfries
DG1 4ZL
United Kingdom

Web www.gla.ac.uk
Phone +44 (0)1387 702001

INSTITUTION STATS

Undergraduates	19,620
Postgraduates	5,480
International Students	10.0%
Student Faculty Ratio	18.8:1
Total Citations	171,970
Avg UG Fees	17,870
Avg PG Fees	19,296

RANKINGS PERFORMANCE

Overall Rankings Position	81
Faculty Level Positions	
Arts & Humanities	68
Engineering & IT	107=
Life Sciences & BioMedicine	75=
Natural Sciences	121
Social Sciences	96=

Lancaster University

CONTACT DETAILS

Address
Bailrigg
Lancaster
LA1 4YW
United Kingdom

Web www.lancs.ac.uk
Phone +44 1524 65201

INSTITUTION STATS

Undergraduates	13,795
Postgraduates	2,545
International Students	14.5%
Student Faculty Ratio	13.9:1
Total Citations	37,936
Avg Fees	17,348

RANKINGS PERFORMANCE

Faculty Level Positions	
Arts & Humanities	311=
Engineering & IT	382=
Life Sciences & BioMedicine	314=
Natural Sciences	286=
Social Sciences	92

University of Leeds

CONTACT DETAILS

Address
Leeds
LS2 9JT
United Kingdom

Web www.leeds.ac.uk
Phone +44(0)113 243 1751

INSTITUTION STATS

Undergraduates	26,515
Postgraduates	9,695
International Students	15.3%
Student Faculty Ratio	22.7:1
Total Citations	138,513
Avg UG Fees	25,475
Avg PG Fees	25,475

RANKINGS PERFORMANCE

Overall Rankings Position	121
Faculty Level Positions	
Arts & Humanities	55=
Engineering & IT	128=
Life Sciences & BioMedicine	186=
Natural Sciences	123=
Social Sciences	108

University of Leicester

CONTACT DETAILS

Address
University Road
Leicester
LE1 7RH
United Kingdom

Web www.le.ac.uk
Phone + 44(0)116 252 2522

INSTITUTION STATS

Undergraduates	9,890
Postgraduates	6,290
International Students	18.5%
Student Faculty Ratio	9.5:1
Total Citations	99,656

RANKINGS PERFORMANCE

Faculty Level Positions	
Arts & Humanities	430=
Engineering & IT	438=
Life Sciences & BioMedicine	207=
Natural Sciences	365=
Social Sciences	183=

UNITED KINGDOM

University of Liverpool

CONTACT DETAILS	INSTITUTION STATS		RANKINGS PERFORMANCE	
Address	**Undergraduates**	16,905	**Overall Rankings Position**	139
Liverpool	**Postgraduates**	4,305	**Faculty Level Positions**	
L69 3BX	**International Students**	13.0%	Arts & Humanities	178=
United Kingdom	**Student Faculty Ratio**	19.6:1	Engineering & IT	165=
	Total Citations	123,680	Life Sciences & BioMedicine	114=
Web www.liv.ac.uk	**Avg UG Fees**	16,825	Natural Sciences	185
Phone +44 (0) 151 794 2000	**Avg PG Fees**	18,060	Social Sciences	167=

Goldsmiths College

CONTACT DETAILS	INSTITUTION STATS		RANKINGS PERFORMANCE	
Address	**Undergraduates**	4,700	**Faculty Level Positions**	
New Cross	**Postgraduates**	2,570	Arts & Humanities	93
London	**International Students**	18.0%	Engineering & IT	463=
SE14 6NW	**Student Faculty Ratio**	7.3:1	Social Sciences	320=
United Kingdom	**Avg UG Fees**	20,152		
	Avg PG Fees	20,342		
Web www.goldsmiths.ac.uk				
Phone +44 20 7919 7171				

Imperial College London

CONTACT DETAILS	INSTITUTION STATS		RANKINGS PERFORMANCE	
Address	**Undergraduates**	7,850	**Overall Rankings Position**	9
South Kensington Campus	**Postgraduates**	4,335	**Faculty Level Positions**	
London	**International Students**	34.8%	Arts & Humanities	118=
SW7 2AZ	**Student Faculty Ratio**	6.6:1	Engineering & IT	4
United Kingdom	**Total Citations**	304,417	Life Sciences & BioMedicine	4
	Avg UG Fees	25,570	Natural Sciences	9
	Avg PG Fees	25,760	Social Sciences	65
Web www.ic.ac.uk				
Phone +44 20 7594 1279				

King's College London

CONTACT DETAILS	INSTITUTION STATS		RANKINGS PERFORMANCE	
Address	**Undergraduates**	14,995	**Overall Rankings Position**	46=
Strand	**Postgraduates**	6,970	**Faculty Level Positions**	
London	**International Students**	18.4%	Arts & Humanities	23
WC2R 2LS	**Student Faculty Ratio**	5.5:1	Engineering & IT	191=
United Kingdom	**Total Citations**	154,385	Life Sciences & BioMedicine	28
	Avg UG Fees	21,859	Natural Sciences	84
Web www.kcl.ac.uk	**Avg PG Fees**	20,129	Social Sciences	80
Phone +44 20 7836 5454				

UNITED KINGDOM

Queen Mary and Westfield College

CONTACT DETAILS

Address
Mile End Road
London
E1 4NS
United Kingdom

Web www.qmw.ac.uk
Phone +44 20 7882 5555

INSTITUTION STATS

Undergraduates	8,225
Postgraduates	2,785
International Students	24.6%
Student Faculty Ratio	5:1
Total Citations	47,403
Avg UG Fees	18,232
Avg PG Fees	18,232

RANKINGS PERFORMANCE

Overall Rankings Position	99=
Faculty Level Positions	
Arts & Humanities	79=
Engineering & IT	276=
Life Sciences & BioMedicine	186=
Natural Sciences	237=
Social Sciences	115=

London School of Economics and Political Science

CONTACT DETAILS

Address
Houghton Street
London
WC2A 2AE
United Kingdom

Web www.lse.ac.uk
Phone +44 20 7405 7686

INSTITUTION STATS

Undergraduates	4,020
Postgraduates	4,795
International Students	61.8%
Student Faculty Ratio	21.1:1
Total Citations	13,065
Avg UG Fees	20,874
Avg PG Fees	29,326

RANKINGS PERFORMANCE

Overall Rankings Position	17
Faculty Level Positions	
Arts & Humanities	19
Engineering & IT	276=
Life Sciences & BioMedicine	397=
Natural Sciences	246=
Social Sciences	3

School of Oriental and African Studies

CONTACT DETAILS

Address
Thornhaugh Street
Russell Square
London
WC1H 0XG
United Kingdom

Web www.soas.ac.uk
Phone +44 (0)20 7637 2388

INSTITUTION STATS

Undergraduates	2,250
Postgraduates	2,205
International Students	45.6%
Student Faculty Ratio	11.4:1
Total Citations	270
Avg UG Fees	19,011
Avg PG Fees	19,011

RANKINGS PERFORMANCE

Overall Rankings Position	70=
Faculty Level Positions	
Arts & Humanities	30
Engineering & IT	390=
Natural Sciences	440=
Social Sciences	95

University College London

CONTACT DETAILS

Address
Gower Street
London
WC1E 6BT
United Kingdom

Web www.ucl.ac.uk
Phone +44 (0)20 7679 2000

INSTITUTION STATS

Undergraduates	12,085
Postgraduates	7,505
International Students	28.8%
Student Faculty Ratio	11.2:1
Total Citations	376,098
Avg UG Fees	23,051
Avg PG Fees	25,190

RANKINGS PERFORMANCE

Overall Ranking Position	25
Faculty Level Positions	
Arts & Humanities	35
Engineering & IT	103
Life Sciences & BioMedicine	16
Natural Sciences	90=
Social Sciences	45

UNITED KINGDOM

Loughborough University

CONTACT DETAILS		INSTITUTION STATS		RANKINGS PERFORMANCE	
Address		Undergraduates	10,660	**Faculty Level Positions**	
Leicestershire		Postgraduates	5,610	Arts & Humanities	398=
LE11 3TU		International Students	19.3%	Engineering & IT	203
United Kingdom		Student Faculty Ratio	9.6:1	Life Sciences & BioMedicine	390=
		Total Citations	11,328	Natural Sciences	390=
		Avg UG Fees	19,296	Social Sciences	447=
Web	www.lboro.ac.uk	Avg PG Fees	19,391		
Phone	+44 1509 263171				

University of Manchester

CONTACT DETAILS		INSTITUTION STATS		RANKINGS PERFORMANCE	
Address		Undergraduates	28,960	**Overall Rankings Position**	40
Oxford Road		Postgraduates	11,025	**Faculty Level Positions**	
Manchester		International Students	17.6%	Arts & Humanities	51
M13 9PL		Student Faculty Ratio	9.8:1	Engineering & IT	41=
United Kingdom		Total Citations	201,395	Life Sciences & BioMedicine	36
		Avg UG Fees	19,011	Natural Sciences	86
Web	www.manchester.ac.uk	Avg PG Fees	19,011	Social Sciences	66=
Phone	+44 (0) 161 306 6000				

University of Newcastle upon Tyne

CONTACT DETAILS		INSTITUTION STATS		RANKINGS PERFORMANCE	
Address		Undergraduates	13,180	**Overall Rankings Position**	133=
NE1 7RU		Postgraduates	5,330	**Faculty Level Positions**	
United Kingdom		International Students	19.6%	Arts & Humanities	204=
		Student Faculty Ratio	14.3:1	Engineering & IT	197=
		Total Citations	106,739	Life Sciences & BioMedicine	86=
		Avg UG Fees	18,726	Natural Sciences	188
		Avg PG Fees	17,167	Social Sciences	261=
Web	www.ncl.ac.uk				
Phone	+44 191 222 6000				

University of Nottingham

CONTACT DETAILS		INSTITUTION STATS		RANKINGS PERFORMANCE	
Address		Undergraduates	24,865	**Overall Rankings Position**	85
Nottingham		Postgraduates	7,755	**Faculty Level Positions**	
NG7 2RD		International Students	18.0%	Arts & Humanities	141=
United Kingdom		Student Faculty Ratio	6.3:1	Engineering & IT	116=
		Total Citations	134,652	Life Sciences & BioMedicine	51
		Avg UG Fees	19,334	Natural Sciences	120
Web	www.nottingham.ac.uk	Avg PG Fees	19,334	Social Sciences	81
Phone	+44 (0) 115 951 5151				

UNITED KINGDOM

Open University

CONTACT DETAILS

Address
Walton Hall
Milton Keynes
MK7 6AA
United Kingdom

Web www.open.ac.uk
Phone +44 1908 274066

INSTITUTION STATS

Undergraduates	154,660
Postgraduates	18,355
International Students	0.0%
Student Faculty Ratio	6.1:1

RANKINGS PERFORMANCE

Faculty Level Positions
Arts & Humanities	82=
Engineering & IT	433=
Life Sciences & BioMedicine	252=
Natural Sciences	394=
Social Sciences	267

University of Oxford

CONTACT DETAILS

Address
Wellington Square
Oxford OX1 2JD
United Kingdom

Web www.ox.ac.uk
Phone +44 (0)1865 270000

INSTITUTION STATS

Undergraduates	15,495
Postgraduates	7,145
International Students	23.9%
Student Faculty Ratio	23.4:1
Total Citations	487,496
Avg UG Fees	28,840
Avg PG Fees	23,707

RANKINGS PERFORMANCE

Overall Rankings Position	3
Faculty Level Positions	
Arts & Humanities	2
Engineering & IT	11
Life Sciences & BioMedicine	3
Natural Sciences	2
Social Sciences	1

Queen's University of Belfast

CONTACT DETAILS

Address
University Road
Belfast
Northern Ireland
BT7 1NN
United Kingdom

Web www.qub.ac.uk
Phone +44 (0) 2890 245133

INSTITUTION STATS

Undergraduates	20,065
Postgraduates	5,480
International Students	10.0%
Student Faculty Ratio	11.4:1
Total Citations	68,954
Avg UG Fees	18,060
Avg PG Fees	18,060

RANKINGS PERFORMANCE

Faculty Level Positions
Arts & Humanities	176=
Engineering & IT	232=
Life Sciences & BioMedicine	109=
Natural Sciences	270=
Social Sciences	265=

University of Reading

CONTACT DETAILS

Address
PO Box217
Reading
RG6 6AH
United Kingdom

Web www.rdg.ac.uk
Phone + 44 (0)118 987 5123

INSTITUTION STATS

Undergraduates	10,170
Postgraduates	4,185
International Students	15.5%
Student Faculty Ratio	14.3:1
Total Citations	59,786
Avg UG Fees	18,441
Avg PG Fees	21,863

RANKINGS PERFORMANCE

Overall Rankings Position	190=
Faculty Level Positions	
Arts & Humanities	132=
Engineering & IT	311=
Life Sciences & BioMedicine	231=
Natural Sciences	221=
Social Sciences	237=

UNITED KINGDOM

Royal Holloway University of London

CONTACT DETAILS

Address
Egham Hill
Egham
Surrey TW20 0EX
United Kingdom

Web http://www.rhul.ac.uk
Phone +44 (0)1784 434455

INSTITUTION STATS

Undergraduates	5,660
Postgraduates	1,990
International Students	26.5%
Student Faculty Ratio	17.2:1

University of Sheffield

CONTACT DETAILS

Address
Western Bank
Sheffield
S10 2TN
United Kingdom

Web www.shef.ac.uk
Phone + 44 (0) 114 222 1255

INSTITUTION STATS

Undergraduates	18,885
Postgraduates	7,170
International Students	17.1%
Student Faculty Ratio	27.3:1
Total Citations	152,354
Avg UG Fees	17,965
Avg PG Fees	15,399

RANKINGS PERFORMANCE

Overall Rankings Position	102=
Faculty Level Positions	
Arts & Humanities	110=
Engineering & IT	93
Life Sciences & BioMedicine	109=
Natural Sciences	181=
Social Sciences	117

University of Southampton

CONTACT DETAILS

Address
University Road
Southampton
SO17 1BJ
United Kingdom

Web www.soton.ac.uk/
Phone +44(0)23 8059 5000

INSTITUTION STATS

Undergraduates	16,185
Postgraduates	7,320
International Students	15.7%
Student Faculty Ratio	10.5:1
Total Citations	120,685
Avg UG Fees	18,156
Avg PG Fees	18,156

RANKINGS PERFORMANCE

Overall Rankings Position	141=
Faculty Level Positions	
Arts & Humanities	209=
Engineering & IT	128=
Life Sciences & BioMedicine	168=
Natural Sciences	159
Social Sciences	142=

University of St Andrews

CONTACT DETAILS

Address
New Barn Lane
GL52 3LZ
United Kingdom

Web www.st-andrews.ac.uk
Phone +44 01242 223707

INSTITUTION STATS

Undergraduates	6,785
Postgraduates	1,675
International Students	33.0%
Student Faculty Ratio	10.8:1
Total Citations	58,568
Avg UG Fees	20,057
Avg PG Fees	20,152

RANKINGS PERFORMANCE

Overall Rankings Position	109=
Faculty Level Positions	
Arts & Humanities	44
Engineering & IT	328=
Life Sciences & BioMedicine	327
Natural Sciences	157=
Social Sciences	212

UNITED KINDOM

University of Strathclyde

CONTACT DETAILS

Address
New Barn Lane
Glasgow G1 1XQ
United Kingdom

Web www.strath.ac.uk
Phone +44 (0)141 552 4400

INSTITUTION STATS

Undergraduates	15,140
Postgraduates	9,165
International Students	10.1%
Student Faculty Ratio	11.7:1
Total Citations	41,035

RANKINGS PERFORMANCE

Faculty Level Positions

Arts & Humanities	328=
Engineering & IT	258=
Life Sciences & BioMedicine	258=
Natural Sciences	300=
Social Sciences	229=

University of Surrey

CONTACT DETAILS

Address
Guildford
Surrey
GU2 7XH
United Kingdom

Web www.surrey.ac.uk
Phone +44 (0)1483 68 9249

INSTITUTION STATS

Undergraduates	9,465
Postgraduates	6,460
International Students	27.6%
Student Faculty Ratio	25.8:1
Total Citations	40,466

RANKINGS PERFORMANCE

Faculty Level Positions

Arts & Humanities	381=
Engineering & IT	205=
Life Sciences & BioMedicine	390=
Natural Sciences	318=
Social Sciences	372=

University of Sussex

CONTACT DETAILS

Address
Sussex House
Brighton,
BN1 9RH
United Kingdom

Web www.sussex.ac.uk
Phone +44 (0)1273 606755

INSTITUTION STATS

Undergraduates	8,935
Postgraduates	3,270
International Students	16.9%
Student Faculty Ratio	15.4:1
Total Citations	74,197
Avg UG Fees	15,855
Avg PG Fees	18,218

RANKINGS PERFORMANCE

Overall Rankings Position	105=
Faculty Level Positions	
Arts & Humanities	62
Engineering & IT	219=
Life Sciences & BioMedicine	328=
Natural Sciences	286=
Social Sciences	61=

Swansea University

CONTACT DETAILS

Address
Singleton Park
Swansea
SA2 8PP
United Kingdom

Web www.swan.ac.uk
Phone +44 (0) 1792 205678

INSTITUTION STATS

Undergraduates	12,080
Postgraduates	2,400
International Students	10.5%
Student Faculty Ratio	17.5:1

RANKINGS PERFORMANCE

Faculty Level Positions

Arts & Humanities	272=
Engineering & IT	358=
Life Sciences & BioMedicine	338=
Natural Sciences	368=
Social Sciences	305=

UNITED KINGDOM

University of Warwick

CONTACT DETAILS

Address
Coventry
CV4 7AL
United Kingdom

Web   www2.warwick.ac.uk/
Phone   +44 (0)24 7652 3523

INSTITUTION STATS

Undergraduates	19,910
Postgraduates	9,885
International Students	25.3%
Student Faculty Ratio	9.3:1
Total Citations	55,054
Avg UG Fees	19,011
Avg PG Fees	19,011

RANKINGS PERFORMANCE

Overall Rankings Position	73
Faculty Level Positions	
Arts & Humanities	37=
Engineering & IT	169=
Life Sciences & BioMedicine	168=
Natural Sciences	65=
Social Sciences	30=

University of York

CONTACT DETAILS

Address
Heslington
York
YO10 5DD
United Kingdom

Web   www.york.ac.uk
Phone   +44 1 90443 0000

INSTITUTION STATS

Undergraduates	8,715
Postgraduates	3,910
International Students	18.5%
Student Faculty Ratio	10.5:1
Total Citations	72,686
Avg UG Fees	18,593
Avg PG Fees	18,593

RANKINGS PERFORMANCE

Overall Rankings Position	124=
Faculty Level Positions	
Arts & Humanities	64
Engineering & IT	245=
Life Sciences & BioMedicine	49
Natural Sciences	281=
Social Sciences	248

UNITED STATES

University of Alabama

CONTACT DETAILS

Address
Tuscaloosa
AL 35487
United States

Web   www.ua.edu
Phone   +1 (205) 348-6010

INSTITUTION STATS

Undergraduates	16,568
Postgraduates	3,754
International Students	4.3%
Student Faculty Ratio	10.4:1
Total Citations	296,465
Avg UG Fees	12,664
Avg PG Fees	12,664

RANKINGS PERFORMANCE

Faculty Level Positions	
Arts & Humanities	328=
Engineering & IT	377=
Life Sciences & BioMedicine	181=
Natural Sciences	381=
Social Sciences	281=

Arizona State University

CONTACT DETAILS

Address
University Drive and Mill Avenue
Tempe
Arizona
United States

Web   www.asu.edu
Phone   +1 480 965 9011

INSTITUTION STATS

Undergraduates	48,826
Postgraduates	11,102
International Students	5.1%
Student Faculty Ratio	19.1:1
Total Citations	110,471
Avg UG Fees	12,828
Avg PG Fees	13,558

RANKINGS PERFORMANCE

Faculty Level Positions	
Arts & Humanities	137=
Engineering & IT	195=
Life Sciences & BioMedicine	231=
Natural Sciences	250=
Social Sciences	213=

UNITED STATES

University of Arizona

CONTACT DETAILS

Address
Tucson
AZ 85721
United States

Web www.arizona.edu
Phone +1 (520) 621-2211

INSTITUTION STATS

Undergraduates	28,368
Postgraduates	7,387
International Students	7.2%
Student Faculty Ratio	14.3:1
Total Citations	291,374
Avg UG Fees	12,978
Avg PG Fees	13,228

RANKINGS PERFORMANCE

Faculty Level Positions
Arts & Humanities	141=
Engineering & IT	250=
Natural Sciences	210=
Social Sciences	280

University of Arkansas

CONTACT DETAILS

Address
Fayetteville,
Arkansas 72701
United States

Web www.uark.edu
Phone +1 479-575-2000

INSTITUTION STATS

Undergraduates	13,817
Postgraduates	2,981
International Students	5.3%
Total Citations	94,677
Avg UG Fees	11,405
Avg PG Fees	13,740

RANKINGS PERFORMANCE

Faculty Level Positions
Arts & Humanities	328=
Engineering & IT	463=
Life Sciences & BioMedicine	338=
Natural Sciences	409=

Boston University

CONTACT DETAILS

Address
One Sherborn Street
Boston
MA 02215
United States

Web www.bu.edu
Phone +1 617 353 2000

INSTITUTION STATS

Undergraduates	17,740
Postgraduates	9,811
International Students	13.0%
Student Faculty Ratio	27.3:1
Total Citations	285,276
Avg UG Fees	29,988
Avg PG Fees	29,988

RANKINGS PERFORMANCE

Overall Rankings Position	66

Faculty Level Positions
Arts & Humanities	139=
Engineering & IT	95=
Life Sciences & BioMedicine	50
Natural Sciences	110
Social Sciences	72

Brandeis University

CONTACT DETAILS

Address
415 South St.
Waltham
MA 02454-9110
United States

Web www.brandeis.edu
Phone +1 781 736 2000

INSTITUTION STATS

Undergraduates	3,200
Postgraduates	1,872
International Students	14.2%
Student Faculty Ratio	10.3:1
Total Citations	51,946
Avg UG Fees	30,160
Avg PG Fees	30,160

RANKINGS PERFORMANCE

Overall Rankings Position	187=

Faculty Level Positions
Arts & Humanities	184=
Engineering & IT	438=
Life Sciences & BioMedicine	119=
Natural Sciences	306
Social Sciences	354=

UNITED STATES

Brigham Young University

CONTACT DETAILS

INSTITUTION STATS

RANKINGS PERFORMANCE

Address	
Provo	
UT 84602	
United States	

Undergraduates	44,658
Postgraduates	3,261
International Students	6.6%
Student Faculty Ratio	17.4:1

Faculty Level Positions	
Arts & Humanities	364
Engineering & IT	328=
Life Sciences & BioMedicine	314=
Social Sciences	320=

Web	www.byu.edu
Phone	+1 801 422 4636

Brown University

CONTACT DETAILS

INSTITUTION STATS

RANKINGS PERFORMANCE

Address	
Providence	
RI 02912	
United States	

Undergraduates	6,014
Postgraduates	1,654
International Students	12.4%
Student Faculty Ratio	26.6:1
Total Citations	160,164
Avg UG Fees	30,672
Avg PG Fees	30,672

Overall Rankings Position	54=
Faculty Level Positions	
Arts & Humanities	48=
Engineering & IT	243=
Life Sciences & BioMedicine	161=
Natural Sciences	99
Social Sciences	109=

Web	www.brown.edu
Phone	+1 401 863 1000

University of California, Berkeley

CONTACT DETAILS

INSTITUTION STATS

RANKINGS PERFORMANCE

Address	
Berkeley	
California	
CA 94720-4	
United States	

Undergraduates	22,880
Postgraduates	8,792
International Students	7.8%
Student Faculty Ratio	10.1:1
Total Citations	621,001
Avg UG Fees	16,476
Avg PG Fees	14,694

Overall Rankings Position	8
Faculty Level Positions	
Arts & Humanities	4
Engineering & IT	2
Life Sciences & BioMedicine	10
Natural Sciences	3
Social Sciences	5

Web	www.berkeley.edu
Phone	+1 (510) 642-6000

University of California, Davis

CONTACT DETAILS

INSTITUTION STATS

RANKINGS PERFORMANCE

Address	
One Shields Avenue	
Davis	
California	
CA 95616	
United States	

Undergraduates	23,113
Postgraduates	4,666
International Students	4.9%
Student Faculty Ratio	21.6:1
Total Citations	322,963
Avg UG Fees	16,476
Avg PG Fees	14,694

Overall Rankings Position	170=
Faculty Level Positions	
Arts & Humanities	135=
Engineering & IT	119=
Life Sciences & BioMedicine	68=
Natural Sciences	144
Social Sciences	188=

Web	www.ucdavis.edu
Phone	+1 (530) 752-0650

UNITED STATES

University of California, Irvine

CONTACT DETAILS	INSTITUTION STATS		RANKINGS PERFORMANCE	
Address	**Undergraduates**	19,862	**Overall Rankings Position**	198=
Irvine	**Postgraduates**	4,096	**Faculty Level Positions**	
California	**International Students**	6.4%	Arts & Humanities	95=
CA 92697	**Student Faculty Ratio**	13.5:1	Engineering & IT	160=
United States	**Total Citations**	220,375	Life Sciences & BioMedicine	193=
	Avg UG Fees	16,476	Natural Sciences	198=
Web www.uci.edu	**Avg PG Fees**	14,694	Social Sciences	281=
Phone +1(949) 824-5011				

University of California, Los Angeles

CONTACT DETAILS	INSTITUTION STATS		RANKINGS PERFORMANCE	
Address	**Undergraduates**	24,946	**Overall Rankings Position**	31
Los Angeles	**Postgraduates**	9,174	**Faculty Level Positions**	
California 90095-1419	**International Students**	7.5%	Arts & Humanities	20
United States	**Student Faculty Ratio**	0.6:1	Engineering & IT	34
	Total Citations	680,796	Life Sciences & BioMedicine	26=
	Avg UG Fees	16,476	Natural Sciences	21
Web www.ucla.edu	**Avg PG Fees**	14,694	Social Sciences	23
Phone +1 (310) 825-3819				

Official University of California, Riverside

CONTACT DETAILS	INSTITUTION STATS		RANKINGS PERFORMANCE	
Address	**Undergraduates**	15,089	**Faculty Level Positions**	
900 University Avenue	**Postgraduates**	1,964	Arts & Humanities	328=
Riverside	**International Students**	5.3%	Engineering & IT	349=
CA United States	**Student Faculty Ratio**	15.7:1	Life Sciences & BioMedicine	338=
	Total Citations	85,591	Natural Sciences	356=
	Avg UG Fees	16,476	Social Sciences	320=
Web www.ucr.edu	**Avg PG Fees**	14,694		
Phone +1 951.827.1012				

University of California, San Diego

CONTACT DETAILS	INSTITUTION STATS		RANKINGS PERFORMANCE	
Address	**Undergraduates**	20,339	**Overall Rankings Position**	44
San Diego	**Postgraduates**	3,743	**Faculty Level Positions**	
California	**International Students**	5.5%	Arts & Humanities	104
CA 92093	**Student Faculty Ratio**	20.2:1	Engineering & IT	48=
United States	**Total Citations**	609,277	Life Sciences & BioMedicine	14=
	Avg UG Fees	16,476	Natural Sciences	36
Web www.ucsd.edu	**Avg PG Fees**	14,694	Social Sciences	118
Phone +1(858) 534-2230				

UNITED STATES

University of California, Santa Barbara

CONTACT DETAILS | **INSTITUTION STATS** | **RANKINGS PERFORMANCE**

Contact	Stats		Rankings	
Address	**Undergraduates**	13,694	**Overall Rankings Position**	141=
3117 Cheadle Hall	**Postgraduates**	2,905	**Faculty Level Positions**	
Santa Barbara	**International Students**	4.7%	Arts & Humanities	187
California	**Student Faculty Ratio**	5.5:1	Engineering & IT	94
CA 93106-2070	**Total Citations**	204,369	Life Sciences & BioMedicine	166=
United States	**Avg UG Fees**	16,476	Natural Sciences	31
	Avg PG Fees	14,694	Social Sciences	251=
Web www.ucsb.edu				
Phone +1 (805) 893-2277				

University of California, Santa Cruz

CONTACT DETAILS | **INSTITUTION STATS** | **RANKINGS PERFORMANCE**

Contact	Stats		Rankings	
Address	**Undergraduates**	13,694	**Faculty Level Positions**	
1156 High Street	**Postgraduates**	1,342	Arts & Humanities	153=
Santa Cruz,	**International Students**	2.8%	Engineering & IT	390=
California	**Student Faculty Ratio**	18.3:1	Life Sciences & BioMedicine	181=
CA 95064	**Total Citations**	112,133	Natural Sciences	236
United States	**Avg UG Fees**	16,476	Social Sciences	393=
	Avg PG Fees	14,694		
Web www.ucsc.edu				
Phone +1 (831) 459-011				

California Institute of Technology

CONTACT DETAILS | **INSTITUTION STATS** | **RANKINGS PERFORMANCE**

Contact	Stats		Rankings	
Address	**Undergraduates**	896	**Overall Rankings Position**	7
1200 East California Boulevard	**Postgraduates**	1,275	**Faculty Level Positions**	
Pasadena	**International Students**	24.6%	Arts & Humanities	212=
California 91125	**Student Faculty Ratio**	20.5:1	Engineering & IT	9
United States	**Total Citations**	335,701	Life Sciences & BioMedicine	25
	Avg UG Fees	25,355	Natural Sciences	8
	Avg PG Fees	25,355	Social Sciences	169=
Web www.caltech.edu				
Phone +1 626 395 6811				

Carnegie Mellon University

CONTACT DETAILS | **INSTITUTION STATS** | **RANKINGS PERFORMANCE**

Contact	Stats		Rankings	
Address	**Undergraduates**	5,529	**Overall Rankings Position**	35=
5000 Forbes Avenue	**Postgraduates**	4,274	**Faculty Level Positions**	
Pittsburgh	**International Students**	24.7%	Arts & Humanities	228=
PA 15213	**Student Faculty Ratio**	18.9:1	Engineering & IT	10
United States	**Total Citations**	114,818	Life Sciences & BioMedicine	67
	Avg UG Fees	30,650	Natural Sciences	89
Web www.cmu.edu	**Avg PG Fees**	28,200	Social Sciences	35
Phone +1 412 268 2000				

UNITED STATES

Case Western Reserve University

CONTACT DETAILS	INSTITUTION STATS		RANKINGS PERFORMANCE	
Address	**Undergraduates**	3,516	**Overall Rankings Position**	60
10900 Euclid Ave	**Postgraduates**	4,019	**Faculty Level Positions**	
Cleveland	**International Students**	14.6%	Arts & Humanities	398=
Ohio 44106-7027	**Student Faculty Ratio**	12.1:1	Engineering & IT	173=
United States	**Total Citations**	255,154	Life Sciences & BioMedicine	121
	Avg UG Fees	26,500	Natural Sciences	365=
Web www.cwru.edu	**Avg PG Fees**	25,400	Social Sciences	305=
Phone +1 216 368 4390				

University of Chicago

CONTACT DETAILS	INSTITUTION STATS		RANKINGS PERFORMANCE	
Address	**Undergraduates**	4,545	**Overall Rankings Position**	11
1101 E. 58th Street	**Postgraduates**	8,262	**Faculty Level Positions**	
Chicago	**International Students**	18.3%	Arts & Humanities	17
IL 60637	**Student Faculty Ratio**	8.5:1	Engineering & IT	132=
United States	**Total Citations**	362,437	Life Sciences & BioMedicine	39
	Avg UG Fees	30,123	Natural Sciences	18
Web www.uchicago.edu	**Avg PG Fees**	31,680	Social Sciences	9
Phone +1773-702-8650				

University of Cincinnati

CONTACT DETAILS	INSTITUTION STATS		RANKINGS PERFORMANCE	
Address	**Undergraduates**	26,314	**Faculty Level Positions**	
2600 Clifton Ave	**Postgraduates**	7,051	Engineering & IT	438=
Cincinnati	**International Students**	6.7%	Life Sciences & BioMedicine	338=
Ohio 45221	**Student Faculty Ratio**	9.9:1	Natural Sciences	498=
United States	**Total Citations**	170,988	Social Sciences	426=
	Avg UG Fees	13,647		
Web www.uc.edu	**Avg PG Fees**	17,031		
Phone +1513-556-1100				

College of William & Mary

CONTACT DETAILS	INSTITUTION STATS		RANKINGS PERFORMANCE	
Address	**Undergraduates**	5,594	**Faculty Level Positions**	
Williamsburg	**Postgraduates**	1,950	Arts & Humanities	398=
VA 23187-8795	**International Students**	3.4%	Engineering & IT	463=
United States	**Student Faculty Ratio**	9:1	Life Sciences & BioMedicine	338=
	Total Citations	26,531	Natural Sciences	472
	Avg UG Fees	20,000	Social Sciences	299=
Web www.wm.edu	**Avg PG Fees**	21,900		
Phone +1 757 221 4000				

UNITED STATES

Colorado State University

CONTACT DETAILS	INSTITUTION STATS		RANKINGS PERFORMANCE	
Address	**Undergraduates**	21,913	**Faculty Level Positions**	
Fort Collins	**Postgraduates**	5,522	Engineering & IT	315=
CO 80523	**International Students**	3.0%	Life Sciences & BioMedicine	252=
United States	**Student Faculty Ratio**	42.3:1	Natural Sciences	237=
	Avg UG Fees	13,527	Social Sciences	354=
	Avg PG Fees	14,109		
Web www.colostate.edu				
Phone +1 970 491 6909				

University of Colorado

CONTACT DETAILS	INSTITUTION STATS		RANKINGS PERFORMANCE	
Address	**Undergraduates**	26,430	**Faculty Level Positions**	
Boulder	**Postgraduates**	5,434	Arts & Humanities	328=
Colorado 80309	**International Students**	3.5%	Engineering & IT	157=
United States	**Student Faculty Ratio**	20.7:1	Life Sciences & BioMedicine	248=
	Total Citations	422,563	Natural Sciences	145
	Avg UG Fees	20,592	Social Sciences	320=
Web www.colorado.edu	**Avg PG Fees**	20,592		
Phone +1 (303) 492-1411				

Columbia University

CONTACT DETAILS	INSTITUTION STATS		RANKINGS PERFORMANCE	
Address	**Undergraduates**	7,233	**Overall Rankings Position**	12
2960 Broadway	**Postgraduates**	12,226	**Faculty Level Positions**	
New York	**International Students**	19.9%	Arts & Humanities	14
NY 10027-6902	**Student Faculty Ratio**	6.8:1	Engineering & IT	75
United States	**Total Citations**	557,977	Life Sciences & BioMedicine	29
	Avg UG Fees	30,260	Natural Sciences	25
	Avg PG Fees	30,532	Social Sciences	14
Web www.columbia.edu				
Phone +1 212 854 1754				

University of Connecticut

CONTACT DETAILS	INSTITUTION STATS		RANKINGS PERFORMANCE	
Address	**Undergraduates**	20,151	**Faculty Level Positions**	
Storrs	**Postgraduates**	6,053	Engineering & IT	438=
Connecticut 06269	**International Students**	5.6%	Life Sciences & BioMedicine	258=
United States	**Student Faculty Ratio**	7.9:1	Natural Sciences	392=
	Total Citations	148,675	Social Sciences	426=
	Avg UG Fees	18,202		
Web www.uconn.edu	**Avg PG Fees**	19,535		
Phone +1 (860) 486-2000				

UNITED STATES

Cornell University

CONTACT DETAILS

Address
Day Hall Lobby
Ithaca
NY 14853
United States

Web www.cornell.edu
Phone +1 607 254 4636

INSTITUTION STATS

Undergraduates	13,625
Postgraduates	4,968
International Students	15.7%
Student Faculty Ratio	17.1:1
Total Citations	492,207
Avg UG Fees	30,000
Avg PG Fees	30,000

RANKINGS PERFORMANCE

Overall Rankings Position	15
Faculty Level Positions	
Arts & Humanities	41
Engineering & IT	28=
Life Sciences & BioMedicine	22
Natural Sciences	15
Social Sciences	22

City University of New York

CONTACT DETAILS

Address
365 Fifth Avenue
New York,
NY 10016-4309
United States

Web www.cuny.edu
Phone +1 (212)817-7000

INSTITUTION STATS

Undergraduates	188,475
Postgraduates	29,212
International Students	7.2%
Student Faculty Ratio	5.9:1
Total Citations	72,158
Avg UG Fees	7,200
Avg PG Fees	10,300

RANKINGS PERFORMANCE

Faculty Level Positions	
Arts & Humanities	167=
Engineering & IT	368=
Life Sciences & BioMedicine	281=
Natural Sciences	365=
Social Sciences	426=

Dartmouth College

CONTACT DETAILS

Address
Hanover
NH 03755
United States

Web www.dartmouth.edu
Phone +1 603 646 1110

INSTITUTION STATS

Undergraduates	4,079
Postgraduates	1,327
International Students	10.8%
Student Faculty Ratio	9.5:1
Total Citations	117,848
Avg UG Fees	30,279
Avg PG Fees	30,279

RANKINGS PERFORMANCE

Overall Rankings Position	61=
Faculty Level Positions	
Arts & Humanities	98
Engineering & IT	377=
Life Sciences & BioMedicine	163=
Natural Sciences	308=
Social Sciences	188=

University of Delaware

CONTACT DETAILS

Address
Gainesville
Florida 32611
United States

Web www.udel.edu
Phone +1 (352) 392-3261

INSTITUTION STATS

Undergraduates	17,843
Postgraduates	3,395
International Students	4.9%
Student Faculty Ratio	23.1:1
Total Citations	88,157
Avg UG Fees	15,990
Avg PG Fees	15,990

RANKINGS PERFORMANCE

Faculty Level Positions	
Arts & Humanities	369=
Engineering & IT	322=
Natural Sciences	368=
Social Sciences	426=

UNITED STATES

Drexel University

CONTACT DETAILS

Address
3141 Chestnut Street
Philadelphia
PA 19104
United States

Web www.drexel.edu
Phone +1 215 895 6700

INSTITUTION STATS

Undergraduates	11,960
Postgraduates	4,689
International Students	8.5%
Student Faculty Ratio	18.8:1
Total Citations	33,681
Avg UG Fees	20,800
Avg PG Fees	28,000

RANKINGS PERFORMANCE

Faculty Level Positions
Arts & Humanities	423=
Engineering & IT	349=
Life Sciences & BioMedicine	310=
Natural Sciences	498=
Social Sciences	464=

Duke University

CONTACT DETAILS

Address
Durham
NC 27708
United States

Web www.duke.edu
Phone +1 919 684 8111

INSTITUTION STATS

Undergraduates	6,301
Postgraduates	4,805
International Students	13.2%
Student Faculty Ratio	16.7:1
Total Citations	475,144
Avg UG Fees	29,770
Avg PG Fees	29,350

RANKINGS PERFORMANCE

Overall Rankings Position	13
Faculty Level Positions	
Arts & Humanities	71=
Engineering & IT	148
Life Sciences & BioMedicine	33
Natural Sciences	109
Social Sciences	42

Emory University

CONTACT DETAILS

Address
201 Dowman Drive
Atlanta
Georgia 30322
United States

Web www.emory.edu
Phone + 1 404 727 6123

INSTITUTION STATS

Undergraduates	6,346
Postgraduates	3,822
International Students	8.9%
Student Faculty Ratio	9.9:1
Total Citations	298,289
Avg UG Fees	28,940
Avg PG Fees	27,770

RANKINGS PERFORMANCE

Overall Rankings Position	56
Faculty Level Positions	
Arts & Humanities	222=
Engineering & IT	377=
Life Sciences & BioMedicine	108
Natural Sciences	310=
Social Sciences	320=

Florida State University

CONTACT DETAILS

Address
Tallahassee
FL 32306
United States

Web www.fsu.edu
Phone +1 850-644-2525

INSTITUTION STATS

Undergraduates	30,373
Postgraduates	7,416
International Students	2.9%
Student Faculty Ratio	14:1
Total Citations	86,464
Avg UG Fees	13,956
Avg PG Fees	18,179

RANKINGS PERFORMANCE

Faculty Level Positions
Arts & Humanities	277=
Engineering & IT	217=
Life Sciences & BioMedicine	314=
Natural Sciences	167=
Social Sciences	250

UNITED STATES

University of Florida

CONTACT DETAILS

Address
Gainesville
Florida 32611
United States

Web www.ufl.edu
Phone +1(352) 392-3261

INSTITUTION STATS

Undergraduates	33,694
Postgraduates	10,581
International Students	6.1%
Student Faculty Ratio	14.7:1
Total Citations	274,068
Avg UG Fees	14,304
Avg PG Fees	19,726

RANKINGS PERFORMANCE

Faculty Level Positions
Arts & Humanities	260=
Engineering & IT	250=
Life Sciences & BioMedicine	258=
Natural Sciences	200=
Social Sciences	213=

George Washington University

CONTACT DETAILS

Address
2121 I Street NW
Washington,
DC20052
United States

Web www.gwu.edu
Phone +1 (202) 994-1000

INSTITUTION STATS

Undergraduates	10,967
Postgraduates	10,884
International Students	7.8%
Student Faculty Ratio	26.2:1
Total Citations	81,413
Avg UG Fees	34,000
Avg PG Fees	15,768

RANKINGS PERFORMANCE

Overall Rankings Position	168=
Faculty Level Positions	
Arts & Humanities	178=
Engineering & IT	250=
Life Sciences & BioMedicine	166=
Natural Sciences	314=
Social Sciences	111

Georgetown University

CONTACT DETAILS

Address
37th and O Streets, NW,
Washington
DC 20057
United States

Web www.georgetown.edu
Phone +1 (202) 687-0100

INSTITUTION STATS

Undergraduates	6,522
Postgraduates	4,037
International Students	10.7%
Student Faculty Ratio	10.2:1
Total Citations	133,585
Avg UG Fees	29,808
Avg PG Fees	27,528

RANKINGS PERFORMANCE

Overall Rankings Position	102=
Faculty Level Positions	
Arts & Humanities	156=
Engineering & IT	463=
Life Sciences & BioMedicine	338=
Natural Sciences	429=
Social Sciences	66=

Georgia Institute of Technology

CONTACT DETAILS

Address
Georgia 30332
Atlanta
United States

Web www.gatech.edu
Phone +1 404.894.2000

INSTITUTION STATS

Undergraduates	11,841
Postgraduates	5,294
International Students	16.7%
Student Faculty Ratio	8.1:1
Total Citations	99,728
Avg UG Fees	20,272
Avg PG Fees	20,244

RANKINGS PERFORMANCE

Overall Rankings Position	145
Faculty Level Positions	
Arts & Humanities	328=
Engineering & IT	22
Life Sciences & BioMedicine	284=
Natural Sciences	76
Social Sciences	281=

UNITED STATES

Georgia State University

CONTACT DETAILS

Address
Atlanta
GA 30302-3965
United States

Web www.gsu.edu
Phone +1 404 651 2000

INSTITUTION STATS

Undergraduates	19,889
Postgraduates	6,708
International Students	5.5%
Student Faculty Ratio	11.8:1
Total Citations	28,501
Avg UG Fees	13,474
Avg PG Fees	16,170

RANKINGS PERFORMANCE

Faculty Level Positions

Engineering & IT	328=
Life Sciences & BioMedicine	310=
Natural Sciences	446
Social Sciences	197=

University of Georgia

CONTACT DETAILS

Address
Athens
GA 30602
United States

Web www.uga.edu
Phone +1 (706) 542-3000

INSTITUTION STATS

Undergraduates	25,019
Postgraduates	6,792
International Students	4.0%
Student Faculty Ratio	8:1
Total Citations	133,862
Avg UG Fees	14,684
Avg PG Fees	17,378

RANKINGS PERFORMANCE

Faculty Level Positions

Arts & Humanities	305=
Engineering & IT	423=
Natural Sciences	347
Social Sciences	426=

Harvard University

CONTACT DETAILS

Address
1350 Massachusetts Ave
Cambridge
MA 02138
United States

Web www.harvard.edu
Phone +1 617 495 1000

INSTITUTION STATS

Undergraduates	9,519
Postgraduates	12,428
International Students	15.6%
Student Faculty Ratio	18:1
Total Citations	1,763,448
Avg UG Fees	27,448
Avg PG Fees	27,488

RANKINGS PERFORMANCE

Overall Rankings Position	1
Faculty Level Positions	
Arts & Humanities	3
Engineering & IT	23
Life Sciences & BioMedicine	2
Natural Sciences	4
Social Sciences	2

University of Hawaii

CONTACT DETAILS

Address
2500 Campus Road Hawai'i Hall
202 Honolulu
HI 96822 United States

Web www.uhm.hawaii.edu
Phone +1 (808) 956-8111

INSTITUTION STATS

Undergraduates	14,251
Postgraduates	5,699
International Students	8.2%
Student Faculty Ratio	9.6:1
Total Citations	123,793
Avg UG Fees	9,888
Avg PG Fees	10,848

RANKINGS PERFORMANCE

Faculty Level Positions

Arts & Humanities	228=
Engineering & IT	423=
Life Sciences & BioMedicine	338=
Natural Sciences	377

UNITED STATES

University of Houston

CONTACT DETAILS

Address
4800 Calhoun Rd.
Houston
Texas 77004
United States

Web www.uh.edu
Phone +1 (713)-743-2255

INSTITUTION STATS

Undergraduates	27,312
Postgraduates	5,915
International Students	8.1%
Student Faculty Ratio	27.1:1
Total Citations	54,372
Avg UG Fees	7,344
Avg PG Fees	6,372

RANKINGS PERFORMANCE

Faculty Level Positions
Arts & Humanities	328=
Engineering & IT	423=
Natural Sciences	256=
Social Sciences	393=

University of Illinois

CONTACT DETAILS

Address
Box 5220
Chicago
Illinois 60680-5220
United States

Web www.uillinois.edu
Phone + 1(312) 996-4350

INSTITUTION STATS

Undergraduates	47,601
Postgraduates	19,067
International Students	9.8%
Student Faculty Ratio	14.1:1
Total Citations	460,725
Avg UG Fees	16,108
Avg PG Fees	15,362

RANKINGS PERFORMANCE

Overall Rankings Position	77
Faculty Level Positions	
Arts & Humanities	218=
Engineering & IT	30=
Life Sciences & BioMedicine	153
Natural Sciences	29
Social Sciences	87

Indiana University

CONTACT DETAILS

Address
107 S. Indiana Ave
Bloomington
IN 47405-7000
United States

Web www.indiana.edu
Phone +1 812 855 4848

INSTITUTION STATS

Undergraduates	83,268
Postgraduates	17,204
International Students	4.5%
Student Faculty Ratio	16.3:1
Total Citations	265,907
Avg UG Fees	12,200
Avg PG Fees	10,334

RANKINGS PERFORMANCE

Faculty Level Positions
Arts & Humanities	128=
Engineering & IT	390=
Life Sciences & BioMedicine	363=
Natural Sciences	200=
Social Sciences	161=

Iowa State University

CONTACT DETAILS

Address
Ames
IA 50011-2011
United States

Web www.iastate.edu
Phone +1 515-294-5836

INSTITUTION STATS

Undergraduates	21,354
Postgraduates	4,618
International Students	8.7%
Student Faculty Ratio	10.5:1
Total Citations	126,892
Avg UG Fees	14,404
Avg PG Fees	15,114

RANKINGS PERFORMANCE

Faculty Level Positions
Engineering & IT	191=
Life Sciences & BioMedicine	221=
Natural Sciences	286=
Social Sciences	464=

UNITED STATES

University of Iowa

CONTACT DETAILS

Address
100 Pomerantz Center rm C210
Iowa City
IA 52242-7700
United States

Web www.uiowa.edu
Phone +1319-335-3500

INSTITUTION STATS

Undergraduates	20,135
Postgraduates	6,182
International Students	6.4%
Student Faculty Ratio	13.2:1
Total Citations	272,439
Avg UG Fees	15,354
Avg PG Fees	15,972

RANKINGS PERFORMANCE

Faculty Level Positions
Arts & Humanities	328=
Engineering & IT	390=
Life Sciences & BioMedicine	252=
Natural Sciences	417=
Social Sciences	239=

Johns Hopkins University

CONTACT DETAILS

Address
1740 Massachusetts Avenue. N.W.
Washington
DC 20036-1983
United States

Web www.jhu.edu
Phone +1202.663.5700

INSTITUTION STATS

Undergraduates	5,710
Postgraduates	12,435
International Students	12.3%
Student Faculty Ratio	7.8:1
Total Citations	803,654
Avg UG Fees	30,140
Avg PG Fees	30,140

RANKINGS PERFORMANCE

Overall Rankings Position	23
Faculty Level Positions	
Arts & Humanities	48=
Engineering & IT	85=
Life Sciences & BioMedicine	6
Natural Sciences	48
Social Sciences	89

University of Kansas

CONTACT DETAILS

Address
Lawrence
KS 66045
United States

Web www.ku.edu
Phone +785 864-2700

INSTITUTION STATS

Undergraduates	21,343
Postgraduates	6,036
International Students	5.8%
Student Faculty Ratio	17.7:1
Total Citations	113,636
Avg UG Fees	12,117
Avg PG Fees	11,018

RANKINGS PERFORMANCE

Faculty Level Positions
Arts & Humanities	305=
Engineering & IT	315=
Life Sciences & BioMedicine	258=
Natural Sciences	440=
Social Sciences	249

University of Kentucky

CONTACT DETAILS

Address
Lexington
KY 40506
United States

Web www.uky.edu
Phone +1(859) 257-9000

INSTITUTION STATS

Undergraduates	18,434
Postgraduates	5,825
International Students	4.9%
Student Faculty Ratio	9.1:1
Total Citations	157,510
Avg UG Fees	11,382
Avg PG Fees	12,530

RANKINGS PERFORMANCE

Faculty Level Positions
Engineering & IT	438=

UNITED STATES

Louisiana State University

CONTACT DETAILS

Address
Baton Rouge
LA 70803
United States

Web www.lsu.edu
Phone +1225/578-2311

INSTITUTION STATS

Undergraduates	26,387
Postgraduates	4,804
International Students	5.7%
Student Faculty Ratio	15:1
Total Citations	157,395
Avg UG Fees	2,855
Avg PG Fees	2,855

RANKINGS PERFORMANCE

Faculty Level Positions
Arts & Humanities	369=
Engineering & IT	406=
Life Sciences & BioMedicine	241
Natural Sciences	281=
Social Sciences	354=

Loyola University Chicago

CONTACT DETAILS

Address
6525 N. Sheridan Road
Chicago
IL 60626
United States

Web www.luc.edu
Phone +1 773 508 3396

INSTITUTION STATS

Undergraduates	8,319
Postgraduates	4,179
International Students	3.2%
Student Faculty Ratio	13.6:1
Total Citations	66,814
Avg UG Fees	21,780
Avg PG Fees	10,908

RANKINGS PERFORMANCE

Faculty Level Positions
Arts & Humanities	260=
Engineering & IT	482=
Life Sciences & BioMedicine	338=
Natural Sciences	476=
Social Sciences	354=

University of Maryland

CONTACT DETAILS

Address
College Park
MD 20742
United States

Web www.umd.edu
Phone +1301.405.1000

INSTITUTION STATS

Undergraduates	25,140
Postgraduates	9,678
International Students	9.2%
Student Faculty Ratio	6.7:1
Total Citations	410,307
Avg UG Fees	17,500
Avg PG Fees	12,618

RANKINGS PERFORMANCE

Overall Rankings Position	111=
Faculty Level Positions	
Arts & Humanities	260=
Engineering & IT	82
Life Sciences & BioMedicine	252=
Natural Sciences	97=
Social Sciences	197=

University of Massachusetts, Amherst

CONTACT DETAILS

Address
Amherst
United States

Web www.umass.edu
Phone +1413-545-0111

INSTITUTION STATS

Undergraduates	18,966
Postgraduates	5,680
International Students	6.4%
Student Faculty Ratio	19.2:1
Total Citations	260,786
Avg UG Fees	9,937
Avg PG Fees	9,937

RANKINGS PERFORMANCE

Overall Rankings Position	124=
Faculty Level Positions	
Arts & Humanities	153=
Engineering & IT	61
Life Sciences & BioMedicine	181=
Natural Sciences	147
Social Sciences	93=

UNITED STATES

University of Miami

CONTACT DETAILS

Address
Coral Gables,
Florida 33124
United States

Web www.miami.edu
Phone +1 305-284-2211

INSTITUTION STATS

Undergraduates	10,104
Postgraduates	3,235
International Students	8.9%
Student Faculty Ratio	4.7:1
Total Citations	165,409
Avg UG Fees	27,384
Avg PG Fees	20,520

RANKINGS PERFORMANCE

Faculty Level Positions

Engineering & IT	390=
Life Sciences & BioMedicine	334=
Natural Sciences	491=
Social Sciences	419=

Michigan State University

CONTACT DETAILS

Address
East Lansing
MI 48824-0590
United States

Web www.msu.edu
Phone +1 517 355 8332

INSTITUTION STATS

Undergraduates	35,408
Postgraduates	8,040
International Students	7.4%
Student Faculty Ratio	16:1
Total Citations	189,155
Avg UG Fees	17,336
Avg PG Fees	15,168

RANKINGS PERFORMANCE

Overall Rankings Position	163

Faculty Level Positions

Arts & Humanities	181=
Engineering & IT	106
Life Sciences & BioMedicine	173=
Natural Sciences	131
Social Sciences	127

University of Michigan

CONTACT DETAILS

Address
4901 Evergreen Road
Dearborn
Michigan 48128
United States

Web www.umich.edu
Phone +1 (313) 593-5000

INSTITUTION STATS

Undergraduates	24,828
Postgraduates	12,184
International Students	11.7%
Student Faculty Ratio	31.9:1
Total Citations	612,751
Avg UG Fees	25,840
Avg PG Fees	27,124

RANKINGS PERFORMANCE

Overall Rankings Position	29=

Faculty Level Positions

Arts & Humanities	39=
Engineering & IT	36
Life Sciences & BioMedicine	55
Natural Sciences	34
Social Sciences	28

University of Minnesota

CONTACT DETAILS

Address
240 Williamson Hall
231 Pillsbury Drive S.E.
Minneapolis
MN 55455-0213
United States

Web www.umn.edu
Phone +1 612-625-2008

INSTITUTION STATS

Undergraduates	46,084
Postgraduates	15,280
International Students	6.0%
Student Faculty Ratio	21.1:1
Total Citations	487,575
Avg UG Fees	12,320
Avg PG Fees	15,272

RANKINGS PERFORMANCE

Overall Rankings Position	187=

Faculty Level Positions

Arts & Humanities	266=
Engineering & IT	119=
Life Sciences & BioMedicine	163=
Natural Sciences	146
Social Sciences	135=

UNITED STATES

University of Missouri

CONTACT DETAILS

Address
721 Lewis Hall,
Columbia
MO65211
United States

Web www.missouri.edu
Phone +1 573-882-4077

INSTITUTION STATS

Undergraduates	20,883
Postgraduates	5,051
International Students	5.2%
Student Faculty Ratio	16.8:1
Total Citations	156,779
Avg UG Fees	15,723
Avg PG Fees	15,761

RANKINGS PERFORMANCE

Faculty Level Positions

Arts & Humanities	397
Engineering & IT	336=
Life Sciences & BioMedicine	385=
Natural Sciences	423=
Social Sciences	320=

Massachusetts Institute of Technology

CONTACT DETAILS

Address
77 Massachusetts Avenue
Cambridge
MA 02139-4307
United States

Web web.mit.edu
Phone +1 617 253 1000

INSTITUTION STATS

Undergraduates	4,136
Postgraduates	6,184
International Students	24.1%
Student Faculty Ratio	20.7:1
Total Citations	541,452
Avg UG Fees	30,600
Avg PG Fees	30,600

RANKINGS PERFORMANCE

Overall Rankings Position	4=
Faculty Level Positions	
Arts & Humanities	21
Engineering & IT	1
Life Sciences & BioMedicine	13
Natural Sciences	5
Social Sciences	12

North Carolina State University

CONTACT DETAILS

Address
Flex Lab, Module 6, Room 1418
Raleigh, NC 27695
1575 Varsity Drive
United States

Web www.ncsu.edu
Phone +1(919) 515-2872

INSTITUTION STATS

Undergraduates	22,754
Postgraduates	6,904
International Students	5.2%
Student Faculty Ratio	7:1
Total Citations	130,230
Avg UG Fees	15,103
Avg PG Fees	15,461

RANKINGS PERFORMANCE

Faculty Level Positions

Arts & Humanities	139=
Engineering & IT	160=
Life Sciences & BioMedicine	334=
Natural Sciences	270=
Social Sciences	320=

University of North Carolina

CONTACT DETAILS

Address
CB #2200, Jackson Hall
Chapel Hill
NC 27599-2200
United States

Web www.unc.edu
Phone +1 (919) 966-3621

INSTITUTION STATS

Undergraduates	16,525
Postgraduates	8,008
International Students	4.7%
Student Faculty Ratio	8.4:1
Total Citations	419,382
Avg UG Fees	16,303
Avg PG Fees	16,661

RANKINGS PERFORMANCE

Overall Rankings Position	123
Faculty Level Positions	
Arts & Humanities	218=
Engineering & IT	195=
Life Sciences & BioMedicine	193=
Natural Sciences	191=
Social Sciences	175

UNITED STATES

University of New Mexico

CONTACT DETAILS

Address
Albuquerque
NM 87131
United States

Web www.unm.edu
Phone +1 (505) 277-0111

INSTITUTION STATS

Undergraduates	25,104
Postgraduates	6,824
International Students	2.8%
Student Faculty Ratio	32.4:1
Total Citations	108,571
Avg UG Fees	4,376
Avg PG Fees	12,203

RANKINGS PERFORMANCE

Faculty Level Positions
Arts & Humanities	212=
Engineering & IT	336=
Life Sciences & BioMedicine	390=
Natural Sciences	394=
Social Sciences	419=

New York University

CONTACT DETAILS

Address
22 Washington Square North
New York
New York 10011
United States

Web www.nyu.edu
Phone +1 (212) 998-4500

INSTITUTION STATS

Undergraduates	20,212
Postgraduates	15,884
International Students	9.7%
Student Faculty Ratio	8.4:1
Total Citations	293,633
Avg UG Fees	28,328
Avg PG Fees	23,304

RANKINGS PERFORMANCE

Overall Rankings Position	43
Faculty Level Positions	
Arts & Humanities	47
Engineering & IT	209=
Life Sciences & BioMedicine	81
Natural Sciences	82=
Social Sciences	29

Northeastern University

CONTACT DETAILS

Address
360 Huntington Avenue
Boston
MA 02115
United States

Web www.northeastern.edu
Phone +1(617) 373-2000

INSTITUTION STATS

Undergraduates	18,571
Postgraduates	3,762
International Students	7.7%
Student Faculty Ratio	10:1
Avg UG Fees	26,750
Avg PG Fees	19,800

RANKINGS PERFORMANCE

Faculty Level Positions
Engineering & IT	406=
Natural Sciences	476=

Northwestern University

CONTACT DETAILS

Address
633 Clark Street
Evanston,
IL 60208
United States

Web www.northwestern.edu
Phone +1847-491-3741

INSTITUTION STATS

Undergraduates	9,115
Postgraduates	7,169
International Students	12.6%
Student Faculty Ratio	12.6:1
Total Citations	350,238
Avg UG Fees	29,940
Avg PG Fees	29,940

RANKINGS PERFORMANCE

Overall Rankings Position	42
Faculty Level Positions	
Arts & Humanities	161
Engineering & IT	98
Life Sciences & BioMedicine	210=
Natural Sciences	130
Social Sciences	41

UNITED STATES

University of Notre Dame

CONTACT DETAILS

Address
317 Main Building
Notre Dame
Indiana - 46556
United States

Web www.nd.edu
Phone +1(574) 631-7367

INSTITUTION STATS

Undergraduates	8,332
Postgraduates	2,560
International Students	8.5%
Student Faculty Ratio	12.7:1
Total Citations	78,891
Avg UG Fees	29,070
Avg PG Fees	28,970

RANKINGS PERFORMANCE

Overall Rankings Position	152
Faculty Level Positions	
Arts & Humanities	103
Engineering & IT	287=
Natural Sciences	252
Social Sciences	188=

Ohio State University

CONTACT DETAILS

Address
Enarson Hall 154 W 12th Avenue
Columbus
Ohio 43210
United States

Web www.osu.edu

INSTITUTION STATS

Undergraduates	44,518
Postgraduates	10,571
International Students	7.1%
Student Faculty Ratio	22.9:1
Total Citations	306,080
Avg UG Fees	15,755
Avg PG Fees	19,615

RANKINGS PERFORMANCE

Faculty Level Positions	
Arts & Humanities	423=
Engineering & IT	123
Life Sciences & BioMedicine	397=
Natural Sciences	180
Social Sciences	150

University of Oklahoma

CONTACT DETAILS

Address
660 Parrington Oval
Norman
OK, 73019-0390
United States

Web www.ou.edu
Phone +1 (405) 325-0311

INSTITUTION STATS

Undergraduates	21,704
Postgraduates	7,396
International Students	5.8%
Student Faculty Ratio	5.4:1
Total Citations	99,537
Avg UG Fees	10,296
Avg PG Fees	10,349

RANKINGS PERFORMANCE

Faculty Level Positions	
Arts & Humanities	328=
Engineering & IT	482=
Natural Sciences	356=
Social Sciences	241

University of Oregon

CONTACT DETAILS

Address
Eugene
OR 97403
United States

Web www.uoregon.edu
Phone +1 (541) 346-1000

INSTITUTION STATS

Undergraduates	16,350
Postgraduates	3,415
International Students	6.0%
Student Faculty Ratio	7.7:1
Total Citations	71,439
Avg UG Fees	15,501
Avg PG Fees	12,798

RANKINGS PERFORMANCE

Faculty Level Positions	
Engineering & IT	438=
Life Sciences & BioMedicine	338=
Natural Sciences	324=
Social Sciences	393=

UNITED STATES

Pennsylvania State University

CONTACT DETAILS

Address
201 Shields Building, Box 3000
University Park
PA 16804-3000
United States

Web www.psu.edu
Phone +1 (814) 865-5471

INSTITUTION STATS

Undergraduates	63,833
Postgraduates	10,310
International Students	4.7%
Student Faculty Ratio	16.5:1
Total Citations	341,477
Avg UG Fees	29,910
Avg PG Fees	16,654

RANKINGS PERFORMANCE

Overall Rankings Position	99=
Faculty Level Positions	
Arts & Humanities	153=
Engineering & IT	90=
Life Sciences & BioMedicine	128=
Natural Sciences	77
Social Sciences	83

University of Pennsylvania

CONTACT DETAILS

Address
100 College Hall
Philadelphia
Pennsylvania / PA 19104-6380
United States

Web www.upenn.edu
Phone +1 215-898-7221

INSTITUTION STATS

Undergraduates	11,958
Postgraduates	8,942
International Students	15.9%
Student Faculty Ratio	26:1
Total Citations	605,674
Avg UG Fees	27,544
Avg PG Fees	29,386

RANKINGS PERFORMANCE

Overall Rankings Position	26
Faculty Level Positions	
Arts & Humanities	45
Engineering & IT	81
Life Sciences & BioMedicine	58
Natural Sciences	55
Social Sciences	24

University of Pittsburgh

CONTACT DETAILS

Address
Pittsburgh
PA 15260
United States

Web www.pitt.edu
Phone +1 412-624-4141

INSTITUTION STATS

Undergraduates	17,181
Postgraduates	3,371
International Students	6.2%
Student Faculty Ratio	31.6:1
Total Citations	435,747
Avg UG Fees	19,500
Avg PG Fees	24,824

RANKINGS PERFORMANCE

Overall Rankings Position	88
Faculty Level Positions	
Arts & Humanities	66
Engineering & IT	214=
Life Sciences & BioMedicine	314=
Natural Sciences	360=
Social Sciences	290=

Princeton University

CONTACT DETAILS

Address
Princeton
NJ 08544
United States

Web www.princeton.edu
Phone +1(609) 258-3000

INSTITUTION STATS

Undergraduates	4,678
Postgraduates	2,030
International Students	17.9%
Student Faculty Ratio	15.2:1
Total Citations	273,573
Avg UG Fees	29,910
Avg PG Fees	29,910

RANKINGS PERFORMANCE

Overall Rankings Position	10
Faculty Level Positions	
Arts & Humanities	9
Engineering & IT	33
Life Sciences & BioMedicine	37
Natural Sciences	6
Social Sciences	13

UNITED STATES

Purdue University

CONTACT DETAILS

Address
West Lafayette
IN 47907
United States

Web www.purdue.edu
Phone +1 (765) 494-4600

INSTITUTION STATS

Undergraduates	43,897
Postgraduates	7,950
International Students	9.6%
Student Faculty Ratio	12.4:1
Total Citations	161,168
Avg UG Fees	16,867
Avg PG Fees	18,980

RANKINGS PERFORMANCE

Overall Rankings Position	127
Faculty Level Positions	
Arts & Humanities	163=
Engineering & IT	40
Life Sciences & BioMedicine	135=
Natural Sciences	119
Social Sciences	200=

Rensselaer Polytechnic Institute

CONTACT DETAILS

Address
110 8th St., Troy,
NY 12180.
United States

Web www.rpi.edu
Phone +1 (518) 276-6000

INSTITUTION STATS

Undergraduates	4,927
Postgraduates	1,769
International Students	13.8%
Student Faculty Ratio	15.8:1
Total Citations	44,387
Avg UG Fees	28,950
Avg PG Fees	28,950

RANKINGS PERFORMANCE

Faculty Level Positions	
Engineering & IT	77=
Life Sciences & BioMedicine	421=
Natural Sciences	269

Rice University

CONTACT DETAILS

Address
6100 Main
Houston
Texas 77005-1827
United States

Web www.rice.edu

INSTITUTION STATS

Undergraduates	2,933
Postgraduates	1,922
International Students	14.0%
Student Faculty Ratio	29.9:1
Total Citations	84,185
Avg UG Fees	18,863
Avg PG Fees	25,600

RANKINGS PERFORMANCE

Overall Rankings Position	102=
Faculty Level Positions	
Arts & Humanities	328=
Engineering & IT	111=
Life Sciences & BioMedicine	310=
Natural Sciences	173=
Social Sciences	320=

University of Rochester

CONTACT DETAILS

Address
Rochester,
NY 14627
United States

Web www.rochester.edu

INSTITUTION STATS

Undergraduates	4,535
Postgraduates	3,371
International Students	14.3%
Student Faculty Ratio	7.5:1
Total Citations	211,580
Avg UG Fees	28,250
Avg PG Fees	28,250

RANKINGS PERFORMANCE

Overall Rankings Position	48=
Faculty Level Positions	
Arts & Humanities	276
Engineering & IT	173=
Life Sciences & BioMedicine	258=
Natural Sciences	286=
Social Sciences	139

UNITED STATES

Rutgers State University

CONTACT DETAILS	INSTITUTION STATS		RANKINGS PERFORMANCE	
Address	**Undergraduates**	37,428	**Faculty Level Positions**	
18 Bishop Place	**Postgraduates**	11,153	Arts & Humanities	128=
New Brunswick	**International Students**	5.7%	Engineering & IT	219=
NJ 08901-8530	**Student Faculty Ratio**	9.7:1	Life Sciences & BioMedicine	258=
United States	**Total Citations**	210,670	Natural Sciences	115=
			Social Sciences	169=
Web www.rutgers.edu				
Phone +1 732/932-7711				

University of South Carolina

CONTACT DETAILS	INSTITUTION STATS		RANKINGS PERFORMANCE	
Address	**Undergraduates**	29,765	**Faculty Level Positions**	
Columbia	**Postgraduates**	6,718	Engineering & IT	303=
SC 29208	**International Students**	3.1%	Life Sciences & BioMedicine	397=
United States	**Student Faculty Ratio**	9.7:1	Natural Sciences	390=
	Total Citations	80,577		
	Avg UG Fees	11,048		
Web www.sc.edu	**Avg PG Fees**	14,920		
Phone +1 803-777-7000				

University of South Florida

CONTACT DETAILS	INSTITUTION STATS		RANKINGS PERFORMANCE	
Address	**Undergraduates**	33,266	**Faculty Level Positions**	
4202 E. Fowler Avenue	**Postgraduates**	8,545	Natural Sciences	447=
Tampa	**International Students**	4.5%	Social Sciences	426=
FL 33620	**Student Faculty Ratio**	20.2:1		
United States	**Total Citations**	104,654		
	Avg UG Fees	14,305		
Web www.usf.edu	**Avg PG Fees**	19,727		
Phone +1 (813) 974-2011				

Smith College

CONTACT DETAILS	INSTITUTION STATS		RANKINGS PERFORMANCE	
Address	**Undergraduates**	2,692	**Faculty Level Positions**	
Northampton	**Postgraduates**	472	Arts & Humanities	305=
Massachusetts 01063	**International Students**	6.3%	Life Sciences & BioMedicine	390=
United States	**Student Faculty Ratio**	10.1:1		
	Avg UG Fees	28,930		
	Avg PG Fees	28,930		
Web www.smith.edu				
Phone +1 (413) 584-2700				

UNITED STATES

University of Southern California

CONTACT DETAILS

Address
Los Angeles
CA 90089
United States

Web www.usc.edu
Phone +1 (213) 740-2311

INSTITUTION STATS

Undergraduates	16,474
Postgraduates	13,004
International Students	17.2%
Student Faculty Ratio	7.5:1
Total Citations	286,762
Avg UG Fees	29,988
Avg PG Fees	24,240

RANKINGS PERFORMANCE

Overall Rankings Position	101
Faculty Level Positions	
Arts & Humanities	197
Engineering & IT	101=
Life Sciences & BioMedicine	119=
Natural Sciences	304=
Social Sciences	151

Stanford University

CONTACT DETAILS

Address
Old Union, Room 141
520 Lasuen Mall
Stanford
CA 94305-3005
United States

Web www.stanford.edu

INSTITUTION STATS

Undergraduates	6,555
Postgraduates	11,267
International Students	21.0%
Student Faculty Ratio	12.3:1
Total Citations	766,457
Avg UG Fees	29,847
Avg PG Fees	29,847

RANKINGS PERFORMANCE

Overall Rankings Position	6
Faculty Level Positions	
Arts & Humanities	15
Engineering & IT	5
Life Sciences & BioMedicine	5
Natural Sciences	7
Social Sciences	7=

State University of New York at Stony Brook

CONTACT DETAILS

Address
Stony Brook
NY 11794
United States

Web www.sunysb.edu/
Phone +1 (631) 632-6000

INSTITUTION STATS

Undergraduates	13,858
Postgraduates	7,228
International Students	9.5%
Student Faculty Ratio	17.2:1
Total Citations	208,067
Avg UG Fees	10,610
Avg PG Fees	10,920

RANKINGS PERFORMANCE

Overall Rankings Position	165=
Faculty Level Positions	
Arts & Humanities	148=
Engineering & IT	209=
Life Sciences & BioMedicine	181=
Natural Sciences	90=
Social Sciences	217=

Temple University

CONTACT DETAILS

Address
Temple University
1801 North Broad Street
Philadelphia
PA 19122
United States

Web www.temple.edu
Phone +1 215-204-7000

INSTITUTION STATS

Undergraduates	23,429
Postgraduates	7,000
International Students	4.7%
Student Faculty Ratio	21.8:1
Total Citations	64,338
Avg UG Fees	15,788
Avg PG Fees	15,936

RANKINGS PERFORMANCE

Faculty Level Positions	
Engineering & IT	368=
Life Sciences & BioMedicine	421=
Natural Sciences	514=
Social Sciences	359=

UNITED STATES

University of Tennessee

CONTACT DETAILS

INSTITUTION STATS

RANKINGS PERFORMANCE

Address
Knoxville
Tennessee
37996
United States

Web www.utk.edu
Phone +1 865-974-1000

Undergraduates	19,640
Postgraduates	6,032
International Students	4.1%
Student Faculty Ratio	11:1
Total Citations	191,494
Avg UG Fees	13,616
Avg PG Fees	14,244

Faculty Level Positions

Engineering & IT	289=
Life Sciences & BioMedicine	385=
Natural Sciences	381=

University of Texas at Austin

CONTACT DETAILS

INSTITUTION STATS

RANKINGS PERFORMANCE

Address
1 University Station
Texas
Austin 78712
United States

Web www.utexas.edu
Phone +1 (512) 475-7348

Undergraduates	37,377
Postgraduates	11,282
International Students	8.8%
Student Faculty Ratio	18.6:1
Total Citations	1,151,255
Avg UG Fees	12,960
Avg PG Fees	11,952

Overall Rankings Position	32
Faculty Level Positions	
Arts & Humanities	46
Engineering & IT	35
Life Sciences & BioMedicine	123=
Natural Sciences	26
Social Sciences	100

Texas A&M University

CONTACT DETAILS

INSTITUTION STATS

RANKINGS PERFORMANCE

Address
302 J. K. W. Administration Building
1113 TAMU
College Station
TX 77843
United States

Web www.tamu.edu
Phone +1 979 845 3631

Undergraduates	35,732
Postgraduates	8,192
International Students	8.2%
Student Faculty Ratio	11.2:1
Total Citations	213,741
Avg UG Fees	11,415
Avg PG Fees	10,284

Overall Rankings Position	150=
Faculty Level Positions	
Arts & Humanities	321=
Engineering & IT	60
Life Sciences & BioMedicine	97=
Natural Sciences	104=
Social Sciences	176=

Tufts University

CONTACT DETAILS

INSTITUTION STATS

RANKINGS PERFORMANCE

Address
Medford
MA 02155
United States

Web www.tufts.edu
Phone +1 (617) 628-5000

Undergraduates	4,912
Postgraduates	3,099
International Students	10.4%
Student Faculty Ratio	14.8:1
Total Citations	203,148
Avg UG Fees	30,377
Avg PG Fees	30,982

Overall Rankings Position	130=
Faculty Level Positions	
Arts & Humanities	175
Engineering & IT	382=
Life Sciences & BioMedicine	177=
Natural Sciences	356=
Social Sciences	390=

UNITED STATES

Tulane University

CONTACT DETAILS

Address
6823 St. Charles Avenue
New Orleans
LA 70118
United States

Web www.tulane.edu
Phone +1 (504) 865-5000

INSTITUTION STATS

Undergraduates	7,952
Postgraduates	3,098
International Students	7.9%
Student Faculty Ratio	18.8:1
Total Citations	95,298
Avg UG Fees	28,900
Avg PG Fees	29,900

RANKINGS PERFORMANCE

Faculty Level Positions

Arts & Humanities	222=
Engineering & IT	390=
Life Sciences & BioMedicine	421=
Natural Sciences	460
Social Sciences	299=

University of Utah

CONTACT DETAILS

Web www.utah.edu
Phone +1 801-581-7200

INSTITUTION STATS

Undergraduates	22,775
Postgraduates	5,814
International Students	5.2%
Student Faculty Ratio	25.7:1
Total Citations	246,200
Avg UG Fees	11,774
Avg PG Fees	9,324

RANKINGS PERFORMANCE

Faculty Level Positions

Arts & Humanities	148=
Engineering & IT	328=
Natural Sciences	265=
Social Sciences	281=

Vanderbilt University

CONTACT DETAILS

Address
Nashville
Tennessee 37235
United States

Web www.vanderbilt.edu
Phone +1(615) 322-7311

INSTITUTION STATS

Undergraduates	6,272
Postgraduates	3,782
International Students	8.6%
Student Faculty Ratio	36.2:1
Total Citations	297,407
Avg UG Fees	29,240
Avg PG Fees	29,240

RANKINGS PERFORMANCE

Overall Rankings Position	53

Faculty Level Positions

Arts & Humanities	266=
Engineering & IT	463=
Life Sciences & BioMedicine	68=
Natural Sciences	219=
Social Sciences	188=

Virginia Commonwealth University

CONTACT DETAILS

Address
Richmond
VA 23284
United States

Web www.vcu.edu
Phone +1 (804) 828-0100

INSTITUTION STATS

Undergraduates	19,021
Postgraduates	7,748
International Students	2.7%
Student Faculty Ratio	9.7:1
Total Citations	117,777
Avg UG Fees	15,904
Avg PG Fees	15,904

RANKINGS PERFORMANCE

Faculty Level Positions

Arts & Humanities	398=
Engineering & IT	463=
Life Sciences & BioMedicine	363=
Natural Sciences	518=
Social Sciences	464=

UNIETED STATES

Virginia Polytechnic Institute

CONTACT DETAILS

Address
VA 24061
United States

Web www.vt.edu
Phone +1 (540) 231-6000

INSTITUTION STATS

Undergraduates	21,330
Postgraduates	5,932
International Students	7.8%
Student Faculty Ratio	5.7:1
Total Citations	80,039
Avg UG Fees	15,206
Avg PG Fees	10,307

RANKINGS PERFORMANCE

Faculty Level Positions

Engineering & IT	71
Life Sciences & BioMedicine	421=
Natural Sciences	300=
Social Sciences	419=

University of Virginia

CONTACT DETAILS

Address
P.O. Box 400132
Charlottesville
VA 22904-4132
United States
Web www.virginia.edu
Phone +1 434 924-7923

INSTITUTION STATS

Undergraduates	14,129
Postgraduates	7,562
International Students	6.8%
Student Faculty Ratio	20.2:1
Total Citations	263,114
Avg UG Fees	21,172
Avg PG Fees	18,672

RANKINGS PERFORMANCE

Overall Rankings Position	130=

Faculty Level Positions

Arts & Humanities	178=
Engineering & IT	235=
Life Sciences & BioMedicine	314=
Natural Sciences	326=
Social Sciences	186=

Wake Forest University

CONTACT DETAILS

Address
1834 Wake Forest Road
Winston-Salem
NC 27106
United States

Web www.wfu.edu
Phone +1 (336) 758-5255

INSTITUTION STATS

Undergraduates	4,128
Postgraduates	1,379
International Students	3.6%
Student Faculty Ratio	16.1:1
Total Citations	123,568
Avg UG Fees	28,210
Avg PG Fees	24,475

RANKINGS PERFORMANCE

Overall Rankings Position	111=

Faculty Level Positions

Arts & Humanities	423=
Engineering & IT	463=
Life Sciences & BioMedicine	258=
Social Sciences	320=

Washington State University

CONTACT DETAILS

Address
PO Box 641067
Pullman,
WA 99164-1067
United States

Web www.wsu.edu

INSTITUTION STATS

Undergraduates	19,281
Postgraduates	3,228
International Students	5.3%
Student Faculty Ratio	29.5:1
Total Citations	94,967
Avg UG Fees	13,163
Avg PG Fees	15,289

RANKINGS PERFORMANCE

Faculty Level Positions

Arts & Humanities	328=
Engineering & IT	315=
Life Sciences & BioMedicine	397=
Natural Sciences	318=
Social Sciences	471=

UNITED STATES

University of Washington

CONTACT DETAILS

Address
Seattle 98195+4
United States

Web www.washington.edu
Phone +1(206) 543-9198

INSTITUTION STATS

Undergraduates	30,790
Postgraduates	10,310
International Students	6.0%
Student Faculty Ratio	18.5:1
Total Citations	749,072
Avg UG Fees	17,400
Avg PG Fees	17,300

RANKINGS PERFORMANCE

Overall Rankings Position	84
Faculty Level Positions	
Arts & Humanities	191=
Engineering & IT	90=
Life Sciences & BioMedicine	60
Natural Sciences	100=
Social Sciences	239=

Washington University in St. Louis

CONTACT DETAILS

Web www.wustl.edu
Phone +1(314) 935-6000

INSTITUTION STATS

Undergraduates	7,350
Postgraduates	4,645
International Students	11.1%
Student Faculty Ratio	23.3:1
Total Citations	481,861
Avg UG Fees	29,700
Avg PG Fees	29,700

RANKINGS PERFORMANCE

Overall Rankings Position	48=
Faculty Level Positions	
Arts & Humanities	228=
Engineering & IT	197=
Life Sciences & BioMedicine	46
Natural Sciences	400
Social Sciences	169=

University of Wisconsin

CONTACT DETAILS

Web www.wisc.edu
Phone +1 608-263-2400

INSTITUTION STATS

Undergraduates	29,078
Postgraduates	8,928
International Students	8.5%
Student Faculty Ratio	10.4:1
Total Citations	501,059
Avg UG Fees	19,254
Avg PG Fees	22,978

RANKINGS PERFORMANCE

Overall Rankings Position	79=
Faculty Level Positions	
Arts & Humanities	82=
Engineering & IT	65
Life Sciences & BioMedicine	123=
Natural Sciences	51
Social Sciences	48

Yale University

CONTACT DETAILS

Web www.yale.edu
Phone +1 (203) 432-4771

INSTITUTION STATS

Undergraduates	5,319
Postgraduates	4,877
International Students	15.9%
Student Faculty Ratio	34.3:1
Total Citations	580,398
Avg UG Fees	29,820
Avg PG Fees	26,800

RANKINGS PERFORMANCE

Overall Rankings Position	4=
Faculty Level Positions	
Arts & Humanities	8
Engineering & IT	57
Life Sciences & BioMedicine	11
Natural Sciences	14
Social Sciences	7=

UNITED STATES

Yeshiva University

CONTACT DETAILS

Address
500 West 185th Street
New York
New York 10033
United States

Web www.yu.edu
Phone +1 (212) 960-5400

INSTITUTION STATS

Undergraduates	2,803
Postgraduates	1,529
International Students	3.6%
Student Faculty Ratio	10.5:1
Total Citations	194,140
Avg UG Fees	22,200
Avg PG Fees	22,178

RANKINGS PERFORMANCE

Overall Rankings Position	172=
Faculty Level Positions	
Engineering & IT	497=
Life Sciences & BioMedicine	363=
Natural Sciences	415
Social Sciences	426=

URUGUAY

University ORT de Uruguay

Web www.ort.edu.uy

INSTITUTION STATS

Undergraduates	3,245
Postgraduates	268
International Students	0.9%
Student Faculty Ratio	10.1:1
Avg UG Fees	4,000
Avg PG Fees	4,550

RANKINGS PERFORMANCE

Faculty Level Positions	
Engineering & IT	482=